Internet Marketing

INTEGRATING ONLINE AND OFFLINE STRATEGIES 2E

Internet Marketing

INTEGRATING ONLINE AND OFFLINE STRATEGIES

Mary Lou Roberts

Atomic Dog
A part of Cengage Learning

CENGAGE
Learning™

Australia • Brazil • Japan • Korea • Mexico • Singapore • Spain • United Kingdom • United States

CENGAGE
Learning™

Internet Marketing, 2e

Mary Lou Roberts

Executive Editors: Michele Baird, Maureen Staudt and Michael Stranz

Marketing Manager: Mikka Baker

Managing Editor: Laureen Ranz

Sr. Marketing Coordinators: Lindsay Annett and Sara Mercurio

Production/Manufacturing Manager: Donna M. Brown

Production Editorial Manager: Dan Plofchan

Premedia Supervisor: Becki Walker

Rights and DPermissions Specialist: Kalina Ingham Hintz

Associate Technology Project Manager: Angela Makowski

Production Editor: KA Espy

Cover Image: Getty Images

Composition House: ICC Macmillan Inc.

© 2008, 2007 Atomic Dog, a part of Cengage Learning

ALL RIGHTS RESERVED. No part of this work covered by the copyright herein may be reproduced, transmitted, stored or used in any form or by any means graphic, electronic, or mechanical, including but not limited to photocopying, recording, scanning, digitizing, taping, Web distribution, information networks, or information storage and retrieval systems, except as permitted under Section 107 or 108 of the 1976 United States Copyright Act, without the prior written permission of the publisher.

For product information and technology assistance, contact us at
Cengage Learning Customer & Sales Support, 1-800-354-9706

For permission to use material from this text or product, submit all requests online at **cengage.com/permissions**
Further permissions questions can be emailed to
permissionrequest@cengage.com

Library of Congress Control Number: 2006907940

ISBN-13: 0-759-39165-3

ISBN-10: 978-0-7593-9165-9

PKG ISBN-13: 0-7593-9278-1

PKG ISBN-10: 978-0-7593-9278-6

Cengage Learning
5191 Natorp Blvd.
Mason, OH 45040
USA

Cengage Learning is a leading provider of customized learning solutions with office locations around the globe, including Singapore, the United Kingdom, Australia, Mexico, Brazil, and Japan. Locate your local office at:
international.cengage.com/region

Cengage Learning products are represented in Canada by Nelson Education, Ltd.

Visit Atomic Dog online at **atomicdog.com**
Visit our corporate website at **cengage.com**

Printed in the United States of America
3 4 5 6 7 11 10 09

The second edition is dedicated to students and practitioners of Internet marketing around the globe who have enhanced my knowledge and understanding of this evolving marketing discipline.

Brief Contents

Contents

Chapter Seven

Customer Acquisition: Search, E-Mail, and Other Marketing Tools 173

Chapter Eight

Customer Relationship Development and Management 197

Chapter Nine

Customer Service and Support in Web Space 221

Part Three   Evaluating Performance and Opportunities   247

Introduction

The first edition of *Internet Marketing: Integrating Online and Offline Strategies* was begun at the height of the Internet bubble, when there seemed to be no limits to Internet success. It was rewritten during the crash that followed as it became clear that bad business models don't work on the Internet either. It was rewritten a third time to try to make it completely correct, current, and engaging. At that point, an exhausted author was willing to believe that the pace of change would slow and the future would be less challenging.

Not so!

In the brief intervening time, search has exploded and Google has taken its place with Yahoo!, Amazon, eBay, and other Internet pioneers as a major brand, competing with the likes of Coke and Sony for global recognition. Broadband has become widely available at home and at work. Rich media, new advertising models, and innovative businesses have developed to take advantage of high-speed transmission to the desktop. Mobile devices are also moving into the broadband age.

Consumers and business users alike have accepted the Internet as an indispensable part of their daily lives. Consumers use the Web for communications, information, shopping, and many other daily tasks. Traditional consumer packaged goods marketers have moved onto the Web because their customers are there. Marketers of services who were early entrants are expanding their offerings. Businesses make use of both the communications and transactional capabilities of the Web. In addition, they have found that the efficiency of virtual value chains is essential to compete in the Internet age. Nonprofit organizations and government agencies have found the Web an effective way to reach and serve their constituencies.

For their part, consumers have not accepted what was offered to them on the new channel in a passive manner. They have aggressively moved out to create their own content and to confront corporations on their own terms. They demand information when, where, and how they want it. Media have responded with content on demand and strategic partnerships that allow content to move seamlessly from one medium to another. Many services are becoming available on mobile devices.

Underneath the steady stream of changes to the current Internet marketspace is the discussion of Internet 2. Its shape is not entirely clear, but it will certainly be faster and is likely to be organized around an ecosystem of content, not Web sites with precisely defined boundaries. This implies change that will continue and perhaps accelerate over the next few years.

Unifying Themes

This text is uniquely positioned to take advantage of the innovation that is inherent in the Internet. The Internet itself is no longer a stand-alone medium, if indeed it ever was. It is most effective if strategies and messages are integrated across media. That viewpoint is pervasive throughout this text. Internet marketing is considered in the context of overall marketing strategy. Throughout, examples show the integrated use of online and offline media to achieve marketers' objectives.

This text also recognizes the Internet as the global phenomenon that it truly is. Coverage of global issues is integrated into the appropriate subject areas. Global data are presented when appropriate, and examples of programs in various countries are seamlessly woven into content coverage. Where Internet-readiness, regulations, or culture affect Internet marketing activities, they are treated separately and specifically.

It is impossible to understand Internet marketing without having a layperson's appreciation of the technology that makes it possible. Technology is also covered in the context of the marketing activities affected by it, not as a separate issue. Complex technological subjects are explained in a manner that can be successfully grasped by those with only introductory or user-level familiarity with computer technology.

Organization of the Text

This second edition of the text contains fourteen chapters, compared with the fifteen in the first edition. What were previously two chapters, each on business models and social and regulatory issues, have been condensed into a single chapter each. An additional chapter on customer acquisition has been added to cover the ever-increasing array of technologies and applications used to reach prospective customers.

The fourteen chapters in this second edition are divided into three parts. Part I, The Foundations of Internet Marketing, contains the introductory chapter and chapters on the value chain, business models, and direct marketing and database fundamentals. Generic objectives of customer acquisition, conversion, and retention form the conceptual framework. Part II, Internet Strategies and Programs, covers the unique aspects of consumer behavior on the Internet and customer acquisition and retention programs. Customer service and support receives the attention it warrants as an important element of marketing strategy. The role of the website in both communications and transactions is approached from a strategic perspective. Part III, Evaluating Performance and Opportunities, covers the essential subjects of Web metrics, social and regulatory issues, and knowledge-based marketing programs. The future is viewed from the perspectives of a pervasive wireless Internet and a converged media environment that makes content available anywhere, anytime, anyplace.

Online and in Print

Internet Marketing: Integrating Online and Offline Strategies is available online as well as in print. The online version demonstrates how the interactive media components of the text enhance presentation and understand. For example,

- Clickable glossary terms provide immediate definitions of key concepts.
- References and footnotes "pop up" with a click.
- Highlighting capabilities allow students to emphasize main ideas. They can also add personal notes in the margin.
- The search function allows students to quickly locate discussions of specific topics throughout the text.
- An interactive study guide at the end of each chapter provides tools for learning, such interactive key-term matching and the ability to review customized content in one place.

Students may choose to use just the online version of the text or both the online and print versions together. This gives them the flexibility to choose which combination or resources works best for them. To assist those who use the online and print version together,

the primary heads and subheads in each chapter are numbered the same. For example, the first primary head in Chapter 1 is labeled 1–1, the second primary head in this chapter is labeled 1–2, and so on. The subheads build from the designation of their corresponding primary head: 1–1a, 1–1b, etc. This numbering system is designed to make moving between the online and print versions as seamless as possible.

Supplements

There is a robust set of supplemental materials available to instructors. It includes an Instructors' Manual, a full set of PowerPoint® slides, and a test bank presented as a Word document.

The Instructor's Manual includes a detailed discussion of each chapter that concentrates on ways to teach the material that make it as engaging as the subject it covers. It also includes suggestions and resources for updating coverage. The resources include content Web sites, online demonstrations and suggestions for using screen captures and live Internet material that will both enliven and update classroom presentations. The discussion is cross-indexed between text headings in each chapter and original PowerPoint® slide numbers for ease of reference. Answers to discussion questions and suggestions for using the end of chapter exercises are included. Inclusion of key terms and end of chapter quizzes from the text also provide for ease of use. Sample syllabi for both undergraduate and graduate Internet marketing courses are included.

The PowerPoint® slides contain comprehensive coverage of each chapter. They provide structure for student coverage of the material and an easy venue for instructors who wish to supplement and update text material. The chapter-by-chapter files are easy to use in the classroom and small enough to upload to course Web sites if instructors wish to provide them for note-taking and study purposes.

The author maintains a personal Web site with resource and supplemental material for her own classes at www.marylouroberts.info. Instructors are welcome to provide this material on their own sites or to have students access it directly. An email newsletter is planned that will offer key updates on a chapter-by-chapter basis prior to the beginning of each semester.

Acknowledgments

Both reviewers and adopters of the first edition have provided insightful comments that have been incorporated into the second edition. Reviewers of the second edition also provided helpful and timely commentary. Thanks to

- Alicia Aldridge, Appalachian State University
- Lewis S. Boyce, Jr., Albertus Magnus College
- Robert Moore, Mississippi State University
- Deborah M. Moscardelli, Central Michigan University

Internet marketers too numerous to mention have contributed their expertise. To all who have shared their work, answered e-mails and phone calls, and met with student groups, a very sincere thank you. Above all, the author would like to acknowledge students, past and present, who have shared their experience and expertise related to subjects throughout the text. In that spirit, the second edition is dedicated to all students of Internet marketing, both in the classroom and on the frontline of Internet marketing practice.

About the Author

Mary Lou Roberts has been a tenured professor of marketing at the University of Massachusetts Boston and held a number of administrative positions there including Director of Development. She is currently an adjunct at the University of Massachusetts Amherst and teaches Internet marketing to a global cadre of students at the Harvard University Extension School. Her Ph.D. in marketing is from the University of Michigan. In addition to *Internet Marketing: Integrating Online and Offline Strategies,* 2nd edition, she is senior author of *Direct Marketing Management,* 2nd ed. (available at www.marylouroberts.info).

She has published extensively in marketing journals in the U.S. and Europe and currently serves on a number of editorial review boards including the *Journal of Database Marketing,* the *Journal of Financial Services Marketing* and the *Journal of Consumer Marketing.* Her current scholarly work deals with information-driven marketing strategies, measurable marketing programs, marketing metrics and consumer-generated and social media.

Dr. Roberts is a frequent presenter on programs of both professional and academic marketing organizations, and has consulted and provided planning services and management training programs for a wide variety of corporations and non-profit organizations. Projects have been conducted for organizations including Chordiant, Citizens Bank, Region 1 of the Environmental Protection Agency, the Cape Cod Commission, the Affinity Group, Inc., the Paralyzed Veterans of America, the Museum of Science and the Massachusetts Audubon Society.

She has been an active member of many professional organizations and has served on a number of their boards. She served several terms as a director of the Boston Chapter of the American Marketing Association and two terms on the national board of the AMA. As a representative of the AMA, Dr. Roberts also served two terms on the advisory committee to the United States Bureau of the Census. She was a member of the Board of Directors of the Massachusetts Audubon Society for fifteen years, serving at various times as a member of the Executive Committee and chair of the Marketing Committee. She continues to be active with that organization as a member of their Advisory Council and Development and Marketing Committee.

Dr. Roberts is will soon be joining marketing firm Infomorphosis as a partner and interactive marketing specialist.

The Foundations of Internet Marketing

Part One

1

Internet Marketing Enters the Mainstream

Chapter One

Source: © Getty

Key Terms

2

Learning Objectives

By the time you complete this chapter, you will be able to:

- Briefly describe how the Internet originated and what makes it unique as a communications and transactions medium.
- Explain the advantages of the Internet for consumers and for businesses of all kinds.
- Understand the generic marketing objectives that form the basis for Internet marketing strategies.
- Describe the basic technical infrastructure of the Internet.
- Discuss the strategic and economic drivers of the Internet.

Wireless access, rich media, pop-ups and pop-unders, streaming media, broadband, HTML, blogging, DSL, bit torrents and more—these are only a few of the Internet-related terms that have entered the marketing vocabulary in recent years. Although these terms scratch only the surface, they suggest how complex marketing has become in the Internet age.

Marketers are caught up in revolutionary change that is fundamentally altering the operations of businesses around the globe. It is important that we understand these deep-seated changes in business processes and strategy before we attempt to specify marketing's roles and responsibilities in dealing with the new milieu. To do that, it will be helpful to understand how the technology got us to where we are today.

1-1 The Evolution of the Internet[1]

The Internet dates back to 1957, when the Soviet Union launched the Sputnik satellite and thereby started the "space race," in which it and the United States competed relentlessly for technological supremacy on the ground and in the skies. In the Cold War era, the fact that the Soviet Union was leading the way with space-focused technology caused U.S. military and defense institutions great concern. To close the gap, President Eisenhower created the Advanced Research Project Agency, or ARPA, which later came under the control of the Department of Defense as the Defense Advanced Research Project Agency (DARPA). DARPA's purpose was to fund scientific research, and the designers of the original ARPA system believed they could use the research mandate to develop an attack-proof communications structure for national defense purposes.

Two breakthroughs in computer science were necessary to support the system DARPA's developers visualized. The first of these was time-sharing, or the ability to run programs of multiple users at the same time on the same computer, using then-scarce computing resources to their fullest capacity. With the advent of time-sharing, the user was not aware that there were multiple programs executing simultaneously because the computer moved back and forth between jobs without user intervention. The second breakthrough was the linking of computers at participating institutions to the **ARPANet**, an early version of today's Internet.

The inspiration for the ARPANet came primarily from the scientist J. C. R. Licklider, who envisioned an "Intergalactic Network" of interconnected communities of scientists who would share computer resources, exchange ideas, and cooperate on scientific projects all from their own individual labs. The ARPANet, which ran on a system of telephone circuits and switching **nodes**, enabled human communication in a time- and distance-independent manner that was completely new but that remains today as the core legacy of this system. By the early 1970s, more than twenty institutions were participating, mostly universities and government agencies, linked by telephone

ARPANet Stands for Advanced Research Project Agency, originally an arm of the U.S. Department of Defense. In the 1950s, the Agency developed a connected system of computers that formed the basis of the modern Internet.

node A communications junction or connection point.

lines and satellites in the continental United States, Alaska, and Hawaii. In 1973, ARPANet became international when connections to University College in London, England, and the Royal Radar Establishment in Norway were established.

The original ARPANet was the exclusive domain of a few scientists who needed to interact with one other and were willing to learn the arcane control language that was required to operate the system. The system had the capacity to handle a large volume of traffic, but it had few users in its early days. To the dismay of some of the **network's** originators, ARPANet became more of a digital post office than a sophisticated research device. The volume of e-mail was far greater than the volume of long-distance computing, and the scientists were enthusiastic about their ability to engage in research collaboration and even gossip over great distances. The ARPANet, which in the 1980s fell under the auspices of the National Science Foundation (NSF), would remain limited to a select few users until the widespread adoption of the personal computer in the middle of the decade.

network A system that transmits voice, data, and video between users.

1-1a Fast Growth Leads to a 1990s Boom

Between 1982 and 1987, the foundations of the modern Internet were laid. One of the essential elements of the Internet that was developed during this period was **TCP/IP** (Transmission Control Protocol/Internet Protocol), the standard language of all Internet computing. During this time, use of the Internet grew rapidly at universities and research and development centers for science and technology. In 1984, there were 1,000 Internet host computers; by 1987, the number had grown to 10,000; by 1990, 300,000. The rapid growth of the Internet contributed to the decommissioning of the ARPANet in 1990, although the NSF continued to operate the telecommunications backbone for the network. NSF banned commercial traffic on the Internet until 1991.

TCP/IP Transmission Control Protocol/Internet Protocol, the communications protocol (standard) of the Internet. It permits the accurate transmission of messages over otherwise incompatible networks.

Prior to 1991, the rapid growth of the Internet made it difficult for users to find information in a timely manner. This obstacle to efficient Internet use changed in 1991 with two important developments: "gopher" search tools and the code for the World Wide Web. With the release of gopher search tools, which were distributed free over the net, users were able to search in a text-only format. That same year the first code for the World Wide Web was posted on a newsgroup by Tim Berners-Lee—today credited as the founder of the modern Internet—scientist at the European Particle Physics Laboratory (CERN) in Switzerland. Berners-Lee's system included a simple language called **hypertext** markup language, or **HTML**. HTML was easy for users to learn—especially in comparison to the majority of programming languages—and can be created on any text editor or word processor. In time HTML was expanded to allow the posting of not only words but also pictures and sound files.

hypertext Allows one document, or one portion of a document, to be linked to another.

HTML Hypertext markup language, one of the foundations of the common Internet platform. HTML describes the structure of Web documents using a type of coding called tags.

1-1b The First Geographical Browser Arrives

In 1993, a graphical **browser** called Mosaic was introduced, and the ordinary computer user could move around the Web in today's familiar point-and-click mode instead of having to learn the cumbersome search terms required by gopher search tools. With the advent of Yahoo!'s commercial Web site in 1995, users could locate information on the Web with relative ease using a dedicated search engine. The Internet's growth rate shot up, both in terms of access points and daily use, and it has continued unabated.

browser A program that allows a user to connect to the World Wide Web by simply typing in a URL.

This phenomenal growth of the Internet during the late 1990s was extraordinary by almost all measures—number of households and businesses connected, number of Web sites, and amount of business conducted over the net were only a few. What did not grow as quickly—in fact, did not grow at all—were profits from the many enterprises that blossomed as part of the emerging Internet economy. Investors around the world bought the hype surrounding the Internet and put their resources in e-business models that appeared to have no hope of a profitable future. The market capitalizations of many

Internet firms soared until they greatly exceeded that of profitable businesses in the physical world. It was also clear that in both the business-to-consumer (B2C) and business-to-business (B2B) arenas, there was a greater number of Internet firms than there was the potential business to support them. It was a situation that could not continue.

1-1c The Internet Bubble Bursts

In mid-2000 and 2001, an upheaval took place. Venture capital became unavailable and many unprofitable, purely Internet-based firms could not survive without it. Stock market values for even the leading Internet firms dropped many-fold. As a result, major suppliers of Internet products and services, telecommunications carriers, and the burgeoning wireless market were all seriously damaged in the eyes of investors. High prices paid for licenses for wireless spectrum by European firms worsened their financial position. Public euphoria about Internet business disappeared and media pundits speculated that e-commerce—business conducted on the Internet—was a short-term phenomenon that had run its course.

However, events since 2002 have proved the naysayers wrong. Consider the following:

- The number of Internet users worldwide was estimated to be 934 million in 2004, with projections showing it growing to 1.08 billion in 2005 and 1.8 billion by 2010.[2]
  - The United States alone has more than 203 million users; China has more than 103 million and Japan has more than 78 million.[3]
  - Although the global penetration of the Internet is only about 15.2%, 30 countries had penetration rates exceeding 50% of all households as of November 30, 2005. Leading the way is Iceland, with penetration of 76.5%, while the Scandinavian countries are close behind. The United States had a household penetration rate of 68.7%.[4]
- The volume of goods sold online is growing at a rapid pace:
  - Online retail sales amounted to $143.2 billion in 2005. That is a growth of 22% in a single year and 6% of total retail spending.[5] Forrester Research expects the double-digit growth to continue, projecting online retail sales of $316 billion, or 12% of total retail sales, by 2010.[6]
    - During the holiday shopping season in 2005, retail giant Wal-Mart had the most visitors to its site—27.7 visitors, an increase of 47% over the previous year. Others in the top ten online retail sites for the season included Target, with 23 million visitors (39% growth), and Best Buy with 17.2 million visitors (30% growth).[7] Their presence in the top ten, along with dominant online retailers like Amazon and eBay, underscores the role Internet marketing is beginning to play in the overall marketing strategies of all kinds of businesses.
  - eMarketer estimated that worldwide B2B e-commerce would exceed $2.3 *trillion* in 2004.[8]

The Internet continues to evolve.[9] A consortium of universities, corporations, and government agencies is developing a network called Internet2. This closed network is currently limited to paying members who are willing to contribute to the development of a better Internet. The current version is said to be about 100 times faster than the public Internet.[10] The concept is being developed around ideas of seamless content that moves freely over various media channels. It places emphasis on consumer control, social networks, and consumer creation of content, topics that are discussed in Chapter 6.[11]

Many of the commercial survivors of the early e-commerce crash were enterprises that had both physical world and Internet presences. Even though the Internet had only recently emerged as part of the public consciousness, businesses like Sabre Holdings had been developing their information-based strategies for many years. Consequently, when the Internet became commercially viable, they were ready to seize the opportunity it offered to improve existing systems and build new ones.

Box 1-1   Sabre timeline.

1957

IBM and American Airlines team up to form the Semi-Automatic Business Research Environment (known as Sabre). It's based on the Semi-Automatic Ground Environment (SAGE)—the first major system to use interactive, real-time computing—which IBM helped develop for the military.

1960

The first Sabre reservation system is installed in Briarcliff Manor, New York, on two IBM 7090 computers. It processes 84,000 telephone calls per day.

1964

The Sabre system, with its nationwide network is completed at a cost of $40 million and becomes the largest commercial real-time data-processing system in the world. It saves American Airlines 30 percent on labor costs.

1972

The Sabre system is upgraded to IBM S/360 and moved to a new consolidated computer center in Tulsa, Oklahoma. It is used for all of American Airlines' data-processing facilities.

1976

the Sabre system is installed in a travel agency for the first time, triggering a wave of travel automation. By the end of the year, 130 locations have the system.

1984

Sabre introduces BargainFinder, the industry's first automated low-fare search capability. Competitors sue American Airlines, saying its Sabre system unfairly gives its flights priority on the displays travel agents see. American agrees to discontinue any preferential treatment of its flights.

1985

Sabre introduces easySabre, allowing consumers with PCs to tap into the Sabre system to make airline, hotel, and car rental reservations.

1989

On May 12, the ultrareliable Sabre system goes down for 12 hours. The cause: a latent bug in disc-drive software that destroys file addresses.

1996

Sabre launches Travelocity.com.

2000

AMR Corporation, the parent of American Airlines, spins off The Sabre Group as an independent company.

2001

Sabre Holdings Corporation begins migrating its massive, 25-year old mainframe system for air-travel shopping and pricing to HP NonStop servers and Linux servers.

Source: Gary Antehes, "Sidebar: Sabre Timeline," http://www.computerworld.com/managementtopics/management/project/story/0,10801,93453,00.html?from=story_packages.

1-2 The Sabre System

What is now the Sabre travel reservation system began quite innocently in the 1960s as an internal system for reservations agents at American Airlines. Only reservations agents, first in the Dallas call center headquarters and soon thereafter at airport terminals, were allowed to access the system. At that time customers who needed to make a flight reservation had only two options: they used a travel agent or they booked reservations directly by calling the airline. Using two IBM 7090 mainframe computers, the Sabre system was able to process 84,000 telephone calls from customers and travel agents each day. Because the information technology (IT) environment was still composed of mainframe computers that required massive amounts of tedious custom programming, the research and development and installation of the Sabre system took 400 man-years of effort and cost almost $40 million. Although return on investment (ROI) was not easy to calculate, by the time the system was fully deployed in 1964 it was saving American Airlines 30% each year in staff time, had an error rate of less than 1%, and was believed to deliver a competitive advantage that would last for 5 to 7 years.

It was not until 1976 that the system was first installed in a travel agency. This gave agents direct access to the system database and allowed them to book reservations without the assistance of the American Airlines call center. By year-end, there were 130 installations and the Sabre system held a market share of 86%. In 1985, the introduction of easySABRE® allowed consumers to use personal computers to access the system for airline, hotel, and car rental reservations. Along the way, various applications had been added to perform tasks such as airline yield management and crew scheduling. In 1988, Sabre began to offer these services to other airlines. By early 2000, Sabre claimed that almost all airlines around the world used one or more of their IT modules to control some aspect of flight and business operations from passenger boarding and cargo operations to sales automation and human resources functions.

By 1996, the Sabre system had become an important business entity in and of itself. It continued its growth by establishing Travelocity.com to offer travel and lodging reservation services on the Internet. AMR, the holding company, which also controls American Airlines, made Sabre a separate legal entity in that year. In March 2000, AMR distributed the 83% of Sabre shares that it still held, making it a fully publicly traded company with revenues of $2.4 billion.

1-2a Becoming an Information Product

To the consumer, Sabre offers direct booking of airline, hotel, and car rental reservations through its Travelocity.com Web site. They also offer a personal page called "My Stuff" that contains all the details about an individual's travel plans and allows the traveler to access information about the destination that ranges from restaurants to weather. It provides access to departure times and gate assignments and to the Flight Tracker service, which allows not only the traveler but also business associates, family, and friends to track flight progress and arrival times. The system is also accessible to a variety of wireless handheld devices.

To the business traveler, it offers a Business Travel Network with all the functionality of the base site and additional features of special interest. Special functions include Repeat a Trip, which allows easy booking of frequently used travel itinerary; a Currency Converter; Flight Paging in which Travelocity.com sends flight status information directly to the traveler's pager; and an Email or Fax Your Itinerary for easy sharing of information with colleagues and family.

To the business, Sabre offers services that assist in the management and containment of employee travel costs. One service, called Get There, allows business travelers to make their own travel reservations from the corporation's list of approved vendors. Business people find it easy to make travel arrangements, and corporations use it to manage costs. For travel agents, Sabre offers a variety of computerized reservations platforms, depending on agency needs, along with consulting and management services.[12]

Business organizations like Sabre were early movers in developing information-driven business processes and marketing strategies. When the Internet opened up new possibilities, they were ready to seize the opportunities. They were among the first to understand that the Internet had created an environment for communications and transactions that was unlike any other that had ever existed. Some of their efforts, like the OnStar system to be discussed later in the chapter, became **information products**.

information product A commercial product that consists solely of data.

1-3 Consumer Adoption of the Internet

Consumers around the world also realized that the Internet provided an unsurpassed forum for communicating and acquiring information. A 2004 study documented the fact that the Internet has become a part of daily life in a relatively few years. The 1,358 adult Internet users surveyed in the United States said that the net affects the way they conduct their everyday life. According to the report:

- 88% of online Americans say the Internet plays a role in their daily routines. Of those, one-third say it plays a major role and two-thirds say it plays a minor role. The activities they identified as most significant are communicating with family and friends and finding a wealth of information at their fingertips.

> **FIGURE 1-1** Internet Activities

According to our February–April 2006 survey, 73%
of American adults use the Internet. That currently
represents about 147 million people.

Here are some of the things they do online:	Percent of internet users who report this activity	Most recent survey date
Send or read e-mail	91	December 2005
Use a search engine to find information	91	December 2005
Search for a map or driving directions	84	February 2004
Look for health/medical info	79	November 2004
Research a product or service before buying it	78	February–March 2005
Check the weather	78	November 2004
Look for info on a hobby or interest	77	November 2004
Get travel info	73	May–June 2004
Get news	68	December 2005
Buy a product	67	May–June 2005
Surf the Web for fun	66	December 2005
Buy or make a reservation for travel	63	September 2005
Look for political news/info	58	November 2004
Go to a Web site that provides info or support for a specific medical condition or personal situation	58	November 2004
Research for school or training	57	January 2005
Watch a video clip or listen to an audio clip	56	November 2004
Look for "how-to," "do-it-yourself" or repair information	55	February–March 2005
Look for info from a government Web site	54	November 2004
Look up phone number or address	54	February 2004
Do any type of research for your job	50	December 2005

Source: Pew Internet & American Life Project Tracking surveys (March 2000–April 2006).

- 64% of Internet users say their daily routines and activities would be affected if they could no longer use the Internet.
- 53% of Internet users say they do more of certain everyday activities simply because they can do them on the Internet. The most popular are "communicating with family and friends" and "looking up information."[13]

Figure 1-1 gives a sense of the many ways in which people make use of the Internet in their daily lives. Does this list correspond with your own usage of the Web and with what you see friends, family, and coworkers doing on a daily basis? If consumers had made the Internet part of their daily lives, could the businesses that serve them be far behind?

1-4 Businesses and Governments Move onto the Internet

As both consumers and businesses make greater use of the Internet for activities ranging from communications to gathering information to completing transactions, organizations of all kinds have responded by making greater use of the Internet for marketing purposes. Internet advertising dropped briefly by 15.8% in 2002 as a result of the dot-com collapse, but since then, it has grown 20% per year. Online advertising revenue was about $12 billion in 2005 and is forecasted to grow another 20% to 30% in 2006.[14]

Unlike the early years of e-commerce on the commercial Internet, when much of the Internet advertising was done by start-ups that vanished along with the bubble, the way is now being led by large corporations who have been heavy advertisers in traditional mass media. According to *Advertising Age,* AT&T Wireless Services increased the number of online advertising items by 1,262% in 2004. Pharmaceutical marketer Schering-Plough followed suit, with an increase of 737%, and consumer credit services firm MBNA Corporation's online advertising grew by 471%. Automobile manufacturers were also among those who increased their online advertising expenditures by substantial amounts.[15]

Lexus, for example, has substantially reallocated its marketing budget for certified pre-owned (CPO) cars in recent years, treating CPO as a third product category in the Lexus line. According to Marv Ingram, national CPO/fleet manager for Lexus:

> [Based on our market research, we found that] approximately 70 to 80 percent of luxury car shoppers use the Internet in the research phase of their shopping process, [and] we created a program that would address these issues.[16]

Like corporations, governmental entities are discovering the power of the Internet to improve their operations and provide services to their citizens. According to a study by consulting firm Accenture, Canada has led the way in online government initiatives for 4 years in a row. Canada's e-government program has two specific goals: to have the most commonly used services online by its citizens and to achieve a 10% increase in citizen satisfaction by 2005. Canadian e-government achievements have consistently been rated above those of other leading countries, including the United States and Singapore. Drivers of its success include regular surveys of the needs of individuals and businesses and the use of focus groups to evaluate the portals that provide access to important government services.[17]

These examples represent a growing realization by traditional bricks and mortar enterprises and government agencies that the Internet can provide a cost-effective addition to their communications channels. A survey of chief marketing officers finds 64% saying that the strategic importance of digital marketing in their firm is high or very high (Diagram a in Figure 1-2), with 39% indicating that more than 20% of their marketing budget would be spent online (Diagram b in Figure 1-2). They are using digital techniques to meet many marketing objectives (Diagram c in Figure 1-2) because of its low cost, speed of delivery, and measurable ROI (Diagram d in Figure 1-2).

The Internet has infiltrated the daily lives of consumers and the strategies of marketers because it offers capabilities that are unique to it as a medium of communications.

1-5 The Unique Characteristics of the Internet

When the Internet began to emerge in the public consciousness in the mid-1990s, no one really believed that it would spread through the global economy as quickly as it has. Consumers were generally indifferent, and business executives thought they had ample time to understand and adapt to the requirements of the new medium. To the surprise of all, it has diffused throughout the world more quickly than any other medium in modern history.

Diffusion theory suggests that rapid adoption implies a relative advantage on the part of the new product or service. The Internet has a number of characteristics that

FIGURE 1-2 Strategic role for digital marketing.

(a) Describe the level of strategic importance placed on the digital marketing in your company.

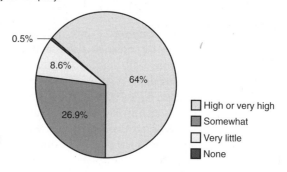

- High or very high
- Somewhat
- Very little
- None

0.5%
8.6%
64%
26.9%

(b) What is the estimated percentage of marketing budget your company spent towards digital marketing this year and in 2004?

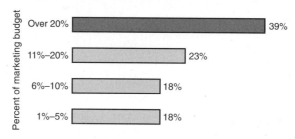

Percent of marketing budget

Over 20%	39%
11%–20%	23%
6%–10%	18%
1%–5%	18%

(c) For what purpose is digital marketing being employed in your company?

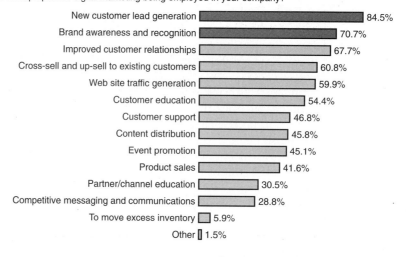

New customer lead generation	84.5%
Brand awareness and recognition	70.7%
Improved customer relationships	67.7%
Cross-sell and up-sell to existing customers	60.8%
Web site traffic generation	59.9%
Customer education	54.4%
Customer support	46.8%
Content distribution	45.8%
Event promotion	45.1%
Product sales	41.6%
Partner/channel education	30.5%
Competitive messaging and communications	28.8%
To move excess inventory	5.9%
Other	1.5%

(d) What are the top three drivers and imperatives for digital marketing in your company?

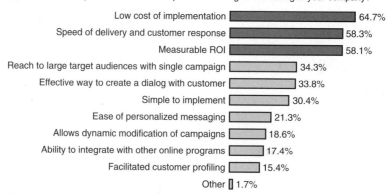

Low cost of implementation	64.7%
Speed of delivery and customer response	58.3%
Measurable ROI	58.1%
Reach to large target audiences with single campaign	34.3%
Effective way to create a dialog with customer	33.8%
Simple to implement	30.4%
Ease of personalized messaging	21.3%
Allows dynamic modification of campaigns	18.6%
Ability to integrate with other online programs	17.4%
Facilitated customer profiling	15.4%
Other	1.7%

Source: CMO Council, "The Digital Marketing Dialog."

differentiate it from any other medium or channel in history and that have contributed to its rapid diffusion. Unique characteristics of the Internet include:

- a single, *common **platform*** for communications and transactions throughout the world. Computer scientists may argue that TCP/IP is not ideal, but its universal acceptance as the Internet standard makes it valuable in a way that far surpasses its inherent functionality. Individuals and corporations can interact with one another over a common network with little additional investment in either software or communications hardware. That creates a medium for communications and a channel for commercial transactions unlike any that has existed in the past.

- a method of information supply that approaches the *"perfect information"* of economic theory. Consumers and business customers alike can obtain information from any Web-enabled organization quickly and at little or no cost. That allows them to broaden the scope of their search activities, which were previously limited to vendors that are geographically nearby or to which they have access through media such as catalogs and television advertisements. Not only is the scope of search increased, but the depth of information that can be obtained on the Internet is much greater than what is available via other media.

- an ***interactive*** nature of communications in this medium that affords an unparalleled opportunity for meaningful dialog with customers and suppliers alike. It also creates the specter of unparalleled intrusion into the private affairs of Internet users.

- a *global* scope. Assuming that the necessary infrastructure is available, any individual, business, or nonprofit organization in the world can connect to the Internet and avail themselves of its functions in exactly the same way as other users. Practical problems of languages, and to some extent cultures, still exist, but the Internet is a global medium to an extent that has never before been true.

- the opportunity for organizations to compete on a level playing field *regardless of size or distance*. Neither the size nor the location of an enterprise is apparent to a visitor to its Web site unless the enterprise chooses to make it so. To that extent, the playing field has been leveled. At the same time, the advantages of ample financial resources and a respected brand name cannot be understated in the increasingly competitive and demanding Internet environment.

- an *"always on"* communications network. It allows consumers and businesses alike to access information, entertainment, and businesses services on a 24/7/365 basis.

- a **"many-to-many"** communications network, as compared with one-to-one networks like the telephone or one-to-many systems like television or radio broadcast.[18]

The combined effect of these unique characteristics is a network that can reach anywhere on the planet, connecting any set of persons or organizations who choose to be connected. The result is strategic opportunities and options that were previously unthinkable. In addition, because incremental costs of adding nodes to the network are negligible, the economics of business processes are being changed in profound ways. According to Mercer Management Consulting, there are four ways in which the Internet affects business processes, not at the margin, but by orders of magnitude:

- *Cost*. An online bank transaction costs $0.04 versus more than $1 for a transaction at a branch, a greater than 25 × factor of improvement.

- *Quality*. The design process for the Boeing 777, being entirely electronic, generated one-tenth the number of errors generated by the prior physical design process.

- *Customer Access*. Whereas a large retail store might be lucky to get 50,000 visitors a month, a leading electronic retailer can get 5 million visitors or more each month—a 100-fold improvement.

platform The hardware and software architecture, including the operating system, on which computers run.

interactive Media or channels that permit two-way communications, for instance, between a marketer and potential customer.

many-to-many A communications system in which there are many recipients of communications and many sources of those same communications.

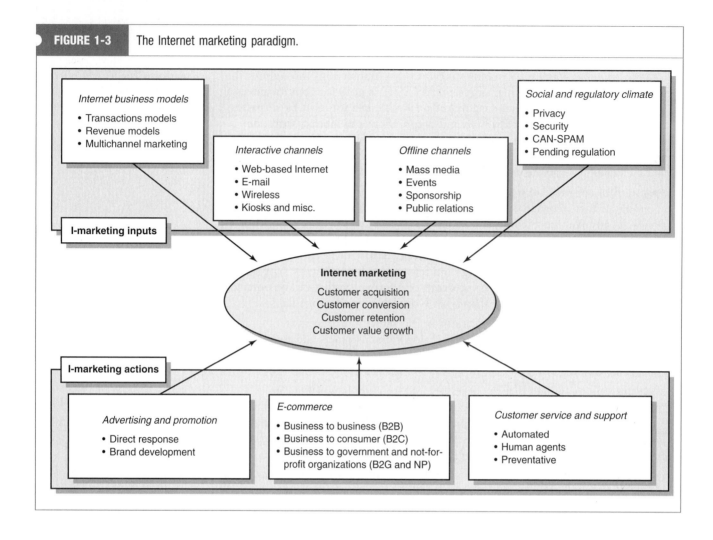

FIGURE 1-3   The Internet marketing paradigm.

- *Choice*. Amazon.com, the Internet's leading retailer, "stocks" more than 4 million books, roughly 25 times the assortment of a Borders superstore.[19]

The Internet is changing business processes in fundamental ways. It is altering the nature of our relationships with customers and other stakeholders and broadening the base of those who interact in meaningful ways with the businesses. It enhances speed and affects timing of activities of many kinds. Above all, it transforms the nature of successful organizations. Hierarchical organizations lack the flexibility to compete in the information-driven economy. Vertical integration no longer offers substantial benefits in either cost or control. Traditional corporate boundaries blur as information moves freely across them, and the most effective organization is often a virtual one.

1-5a Marketing in the Unique Internet Environment

In this environment, marketing takes on new and challenging roles. The nature of the Internet marketing milieu is portrayed in Figure 1-3.

The milieu in which Internet marketing takes place is seen as a complex environment in which marketers attempt to achieve four distinct generic goals:

acquisition The process of obtaining new customers.

- Customer **acquisition** is a foundation goal of all marketers. To grow and thrive, all businesses must attract a continuing stream of new customers. Internet marketing adds another communications channel and a variety of techniques to the customer acquisition effort.

- Customer **conversion** is the process of changing visitors, shoppers, or prospects into actual customers. It requires persuading the customer who has simply made contact, say by visiting a Web site, to make a purchase or to engage in a set of interactions that will eventually result in a purchase.

- Customer **retention** involves turning the newly found customer into a loyal one who will remain with the enterprise over an extended period. Marketers have learned that it is cheaper to retain customers than to acquire them and that they must therefore focus some of their activities specifically on retention.

- Growth in **customer value**, that is, the equity that exists in the enterprise's customer base, is the end goal of the acquisition, conversion, and retention process. Marketers have discovered that not all customers are equally profitable. Internet marketers can track customer behavior, calculate the profitability of individual customers, and improve the value of the overall customer base.

The actions that permit marketers to achieve these generic goals take place in an increasingly complex environment. It is made up of an external environment that affects marketing activities of all kinds and of the actions that marketers themselves take. These can be characterized as the inputs and actions of Internet marketing.

1-5b The Marketing Inputs and Actions for the Internet Environment

In the information-driven Internet economy, marketing decisions are made in an increasingly complex environment characterized as producing the I-Marketing Inputs displayed in Figure 1-3. These inputs are the specific environmental factors that affect the way Internet marketing is done.

The inputs include the following:

- The business models that are prominent on the Internet.
  - *Transactions* models are the way in which Internet businesses organize to carry out exchange, whether it be content or commercial transactions.
  - **Revenue models** are the various streams of revenue that businesses can employ to support their activities. The importance of online activities in the development of supplier/manufacturer/customer value chains are discussed in Chapter 2. Both transactions and revenue models are discussed in Chapter 3.
  - **Multichannel** marketing is the driving force behind many business models. It is discussed as it affects customer acquisition in Chapters 6 and 7, customer retention in Chapter 8, and customer service and support in Chapter 9. Multichannel marketing requires the integration of both offline (physical world) and online (interactive) channels.
- The *interactive* channels that permit Internet communication and commerce include the following:
  - *Web site* on the Internet. The creation of Web sites that produce satisfying customer experience is discussed in Chapter 10.
  - *E-mail marketing* has become an important technique for customer acquisition in Chapter 7 and especially for customer retention in Chapter 8.
  - *Wireless marketing* over the Internet is a burgeoning channel that is discussed in Chapter 14.
  - There are a number of *other interactive channels,* with kiosks being the most rapidly growing around the world, that are discussed in Chapter 7.
- The *offline* channels—including the **mass media** of print and broadcast, marketer-created events, sponsorships, and public relations—that represent an important part of the integrated communications process. They are discussed as they impact online channels and multichannel marketing throughout the book.
- The *social and regulatory* issues that have become increasingly important as the Internet has achieved a place among the major communications channels. Issues

conversion The process of moving a prospect from consideration to purchase.

retention Preventing existing customers from defecting to another supplier.

customer value The worth of a single customer to the enterprise.

revenue model The way or ways in which a firm makes its money from marketplace transactions.

multichannel Using more than one channel of distribution to reach the customer.

mass media Media that are characterized by large audiences and relatively few sources of messages, often referred to as one-to-many communications channels.

including consumer data privacy and security in Chapter 12 have a great deal of impact on marketer actions, and are discussed in detail later. Other social and regulatory issues, such as e-mail spam and the efforts to combat it, are discussed in the context of the channel or technique.

The *Actions* that marketers can take to avail themselves of the Internet as a powerful channel for communications and transactions include:

- *online advertising and promotion* that can be used to incite the viewer to immediate action or to build the image of the brand. Many kinds of online advertisements exist, ranging from static banners to full-page rich media ads to ride-along ads. These are discussed in Chapter 6. Other types of online promotional activities such as email marketing, sponsorships, events and optimized press releases will be discussed in Chapter 7. Each of these techniques has a potential role in either encouraging the visitor to take immediate action or developing the brand image.

e-commerce Buying and selling goods and services online.

- **e-commerce**, which refers to commercial transactions on the Internet. Consumer, business, not-for-profit, and governmental marketers are all using the Internet for transactions ranging from purchase of goods and services to renewal of driver's licenses to contributions to charitable causes. E-commerce issues are discussed in various contexts throughout the book.

- *customer service and support,* which is taking its place as a key marketer activity, largely as a result of the emphasis on customer retention. Through judicious use of the Internet, the quality of customer service can be improved while simultaneously decreasing the cost to deliver. Customer service and support is the subject of Chapter 9.

The marketing inputs and actions are the focus of this text. No single input or action, however, is particularly effective on its own. *The strategic imperative is to integrate all marketing activities, online and offline, into a seamless whole.* That is the message that pervades discussion of concepts and the real-world examples that are given throughout this text.

To understand the environment in which the Internet marketing activities take place it is important to understand the basics of the technical infrastructure that supports them. This is often referred to as "the Internet infrastructure stack" because it is, in fact, a set of interrelated technologies that build and depend on one another to create the network we know as the Internet.

infrastructure stack A term used to describe the various layers of hardware, software, and purchased services that make up the network on which the Internet runs.

telecommunications The network of copper land lines, fiber-optic cables, and wireless transmitters that allows voice, data, text, graphics, and video to be transmitted over long distances.

broadband High-speed transmission over telecommunications networks.

hosting Locating a Web site on the servers that will make it available to the Internet. Hosting can be done internally or by specialty suppliers that offer hosting and associated services such as Web metrics.

1-6 The Internet Infrastructure Stack

The technical infrastructure of the Internet is portrayed in Figure 1-4. Forming the backbone of the **infrastructure stack** is the **telecommunications** connection, either narrowband or **broadband**. Telecommunications services, both wired and wireless, are provided by a variety of carriers in an atmosphere that is increasingly competitive as a result of deregulation efforts around the world.

1-6a Hosting

A Web site must be housed on a server, an operation commonly called **hosting**. The server that hosts the site must be connected to the network and is dedicated wholly or in part to performing the functions needed to operate the site. Many organizations, primarily those with either high levels of technical expertise or small Web sites, perform this function internally. Other organizations, both large and small, choose to outsource this highly technical function to external services firms that provide the hosting function.

FIGURE 1-4   The Internet infrastructure stack.

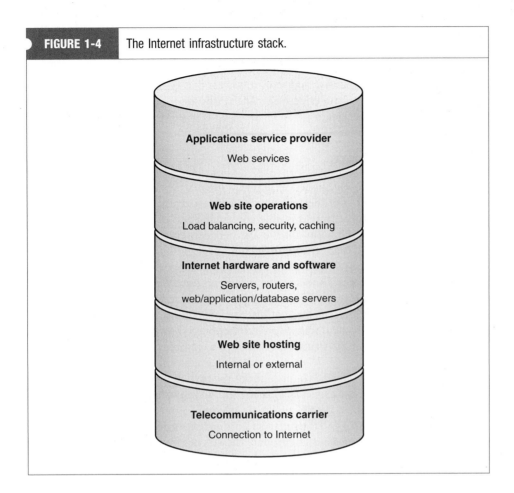

One reason for the increasingly common decision to outsource Web site hosting is the

1-6b Hardware and Software

One reason for the increasingly common decision to outsource Web site hosting is the large investment required in specialized *Internet hardware and software*. The hardware includes computers needed to serve Web pages to visitors as well as increasingly large amounts of either computer or network-based storage required to hold the content and databases that drive Web services. It also includes a great deal of specialized telecommunications hardware—items such as fiber-optic cables, routers, and bridgers,[20] for example. Both the computer and telecommunications hardware are driven by specialized software necessary to connect to the Internet and to run the specific applications programs that drive the functionality of the site.

1-6c Operations

The next level on the stack is the *operation* of the site, that is, the day-to-day work of keeping the system running and of fine-tuning it to provide a high level of uptime and fast and dependable downloading of pages to users. This is a purely technical part of the Web infrastructure, and marketers do not need specialized knowledge of the daily operational issues. They do, however, need to exhibit consistent concern about the efficient operation of the site because that is a necessary element of providing a good visitor experience.

1-6d Service Providers and Outsourcing

At the top level of the stack is the *applications service provider, Web services solution,* or *other outsourcing options*. Applications services providers (ASPs) provide network access to the software applications that are needed for Web site functionality. This can include applications like data warehousing and personalization, both of which are discussed in later chapters as important parts of Internet marketing programs. Organizations can choose to purchase or license applications like this and run them internally, but they are expensive and require a great deal of technical skill to integrate with other software and to run effectively. ASPs, who essentially "rent software," are discussed as a business model in Chapter 3.

1-6e Services and Strategies

Web services is a term loosely applied to applications that let diverse pieces of software interact with one another over the Internet. Because enterprises have large investments in software solutions, and because it is time-consuming and expensive to change them, the concept of systems that allow interaction between enterprises without changing software is attractive. This is an enterprise integration technique discussed in Chapter 2. There are many other ways of outsourcing activities that support Internet marketing. For example, there are companies who serve advertisements onto Web sites, vendors of e-mail software and services, and companies who supply customer service and support solutions of various types. Issues of outsourcing Internet marketing activities as opposed to conducting them in-house are discussed at various points throughout the book.

In fact, the entire infrastructure stack implies a complex set of "make or buy" decisions with regard to the Web site and the execution of Internet marketing programs. This subject is referred to throughout the text. At this point, it is sufficient to recognize the reasons for the existence of this issue. An important driver of outsourcing is the lack of the specialized technical experts needed to develop and maintain these systems. Both the personnel and the infrastructure are expensive, and unless they can be fully utilized, it is more economical to procure the services from outside firms. Finally, a carefully reasoned outsourcing strategy can permit the organization to concentrate on its own areas of product and marketing expertise, leaving many of the essential but bothersome technical details to others. That means that the organization can react with more speed and precision to both problems and opportunities.

Throughout the text the critical importance of organizational flexibility and speed in bringing products and services to market is emphasized. As a commercial medium, the Internet is still in its early stages, and experimentation and change are everywhere. For the foreseeable future, managers will live in a milieu characterized by constant change. In large part their success will be determined by their ability to react swiftly and in a meaningful way to environmental change. Yet, in the midst of ongoing change, there are strategic and economic drivers that establish the ground rules for success in the Internet economy.

1-7 Drivers of the Internet Economy[21]

There are many versions of the drivers and many books and articles devoted to a single aspect of the Internet economy. The list of drivers in Table 1-1 incorporates a variety of perspectives into a comprehensive set of dimensions.

Taken together, the drivers presented in Table 1-1 describe an information-driven macroenvironment that differs in many respects from the resource-based economy of the past.

1-7a Driver One—Information Produces the Greatest Value, Either as Added Value for Existing Products or Services or in the Form of Information Products

The focus of economic activity has switched from the production of physical goods to the manipulation of information that increases customer value. Many Internet businesses have been built on the concept of using information to provide greater

TABLE 1-1	Drivers of the Internet Economy

1. Information produces the greatest value, either as added value for existing products or services or in the form of information products.
2. Distance does not matter in many types of communications and transactions.
3. Speed is of the essence.
4. People are the key assets in Internet enterprises.
5. Growth in the network causes exponential increase in value.
6. Marketers can deal with customers on a one-to-one basis.
7. Demand can be predicted with greater accuracy.
8. Cost patterns change as transaction and coordination costs shrink for businesses, and consumers recognize that switching costs are low.
9. Consumers have power in information-rich channels.
10. An information economy is characterized by choice and abundance.

customer satisfaction. Jed Smith, the founder of online retailer drugstore.com, saw the health and beauty aid sector as presenting a number of opportunities to use information to enhance value. These over-the-counter products have a major information component that consumers wanted and were willing to acquire over the net. The industry was large, cumbersome, and extremely slow. Smith believed that technology could be used meet consumers' needs in a more efficient manner. He opened drugstore.com in 1999 with "a clear mission: to serve the health, beauty, and wellness consumer with selection, convenience, information, personal service, and a trustworthy and reliable pharmacy."[22] In 2000, drugstore.com acquired Beauty.com, a marketer of upmarket beauty products, and in 2003, it acquired VisionDirect, the Web's second largest retailer of contact lenses. It also has marketing partnerships with a number of online and offline merchants, including Amazon.com, retail drug chain Rite-Aid, and GNC, a marketer of vitamins and supplements. Chief Marketing Officer Kathy Gersch says that 95% of the customers who come to drugstore.com through their partners are new customers, making partnerships an important customer acquisition technique.[23]

Drugstore.com describes the value proposition they offer to consumers as being composed of the following:

- Convenience. Drugstore.com provides the ability to shop 24/7, supported by things like e-mail reminders and onsite shopping lists. One strategic partnership allows consumers to order their prescriptions online and pick them up at a nearby Rite-Aid pharmacy.

- Selection. As an Internet retailer, drugstore.com can offer more products than a traditional retailer—three to four times as many, according to the company's Web site.

- Information. Adding value by offering more information than consumers find at retail stores has been a hallmark of drugstore.com from the beginning. They offer content that includes editorials, product comparisons, and encyclopedias of vitamins and herbs. Directly relevant information, such as product comparisons, is located near the point of purchase to facilitate immediate decisions.

- Shopping experience. Personalizing and providing features that make shopping easier are ways in which drugstore.com uses the interactivity of the Internet. A shopping list records previous purchases for easy repurchase. It recommends substitute items if something on the list has been discontinued. The shopper can set up a personalized store stocked with favorite products or brands. This provides convenience for the shopper and a great deal of purchase pattern information for drugstore.com. It is a large site, so to reduce the frustration of, "I know I saw the product, but I can't find it again," there is a "recently viewed areas" section that allows the visitor to efficiently return to places where he or she has recently shopped. The visitor can also clear this area if desired.

- Confidentiality. Shoppers who patronize drugstore.com and its affiliates can shop without discomfort or embarrassment for personal items such as laxatives, tampons, condoms, and even sex toys. The site allows for a mostly anonymous shopping experience and ships in discreet packages.

Drugstore.com also offers the experience found in physical drugstores. There are coupons, sales, and various types of promotion. If the shopper wishes, drugstore.com will e-mail information about promotions and new products and services can be delivered in the form of an electronic newsletter.

There is a potential downside to all this information, however. For many years, existing businesses and industries have been drowning in data, finding it difficult to turn these data into useful information. For example, the average supermarket carries between 30,000 and 40,000 items, and keeping track of all of the various kinds of stock has traditionally proved very difficult. Various technologies and applications tried to improve the situation, but the only accepted standard was the **Universal Product Code** (UPC) and checkout scanners. In fact, while those developments did permit closer tracking at all levels of distribution, they only added to the deluge of data that was more than manufacturers, distributors, or retailers could meaningfully utilize. The connectivity of the Internet offered a potential solution by allowing enterprises to connect to their suppliers in a way that makes effective use of the data and provides better service to customers. Today, **RFID (radio frequency identification)** tags are making the process more open and precise.

When it comes to the Internet, the best product and service candidates are ones that either have a major information component like travel services, as in the Sabre example, or where information can be added in a way that improves the buying experience and/or decreases risk, as in the health and beauty aid market.

UPC Universal Product Code; codes embedded in bars and printed on items of merchandise. The codes can be read by checkout and handheld scanners.

RFID Radio frequency identification tags; tiny computer chips that can be affixed to any item of merchandise which then transmits data to a radio transponder.

1-7b Driver Two—Distance Does Not Matter in Many Types of Communications and Transactions

Limitations imposed by distance on the acquisition of knowledge and commercial exchange have been reduced or, in some cases, completely eliminated. Buyers and sellers can connect directly with one another, and economies of knowledge replace the economies of scale that were the foundation of the modern corporation and the rationale for vertical integration of the stages of production and distribution.

The markets that are created in this electronic world are about convenience and communities of interest, not about proximity and rules for allocating resources. The downloading of music and other entertainment in recent years provides an excellent example of both the opportunities and the problems. The spectacular rise, and equally rapid decline, of file sharing service Napster highlighted the ability of the Web to provide downloadable products without regard to distance. Music lovers were delighted to be able to obtain the music they wanted from any other registered Napster user whenever and wherever they wanted it. The Napster model, however, also operated without regard to intellectual property issues (discussed in Chapter 12). Seeing the danger of greatly reduced revenue, the entertainment industry forced the shutdown of Napster as a free file-sharing service. However, similar services still remain in operation, and the issues of how to handle such business models continue to evolve.

The Napster experience demonstrated clearly that consumers wanted to both download music and have the option of downloading only the songs they wanted, instead of having to purchase entire CDs. In 2003, Apple entered the market with its iTunes music store, which offers individual tracks for 99 cents and entire albums priced at

$9.99. Observers suggested that iTunes would have little impact because, at the time of introduction, it could be used only on Mac computers. Nevertheless, in the first week 1 million tracks were downloaded by Apple users, and within a few months a version for Microsoft's Windows operating system was introduced. Just 3 days after the Windows version debuted, 1 million copies of the software and 1 million songs had been downloaded by Windows users. That number had grown to 850 million by the end of 2005. At that time the video iPod was only a few months old, but Apple had already sold 8 million videos. At the MacWorld conference in January 2006, Apple announced an accessory that would allow users to play radio stations on their iPods.[24] These are examples of the convergence of devices and media that are discussed in Chapter 14.

iTunes is a high-volume, but not a high-profit, business. After paying royalties to the music label and operating costs, Apple probably only realizes about 10 cents per track. Why is it worth the effort? The answer is simple: to sell iPods.[25] Apple confirmed long-standing industry speculation when Steve Jobs announced the iPhone at the Macworld 2007 conference. The news was immediately spread by bloggers and Apple itself posted Jobs' keynote speech on its Web site,[26] where it was accessible to the entire Internet population.

1-7c Driver Three—Speed Is of the Essence in Doing Business on the Internet

Internet customers have come to expect real-time access to suppliers who can offer a huge selection of products and fulfill their orders accurately and swiftly. iTunes not only offers the convenience of buying from home and the ability to control exactly what tracks are purchased but also offers immediate gratification for the eager music buyer. Auction firm eBay provides a marketplace for individuals and small firms to buy and sell with ease in real time. The auction, with most listings lasting only a few days, was eBay's sole transaction mechanism in the beginning. Soon, however, the impatience of buyers and sellers alike caused them to offer a firm-price "Buy It Now" feature.

The same concern with speed is evident in B2B markets. For example, businesses that work on the trans-Alaskan pipeline have found that whereas they once had to order bear repellant from mail-order catalogs or specialized suppliers in the lower forty-eight states, they can now order directly from manufacturers, saving time and money.

In another case, a company called FindMRO was established as the Internet arm of industrial supply house Grainger. The company specializes in hard-to-find maintenance, repair, and operating supplies for businesses of all kinds and sizes. They represent more than 12,000 different suppliers. FindMRO takes product requests over the Internet or telephone, locates a supplier, and responds with a price and availability quote within 1 business day. They handle the entire purchase process for the buyer. Goods are shipped directly from the supplier to the purchaser using one of a variety of UPS shipping options depending on the urgency of the need. The streamlined purchase process saves both time and effort on the part of the buyer.[27]

Speed can be enhanced by the addition of information throughout the enterprise. Collaborative processes for product development can reduce cycle time and move products into the marketplace more quickly. Streamlined business processes and connections between buyers and sellers in all kinds of markets move products through those markets quickly and efficiently. Online customer advisory panels can produce rapid feedback on a variety of marketplace issues. Customers can obtain service 24/7 from anywhere in the world. It is, however, important to note that firms have increasingly recognized that "getting it right" is more important than "getting it fast."

1-7d Driver Four—People Are the Key Assets in Internet Businesses

This may sound like a trite statement to many members of the Internet age, but it has not always been true. The principles of scientific management, best exemplified by the productivity principles of Frederick Taylor and the assembly line practices of the Ford Motor Company, focused on the task, not the worker. According to influential management theorist Peter Drucker, the former Chairman of the Leader to Leader Institute:

> The most valuable assets of a 20th-century company were its *production equipment*. The most valuable asset of a 21st-century institution, whether business or nonbusiness, will be its *knowledge workers* and their *productivity*.[28]

knowledge worker A person who uses brains, not brawn, to earn a living. Most Internet-related workers fall into this category.

Managers of **knowledge workers** have long recognized that skilled employees are the only asset that walks out the door each evening—and may not return in the morning. They also know that in order "To do effective knowledge work, people must be motivated, have trust in their fellow workers and company, and have a real sense of commitment, not just compliance, to achieving team goals."[29]

gen X The population cohort born after the Baby Boom, in the 1960s and 1970s. There is considerable debate about the exact beginning and ending dates.

Many of these mature knowledge workers come from the **Generation X (Gen X)** age cohort of young adults born from 1964 to 1979. They present unfamiliar challenges to managers, most of whom are from the **Baby Boom** generation (1945 to 1963). A consultant at Booz Allen & Hamilton profiles Gen X workers as follows:

baby Boom The population cohort born between 1945 and 1963.

> They want to come and go as they please, wear what they like, work the hours that suit them—and not too many, thank you—because they value a balanced life more than piling up possessions. They want to work in small groups and be a part of every decision. Direct orders set their teeth on edge. You must explain why you want them to do something or, better, show them by example. You earn their respect by doing what they do.[30]

gen Y The population cohort born between 1981 and 1995.

To further complicate matters, **Generation Y (Gen Y)**, people born between 1981 and 1995, are now entering the workforce as a younger set of knowledge workers. They have still another set of expectations. According to Rod Fralicx, global employer research director at Mercer Human Resource Consulting:

> Employers were finally getting a handle on the needs and expectations of their Generation X workers, who differ considerably from other workers such as the 'Baby Boomers,' and now along comes Generation Y. Employees age 18–24 clearly have different views and expectations than older employees, even when compared to Generation X employees. This will require different management approaches to recruit them, retain them, and keep them engaged.[31]

Moore's Law In 1965, Gordon Moore, one of the founders of Intel, predicted that computing power would double every 18 months while the cost of producing it fell by 50%. That prediction has been borne out, and the result is a reduction of roughly 60 million times in the cost of storing a single item of data.

A survey of 2,600 workers in the United States showed the Gen Y segment to be less satisfied with both their jobs and their organizations than older age groups. Figure 1-5 shows that they were more satisfied with some aspects of their jobs—balance between work and personal life, training opportunities, helpful performance reviews, managerial availability, and the firm's reputation for customer service. The younger workers were less satisfied than the older workers with cooperation between work groups, fair treatment, and the opportunity to do challenging and interesting work.[32]

1-7e Driver Five—Growth in the Network Causes Exponential Increase in Value

Metcalfe's Law In 1994, Robert Metcalfe, inventor of Ethernet and one of the founders of the 3Com Corp., stated that the power of a computer is proportional to the square of the number of computers that are connected to it. That results in a geometrical increase in value each time a new computer is connected to the network.

The network itself is growing rapidly, fueled by decreasing costs and increasing productivity. **Moore's Law** describes the increase in productivity coupled with the decrease in costs that makes computing power widely available today. **Metcalfe's Law** portrays the exponentially increasing power of the network.

Initially, networks were merely computers and printers connected to one another. But today, many items have simple silicon chips that transmit streams of information. Your cell phone is recognizable as such an instrument, whether it is Internet-enabled or not. So is your rice cooker, especially if it uses fuzzy logic algorithms to ensure perfect rice. The time is coming closer when many of these items will be connected, through the Internet and increasingly through wireless systems. Electrolux in Sweden

| FIGURE 1-5 | Attitudes of worker age cohorts toward their work. |

Significant attitude gaps among employees by age (% of favorable responses)

	All	18-24	25-34	35-44	45-54	55-64
In my organization, employees are able to maintain a healthy balance between their work and personal lives.	47%	67%	48%	48%	43%	47%
I am able to take time away from my job to participate in training.	52%	67%	48%	53%	52%	52%
My last performance review was helpful in identifying actions I could take to improve my performance.	55%	73%	60%	56%	51%	55%
My manager does a good job of being available when needed.	56%	75%	59%	62%	51%	49%
My organization has established a good reputation for customer service.	65%	83%	64%	63%	67%	66%
My work group gets the cooperation it needs from other work groups to achieve our business objectives.	47%	30%	46%	48%	45%	47%
Personally, I feel that I am treated fairly in my organization.	64%	44%	65%	63%	64%	64%
My job gives me the chance to do challenging and interesting work.	75%	64%	75%	76%	74%	75%

Source: Mercer Human Resource Consulting, 2002 People at Work Survey.

already makes a "smart" refrigerator that keeps an inventory of staple items and has the capability of contacting a delivery service to order more when supplies run low.

When the chips are connected, important benefits follow. General Motors first introduced its OnStar system on its Cadillac line and soon made it available to other automobile manufacturers. The system uses a mix of technologies to enable the driver to perform activities ranging from summoning assistance in an emergency, to locating a stolen car, to requesting that doors be remotely unlocked. Optional services available through OnStar include a personal concierge who will recommend entertainment and shopping activities. Through a partnership with Verizon Wireless it offers personal calling and voice activation services to increase the convenience and safety of the system.[33] Other automobile manufacturers, including Acura, Audi, and Volkswagen, have licensed the system for use in their cars. In 2003, GM announced that the OnStar unit had achieved profitability.[34] GM reported almost 4 million subscribers to the personalized 24-hour service in 2005. Their subscribers made 9.5 million hands-free OnStar calls, and the system received 43,000 calls to unlock car doors and 15,000 emergency calls in 2005. It also introduced a premium service that performs remote diagnostics on vehicle systems and e-mails a report to the subscriber.[35] Clearly the system has potential for generating a great deal of data, and GM must constantly be sensitive to issues of customer privacy.

1-7f Driver Six—Marketers Can Deal with Customers on a One-to-One Basis

As the first truly interactive medium, the Internet allows even the largest companies to deal directly with each customer as an individual person or business. As the OnStar system illustrates, customers are coming to expect interactions that satisfy their individual needs at the time they are needed. However, just because the technology exists to allow companies to deal effectively with individuals does not mean that most companies do it well. A select few, though, do it brilliantly.

FedEx owes its current success to its vision of using technology to provide greater customer satisfaction. As such, it was one of the first to understand the power of providing information to customers that allowed them to meet their own needs at the time they choose. By providing free tracking software to its customers, FedEx literally allows customers access to a portion of its operational database to schedule shipments, track the progress of shipments, and confirm delivery, and customers are happier with FedEx because they have the information they need at their fingertips. FedEx saves money with the process because incremental Internet inquiries are virtually free as compared with several dollars for a call to a customer service representative. In the end, both the company and its customers are better off because representatives are freed from most routine calls and are able to deal with troublesome or complex issues that require skilled human intervention.

The announcement in late 2003 that FedEx would purchase Kinko's opened a wide new array of possibilities, especially for serving the small and home-based business markets. The new FedEx Kinko's allows the customer to submit print jobs directly from his or her computer to a selected FedEx Kinko's location, choose from many printing formats, arrange to pick up from the retail location or have FedEx conveniently deliver, then pay for it all with a commercial account credit card that had been distributed by surface mail.

FedEx Kinko's offers free software to support this service, just as they do to support FedEx tracking. The credit card also provides a physical mailing address that Kinko's can use to promote products like the direct mail services it offers to small to medium-sized marketers. Orders placed over the web provide email addresses that can be used to promote products like its basic "File, Print FedEx" service (http://www.fedex.com/us/officeprint/main/?link=1&lid=Office+Print+Services.)

Other marketers are using a combination of media to reach individual customers in a targeted manner. The television shopping channels provide an excellent example of multichannel marketing (to be discussed as a business model in Chapter 3). Their primary transactions channel is television and the three largest—HSN, QVC and ShopNBC—all stream their television programming live on their Web sites. In case you missed it when it was shown live, they archive video clips on their sites so you can see featured products at another time. All permit viewers to sign up for product- or vendor-specific emails so they will know, for example, when automobile care supplies or Gateway computer equipment is being featured. Some also use direct mail to alert good customers to upcoming product events that are likely to be of interest. The direct mail can direct the reader to the Web site for advance shopping—a customer retention strategy that offers a special privilege at the same time it drives the purchaser to the lowest-cost channel. All of this is based on individual contact with—and individual knowledge of the purchasing habits of—their customers.

There are numerous opportunities for marketers to deal directly with customers in ways that improve the customer experience and add to the marketer's store of knowledge about the customer. Various approaches will be discussed throughout the text.

1-7g Driver Seven—Demand Can Be Predicted with Greater Accuracy

Internet channels tend to be shorter because some intermediaries become less prominent, especially ones whose primary business has been in moving information, such as retail travel agents. The speed with which information is exchanged, both within and between organizations, is also greatly increased. Even in the absence of other developments, shorter channels that operate more efficiently bring producers closer to customers and improve demand forecasting. As is discussed in Chapter 2,

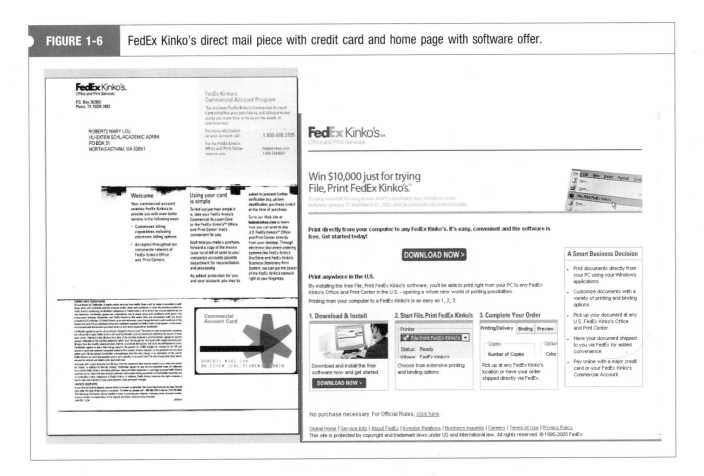

| FIGURE 1-6 | FedEx Kinko's direct mail piece with credit card and home page with software offer. |

enterprises like Dell have gone much further in streamlining channels in ways that make customer demand highly predictable.

1-7h Driver Eight—Cost Patterns Change as Transaction and Coordination Costs Shrink for Businesses, and Consumers Recognize That Switching Costs Are Low

In electronic marketplaces **transaction** and **coordination costs** are greatly reduced or even eliminated. Economists describe these costs as "friction" in an economic system. Friction includes nonproductive costs of preparing and coordinating agreements between parties to a transaction as well as higher costs caused by lack of knowledge about competitive prices. In a frictionless economy, there is no reason for huge, vertically integrated enterprises. They are replaced with confederations of enterprises, linked by the electronic network. Each enterprise in this system can concentrate on its core expertise, moving information seamlessly across corporate boundaries. The economic friction that remains is the cost of physical logistics for products that cannot be digitized and transmitted across the network. Even this cost, however, can be greatly reduced by the network, as we will see in various examples throughout the text, especially in Chapter 2.

Transaction cost theory was not born out of the Internet. As early as 1937, University of Chicago economist Ronald Coase described the firm's main role as being an allocator of resources. When an effective market is available to make price knowledge widely accessible, regardless of time or distance, the market becomes better able to allocate resources than the firm, and a primary reason for the firm's existence begins to disappear. In 1981, Stanford economist Oliver Williamson

transaction costs The costs of making and fulfilling sales, often referred to as "friction" in channels of distribution. They include both search and distribution costs.

coordination costs The costs incurred in transmitting information that permits economic exchange.

popularized this theory in a paper titled "The Modern Corporation," and in 1991, Coase won the Nobel Prize in economics for changing the way economists think about the nature of the corporate firm.[36]

Downloading music from iTunes is a good example of costs being wrung out of the physical distribution system by electronic commerce. When travel networks like Sabre's Travelocity begin to charge for paper tickets to encourage travelers to use e-tickets, they are also capitalizing on the decreased transactions costs made possible by the Internet.

1-7i Driver Nine—Consumers Have Power in Information-Rich Channels

Consumers have great power in new economy channels, and they exercise it fearlessly. Silicon Valley consultant Regis McKenna was one of the first to identify the phenomenon of endlessly escalating customer expectations. He gives the following advice to managers:

> New consumers are never satisfied consumers. Managers hoping to serve them must work to eliminate time and space constraints on service. They must push the technological bandwidth with interactive dialogue systems—equipped with advanced software interfaces—in the interest of forging more intimate ties with these consumers. Managers must exploit every available means to obtain their end: building self-satisfaction capabilities into services and products and providing customers with access anytime, anywhere.[37]

What this all boils down to is that customers want to be in control. They want to control when and where they make contact. They want to control what they consume through personalized communications and customized products. They want their privacy and full disclosure of purchase conditions and information collection and use. They want it all in a neat package that allows them to complete their task quickly and effortlessly. To top it off, they want to receive any service and support they need in the same 24/7/365 fashion. If the bar is continually being raised in terms of what makes for overall customer satisfaction, then this is a formidable challenge indeed!

The following report from the 2004 International Advertising Association World Conference in Beijing illustrates how much impact individual consumers like the Neistat brothers can have on the actions of a large corporation like Apple using a combination of online and traditional methods. According to Rance Crain, publisher of *Advertising Age:*

> [. . . .] two ordinary consumers, the Neistat brothers, created a Web site and film to protest that Apple's iPod battery couldn't be replaced and lasted only 18 months. The film, "iPod's Dirty Secret" (using iMacs to produce it) showed the brothers stenciling their findings about the iPod battery all over Apple's poster ads for the product. The Web site generated over 15 million hits from around the world and forced Apple to change the battery.[38]

The film still exists on the Web, long after Apple improved the iPod battery, along with other films by the Neistat brothers.[39] This is one example of consumer-created content that is on the increase all over the Web. We discuss the marketing implications of this phenomenon in Chapters 6 and 14.

1-7j Driver Ten—An Information Economy Is Characterized by Choice and Abundance

A resource-based economy runs on natural resources, which are consumable and generally irreplaceable. These resources increase in price as demand increases and supply becomes scarce. Information resources, on the other hand, become more valuable the more they are used. They do not become more scarce with use; they become more plentiful.

The markets that are created in this electronic world are about convenience and communities of interest, not about proximity and rules for allocating resources. A prime example is eBay. eBay bills itself as "The World's Online Marketplace" and describes its mission as being able "to provide a global trading platform where practically anyone can trade practically anything."[40] In 2004, eBay was described as the fastest-growing enterprise in business history. It had 48 million active users around the world and was expected to provide $3.2 billion in operating revenues and $1 billion in profit that year. According to *Fortune,* "eBay has such high margins partly because it has no factories or inventory, but also because its customers do the work."[41] Their financial report indicates that there were 404.6 million new listings in the fourth quarter of 2004 alone.[42] As eBay promotes its global presence and becomes a major closeout site for large corporations, including The Sharper Image, Sears, and IBM, the business model seems infinitely scalable.[43]

Summary

The advent of the Internet has altered the business landscape with astounding speed and power. In that changed terrain, the role of marketing has also undergone dramatic upheaval.

Customers, both consumer and business, have access to voluminous amounts of information and many competitive offerings. Their expectations in terms of both product quality and customer service are high. The number of choices available to customers is very great, as is their ability to acquire information and change suppliers. Marketers must meet ever-increasing expectations, master a new medium, and drive costs down in order to offer competitive prices—all at the same time.

Marketers engage in a variety of activities to accomplish their goals. These fall into the basic categories of customer acquisition, conversion, retention, and building customer value. Gone are the days when marketers could appeal to a mass market using more intuition than information. Gone also are the days when marketing escaped the rigorous accountability applied to other parts of the firm.

Marketing has become an information-driven, technology-enabled endeavor with many new tasks and techniques. Increasingly, it works in a virtual environment composed of business alliances, outsourced services, and virtual value chains. Success in this setting requires an understanding of the basic technological infrastructure and the strategic and economic drivers that underlie Internet activity.

Understanding the new techniques, while keeping a focus on sound marketing strategy in both cyberspace and the physical world is the purpose of this book.

Quiz

1. _____ is the communications protocol that provides the common "language" of Internet computing.
   a. HTML
   b. TCP/IP
   c. The graphic browser

2. _____ is the feature of the World Wide Web that allows users to move easily from one document to another.
   a. Hypertext
   b. Telecommunications
   c. Common platform

3. Household penetration of computers is less than 50% in _____.
   a. Denmark
   b. China
   c. the United States

4. The Sabre System is an example of _____.
   a. a new service made possible by the Internet
   b. an information product
   c. a product targeted solely at the consumer market

5. Objectives that can be appropriate for Internet marketing include _____.
   a. acquiring as many customers as possible
   b. decreasing the need for customer service
   c. building loyal customer relationships.

6. Which of the following is *not* an element of the Internet infrastructure stack?
   a. Web site content
   b. operations like load balancing and security
   c. connections to the telecommunications backbone of the Internet

7. One of the following is *not* a unique characteristic of the Internet?

   a. one-to-many communication
   b. allows almost perfect knowledge about products and services
   c. interactivity

8. Which of the following is *not* a strategic driver of the Internet economy?

   a. Making it possible to deal with customers on a one-to-one basis.
   b. Employees can easily be substituted for one another.
   c. Speed is essential to successful Internet operations.

9. Marketplace power has shifted in the direction of customers because customers _____.

   a. are represented by larger business enterprises
   b. have a myriad of choices in the marketplace
   c. are willing to wait for their questions to be satisfactorily answered

10. OnStar is an example of _____.

   a. a public network
   b. a dot-com business enterprise
   c. the power of the network to communicate and provide services

Discussion Questions

1. The origins of the Internet and the World Wide Web are unusual in the history of commercial media. What makes them unusual, and what qualities does that impart to the medium?

2. The terms *information-rich products* and *information products* are used frequently in this chapter. Explain the meaning of each concept and give an example or two of each.

3. Discuss the role the Internet plays in the lives of consumers and businesses. Has it changed the lives of consumers in any meaningful way? Has it changed the way businesses operate in any significant fashion? Can you give examples of the impact of the Internet in either B2C or B2B markets?

4. The Internet marketing paradigm includes both marketing inputs and marketing actions. Discuss the major components of both the inputs and the actions.

5. What is the Internet infrastructure stack? What is the relevance of this technological concept to marketers?

6. This chapter emphasizes throughout that business and marketing processes are changing in fundamental ways as a result of the Internet. Choose one specific driver of change and identify ways in which it is altering the way businesses conduct their daily and strategic activities.

Internet Exercises

1. Select an organization (corporate or not-for-profit) with which you are somewhat familiar that uses both online and offline channels. Discuss two or three specific examples of how it is taking advantage of the strategic change drivers.

2. Select three different Web sites that you will follow for the semester. Your instructor may make several different assignments based on these sites, so you should choose sites of substance, although they do not have to be large. Each site should, however, be a brand site, not a site for a mega corporation. Following at least one not-for-profit site can add to the learning experience.

   If you can sign up for free newsletter from the sites you select that will help you understand the various elements of their online strategies and may also give you insight into how their multichannel marketing is carried out.

   If the company has retail outlets nearby, you should also consider a visit to the retail site, looking for ways in which the firm is integrating marketing activities on and off the Internet.

3. Select a company that uses at least two of the following three channels—Internet, retail, and direct marketing (e.g., catalogs). Conduct an ongoing analysis of their situation and strategy.

4. Consider creating a blog to record your insights and discoveries as you move through the Internet marketing course. Blogs are discussed in Chapter 6. Directions for creating your own blog can be found on free blog sites like Blogster.

Notes

1. Material in this section was taken from "Timeline: PBS Life on the Internet," http://www.pbs.org, nd; Michael Hauben, "History of ARPANET," http://www.dei.isep.ipp.pt/docs/arpa.html, nd;PBS Home Video, "A Brief History of the Internet, Vol. One, Networking The Nerds," 1998; Jeffrey Veen, "The History of HTML," http://hotwired.lycos.com/webmonkey.

2. "Web Worldwide," accessed 1/9/06, http://clickz.com/stats/web_worldwide/.

3. "Top Ten Countries with Highest Number of Internet Users," *Internet World Stats*, http://www.internetworldstats.com/top10.htm#pop.

4. "Countries with the Highest Internet Penetration Rate," *Internet World Stats*, http://www.internetworldstats.com/top10.htm#pop.

5. Antone Gonsalves, "Online Spending Reaches 6% of Total Retail Sales," January 5, 2006, *Information Week*, http://www.informationweek.com/shared/printableArticle.jhtml?articleID=175802174.

6. Melody Vargas, "Online Retail Sales Projections," August 23, 2004, About.com, http://retailindustry.about.com/b/a/109188.htm.

7. "Double-Digit Increases in Visits to Shopping Sites," December 30, 2005, Marketing Vox, http://www.marketingvox.com/archives/2005/12/30/doubledigit_increases_in_visits_to_shopping_sites/index.php.

8. "Worldwide B2B E-Commerce to Surpass $1T in 2003," *eMarketer*, March 20, 2003, www.emarketer.com.

9. For Internet history frequently updated see Hobbes' Internet Timeline, http://www.zakon.org/robert/internet/timeline/, and The Living Internet, http://www.livinginternet.com/.

10. "Internet2 Is Higher-Tech Version of Regular Internet," USA Today, April 13, 2005, http://www.usatoday.com/tech/news/techinnovations/2005-04-13-qa-internet2_x.htm.

11. Tom O'Reilly, "What Is Web 2.0," September 30, 2005, Tim.OReilly.com, http://www.oreillynet.com/pub/a/oreilly/tim/news/2005/09/30/what-is-web-20.html.

12. "About Us," http://www.sabre-holdings.com; "History," http://www.sabretravelnetwork.com/about/history.htm;Gary H. Anthes, "Sabre Flies to Open Systems," May 31, 2004, *Conmputerworld*, http://www.computerworld.com.

13. Deborah Fallows, "The Internet and Daily Life," http://www.pewinternet.org/pdfs/PIP_Internet_and_Daily_Life.pdf.

14. Mile Shields, "Forecast 2006," *MediaWeek*, http://www.mediaweek.com/mw/news/recent_display.jsp?vnu_content_id=1001772508.

15. Kris Oser, "Old-Line Marketers Drive New Surge in Online Ad Spending," AdAge.com, May 26, 2004, http://www.adage.com.

16. Jim Meskauskas, "Lexus Shifts Ad Dollars from TV to Web," *iMedia Connection*, March 4, 2004, http://www.imediaconnection.com.

17. GraemeGordon, "Congratulations Canada! We Are Number One, Again!" 2004, http://www.accenture.com.

18. See Donna L. Hoffman and Thomas P. Novak, "Marketing in Hypermedia Computer-Mediated Environments: Conceptual Foundations," *Journal of Marketing*, 60 (July 1996), 50–68, for an in-depth discussion of the Internet as a communications medium.

19. John J. Marshall, Richard S. Christner, and Erich Almasy, "The real point of going digital," *Mercer Management Journal*, 11, 1999, p. 38.

20. Routers are specialized computers or software that transfer data on a network. Bridgers work within local area networks (LANs) to connect various parts of the network, regulate traffic, and switch data. Both fall under the heading of specialized telecommunications devices.

21. Adapted from "10 Driving Principles of the New Economy," *Business 2.0*, March 2000, pp. 198–284, and "Our 10 Principles of the New Economy, Slightly Revised," *Business 2.0*, August/September 2001, p. 85.

22. http://investor.shareholder.com/drugstore/corporate_profile.cfm, accessed June 12, 2006.

23. Paul Demeny, "Drugstore's Vitamin Boost," http://www.internetretailer.com, March 2005.

24. Nick Wingfield, "Apple Unveils iMac Running on Intel Chips," January 10, 2005, *Wall Street Journal*, http://online.wsj.com/article/SB113691345019542844.html?mod=djemalert.

25. "The 99c Solution," Time.com, *Coolest Inventions*, 2003.

26. http://events.apple.com.edgesuite.net/j47d52oo/event/.

27. "FindMRO Delivers Hard-to-Find Products—Fast," nd, http://www.ec.ups.com/ecommerce/clicks/findmro.html.

28. Peter F. Drucker, *Management Challenges for the 21st Century* (New York: HarperBusiness, 1999), p. 135.

29. Don Tapscott, "Minds Over Matter," *Business 2.0*, March 2000, p. 222.

30. David Berreby, "The Hunter-Gatherers of the Knowledge Economy," Third Quarter 1999, http://www.strategy-business.com.

31. "New Generation of Workers Has Different Views, Expectations," July 2003, Mercer Human Resource Consulting, http://www.mercerhr.com/pressrelease/details.jhtml/dynamic/idContent/1101090.

32. "New Generation of Workers Has Different Views, Expectations," July 2003, Mercer Human Resource Consulting, http://www.mercerhr.com/pressrelease/details.jhtml/dynamic/idContent/1101090.

33. http://www.onstar.com/us_english/jsp/plans/direct_conn.jsp.

34. "GM Finally Profiting from OnStar," February 27, 2003, http://www.boston.com.

35. "Press Room," accessed 1/9/06, http://www.onstar.com.

36. Edward J. Romar and Mary Lou Roberts, "Partnerships, Alliances and the New Economy: Towards a Typology of Web-Based Relationships," Proceedings of the 2001 Macromarketing Conference; Oliver E. Williamson, "The Modern Corporation: Origins, Evolution, Attributes," *Journal of Economic Literature*, 1981, 1537–1569; David Warsh, "Nobel Winner Coase Blends Theories of Economics, Law," *Boston Globe*, October 16, 1991, p. 63; Ronald H. Coase, "The Nature of the Firm," *Economica*, 1937, 386–405.

37. Regis McKenna, "Real Time: Preparing for the Age of the Never Satisfied Customer," Boston, Harvard Business School Press, 1997, p. 56.

38. Rance Crain, "The Growing Impact of Consumers' Web Publishing," November 1, 2004, http://www.advertisingage.com.

39. http://www.neistat.com.

40. http://pages.ebay.com/aboutebay/thecompany/companyoverview.html.

41. Patricia Sellers, "eBay's Secret," October 18, 2004, http://www.fortune.com.

42. eBay Inc. "Announces 4th Quarter and Full Year 2004 Results," http://investor.ebay.com/releases.cfm.

43. Adam Lashinsky, "There's No Stopping eBay," February 9, 2004. http://www.fortune.com.

The Internet Value Chain

Chapter Outline

Source: © Getty

Key Terms

application programming interfaces (p. 45)
build-to-inventory (p. 32)
build-to-order (p. 34)
bar code (p. 46)
channels of distribution (p. 31)
cycle time (p. 38)
dealer (p. 31)
distributor (p. 30)
electronic data interchange (p. 42)
electronic product code (p. 47)
enterprise resource (p. 43)
extranet (p. 31)
friction (p. 36)
HTML (p. 44)
inventory turns (p. 31)
just in time (p. 36)
legacy (p. 44)
logistics (p. 32)
margin (gross margin) (p. 33)

mirroring (p. 40)
portal (p. 41)
protocol (p. 44)
radio frequency IDs (also RFID tags, smart tags) (p. 45)
RFID (p. 41)
scalable (p. 41)
SKU (p. 47)
Six Sigma (p. 41)
supply chain (p. 31)
total cost of ownership (p. 44)
value (customer value, customer perceived value) (p. 32)
value-added network (p. 42)
value chain (p. 32)
virtual value chain (p. 33)
visibility (p. 39)
Web services (p. 44)
XML (p. 44)
Y2K (p. 44)

Learning Objectives

By the time you complete this chapter, you will be able to:

- Distinguish between the following concepts: supply chain, value chain, and virtual value chain.
- List the business processes that are necessary to manage the supply chain.
- Identify the core marketing processes.
- Explain the role of information in, first, integrating the value chain and, later, making it virtual.

- Define EDI, ERP, and Web services and explain their role in integrating the value chain.
- Discuss the potential of RFID technology in supply chains.
- Know the benefits of supply chain integration.

2-1 The Transformation of Herman Miller—A Case Study

In 1995, furniture-maker Herman Miller was a business in trouble. The company had prospered for more than 70 years as a manufacturer of high-end, ergonomic office furniture systems. Their products were marketed to large corporations through a sales force of 300 and more than 240 contract office furniture dealers. Despite their trophy case of design awards and their reputation as one of the most agreeable employers in the country, though, lead times to fill customer orders were long, delivery was haphazard, and customer service was poor. There was a measurable decline in customer satisfaction, and expenses were out of control. Sales were up slightly, but profits fell by nearly 90% in a single year. The disarray led to the exodus of almost 200 employees that year, including the chief executive officer (CEO).

The nature of Herman Miller products only increased the complexity of the situation. The company processed more than 3,000 orders for furniture and accessories each week. The furniture was sold as a system that required orders to be held until complete: if a single item was missing, the order could not be shipped. The required coordination between eight separate manufacturing plants was missing. Mark Doublas, project manager at Herman Miller, explains that the situation suffered from a complete breakdown of synchronization, leading to high inventory and storage costs, as well as low customer satisfaction:

> We'd get in one item one day, then the panels would come in the next day, then a few days later the chairs would come in. This meant we had three or four weeks of finished goods waiting for the rest of the order. [...] When all this waiting time was factored in, we were looking at very extended internal lead times of 8 to 12 weeks. [...] Add at least another month on the end of that in the **distributor** network, and you get a very slow product pipeline.[1]

distributor An intermediary in B2B channels of distribution that is roughly equivalent to the wholesaler in business-to-customer channels.

As the first step in resolving the problem, Herman Miller implemented planning software to improve production scheduling and delivery with the specific goal of improving customer satisfaction through better, faster service. The software allowed creation of a firm completion date for each project by querying each plant about when it could build the ordered items. Each item was then synchronized to the longest production date, with a rule of not building any item more than 3 days before that date. Within 18 months, striking results were achieved:

> the company had boosted delivery performance—i.e., on-time shipments—from 70% to 99%. It decreased lead time by 22%, and now ships 30% of orders directly to

customers, bypassing distribution center layovers and handling. The company reduced finished goods waiting time to two days and eliminated $50 million to $70 million in pipeline inventory. Other impressive milestones; a 40% increase in throughput and a 100% increase in **inventory turns.**[2]

The savings on the initial project represented a three-fold return on the original investment of almost $6 million.

2-1a Birth of SQA

Five years after the transformation began, Herman Miller had a fully integrated, Internet-based division, initially designed to serve the small business market it had previously ignored. The division was initially called SQA for "simple, quick, and affordable." Their delivery objective was 2 weeks, compared with 6 to 8 weeks for the company as a whole. Salespeople produced the three-dimensional office design on a laptop at the client's location, and the system was immediately activated:

> When an order is completed, it is zapped via the Web to an SQA factory in Michigan or in California. As soon as the order is transmitted, another program schedules a manufacturing date and reserves space on a truck that will deliver it a week or two later. Within two hours, the dealer and customer receive an e-mailed confirmation of the delivery and installation time.

The company developed another program to give its network of more than 500 suppliers access to its ordering system on the Web. This allowed companies that make chair coverings or laminated surfaces to check what the factory's needs will be weeks in advance. As soon as inventories are expected to drop below a certain level—usually a day's worth of production—the supplier sends more. Companies that perform consistently below expectations are warned and eventually face termination of their contracts.[3]

The customer's order is delivered and installed anywhere from 3 days to 2 weeks after the date of the sale, with a 99% on-time record. Other benefits of the system include an inventory turn of 40 times a year as compared with the industry average of less than 20. Order entry errors are almost nonexistent, as opposed to 20% for manual systems. Because the system is so efficient, it has opened the small business market, previously viewed by the company as uneconomical, to Herman Miller. It is also being used as a blueprint for the rest of the corporation. "SQA was the petri dish, and now we're reinventing the entire company," says CEO Gary Van Spronsen.[4]

2-1b Evolution to eZconnect

Herman Miller's next step was to fully integrate the customer into the system, a process that gave a new name to the process: eZconnect. The company's **channels of distribution** were an important consideration in this phase. Herman Miller office systems are sold and installed by dealers in more than 40 countries, supported by design centers and regional sales offices. The goal was to support the **dealer** channel, not compete with it. The result is a series of secure Web sites restricted to customers that complement Herman Miller's public site. Another secure site hosted by the company, called Kiosk dealer services, provides dealers with access to product information and training. Dealers provide passwords to their customers, giving them access to the eZconnect site, where they find a customized online catalog with products and pricing just for that customer account. Customers may place orders on the site, and their orders are submitted through their local dealer. As a result, Herman Miller provides customers anywhere in the world the convenience of online ordering designed to meet their unique needs coupled with the necessary installation and support services of their local dealers. The businesses of dealers are streamlined and supported in the process. This set of secure Web sites is completed with an **extranet** for Herman Miller suppliers where the operations of the **supply chain** take place.[5]

inventory turns The number of times inventory is sold (turns over) in a year.

channels of distribution The intermediaries through which products and information about transactions move in the course of a single exchange.

dealer An intermediary in B2B channels of distribution that is roughly equivalent to the retailer in business-to-customer channels.

extranet A corporate information system that is made available to business partners who are able to access portions of the system for which they have passwords.

supply chain The downstream portion of the value chain, the channel from suppliers to producers.

value chain The integrated channel that stretches from suppliers through the producer and on to the end users.

build-to-inventory The generic business model in which demand is forecasted and products are made and stocked in inventory based on the forecast.

logistics The business function that controls the flow of products, information, and other resources from their point of production to the place where they are needed for further production or for sale.

value (customer value, customer perceived value) Essentially the usefulness (economic utility) of the product less its price.

This extended example captures the essence of the Internet-based **value chain.** On the demand side, it is focused on customer needs, going so far as to customize products and information resources for individual customers. Needs are determined and then products are manufactured, not the reverse. In fact, as in the Herman Miller example, often the order is placed before manufacturing begins, a reversal of the traditional **build-to-inventory** model. On the supply side, vendors become an integral part of the process, acting on information from electronic manufacturing and distribution systems, not on the basis of paper orders. The system completely integrates the activities of both dealers and suppliers with those of the manufacturer, and, at its best, focuses all activities on value creation for the customer. It lowers the costs of process at every possible point. It wrings costs out of the process at every possible point.

There are a number of concepts that are important to understanding the evolution of the value chain and what makes value chains effective in the Internet environment.

2-2 Value Chain Concepts

Michael Porter popularized the concept of the value chain in the early 1980s. The familiar graphic, which identifies primary activities as inbound **logistics**, operations, outbound logistics, marketing and sales, and service and recognizes the support activities of infrastructure, human resources, technology, and procurement, provides a useful basis for understanding *how the enterprise produces value for its customers.*

In the last few years, the term *value chain* has been widely used in a different way. In the context of the automation of business processes and later the Internet, the term *value chain* has come to mean the *seamless, end-to-end integration of activities throughout the channel of distribution.* In essence, this value chain concept incorporates two familiar business processes—the supply chain and the channel of distribution (Figure 2-1). Companies are moving, first, to integrate the supplier-facing side of their channels—the supply chain. Only a few have moved to integrate on the customer-facing side, the channel of distribution.

2-2a Core Marketing Processes

Figure 2-2 blends several concepts that help clarify some of these issues by focusing on the manner in which an enterprise creates **value.** The primary business processes are those identified by Porter and take place at the corporate level. As you can see, the marketing and sales function represents one of several fundamental business processes.

Marketing itself has three core processes: supply chain management, product development and management, and customer relationship management.[6] Supply chain management is discussed in this chapter in the context of creating the value chain. The implications of the Internet for product development and management are

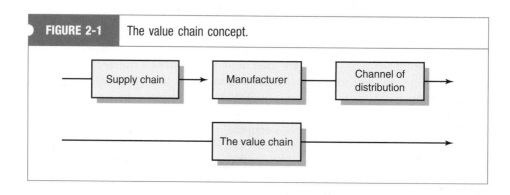

| **FIGURE 2-1** | The value chain concept. |

Otis Elevator has been integrating with customer infra-structure for many years. In 1988, it introduced the first Remote Elevator Monitoring (REM®) system. REM is a diagnostic system that monitors the performance of Otis elevators and other brands with which Otis has service contracts. It monitors both the usage level and individual systems within the elevator. The system schedules regular maintenance calls based on the level of usage. If it detects an urgent problem, it reports the condition to a 24-hour communications center, which in turn dispatches a repair person with the required tools and parts. According to Otis, the system identifies most problems before they occur, minimizing elevator downtime. By analyzing all the hundreds of systems in an elevator, the company also maintains that the number of service calls are minimized and performance is optimized. Reports covering both scheduled and REM-based service calls are available online. The remote monitoring of elevators is an example of the **machine-to-machine** business model discussed in Chapter 3.[7]

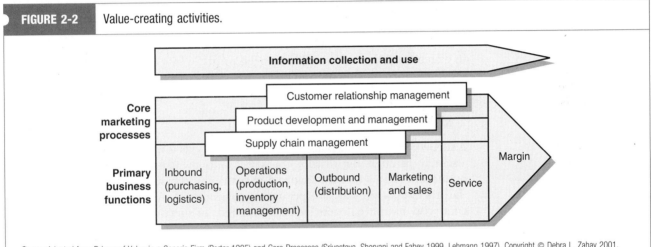

FIGURE 2-2 Value-creating activities.

Source: Adapted from Drivers of Value in a Generic Firm (Porter 1985) and Core Processes (Srivastava, Shervani and Fahey 1999, Lehmann 1997). Copyright © Debra L. Zahay 2001. Adapted from Prof. Debra L. Zahay.
Rajendra K. Srivastava, Tasadduq A. Shervani, and Liam Fahey, "Marketing, Business Processes, and Shareholder Value: An Organizationally Embedded View of Marketing Activities and the Discipline of Marketing," *Journal of Marketing,* 1999, 168–179.

covered in Chapter 5; and customer relationship management is the subject of Chapter 8.

This conceptualization also emphasizes the importance of information in value creation. In early stages, information fosters integration between members of the value chain. In later stages, it permits the development of a **virtual value chain** and the creation of new types of value.

Taken together, all the elements of the process determine the **margin** realized by the firm. Using e-business techniques can increase margins in a number of ways. Enterprises have generally focused on the supply side first because there are large savings to be realized from streamlining the procurement process. These savings can be passed on to customers in the form of price reductions, or they can increase margins and therefore profitability. Turning to the demand side, many of the same e-business techniques can increase the speed and decrease the cost of fulfilling customer orders. This, too, may decrease operating costs. Better servicing of customer orders may also provide an opportunity to charge premium prices.

Whether a value chain focuses on physical products, services, or information products, it should no longer be viewed as a simple linear entity. In its linear form, it is made up of a complex set of interlocking activities. Although it is not often specified, the assumption is that most activities are carried out internally by a somewhat

virtual value chain The term given to an integrated supply chain in which all transactions are conducted electronically.

margin (gross margin) Essentially sales minus cost of goods sold; margin is the amount that must cover operating expenses, including marketing expenses, and profit.

self-contained business entity interacting with an external environment. This is an "old economy" perspective, one that leads to vertical integration. However, as the chain evolves, it becomes a network of fluid partnerships that constantly rearrange themselves to accomplish necessary tasks in the most economical manner. This as a "new economy" concept in which overall value is optimized, not the value of one link in the chain.

It is also important to recognize that businesses in a network are not simply free-floating entities, in constant motion like tiny fish in a pond. They move with a purpose, each to accomplish the task at which it is most proficient. Therefore, we need to understand the tasks that must be accomplished, not at the high level of a Porter-like value chain, but at the granular level of daily business tasks that must be understood, automated where possible, and integrated into a chain that seamlessly delivers value to the customer. To do this, we need to explore three separate but related concepts:

- The supply chain
- The value chain
- The integrated value chain

As we examine these concepts, we will recognize them as an evolutionary hierarchy in which firms like Herman Miller need to begin by getting their supply chain in order and then moving on to higher levels of customer integration and system-wide effectiveness.

2-2b The Supply Chain

A supply chain maps the physical movement of goods from initial production through assembly through the distribution process to the customer. Table 2-1 lists the business processes that are involved in managing the supply chain. As you look at the processes, which have an operations management flavor, keep in mind that a single enterprise may have dozens or even hundreds of suppliers whose activities must be coordinated.

Because supply chain management is such a complex task, enterprises can realize large cost savings from integrating and improving it, with best-in-class companies spending 5% to 6% less of their total revenue on supply chain costs than their median industry counterparts. They can also realize major improvements in process elements ranging from inventory (25% to 60% improvement) to overall productivity (10% to 16% improvement).[8] The classic example of a tightly integrated value chain is Dell Computer and its **build-to-order** model, which we discuss later in this chapter. Zara, the European clothing chain, provides an example of combining customer information with supply chain integration to succeed in the ever-changing world of fashion (Box 2-2).

build-to-order A business model, most often attributed to Dell, in which products are built only after an order has been received.

> **TABLE 2-1** Supply Chain Management Processes

1. Selecting and qualifying desired suppliers
2. Establishing and managing inbound logistics
3. Designing and managing internal logistics
4. Establishing and managing outbound logistics
5. Designing work flow in product-solution assembly
6. Running batch manufacturing
7. Acquiring, installing, and maintaining process technology
8. Order processing, pricing, billing, rebates, and terms
9. Managing (multiple) channels
10. Managing customer services such as installation and maintenance to enable product use

Source: Rajendra K. Srivastava, Tasadduq A. Shervani and Liam Fahey, "Marketing, Business Processes, and Shareholder Value: An Organizationally Embedded View of Marketing Activities and the Discipline of Marketing," *Journal of Marketing*, 1999, 170.

Zara, a division of Spanish conglomerate Inditex Group, is a trendy women's apparel store with 739 stores in 54 countries as of mid-2005.[9] Its growth and financial results have captured the attention of investors in recent years because they have far outstripped those of other fashion retailers.

Zara's success comes from two key drivers. First is its fashion appeal. Customer trends are constantly monitored. Store employees, using handheld devices, roam the stores, asking customers what they like, don't like, and are looking for but don't find. That information is transmitted to the design team, which immediately begins to sketch new items. At the end of each day, store managers provide sales reports to headquarters, giving constant updates on what merchandise is and is not selling.

The second driver is the ability of Zara's supply chain to produce new items and get them into stores in just 2 weeks. This enables Zara to provide customers with up-to-date designs that mimic the hottest haute couture products even while the couture designs are still in vogue. Competitive fashion chains often take 6 to 8 months to spot a trend and react to it by producing more of desired items and quickly disposing of unpopular ones. Both types of reaction are key to success in the fashion industry.

How has Zara designed a supply chain that supplies desired merchandise so quickly and so effectively? First, it owns many of its own production facilities, making about 40% of its own fabric in highly automated factories in Spain and Portugal, and it actually makes about 60% of the

garments it sells, rather than having items outsourced to manufacturers in Eastern Europe or Asia. Inventory reaches stores quickly. To serve the United States, where it has relatively few stores and no physical distribution facilities, Zara ships new merchandise to stores by air as often as three times each week.

The Zara Web site reflects the customer orientation and the localization of this global enterprise. Language options of English and Spanish are offered on the opening screen (Figure 2-3). To support the global nature of its business the Zara site has localization features that allow the customer to easily locate stores and to determine what types of merchandise are available in stores in that geographical area. The site is designed to draw customers into stores; it is not an ecommerce site.

According to Prof. John Gallaugher, "The genius of the Zara model is that they ask their customers what they want, and then they give it to them." He goes on to say, "The Zara model is particularly troubling for rivals. Not only is it wildly successful, but it's brutally difficult for established competitors to copy. That translates into a fairly sustainable advantage."[10]

Other industry experts add that "trying to predict what consumers will want to buy nine months out is dicey. 'Regardless of what you're trying to predict, the closer you are to the event the more accurate your prediction will be'... explains Brian Hume, president of Atlanta based Martec International. The amount of risk involved in committing to [the production of] a fashion item in March

FIGURE 2-3   Zara opening screen.

Source: http://www.zara.com.

continued

Case in Point 2-2 *Continued*

that won't appear on a store rack until August is enormous."[11]

The importance of supply chain excellence in every area of time-sensitive industry is well summarized by Jani Friedman of Freeborders, a San Francisco software firm that serves the retail outsourcing trade. According to Ms. Friedman, "Speed to market is the Holy Grail. Retail companies that figure it out will have a significant increase in revenue because they'll sell more trend items at full price, which drives profitability."[12]

By following this approach, both supplier and customer win. But it requires that the supplier take a broader perspective, looking at the customer's demand chain as well as its own supply chain. This is another example of managing business processes beyond corporate boundaries, and moves us toward the concept of a value chain.

2-2c The Value Chain

To create optimal value, a company must examine the entire supply chain, from initial production to final consumption, to understand where costs are incurred in the process. Consultants at Bain & Company liken it to the game Jenga, in which players must remove as many blocks as possible from a tower, using them to build additional structures, all without causing the original structure to come crashing down. This seems an apt analogy.

They identify four key factors in this effort:

- Information search costs
- Transaction costs
- Fragmentation of the customer marketplace
- Standardization of products

friction The economic term that describes the presence of information search and transactions costs, which do not add value, in a channel of distribution.

Together information and transaction costs typically account for more than 40% of total costs. Economists characterize these costs as "**friction**" in channels of distribution, and they offer ripe targets for cost reduction in value chains.

Integrated value chains represent an important step in managing both the supply-facing and the customer-facing sides of the business. Dell's integrated value chain operates almost entirely in Internet space, hence the term *virtual value chain*.

2-3 Dell's Direct Model

Dell Computers is one of the classic examples of creating a value chain in Internet space, one that is not a series of links, but a network of interconnected enterprises, both supplier and customer. Before Dell's direct model became a force in the industry, personal computers met all four of the categories established by Bain. Search and transaction costs were high, especially for the small business or individual customer. The fragmented market ranged from the individual customer buying a single unit to the very large corporation, which might purchase several hundred computers each month. Even very large customers tended to settle for a standard product because it was cheaper to buy in a large, standardized lot until Dell.

just in time A set of production management techniques that requires production close to the time of demand, reducing work-in-process inventory and the overall cost of production.

Figures 2-4a and 2-4b are a representation of the traditional value chain in the personal computer industry versus the Dell value chain. It is particularly important to note that "Distribution" does not exist as a separate step in Dell's JIT (**just in time**) production environment. The flexible manufacturing approach allows Dell to customize a computer for an individual customer. It also allows Dell to ship directly to its customers, increasing inventory turns, decreasing inventory obsolescence, and decreasing the number of hands that touch each machine.

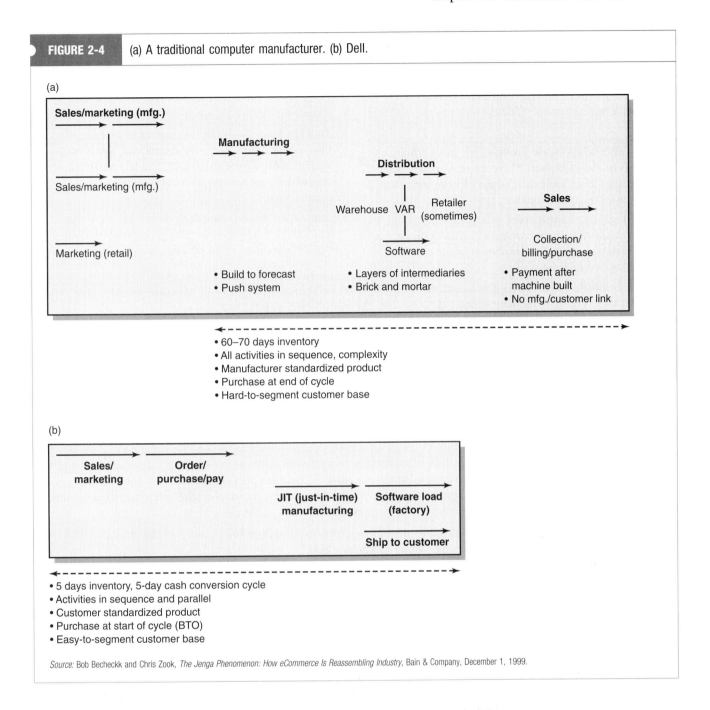

FIGURE 2-4   (a) A traditional computer manufacturer. (b) Dell.

(a)

Sales/marketing (mfg.)

Sales/marketing (mfg.)

Marketing (retail)

Manufacturing

Distribution

Warehouse VAR Retailer (sometimes)

Software

Sales

Collection/billing/purchase

• Build to forecast
• Push system

• Layers of intermediaries
• Brick and mortar

• Payment after machine built
• No mfg./customer link

• 60–70 days inventory
• All activities in sequence, complexity
• Manufacturer standardized product
• Purchase at end of cycle
• Hard-to-segment customer base

(b)

Sales/marketing

Order/purchase/pay

JIT (just-in-time) manufacturing

Software load (factory)

Ship to customer

• 5 days inventory, 5-day cash conversion cycle
• Activities in sequence and parallel
• Customer standardized product
• Purchase at start of cycle (BTO)
• Easy-to-segment customer base

Source: Bob Becheckk and Chris Zook, *The Jenga Phenomenon: How eCommerce Is Reassembling Industry,* Bain & Company, December 1, 1999.

In naming Dell "America's Most Admired Company" for 2005, *Fortune* magazine pointed out that Dell is now the worldwide leader in personal computer market share, with 17.6%. Its worldwide revenues are growing at a rate of 19%, 7 points higher than the rest of the industry, and it has a net margin of 6% while others are closer to 1%. Why? "Because operating expenses—e.g., selling, general and administrative—are so low, a direct result of the cost-effectiveness of selling directly to customers rather than through a middleman." In addition, Dell carries only 4 days of inventory, compared with IBM, which carries 20 days' worth, and Hewlett-Packard, which carries 28 days' worth.[13] *Fast Company* magazine adds that "Dell has replaced inventory with information, and that has helped turn it into one of the fastest, most hyperefficient organizations on the planet."[14]

Dell also uses information to create customer value. One primary mechanism for doing this is its Premier Pages. Each business customer, from a Fortune 500 enterprise

Case in Point 2-3 The Dell Direct Model

According to Dell.com, the Dell direct model "starts and ends with our customers." The five tenets of the model are as follows:

- **A direct relationship provides the most efficient path to the customer.** There are no intermediaries. Instead Dell has sales and services forces organized around customer segments.

- **Dell acts as a single point of accountability,** although, as this chapter describes, many components of their systems are manufactured by others. This increases customer satisfaction.

- **The build-to-order model** gives customers exactly what they want without maintaining expensive inventory that quickly becomes obsolete. Customers receive the latest technology at the best prices.

- **Dell is a low-cost leader** because of its efficient supply chain and manufacturing operations, collaboration with industry partners that results in the use of standards-based technology, and business process improvements.

- **Standards-based technology** gives customers choice and flexibility not possible with proprietary technology developed and sold by a single enterprise.

Source: Direct Model, http://www1.us.dell.com/content/topics/global.aspx/corp/background/en/directmodel?c=us&l=en&s=corp&~ck=mn.

to a small local business, can have its own secure page on the Dell site. This includes the products that have been approved for purchase by the firm and support information for those specific products. Products not approved for purchase are not even seen, making life easier for the purchasing department. In addition, employees with purchasing authority can simply log on and make their purchase without going through purchasing, saving time for both. Dell also wins because purchases are driven to the Web site, where transactions are cheaper. This service is feasible for even a small business because Dell's telephone representatives have easy-to-use templates that allow them to set up a page by simply entering information provided by the customer over the phone. Many companies have copied this process; remember the reference to "customized online catalog" in the Herman Miller example.

2-3a In the Words of Michael Dell

Dell Founder and Chairman Michael Dell identifies strong customer relationships, speed, and business focus as the key elements of competitive advantage in the Internet economy. Dell has developed its direct sales model, which was initially focused on the business-to-business (B2B) market, into a direct relationship model that produces unusually close ties with its customers. It focuses on customer relationships and its build-to-order model to achieve speed (reduced **cycle times**) and maintain its strong financial performance.

cycle time The time from beginning to completion of a business process; for example, the time it takes to fill a customer's order.

Michael Dell is a leading advocate of value chain integration. Observations from speeches to industry groups and college students articulate his vision as follows:

- *On value chain integration:* "The concept of virtual integration essentially describes how we have integrated with our suppliers and partners as one enterprise, as opposed to trying to build all those things ourselves.... Figuring out what we really do well and then partnering with the best in the industry has made a huge impact on our success."[15]

- *On business focus:* "Because of our close relationships with customers, we have access to an enormous amount of information about what they like and don't like. We build our business around customer segments.... Most companies in our industry run from a product and technology driven process. Our customer focus gives us a very different outlook than others have in our industry."[16]

- *On customer relationships:* "We look at things like the customer experience and measurements that tell us how we're doing for our customers throughout the lifecycle of the ownership experience. We look at different elements of the service level that we provide to our customers."[17]

- *On customer value:* "Customers may have a unique image or set of programs they wanted loaded on their computer system. They can upload that into a special place on Dell.com and then every time a computer is built for them that software goes on the computers that they order. And, of course, you can do that millions and millions of times . . . that allows us to continue to scale our costs, be more efficient, and bring more value to users."[18]

- *On speed:* "Speed is very important to us, as is agility. Our customer teams can adjust promotions and advertising immediately to drive volume in specific areas of the business."[19]

- *On metrics that drive the business:* "We get real-time information. At 3:00 or 4:00 a.m. every day, I get an automated report that tells me exactly what we sold the prior day by product, by customer, by region . . . compared to last quarter or last year, every product line and all kinds of data. And that data goes out throughout the organization so that our teams can understand what's happening . . . they may see by 10:00 a.m. we're not getting enough calls in, so we'll send more ads out and drive up the leads coming in, [or] change the pricing dynamic. If we introduce a new product, we know within a week or two whether it's going to succeed."[20]

- *On global expansion:* "We have only six percent market share in an $800 billion market. There are enormous opportunities for us to grow across multiple dimensions in terms of products, with servers, storage, printing, and services. . . . China is the fourth largest market for Dell in the world. They have an enormous population and need technology."[21]

Jack Welch, the legendary former CEO of GE, sums it up: "No one has pulled the levers of cost, quality, and service better than Dell."[22]

2-4 Creating a Virtual Value Chain

As the Herman Miller, Zara, and Dell examples illustrate, integrating the complex value chain process and moving it onto the Web is a formidable task. The three steps shown in Figure 2-5 represent basic steps in the process. Highlights from the value chain development of consumer snack maker Frito-Lay and business services provider FedEx help illuminate the process.

2-4a Visibility

The first step in creating a value chain is for the enterprise to provide **visibility** or translate all of the relevant information about all activities in the supply chain to all employees who need it. Frito-Lay created visibility for its supply chain when it gave handheld order-entry computers to its route salespersons. Inside the retail store, the reps were able to use the devices to record store-level inventory data, which was immediately transmitted to Frito-Lay headquarters by satellite. This system not only improved management's ability to forecast demand and inventory levels but also permitted reps to make price changes in the field to respond to local market conditions. Data about competitor promotional activity were also collected in the field and transmitted to headquarters. Although the initial investment was substantial, Frito-Lay's director of information systems reported that it paid back the cost every year in savings on inventory that had gone stale on retail shelves or in the distribution pipeline.

    FedEx pioneered visibility for its service operations when it introduced COSMOS (Customer Operations Service Master Online System) in 1979. The following year it added DADS (Digital Assisted Dispatch System) to transmit package pickup requests to couriers while they were on the road. In 1986, it added

visibility The ability to obtain supply chain information, especially about goods in transit, in an easy and timely fashion.

FIGURE 2-5	Creating a virtual value chain.

Figure content:

Frito-Lay		
Late 1980s—Gives handheld computers to route salespeople and builds data warehouse; store-level data transmitted daily to central information system	Late 1990—With parent company PepsiCo and Tropicana Products unit, has consolidated system to monitor and maintain store-level inventory and to develop common promotions	2000—Builds knowledge management portal to make customer knowledge consistent and available and to foster collaboration among employees 2004—Prepares to incorporate radio frequency identification (RFID) tags into its supply chain systems
 **Visibility** Enterprises are able to "see" supply chain processes more clearly through their information systems.	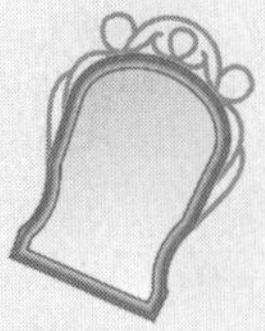 **Mirroring** Enterprises create a parallel system in which information "mirrors" the physical activities of the supply chain.	 **More value to customers** Enterprises use information to deliver value to customers in different ways and to create new value.
FedEx		
Early 1980s—Launches digital assisted dispatch system (DADS) to transmit information to couriers on the road	Middle 1990s—Introduces software that allows customers to manage shipping from desktops and follows with a variety of e-business tools	2002—Announces ability to track FedEx shipments from wireless devices 2004—Purchases Kinko's, creating the "File, Print, FedEx Kinko's" service

Super Tracker, a handheld barcode scanning system, and became able to manage its package delivery operations in real time. It was time for these companies to implement the next stage.

2-4b Mirroring

mirroring Using information to present a complete and timely picture of activities in the value chain.

The second stage is called **mirroring,** the ability to create information systems that provide a complete picture of the supply chain at a given point in time. Leading-edge companies like Frito-Lay and FedEx have not only created systems that provide a complete real-time view of their supply chains but also shared this data with their customers.

At Frito-Lay, mirroring takes the form of electronic sharing of store-level inventory and pricing data with the retailer through the use of handheld computers given to store reps. By ensuring that the manufacturer and the customer have precisely the same data, the system substantially reduces procurement costs and errors.

In 1992, FedEx began providing free software that allowed customers to schedule shipments and track packages using dial-up connections. In 1994, it launched fedex.com, a Web site on which customers could access many services, including real-time package scheduling and tracking. Customers were able to see the FedEx information in real time, providing a degree of control that led to increased customer satisfaction. For FedEx, it greatly decreased the number of routine inquiries to the telephone call center and substantially reduced the cost of that function.

2-4c Enhancing Customer Value

The direct customers of Frito-Lay are, of course, retail grocery outlets of various kinds. Beyond the cost and time savings their information-driven store replenishment system is able to offer, Frito-Lay is able to offer services such as merchandising plans tailored to local conditions, tailored promotional programs, and other types of merchandising incentives. Their corporate knowledge **portal** makes it easier to deliver these benefits in the field. Frito-Lay's information system has been merged with that of its parent company, PepsiCo, and its Tropicana Products unit since the late 1990s, and that offers further opportunities for integrated promotional programs. When radio frequency identification (**RFID**; discussed in detail later in this chapter) tags are embedded in individual product packages, it will be possible to track inventory from factory through retail store with total precision.

FedEx also delivers new types of value to customers in various ways. In recent years it has become an integral part of many other Web sites, allowing customers to schedule shipments without leaving their own site. It offers specialized services on its own site, including the free FedEx Global Trade Manager. This service helps small and medium-size businesses deal with some of the difficulties of international commerce by allowing shippers to identify and prepare appropriate import/export forms.[23] The acquisition of Kinko's in December 2004 created new options for FedEx to serve customers. Businesses large or small can now transfer a file from a personal computer to a Kinko's, which will print and FedEx the document according to the sender's instructions, as illustrated in Chapter 1.

2-5 Benefits of an Integrated Value Chain

The kind of integrated value chains exemplified by Frito-Lay and FedEx have five key characteristics:

- They are customer-centric, focusing on customer needs as well as supply chain and logistics issues.
- They encompass both the demand chain and the supply chain, from customers' customers to suppliers' suppliers.
- They are designed to compete as an extended enterprise, bringing customers and suppliers into the system through real-time information flows.
- They increase customer value added by provision of information and customer service and support.
- They offer the opportunity to create specialized value propositions for individual customers.[24]

In the Internet economy, customer value has taken on a special meaning. The quality of products is still unquestionably important. However, the stark truth is that many companies have mastered the art of product quality. They spent much of the last 10 to 15 years learning to produce products at or near the **six-sigma level** of quality (no more than 3.4 defects per million according to the American Society for Quality). That kind of quality has become expected and even standard in many applications. It is necessary, but no longer sufficient. Bix Norman, the originator of the SQA concept at Herman Miller, says:

> "A product's a product.... It isn't about product, it's about simplicity and how fast you can get it.... If you looked at our industry from a customer's viewpoint of what it was like to buy and get office furniture, you'd find that it was just a big, huge pain."[25]

Customers want performance, reliability, speed, and convenience. In order to deliver, enterprises must be agile, reacting quickly to changes in customer demand, as shown by the Zara customer feedback model. They also must be **scalable,** that is, able to grow as needed without the need to replace entire old systems with completely new ones. Information must flow freely and quickly in all directions inside the value chain often using corporate extranets that permit secure exchange of data.[26]

The economic upheaval that began in 2002 may have slowed business integration for a time, but the pace of change has once again accelerated, as is described in the

portal A large site with multiple services, ranging from news to directories to searches, that acts as an entry point onto the Internet.

RFID Radio frequency identification technology allows the identification of tagged goods from a distance with no intervention by a human operation.

six sigma The quality management technique that results in near-perfect products, technically results that fall within six standard deviations from the mean of a normal distribution.

scalable The degree to which an information system can grow with demand without completely replacing the system.

final section of this chapter. In this environment, both management vision and organization-wide execution are necessary to create an integrated value chain and transform it into a network that benefits all parties. Many kinds of supporting services are required as companies undergo these kinds of transformations. Most of these are specialized and beyond the scope of this book. However, three types of processes and their enabling software need to be understood to have a satisfactory grasp of the scope and nature of value chain integration.

2-6 EDI, ERP, and Web Services

Electronic data interchange, the oldest of the processes, provides a way of automating the supply chain. *Enterprise resource planning* is a broader term that describes systems stretching back into the production process and forward into the order processing and distribution systems. Web services is a new entry into the process automation space. Here is an overview of each, and how they play into the Internet marketing mix.

2-6a Electronic Data Interchange

electronic data interchange
The general term used to describe the digitizing of business information like orders and invoices so that they may be communicated electronically between suppliers and customers.

Electronic data interchange (EDI) has been available and in use by large corporations and their suppliers for more than two decades. The term is representative of the process; essentially EDI enables paperless transaction processing. Despite the benefits of speed, error reduction, and lowered costs that it offers, the cost and difficulty of implementing the technology has slowed its adoption. In particular, the cost of an EDI installation put it out of the reach of small businesses in the early years.

In general, the steps in an EDI transaction are as follows:

- The order is entered into the system and an electronic purchase order is generated. This purchase order contains all the information of a paper purchase order. In addition, it may contain information required by the purchaser, such as stocking information needed by a retailer.

value-added network
Connectivity between computer systems that adds additional functions to ensure the quality and security of the data transmitted.

- The order is sent to the seller, either directly or through a proprietary **value-added network** (VAN).

- The order enters the seller's order entry and processing system.

- An electronic acknowledgment is sent to the purchaser.

- The seller's system generates fulfillment instructions to its warehouse, which fills the order and prepares it for shipping.

- An electronic invoice is prepared by the seller and transmitted to the purchaser.

- Payment for the goods is transferred by means of a secure electronic payments system.

One supplier of services estimates that more than 80,000 companies use EDI systems.[27] Because large firms can require that their suppliers use EDI to deal with them, this multiplies the number of users many-fold.

Wal-Mart has always required that its suppliers do business with them electronically. In 2002, it mandated that suppliers use an Internet-based platform, replacing the older and more expensive VANs. A consultant with the Giga Information Group notes that "they [Wal-Mart] are big enough to tell people what to do if they want to do business with them. . . . They can also afford the staff and the technical people to monitor the thousands of connections that will now be coming in." Wal-Mart replies that customers will ultimately be the beneficiaries. "Any savings gets driven right to the bottom line," the spokesman said, adding that Wal-Mart is just gearing up to roll this new program out to its suppliers and will work closely with them to make it a success. "We look to take out any cost we can." Wal-Mart has more than 14,000 suppliers who process more than $217 billion worth of transactions via EDI annually.[28]

In the early days of EDI, software packages alone cost tens of thousands of dollars. Their use required extensive, and expensive, systems integration, as well as skilled technicians to operate the system. Today, there are many hosted EDI applications that are more affordable to the small and medium-sized business without an extensive information technology (IT) workforce. In fact, a small industry has grown up around providing EDI services for Wal-Mart and for the U.S. government, which also mandates EDI use for much of its procurement activity. One of the suppliers estimates that it costs $70 or more and takes up to 10 days to process a paper order, whereas an EDI order can be processed for a dollar or less and requires only 1 day. Quality is improved because manual and repetitive order entry is eliminated. Faster order processing also decreases inventory cost for suppliers.[29]

The universal platform provided by the Internet has fueled growth in EDI that seemed unlikely before the Internet, although corporations have expressed concerns about security when moving from a closed VAN environment to the open environment of the Internet. However, leaders in the supply chain arena like Wal-Mart and GE require that their suppliers be EDI-compliant, using software that interfaces smoothly with their internal systems. That represents the second key issue. Speedy transfer of data between companies is only part of the picture. Internal processes must also be automated in order to achieve the full benefit of an integrated value chain. Enterprise resource planning is the technique most often used to achieve information integration inside the organization.

2-6b Enterprise Resource Planning

Enterprise resource planning (ERP) is the name given to modular software systems that are aimed at automating all business processes within an organization. Such a system requires nothing less than creating a digital record of every business transaction in a totally integrated enterprise-wide system.

The goal of ERP is to tie together systems that have formerly run independently, often on mainframe computers, into an integrated system that gives a complete view of corporate activity from the perspective and desktop of the relevant decision maker. The human resources professional needs one view of personnel data; the manufacturing planner needs to see the same data through a different lens. The marketer needs access to enterprise data, including personnel availability, as well as access to a wealth of marketing-specific customer and promotional data.

According to the ERP Resource Center, there are five basic reasons for an organization to embark on an ERP project:

- To *integrate financial information* so that all users work from a single information source.

- To *integrate customer order information* so that it moves seamlessly between all functions from order intake to customer fulfillment to inventory monitoring. This also presents the opportunity to make this information visible to the customer.

- To *standardize and speed up manufacturing processes* in an effort to increase productivity and decrease costs.

- To *reduce inventory* by speeding up the internal movement of work-in-process and finished goods inventory. An ERP system, however, is not a substitute for supply chain management software.

- To standardize *human resources information*, especially important at merged companies where the previously independent firms used different human resources systems.[30]

If you are able to enroll for classes online or to check your grades online at the end of the semester, the enabling system is most likely the result of an ERP initiative. It has

enterprise resource Planning that integrates all aspects of the business from manufacturing resource planning and scheduling through service functions like human resources.

not all been smooth sailing at many institutions, however. Many schools faced the same situation:

> By the mid-1990s, most college administrative systems were a disconnected mess of **legacy** applications. Forward-thinking administrators knew that they needed to graduate their aging homegrown systems. College administrators loved the idea of having an HR management, financial and student administration system that could unite offices and departments.[31]

Colleges and universities almost universally opted for ERP software. Many of them were originally motivated by the same concern as commercial firms—that their systems would crash on January 1, 2000 **(Y2K).** Their legacy systems were often either homegrown or built on commercial software that had been substantially modified over the years. Most lacked the number of skilled IT people required to develop a system from scratch, even if there had been sufficient time. Consequently, they opted for the installation of ERP software. Few have found it easy. Students and staff have found themselves unable to access systems that provided key information, such as room assignments, or services, such s financial aid awards. IT administrators have been faced with system malfunctions or crashes at peak load times, such as when students return to campus in the fall. Administrators have been confronted with longer time frames and higher costs than they originally anticipated.[32] You may have experienced difficulty with some of these systems yourself in registering for classes or downloading documents for class. You can be assured that the higher education experience has not been substantially different from that of many corporations.

The need for integration is compelling, but the difficulties are substantial. It may take several years for an integration project to be completed. A study of sixty-three corporations by the Meta Group estimated the average **total cost of ownership** (TCO) of an ERP installation to be $15 million, with an astounding range of $400,000 to $300 million. They found that it took 8 months after system completion to see any financial benefits. At that point, the median annual cost saving was estimated at $1.6 million.[33] It is even harder to measure the benefits to staff and customers—ranging from a student's ability to register for classes online to a corporate customer's ability to track an order from his desktop computer. Put another way, integrating internal systems is a necessary precursor to providing customer value through visibility of supply chain processes.

However, the costs and difficulties of implementing EDI and ERP have given rise to another set of technologies aimed at the same issues. This set of technologies has come to be known by the entirely nondescriptive name of Web services.

2-6c Web Services

Web services is an emerging discipline, and many companies are eager to sell software and services into this market. Consequently, there is a great deal of hype and considerable confusion over just what the term means. The basic idea, however, is to enable different computer systems—read that various elements in the supply chain—to communicate with one another using accepted telecommunications protocols and programming languages (e.g., **HTML** and **XML**). This is intended to eliminate the need for expensive software and systems integration that are needed with both EDI and ERP.

The basic toolkit for Web services includes a messaging **protocol,** definitions of the interfaces that programmers need to write applications that communicate with customer or supplier applications, and a directory of Web services for programmers. Using these components, programmers can construct applications that can locate and communicate with other applications without extensive custom programming and systems integration. Notice that this list does not include security protocols, and this is a concern to managers who are considering allowing suppliers and customers access to their internal records. Beyond these simple statements, the description of Web services quickly becomes highly technical and difficult for the

---

legacy Existing information systems, usually ones running on mainframe computers or minicomputers.

Y2K The acronym given to the fear that, because of shortsighted design of early computer programs, many software applications for critical businesses like utilities and banks would cease to function at midnight on January 1, 2000.

total cost of ownership How much it actually costs to own a piece of technology, including items like the original cost, upgrades, maintenance, technical support, and training.

Web services Applications that allow enterprises to exchange information over the Internet using open (public) standards; this permits otherwise incompatible systems to interact with one another without human or programming intervention.

HTML Hypertext markup language, one of the foundations of the common Internet platform; describes the structure of Web documents using a type of coding called tags.

XML Extensible markup language; like HTML, XML uses tags to code documents—technically, it defines data elements on a page; practically, it allows the creation of documents that can be filled out and transmitted electronically.

protocol A set of rules that govern the sending and receiving of data.

layperson to follow. An example using a familiar firm may help to make the situation clearer.

You know Amazon as one of the premier retailers of the Internet. You may also be aware that when Amazon began, no robust e-commerce software was available. They had to develop their own. Over the years, that has evolved into a platform for doing business with Amazon, the B2B aspect of their model. According to their Web site, "Amazon Web Services (AWS) provides software developers direct access to Amazon's ever-growing technology platform and product data. Developers are empowered to innovate and build businesses by creating dynamic, highly-effective Web sites and Web applications."

Amazon Web Services is an open system that gives software developers access to their code so the developers can write programs that interface with internal Amazon systems. They list several groups of users who will benefit from their open system:

- Associates: Our Associates program (to be discussed in Chapter 3) enables Web sites to link to Amazon.com and earn referral fees for sales that they drive through their links. Many Associates are now using the Amazon E-Commerce Service to build more effective links to our store, thus enhancing their sites and earning more money.

- Sellers and Vendors: Amazon has thousands of third-party sellers who offer their products on our Web site. Using the Amazon E-Commerce Service, these sellers can easily manage large quantities of inventory on our platform and download the latest product information to make sure that their products are competitively priced.

- Developers: Among the tens of thousands of developers who have signed up for our Web Services program, many are now creating solutions to help other people work with Amazon. These solutions are powered using our Web Services APIs **(Application Programming Interfaces)**.

application programming interfaces A set of programming tools including small modules of software and communications protocols used as building blocks in building software applications.

Participation in the program is "easy and free." The software developer registers for the program, downloads free code samples, reads the online documentation, and begins to write the software.[34] Developers can also gain access to the database for Amazon's own site. This includes things like product data and images that allow developers to build virtual stores to sell Amazon's products. Developers, however, do not gain access to Amazon's extensive database of customer information.[35]

In true Amazon fashion, they continue to push the envelope in terms of expanding the services they offer to other marketers. An increasing number of online retailers, ranging from Borders bookstore and Target to British department store chain Marks & Spencer, are using the Amazon e-commerce platform to conduct their online business.[36]

Web services technology can be used to tie together incompatible applications inside the enterprise or, as in this example, to make internal systems visible and accessible to outsiders. The use of common services accessed on the Web has the potential to be easier than the complex software and process integration projects represented by EDI and ERP, but it will not be a panacea for all supply chain integration issues.

2-7 The RFID Future

Increasing the speed and reducing the cost of supply chain operation continues to be the focus of both business and technological innovation. Consider the following scenario:

> Somewhere in Neuss-Norf, Germany, a customer is approaching NCR's new FastLane self-checkout machine. Using **radio-frequency IDs**, or **smart tags**, on every item, the customer's groceries are being scanned on-the-spot and tallied

radio frequency IDs (also RFID tags, smart tags) Tiny silicon chips with antennae that can receive and transmit information.

Source: http://www.canadaid.ca.

The Canadian Cattle Identification Program is an industry trace-back system designed for the containment and eradication of animal disease.

Source: http://en.wikipedia.org/wiki/Electronic_toll_collection.

Many ETC systems use transponders like this one to electronically debit the accounts of registered cars without their stopping.

bar code The printed, machine-readable set of black lines and white space that identifies products according to the universal product code (UPC).

up—no need to take them out of the cart. At the same time, the **RFID tags** are being automatically disabled so security sensors will know the customer isn't shoplifting.[37]

Self-checkout is available at supermarkets and mass marketers around the world. Goods are marked with **bar codes** that are passed over scanners that read identifying data and price. So what is so new about the prototype system at the RFID Innovation Center? It uses RFID tags, essentially computer chips, as the data storage device. RFID tags open a wide range of supply chain possibilities over and above the ubiquitous bar codes. First, these tiny tags can hold more data than a bar code. Second, they do not have to be passed directly over a scanner, but can transmit data from a distance as individual items or containers full of individually tagged items move from one location to another. RFID tags are already being used in libraries, in bookstores, and on employee and student ID badges, as well as in car keys, electronic toll passes, and tracking bracelets for prisoners.

RFID technology is not new. It was used by the British in World War II to identify friendly aircraft. The OnStar System discussed in Chapter 1 is an example of RFID technology, as is Mobil's Speedpass system. Other applications on the horizon range from chips replacing bar codes on consumer packaged goods to implanted chips that can track lost pets using the Global Positioning System (GPS) in the owner's mobile phone.

> **FIGURE 2-6**   RFID schema.

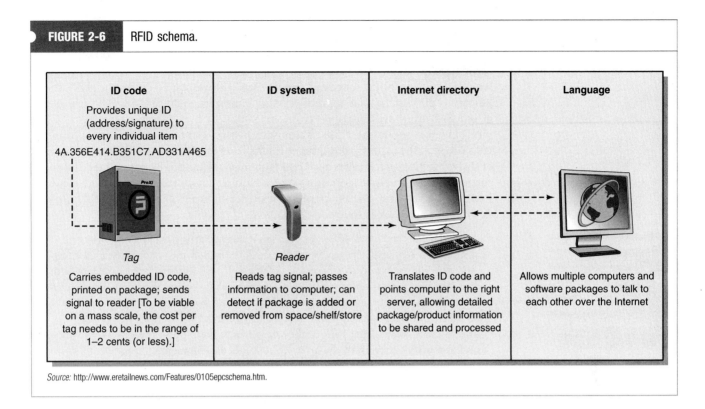

ID code	ID system	Internet directory	Language
Provides unique ID (address/signature) to every individual item 4A.356E414.B351C7.AD331A465 *Tag*			
Carries embedded ID code, printed on package; sends signal to reader [To be viable on a mass scale, the cost per tag needs to be in the range of 1–2 cents (or less).]	*Reader* Reads tag signal; passes information to computer; can detect if package is added or removed from space/shelf/store	Translates ID code and points computer to the right server, allowing detailed package/product information to be shared and processed	Allows multiple computers and software packages to talk to each other over the Internet

Source: http://www.eretailnews.com/Features/0105epcschema.htm.

An RFID system begins with a tag, which contains a chip with a unique identifying code called an **electronic product code.** The format of the code and the number of characters it contains permit an almost infinite number of IDs. Consequently, each individual product can be given its own identifier, including all the data in the retail **SKU.** The tag also contains a tiny antenna. As the product moves from one place to another a reader captures the data on the tag. The tag reader (or interrogator) captures data from as far as 20 feet away without the intervention of a human operator. The data are passed to a host computer which can process and transmit the data.[38] Figure 2-6 represents the basic process.

The Store of the Future prototype specifies a number of supply chain elements that can benefit from the use of RFID technology:

- Delivery of goods to the retail store warehouse. RFID is used to check to ensure that the incoming goods match the order.

- Warehouse management. The tracking system shows exactly which products, at the SKU level, are stored in the warehouse.

- Movement of goods to the retail store. When goods are moved to the store back room or onto the floor, the system records their location.

- Intelligent shelves in the store. Shelves are equipped with readers that record product movement and notify store staff when the shelf needs to be restocked.

- Tags can be used for promotion. Tags on CDs, DVDs, and videos allow customers to watch trailers of films or sample music CDs at the point of purchase.[39]

Technology to perform most of these activities has been available for a number of activities. RFID allows them to be performed in seamless fashion from the time the product leaves the factory until the time the consumer purchases the product and deactivates the tag. Put another way, the manufacturer knows where the product is at all times, whether it is in transit or in inventory at some point in the physical distribution system.

electronic product code
Made up of header information, manufacturer identification, product identification, and serial number in a way that provides unique identification number for more than 16 million manufacturers and SKUs as compared to 100,000 manufacturers and SKUs for the Universal Product Code (UPC).

SKU An identifying code assigned by the retailer that describes a specific item by product, size, color, flavor, or any other relevant feature.

2-7a RFID Mandates

On June 11, 2003, Wal-Mart announced that it would require its top 100 suppliers to use RFID tags on products going into three Texas warehouses and the 150 stores they serve by January 2005. A second tier of suppliers was expected to tag products by January 1, 2006. One analyst predicted that Wal-Mart could save $8.4 billion, mostly in reduced inventory and labor costs, by 2007.[40] Chief information officer (CIO) Linda Dillman points out, "That's almost more than our total profit as a company."[41] Nevertheless, she expects substantial benefits from improvements like better stocking of shelves at peak traffic times and reduction in shoplifting. The first tagged products, part of a test with eight large suppliers, including Procter & Gamble and Hewlett-Packard, arrived at a Dallas distribution center in April 2004. The *RFID Journal* describes the process as follows:

> Tagged pallets and cases of those products will arrive at Wal-Mart's regional distribution center, where readers at the dock doors will automatically scan the tags. The data will be passed to an application that will alert the retailer's operations and merchandising teams and the products' suppliers that the specific shipment has arrived.
>
> At the distribution center, cases will be removed from the pallets and processed, as usual, and then trucked to the seven participating Wal-Mart stores. When tagged cases arrive at the back of the seven stores, the tags on the cases will be read and automatically confirm the arrival of the specific shipment.[42]

Wal-Mart expects to read tags at the distribution center and back doors of the participating stores with 100% accuracy. The tags will be embedded in packaging, which will be removed and disposed of by the consumer. The EPC global symbol will be on the package, and signage in the store will alert customers to the presence of tags on some products. Dillman stresses Wal-Mart's attention to the customer privacy issue: "'We certainly understand and appreciate consumer concern about privacy,' Dillman said. 'That's why we want our customers to know that RFID tags will not contain nor collect any additional information about consumers. In fact, for the foreseeable future, there won't even be any RFID readers on our stores' main sales floor.'"[43]

2-7b Moving into the Future

Other large retailers including mass merchandiser Target and supermarket Albertson's have announced RFID initiatives and others are considering it. The U.S. government also mandated that suppliers to agencies, including the Department of Defense, begin using tags in 2005.[44]

In the United Kingdom, supermarket giant Tesco has cooperated with Gillette on an in-store test of RFID technology. Gillette was concerned about razors not being restocked at retail in a timely fashion, leading to lost sales. In addition, its Mach3 razor has been a particular target of shoplifters. Consequently, in late 2002, Gillette announced that it would purchase up to 500 million tags, attaching them to products near the point of manufacture instead of later in the supply chain, where bar codes are usually added. Some of the tags were to be used in the early phases of the Wal-Mart supplier mandate; others were used on goods shipped to Tesco.

In addition to inventory management, Tesco was interested in testing various store security measures. For the test Tesco installed "smart shelves" in their Cambridge, England, store. The shelves can read the tags and send a message to a store computer when the stock is low or when a large number of products are removed at once, suggesting theft.

The *Guardian* newspaper ran an article on the uses of RFID in the big grocery stores entitled "Tesco Tests Spy Chip Technology." According to the article:

> tags in the razor blades trigger a CCTV [closed circuit] camera when a packet is removed from the shelf. A second camera takes a picture at the checkout and security

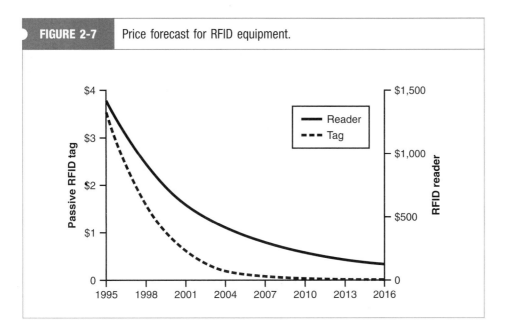

FIGURE 2-7 Price forecast for RFID equipment.

staff then compare the two images, raising the possibility that they could be used to prevent theft.[45]

The article quoted a Tesco spokesman as saying that customers know there are closed circuit TV cameras in the store. He asserted that shelf stocking information was the object of the test. Still, the manager of the Cambridge Tesco told the paper that he had reported a shoplifter to the police. The disclosure prompted protests outside the Tesco store, and the test was concluded later that month. At the same time, Tesco was reported to be testing tags on DVDs in its other locations throughout Britain.[46]

The gradual rollout of RFID technology continues, motivated by the potential for large cost savings. The rollout is slowed, however, by the current prices for RFID tags, readers (Figure 2-7), and the associated networks. At 50 cents to a dollar, tags are not economically feasible for low-margin goods such as most of those found in supermarkets and mass merchandisers. When they reach as little as 1 cent per tag, as is predicted to occur within the next several years, it will become feasible to tag individual products.

2-8 The Benefits of Business Integration

Moving from a linear supply chain to a web of interlocking partnerships that work together to create maximum customer value is essential to success in the Internet economy. The dominant characteristics of these new organizational modes can be summarized as the "four V's" of business integration:

- *Velocity.* Customers demand better products and services and expect to receive them more quickly and with complete accuracy.
- *Visibility.* Transparency of information between customers and all value chain members creates a self-service model that speeds flows and improves customer satisfaction.
- *Variability.* Customers want products manufactured and delivered according to their individual requirements.
- *Volume.* Achieving profitable scale and scope in an environment that requires marketing to individual customers is essential.[47]

Technology is essential to achieve the benefits of organizational integration, but technology alone does not present a solution. Achieving the desired outcomes requires relentless focus on the needs of the consumer, achieving internal efficiencies of time and cost, and managing across organizational boundaries to achieve maximum impact.

Summary

The supply chain of the past cannot meet the requirements of the Internet economy. Neither can a "one size fits all" product that is pushed through channels using conventional marketing promotional and pricing techniques. In some cases, such as configuring internal and external networks, the final product is inherently a custom proposition. In others, such as office furniture systems, prospering in a competitive marketplace requires using a set of products to meet customer needs in an individualized manner.

The supply chain has evolved into a virtual value chain made up of interconnected relationships. Each member contributes its core capability and the final product is delivered to the customer as a single strong and recognizable brand. This represents a revolution in business organization and management that few enterprises have yet achieved. As examples throughout this chapter have emphasized, it is an achievement that can be years in the making.

Enterprises will often begin by creating information systems that allow them to visualize all aspects of the value chain, first as a snapshot in time and then in real time. They can then progress to the creation of information systems

that fully mirror the activities of the value chain. That information will first be of use to management in controlling, forecasting, and planning. It will generate additional value if it is shared with customers. That will be the first step in delivering value to customers in ways that are faster and more convenient. It can be followed by the creation of entirely new kinds of customer value.

None of this is easy. It is likely to require reengineering of existing business processes and major projects to integrate internal systems and to communicate across organizational boundaries with both suppliers and customers. Existing technologies like EDI and ERP will be part of this process. Web services offer the potential for achieving the benefits of integration without time-consuming and costly integration projects. RFID technology holds great promise for providing the data that will speed and smooth the operation of the supply chain for manufacturers, distributors, and retailers alike.

Despite the complexity of these undertakings, this is clearly the direction in which all enterprises need to be moving with a sense, not of deliberation, but of urgency.

Quiz

1. Herman Miller realized _____ as a benefit of its value chain improvements.
   a. ability to maintain a larger inventory of finished products
   b. improvement in the time it takes to deliver an order to a customer
   c. decrease in turnover of inventory

2. The value chain incorporates _____.
   a. the concept of vertical integration
   b. distinct divisions between entities in the supply chain
   c. channels of distribution that reach the ultimate customer

3. The core processes of marketing include _____.
   a. supply chain management
   b. customer communications
   c. order processing and inventory management

4. _____ is *not* a feature of an integrated/virtual value chain.
   a. Increased customer satisfaction
   b. Increased quality of products and services
   c. Paper forms move through the same process as electronic information

5. Zara is successful in the highly competitive fashion industry because it _____.
   a. outsources production to low-wage countries
   b. is able to get the fashion consumers want into stores quickly
   c. relies on formal surveys of consumers to judge what will be popular next season

6. Major components of supply chain costs do *not* include _____.
   a. information search costs
   b. software costs
   c. transaction costs

7. Dell promotes customer loyalty by _____.
   a. Premier Pages
   b. frequent telephone calls
   c. comprehensive satisfaction surveys every business quarter

8. One of the ways in which the Internet is changing business is _____.
   a. increasing the need for speed and agility
   b. making market share less important
   c. increasing the reliance on hierarchical organizations

9. Which of the following is *not* an example of an integration process that is used in the creation of virtual value chains?
   a. EDI
   b. Web services
   c. XML

10. _____ allows supply chain partners to use the common platform of the Internet to exchange data without extensive back-end integration.
   a. ERP
   b. EDI
   c. Web services

11. RFID is a 21st-century technology that is destined to revolutionize supply chains.
   a. true
   b. false

12. RFID technology involves _____.
   a. tags that store more information than bar codes
   b. tags that can be read from a distance without intervention by a human operator
   c. both a and b

Discussion Questions

1. Differentiate between three key concepts—supply chain, value chain, and integrated value chain.
2. Marketing has three core processes—one of which is supply-facing, one of which is essentially internal, and one of which is customer-facing. Do you agree with this statement? Explain why or why not.
3. What are the business practices used by Zara that have made it responsive to customer needs and successful financially?
4. What stages is an enterprise likely to go through en route to a virtual value chain?
5. Discuss integrative elements Dell has employed on (a) the supply side and (b) the customer side.
6. How does the combined use of EDI and ERP facilitate the development of an integrated value chain?
7. What potential advantages does Web services have to offer over EDI and ERP?
8. What is RFID technology? In what ways can it improve supply chain functioning?

Internet Exercises

1. Select an industry (e.g., automotive) or a specific company (e.g., Ford) and identify elements of its value chain. Where can information be used to decrease costs or increase customer satisfaction or both?
2. Think about how you bought the text and other material for this class. It might have been at the college bookstore, at a local supplier, over the Internet, or some combination of all three. Identify the elements of the value chain that were necessary to get these products to you, the final customer.
3. Spend some time on the Web site for your school, college, or department. How is that organizational unit using its Web site to help students visualize institutional processes, mirror activities carried on in the physical world, and increase the strength of relationships with students and potential students? What more could it do in each of these areas?
4. Locate a news article on a marketing application of RFID technology different from those described in the chapter. Be prepared to discuss the application in class, being specific about how it is improving a supply chain or other marketing process.

Notes

1. Lisa H. Harrington, "A Tale of Two Planners," April 3, 2000, http://www.industryweek.com, p. 2.
2. Lisa H. Harrington, "A Tale of Two Planners," April 3, 2000, http://www.industryweek.com, pp. 3–4.
3. David Rocks, "Reinventing Herman Miller," *Business Week e.biz*, April 3, 2000, p. 96.
4. David Rocks, "Reinventing Herman Miller," *Business Week e.biz*, April 3, 2000, p. 90.
5. My Herman Miller, http://www.hermanmiller.com/CDA/SSA/PN/Category/1,1793,a7c647,00.html.
6. Rajendra K. Srivastava, Tasadduq A. Shervani, and Liam Fahey, "Marketing, Business Processes, and Shareholder Value: An Organizationally Embedded View of Marketing Activities and the Discipline of Marketing," *Journal of Marketing*, 1999, 168–179.
7. e*Service, http://www.otis.com/eservice/front/1,1417,CLI1_RES1,00.html.
8. Scott Stephens, "Supply Chain Council & Supply Chain Operations Reference (SCOR) Model Overview," PowerPoint presentation, May 2000, http://www.supply-chain.org.

9. http://www.zara.com.

10. "The Secret to Zara's Success," *Stores*, March, 2004, http://www.stores.org.

11. Susan Reda, "Retails Great Race; Getting Fashion to the Finish Line," *Stores*, March 2004, http://www.stores.org.

12. Susan Reda, "Retails Great Race; Getting Fashion to the Finish Line," *Stores*, March 2004, http://www.stores.org. Other sources for this section: Robert D'Avanzo, "The Reward of Supply-Chain Excellence," December 2003, http://www.optimizemag.com; Eric Wahlgren, "Fast, Fashionable—and Profitable," *Business Week*, March 10, 2005, http://www.businessweek.com.

13. Andy Serwer, "The Education of Michael Dell," February 22, 2005, http://www.fortune.com.

14. "Living in Dell Time," November 2004, p. 86, http://www.fastcompany.com.

15. "Michael Dell Remarks," Rotman Integrative Thinking Seminar, University of Toronto, Toronto, Ontario, September 21, 2004, http://www1.us.dell.com/content/topics/global.aspx/corp/michael/en/speeches?c=us&l=en&s=corp&~ck=mn.

16. "Michael Dell Remarks," Rotman Integrative Thinking Seminar, University of Toronto, Toronto, Ontario, September 21, 2004, http://www1.us.dell.com/content/topics/global.aspx/corp/michael/en/speeches?c=us&l=en&s=corp&~ck=mn.

17. "Michael Dell Remarks," Southern Methodist University Evening Lecture, Dallas, Texas, May 10, 2004, http://www1.us.dell.com/content/topics/global.aspx/corp/michael/en/speeches?c=us&l=en&s=corp&~ck=mn.

18. "Michael Dell Remarks," Southern Methodist University Evening Lecture, Dallas, Texas, May 10, 2004, http://www1.us.dell.com/content/topics/global.aspx/corp/michael/en/speeches?c=us&l=en&s=corp&~ck=mn.

19. "Michael Dell Remarks," Southern Methodist University Evening Lecture, Dallas, Texas, May 10, 2004, http://www1.us.dell.com/content/topics/global.aspx/corp/michael/en/speeches?c=us&l=en&s=corp&~ck=mn.

20. "Michael Dell Remarks," Penn State University, School of Information Sciences and Technology, September 3, 2004, http://www1.us.dell.com/content/topics/global.aspx/corp/michael/en/speeches?c=us&l=en&s=corp&~ck=mn.

21. "Michael Dell Remarks," Rotman Integrative Thinking Seminar, University of Toronto, Toronto, Ontario, September 21, 2004, http://www1.us.dell.com/content/topics/global.aspx/corp/michael/en/speeches?c=us&l=en&s=corp&~ck=mnhttp://www1.us.dell.com/content/topics/global.aspx/corp/michael/en/speeches?c=us&l=en&s=corp&~ck=mn.

22. Andy Serwer, "The Education of Michael Dell," February 22, 2005, http://www.fortune.com.

23. Jeffrey F. Rayport and John J. Sviokla, "Exploiting the Virtual Value Chain," *Harvard Business Review*, November–December 1995, 75–85; Ronald Fink, "Data Processing: PepsiCo," *Financial World*, September 29, 1992, 52; Julia King and Thomas Hoffman, "The Next IT Generation," April 6, 1998, http://www.computerworld.com; Julia King, "Pepsi CIO Aims to Join New Economy," July 10, 2000, http://www.computerworld.com; Esther Shein, "The Knowledge Crunch," May 1, 2001, http://www.cio.com; http://www.fritolay.com; Joanie M. Wexler, "Cosmos2: Fedex's Next Generation," *Computerworld*, February 11, 1991, 29; Alice LaPlante, "Federal Express Gives Clients On-Line Access to Tracking System," *InfoWorld*, November 16, 1992, 108; Monua Janah and Clinton Wilder, "Special Delivery," October 27, 1997, http://www.informationweek.com; Mike Drummond, "Wireless at Work," February 2001, http://www.business2.com; http://www.fedex.com.

24. John H. Dobbs, "Competition's New Battleground: The Integrated Value Chain," Cambridge Technology Partners, nd, http://www.ctp.com, p. 5

25. David Bovet and Joseph Martha, Value Nets: Breaking the Supply Chain to Unlock Hidden Profits (New York: John Wiley & Sons, 2000), p. 171.

26. David Bovet and Joseph Martha, Value Nets: Breaking the Supply Chain to Unlock Hidden Profits (New York: John Wiley & Sons, 2000), pp 5–7.

27. "Overview of EDI," Covalent Networks, nd, http://www.covalentworks.com.

28. Richard Karpinski, "Wal-Mart Mandates Secure, Internet-Based EDI for Suppliers," *InternetWeek*, September 12, 2002, http://www.internetweek.com.

29. Hanna Hurley, "EDI Takes to the Internet," *Network*, October 1, 1998, http://www.cma.zdnet.com; "EDI Legacy Systems: Make the Old Work with the New," June 11, 2003, http://www.techrepublic.com; "Overview of EDI," "How EDI Works," Covalent Networks, nd, http://www.covalentworks.com.

30. Christopher Koch, "The ABCs of ERP," ERP Resource Center, *CIO Magazine*, http://www.CIO.com.

31. Thomas Wailgum, "Big Mess on Campus," *CIO Magazine*, May 1, 2005, http://www.CIO.com.

32. Thomas Wailgum, "Big Mess on Campus," *CIO Magazine*, May 1, 2005, http://www.CIO.com.

33. Christopher Koch, "The ABCs of ERP," ERP Resource Center, *CIO Magazine*, http://www.CIO.com.

34. http://www.amazon.com/gp/browse.html/103-7808876-6181457?%5Fencoding=UTF8&node=3435361.

35. Christopher Saunders, "Amazon Improves Access for Developers, Associates," October 5, 2004, http://www.ecommerce-guide.com.

36. Matt Hines, "Amazon to Provide Marks and Spencer's E-Commerce," April 19, 2005, http://networks.silicon.com/webwatch/0,39024667,39129677,00.htm.

37. "Inching Toward the RFID Revolution," *Business Week Online*, August 31, 2004, http://www.businessweek.com.

38. RFID, nd, http://www.techweb.com/encyclopedia/defineterm.jhtml?term=RFID; RFID, nd, http://en.wikipedia.org/wiki/RFID.

39. http://www.future-store.org/servlet/PB/s/19vt49w1qjrt1h1c1dcin1mt9m9klrz40c/menu/1002220_l2/1116872629407.html.

40. "Bar Codes Better Watch Their Backs," *Business Week Online*, August 31, 2004, http://www.businessweek.com.

41. Laurie Sullivan et al., "Linda Dillman on RFID," *Information Week*, September 13, 2004, http://www.informationweek.com.

42. Mark Roberti, "Wal-Mart Begins RFID Rollout," April 30, 2004, http://www.rfidjournal.com.

43. Mark Roberti, "Wal-Mart Begins RFID Rollout," April 30, 2004, http://www.rfidjournal.com. Other sources for this section are: "Bar Codes Better Watch Their Backs," *Business Week Online*, July 14, 2003, http://www.businessweek.com; "Other Large Retailer Announce RFID Plans," *Secure ID News*, August 20, 2004, http://www.secureidnews.com.

44. Mary Catherine O'Connor, "Federal RFID Spending to Rise Sharply," *RFID Journal*, March 1, 2005, http://www.rfidjournal.com.

45. Alok Jha, "Tesco Tests Spy Chip Technology," July 19, 2003, http://www.guardian.co.uk.

46. "Gillette to Buy 500 Million EPD Tags," *RFID Journal*, November 15, 2002, http://www.rfidjournal.com; "RFID Issues and News," nd, http://www.spychips.com/index.html; Alorie Gilbert, "Major Retailers to Test Smart Shelves," CNET, January 8, 2003, http://msn-cnet.com.com.

47. Kevin P. O'Brien, "Value-Chain Report," April 3, 2000, http://www.industryweek.com.

Business Models
and Strategies

Source: © Getty

Chapter Outline

Key Terms

affiliate (p. 61)

Applications Services Provider (ASP) (p. 62)

auction (p. 58)

barter (p. 58)

blogs (p. 64)

business plan (p. 55)

collaborative filtering (p. 60)

consortia (p. 70)

domain name (p. 62)

80/20 rule (p. 62)

extranet (p. 74)

infomediary (p. 66)

Intranet (p. 74)

licensing (p. 57)

machine-to-machine (M2M) (p. 72)

market segment (p. 55)

MMS (p. 73)

monetize (p. 57)

open source (p. 73)

operating system (p. 73)

peer-to-peer model (p. 74)

portal (p. 74)

predictive model (p. 60)

proprietary systems (p. 57)

reverse auction (p. 58)

RSS (Rich Site Summary or, more commonly, Really Simple Syndication) (p. 57)

Sarbanes Oxley Act (p. 62)

search engine (p. 74)

server (p. 74)

syndication (p. 57)

telematics (p. 73)

value-added services (p. 59)

value proposition (p. 55)

vertical markets (p. 62)

Voice Over Internet Protocol (VOIP) (p. 74)

Our examination of value chains made it clear that organizations that existed before the advent of the Internet can take advantage of the opportunities it presents just as pure-play Internet firms can. They may, however, do so in different ways. A set of business models is emerging, most of which meld the best of both the Internet and physical worlds.

3-1 Understanding Business Models

A Google search for the term *business model* returns more than 50 million hits. Even so, there is no commonly accepted definition of the term. Why is that? First, the discussion of business models was at its height during the Internet bubble when serious analysis was often not a major consideration. Second, the term does not seem to belong to any specific business discipline like marketing or strategy and therefore is used by different people with slightly different meanings. Michael Rappa's definition is one of the most often quoted: a "business model is the method of doing business by which a company can sustain itself—that is, generate revenue. The business model spells out how a company makes money by specifying where it is positioned in the value chain."[1]

A more detailed definition is set forth by Ethiraj, Guler, and Singh. They define a business model as "a unique configuration of elements comprising the organization's goals, strategies, processes, technologies, and structure, conceived to create value for the customers and thus compete successfully in a particular market." They go on to say that a business model describes the core value proposition, sources and methods of revenue generation, the costs involved in generating the revenue, and the plan and trajectory of growth.[2]

Both these definitions are typical descriptions of Internet business models, which focus on the ways the enterprise generates revenue. Perhaps the reason for this emphasis is that the revenue side of the business is the most changed by the Internet. Although it is true that the basic cost elements that you would find on any business's income statement are little changed by the Internet, it is a great mistake to ignore the cost side of the business equation. Cost *elements* do not change, but the relative *weights* of various costs may change significantly. Comparing catalog marketers to retailers gives a good example. Most retailers spend extensively on their stores, both to permit attractive presentation of merchandise and to offer the shopper an enjoyable experience. Most retailers today, like Zara, try to have as little as possible in the way of warehouse facilities, preferring to receive shipments directly from the manufacturer. Pure catalog merchants do not have stores, except possibly for an outlet or two. They do, however, have large investments in and operating expenditures on warehousing and order fulfillment facilities. Many contemporary marketers have major efforts in both retail and catalog channels (J. Crew, Sharper Image, and Crate and Barrel are good examples). They find it necessary to have separate management and accounting groups for retail and catalog because the two channels are operationally so different.

3-1a Functions of Business Models

Henry Chesbrough and Richard Rosenbloom go on to explain that the functions of a business model are to:

- articulate the *value proposition*, that is, the value created for users by the offering based on the technology;
- identify a *market segment*, that is, the users to whom the technology is useful and for what purpose;
- define the structure of the *value chain* within the firm required to create and distribute the offering;
- estimate the *cost structure* and *profit potential* of producing the offering, given the value proposition and the value chain structure chosen;
- describe the position of the firm with the *value network* linking suppliers and customers, including identification of potential partners and competitors; and
- formulate the *competitive strategy* by which the innovating firm will gain and hold competitive advantage over rivals.[3]

Although this description does a great deal to aid our understanding of business models, it also poses a danger. By making more explicit the various elements of a business model, it begins to sound like a **business plan.** *A business model and a business plan are two distinctly different entities.* A business model is a conceptual description that may have been given a name like "aggregator." A business plan is a detailed document that is prepared for strategic guidance and to aid in the acquisition of resources, either internal or external. Some similarity of content exists between the two, but they are not synonymous. Recognizing this issue, Chesbrough and Rosenbloom go on to specify the differences between a business model and a strategy:

- A business model focuses on creating value for the customer and delivering that value to the customer.
- It focuses on creating business value that can be translated into value for the shareholder.
- It requires that managers use technical inputs to create economic results in a context of technological and market uncertainty.

Their final point puts the business model concept firmly in the arena of business innovation including Internet-based businesses. It also reinforces the focus on value creation by the firm as a key element of an Internet business model.

3-2 The Value Proposition

That leads us squarely to another term that is used frequently but not defined with any degree of precision. In this case, it seems to be because marketers follow the definition of economic value, which is essentially the value of ownership and use less the cost of the item. The term *value proposition* has come to mean the value delivered by the firm to a specific, targeted customer segment. From that rather simple beginning, marketers can study the drivers of value in a particular market. Osterwalder and Pigneur have a simple framework that is useful in that process (Figure 3-1). It combines consideration of the needs of the target customer, which define the nature of the value desired, with an understanding of the core capabilities of the enterprise, which determines the value that can be delivered.[4] Data can be obtained and used to understand both target customer and organizational capabilities, making developing a value proposition an information-driven marketing activity.

Renowned strategist Kenichi Ohmae puts it strongly. He urges marketers to "provide value to customers rather than aping the competition." He tells the following story to illustrate his point:

value proposition Customer value delivered to a specific target market.

market segment A portion of a total market that is homogeneous in terms of demographics, behaviors, lifestyles, or other variables of interest to the marketer.

business plan Written statement of how an owner, often an entrepreneur, intends to execute all business functions to successfully achieve objectives.

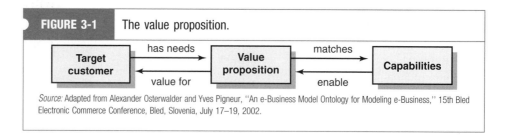

FIGURE 3-1   The value proposition.

Target customer → has needs → Value proposition → matches → Capabilities
Target customer ← value for ← Value proposition ← enable ← Capabilities

Source: Adapted from Alexander Osterwalder and Yves Pigneur, "An e-Business Model Ontology for Modeling e-Business," 15th Bled Electronic Commerce Conference, Bled, Slovenia, July 17–19, 2002.

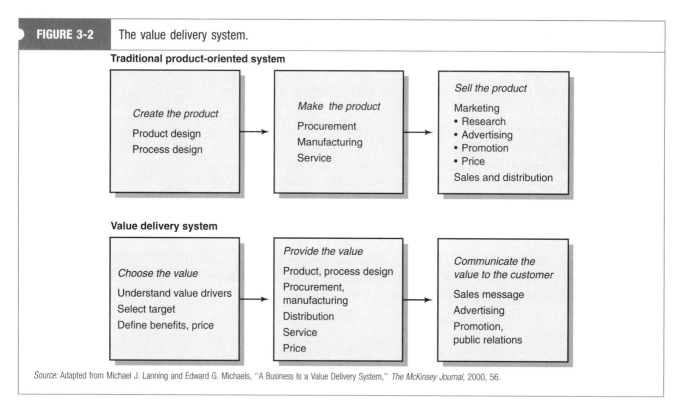

FIGURE 3-2   The value delivery system.

Traditional product-oriented system

Create the product

Product design
Process design

→

Make the product

Procurement
Manufacturing
Service

→

Sell the product

Marketing
• Research
• Advertising
• Promotion
• Price
Sales and distribution

Value delivery system

Choose the value

Understand value drivers
Select target
Define benefits, price

→

Provide the value

Product, process design
Procurement,
manufacturing
Distribution
Service
Price

→

Communicate the value to the customer

Sales message
Advertising
Promotion,
public relations

Source: Adapted from Michael J. Lanning and Edward G. Michaels, "A Business Is a Value Delivery System," *The McKinsey Journal,* 2000, 56.

Some time back, a Japanese home-appliance company was trying to develop a coffee percolator. Executives were asking, "Should it be a General Electric-type machine? Should it be the drip-type of the kind Philips makes? Larger? Smaller?" I urged them to ask a different question: "Why do people drink coffee?" The answer came back—good taste. After further research, the company found that this "good taste" had a few critical components: water quality, coffee-grain distribution, time elapsed between grinding and brewing. Certain things mattered more than others. That got the company thinking differently about the percolator's essential features. Suddenly, it had to have a built-in dechlorinator and, of course a built-in grinder.[5]

Ohmae's story makes two important points. One is, of course, to do marketing research to learn what consumers want. The second is to ask the right research question. The primary motivation for drinking coffee, which we assume they knew from previous research, was good taste. When the appliance company asked consumers what makes coffee taste good, they uncovered the drivers of customer value in a coffee-making machine—water quality, distribution of the coffee grains, and freshness of the ground coffee. Having asked the right questions and received the answers directly from customers, they were ready to design a product that delivered superior value.

Ohmae's colleagues at McKinsey have a simple graphic that highlights the difference between the traditional approach and the value delivery approach (Figure 3-2). The traditional approach is clearly product-oriented. The product is developed, manufactured, and sold through channels—the build-to-inventory model of Chapter 2. The value delivery system puts the focus on the customer—first defining the value drivers desired by customers, next creating a product and a marketing strategy that delivers the value, and finally communicating that value to the customer. That does not necessarily imply either the build-to-order or the direct models discussed in Chapter 2, but it does recall Michael Dell's relentless focus on the customer.

As Ohmae's story illustrates, the value drivers for each product will be specific to that product. It is also important to remember that the value that the enterprise is able to deliver is dependent on its own core capabilities. Having developed a value proposition, the firm must then understand how it can obtain revenue from it, that is, how to **"monetize"** the offering in Internet terms.

monetize Jargon used to describe the concept of first creating a content-rich Web site and then being able to sell advertising to support it.

3-3 Internet Revenue Models

Businesses can realize revenue on the Internet in several ways. Table 3-1 contains examples of firms that use each type. Important Internet revenue models include the following:

- *Access* to the Internet. All users must have an on-ramp to the Internet. They can access the Internet either through a dial-up connection or, increasingly, through a broadband connection.

- *Advertising* revenue. In Chapter 1 we discussed the explosive growth of advertising on the Internet. Nevertheless, few sites can sustain themselves on advertising revenue alone.

  - *Sponsorship revenue.* Content on a Web site or in an e-mail can be sponsored, providing another type of advertising opportunity.

- *Donations.* Not-for-profit marketers raise substantial sums of money through their Web sites. In addition, a number of large sites exist on services donated by the Internet community.

- *Membership or subscription revenue.* In the early days of the Internet, most content was free. Much of it still is, but increasingly content-oriented sites are charging for the content they provide.

- *Sale or licensing of software or systems.* **Proprietary systems** may become an important source of competitive advantage, and some firms will guard them closely. Others, however, will find additional revenue opportunities in sale or licensing of specialized software. It is important to remember, though, the example from Chapter 2 of Amazon's free provision of Web services to other software developers.

proprietary systems Software or networks that are the exclusive property of the firm that developed them and that cannot be used by others without permission.

- *Software-based services.* In Chapter 2 we discussed the fact that many firms are using hosted software solutions to avoid owning and maintaining their own software.

- **Syndication** or **licensing** *of content.* Physical-world publishers have content they can migrate onto the Web, and many of them are creating additional Web-only content to add to the attractiveness of their site. They are actively marketing this content to other sites through **RSS** feeds. Software firms may choose to license their product to users instead of selling it outright. They may collect revenue based on the number of users, as the creators of most business-to-business (B2B) software products typically do, or they may charge on a usage basis as search engines often do.

syndication Sale of content to multiple customers, each of whom then integrates it into their own products.

licensing Legal permission to own or use a product or piece of content.

- *Transactions revenue.* Sites of all kinds, whether it is their major objective or not, are realizing revenue from transactions. They may be selling products ranging from clothing to computers or services that vary from employment listings to credit cards. They may be selling their own products or services; they may be affiliates of large sites like Amazon, or they may operate from a larger site like eBay. There are three identifiable types of transactions:

RSS (Rich Site Summary or, more commonly, **Really Simple Syndication)** Technology that allows the owner of content to share it with other Web sites.

	TABLE 3-1	Internet Business Models			
	Primary Revenue Model	**Secondary Revenue Models**	**B2C Examples**	**B2B Examples**	**Nonprofit/ Government Examples**
Aggregator	E-commerce	Advertising, membership	Amazon	Grainger Industrial Supplies	
Applications services provider	Software-based services	Access, advertising, membership, value-added services	TurboTax	MicroSoft Office Live	Convio
Content provider	Advertising	E-commerce, sponsorship, syndication	WSJ.com	InternetRetailer.com	Cancer.gov
Fund raiser	Donations	Membership, e-commerce			RedCross.org
Infomediary	E-commerce	Advertising, sponsorship	AnnualCredit Report.com	InfoUSA.com	
Marketplace	Auction, reverse auction	Advertising, membership, sponsorship	eBay.com	Exostar.com	Craigslist.org
Machine-to-machine	Software-based services, value-added services	E-commerce	McAfee.com (PC security software)	Dell.com	
Multichannel/bricks and clicks	E-commerce		Staples.com	HomeDepot.com	Momastore.org (Museum of Modern Art)
Open source	Donations		Wikipedia.org	Linux.org	
Peer to peer	Donations		Kazaa.com		
Portal	Advertising	E-commerce, membership	Yahoo!	Chemlink.com.au (Australian Chemical Industry)	Ecitizen.gov.sg (government of Singapore)

auction A preexisting business model that operates successfully on the Internet by announcing an item for sale and permitting multiple purchasers/suppliers to bid on them under specified rules and conditions; see also *reverse auction*.

reverse auction Auction in which there is a single purchaser with multiple suppliers bidding for the opportunity to supply the product or service.

barter Trading goods or services without money changing hands.

- *Auction/reverse auction.* The traditional auction, in which many buyers compete for the product of a single seller, is commonly seen in the physical world for products as diverse as fine art and agricultural commodities. The reverse auction, in which many sellers compete for the business of one seller, is an important facet of B2B activities on the Internet.
- *Barter.* Barter does not produce revenue directly, but it is a common practice in B2B markets and is found in business-to-customer (B2C) markets. It simply describes the direct exchange of goods or services without money changing hands.
- *E-commerce.* E-commerce describes the most common type of economic exchange, the one in which a purchaser pays the seller for the goods or services. E-commerce is ubiquitous in B2C, B2B, and governmental and nonprofit markets.

- *Value-added services revenue.* The Internet provides an opportunity for firms to charge for services that complement their primary offering. For example, a B2B auction site may offer credit verification services to support transactions that take place on its site.

value-added services Services that make the original product more valuable and help generate additional revenue.

These revenue models are not mutually exclusive. Many firms do, in fact, pursue multiple revenue streams, and it seems likely that, going forward, most sites will need to do so in order to be viable. Chances are that additional revenue models will be revealed in this process. The challenge for all Internet marketers is to choose a value proposition that taps into viable revenue streams.

3-4 Identifying Business Models

Now that we understand the basics of business models, it is time to look at Internet business models. Here again, we face the problem that there is no commonly accepted set of models. Worse, various authors have given different names to the same model. Table 3-1 gives an overview of the most common models, using one widely used name. It shows the primary and secondary revenue models for each business model and gives examples of each in B2C, B2B, and nonprofit/government sectors.

3-4a Aggregator

Tapscott, Ticoll, and Lowy say that aggregators "organize and choreograph the distribution of goods, services, and information. They intermediate transactions between producers and consumers, creating value for both and for their shareholders. An [aggregator's] value proposition depends on six complementary variables: selection, organization, price, convenience, matching, and fulfillment."[6]

This is a familiar model, not unlike the catalog model of direct marketing. Most retailers, both online and offline, are aggregators who combine merchandise from a variety of suppliers into an edited selection for their customers. Among those who have made successful moves onto the Web are cataloger L.L. Bean (http://www.llbean.com) and retailer Neiman Marcus (http://www.neimanmarcus.com). The aggregation of physical products is a common business practice, and the aggregation of services is also widespread.

Amazon is generally acknowledged to be the initiator of many aspects of current Internet business models. In Chapter 2 we discussed the Web services that Amazon offers other businesses. It is best known, however, as an e-tailer, first of books, videos, and DVDs, and in later years of many diverse product lines. In fact, Amazon has the immodest vision of being the place "where people can come to find and discover anything they might want to buy online,"[7] suggesting that it views itself as the ultimate aggregator. As the number of merchandise lines has increased beyond books, the site has been carefully organized by product category in a way that is simple to decipher and use. In mid-2005 the site had thirty-one product categories from Apparel and Accessories to VHS.

An identified customer who has shopped at Amazon before is greeted by name on a personalized home page when later visiting the site (Figure 3-3). The credit card offer and Father's Day promotions shown in Figure 3-3 are generic and seen by all visitors. Father's Day is obviously seasonal; the promotion for Watergate-related tapes and books was related to then-current news. Notice that the page in Figure 3-3 has direct access to individual information in "Your Favorites" and "Joe's Store." Joe also has a "Watch List" that notifies him of new releases by a favorite musician. More of the left-hand navigation bar is shown in the second column of Figure 3-3. It shows "Featured Partners," some of whom use their Amazon store as their primary e-commerce site. In

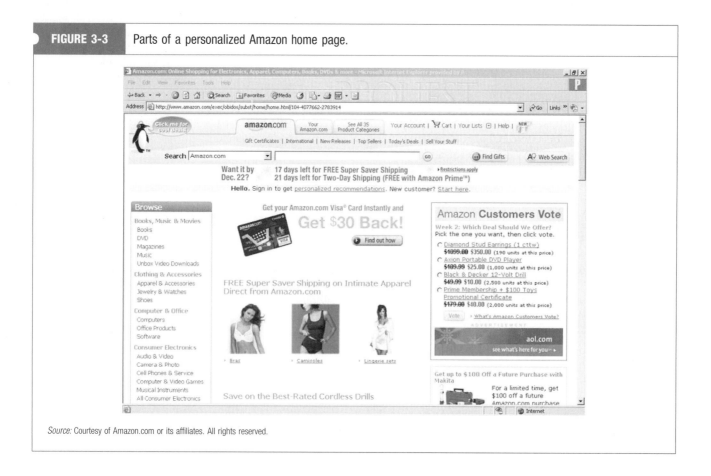

the "Make Money" section, there are links to business services of various types, and in "Special Features," there are links to various consumer services. The home page, and the entire Web site for that matter, features clean design and easy-to-follow navigation and is information rich.

One of Amazon's early innovations was the use of customers to provide some of the content on the site. From the beginning, Amazon had only a few professional reviewers who could not pretend to be familiar with all the books offered. Consequently, Amazon asked visitors to review books—and then asked readers to rate the usefulness of the reviews. As the number of product lines expanded, Amazon extended the reviewing option to them. Content is greatly expanded beyond what Amazon could manage on its own, and every visitor, whether that person buys a product or not, has a chance to interact with and become involved in the site.

predictive model Relevant variables and associated response factors or probabilities are used to estimate the likelihood of occurrence of a specific behavior, given the existence of a given level of the specified variables.

Amazon was also one of the first to give personalized recommendations based on the customer's purchase pattern. If, for example, the customer buys several books on advertising and marketing communications, the recommendations for other advertising and marketing communications books are usually quite accurate. If, however, the customer throws in a purchase from a completely different category— say, a book on spirituality—the **predictive model** tends to become a bit confused. The information, however, remains an interesting and potentially useful adjunct to a visit.

collaborative filtering Software used to make recommendations based on the stated preferences and purchase history of other visitors to the site.

Amazon also uses **collaborative filtering** technology (software that performs statistical analysis to determine patterns of activity) to generate personalized recommendations for products on their site. The user gets an individualized recommendation, "People who bought *Internet Marketing* also bought *E-Commerce*." It also produces "Purchase Circle" recommendations: "This DVD is also popular at

FIGURE 3-4	Search results from the Amazon A9 search engine.

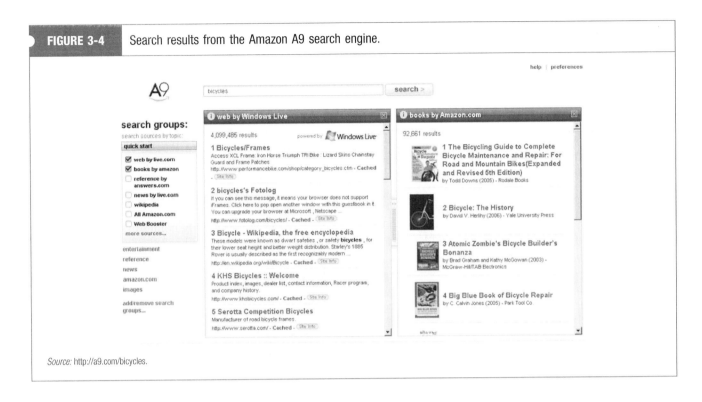

Source: http://a9.com/bicycles.

The Acme Corporation," or "See what types of lawn furniture are most popular this year." The "My Store" feature includes recommendations, new product releases, and bargains, all based on the customer's purchase history. If customers wish to improve those recommendations, they sign in and have the option of editing their purchase histories, selecting favorite Amazon stores or products, or rating products that they own.

From the beginning, Amazon offered a huge selection of books, so a good search engine for the site was important. It later added the ability to "search inside the book," allowing visitors to sample some of the content before they bought. In 2004, it extended its reach beyond its own site and onto the Web. It set up a division called Alexa and in 2004 debuted the beta version of A9, a search engine based on Google functionality that is able to display a much richer set of information. Figure 3-4 shows the result of a search for bicycles. The functionality that is activated produced the usual search results, both paid and organic in the first column, books about bicycles in the second column, image links to various bicycle products in the third column, and a map of the closest bicycle dealers to the searcher in the fourth column. Other functions are available on the right-hand menu. Following the B2B model described in Chapter 2, Amazon is making the A9 software available to other developers for use on their sites.

Just as the disappearance of economic friction in value chains fosters efficient relationships among a large number of other firms like Amazon's Featured Partners, it also permits the development of new business processes and models. **Affiliate** marketing is a creature of the Internet that would not be possible if transaction and coordination costs were a significant factor. Whether it is a business model or a customer attraction technique is an open question, but affiliate programs have become an important aspect of e-commerce on the Internet.

Amazon began its program in 1996 and had more than 900,000 affiliates—called "Associates"—as of early 2005. Signing up as an Amazon associate is a simple, automated three-step process. A representative of the potential affiliate Web site fills out a brief form and gains access to the instructions for creating links to the Amazon

affiliate A Web site that agrees to post a link to a transactional site in return for a commission on sales made as a direct result of the link.

site and to the reports of the resulting activity that are produced for each affiliate on a daily basis. When the links are activated, the affiliate site begins to earn revenue from referral sales made on Amazon. The affiliate site can make as much as 10% commission on sales made on Amazon from the referring site. Checks or merchandise credits are sent to the site quarterly. It is generally understood that most affiliates of any site do not produce a large volume of sales. The **80/20 rule** holds true; about 80% of the affiliates are low volume, and only 20% produce significant volume. However, the automated system makes it possible to handle a large number of affiliates in a cost-effective fashion. Amazon does not disclose the proportion of sales that are achieved through Associate referrals—nor does it attempt to estimate the advertising value derived from the presence of the Amazon logo on more than 900,000 Web sites!

Many of the customer services listed in Figure 3-3 are common retailing services, like a wedding registry. Amazon has also introduced a number of services unique to the Web. One that has been widely emulated is its patented 1-Click® process that "remembers" the customer's purchasing information and mailing list, eliminating the need to fill out lengthy forms. The books and many of the products Amazon sells are standardized; its customer-friendly services make the customer experience non-standard and encourage repeat transactions.

3-4b Applications Services Provider

An **applications services provider (ASP)** is an Internet services company that offers access to software applications and other services. Their customers are both small businesses that cannot afford to own or manage the software and large enterprises that prefer to outsource some technical services. That describes the primary market, but applications services are also available to consumers. For example, Adobe offers a service that allows subscribers to create PDF files online instead of owning the Adobe Acrobat software themselves.

It is tempting but far too simplistic to say that ASPs simply "rent" software to clients on a usage fee basis. It is more accurate to say that they offer services on demand and charge on a usage basis, essentially acting like a utility. ASPs range from large to small and from general business/e-commerce to specialized software applications for **vertical markets.** They may also offer various services, such as **domain name** registration, Web site hosting, Internet access, and submission to search engines.

The following examples give a sense of the types of offerings already present in a business model that has only been in evidence since 1998:

- Corio, a division of IBM, is one of the largest ASPs, focusing on enterprise applications and high-end e-commerce solutions for Global 1000 firms. According to the Corio site, "Experts estimate that for every dollar spent on enterprise software, five or more dollars is spent to run the solution."[8] Corio's solution has modules that cover various information technology (IT) activities, from implementing new projects to archiving files to providing compliance documentation for the **Sarbanes Oxley Act** of 2002, which mandated various kinds of financial disclosure by U.S. corporations. These solutions work *with* enterprise resource planning (ERP) software like PeopleSoft, they do not *replace* it. Use of their hosted solutions removes some of the onerous IT task of keeping the ERP system working at an optimal level and providing the reports needed by managers throughout the organization.

- At the other end of a general provider/specialized provider of ASPs are firms that serve one vertical market. ASPDirectory.com lists more than thirty such firms. ASPs listed include the following:
  - Constructw@re is the leading ASP for the construction industry, providing Internet-based project management, collaboration, and e-commerce solutions.[9]

80/20 rule Pareto principle. The rule of thumb that states that 20% of a phenomenon (customers) tends to product 80% of the results (profits).

Applications Services Provider (ASP) Provides access to software-based services to clients.

vertical markets Business markets that concentrate on a specific industry sector or business function.

domain name A unique name on the Internet.

Sarbanes Oxley Act U.S. law passed in 2002 that mandates standards for financial disclosure and corporate governance.

- CTI is the leading provider of fully integrated property management, portfolio accounting, leasing, and forecasting ERP software solutions to the global commercial real estate industry via the Internet.[10]
- ELF Technologies provides innovative legal software and services to help insurance claims departments, corporate law departments, and law firms measurably improve the handling and management of legal work.[11]

And so it goes, with over fourteen industry segments and more than thirty specialist ASP firms. Another directory lists 173 firms headquartered in various parts of the world that serve nine different vertical markets.[12] The profusion of ASPs serving verticals parallels the structure of business markets in general, where the needs of different industry sectors vary greatly and require specialized products and services.

3-4c Content Provider

The content model is the traditional media model in which content is provided free (radio and network television) or at a price far below total cost of production (magazines and newspapers) and advertising provides the primary revenue stream. This heritage probably explains why it was the original Internet business model. In the days before avenues to profitability on the Internet were clear, the goal was to attract a sizeable customer base, which would, in turn, attract advertisers, leading to profitable advertising-supported Web sites. This was described as "monetization," and it was the shining goal of content businesses during the early years of the Internet. For most sites, however, the advertising revenue stream alone was not enough.

There are several reasons why advertising revenue is often insufficient to produce profitable operations. First, sites that attract a relatively untargeted visitor base (general news, for example) cannot command a high CPM (cost per thousand advertising impressions), even if they have a large audience. Second, many advertisers have not been satisfied with "click-through" rates, even though they often approximated response rates in traditional direct marketing, as we discuss in more detail in the next chapter. Third, the barriers to entry in the Web world are very low, and there is always a huge amount of advertising inventory, which also depresses advertising rates. There are sites with substantial revenue streams from advertising, but you will find few, if any, that support themselves on advertising alone.

Large, general-purpose (or, perhaps more precisely, mass-targeted) sites quickly found their advertising revenue to be insufficient and took action to increase their sources of revenue. Some added classified advertising or auction services. Others added "tiers" of paid subscription services to their free content; a few became subscription only. Still others developed their own e-commerce activities or offered e-commerce functionality to small businesses that did not want to maintain their own transactional sites. In the process, many became portals, to be discussed as a separate model later in this chapter.

The *New York Times* has been a leader among free content sites through NYTimes.com. However, it may have signaled another trend when it announced its intention of making some premium content available by subscription only beginning in September 2005. This is only one part of a "monetization plan" according to remarks attributed to Martin Nisenholtz, senior vice president of digital operations. He stated that in mid-2005, about 85% of NYT visitors came into the site through their home page. However, their fastest-growing visitor source was links from other sites, like Yahoo!, which receive news feeds from NYT and display links directly to *Times* content. The *Times* expects that source of visitors to continue to grow rapidly and is developing new models to encourage the trend.

The premium subscription model is not new, and like other sites, the NYT expects to be able to charge a higher CPM for advertising on those pages because the subscribers will be upscale. However, their concept of "information affiliates," patterned after the affiliate model used by Amazon and others, is new. The early-stage

blogs Short for Web logs; records of personal experiences posted on the Web and publicly accessible.

concept had two basic components. The first was to promote RSS feeds of NYT content. The second was to encourage bloggers to link to NYTimes.com in return for revenue from advertising placed on their **blogs.** Both components represent relatively new developments (business models?) on the Internet and deserve some explanation.

RSS feeds are the method of choice for implementing content syndication on the Web. Syndication as a revenue stream for news organizations is not new—witness well-known opinion columnists and cartoonists whose work is distributed to many local newspapers by syndication services. RSS, however, is a technology that makes content feeds available to other Web sites, blogs, or the desktop of an individual user. The content is provided free (see Figure 3-5 for the content use guidelines of tech news site CNET). Receiving the feed requires an RSS reader, a piece of software that can be downloaded free or at minimal charge, depending on the reader chosen. Then the Webmaster, blogger, or user identifies the news feeds he or she wants and begins receiving them. The example of the *New York Times* and the usage guidelines from CNET make clear that the point of providing this free content is to bring more visitors to the content site.

What, then, is a blog, and why has the blogosphere become important in Web space? Blogs are essentially electronic journals in which the owner records personal experiences, observations, and opinions, often on a daily basis. They are generally created and hosted on free sites, although some professionals use fee-for-service sites with more functionality. They are publicly available on the Internet. Does this sound a bit like reading someone's personal diary? It does, and that is often the intent. Readers can comment on postings or ask questions, so blogs encourage dialog, adding interactivity as a way to appeal to readers and keep them coming back. Including an

FIGURE 3-5	Conditions for accessing RSS feed.

Usage guidelines
We share, be fair

We encourage you to use these feeds, so long as you do not post our full-text stories, and so long as you provide proper attribution to CNET.

Whenever you post CNET content on your web site or anywhere else, please provide attribution to CNET Networks, either as text (CNET is our site name) or with a graphic (we reference a small 88×31 logo in each feed for this purpose) if you use the feeds publicly—meaning, where anyone but yourself will read them.

CNET reserves all rights in and to the logo, and your right to use the logo is limited to providing attribution in connection with the RSS. We don't require anything dramatic, but we do ask that you always note the source of the information.

Source: http://www.cnet.com/4520-6022_1-5115040-1.html?tag=cnetfd.ft.

RSS feed on the blog increases the richness of its content and may help encourage repeat visits. Blogs have characteristics of Web sites that allow them to be indexed on the major search engines. That begins to explain why blogs are interesting to Web businesses as diverse as Google and the *New York Times*. Blogs have readers that, through RSS feeds, can be attracted to the content site. It is also possible for the content site to put ads on the blog, providing a (usually small) revenue stream for the blogger—a genuinely win-win situation.[13]

Content sites have come a long way from early ventures that expected to build huge sites full of content, attract huge numbers of visitors, and make huge amounts of money through advertising. Multiple revenue sources are essential, and as the previous example illustrates, the Web is offering opportunities to monetize content that are new and different from those of the physical world, at least in their execution.

3-4d Fund-Raiser

In the early days of the commercial Internet it was considered highly improbable that nonprofit organizations would be able to raise money on the Internet. Time, and a relatively short amount of it, has proved that early prediction to be incorrect. Two events that took place in 2004 conclusively established the power of Internet fund-raising: the American presidential election and the tsunami that hit Southeast Asia.

The 2004 U.S. presidential election saw a massive change in the way politicians used the Internet for campaigning and fund-raising purposes. According to financial analysis site Bloomberg.com, political fund-raising totaled $4.8 billion, up 55% from the previous presidential election in 2002. For the first time, the Internet figured prominently in the election, as political bloggers swarmed onto the Web (the same was true in the 2005 British election[14]) and as the Internet became an important venue for political fund-raising. Alexis Rice, fellow at the Johns Hopkins Center for the Study of American Government, said that "the way campaigns grew this time was in online fund raising." She went on to state that after Vermont Governor Howard Dean raised more than $20 million in his unsuccessful presidential campaign, both of the major party nominees took notice. Democratic nominee John Kerry raised $82 million, and President George Bush raised $14 million online.[15]

Senator John Kerry has continued to use approximately 3 million e-mail addresses he collected over the course of the political campaign. E-mails to his supporters have focused on issues such as children who are not covered by health insurance and have used leading-edge technology like streaming video of television ads embedded in the e-mail. The extent to which this extensive e-mail list will become a basis for future political fund-raising is unknown, but it could offer a powerful head start.

When the devastating tsunami hit Southeast Asia in December 2004, concerned businesses and individuals turned immediately to the Internet for information on ways to help. Relief organizations from around the globe quickly mobilized to raise funds for disaster relief. Based on the previous experience of numerous successful nonprofits, the Internet played an important role in their efforts. One month later the *Chronicle of Philanthropy* reported results for a number of organizations in the United States. Here is a small sample:

- The American Red Cross, in Washington, raised $236.2 million, more than $84 million of which was donated online. The organization's total includes $18.3 million donated during a 2-hour telethon broadcast on NBC on January 15.

- The U.S. Fund for Unicef, in New York, received $68 million for its relief efforts, $35 million of which was donated online.

- Catholic Relief Services, in Baltimore, brought in $51.1 million, $12.1 million of which was donated online.

- Doctors Without Borders, in New York, raised more than $20 million, $16 million of which was contributed over the Internet.[16]

These are only a few of the examples given, but they make an important point. The donations raised online as a percentage of total donations varied a great deal by organization. This may be partly due to the way in which the organization appealed to donors. It is also the result of the donor base of the respective organizations; some are more comfortable with the idea of donating money over the Internet than others. As more consumers become comfortable giving their credit card number over the Internet to purchase goods and services, it is quite likely that they will feel more comfortable giving money to philanthropic organizations and colleges and universities in the same way.

3-4e Infomediary

infomediary Intermediary in channels of distribution that specializes in the capture, analysis, application, and distribution of information.

In the early days of the Web, the term **infomediary** was used to describe a trusted intermediary who managed the personal data of consumers. The current use of the term is much broader, covering virtually any third party that manages and distributes data on the Internet. Two definitions underscore the lack of precision in the use of the term:

- An infomediary is a firm that acts as a filter between companies and consumers. Individuals provide infomediaries with personal information and in turn receive targeted ads. Companies pay these infomediaries for the information that they collect.[17]

- An infomediary is a Web site that gathers and organizes large amounts of data and acts as an intermediary between those who want the information and those who supply the information.[18]

Canadian financial services firm Stockgroup Media is a good example of an infomediary of the second type. Beginning as a Web developer for small, often natural resource–based companies, the founders realized that there was a need to help these companies connect with capital markets. They quickly broadened the business concept to include provision of various kinds of financial information. Today they supply that information to publishers and financial services providers. They use their own proprietary software to stream information to their clients. They also offer disclosure and advertising services. They have specialized Web sites, including SmallCapCenter.com, which focuses on emerging companies, and Stockhouse Network, a financial news site.

The information-based services of Stockgroup Interactive provide information to clients and offer services such as Web site hosting and advertising that allow its clients to market themselves with a level of technological sophistication that would not otherwise be available to many small businesses. Many other sites like them exist on the Web—sites that specialize in data, often serving vertical business markets.

There is also another group of infomediaries whose existence as a category predated the Internet and who occupy a distinct niche within the B2B space. They are the providers of marketing data, especially sales leads. A few of many examples:

- PostMasterDirect is a division of NetCreations specializing in e-mail list management, brokerage, and delivery. For e-businesses, it parallels the services long offered to the direct mail industry by list managers and brokers.[19] PostMasterDirect collects opt-in e-mail addresses from a large network of partner sites and markets them to other Internet businesses who wish to run e-mail campaigns. They place emphasis on marketing only permission-based lists, a subject discussed in Chapter 4.

- Harte-Hanks Market Intelligence is a business within the direct marketing services firm Harte-Hanks. It has an extensive B2B database (the Ci Technology Database) that is used by technology and telecommunication companies to provide sales leads for initial prospecting as well as company reports and profiles (see Figure 3-6) which can prove useful throughout the sales cycle. The parent company also sources

| FIGURE 3-6 | Corporate profile data. |

CI TECHNOLOGY DATABASE
The source for market intelligence.

H C N Mortgage Inc

| 415 E. 11th St. Ste 2901
Irvine, CA 92614-0510
UNITED STATES
Phone: (949)260-5446 | **Mailing Address:**
415 E. 11th St. Ste 2901
Irvine, CA 92614-0510
UNITED STATES | Site ID: 223581900
www.hcnmortgage.com
Standard Site |

THIS IS A FICTITIOUS SITE AND IS FOR DEMONSTRATION PURPOSES ONLY

Information on this Site

ECONOGRAPHICS

Employees:	500	Channel	No
IT Employee Range:	10-24	Enterprise Status:	Branch
Estimated Revenue ($M):	239	Metro/Code: Orange County -CA	5945
Fiscal Year End:	Dec		
Industry (SIC):	6163		FIN-MORTGAGE BANKERS
Industry (NAICS):	522310	FIN- Mortgage and Nonmortgage Loan Bankers	

SITE UPDATES

Demographics/Contacts Update:	Jan 05	Technology Infrastructure Update: (NEW)	Sep 04
Network/Comm Equip. Update:	Oct 04	Application Software Update:	Nov 04

Business Functions Performed at this Site

BUSINESS ACTIVITIES

Accounting:	Yes	Customer Support:	Yes
Sales:	Yes	Call Center;	No
Marketing:	No	Manufacturing:	No
Human Resources:	Yes	Engineering:	No
Purchasing:	Yes		

Summary of Technology at this Site

Total PC's:	440	Total Servers: (NEW)	40
>Desktop PC's:	430	Total Printers:	150
>Portable PC's:	10		
Primary Desktop Vendor:	HP	Phone System Installed:	Avaya
Primary Portable Vendor:	TOSHIBA	Toll-free Number at this Location:	Yes
		Wireless Presence: (NEW)	Yes
Internet Users:	250 - 499		
Source for Mgmt of Computers & Systems:			Local
Planning a Major Move / Renovation Next 12 Months:			No

Site Technology Totals

PC

Total PC's:	440	PC Purchasing Decisions:	Local
>Desktop PC's:	430	Primary Desktop Vendor:	HP
>Portable PC's:	10	Primary Portable Vendor:	TOSHIBA
Total Planned PC's:	5	Total High Performance Workstations: (NEW)	0

SYSTEMS/SERVERS

Total Servers:	40	Operating Systems:	WIN2000, WIN/XP
>Intel/AMD Servers: (NEW)	36	Primary Server Vendors:	HP
>Unix/RISC Servers: (NEW)	0	Total Planned Servers:	0
>IBM Midrange Servers - iSeries/AS400: (NEW)	0	Server Purchasing Decisions:	Local
>Other Proprietary Servers:	4		
>IBM/PCM Mainframes: (NEW)	0		

SOFTWARE

RDBMS:	SQL-SERVER	Development Totals:	JAVA
Accounting Vendor: (NEW)	Oracle	CRM Vendor: (NEW)	Siebel
Groupware Vendor:	Lotus	Planned Open Source: (NEW)	Yes

FIGURE 3-6	Continued

STORAGE	Total Site Storage Capacity:	50 TO 249 GB	Primary Storage Vendor: NEW	EMC
	Storage Area Network Presence: NEW	Yes	Network Attached Storage Presence: NEW	No
	Direct-Attached Storage Presence:	Yes	Tape Library Presence: NEW	No

PERIPHERALS	Total Printers:	150	Total High Speed Production Printers:	100

E-BUSINESS	Internet Users:	250 - 499	Access Type:	T1/T3

LAN	Wireless LAN Presence: NEW	Yes	Nodes:	500
	Wireless LAN Users:	450		

NETWORKS	Private Network Remote Locations:	0	Long Distance Provider:	SBC
	Monthly Long Distance:	$3,000	Primary Line Carriers:	MCI, SBC
	Network Purchasing Decisions:	Local	Dial Lines:	50
	Host or Remote Site Status	Neither	Number of Remote Locations:	0
	Tie/Lease Dedicated Access Lines:	2	T1 Lines:	3
	Tie/Lease Private Net Lines:	0	ISDN Lines:	0
	800/Wats Lines:	30	Total Data Lines:	0
	Maximum Data Line Speed:	0Mbps	Long Dist Purchase Decisions:	Local

COMM EQUIP	Prim. Phone System Vendor:	AVAYA	Phone Extensions:	500
	Call Center:	No	Planned Phone System:	Avaya
	Telco: VERIZON NEW YORK INC - NY	5170	LATA: LOS ANGELES CA	730
	Phone System Purchase Decisions:	local		

Contacts / Functions

CONTACT/FUNCTIONS		
Mr. Robert S. McCoy CEO/Chairman 949/260-2901		General Manager/President
Ms. Jean Davis Head of Operation/Technology 949/260-2901		Senior Information Systems Telecommunications Manager
Ms. Shwetha Thompson Webmaster 949/260-2901		Webmaster/Internet App Manager
Mr. Paul George IT Manager 949/260-2901		Data Communications Manager
Mr. George Mattingly Network Service Manager 949/260-2901		Network/Security Manager

Standard Functional Contact Summary

Business Functions:

General Manager/President

Technical Functions

Senior Information Systems Manager
Network/Security Manager
Data Communications Manager

Personal Computer Manager
Telecommunications Manager
Webmaster/Internet Applications Manager

Source: http://www.hartehanksmi.com/content/pdf/STANDARD_Profile%202005.pdf.

other lists for rental, among them e-mail lists, and provides a wide array of direct and interactive marketing services including creative development.

- InfoUSA is a traditional third-party list supplier to the direct marketing industry. It now includes e-mail lists in its product offering. According to its Web site, InfoUSA is "the leading compiler of several proprietary databases [that] capture detailed information on the majority of businesses and consumer households in the United States and Canada." InfoUSA has more than 600 full-time employees who create and update these databases using public records, including the yellow and white pages, court and tax records, newspapers, and other sources.[20]

These firms qualify as infomediaries, although they are rarely included in discussions of Internet intermediaries. They are part of the basic marketing services infrastructure used by businesses of all sizes and in all industrial sectors. They have their roots firmly in corporations that are experienced and successful in the physical world. These firms are likely to grow and add services, especially ones based on the Internet, but it is not clear that their business models will undergo major changes.

3-4f Marketplace

Marketplaces have been part of the human experience for thousands of years. All over the world there are central spaces where buyers and sellers meet to purchase and exchange goods. Given the pervasiveness and longevity of the physical business model, it is perhaps not surprising that the e-marketplace has become an important business model on the Web in both the B2C and B2B spaces.

B2C Marketplaces

The most famous of those marketplaces is certainly eBay. More than 125 million people worldwide use the site. At any time millions of items are listed for sale, and more than $1,000 in transactions takes place every second.[21] In 2004, the International Data Corporation reported that 24% of all e-commerce in the United States took place on eBay. eBay has local sites that serve Australia, Austria, Belgium, Canada, China, France, Germany, Hong Kong, India, Ireland, Italy, Malaysia, the Netherlands, New Zealand, the Philippines, Singapore, South Korea, Spain, Sweden, Switzerland, Taiwan, and the United Kingdom, as well as the United States. In addition, eBay has a presence in Latin America through its investment MercadoLibre. com. In 2004, Asia was its fastest-growing region, with strong growth also seen in Europe.[22]

How and why has eBay evolved from a tiny site where Pierre Omidyar's girlfriend could trade Pez candy dispensers to a force in the global economy? On the emotional side, eBay seems to speak to a human need to meet and trade items of interest. On the practical side, it provides a place for as many as 150,000 small businesses to offer their wares.[23] To do that, eBay has been required to build an extensive infrastructure, not only of technology, but also of services.

Do you want to increase your visibility and volume on eBay? Click on the Power Seller link for tips on doing just that. Is your goal to establish a small business on eBay? Visit the Small Business Center link to learn how. Do you want to sell things on eBay but don't have the time or the skills? See the Trading Assistant Link and get the help you need. And so it goes, with a constantly growing set of services for buyers and sellers. There is also a page for developers that offers Web services to help them create software for high-volume or specialized selling on eBay. Does that sound familiar? It is exactly the same model used by Amazon, discussed in Chapter 2, that encourages smaller sites to use its platform and integrate with its site.

When eBay was founded, it offered only the auction model of transactions. When its administrators learned that some buyers did not want to participate in auctions, they began to offer a "Buy It Now" option, in which customers can purchase items immediately, without going through the auction process. They also realized that customers were actually selling used cars on eBay by listing them in the Toy Cars section. eBay Motors was launched and now accounts for 30% of the dollar volume of sales on the site.[24] Among its other skills, eBay has become a master at listening to its customers and reacting quickly to their wants and needs.

B2B Marketplaces

Since the B2B buying process tends to be somewhat long and often complex, and since the process of locating suppliers can be onerous and expensive, marketplaces quickly took hold in the B2B space. The marketplace is able to reduce information search costs for buyers by maintaining a selected set of potential vendors that have been prequalified for expertise and reliability. It is able to provide sales leads for sellers because it has a set of member firms, usually in a vertical market, that need particular kinds of goods and services.

Three different kinds of B2B marketplaces exist:

- *Public marketplaces* serve any qualified purchaser or supplier.
- *Private exchanges* serve only a single firm.

consortia B2B marketplaces sponsored by a group of otherwise competitive enterprises in a specific industry.

- Industry exchanges, often called **consortia,** serve several competitor firms in a given industry, for example, Exostar in the airline industry.

Most B2B marketplaces offer the opportunity for participating sellers to post their online catalogs for simple e-commerce transactions. The primary transaction mechanism, however, is the reverse auction.[25] In the early days, B2B marketplace sites loudly trumpeted huge savings realized by purchasers on their site. Buyers' savings, however, translated into decreases in margin on the part of sellers. Marketplaces tried to compensate by trying to get most of their own revenue from buyers in the form of commissions on purchases, membership fees, and value-added services. However, it appears that the pressure on sellers created an unsustainable situation because most of the sites of the Internet bubble days have quietly gone out of business or have been acquired by and their technology integrated into other sites.

The exception seems to be in e-government, which has the purchasing power, and perhaps an appeal to corporate citizenship, that makes reverse auctions a continuing presence in that marketspace. The government of Australia has an Online and Reverse Auctions resource center that gives links to government auctions and reverse auctions in the United States and United Kingdom. The British government has a site that provides information and services for government agencies that want to set up e-auctions. This suggests that one of the key motivators for e-government around the world is access to low-cost procurement, using the reverse auction as one key component.

3-4g Multichannel/Bricks and Clicks

The terms *bricks and clicks* and *clicks and mortar* are frequently used to describe the business model that includes a physical retail store (or stores) and an e-commerce Internet site. That is not, however, a complete description of the business models of these firms. For example, Abercrombie & Fitch has stores, a transactional Web site, and a magazine, and it issues seasonal catalogs. Other retailers include a telephone call center as part of the mix. Whatever the exact components of the channel mix, *multichannel* is the most accurate term to describe this type of infrastructure.

One of the best examples of the challenges and opportunities involved in trying to integrate physical and online strategies is discount brokerage Charles Schwab. Schwab founded the brokerage that bears his name in 1975 after the Securities and Exchange Commission eliminated fixed-rate commissions on stock brokerage trades. To eliminate the conflict of interest inherent in the practice of compensating brokers based on their clients' trades, Schwab employed salaried brokers. The discount brokerage did not offer investment advice or actively manage client portfolios. It provided an objective environment in which consumers could make their own investment decisions and experience superb customer service. In the mid-1990s, the cost to execute a trade at Schwab averaged $80 as compared with trades executed through full-service brokers, which could cost hundreds of dollars. It offered a wide variety of financial services products and conducted business in more than 200 retail branches and a full-service telephone call center, making it a multichannel marketer before the dawn of the Internet.

Dawn Lepore, who was then chief information officer (CIO) at Schwab, recounted the evolution of their online trading capability in a speech in 1999:

> When we saw the opportunity to plunge into online investing in 1985, we took it and introduced a software product called the "Equalizer®." [...] With the advent of Windows, we were able to build a much more user-friendly software trading product called Streetsmart®, which became a big success with about 200,000 to 300,000 customers.
>
> By the end of 1995, we had created e.Schwab™ [and by] mid-'96, we felt that Internet technology was strong enough, and we added Web trading. This was a dramatic event. It was the equivalent of having a whole new world-wide free telephone system available overnight.[26]

e.Schwab was created as a separate division within the company, and its managers reported directly to the chief executive officer (CEO). There were two primary reasons for making Schwab's Internet operation a separate entity in the early days of online trading. The first was competition. Pure-play Internet brokerages were springing up right and left and offering deep discounts. To compete against these houses, Schwab had to offer a significantly lower price point for its services. The second reason was to try to wall off the online division so that in the case of a failure, the resulting losses and debt would have the minimal possible impact on the image of the parent firm, a common strategy in the early days of the Internet. Schwab quietly developed the new division and launched it with an announcement at a shareholder's meeting unsupported by any media advertising—another risk reduction strategy. A member of the development team recalls:

> "We were totally unprepared. Customers began voting with their keyboards, and in two weeks we reached 25,000 Web accounts—our goal for the entire year." By the end of 1997, all online accounts, both at e.Schwab and at regular Schwab, had grown to 1.2 million. Online assets mushroomed 94%, to $81 billion. . . . Schwab executives were ready to declare victory.[27]

Customers, however, were not. The brokerage had a number of initial problems to overcome. Customers were required to communicate with e.Schwab almost exclusively through e-mail; Schwab personnel in retail offices and the telephone call center could not help e.Schwab customers except for one free phone call each month. Existing customers who did not want to give up the option of personal contact could not take advantage of the low transaction fees available to electronic customers. Charles Schwab himself admitted publicly that the company's approach was not customer-friendly and could not be sustained. It was evident that the retail and electronic divisions had to be integrated into a single entity in order to offer a seamlessly satisfactory customer experience in any channel customers chose to use.

However, the financial implications of integrating the two divisions and instituting a flat charge of $30 per trade were immense. Schwab executives believed they risked a decrease of as much as $100 million in revenues, but they also believed they had no alternative. Schwab essentially bet its company on total integration. Revenues did initially decline, but within a year, online assets nearly had doubled. The number of online accounts also doubled and then doubled again the following year.

The unfortunate thing about having a strategy that works is that competition can easily observe, imitate, and even embellish on the successful strategy. A few of the discount brokerages founded as a direct result of the Internet boom have survived the bust and have become serious competition to Schwab. Within a few years of Schwab's initial foray into a broadly integrated bricks and clicks brokerage, the model had to be revised again. The necessary change was from a discount brokerage that provided no investment advice to a new model that might be described as hybrid—"More advice than a discount firm, but a different cost structure, a different pricing structure, and without the fundamental conflicts of interest that are so inherent in the structure of most Wall Street firms."[28]

The extent of the challenge inherent in formulating still another business model became clear in August 2004, when Charles Schwab reassumed full control of the firm that bears his name. The importance of his image and stature to the Schwab brand was made clear in the "Ask Chuck" advertising theme, seen on television, in magazines, and on the firm's Web site. It also emphasizes the fact that the sometimes wrenching changes brought on in some industries by the Internet have not yet ended.

3-4h Machine-to-Machine

machine-to-machine (M2M)
A business model in which automated systems allow computers and specialized devices to communicate with one another without direct human intervention.

Machine-to-machine (M2M) is another business model that may achieve prominence in the years to come. The example of the embedded chip in the elevator in Chapter 2 is an early illustration of what we may expect to see in the coming years.

Most of the M2M activity will be wireless based: a number of industry sectors are likely to make extensive use of M2M communications over the next few years (Figure 3-7). There are many examples of possible M2M applications:

- In B2B markets:
  - e-Suds.net offers laundry owners a comprehensive system that enables coin-free transactions, tracks cash receipts, allows customers to check availability and status, and schedules service for machines on an as-needed basis. As you might imagine, e-Suds has a specialized product for the college and university dormitory market.[29]

FIGURE 3-7   Forecasted M2M applications.

	Utility meters	Household appliances	Vending machines	Security systems	Elevators	HVAC* systems	Billboards	Amusement machines	Industrial machines	Photocopiers	Traffic signs	Trucks
Service and maintenance	✓	✓	✓		✓	✓	✓	✓	✓	✓		✓
Home automation	✓	✓		✓		✓						
Building automation	✓			✓	✓	✓						
Infotainment		✓	✓				✓	✓			✓	
Pay as you use	✓									✓		✓
Transportation and logistics				✓					✓		✓	✓

*heating, ventilation, air conditioning

Source: Adapted from *Machine-to-Machine: Let Your Machines Talk,* Nokia, 2004.

- Automobile manufacturers are increasingly including **telematics** in automobiles, allowing manufacturers to maintain a centralized database that tracks each car and provides options like remote diagnosis of equipment problems. Comprehensive data on the automobile are available to any dealer at the time of servicing. Since the data cover the life of the car, they are available to purchasers of second-hand automobiles.[30]
- In B2C markets:
  - In Europe, Swedish manufacturer Electrolux has developed several "concept refrigerators" over the years. The current version allows cell phone users with **MMS** service to take a picture of the interior contents of their refrigerator from a remote location, presumably a supermarket.[31]
  - In the United States, LG Electronics offers a refrigerator with an Internet-enabled plasma television screen. The refrigerator self-monitors for equipment problems, informing the owner by e-mail and, if necessary, providing contact information for the nearest service center.[32]

As you can see, wireless technology is an important component of M2M interaction. Other standard and emerging applications of wireless are explored in more detail in Chapter 14.

3-4i Open Source

Open source projects are carried out by a group of volunteers. At least the basic product created as a result of this collaboration is available free to all users. Many open source products are sold by businesses that provide the free source code but also include proprietary software utilities and a technical support package. For example, Linux, the popular **operating system,** is available both free of charge from http://www.linux.org or for a fee from a number of software developers.

Some examples of open source sites or products that are widely used by both consumers and technicians include the following:

- Wikipedia (http://en.wikipedia.org/wiki/Main_Page) bills itself as a free encyclopedia. Although not all definitions and articles found in Wikipedia are completely accurate and may have been written or edited by nonexperts, it is often a good source for up-to-date information on the Internet and Web trends. In fact, many of the definitions in this text are based on material in Wikipedia. Its content is provided by volunteers, and donations are solicited to purchase and maintain the system necessary to provide it.
- dmoz (http://www.dmoz.org) describes itself as a human-edited directory or catalog of Web sites. It invites people with relevant expertise to become editors and participate in the project.
- Firefox (http://www.mozilla.org/firefox/) is an open source Internet browser that has evolved from the original Netscape browser. It allows users to extensively customize their browsers and actively recruits software developers to assist in maintenance and in developing new functionality. Firefox quickly developed a strong following among personal and corporate users because of its high security capabilities, gaining significant market share within a few weeks of its official launch.
- OpenOffice (http://www.openoffice.org/) is a suite of business applications that works on a number of platforms, including Microsoft Windows, Sun Solaris, and Linux. It is also available in many languages. The site recruits users with computer expertise to try out beta versions of offerings and encourages developers to contribute to the open source software.

These are only some of the many ongoing open source projects. They recall the freewheeling early days of the Internet, when commercialism was suspect and group

telematics Sending, receiving, and storing data using telecommunications devices.

MMS wireless telecommunications services that allow graphics, audio clips, and video clips to be transmitted over cell phones.

open source Freely available content that is produced collaboratively by volunteers.

operating system The master piece of software that runs the computer and all the applications used on it.

projects resulting in freeware and shareware were the norm. From a practical point of view, these endeavors also contribute to the constant innovation that is the nature of the Internet.

3-4j Peer-to-Peer

peer-to-peer model
Transmission of files directly from one user to another.

The Internet public became aware of the **peer-to-peer** (P2P) **model** in early 2000, when a legal ruckus over Napster, a popular software for downloading music files, became a media event. Napster was already well known among teens and young adults and became more widely known when colleges began to filter Napster's file-sharing software from their networks. The music files that students were downloading in computer labs and dorm rooms were clogging networks and devouring storage space allocated for research and legitimate files. In addition, Napster raised complex issues involving copyright and intellectual property laws. The music industry's unwavering opposition to Napster based on these grounds forced its sale to European media giant Bertelsmann Media Worldwide, followed by a transition to a subscription-based business model.

Napster was not alone in its quest to offer file-sharing software in a P2P format. Gnutella and Kazaa were but two other entries into the field of P2P file sharing using free software easily downloadable from the Web. These services allow all types of files, not just digital audio, to be shared between users. Many services are offered, from **Voice Over Internet Protocol (VOIP)** phone calling (online telephone communications) to self-publishing to messaging to video services. The software used by services such as Gnutella and Kazaa both effectively establish each individual user's computer as a **server,** making it relatively impervious to shutdown by an outside agency.

Voice Over Internet Protocol (VOIP) Internet telephony; the ability to make calls over any IP network.

server A computer from which other computers request files.

intranet Corporate network accessible only to employees and outsiders with authorization.

extranet Corporate networks linked together to share designated information.

Although it is much less newsworthy, P2P is alive and well—legally—in business markets. The sharing of supply chain information discussed in Chapter 2 is an example of business-to-business P2P file sharing. B2B marketplaces provide a forum for users to exchange ideas and information, and corporate **intranets** host busy traffic in files moving around the world. **Extranets** link corporate information resources to those of strategic partners and suppliers. Sharing information within corporate enterprises and with external partners is a key part of the networked economy, and it will support the continued growth of P2P in the business space.

3-4k Portals

portal A large site with multiple services, ranging from news to directories to searches, that acts as an entry point onto the Internet.

search engine Software that allows users to search for content based on keywords.

A **portal** is traditionally defined as a gateway, often an imposing one. On the Internet, the term has come to mean a site that serves as an entrance ramp onto the Internet through a **search engine** and links to content. Many sites describe themselves as portals. Some serve particular interests, like health or sports information. Others serve vertical business markets, as was suggested earlier in this chapter. Still others serve particular technologies; for example, some portals give access to wireless services and content. One of the first and best known portals is Yahoo! Its story is in many ways the story of the commercial Internet.

Yahoo! was the brainchild of two graduate students working out of a trailer at Stanford University. David Filo and Jerry Yang were Internet aficionados who wanted a way to keep track of all the Web sites they liked to visit. They created software that allowed them to list and link to their favorite sites. This was the origin of Yahoo!—a directory of sites that had been located and cataloged by human beings.

Word of the directory, originally called "Jerry and David's guide to the World Wide Web," quickly spread among early Internet users, who took advantage of its listings and contributed additional content. The directory soon outgrew the capacity of the university network and moved into offices at Netscape, the original graphical browser,

| FIGURE 3-8a | Yahoo page from October 1996. |

Source: http://web.archive.org/web/19961020022754/http://www9.Yahoo!.com/.

then in its heyday. The name Yahoo! stands for "Yet Another Hierarchical Officious Oracle," and Filo and Yang also selected the name because they liked the dictionary definition of a yahoo: "rude, unsophisticated, and uncouth."

Yahoo! quickly added other services, transforming it from a directory of sites into what is generally regarded as a portal. *Wired* magazine quibbles with that definition:

> It's just not easy to say what Yahoo! is. It's a chat room, a news service, a travel agent, an auction house, and a financial portal, not to mention an ISP and a fantasy sports league. It doles out health information along with music videos and movie trailers. Yahoo! is about everything, so it's forgivable to think it may stand for nothing. Is the company offering specialty services or mass appeal? Is it narrow and wide or shallow and deep? "Actually, we are both horizontal and vertical," COO Dan Rosensweig says, rather unhelpfully.[33]

As the number of Yahoo!'s services grew, the site expanded and required new design configurations. Figure 3-8a shows a page from Yahoo!'s first month of operation. It is a simple page, with most of the content being links. There was little or no ability to personalize services or individualize pages. By 2001, the site had a much richer set of offerings and the home page had a more attractive presentation (Figure 3-8b). Along with links to a wide variety of content, Yahoo! was offering free e-mail, personalized pages, and a free trial of a Yahoo! store.

The content, the services, and the localized Web sites add up to one of the most globally recognizable sites on the Web. By 2005, Yahoo! had more than 165 million registered users and served 345 million unique visitors each month in thirteen different languages. It is generally considered the most recognizable global brand on the Internet.

Yahoo!'s success did not come easily or smoothly. Advertising revenue alone was insufficient to maintain the site from the time it was commercialized. When the Internet bubble burst in 2002, many of the Internet firms that had been aggressive advertisers went out of business, reducing advertising revenue substantially. Yahoo! continued to add services to attract more visitors and return visits, thereby increasing the amount that could be charged for advertising. Other services—like premium e-mail, e-commerce business services, and bill-paying services—produce their own revenue streams. In 2003, Yahoo! acquired the Overture search engine. One year later, this paid search feature accounted for a significant part of the firm's $3.6 billion in revenue. Online advertising began to grow again at about the same time, and Yahoo! was viewed as prime advertising space.

In Yahoo!'s own words:

> Our mission is to be the most essential global Internet service for consumers and businesses. How we pursue that mission is influenced by a set of core values—the standards that guide interactions with fellow Yahoo!s, the principles that direct how we service our customers, the ideals that drive what we do and how we do it. Many of our values were put into practice by two guys in a trailer some time ago; others reflect ambitions as our company grows.[34]

Yahoo!'s goal to be the most essential service on the global Internet brings it into direct conflict with a newer entrant. Google has a similar vision but a very different business model that is discussed in Chapter 7. It seems clear, however, that Yahoo! is not only an Internet survivor—it has also prospered as a portal that offers a vast array of Internet-based services.[35]

3-5 The Future of Business Models

There has been significant upheaval in the Internet business model landscape over the past few years. When the changing landscape is carefully examined, two major patterns appear.

First, the basic nature of the models present has not changed a great deal. The same models are in evidence now that were present in the earlier days of the Internet. However, the prominence of various models has changed. For instance, when Internet use was growing at a spectacular rate, simply providing access as a dedicated Internet service provider (ISP) was considered a viable business model. Now ISP services have become components of much larger and further developed business models. Likewise, in the early years, the Web was home to hundreds of B2B marketplaces, far too many to gain sustainable market share. The number of marketplaces has greatly decreased, although the early B2B models are still clearly viable in both B2B and B2C markets, as evidenced by eBay.

Second, there was initially a widespread belief that a sufficient quantity of content on a Web site would draw enough visitors to produce the advertising revenue required to support the business. This has proved not to be true, and sites have found it necessary to develop multiple revenue streams to achieve and maintain profitability.

The evolution of the Internet business model continues, and there may even be new business models as time goes on. Some may be counterparts of physical-world business models, as are many of the current Internet models. Some may actually be new models that take advantage of the unique characteristics of the Internet.

Summary

Internet business models shape the way enterprises are configured to create value for customers and to deliver that value in a profitable way on the Internet. A business model is a conceptual description of the business. Business models on the Internet have been given a set of names, although there is no commonly accepted set of names or classifications of types of business models. The emphasis on the value proposition, however, is characteristic of all discussions of Internet business models. The drivers of value are customer wants and needs. It is up to the business to uncover the relevant wants and needs and design products

and services that meet those needs and fit with their core expertise. This is a customer-centric—not a product-centric—approach. There are a number of commonly accepted business models—aggregators, applications services providers, content providers, fund-raisers, infomediaries, marketplaces, M2M protocols, multichannel systems, open source offerings, P2P networks, and portals. Most of them can be found in both B2C and B2B marketspaces. Internet businesses can generate revenue in a number of ways—by providing Internet access or selling advertising and sponsorships; through donations, memberships or subscriptions, the sale or licensing of software or systems; by providing software-based services; through syndication or licensing of content, transactions, and value-added services. Few Internet businesses find it possible to sustain themselves on a single revenue stream; most find it necessary to employ several revenue-generating approaches to achieve sustained profitability. The evolution of business models on the Internet continues. It is likely that different models may achieve prominence at different periods of time and possible that entirely new models may emerge as the Internet matures.

Quiz

1. _____ is an important element of any business model.
   a. Financial forecasting
   b. Value proposition
   c. Competitive analysis

2. The value proposition concept only restates the way marketers have approached product development and marketing strategy all along.
   a. true
   b. false

3. Revenue models for online businesses include_____.
   a. memberships and subscriptions
   b. syndication of content
   c. both a and b

4. Music file-sharing is an example of which Internet business model?
   a. machine-to-machine
   b. peer-to-peer
   c. online catalog

5. Which of the following are issues that are confronted in the bricks and clicks model?
   a. deciding whether to establish the e-business under the same brand as the offline business
   b. concern over cannibalizing the online business
   c. both a and b

6. _____ is making recommendations to visitors based on preferences generated by the purchases of similar visitors.
   a. Collaborative filtering
   b. Collaboration
   c. Co-creation

7. _____ markets are focused on a single market sector.
   a. Horizontal
   b. Vertical
   c. Exchange

8. The key function of an ASP is to _____.
   a. manage and distribute software-based services and solutions
   b. own all the hardware and software that clients need to do e-business
   c. develop new software applications for its clients

9. RSS feeds are _____.
   a. a method of generating revenue from Web site content
   b. used by large corporations to transmit information over the Internet
   c. a method of syndicating content

10. Open source models are rarely used because all Web sites want to monetize their content.
    a. true
    b. false

11. _____ is the business model used to describe a site that provides easy access to large amounts of content on the Web.
    a. Portal
    b. Infomediary
    c. Machine-to-machine

12. Nonprofit organizations and government at all levels can make effective use of the Internet.
    a. true
    b. false

Discussion Questions

1. Why is the concept of the business model important? In what ways is it useful?

2. How does the value proposition change a firm's approach to creation of new products and new marketing strategies?

3. Some firms choose to generate revenue by selling or licensing their proprietary software. Others choose an open systems approach and distribute it free of charge. What do you think drives the decision?

4. How have Internet revenue models evolved from the original content/advertising/monetization model? In your opinion, which model(s) offer the best opportunities for sustainable long-run profitability? Why?

5. How has the presence of the Internet affected both fixed and variable costs for multichannel businesses?

6. How has the approach to content changed over the life of the commercial Internet?

7. The text implies that multichannel retailers are more likely to experience long-term success in the Internet economy than are pure-play Internet retailers. Do you agree with this statement? Why or why not?

Internet Exercises

1. Choose one of the Web sites you are following for a detailed study of the business model it represents. Carefully examine the way(s) in which it obtains revenues, and try to find out from its own reports or from industry sources what its current revenue is and what weight is given to each of its revenue streams. Then make your assessment of the manner in which the enterprise (both the Web site and any physical-world business components) creates value for its target customers. Be prepared to present your analysis in class.

2. Choose a business that you believe fits into one of the business models in Table 3-1. Research the elements of its business model and examine the site in considerable detail. Be prepared to discuss both the revenue and cost models of your chosen business and to explain how it creates value for its target customers.

3. Think again about the retail entity from which you bought the material for this class. Analyze all of the ways in which that enterprise attempts to create value for its customers. Also consider the nature of its revenue model and whether it has only a single revenue stream or multiple sources of revenue.

4. Choose one of the business models from Table 3-1. Construct your own hypothetical business around the model. How would you go about developing a value proposition for the business? What would the viable revenue streams be? Why?

Notes

1. Michael Rappa, "Business Models on the Web," http://digital enterprise.org/models/models.html.
2. Sendil Ethiraj, Isin Guler, and Harbir Singh, nd, "The Impact of Internet and Electronic Technologies on Firms and Its Implications for Competitive Advantage," Working Paper, The Wharton School, University of Pennsylvania, pp. 18–19.
3. Henry Chesbrough and Richard S. Rosenbloom, "The Role of the Business Model in Capturing Value from Innovation: Evidence from Xerox Corporation's Technology Spin-off Companies," *Industrial and Corporate Change*, Volume 11, Number 3, 2002, pp. 533–534.
4. Alexander Osterwalder and Yves Pigneur, "An e-Business Model Ontology for Modeling e-Business," 15th Bled Electronic Commerce Conference, Bled, Slovenia, July 17–19, 2002.
5. Kenichi Ohmae, "Getting Back to Strategy," *Harvard Business Review*, November–December 1988, pp. 2–8. Accessed from *The McKinsey Quarterly*, http://mckinseyquarterly.com/article_page.aspx?ar=1055&L2=21&L3=37.
6. Don Tapscott, David Ticoll, and Alex Lowy, Digital Capital: Harnessing the Power of Business Webs (Boston: Harvard Business School Press, 2000), p. 67.
7. http://www.amazon.com.
8. http://www.corio.com/spd.cfm?spi=solutions.
9. http://www.asp-directory.com/directory/vertical_market/construction/index.shtml.
10. http://www.asp-directory.com/directory/vertical_market/other/index1.shtml.
11. http://www.asp-directory.com/directory/vertical_market/legal/index.shtml.
12. http://www.aspstreet.com/directory/d.taf/cid,63.
13. Pamela Parker, "NYTimes.com: Online Ads Aren't Enough," May 16, 2005, http://www.clickz.com; Rebecca Lieb, "RSS Sparks Feeding Frenzy," May 20, 2005, http://www.clickz.com.
14. See "Blogging Blossoms in British Election," Reuters, 2005, accessed on http://www.bizreport.com/news/8889/.
15. Jonathan D. Salant, "Internet Donations Spur 55% Rise in 2004 Fund Raising (update)," December 31, 2004, http://www.bloomberg.com/apps/news?pid=10000176&sid=aWBZ16tiOIi8&refer=us_el.
16. Nicole Wallace, "$597-Million Raised by U.S. Charities for Tsunami Relief," January 26, 2005, http://philanthropy.com/free/update/2005/01/2005012602.htm.
17. "Business to Consumer Electronic Commerce," http://en.wikipedia.org/wiki/Business-to-consumer_electronic_commerce.
18. "Infomediary," http://www.webopedia.com/TERM/I/infomediary.html.
19. For a discussion of how list managers and brokers operate, see Chapter 4, "Mailing List Processing and Selection," in Mary Lou Roberts and Paul D. Berger, *Direct Marketing Management*, available for free download at http://www.marylouroberts.info.
20. "Company Profile," http://ir.infousa.com/phoenix.zhtml?c=96263&p=irol-homeProfile&t=&id=&.
21. "eBay's Bid for Success," January 5, 2005, http://www.CBSNews.com.
22. "eBay Outlines Global Strategy at Conference," http://investor.ebay.com/releases.cfm.
23. "eBay's Bid for Success," January 5, 2005, http://www.CBSNews.com.

24. "Anniversary Lessons from eBay," *The Economist,* June 9, 2005, http://www.economist.com/printedition/displaystory.cfm? Story_ID=4055579.

25. See Sandy D. Jap, "An Exploratory Study of the Introduction of the Online Reverse Auction," July 2003, *Journal of Marketing, 67,* 96–17.

26. "E-Commerce Is More Than Dot Com," speech by Dawn Lepore, Vice Chairman, EVP & CIO, Charles Schwab, Inc., May 1999.

27. Erick Schonfeld, "Schwab Puts It All Online," *Fortune,* December 7, 1998, http://www.fortune.com.

28. "What I Learned during the Economic Slump," *Context,* Winter 2002–2003, http://www.contextmag.com.

29. http://www.usatech.com/laundry_overview.php.

30. "Building Brand Loyalty by Improving the Customer Experience," January 2003, http://www.oracle.com.

31. Elisa Batista, "Chilly Forecast for Smart Fridge," August 2, 2003, http://wired-vig.wired.com/news/print/0,1294,59858,00 .html.

32. Jeff Fila, "LG Announces Multimedia Refrigerator," http://news.designtechnica.com/article4127.html.

33. Michael S. Malone, "The UnGoogle (Yes, Yahoo!)," March 2005, http://www.wired.com.

34. http://docs.yahoo.com/info/values/.

35. Additional sources for this section: Jim Hu, "After 10 Years, Yahoo Still Searching," March 2, 2005, http://www.cnet-news.com; David Callum, "Yahoo Feature," 2004, http://www.akamarketing.com.

The Direct-Response and Database Foundations of Internet Marketing

Chapter Four

Chapter Outline

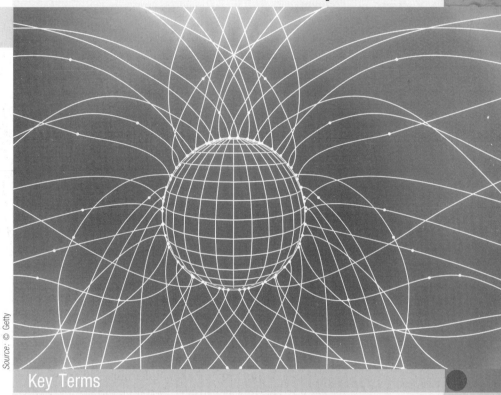

Source: © Getty

Key Terms

Learning Objectives

By the time you complete this chapter, you will be able to:

- Explain the ways in which the Internet is a direct-response medium.

- Distinguish between acquisition, conversion, and retention strategies.

- Explain the concepts of offer, customer lifetime value, and testing.

- Explain the role of a customer database in the development and execution of Internet marketing programs.

- Describe a data warehouse and how it is used by marketers.

- Define *data mining* and explain why it is important in making marketing decisions.

- Describe how strategies can become more customer focused by using information-driven marketing.

4-1 The Internet as a Direct-Response Medium

The Internet is in many ways a direct-response medium. Why? Certainly it is an interactive medium, allowing two-way dialog between marketer and prospective customer. But the Internet presents even more powerful opportunities to the shrewd marketer. From the consumer's perspective, it permits a seamless purchase process. From the marketer's perspective, the Internet allows fine-tuning of marketing programs in ways previously unimaginable. There are four important characteristics—the four I's—that describe the ways in which marketing efforts are powerfully affected by the capabilities of the Internet (Figure 4-1).

The Internet, more than any other current medium, allows *interactivity*. Marketers can initiate two-way communications with prospective customers by sending offers to them and tracking their response or by initiating direct communications by way of surveys, chat rooms, or other Internet-enabled techniques. The potential exists for all marketing activities on the Web to be *information driven*. Every action a Web site visitor makes—from sending an e-mail query to purchasing a product—is a potential piece of data for the marketing database that drives targeted promotional activities. The Internet fosters *immediacy* in a variety of ways. Marketers can reply directly to customer queries, using human agents or automated systems. The Internet makes it cost-efficient to construct offers that appeal to a specific market segment or to make offers that are seasonal or that are triggered by a particular event, for example, synchronizing a team sportswear sale with the NCAA basketball finals. Internet promotions can also be *involving*. Marketers are increasingly using streaming video and games in Internet advertising to attract and involve prospective customers. A

| FIGURE 4-1 | The four I's of Internet marketing. |

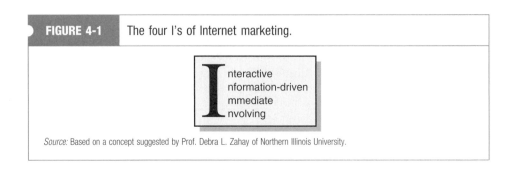

Interactive
Information-driven
Immediate
Involving

Source: Based on a concept suggested by Prof. Debra L. Zahay of Northern Illinois University.

good direct-response offer incites prospects to take action—either to request information or to make a purchase on the spot.

Some marketers have learned to combine brand marketing with direct-response marketing. Procter & Gamble, best known as for its use of mass media and mass distribution channels, was a user of direct response even before the advent of the Internet. Figure 4-2a shows part of the page for what Procter & Gamble calls the Cheer family of brands. One family member is Cheer Free, which does not contain perfumes and dyes. This is important to the small segment of people who are allergic to those additives and can have intense reactions to products washed in detergents that contain them. When Cheer Free was introduced more than two decades ago, Procter & Gamble knew that mass market techniques would not be cost-efficient. Consequently they used promotional techniques like free samples and coupons to build a mailing list of households that needed this product. Using this list, they were able to promote directly to these households by mail, a targeted and cost-effective solution.

Procter & Gamble quickly learned to use the Internet in much the same way. Its extensive site has pages for nearly 300 brands, many of which are global and some of which are available only in certain countries. Its pages for products sold in the United States link to a companion site, P&G brandSAVER (Figure 4-2b), where visitors can find all sorts of promotional offers. Whether the offers are for coupons, free samples, or contests and sweepstakes, all of these sales promotions have the objective of inducing consumers to take immediate action. Whatever response the promotion requests, the data collected through it provide P&G with customer information and e-mail addresses. The page also promotes marketing activities in other media, such as a newspaper insert called brandSaver, and seasonal tie-ins with promotions on the

---

FIGURE 4-2a   P&G new products page.

Source: © Procter & Gamble

FIGURE 4-2b   P&G brandSAVER page.

Source: © Procter & Gamble

Travel Channel and on the Web. Their integration of multiple channels of communication is clearly evident on this page.

The Internet offers companies like P&G the special ability to manage promotional activities for small segments, like the people with specific needs, and to react quickly to new promotional opportunities. Both ads and content can be dynamically targeted toward certain segments of the potential consumer base by using basic techniques developed by early direct marketers. The effectiveness of promotional programs can be tested in real time and adjustments can be made almost instantaneously. In fact, many of the time-honored tools of direct marketing are transferable onto the Web in fairly straightforward ways. It is critical for marketers to understand direct marketing methodology to develop and refine successful Internet marketing programs.

4-2 Generic Direct Marketing Strategies[1]

acquisition The process of obtaining new customers.

conversion The process of moving a prospect from consideration to purchase.

retention Preventing existing customers from defecting to another seller.

Essentially there are three types of direct marketing strategies that parallel a basic customer life cycle (Figure 4-3). First, a customer is acquired. This state represents trial of a product or service. In the **acquisition** stage, the customer has made a single purchase, or perhaps engaged in free use as a result of a sample or demonstration, but is not yet committed to the brand.

The second stage is **conversion**, so called because in this step the prospect converts to customer. This may require one to three purchases, enough to form a habitual purchasing pattern. The final stage is **retention**, in which the customer continues to make purchases, a situation we might call behavioral loyalty. Even better, in this stage the

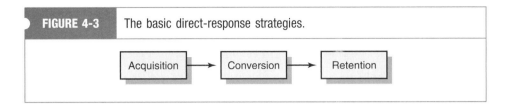

FIGURE 4-3   The basic direct-response strategies.

Acquisition → Conversion → Retention

customer begins to exhibit loyalty in an attitudinal sense, which may result in behaviors ranging from rejecting competing offers to becoming an advocate for the product.

Each of the basic strategies requires a different type of effort on the part of the marketer. *Acquisition* is roughly equivalent to the awareness stage of general advertising with an action component added. It requires a conscious attempt to get the attention of the prospective customer through media placement and creative execution. Direct marketers often add an incentive to clinch the trial. We discuss customer acquisition on the Internet in detail in Chapters 6 and 7.

The *conversion* step is focused on getting the customer to make additional purchases, often the three that psychologists recommend to establish a habitual behavior. Product and service satisfaction is critical to achieving this goal. Customer contact, through media ranging from personal selling to newsletters, is often useful. Sequential incentives have also been used with good results. For example, a bank that wanted its customers to make more deposits at ATMs sent them a series of three checks, each of which could be used only with a series of ATM deposits. The first check was for $5, the second was for $3, and the third was for $1. The incentives were not only sequential, they decreased in value as the presumed habit formation was taking place. It is hard to prove habit formation, but in this case it seems reasonable to assume that many customers, after three successful deposits, recognized that it is safe to make deposits through ATMs. This was a sensible, low-cost conversion program aimed at achieving a worthwhile business goal. Its only visible drawback was that the bank did not make good use of its customer database. It sent the checks to customers who regularly made ATM deposits as well as to those who never deposited through an ATM!

Finally, it is important to *retain* customers to create the highest possible **customer lifetime value** (CLV). Retention is most often the result of adding value to the customer purchase and use experience and superior customer service. A planned program of customer contact, carried out at appropriate points in the purchase cycle, can also be a useful component of retention programs. We discuss retention in detail in Chapter 8.

customer lifetime value The net present value of a future stream of net revenue from an identified customer.

4-3 Critical Strategy Elements

The marketing mix that supports direct marketing programs uses slightly different terminology from the traditional four P's of most marketing approaches. They are as follows:

- The offer—product, price, positioning, and any other product-related elements that make up the complete proposition presented to the prospective customer
- The list—the targeting vehicle
- The media used—with the understanding that any medium can be a direct-response medium with the proper implementation
- The creative execution—which tends to play a secondary role in this action-oriented context
- The service and support—long recognized as a key element in this environment where the shopping experience and many sensory stimuli are not present

These elements are all required to implement any direct-response program. It is, however, especially important to understand the role of the offer in developing Internet marketing strategies.

4-3a Offers That Incite to Action

The first rule of direct marketing is that the initial offer must include a call to action. It must tell the prospect exactly what the marketer wants him or her to do and it must make it easy for the person to take that action. This sounds like a simple notion, but it is easy to let the call to action become buried in Web site pyrotechnics or poor design. All too frequently, a visitor is willing to take action but cannot find a response form, finds that the form doesn't work, or finds the questions on the form to be intrusive or simply too onerous. Action that is not taken when the impulse burns strong will probably never be taken.

A particular Internet marketing program has one of three action objectives—to get the visitor to remain on the site longer, to entice visitors to request additional information, or to achieve a sale:

CPM Cost per thousand exposures; the primary pricing mechanism for many media, including the Internet.

- *To get the visitor to remain on the site longer* and explore more of what the company has to offer. This is referred to as site "stickiness," and it has a direct bearing on the **CPM** (cost per thousand) rates that sites are able to charge for their advertising space. If the site does not have a transactional component, this may be a terminal objective. In the more common situation, in which sites are trying to achieve transactional as well as advertising revenue, this may be a first-stage objective with one of the other two objectives as the primary objective.

- *To entice visitors to request additional information about a product or service.* This is the conventional lead-generation objective long used in both business-to-customer (B2C) and business-to-business (B2B) markets. When automobile manufacturers send to a carefully selected mailing list inviting consumers to come to their nearest dealership and test drive a new model, they are engaged in a multiple-step B2C lead-generation and conversion program. When a software firm offers a free online demonstration of its new release, it is engaged in a B2B lead-generation program. If the site requires the visitor to register and provide an e-mail address to get the information desired, it is building an e-mail list of people who have qualified themselves by indicating their interest in the product. These are clearly more qualified prospects than individuals who have the correct demographics with known or unknown buying habits that the car manufacturer or software developer obtains from a list rental firm.

landing page A Web page designed to receive visitors who are coming to the site as a result of a link from another site.

Consider the **landing page** for Pepperdine University's part-time MBA program (Figure 4-4a), which is linked to from the school's paid ad on Google. When a prospective student clicks through to the Pepperdine site via an ad for an MBA program, this shows interest. It behooves the school to capture the person's contact information to continue to promote the program to him or her. Asking a site visitor to fill out this a form requesting such contact information on a landing page in order to gain access to a site's main content is common practice on the Web and considered acceptable by many users. However, some users will balk at providing this kind of information when they see a form that asks for it and immediately leave the site. Does the fact that these people do not want to provide contact information mean they are less interested than the ones who do? This is unclear, but what is obvious is that this is a risk many organizations are willing take to obtain contact information for people who show interest in their site. In the case of the Pepperdine MBA program, printed material about the program is openly offered and prospects knows they will have to provide an address to get it. Filling out the form to obtain an important piece of information is a reasonable trade-off to most genuinely interested prospects.

| FIGURE 4-4a | A typical landing page. |

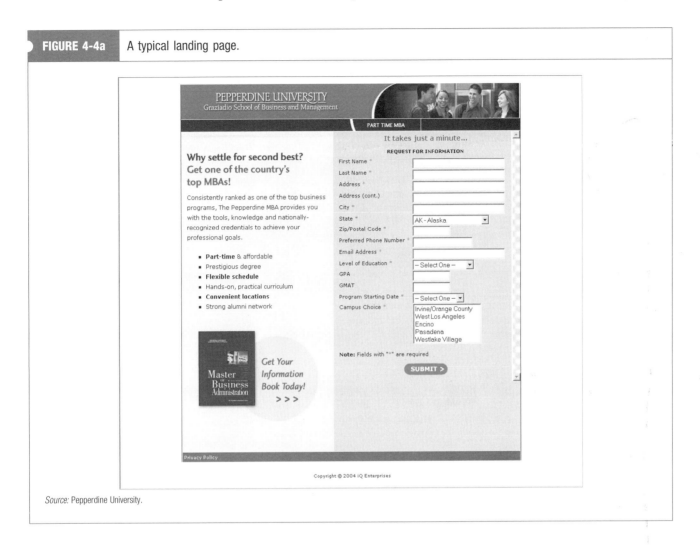

Source: Pepperdine University.

In the case of carefully considered customer actions like enrolling in an MBA program, a multiple-step program is usually necessary to complete the transaction. However, in other cases the customer is seeking information to make a purchase. Making the sale is the final generic direct-response objective.

- *To achieve a sale.* When the product and the purchasing situation are appropriate for a one-step sales effort, the actual sale becomes the objective. The Sony Web page in Figure 4-4b was also accessed from a paid ad on Google. However, in this case Sony's objective is to make an immediate sale, and the technique is different. Instead of a landing page constructed to get information for follow-up marketing efforts, the Sony ad simply takes the prospect directly to the page of interest in the site. Notice, however, that it does not just lead the person searching for digital cameras to the Sony home page, but rather takes the searcher directly to the products he is interested in.

One of the key tools for achieving offers that compel action is the **incentive**. Different objectives call for different incentives. A lead-generation offer typically includes an information incentive, whereas a sales offer is more likely to include something tangible. The general rule is that a tangible incentive should be related to the product, such as giving away a free seasonal candle with an order for Christmas decorations. The Sony page offers several price-oriented, nontangible promotions—price reductions, rebates, and combined offers, for example. It also offers a financing plan with the purchase of the digital camera. In addition, Internet marketers have

incentive A reward offered by a marketer to a prospective customer in return for furnishing information or making a purchase.

FIGURE 4-4b   Sony cameras.

Source: Sony.

learned in recent years that free shipping is another compelling incentive. All of these are powerful incentives that encourage immediate purchase. Direct marketers have long known that action delayed is often action not taken, so Internet marketers have been quick and eager to provide the kinds of extra motivation needed to turn a visit into a transaction.

Another tool that is a key part of the offer is the **brand**. We cover building online brands in greater detail in Chapter 6, but it is worth pointing out here that in designing the offer, the marketer must consider the strength of the brand. The stronger the brand, the easier it is to get a prospect to accept a good offer. If the brand is unknown, it may be harder to compel action. How can smaller brands combat this disadvantage? Offering a bigger incentive is one option. Another is to make use of another important tool—risk reduction. Risk is reduced when a strong guarantee is offered. Customer testimonials and third-party endorsements are also useful. Ultimately, though, the best way to reduce potential buyers' perceived risk is to build a strong and trusted brand.

Much has been written about the issue of trust on the Internet. There is no doubt that marketers need to build trust between their companies and brands and their prospective customers. In the longer term, trust will be achieved by the way the marketer does business—prompt and accurate fulfillment, returns and service practices, and guardianship of the customer's privacy. The immediate issue for the marketer without an established brand, however, is how to create a sense of confidence that will make the prospect feel reasonably comfortable about conducting a transaction. In its early days, Amazon.com recognized that even though it was making Herculean efforts to establish its brand, many customers were reluctant to give their credit card numbers over the Web. Amazon.com posted a prominent guarantee that promised to reimburse any losses customers incurred as a result of transmitting their credit card information to the company. This was appropriate for its time, and as consumer trust has grown, the notice has been replaced with a free shipping offer for many Amazon purchases.

A good offer is designed to compel immediate response from the prospective customer and lays a strong foundation for future marketing efforts to a targeted, identified customer. To do this cost effectively, the marketer must understand front-end vs. back-end issues.

brand A name, term, sign, symbol, design, or a combination thereof intended to identify the goods and services of one seller or a group of sellers and to differentiate them from those of the competition.

4-4 The Front End vs. The Back End

Direct marketers have long used the terms **front end** and **back end**, although no single precise definition exists. It is useful to think of front-end activities as being everything that occurs as part of making the sale. The back end comprises all of the postsale activities, including order fulfillment and customer service. Marketers understand the front end well; that is their historical domain.

Internet marketers, however, have tended to ignore the importance of the back end. They have concentrated on what customers see—the acquisition activities on the front end—to the exclusion of what they do not see—the back-end functions. The problem with that perspective is that it is the back-end activities that create lasting customer satisfaction and lead to customer retention.

It is also worth noting that this is an arena in which established direct marketing firms had an initial advantage over established bricks-and-mortar retailers. Established direct marketers have the infrastructure and the processes for effective order fulfillment and customer service in place. Established bricks-and-mortar businesses have infrastructure and processes that are precisely the opposite of what is needed on the Web. Their back-end systems are designed to meet the needs of a series of stores, not to fulfill the orders of individual customers. Many direct marketers have long concentrated on establishing superb customer service facilities, recognizing the

front end All the marketing and promotional activities that occur before a sale is made.

back end The activities that are required to satisfy the customer after a sale is made, including fulfillment and customer service.

importance of this element in the absence of the store shopping experience. The extent to which many established retailers have slighted customer service functions is well recognized, although an outstanding few, like Neiman Marcus and Nordstrom, have systems that seem to have transferred well into the Web environment. It is, however, worth noting that both had successful catalog operations before moving onto the Internet. The established bricks-and-mortar firm that has no experience in direct marketing not only will require a different infrastructure to be successful at Internet marketing but also will need a change of mind-set in several important areas.

A number of other perspectives that are important in the direct marketing environment must be adopted to achieve long-term success in the Internet space. One is the concept of lifetime value of a customer.

4-5 The Role and Importance of Customer Lifetime Value[2]

It has long been a truism that the role of marketing is to create a customer, not just a sale. That is true, but it has been an elusive goal for many mass media marketers. Being unable to identify their end customers, mass marketers could not interact directly with them and engage in specific attempts to increase their long-term value. This represents another direct marketing technique that is now available to all marketers who make informed use of their Web sites.

The basic idea of CLV is that if the marketer understands what it costs to acquire, maintain, and service a customer, he or she can make a reasoned decision about how much to spend to market to that customer. The underlying model is simple:

$$\text{Net Customer Revenues}$$
$$\text{Less:} \quad \frac{\text{Cost of Goods Sold}}{\text{Gross Margin}}$$
$$\text{Less:} \quad \frac{\text{Cost of Servicing}}{\text{Customer Revenue}}$$
$$\text{Times:} \quad \frac{\text{Cost of Capital}}{\text{Net Present Value of Customer Revenue Stream}}$$

The calculation takes into account the amount of time the customer is likely to persist with the firm. It usually takes as much as 3 years' worth of data collection to calculate CLV with a reasonable degree of accuracy. After 5 years, the discount for the cost of capital becomes so high that future revenue streams have little value, so 3 to 5 years is usually satisfactory. Notice that data must be collected for as long as 3 years in order to begin developing CLV and marketing programs based on it.

Venkatesan and Kumar use a graphic (Figure 4-5) that helps make these issues clear.[3] Characteristics of the customer that include switching cost, involvement with the product category or brand, and the customer's purchase history are used to predict future purchasing frequency and the profit obtained from it. The cost of communicating with the customer determines marketing costs. The contribution margin from each customer is determined, and the amount of communications with the customer across all channels is taken into account. The profit from the customer is based on the frequency of purchasing at a particular contribution margin (revenue times contribution percent) less the costs of marketing to the customer. The discount rate is applied and the net present value of a future stream of profits— CLV—is computed. Then the marketer determines actions that can be taken to increase CLV.

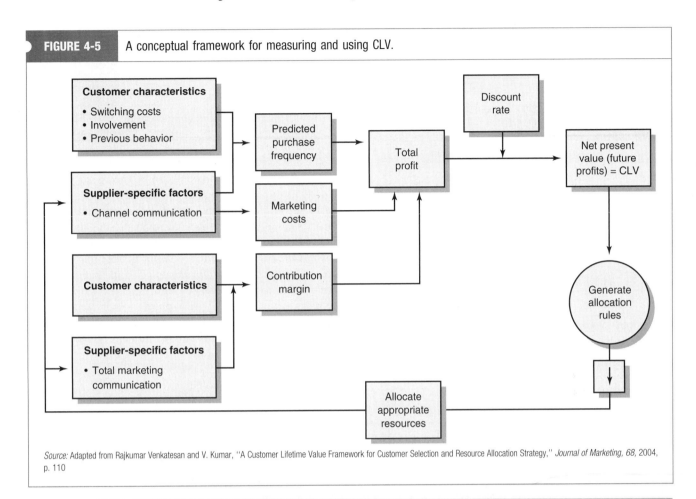

FIGURE 4-5   A conceptual framework for measuring and using CLV.

Source: Adapted from Rajkumar Venkatesan and V. Kumar, "A Customer Lifetime Value Framework for Customer Selection and Resource Allocation Strategy," *Journal of Marketing, 68,* 2004, p. 110

Case in Point 4-1    Safeway—A CLV Example

The actual calculation of CLV is less straightforward than the basic model may suggest. There are a number of questions even after the availability of the necessary customer-level data has been confirmed. What is the typical life span of a customer in this particular situation? How much time is required to achieve a reasonable level of accuracy in predicting purchase frequency and contribution margin across multiple purchases in multiple time periods? Even identifying the relevant revenues and costs is not as easy as it sounds.[4] This example will help explain the concept and its application.

Consultant Arthur Hughes gives an example that is based on the experience of the Safeway supermarket chain.[5] Supermarkets have notoriously thin gross margins, and Safeway was concerned that they spend their scarce promotional resources in the most effective way. They turned to a CLV analysis for guidance. Table 4-1 presents the first stage of that analysis.

Assume that the firm acquires 5,000 new customers in Year 1 and that the goal is to track their value over 3 years, generally considered a minimum for calculating customer value. These customers make 0.64 visits per week, purchasing an average of $33 each trip. Direct costs are

83% of total sales, and labor and benefits for marketing personnel are another 11%. Safeway spends $16 on a shopper loyalty card program for each customer in the first year and $8 in succeeding years. Advertising is 2% of total sales. The following calculations are then done:

Total sales	$5,280,000
Less: Total costs	$5,148,800
Equals: Gross profit	$131,200
Times: Discount rate	1.0
Net present value of first-year revenue	$131,200
Lifetime value of a customer in Year 1	$26.24

The item that needs particular attention—both in terms of computation and of meaning—is the **discount rate**. A discount rate is necessary because a future stream of revenue is worth less than revenue received in the current year. Consequently, in Year 1 the discount rate is 1.0. For subsequent years, the rate is calculated using the formula

$$D + (1 + i)^n$$

Case in Point 4-1   *Continued*

TABLE 4-1	Baseline Consumer Lifetime Value Calculation

Lifetime Value Before New Programs			
	Year 1	Year 2	Year 3
Customers	5,000	3,500	2,590
Retention rate	70.0%	74.0%	80.0%
Visits/week	0.64	0.69	0.78
Average basket	$33	$45	$55
Total Sales	**$5,280,000**	**$5,433,750**	**$5,555,550**
Cost percent	83.0%	80.0%	79.0%
Direct costs	$4,382,400	$4,347,000	$4,388,885
Labor + benefits 11%	$580,800	$597,713	$611,111
Card program $16, $8	$80,000	$28,000	$20,720
Advertising 2%	$105,600	$108,675	$111,111
Total Costs	**$5,148,800**	**$5,081,388**	**$5,131,826**
Gross profit	$131,200	$352,363	$423,724
Discount rate	1.00	1.20	1.44
NPV profit	$131,200	$293,635	$294,253
Cumulative NPV profit	$131,200	$424,835	$719,088
Lifetime value	$26.24	$84.97	$143.82

Source: http://www.dbmarketing.com.

where *D* is the discount rate, *i* is the current interest rate plus a risk factor, and *n* is the number of years that will elapse before the revenue is realized. When the gross profit for any given year is multiplied by the discount rate for that year, the result is the **net present value** (NPV) of the gross profit for that specific year.

Looking back at the baseline table, we see that the retention rate of these customers is 70% in the first year. That means that of the 5,000 customers acquired in Year 1, 3,500 will persist as customers into Year 2. As presumably satisfied customers they will visit the store somewhat more frequently, buy a bit more, and cost a bit less to serve. Following through to the end of Year 2, the value of an original customer in Year 2 is $84.97 (the

cumulative net present value of the profit stream, $424,835, divided by 5,000). Using the same reasoning, the customer value is $143.82 when a customer acquired in Year 1 persists to Year 3.

The first step in working with CLV is usually to identify additional marketing efforts that can be used to increase customer value. Activities that come under this heading include up-selling and cross-selling. *Up-selling* means activities designed to persuade customers to buy more, either in volume or in higher-priced items or both. *Cross-selling* refers to programs that attempt to sell other products to the customer; for example, a bank that markets certificates of deposit (CDs) to high-value checking account customers. This type of program is, in fact, particularly attractive in industries such as financial services where customers frequently have a number of financial products scattered among the offerings of many financial services providers. The attractiveness of persuading customers to consolidate their holdings with a single provider is obvious. That phenomenon has come to be known as "share of wallet" in the financial services industry or, more generally, "share of customer." Many marketers would argue that this is a better metric of marketing success than the more commonly used "share of market." Other types of retailers, like supermarkets, are also testing programs to increase customer value.

Returning to Arthur Hughes' example, he points out that Safeway had determined that it could spend a maximum of $2 per customer per month on customer relationship management. That is not a great deal of money, and it is imperative that it be used wisely. Safeway, for example, tried giving targeted customers an ice cream cone on their birthdays and measured incremental sales that resulted from that trip to the store. Retailers have also experimented with programs like the following:

- Customer-specific pricing, where members get cheaper prices on certain items
- Rewards for larger total purchases
- Rewards for frequency of purchase
- Rewards for shopping on slow days
- Personal recognition and relationship programs

What if the company took the major step of cutting its advertising budget in order to divert money to the customer relationship program? In Table 4-2 Hughes presents some possible results.

Assume that the company has cut advertising to 1% from the 2% in Table 4-1. That money is shown in the

Continued

Case in Point 4-1 *Continued*

TABLE 4-2	Increase in Customer Value Using Targeted Programs

Lifetime Value Using Customer Management Program

	Year 1	Year 2	Year 3
Customers	5,000	3,750	2,963
Retention rate	75.0%	79.0%	85.0%
Visits/week	0.68	0.73	0.82
Average basket	$38	$50	$61
Total Sales	**$6,120,000**	**$6,843,750**	**$7,409,213**
Cost percent	83.0%	80.0%	79.0%
Direct costs	$5,079,600	$5,475,000	$5,853,278
Labor + benefits 11%	$673,200	$752,813	$815,013
Card program $16, $8	$80,000	$30,000	$23,700
Customer-specific marketing	$61,200	$66,438	$74,092
Advertising 1%	$61,200	$68,438	$74,092
Total Costs	**$5,955,200**	**$6, 394,688**	**$6,840,176**
Gross profits	$164,800	$449,063	$569,037
Discount rate	1.00	1.20	1.44
NPV profit	$164,800	$374,219	$395,165
Cumulative NPV profit	$164,800	$539,019	$934,183
Lifetime value	$32.96	$107.80	$186.84

Source: http://www.dbmarketing.com.

"Customer-Specific Marketing" line in Table 4-2. All the rest of the cost and CLV calculations are the same. Notice, however, that the top portion of the table changes. In Year 1 the retention rate goes from 70% to 75%. Visits per week increase from 0.64 to 0.68. The average basket (sale) increases from $33 to $38. As a result of the increase in number of visits per week and average sale, the customer lifetime value for Year 1 goes from $26.24 to $32.96. Because the retention rate has gone up, the company starts Year 2 with 3,750 customers instead of 3,500. This increases the revenue stream. Visits per week and average sale go up as compared with Year 2 without the targeted programs. The same reasoning follows for Year 3. At the end of Year 3 the NPV of the net revenue stream is $934,183. Divided by 5,000—the original cohort of customers who have now been tracked through 3 years—the CLV is $186.84.

Table 4-3 shows the increase in CLV that results from the targeted programs. Because the cost of the targeted programs came out of the amount previously budgeted for advertising, there is no increase in marketing cost. The gain is therefore incremental profit.

TABLE 4-3	Gain in Customer Value From Using Targeted Programs

Effect of Adoption of New Programs

New life time value (LTV)	$32.96	$107.80	$186.84
Previous LTV	$26.24	$84.97	$143.82
Gain	$6.72	$22.83	$43.02

Source: http://www.dbmarketing.com.

4-5a Uses of CLV

The Safeway case study is a very simple example compared to the reality of customers being acquired and leaving at various times, a multiplicity of marketing programs occurring at the same time or in sequence, and the activities of competitors, which may have important effects on variables such as retention rates. It also assumes that all customers are equally desirable prospects for targeted programs. That is usually not true. Banks, for example, sometimes find that their highest-value customers are not desirable targets for additional marketing effort because they are already giving the bank as much of their business as they are likely to give. At the other end of the scale, many enterprises find that their lowest-value customers are unlikely to upgrade

discount rate The interest rate at which a person or a business borrows money. In the calculation of CLV a substantial risk premium is usually added to the market interest rate.

net present value The current value of a future revenue stream.

enough to make the marketing expenditures worthwhile. An overriding issue becomes, "How much should I spend to acquire customers who fit a certain profile?"

The acquisition problem is commonly stated as, "Who are my best customers, and how can I acquire more like them?" To that we should add, "And how much should I spend on the acquisition?" Identifying best customers is another time-honored direct marketing technique based on a simple **RFM** (Recency × Frequency × Monetary value) model. This model does a remarkably good job of segmenting a customer database according to value in many industry sectors.[6] The issue of acquiring more customers like the best customers can be as simple, in the traditional direct marketing environment, as renting lists with similar characteristics and mailing to them. As we build databases of customer activities on the Internet, the same principles will apply. To speed the process of acquiring many years of customer data, marketers have increasingly turned to predictive modeling to profile the best potential customers and to estimate a suitable acquisition cost target. We will give a brief introduction to predictive modeling in the last part of this chapter.

Many CLV-based marketing approaches are directly transferable onto the Web, where their value is often magnified. What if, based on available data and models, the marketer could know within seconds what the prospective value of a site visitor is and consequently could generate an offer that is both optimally cost-effective and attractive to the prospect—all done on the fly, so quickly that the viewer is unaware of the background mechanics?

One application is site content personalization. Based on either **opt-in** databases or **anonymous profiles**, it is possible for marketers to recognize visitor characteristics when the person enters the site and display content accordingly. This may mean selecting banner ads or ad content based on what is known, or it can also lead to individualized display of site content. At least one vendor says that its software "not only customizes the Web content to match the individual's profile throughout the online engagement but also supports sales tactics such as cross-sell and up-sell.[7]"

Another application can be to create customized offers. It is said that at least one online financial services site is able to combine information from a customer credit card application with data and models in its supporting database and present that customer with a personalized credit card offer within less than a minute. Not only does this place a compelling offer in front of the applicant, it also helps the credit card issuer manage risk. The opportunities to customize offers based on past purchase history or segment profiles would seem to be almost limitless.

At the other extreme, CLV analysis will show some customers to be unprofitable. That presents two basic options. If additional analysis indicates that one or more subsegments have potential to become profitable, marketing programs should be developed with this objective. If, as is often the case, other subsegments appear to have little probability of becoming profitable, one of two actions must be taken. The first is to cut costs—either of acquiring customers in this segment or by reducing costs to serve them. For example, these customers may be offered only self-service options via telephone or Web, with personal service options reserved for profitable customer segments.

Some of these applications raise the specter of overstepping the bounds of customer privacy, a subject that is covered in detail in Chapter 12. As long as we can manage issues of customer privacy, however, strategies based on knowledge and enhancement of CLV provide exciting prospects for Internet marketers.

The almost limitless possibilities opened by this type of information-based customization call into play another important direct marketing technique, that of testing.

4-6 Testing Direct-Response Programs

Testing in a timely and statistically valid manner is another advantage that direct marketing has traditionally held over mass media marketing. Direct marketers are able to track each response; they therefore know whether programs are performing

RFM Recency × Frequency × Monetary value; a direct marketing model for assessing the worth of a customer.

opt-in Communication that has been actively requested by the Internet user; it becomes "double opt-in" when the marketer sends an e-mail that requires the user to confirm the request before it is activated.

anonymous profile A customer profile created without knowing the name or e-mail address of a Web site visitor from data captured during Web site visits.

satisfactorily. In addition, some direct-response media—mail, for example—have lent themselves well to controlled testing of different offers or different creative executions. On a broader scale, offer placement in different media can also be tested. Again, this set of direct marketing tools is directly transferable to the Internet space, which offers even greater potential for evaluating and refining marketing efforts on a timely basis. Rick Fernandes of webloyalty.com describes an offline campaign as slow and vague, taking several months to establish a baseline and even longer to adjust the marketing materials, without any guarantee of a prospect reading or responding to the offer:

> In an offline campaign, a fortunate marketer can create and launch a new campaign in eight to 10 weeks. Orders begin to trickle in and maybe 80 percent of orders are in 90 days later. So a baseline is established five to six months after the idea is crystallized.
>
> To improve the baseline performance, you can try to improve the quality of the list to determine if the offer was effective. Perhaps you could improve the order process. You can systematically test variables to determine critical paths, but it's hard, costly and time consuming. You basically drop the mail and hope for the best.
>
> Now consider an e-mail marketing campaign. There's not that much left to chance. Did your message get delivered? How many opened it? Which version of your e-mail was most effective? Did those graphics in the e-mail help or hurt? Once they got to your site, did they go past the home page? Where else did they go? How long were they there?
>
> You receive answers immediately, and if the test is not meeting expectations, you can drop it or do major surgery on it before you do yourself any real economic damage.[8]

The simplest kind of direct marketing test is an **A/B split**. The target group is divided into two groups, often simply putting the first entry into group A, the second entry into group B, the third entry into group A, and so forth. This is satisfactory as long as you have a list that is stored in a systematic manner, say a group of physical addresses stored according to zip code. Group A is then exposed to one version of the variable and Group B, to another. For example, you might be testing different subject lines for an e-mail promotion, because subject lines have a substantial impact on whether the e-mail is opened. Group A gets one version of the subject line; Group B gets the other. Nothing else about the e-mail content or delivery is changed. The difference in the opening rate between the two e-mails can be attributed to the different subject lines. Another variant of the A/B split is to make Group A the control. In the case of the e-mail subject line, the control would be the subject line that had produced the highest open rate in the past. Group B would receive a new subject line to see whether the old or the new subject line produced the best open rate.

Direct marketing testing, whether it uses a simple A/B split or a **complex experimental design**, is both a marketing and a statistical process. In the case of the e-mail subject line, the issue is not whether the open rate is higher for one subject line or the other; the issue is whether the open rate is (statistically) *significantly* higher than the other. Table 4-4 summarizes the marketing approach. Paralleling the marketing activities is a set of statistical activities—establishing hypotheses, choosing the significance level, computing the sample size, and specifying the decision rule—that the student recognizes as the classic hypothesis testing process from statistics and marketing research courses. Both the marketing and the statistical activities are necessary in order to have a valid test on which to base decisions.

Some marketers test some variable on every marketing program they run. They do so because they want to keep learning about what works for their target audience. Others do so only when they have an important marketing question to answer. An example taken from food products manufacturer Hormel illustrates most of the steps in the marketing testing process.

A/B split Presenting one offer, creative execution, and so forth, to one group of customers or prospects and another version of the same offer, creative execution, and so on, to another group of customers.

complex experimental design Test designs that permit testing of more than one variable at a time without sacrificing statistical validity.

TABLE 4-4	The Testing Process

Reasons for Conducting a Test
- Standard practice ("We test all marketing programs.")
- Strategy questions ("Which subset of lapsed customers can be reactivated?")
- Tactical questions ("Which incentive works best with this offer?")

Design the Test
- What marketing variables to test (new offer, different creative execution, new list, etc.)
- Type of test (against control, A/B split, complex experimental design)
- Sample (entire population or random sample; sample size)

Establish Test Metrics
- Test criterion (variable on which test is judged)
- Decision rule (the values of the variable on which the decision will be based)
- Cutoff date
- Ranges for success/failure/continued testing
- Timing and nature of reporting (online, on demand, formal report)

Execute and Monitor the Test
- Ensure that test is conducted according to specifications
- Record results
- Monitor competitive/environmental activity that might affect results
- Record any deviations from testing plan

Analyze and Report Test Results
- Which version performed best?
- Was the difference
  - Statistically significant?
  - At an acceptable level of risk?

Make Marketing Decisions
- What changes, if any, should we make to our marketing efforts?
- Should we repeat the test? test new variables?

4-6a A Testing Example

Hormel uses coupons delivered through newspaper inserts as a key part of its marketing strategy for its meat product Spam. They saw newspaper readership figures declining and couponing on the Web increasing, so they realized they needed to explore the Web for couponing purposes. They did not want to distribute their own coupons, fearing that an e-mail campaign for Spam would be picked up by jokesters, to the detriment of their product's image. Consequently, they chose a couponing firm that maintained its own Web site and had an opt-in list of homemakers who wished to receive coupon offers by e-mail. They also designed the test to promote several Hormel products, not Spam alone. The first campaign featured eight products; the second featured seven.

To avoid introducing sampling as a variable, both campaigns were sent to the same group of registered coupon-site users that was supplied by the marketing services firm. Each campaign was made up of the following:

1. An e-mail featuring the Hormel products
2. An ad featuring the Hormel products in the firm's regular member e-mail newsletter
3. Ads that were placed on various pages in the firm's site

Each e-mail or ad had a separate landing page on which customers could request coupons. This permitted precise tracking of the response rate to each piece of promotion. In addition, they sent a twenty-five-question e-mail survey to members of the list who definitely had seen the campaigns and to a control group of members who did not receive either campaign.

A Hormel executive was quoted as saying that the redemption rate for the e-mail coupons "far exceeded" that of coupons delivered in other media, primarily newspapers. In addition, the careful tracking found no evidence of fraud and the e-mails did not become the butt of Internet jokes. They survey found that:

- almost 30% of participants were not familiar with the Hormel family of products before they received the e-mail offers.

- 27% did not get the Sunday newspaper or did not use it for coupons.

- 37% indicated they would prefer accessing grocery coupons on the Internet instead of in newspapers.

- the multicoupon offer worked. Nearly 50% of the consumers who took action printed three or more coupons; 30% printed four or more; 20% printed five or more.

- 53% of consumers who reported redeeming a coupon said they also purchased at least one more Hormel products without a coupon.[9]

Each company will have its own concerns and its own marketing variables to test. The Hormel example, however, is a good illustration of the useful information that a test can produce. The marketing research was a particularly useful supplement in this instance. However, it is important to remember that testing and marketing research are two different things. Testing involved creating a marketing program, delivering it to people who meet the profile of the target market, and tracking the actions consumers take as a result. Put another way, testing furnishes behavioral data—what customers did or did not do. This is different from using marketing research to ask people what they would do in a particular situation. Both have their uses, as the Hormel example illustrates. However, testing on the Internet provides an unparalleled opportunity to measure actual marketing-related behavior in a realistic context. Whatever the type of test, it should be carried out according to the principles of experimentation summarized in Table 4-5.

> **TABLE 4-5**   Basics of Experimentation in Marketing

Experimentation, as practiced in marketing environments, is based on scientific method as taught in social sciences like psychology and, less directly, in the natural sciences either in the laboratory or in the field.

Three basic ideas are necessary to an understanding of experimentation:

- *Experimental treatment.* The experimental treatment is the stimulus applied to subjects in the experiment. In a laboratory situation, a new version of a Web page could be tested. In a field setting, it might be a revised format for an e-mail newsletter.

- *Control group.* To measure the effect of the experimental treatment, there must be a group of experimental subjects who do not receive it. This is the control group. The control group, for example, would be exposed to the existing Web page or the current e-mail newsletter. They would have no knowledge of the proposed revision.

- *Experimental group.* There is also a group of subjects who are exposed to the experimental treatment. This is the experimental group.

Putting it very simply, and avoiding all the statistics involved, the results of the experiment are determined by comparing the control group, who received the existing stimulus, to the results for the experimental group that received the experimental treatment.

Results are measured on variables specified by the researcher. The Web page could be measured on variables such as ease of use and attractive appearance. The e-mail newsletter could be measured on response as represented by variables ranging from click-through to the shopping page to actual purchases.

4-7 The Database Imperative

database A set of files (data, video, images, etc.) organized in a way that permits a computer program to quickly select any desired piece of content.

The distinctive tools and techniques of direct marketing all have a great deal to offer in the interactive marketing setting created by the Internet. The foundations of virtually all the capabilities that differentiate direct-response marketing from mass media marketing reside in company- or product-specific marketing **databases**. These are the repositories of all customer-related knowledge and the source of data for analytical activities. Databases are the knowledge resources that to some extent can compensate for the churn of human resources in many contemporary firms.

Correctly conceptualized, this tool is not "the marketing database." When marketers refer to "the marketing database," they are generally referring to the customer database. However, there are actually numerous databases that should all be linked through some type of a central repository, such as a data warehouse, so that information can be provided on demand to decision makers and operational personnel. Figure 4-6 provides a hypothetical mapping of a typical database system, indicating the nature of the data in each and its primary source.

From the marketer's viewpoint, the data warehouse can be conceptualized as having four basic components. The marketing management databases drive marketing programs, and the marketing support databases provide additional data that are important for decision-making purposes. Other areas of the business contribute databases that are crucial to the functioning of marketing programs and customer service, including the order-processing database and the inventory database, both of which are essential to good customer service. The sales force management and project databases also provide important marketing-related information. Finally, externally purchased or linked databases provide additional valuable data, such as commercial scanner databases that track product movement. There are numerous database products that marketers can overlay onto the customer database to increase its predictive power. The Prizm **geodemographic** systems from Claritas are a good example of this type of external data product: these products offer data on household segmentation using demographic, lifestyle, and geographic data. A variety of other databases are available from third parties; these are important information resources to specific industry sectors. For example, the data of the large credit bureaus are used in proprietary credit scoring models by banks and other credit issuers.

geodemographic The analysis of demographic data by zip/ postal code to find market segments.

Some marketers may require fewer databases for effective decision making and operations, but a large company may have dozens of databases that need to be integrated to give a full view of the customer. Unfortunately, the technological reality of such multitudinous databases is that the individual databases involved are often not neatly interconnected through a data warehouse. Instead, they sit on various desktops, connected to one individual or unit, and act as isolated islands of information. When this is the situation, marketers are unable to make effective use of the information resource for marketing or customer service.

The difficulty of integrating many databases that have a variety of data structures and that reside on a variety of different platforms can hardly be understated. However, integrating the databases into a data warehouse is a technical task, and the job of the marketer is to determine what data need to be in the central repository and to champion its creation. This requires the marketer to ask, "What can accessible database information accomplish for the business?" In answering that question, let's focus for the moment on the combined customer/prospect database.

4-7a What Benefits Does a Customer Database Confer?

Keeping in mind that the customer database is the repository of all institutional knowledge about the customer, there are a number of marketing activities that can be done only with the assistance of a database and others that can be done more effectively. We will first look at database utilization from a traditional direct

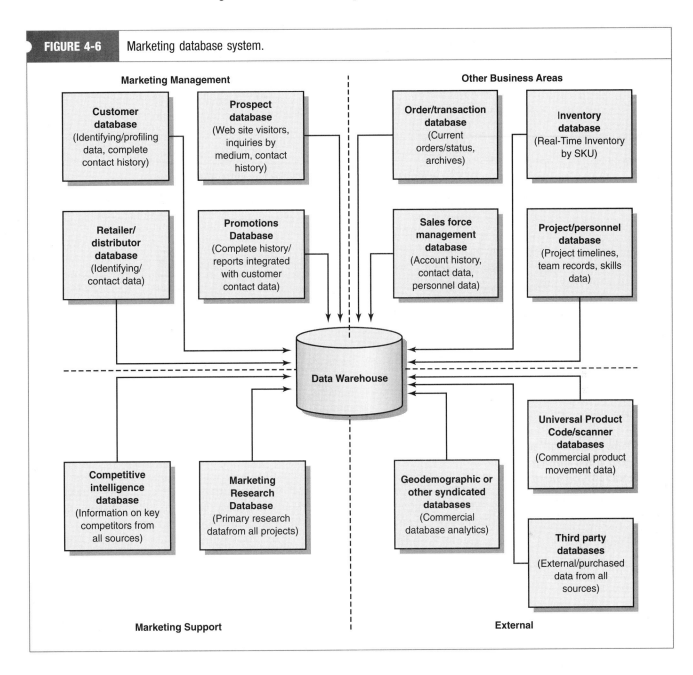

FIGURE 4-6   Marketing database system.

marketing perspective and then take a brief look at the newer technique called *data mining*.

Database use can be approached in two different ways. One involves analytics—any statistical technique that compresses the vast amount of data into summary statistics that are useful either for managerial decision making or for program execution. The second approach can be a stand-alone approach or a follow-on to analytics. It involves using individual data items or summary statistics to execute marketing programs. Figure 4-7 presents an overview of both types of use in a hierarchical format. The Programmatic Uses portion is not absolute; it is rather a suggestion of the types of uses at each analytical level that are generally more appropriate.

Although it is possible to develop marketing programs around a single data item—an offer to all women in the database, for example—it would be unusual for this to be

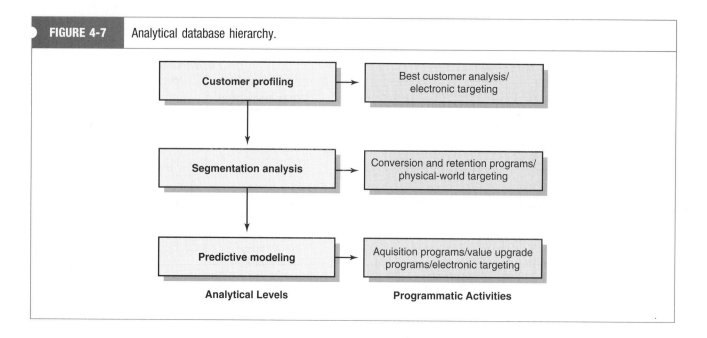

FIGURE 4-7 Analytical database hierarchy.

profile A summary of the distinctive features or characteristics of a person, business, or other entity.

an optimal use of the database. It is more likely that a **profile**, using either RFM or a special-purpose data model, will produce more precise marketing action. This action is most likely to take the form of targeting individuals who have been identified as potential best customers for a particular marketing program. It is described as "electronic targeting" because the capabilities of the Web allow customers to be identified and targeted with individualized content one at a time.

At the second level of complexity in analytical terms is statistical analysis, which has an important use for segmentation purposes in a database environment. When the application requires selection of a group of potential best customers out of the larger database, this will be the approach taken. Because this leads to segmentation marketing, it is an approach that is generally more appropriate for the physical world in which targeting customers individually is usually cost prohibitive. In addition, because the focus is on existing customers who reside in the database, it is particularly suitable for conversion and retention programs. The most often used analysis at this level is some form of **regression**, ranging from simple linear regression to more complex nonlinear models. **Cluster analysis** is also used for segmentation purposes. It is worth noting that these commonly used statistical techniques are often described as models, and they produce results that aid in understanding the relationships between variables that affect customer behavior and hence are a necessary precursor to formal model building.

regression Statistical technique that predicts the level of magnitude of a dependent variable based on the levels of more than one independent variable; also called *multiple regression*.

cluster analysis Classifying objects or people into mutually exclusive and exhaustive groups on the basis of two or more classification variables.

predictive modeling Using relevant variables and associated response factors or probabilities to estimate the likelihood of occurrence of a specific behavior, given the existence of a given level of the specified variables.

The line between segmentation analysis and **predictive modeling** often seems blurry in actual practice, but the conceptual distinction is clear. Segmentation analysis uses statistical models to group customers on the basis of characteristics (demographic and lifestyle) and product-related behaviors. Predictive modeling uses these data to build models that predict future customer or prospect behavior. The most commonly used type of predictive modeling is response modeling in which the statistician constructs a model that predicts the likelihood of response to a given program on a customer-by-customer basis.

At the most complex level of analysis, then, is predictive modeling, in which marketing scientists attempt to predict future customer behavior. Since the result is often a discrete variable like "probability of response," the members of the database can be rank-ordered from highest to lowest probability to develop the most cost-effective programs. Often this would be some type of upgrade program. An example would be a program to encourage subscribers to a free e-mail newsletter to take out a paid subscription to a companion magazine. Using purchased databases, it is also possible to identify prospects who have the same characteristics and purchase-related behaviors as the best-performing customers and develop a cost-effective acquisition program.

The programmatic applications on the right side of Figure 4-7 are not rigid rules. Various analytical techniques can be used to support each one of the programmatic activities. Choice of technique often depends on either the type or the quality of data available, precision of results required, or both. To a great extent choices also depend on our ability to deliver individual strategies at the customer level.

4-7b Using the Customer Database

Customer transactions data is a by-product of Internet marketing, as we discuss in detail in Chapters 5 and 11. The challenge is to capture it and use it effectively for marketing decision making. Even before the Internet, some companies that were not traditional direct marketers began to build and use customer databases in ways that improved their marketing programs. One interesting example is Harrah's, the gambling and entertainment mecca.

In the mid-1990s, Harrah's made a far-reaching strategic decision. While its casino competitors were pouring money into lavish physical facilities in Las Vegas, Atlantic City, and other prime gambling venues, Harrah's decided to place its bets on a customer loyalty program backed by superior customer service and satisfaction at all its properties. In 1997, they rolled out their Total Rewards program, based on airline frequent-flyer programs. Their player card tracked all the activities—gambling, entertainment, dining, hotel stays—of a customer who was visiting a Harrah's property. They used the data gathered to build a comprehensive database of individual patronage of all twelve Harrah's properties. Building the database across properties and their differing information technology (IT) platforms was not easy; persuading property managers to cooperate and to make use of the data for cross-property promotions was even more difficult.

All casinos assumed that players were loyal to specific properties, and, on this assumption, each of the twelve Harrah's locations had run their marketing programs independently. That included having their own individual player's cards and separate databases. Headquarters had to convince the property managers of the merits of a centralized database and marketing programs to encourage cross-property visits.

The outcome was quickly evident. In 2 years, their cross-market revenues increased by 72% and almost 10% of their profits could be traced to cross-market visits.[10] This was an impressive short-term result, but more was to come as Harrah's began to mine the database of information they were capturing about their customers.

4-8 The Power of Data Mining

The opportunities presented by the customer database are great, but you may have seen a recurring theme running through the preceding sections. The traditional approach to database marketing requires that data be captured, housed in a database, analyzed, and modeled. For databases of moderate size, this approach, using simple tools like **Excel macros** or multiple regression, works well. However, data warehouses like Harrah's, which contained about 300 **gigabytes** of customer transactions and preferences data by 2003,[11] quickly become unwieldy, and more powerful tools are needed. These tools go under the broad heading of **data mining**.

Simply put, data mining is used to produce customer information not previously known, or perhaps even previously hypothesized, from large databases. How does it

excel macros Functions or formulas that have been created and saved inside an Excel worksheet so that they can be called and executed as needed.

gigabyte One billion bytes of data; a byte is a binary unit that holds one character of data.

data mining The analytic process and specialized analytic tools used to extract meaning from very large data sets.

do this? The simple answer is that data mining produces new knowledge because it looks for patterns in data that might not be revealed by traditional statistical analysis. Techniques like decision trees and neural networks may be used, as well as techniques commonly used in marketing research, such as regression and cluster analysis.

One of the important aspects of data mining is that marketing managers do not have to deal directly with the complex analytics. They also do not have to request programming assistance from the IT department to obtain information from the data warehouse through the data mining routines. The software includes easy-to-use interfaces that permit managers to ask questions, often in natural language, such as "What were sales yesterday in the northeastern region?" The manager can specify how the information is to be provided—a numerical report and a graphic are common options.

In the case of Harrah's, management made a conscious decision to let customer data suggest marketing strategies, instead of developing strategies and then looking for data to execute them. They already knew from their marketing research that customers who carried their loyalty card only spent about 36% of their annual gaming budget at Harrah's.[12] Extensive mining of their enterprise data warehouse revealed more useful information:

- Of all their patrons, 26% generated 82% of the revenue.
- These patrons were not the "high rollers" portrayed in books and movies. They were more likely to be middle class or professional, to be middle-aged or retired, to have discretionary time, and to prefer playing slot machines.
- They responded better to an offer of free chips than to the more traditional casino offers of free rooms, meals, and entertainment.
- Customers who were satisfied with the Harrah's experience increased their spending by 24% per year. Those who were dissatisfied decreased it by 10%.

Using the results of its data mining, Harrah's was able to construct and test a predictive model of "customer worth," a theoretical forecast of how much a customer could be expected to spend over the long term. This is CLV by a different name. They used the estimate of customer worth to create three tiers of rewards. The highest-level Diamond cardholders, for example, were assigned personal hosts and rarely if ever had to stand in line for anything, from checking into the hotel to visiting a restaurant for a meal. Platinum customers stood in visibly shorter lines. Gold cardholders (the lowest level) or customers without a player's card stood in lines and watched the Diamond and Platinum customers sail on by. Harrah's dubbed this "aspirational marketing," and it worked to give customers an incentive to spend more in order to move up to a higher service level.[13]

Many businesses might be envious of this ability to segment customers on the basis of their potential profitability and to develop targeted strategies that maximize that profitability. Note, however, that it has taken Harrah's almost a decade to get to this point. That is a strong statement about why the capture and wise use of customer information can lead to sustainable competitive advantage.

A final example illustrates data mining used in a different context. Would you believe that the NBA has a sophisticated application based on data mining? The Orlando Magic was one of the first teams to begin using statistical software to look for patterns in the huge amount of data collected for each game. However, an average game had about 200 possessions, and there are about 1,200 NBA games each year. The sheer volume of data was so overwhelming that initial efforts provided only the basic kind of stats that could be found in any newspaper.

Enter an IBM strategic partner by the name of Virtual Gold and a data mining application called Advanced Scout, specifically tailored for the use of NBA coaches and scouts. After two devastating losses to the Miami Heat in the 1997 finals, the coaches of the Magic turned to Advanced Scout. According to Virtual Gold press material:

> Advanced Scout showed the Orlando Magic coaches something that none of them had previously recognized. When Brian Shaw and Darrell Armstrong were in the game,

something was sparked within their teammate Penny Hardaway—the Magic's leading scorer at that time. Armstrong received more play-time and hence, Hardaway was far more effective. The Magic went on to win the next two games and nearly caused the upset of the year. Fans everywhere rallied around the team and naysayers quickly replaced their doubts with season ticket purchases for the following year.[14]

The software application is used in tandem with video recording of games to help coaches uncover patterns they otherwise might miss. A technology note from UCLA's Anderson School of Management explains a bit more about how it works:

> An analysis of the play-by-play sheet of the game played between the New York Knicks and the Cleveland Cavaliers on January 6, 1995 reveals that when Mark Price played the Guard position, John Williams attempted four jump shots and made each one! Advanced Scout not only finds this pattern, but explains that it is interesting because it differs considerably from the average shooting percentage of 49.30% for the Cavaliers during that game.
>
> By using the NBA universal clock, a coach can automatically bring up the video clips showing each of the jump shots attempted by Williams with Price on the floor, without needing to comb through hours of video footage. Those clips show a very successful pick-and-roll play in which Price draws the Knick's defense and then finds Williams for an open jump shot.[15]

Again, this is a data mining application that has been a decade in the making. The future will undoubtedly bring many other uniquely useful applications of data mining to help firms uncover the meaning in their huge data warehouses of customer information, but no one should expect that this is a quick and easy solution to the issue of huge warehouses of customer data that hide strategic nuggets of great value.

4-9 The Hierarchy of Interactive Strategies

Marketing on the Internet offers many possibilities for data analysis and strategy development that marketers have only been able to wish for in the past. At the same time, it presents many demands, both technological and strategic. Successful Internet strategies appear to be moving up a hierarchy in which each stage allows more persuasive communication with the prospective customer and more compelling ways in which to create value for that customer. Each stage also places increasingly rigorous requirements on marketing strategies and operations, as well as on the associated technology. The hierarchy is shown in Figure 4-8.

The underlying rationale is that as marketers learn more about their customers they can develop more focused strategies and more targeted promotional efforts. Take as an example the new Web site of a hypothetical business that had not previously developed a customer database for marketing purposes. The firm undoubtedly has some *informational* marketing material that it can make available to customers as it begins to experiment with a corporate site. A B2C firm might adapt advertising material, especially from print media, as site content. A B2B firm is likely to have sales support material that will provide initial content—hence the derogatory term *brochure ware*. A rather static, informational site may be a viable beginning, but the business needs to have a plan to move beyond that to tap the power of the Internet.

A reasonable next step is to add some *interactivity* to the site, both to engage the visitor's attention and to provide reasons for the visitor to return. Even frequently purchased consumer products that require traditional distribution channels supported by mass media can develop sites that are worthy of consumer attention. The Procter & Gamble sites shown in Figure 4-2a are good examples. B2B companies provide valuable information like detailed product specifications and real-time order tracking to increase their level of on-demand customer service. E-government sites allow

FIGURE 4-8   Hierarchy of customer-focused marketing strategies.

citizens to handle many of the details of everyday interaction with government agencies, like renewing driver's licenses.

At some point in the informational or interactive stages, the business needs to begin to collect the names and e-mail addresses of visitors as it looks ahead to personalized communication. You can be sure that the landing page of Pepperdine University that captures information from visitors interested in their part-time MBA program (Figure 4-4a) will be used for follow-up promotion to those people. On the basis of the data captured on that form, follow-ups may be personalized by name, prospective starting date, or campus location. Every organization needs to think about how it can capture the e-mail addresses of visitors who are genuinely interested in their product and are willing to receive additional communications. This is the beginning of the conversion process, discussed in more detail in Chapter 11. Before an organization begins to collect data, it must think carefully about how the data will be used to add value to the customer experience, as well as to provide data for better marketing decisions. Put another way, it needs to collect useful data that visitors are willing to provide.

Moving to a *transactional* site is a big step. Transactional sites require specialized technology such as shopping carts. They require the integration of back-end data—inventory databases for in-stock status, for example. The site must be sure that effective security software and procedures are in place before any transactional features are activated. These and other possible requirements are demanding in terms of both technical complexity and smoothly functioning internal business processes. This is a good point for the business to stop and recognize that any process that is not smooth, error free, and customer friendly in the physical world should be reengineered *before* it is moved to the Internet, where its flaws are likely to be magnified many times over.

Once solid transactional functionality is in place, the site may turn to *personalization* as a reasonable next step in its attempts to attract and, especially, to retain customers. Specific personalization techniques are discussed in Chapter 8 in the context of customer relationship management. The options range from simple greeting of a return visitor by name to the construction of individualized pages with content and functionality specified by the customer. Personalization is one technique long used by traditional direct marketers in which the Internet vastly expands the opportunities for meaningful marketing actions.

Another step a site might take is to offer *customization*. At this point, the site would have so much information about individual customers that individualized products or services can be created. For example, using their own data and additional third-party data such as credit history, credit card issuers can craft virtually individualized credit card offers for customers. In some instances, you can also choose the physical card design or select an affinity card from your school or a nonprofit organization. This is a time-honored physical-world strategy that was easily migrated onto the Web.

4-9a A Customization Example

As Figure 4-9a shows, the site can allow the customer to customize his or her own product in a way that takes advantage of the Web's unique capabilities. NIKEiD is a companion to the main Nike site dedicated to the single task of helping customers design and purchase their own versions of popular Nike styles.

The customer can start with an available model and change elements or start with a plain shoe. He or she then chooses the size and the color for each part of the shoe. The customer has the option to put personal identification of eight characters or less, in a color of his or her choice, on the back of the shoe. Having created the running shoe of his or her dreams, the customer can then look at it from all perspectives. If not yet ready to purchase, the customer can save the customized shoe in "My Locker." To set up this personal storage space on the NIKEiD site, the customer must, of course, provide a small amount of personal information.

This is an interesting, perhaps appealing, process. Is it an indication of the type of customized products we will see more of in the next few years? Probably. Does it create real value for customers? You decide.

These stages are reasonable and observable in current Internet space. At the same time, the order is not fixed. Personalization may be interchangeable in order with the transactional stage. Content-rich sites—portals, for example—may choose to

| FIGURE 4-9a | Start with a blank shoe. |

FIGURE 4-9b Choose your colors.

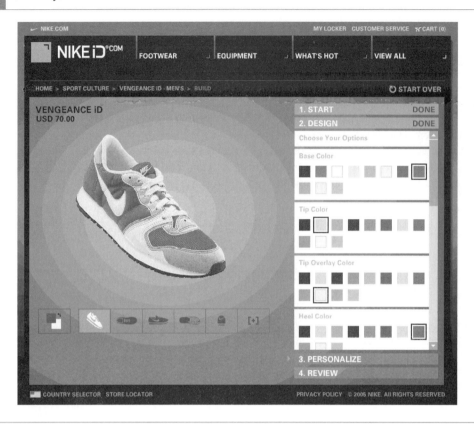

FIGURE 4-9c Examine your finished product.

Source: www.nikeid.nike.com

personalize the visitor experience in order to retain visitors and build the critical mass for transactional activities. On the other hand, e-tail or B2B sites may transact first and then create personalized shopping experiences for consumers or accounts to encourage repeat purchases. A site like NIKEiD may even be a vehicle for new customer acquisition if the offer is sufficiently compelling. Companies need to carefully consider, and rigorously test, the various options that are available for bringing customers to their site and persuading them to transact or to identify themselves as a lead for a future transaction.

Summary

Good Internet marketing has an existing marketing discipline—direct marketing—from which to draw tools and techniques that have been developed and honed in other media. The Web permits faster and more precise execution of many existing direct-response marketing techniques, and it will allow the development of other approaches that would not be cost-effective in physical-world media. The Internet marketer can profit from the knowledge of both front-end and back-end marketing requirements that successful direct marketers have accumulated. This is truly a "do not reinvent the wheel" situation in which marketers who recognize the direct-response foundations of Internet marketing can enjoy a very steep learning curve.

A number of the tools and techniques of direct marketing find direct applicability on the Internet. The offer, which is made up of product, positioning, price, and incentives, is one. A compelling offer is necessary in any marketing environment, and it is especially important on the Web, where the contact is impersonal and the time devoted to any marketer-initiated communication is usually minimal. CLV is becoming increasingly important in both acquisition and retention programs as Internet marketers make use of their ability to capture detailed customer activity and purchase data. Testing is become increasingly important as marketers understand the opportunities offered by the Internet to test alternative marketing approaches in a speedy and reliable manner. All of this is made possible by the existence of "the marketing database," actually a complex system of databases with customer, promotional, and marketing operations data, often contained in a data warehouse.

Some marketing programs will be driven by single pieces of marketing data like "registered on baseball Web site." Still others will be driven by profiles or the results of complex analytics, for example segmentation by CLV, or predictive modeling.

Many, if not most, of these marketing programs will be driven by the goal of increasing CLV as the most direct route to increasing the effectiveness of the marketing effort.

Quiz

1. The four I's of Internet marketing include _____.
   a. involving and interactive
   b. integrated and immediate
   c. information driven and intuitive

2. The basic direct-response strategies are _____.
   a. attraction, conversion, and retention
   b. acquisition, conversion, and retention
   c. attraction, commitment, and loyalty

3. Important characteristics of a direct-response offer include _____.
   a. a call to action
   b. incentive to encourage action
   c. both a and b

4. Objectives of a direct-response marketing program can include _____.
   a. creating awareness of a product or service
   b. generating sales leads
   c. developing brand image

5. Which of the following is a true statement about the front end of marketing?
   a. It describes marketing activities that take place before the product is introduced to the market.
   b. It includes the activities that are most likely to produce satisfied customers.
   c. Front-end activities are the most visible aspects of marketing.

6. Among the uses of CLV data by Harrah's is _____.
   a. to drive programs that increase customer value
   b. to provide a powerful way to segment markets
   c. both a and b

7. Which of the following statements about testing in the Internet environment is true?
   a. Testing provides information that is not ordinarily available to marketers in the mass media environment.

b. Testing requires a substantial amount of marketing research.

c. Both a and b statements are true.

8. _____ is a simple type of test frequently used in various marketing media.
   a. Factorial design
   b. A/B split
   c. Control group

9. Which of the following is a true statement about data mining?
   a. Data mining can uncover previously unsuspected patterns in the data.

b. Marketers require the assistance of statisticians to get information from data mining routines.

c. Data mining routines were developed specifically to deal with the massive amounts of data available from the Internet.

10. Among the interactive strategies marketers can pursue are _____.
    a. transaction, personalization, and collaboration
    b. information, transaction, and personalization
    c. interaction, profiling, and customization

Discussion Questions

1. How does "the offer" differ from "the product" of traditional mass media marketing?

2. Explain the customer lifetime value (CLV) concept. Thinking about a specific firm, how could it use the concept of CLV to increase the overall profitability of its customer base?

3. How is testing different from marketing research?

4. Why and how does testing offer opportunities to Internet marketers?

5. What are some types of analytics that are supported by the customer database?

6. Explain the related concepts of data warehousing and data mining.

7. What do you think the future is for customized products? Think of an example of a product that could reasonably be customized and explain why the target customer would find value in the customization.

Internet Exercises

1. Register at a B2C Web site—one of those you chose to track for the semester if one is appropriate. If not, choose another site for this exercise.

   a. Carefully consider the potential value of the data captured on the registration form. If the option in presented, you may want to configure a personal page, especially if you have not done so before. Then spend a few minutes getting acquainted with the site. What other customer data of value could the site have added to its database as a result of the time you spent there? Would you have been willing to provide that data?

   b. Keep a log of contacts that result from this registration. Bear in mind that contacts may come from the sponsor of the site itself and others may come from marketers with whom the site shares its lists, depending on options you choose in the registration process.

2. Consider the four I's shown in Figure 4-1. Locate a site that makes good use of one, some, or all of the I's. How do these characteristics affect customer experience on the site?

3. Choose a Web site that permits personalization—portals or large content sites are a good choice. Personalize your own page on the site. Think about the kinds of customer data that are produced as you use your personalized page on this site. How can the site use this data to engage in targeted marketing? Also think about the benefits to you, the user, of having a personalized page on the site you have chosen.

4. Visit a Web site that you patronize frequently, one from which you have purchased something, if possible. Identify two marketing elements that could usefully be tested. How would you go about setting up one of these tests?

Notes

1. Concepts in this chapter are based on Mary Lou Roberts and Paul D. Berger, *Direct Marketing Management,* 2nd ed., available for free download at http://www.marylouroberts.info.

2. For an extensive discussion and computational appendix, see Mary Lou Roberts and Paul D. Berger, "Profitability and Lifetime Value," *Direct Marketing Management,* pp. 179–201, http://www.marylouroberts.info.

3. Rajkumar Venkatesan and V. Kumar, "A Customer Lifetime Value Framework for Customer Selection and Resource Allocation Strategy," *Journal of Marketing,* 68, 2004, 110.

4. Details can be found in other articles in journals that deal with issues of data manipulation. A classic article is Robert Dwyer, "Customer Lifetime Valuation to Support Marketing Decision Making," *Journal of Direct Marketing,* 8, No. 2, 1989, 73–81. Recent publications in relevant journals include Paul D. Berger, Bruce Weinberg, and Richard Hanna, "Customer Lifetime Value Determination and Strategic Implications for a Cruise-Ship Company," *Journal of Database Marketing and Customer Strategy Management,* 11, No. 1, 2003, 40–52; Wernar J. Reinartz and V. Kumar, "The Impact of Customer Relationship Characteristics on Profitable Lifetime Duration," *Journal of Marketing,* 67, January 2003, 77–99.

5. This example is based on Arthur Middleton Hughes, "Building Successful Retail Strategies," Database Marketing Institute, February 5, 2002, http://www.dbmarketing.com.

6. For more detail and an example, see Arthur Middleton Hughes, "How to Succeed with RFM Analysis," nd, http://www.dbmarketing.com/articles/Art106.htm.

7. http://www.responselogic.com.

8. Rick Fernandes, "Reap the Web's Testing Capabilities," *iMarketing News,* April 10, 2000, 28 .

9. "Hormel's SPAM Tests Email Marketing," August 24, 2004, http://www.marketingsherpa.com.

10. Jill Griffin, "How Customer Information Gives Harrah's a Winning Hand," *The CEO Refresher,* 2003, http://www.refresher.com/!jlgharrahs.html.

11. Gary Loveman, "Diamonds in the Data Mine," *Harvard Business Review,* May 2003, 2.

12. Gary Loveman, "Diamonds in the Data Mine," *Harvard Business Review,* May 2003, 3.

13. Gary Loveman, "Diamonds in the Data Mine," *Harvard Business Review,* May 2003, 1–5.

14. "IBM in Partnership with Virtual Gold Helps NBA Coaches Score Big with IBM Data Mining Application," nd, http://www.virtualgold.com/customers_sstories.html#success_AdvancedScout.

15. Bill Palace, "Data Mining: What Is Data Mining?" nd, http://www.anderson.ucla.edu/faculty/jason.frand/teacher/technologies/palace/datamining.htm.

Internet Strategies and Programs

Part Two

Understanding the Internet Consumer

Chapter Five

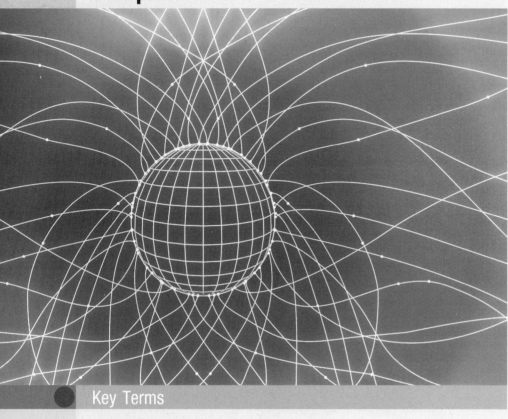

Source: © Getty

Key Terms

choiceboard   (p. 139)
convenience sample   (p. 131)
incidence   (p. 131)
skip patterns   (p. 131)
SKU   (p. 135)

Chapter Outline

Learning Objectives

By the time you complete this chapter, you will be able to:

- Identify the stages of Internet consumer behavior.
- Discuss the types of activities consumers engage in during each stage.
- Describe some of the characteristics of Internet users and purchasers and explain where this data can be found.
- Discuss the differences and similarities between traditional marketing research and online data capture.

- Explain the nature and importance of online data capture.
- Identify key types of consumer data that can be collected online.
  - By third-party suppliers
  - By the enterprise itself
- Understand how research and product development activities are being made better and faster by the use of online research techniques.

5-1 The Internet Consumer Behavior Challenge

As the history of the Internet makes clear, the original ARPANet was populated almost exclusively by scientists, and the early Internet was the province of technicians who were willing to deal with a user-unfriendly communications environment. As discussed in Chapter 1, the launch of Mosaic, the original Web browser, opened the floodgates to the most rapid market penetration by the Internet of any technical innovation in history.

It is the very speed of change that makes understanding the Internet consumer so challenging. In just a decade, the Internet has gone from an unknown to a mass market phenomenon. Growth has been rapid in all developed economies, to the point that Internet access has reached saturation in many countries. Central and South America, Asia, and Africa have pockets of rapid growth. Internet watchers are especially interested in developments in the populous countries of India and China.

The rapidity of overall growth and the shifting nature of high-growth geographic areas, demographic characteristics, and use behaviors have several important implications for marketers:

- The character of the Internet has changed from a geeks-only milieu to a place populated by people of all ages and levels of technical prowess. Although the Internet is still a mostly unregulated medium, it has taken on a more mainstream quality, much to the dismay of some of its original inhabitants. Newer participants are often disturbed by the nature of some of the content and the ease with which it can be accessed. This is especially true of parents, many of whose children have greater technological sophistication than they do. The tension between complete freedom of expression and the need to protect the more vulnerable users is inherent in the Internet.

- The explosion of consumer-created Internet content in recent years has changed the dynamics of Web usage. This has been especially important for certain segments, notably younger Internet users.

- Because of the speed with which the Internet changes, any statistic will be outdated before the ink hits the paper. In this chapter—indeed throughout the book—care has been taken to use the most timely data available and to provide dates that help the reader judge their currency. There is, however, no substitute for continuous use of the Web to access the most current statistics and predictions.

Many of the sources in this chapter provide excellent resources for obtaining the most current available information on many aspects of Web-related behaviors.

The first part of this chapter covers a model of consumer behavior on the Internet and discusses what we currently know about consumer activities in various stages. The second part discusses the ways in which marketers can learn more about their Internet customer base. Let's begin by looking at a model of consumer behavior that takes into account the decision-making process that consumers follow in the Internet environment.

5-2 A Model of Consumer Behavior on the Internet

We are all familiar with the traditional model of the consumer decision process, which can be summarized as follows:

Problem recognition > Information search > Choice process > Purchase > Postpurchase behavior

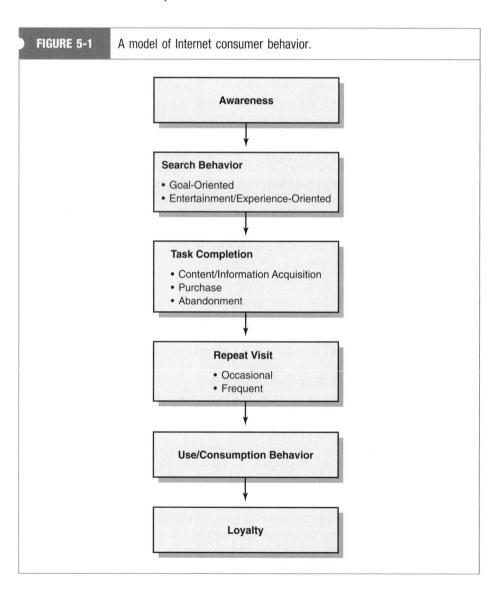

| FIGURE 5-1 | A model of Internet consumer behavior. |

Awareness

Search Behavior
- Goal-Oriented
- Entertainment/Experience-Oriented

Task Completion
- Content/Information Acquisition
- Purchase
- Abandonment

Repeat Visit
- Occasional
- Frequent

Use/Consumption Behavior

Loyalty

This process is so generic that it can be applied to consumer behavior in any channel, including the Internet. However, it has several disadvantages in that context:

- Because of its generic nature, the traditional model does not lend itself to explicit measurement, especially to the kind of metrics available on the Web, which we discuss in detail in Chapter 11.

- The traditional consumer decision process model focuses on acquisition, with little attention to long-term relationship building. Relationship models tend to focus on activities after the customer has been acquired, not at the beginning of the process. Consequently, we combine a number of current perspectives into a comprehensive model of buyer behavior on the Internet. Then we examine existing studies to see how much is known about consumer activities at each stage. To conclude the first part of the chapter, we compare several studies of consumer Internet market segments.

5-2a Stages of Internet Consumer Behavior

Figure 5-1 shows the comprehensive model of Internet consumer behavior. It has all the elements of the traditional model, although they are arranged differently. It also includes elements of relationship building after the initial sale.

Awareness

The model begins with the consumer (see Box 5-1) becoming aware that content or products can be obtained via the Internet. Awareness can be created using any available online or offline medium.

Case in Point 5-1   Profile of the Global Internet Population

Estimates suggest that the world Internet population is hovering around 1 billion as of late 2005. ClickZ Stats quotes the Computer Industry Almanac estimate of 1.08 billion and a projection of 1.80 billion by 2010.[1] Miniwatts International, Ltd., gives an estimate of over 972 million. They break it down geographically and list the number of Internet users in selected countries as follows:[2]

Asia	332,590,713
China	103,000,000
Japan	78,050,000
India	39,200,000

Overall, Asia has a household penetration rate of only 9.2%. Japan has 60.9%, China has 7.9%, and India has 3.6%.

Europe	285,408,118
Germany	47,127,725
United Kingdom	37,800,000

Household penetration is highest in the countries of the European Union (EU) at 49.3%. Among the larger

countries in Europe, Denmark leads with penetration of 69.5%, and many EU member countries have penetration percentages ranging from the high 20s to the 40s. Tiny Iceland has a penetration rate of 76.5%.

North America	224,103,811
United States	203,576,811
Canada	20,450,000

Household penetration is 67.7% in the United States and 63.8% in Canada.

Latin America/Caribbean	72,953,597

This region has a penetration rate of only 13.3%. Among larger nations in the region, Brazil has 22,320,000 users and Mexico has 16,995,400. Chile has a household penetration rate of 36.1% and Costa Rica has 23.2%.

Oceana/Australia	17,690,762
Australia	13,991,612
New Zealand	3,200,000

continued

Overall the region has a penetration rate of 52.9%, with New Zealand having 77.6% and Australia 68.2%.

Africa   23,917,500

Few countries in Africa have a penetration rate of 10% or more, but the continent had the highest rate of growth in Internet use between 2000 and 2005.

Middle East   16,163,500
Iran   5,500,000
Israel   3,200,000

The penetration rate is 45.8% in Israel, 36.9% in the United Arab Emirates, and only 8% in Iran.

Data, frequently updated, on global Internet use can be found at Web Worldwide (http://www.clickz.com/stats/web_worldwide/) and Internet World Stats (http://www.internetworldstats.com/stats.htm).

The Computer Industry Almanac estimates that there will be 215 million broadband Internet subscribers

worldwide in 2005. The top five countries in terms of number of subscribers are as follows:[3]

United States	46,900,000
China	35,900,000
Japan	26,400,000
South Korea	13,100,000
France	9,600,000

As a comparison, Informa Telecoms Media estimated that there will be 2.14 billion cell phone users worldwide by the end of 2005,[4] and IDC estimated 1.7 billion.[5]

A Computer Industry Almanac forecast predicted that by 2007, 56.8% of users would be accessing the Internet on wireless devices. In Europe, 67% and in the Asia-Pacific region 60.4% of Internet users would be wireless. In the United States, the penetration of wireless Internet use is expected to be only 46.3%.[6]

The process of building awareness is facilitated by a trusted brand, either through online branding activities or as a result of an established offline brand. On the Web, the awareness stage can be very brief, as when a consumer sees a banner ad with a compelling message and clicks on it, thereby initiating a visit to a site. On the other hand, it can be an extensive process, as brands from Amazon to eBay to Yahoo! can attest. In Chapter 3 we illustrated both the opportunities and the problems inherent in moving the awareness and brand recognition of Charles Schwab and the firm that bears his name to the Internet. Whatever the specific situation, some level of awareness is necessary before the Internet user moves into the search behavior stage.

Search Behavior

In their analysis and formulation of communication in computer-mediated environments, Hoffman and Novak indicate that there are two basic types of Internet search behavior, each of which has subtypes:[7]

- *Goal-oriented* search behavior, in which the user has an objective of some kind. The objectives may be categorized as follows:
  - *Task completion,* the desire to accomplish a specified task or complete a specific activity.
  - *Prepurchase deliberation,* in which the user engages in information search related to a specific product or service.
- *Experiential* search behavior, in which activities are not task-oriented but are guided by the process itself.
  - *Build information bank,* in which the user accumulates information for long-term use.

- *Opinion leadership,* in which the user searches for information that will be used in her role as an opinion leader.
- *Recreation,* in which the user finds entertainment in using the computer to search out new information or activities.

The U.S. Census Bureau has been tracking Internet behaviors for a number of years (Figure 5-2). The 2003 Current Population Survey found about 60% of U.S. adults using the Internet, compared with only 22% in 1997. In 1997, 2001, and 2003, using e-mail was the most common activity, with obtaining information about products and services a close second. Searching for news, weather, and sports and searching for information on government services were also common activities. Notice that the percentage of respondents purchasing a product or service on the Internet has gone from just over 2% in 1997 to over 32% in 2003. Notice also that many activities, from playing games to searching for a job to making an Internet phone call, have been included in the survey only since 2001. All of this supports the premise that the Internet is maturing as a medium of both communication and commerce. Notice also that all of the activities are clearly goal related. People tend to go onto the Internet for a reason, even if the reason is purely for entertainment.

A study by the Pew Foundation highlights some differences in Internet usage between U.S. men and women. Men log in more often, spend more time online, and are more likely to be broadband users and to engage in online transactions, including bill paying, auctions, and stock trading. Women are more likely to be intensive users of e-mail, especially to nurture relationships. Men and women are equally likely to buy things online and to engage in online banking. The Pew Foundation concludes that male and female Internet usage is more alike than different, driven by their desire for efficiency. According to the Pew Foundation, "Both men and women approach with gusto online transactions that simplify their lives by saving time on such mundane tasks as buying tickets or paying bills."[8] Users value the convenience of the Internet for performing many tasks, with communication and searching for information leading the list, as has been true from the beginning of the Internet.

The same pattern of usage holds true in Europe (Figure 5-2). The 2006 media use tracking study by the European Interactive Advertising Association surveyed 7000 Internet users across Europe. Residents of the EU and Norway were most likely to visit search engines, followed closely by e-mail pages. News pages were in third place, which parallels the pattern of activity in the United States on the top three Internet activities. From there, the pattern of usage frequency diverges, although Internet users on both continents ultimately perform the same tasks. The European study breaks out usage patterns for young people, ages 15 to 24. Not surprisingly, they are heavier users of all entertainment categories.

Task Completion

On the Internet, it is reasonable to define one successful outcome of the consumer behavior process as acquiring information, whereas in the physical world, we define it only as a purchase. Keep in mind also that because our traditional model of consumer behavior focuses on a single purchase episode, the purchase comes near the end of the process. In the Internet environment, it is wise to define a single purchase only as an intermediate step. A successful outcome from the marketer's perspective is not achieved until the user becomes a repeat user or, better, a loyal customer. See Case in Point 5-2 for data on e-commerce in selected countries.

Figure 5-2 makes it clear that, even in the United States, where Internet use is well developed, communication in general and information acquisition in particular are the primary activities of Internet consumers. Actual purchase is further down on the list. In addition, activities that are engaged in by fewer people often require high-speed

FIGURE 5-2   Online activities of Internet consumers.

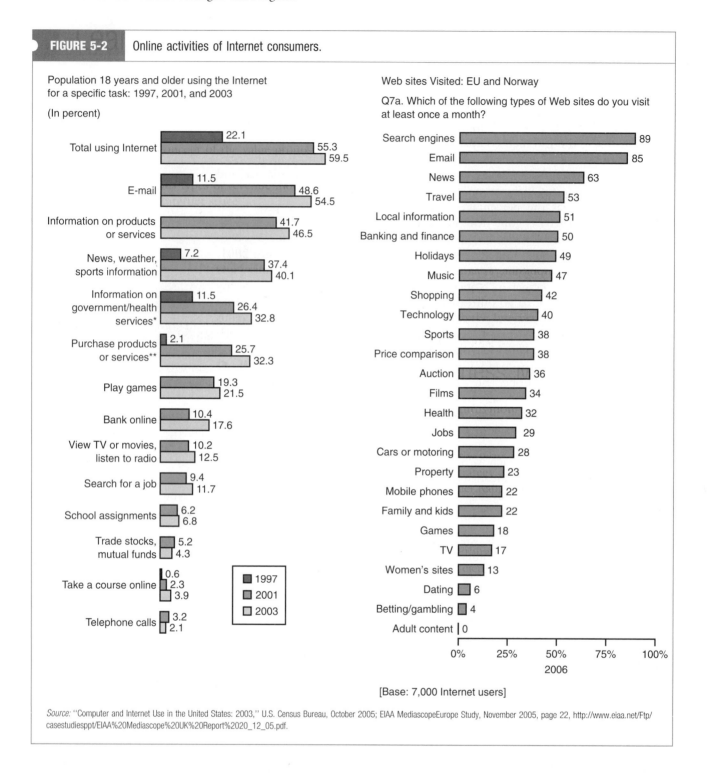

Population 18 years and older using the Internet for a specific task: 1997, 2001, and 2003

(In percent)

Activity	1997	2001	2003
Total using Internet	22.1	55.3	59.5
E-mail	11.5	48.6	54.5
Information on products or services		41.7	46.5
News, weather, sports information	7.2	37.4	40.1
Information on government/health services*	11.5	26.4	32.8
Purchase products or services**	2.1	25.7	32.3
Play games		19.3	21.5
Bank online		10.4	17.6
View TV or movies, listen to radio		10.2	12.5
Search for a job		9.4	11.7
School assignments		6.2	6.8
Trade stocks, mutual funds		5.2	4.3
Take a course online	0.6	2.3	3.9
Telephone calls		3.2	2.1

Web sites Visited: EU and Norway

Q7a. Which of the following types of Web sites do you visit at least once a month?

Web site type	Percent
Search engines	89
Email	85
News	63
Travel	53
Local information	51
Banking and finance	50
Holidays	49
Music	47
Shopping	42
Technology	40
Sports	38
Price comparison	38
Auction	36
Films	34
Health	32
Jobs	29
Cars or motoring	28
Property	23
Mobile phones	22
Family and kids	22
Games	18
TV	17
Women's sites	13
Dating	6
Betting/gambling	4
Adult content	0

0%   25%   50%   75%   100%

2006

[Base: 7,000 Internet users]

Source: "Computer and Internet Use in the United States: 2003," U.S. Census Bureau, October 2005; EIAA MediascopeEurope Study, November 2005, page 22, http://www.eiaa.net/Ftp/casestudiesppt/EIAA%20Mediascope%20UK%20Report%2020_12_05.pdf.

Internet connections. Viewing movies, taking online courses, and Internet phone calls are examples of activities that can be frustrating on slow connections. Activities that require high bandwidth are forecasted to increase as more users get broadband connections. Finally, some tasks that require a high level of trust in the security of Internet transactions, like online banking and stock trading, are also performed by a smaller proportion of the Internet-using population.

Abandonment of virtual shopping carts is an aspect of online purchasing activities that has received considerable attention. Shopping carts are often abandoned in the online world. There are a number of reasons that recur in research on cart abandonment. Two of the most important are difficulty in using the site and shipping and handling costs. Making the site easier to navigate and ensuring that customers can purchase easily are both important. Marketers use site metrics and usability tests to improve their sites, both of which are discussed in Chapter 11. Price, in general, can also be an issue, especially because consumers often come to the Web looking for a bargain. Finally, many consumers may be "just looking" with the intention of purchasing offline. However, if abandonment is frequent, it suggests a potential problem with the site. One such problem is requiring consumers to put a product in the shopping cart before they can see the price. Cart abandonment is an important metric for many e-commerce sites, but it should be interpreted with care. Abandonment also needs to be studied in the context of multichannel consumer behavior because consumers like to move back and forth between channels for both product research and purchasing.

Case in Point 5-2   Profile of Global E-Commerce

Forrester Research estimated that U.S. retail e-commerce will grow from $172 billion in 2005 to $329 billion in 2010, a 14% compounded annual growth rate.[9]

- In late 2005, more than 75% of U.S. Internet users reported that they had made purchases online.

- Almost 63% said the Internet was their main source of product information, followed by print media at just under 11%.[10]

Statistics Canada reported total e-commerce sales in 2003 to be $19.1 billion Canadian, with business-to-business (B2B) making up the largest portion. Business-to-customer (B2C) sales made up $5.5 billion of the total and grew more than 50% between 2002 and 2003.[11]

E-commerce forecasts quoted by eMarketer for selected European countries for 2008:[12]

	Euros
Germany	89.4
United Kingdom	69.8
France	59.0
Italy	39.6
Spain	16.2

A.C. Nielsen reported that for April–May 2005, German buyers averaged 6.7 purchases, U.K. purchasers averaged 6.4, French purchasers averaged 4.2, Italian purchasers averaged 4.4, and Spanish purchasers averaged 4.8.[13]

The Irish Commission for Communications Regulation reported that 20% of Irish Internet users, some 250,000 people, will spend about 200 Euros online, for a total of 55 million Euros in online holiday shopping in 2005.[14]

Forrester Research data showed growth of 19.7% in the number of Internet users in selected European countries who shopped online from the second quarter of 2004 to the second quarter of 2005. The United Kingdom and Germany led in absolute numbers, with 22 million Internet shoppers each. In the United Kingdom, the percentage of users who purchased online was 71%, a figure that almost matches that of the United States. France and Italy each experienced growth rates of 40% in online shopping during that 12-month period.[15]

In 2004, the number of businesses that had Web sites (not necessarily e-commerce enabled) varied by country:[16]

Sweden	82.1%
Japan	78.4%
United Kingdom	66.3%
Canada	63.9%
Australia	49.4%

Miscellaneous U.S. e-commerce statistics:

- Of total customers, 18% make 46% of online purchases (Neilsen//NetRatings).[17]

- The average Internet consumer spent $368 in the first quarter of 2005; the average blog visitor spent $390 (ClickZ).[18]

- Women made up 52% of the online population in 2005. By 2008, there will be 10 million more women online than men. Women influence three-fourths of online purchases, and categories like jewelry and furniture that have special appeal to women are the fastest growing.[19]

Search versus Purchase

The relationship between search and purchase is one of the most complex aspects of the multichannel retailing environment. The volume of search is not in question. The Pew Foundation reported in November 2005 that 60 million Americans used search on a typical day, about 41% of the Internet-using population.[20] Nielsen//NetRatings reported that more than 5.1 billion searches were conducted in October 2005, a growth of 15% between June and October.[21] They also reported data for the holiday season that indicated a growth in online shopping trips of about 33% over the same time period in 2004.[22] By any measure, both search and shopping on the Internet are experiencing rapid growth. It would be easier for marketers if there were a direct, linear relationship between search and subsequent purchases, online or offline or both. Such, however, is not the case.

One of the earliest studies of this issue was conducted by market research firm comScore in the first quarter of 2004. They followed the activities of Internet users who conducted a search on consumer electronics or computers during that period. Twenty-five percent of the searchers actually made a purchase. A remarkable 92% of those purchases were made offline. Of the 8% who made purchases online, most purchased in a subsequent Internet session, not the session in which they conducted the search. They also found that most consumers continued to use the type of search term with which they had started, either a generic keyword or a brand name, throughout their purchase decision process.[23]

Later comScore joined with ad serving firm DoubleClick to study a broader set of product categories. They studied purchasing on thirty Web sites in four categories—apparel, sport/fitness, computer hardware, and travel. They summarized their findings as follows:

- Search played a role in roughly half of the online purchases.
- The majority of prepurchase searches were conducted using generic keywords, not brand names.
- The closer to purchase, the more likely the consumer was to use brand names.
- Most purchasers completed their search well in advance of the actual purchase; 54.7% concluded their search 2 weeks before their purchase.
- Across all four categories, only 23.8% searched and purchased in the same online session.[24]

The influence of media other than the Web on purchases is equally complex. Figure 5-3 shows two different perspectives. BIGresearch tracked users of six different search engines who purchased electronics and home improvement products. Their data showed that word of mouth and reading an article had the most influence overall. Broadcast advertising, newspaper inserts, and Internet advertising also had an impact.

DoubleClick studied four media and purchases in ten product categories over a 6-month period. They found that the Internet played a role in virtually all purchases but that the amount and timing of impact varied by product category (see Figure 5-3). When they analyzed the results by industry they found that:

- purchases of travel services were most influenced by Web sites, with travel sites scoring highest and travel companies second highest.
- purchasers of telecommunications products were most influenced by word-of-mouth communication, followed by salespersons.
- purchasers of personal and home care products were most influenced by seeing the product in the store, with product coupons a distant second.[25]

The message to marketers is that there is no rule of thumb about the impact of search and online promotion that applies to all consumers or to all product categories

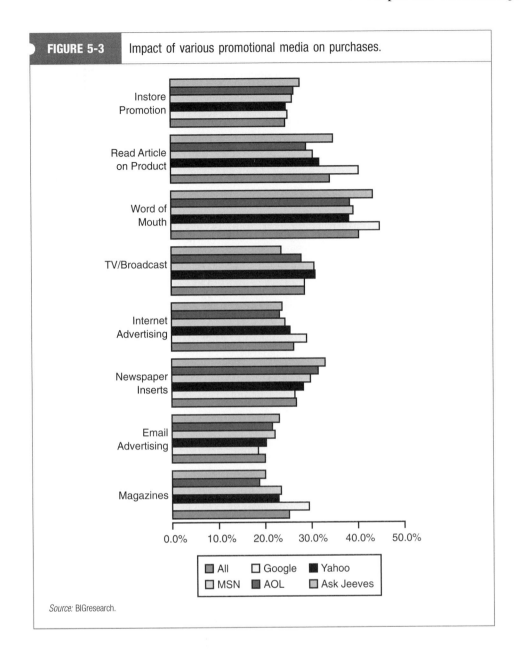

FIGURE 5-3 Impact of various promotional media on purchases.

Source: BIGresearch.

or to all marketing channels. Marketers must carefully monitor what customers do both on and off their Web sites. They must also monitor the impact of offline channels on their customers to reveal the purchasing process that is most common for each segment of their customers for each product they sell.

Well-managed Web sites constantly monitor the traffic on their sites. Many metrics are available to them, which we discuss in detail in Chapter 11. Table 5-1 gives sample statistics on overall Web usage in the United States and the United Kingdom for one specific month. The U.S. data are shown for home use only, and the U.K. data are shown for combined home and work usage.

The same metrics, and many more, are available to individual Web sites so that they can gauge their success in important measures like achieving repeat visits and encouraging visitors to remain on the site and on individual pages longer. Table 5-1a and b shows publicly available aggregate data, not individual site statistics. Site statistics that report activities of visitors on a specific site are available only to that site, and they are important measures of competitive success. Individual sites, however, cannot get competitor data like the "top 10 parent companies" shown in Table 5-1c and d. Those can be obtained only by a third-party measurement service that has the ability to track the activities of users across all sites. In the second section of this chapter, we discuss how both individual sites and third-party measurement services obtain metrics.

TABLE 5-1	Sample Visitation Statistics

(a) United States: Average Web Usage, November 2005 Home Panel

Sessions/visits per person	33
Domains visited per person	62
PC time per person	29:40:04
Duration of a Web page viewed	00:00:48
Active digital media universe	142,704,415
Current digital media universe estimate	203,714,533

(b) United Kingdom: Average Web Usage, November 2005 Home/Work Panel

Sessions/visits per person	37
Domains visited per person	78
PC time per person	34:28:34
Duration of a Web page viewed	00:00:42
Active digital media universe	26,650,849
Current digital media universe estimate	36,306,618

(c) United States: Top 10 Parent Companies, November 2005 Home Panel

Parent Name	Unique Audience (000)	Reach (%)	Time per Person
Microsoft	95,714	67.07	01:22:50
Yahoo!	87,243	61.14	02:16:36
Time Warner	84,475	59.20	03:58:15
Google	71,476	50.09	00:28:44
eBay	48,018	33.65	01:33:57
InterActiveCorp	39,923	27.98	00:20:03
Amazon	33,160	23.24	00:22:02
Walt Disney Internet Group	26,714	18.72	00:34:38
Viacom International	26,469	18.55	00:46:45
RealNetworks	25,380	17.78	00:40:00

TABLE 5-1	Continued.

(d) United Kingdom: Top 10 Parent Companies, November 2005 Home/Work Panel

Property Name	Unique Audience (000)	Reach (%)	Time per Person
Microsoft	20,224	75.89	02:31:47
Google	18,031	67.66	00:35:51
Yahoo!	13,856	51.99	01:20:48
eBay	13,784	51.72	02:09:23
BBC	11,124	41.74	00:44:05
Amazon	9,599	36.02	00:19:55
Time Warner	8,454	31.72	03:20:12
InterActiveCorp	7,548	28.32	00:09:31
HM Government	6,179	23.18	00:14:29
Apple Computer	5,708	21.42	00:40:57

Source: Nielsen//NetRatings, http://www.netratings.com/news.jsp?section=dat_to&country=us.

Use and Consumption Behavior

Purchase is followed by product use or consumption behavior, whether it is a tangible product, an intangible service, or a piece of information. Remember that consumption of information does not destroy the information in question as consumption of a physical product does. In fact, on the Internet, useful information is often shared with a group of friends or colleagues, thereby increasing its value. In either case, the information or the product itself either proves useful to the consumer or does not prove to be satisfactory. Product satisfaction is frequently studied as part of the marketing research process, to be discussed in the second section of this chapter. Satisfaction with the Web site experience is also an important measure of good Internet marketing.

Since 1994, the American Society for Quality and the Stephen M. Ross School of Business at the University of Michigan have partnered to conduct the American Customer Satisfaction Index. Figure 5-4 shows the major categories of questions asked in their quarterly survey. Consumers are queried about their expectations of and their experiences with product and service quality and their reactions to price increases and decreases.[26] This produces a score for the perceived value of the product category (e.g., automobiles) or the business. Expectations, experience, and perceived value are combined to produce a satisfaction score, which are the data that are publicly reported. The data in the survey have been shown to be predictive of corporate earnings because they are linked to customer retention and customer willingness to tolerate price changes.[27]

The results of the index, announced every fiscal quarter, measure satisfaction with both corporate and governmental institutions and have become a recognized measure of consumer confidence in the economy. Satisfaction with Internet sites is measured annually by a commercial partner, ForeSee Results. They report satisfaction with e-business sites (search engines, portals, and news and information sites) and e-commerce (retail, travel, auctions, and brokerage sites). Satisfaction with Internet institutions continues to increase, reaching 75.9 for e-business and 78.6 for e-commerce, compared with 73.0 for all forty-one industries included in the survey.[28] The survey is an index, so scores can range between 0 and 100.

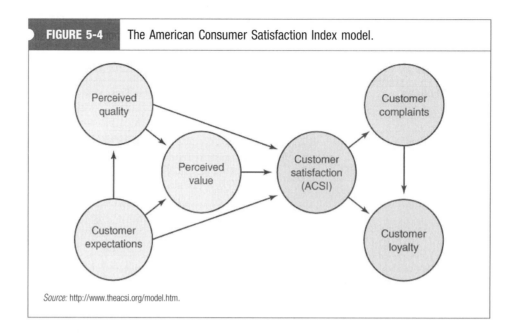

FIGURE 5-4 | The American Consumer Satisfaction Index model.

Source: http://www.theacsi.org/model.htm.

TABLE 5-2 | Retail Web Site Satisfaction Scores

	Average Satisfaction for Category	Highest in Category	Score	Lowest in Category	Score
Books/CDs/videos/DVDs/toys/hobbies	81	Netflix.com	85	ToysRUs.com	77
Drugs/health and beauty	78	Avon.com	80	Quixtar.com	77
Apparel and accessories	78	LLBean.com	84	BananaRepublic.com	73
Flowers/gifts/jewelry/food	76	HarryandDavid.com	80	FTD.com	74
Computers/electronics	76	Newegg.com	82	CompUSA.com	71
Mass merchants/office supplies	76	Amazon.com	84	Kmart.com	69

Source: Adapted from Enid Burns, "Customer Service Trumps Price," http://www.clickz.com/stats/sectors/retailing/article.php/3509301#table3; and "Satisfaction with Online Shopping Dips," December 23, 2005, http://www.clickz.com/stats/sectors/retailing/article.php/3573346.

Results of 2005 e-business surveys are summarized in Table 5-2. Scores for the forty Internet sites surveyed in the first study ranged from the high for Netflix, 85, to the low for the Kmart site, 69. Overall, pure-play Internet businesses like Netflix and Amazon scored higher, but successful multichannel retailers like L.L. Bean also did well. The scores for individual firms represent a substantial spread on a 100-point index, and the correlation between satisfaction scores and corporate profitability makes the differences important. According to Larry Freed, president of ForeSee Results, "For retailers who improve their site experience, there will be a pretty significant payback in terms of the behavior and loyalty of their customers."[29]

When ForeSee surveyed consumers in the important weeks leading up to the 2005 Christmas holiday season (see Table 5-2), they found overall satisfaction scores hovering around 75 on the index throughout the time frame. Consumers reported most satisfaction with the quality of the products they bought online and least with price. The ordering process and delivery of orders, two key measures of the back-end performance of an e-tailer, received scores exceeding 80 throughout. The aggregate statistics suggest that online retailers are doing a reasonably good job on both the marketing front end and the fulfillment back end of e-commerce.

If the consumer found both the Internet experience and the actual use of the product or the information satisfactory—and assuming a continuing need for the product or service—the consumer is likely to return to the Web site at some point. The frequency with which the consumer returns depends on personal circumstances (e.g., the availability or lack of shopping resources nearby) and the consumer's predisposition toward conducting affairs on the Internet. The usage data in Figure 5-4 shows frequent Internet sessions, ranging from twenty-one per month in the United States to thirteen per month in Australia. It also shows a considerable number of sites visited in each session, although it does not distinguish between information search and purchasing. The frequency of use suggests some level of satisfaction with Internet use. At the level of individual enterprises, however, occasional visits to a site may not create a strong enough bond between the customer and the enterprise for true loyalty to develop. If the consumer visits frequently, and continues to experience satisfactory outcomes, a state of loyalty may ensue.

There is a large stream of literature in marketing that discusses the nature of brand loyalty, and it seems entirely applicable in the Internet space. Loyalty is most often measured by repeat purchases in the physical world. We can add frequent visits to the site in Internet space as a behavioral measure of loyalty. If, however, a better product or Web site comes along or if—even more likely—a more substantial incentive lures the consumer away, behavioral loyalty is likely to be transient. Only if consumers become loyal in an attitudinal sense are they likely to be resistant to the appeals of other marketers and/or to engage in word-of-mouth communication that extols the benefits of product, service, or site. This final state has been given many names in relationship marketing models over the years, but whatever it is called, it is clearly the objective to which Internet marketing programs aspire.

In tracing the stages of consumer behavior on the Internet we see a number of implications. The United States has been the leader in developments on the Internet in its early years. The development of the Internet as a consumer medium in other countries appears to be paralleling that of the United States in many ways, like the types of usage shown in Figure 5-2. The United States, however, is a laggard in the development and use of the wireless Internet, as we discuss in Chapter 14. In general, the U.S. dominance in everything from use of the wired Internet to e-commerce seems to be slowly disappearing, creating a truly global marketplace. However, there are still substantial differences from one country to another that are caused by both infrastructure and culture. The savvy marketer takes advantage of the global marketplace but recognizes the differences that exist between countries.

5-3 Internet User Segments

In the same way, differences exist between Internet users within countries. Marketers must recognize the variations between segments in order to mount successful Internet marketing programs. The approach to segmentation in the offline world also applies online. Segmentation approaches can be grouped into categories with multiple variables in each. Some examples of effective segmentation according to U.S. data include the following:

- Geographic
    - Residents of rural areas are less likely to be online than urbanites.[30]
- Demographic
    - Teenagers
        - They spend much of their Internet time communicating with peers through instant messaging, blogs, and social networking sites.[31]
        - They increasingly see e-mail as a way to communicate with adults, not peers.[32]

- They play games, get news, make purchases, and get health information online.[33]
- They are heavy consumers of music and related merchandise.[34]

- Seniors
  - Less than one-third of people older than 65 have ever gone online.
  - Health information is popular among seniors and persons age 50 to 64.
  - Seniors with a high school degree or less or an annual income less than $20,000 are less likely to have gone online.[35]

Age, affluence, and education have been important to Internet use since the beginning. However, one variable that was important in the early days—length of time online—has become relatively unimportant. According to the Pew Foundation, that is because they were finding fewer "newbies."[36]

Segmenting by user behavior is useful offline and it is powerful in the online environment, so much so that a type of advertising targeting has grown up around it. We discuss behavioral advertising in Chapter 6.

Lifestyle is the final category in most segmentation schemes. Consultants in the marketing practice at McKinsey present a segmentation scheme that describes the styles of U.S. Internet users. Their segments are as follows:

- *Connectors* (36%) are relatively new to the Internet. They use it to connect and communicate, but their loyalty is to offline brands.
- *Simplifiers* (29%) use the Internet to make their lives more convenient. They require superior customer service from beginning to end.
- *Routiners* (15%) use the Internet as a regular source of information but are not generally online purchasers.
- *Surfers* (8%) spend the most time online, using it for a variety of tasks, including purchasing.
- *Bargainers* (8%) search for the best deals online. They use the Internet for both entertainment and shopping.
- *Sportsters* (4%) use the Internet almost exclusively for sports and entertainment information.

Because their reasons for and ways of using the Internet differ, different segments must be marketed to in different ways. Simplifiers, surfers, and bargainers are core segments for e-commerce, but simplifiers are clearly looking for convenience and bargainers value low price most highly. Routiners and sportsters can be encouraged to make purchases offline. Connectors may be a potentially profitable segment if they can be enticed to purchase online.[37]

Internet marketers should follow the advice given to offline marketers. They must study the market segments for their own product category and even for their brand to find the most effective segmentation approaches. Conventional marketing research can be used, but the Internet offers some interesting—and potentially cheaper—alternatives. The various types of data available to Internet marketers are discussed in the second half of this chapter. Using site metrics to uncover visitor segments is covered in Chapter 11. In Chapter 6, we discuss the use of standard segments for behavioral targeting. This all implies a robust set of options for Internet marketers to identify and effectively communicate with their target audiences. The challenge for marketers is to identify the right options and execute them with precision.

The segment missing from this schema could be called the unconnected. These are people who do not have access to the Internet. *Ad Age* quotes a Mediamark Research study that says the group comprises about 21% of the U.S. population. They are less affluent and less well educated than their online counterparts. Age is less a determinant of being unconnected. According to this study, it may be more an attitude toward technology. When respondents were asked, "Is life better today than 50 years ago due to advanced technology?" only 13% replied that "Life is worse today." Of respondents who had no cell phones, 15% replied that life was worse, whereas of those who had no Internet connection, 18% said life was worse.[38] The implication is that there is a segment of the population that will never choose to go online.

5-4 Crossing the Digital Divide

Long before the advent of the Internet, there was concern that lack of access to technology would accentuate the economic divisions between "haves and have nots." This is often referred to as the "technology gap," and it is a special concern in the context of developing nations. The United Nations Commission on Science and Technology for Development provides benchmarking measures to gauge the status of the information technology and communications infrastructure in a country. They post studies and reports on their Web site (http://stdev.unctad.org).

What has been called the "digital divide" is a more specific manifestation of the gap in technology access between rich and poor. That term was coined by the Department of Commerce in the early 1990s, and for a time it did tracking studies of the demographic characteristics that described access, or lack thereof, to the Internet. Throughout, the chief variables tended to be age, income, education, and rural/urban residence. There were also ethnic differences, which have largely disappeared in recent years.[39] The second and last major Commerce Department study is dated 1997, which is significant.

As the Internet has become mainstream and prices for technology have gone down, the income gap in Internet access has tended to disappear. Perhaps interest in the so-called digital divide also waned because of the intensive, and largely successful, efforts to see that all schools and public libraries in the United States and other developed countries provided access to the Internet. It is correct to argue that most people who want access to the Internet can get it in most developed nations. It would, however, be incorrect to argue that—especially for school-age children—access outside the home is the same as access at home.

The fact is that there is still a gap, but its nature has changed. In an October 2005 study, the Pew Foundation argues that the real gap is now between those who have broadband access and those who do not. According to them, "Now that the majority of the heaviest internet's users have upgraded from dial-up to high-speed access at home, broadband access is becoming a stronger predictor of online behavior than a user's level of experience"[40] (Table 5-3).

Dial-up users use all the important Internet services studied at a significantly lower rate than do broadband users. It does not appear that the type of broadband connection makes any difference. The Pew study seems to agree that it will be difficult to convince the 22% of the American population who are currently unconnected to connect to the Internet. They point out that about 40% of the population have a rather tepid connection via their dial-up lines and their relatively infrequent use. The 33% who are the heaviest users are highly and consistently engaged with the Internet. They are more likely to be younger than 50 years of age and to have completed college. They constitute an Internet elite that may, in fact, represent a subtler and more enduring Internet divide.

As noted earlier, ethnic differences in Internet use in the United States have lessened considerably in recent years. A study of African Americans online by eMarketer in late 2005 found that 50% to 60% of African American households had Internet access, compared with 70% of white households. Commenting on the study, its author worried that the gap that remains may be by choice. They quote a statement by Bruce Moore, president of the NAACP. "'Some of the digital divide is self-imposed," Bruce Gordon, head of the NAACP, told Businessweek in October 2005. "A computer and a DSL line don't cost that much anymore. We need to convince

TABLE 5-3	Differences in Frequency of Various Internet Activities by Connection Type		
		Home Dial-Up Users (%)	Home Broadband Users (%)
Get news online		68	82
Buy a product online		59	81
Bank online		35	59
Download computer programs		35	47
Play online games		33	41
Read someone else's blog		20	35
Participate in an online auction		19	39
Download music		17	33
Create a blog		4	11

Source: http://www.pewinternet.org/pdfs/PIP_Digital_Divisions_Oct_5_2005.pdf, p. 12.

more households to buy computers and go online.'"[41] The issues may, indeed, be subtler than income or even education would predict.

With that in mind, we end this section of the chapter with two warnings about the publicly available data on consumer behavior on the Internet. First, although identifiable patterns of Internet use are forming around the globe, specific data are subject to rapid obsolescence. It is important for Internet marketers to follow at least some of the key indicators on a regular basis. These data are essential because it is a primary rule of marketing intelligence to answer as many questions as possible with available data, and only then to supplement it with marketing research. Second, it is important to become familiar with suppliers of commercial data, whether free or in the form of paid reports. The quality of commercial data can vary, and the experience and reputation of the supplier is important.

5-5 Understanding the Internet Consumer through Enterprise Data

Even though there is a wealth of publicly available data, it will rarely answer all the marketer's detailed questions about marketing specific products and executing specific programs. To answer specific questions, marketers have always found it necessary to turn to marketing research. Database marketing, fueled by the rich consumer data available on the Internet, has added another category of data—online data capture. Whether data capture and analysis is performed by the enterprise itself or by third-party data suppliers, data taken directly from the Internet behavior of visitors and customers has become a staple of the marketing effort. This is true of firms that were once traditional mass media marketers as well as of firms that have a history of direct-response and database marketing. The data are more immediate and more detailed than marketing research, creating a rich record of individual customer behavior that can be used for planning and executing marketing programs.

With that in mind, let's begin our discussion of enterprise data with the familiar subject of marketing research. Then we conclude the chapter with a discussion of online data capture.

5-6 Conventional Marketing Research

Traditional marketing research has generally been organized around concepts that include the types of data and methods of data collection.

- Data types:
  - Primary data are data collected by the marketer for an identified project. Primary data, properly collected and analyzed, are directly relevant to the objectives and research questions of the project. It often takes several months for the completion of a primary research project and can cost tens or even hundreds of thousands of dollars.
  - Secondary data are relevant data, both internal and external, that were collected for purposes other than the current project. It is both faster and cheaper to obtain secondary data, but it may not provide complete or in-depth answers to the research questions.
- Methods of data collection:
  - Survey research employs questionnaires to collect data from respondents using various kinds of structured questions. It produces quantitative data that can be analyzed in a variety of ways, including statistical tests and models. Samples can be chosen carefully to be statistically representative of target populations. Survey data have the advantage of using widely understood collection and analytic techniques. It is very good for getting at the "whats" of consumer attitudes and behavior, but does not always produce in-depth understanding of the "whys."
  - Qualitative research uses a variety of interview techniques to understand issues in the words of consumers themselves. Techniques include personal interviews and focus groups. It is better at the "whys" of consumer behavior than it is at drawing a complete picture of the "whats." It can produce a deep understanding of how consumers think and feel, but it is based on small and sometimes unrepresentative samples. It requires researchers skilled in interviewing, group dynamics, and the analysis of qualitative data to gain the benefits and avoid the potential pitfalls of qualitative research.
  - Experimental research, discussed in Chapter 5 as the methodology for testing on the Internet, has received less use in the marketing arena.[42] However, it is used in advertising laboratories to test ad concepts and executions. This is similar to its use in testing Web site usability, to be discussed in Chapter 10.

5-6a Marketing Research on the Web

Traditional marketing research[43] has moved onto the Internet with a vengeance. An industry newsletter estimated that only 10% of marketing research spending was online in 2000. That had grown to 23.6% in 2003 and was estimated to be 33% by 2006.[44] That does not, however, represent the complete picture of Internet-enabled marketing intelligence. The other part of the equation are data captured as a result of Internet activities by consumers and marketers. This is characterized in Figure 5-5 as "Online Data Capture." There are two basic types of online data—usage data and transaction history—and two ways in which the data can be captured—by the site itself or by a third-party supplier. Traffic and audience data, detailed data about what Internet users do while they are on a Web site, can be collected either by the enterprise itself or by third-party data suppliers (independent infomediaries who are not part of either the buying or selling side of the transaction). Detailed purchase history (exactly what product, what model, how many items, payment method, and many other possible variables) is collected by the enterprise because only the record of the actual transaction has data at that level of detail. Customer interactions data like response to an e-mail campaign, although not unique to the Web, has achieved great importance

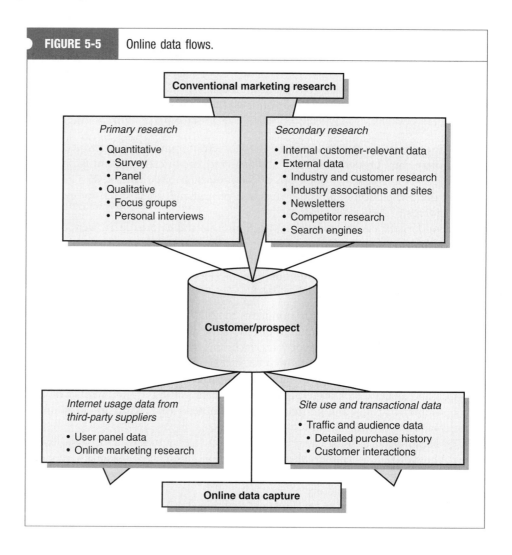

FIGURE 5-5   Online data flows.

Conventional marketing research

Primary research
- Quantitative
  - Survey
  - Panel
- Qualitative
  - Focus groups
  - Personal interviews

Secondary research
- Internal customer-relevant data
- External data
  - Industry and customer research
  - Industry associations and sites
  - Newsletters
  - Competitor research
  - Search engines

Customer/prospect

Internet usage data from third-party suppliers
- User panel data
- Online marketing research

Site use and transactional data
- Traffic and audience data
- Detailed purchase history
- Customer interactions

Online data capture

there and can be collected by the enterprise or by the supplier of the service (e.g., an e-mail marketing supplier).

All these data must be incorporated into the central database or data warehouse if marketing programs are to be successful. In the words of the industry, this provides a "360° view of the customer"—a complete picture of the person's dealings with the enterprise.

Conventional marketing research has moved onto the Internet with a vengeance because there are significant advantages to online marketing research. Online data capture is the natural evolution of the database marketing practiced by direct marketers. It has been expanded and modified by the capabilities of the Web. For a complete understanding, we need to first discuss the benefits of Internet-based marketing research and how both quantitative and qualitative research is conducted on the Web. We then discuss online data capture. This chapter concludes with a discussion of product development research on the Internet, a particularly promising blending of conventional and Internet-based research techniques.

Our traditional ways of doing marketing research can be improved in several ways by the Internet. A study in late 2004 that included both U.S. and European marketing research managers gave reasons for using online research as follows:

- Time advantages, 73%. Online questionnaires can be developed and sent to a chosen sample of potential respondents in only a few days, whereas mail surveys are likely to take several weeks. Telephone surveys are quicker than mail, but the time is still measured in weeks, not days. Qualitative research like focus groups can also be arranged and executed more quickly on the Web.

- Analysis of data is also quicker on the Web. Data is captured automatically and fed directly into the research database. This is not only fast, it prevents many errors that occur in manual data entry. Analytics are preprogrammed. This allows managers to view results in real time if they desire and to receive data tables within hours after data collection is completed.

- Competitive pricing, 71%. Online surveys are cheaper to field because they avoid the costs of printing and mailing or of administration in a telephone call center. In qualitative research, costs such as travel and interviewing facilities can be avoided. There are, however, programming costs associated with preparing online surveys.

- Use of multimedia elements, 59%. Online research provides the opportunity to include rich media such as graphics, animations, and video clips. This can be useful to show everything from product concepts to rough promotional executions to proposed Web pages.

- Access to complex target groups, 53%. Large online panels can be accessed to build samples with detailed and low-**incidence** characteristics.

incidence A marketing research term that describes how often a particular characteristic occurs in a specified population.

- Access to respondents internationally, 49%. The reach of the Web is useful to both quantitative and qualitative researchers.

- Possibility to recruit big samples, 45%. The cost advantages, as well as the availability of large online panels, permit large samples when required.

- Approach adapts well to online, 44%. All the usual types of questions can be included, and **skip patterns** ("If the answer is Yes, continue. If the answer is No, skip to Question 11," for example) can be programmed in. If complexity in a questionnaire is invisible to the respondent, the questionnaire is easier to answer and the likelihood of errors or incomplete responses is decreased. Standard interviewing and focus group moderating techniques also work on the net.[45]

skip patterns The marketing research term that describes survey questions that branch; that is, the next question is dependent on the answer to the previous one.

In short, *most of the methodology of conventional marketing research is directly transferable onto the Web*. Let's look first at quantitative survey research and then at qualitative research on the Web to understand the ways in which this is true.

Survey Research on the Internet

Internet users can be included in surveys either by attaching a pop-up survey to a page on the Web site or by deploying questionnaires over the Internet. Pop-ups have the advantages of being quick and cheap. They annoy users, but they continue to be reasonably successful and marketers continue to use them. The sample obtained is clearly a **convenience sample**. More detailed questioning can be done by e-mail surveys, use of HTML forms, or downloadable interactive surveys.[46] Any one of the three uses traditional offline question types. They can request information from a tightly controlled sample either from the customer database or from a research panel. In that sense, they are closer to traditional mail surveys than are pop-ups. Marketers are not forthcoming about research response rates either offline or online, but it is easy to surmise that the low response rates of the offline world are mirrored in the online world.

convenience sample As the name suggests, a sample that is easy to obtain; convenience samples do not permit generalization to a larger population, as random samples do.

Whether marketers decide to use pop-up or more detailed questionnaires, there are software packages that allow marketers to develop and analyze the surveys themselves. Technically, the software packages generally work well. Whether they produce valid results in the hands of inexperienced researchers is open to question. Many online marketing research firms will design, execute, analyze, and report the research results. Many of them are divisions of well-established offline research firms and have the credibility and resources associated with those firms.[47] Whether marketers choose to field surveys themselves or to use a supplier depends on the marketers' training, budget, and time constraints.

Use of the term *survey* implies that there is a defined population from which a sample is drawn. Traditionally, sample members are contacted and their cooperation in the survey is requested. This is what most people mean when they say "survey research." There is, however, another method—the consumer panel.

Panels on the Internet

For many years, several large marketing research firms like Market Facts and Louis Harris and Associates have maintained large consumer panels from which they could draw samples for specific marketing research projects. In an earlier section of this chapter, you saw data tables that were obtained from the Nielsen//NetRatings online panel. Although there has been criticism, primarily the charge that panel members become "professional respondents," panel-based research is often the only feasible alternative when the marketer needs to find a sample that matches a demographic, lifestyle, or behavioral profile. Standard panel methodology is one of the techniques that has not only been transferred onto the Web but has also benefited from the speed and accessibility it provides.

Harris Interactive is one of the largest suppliers and counts the number of its panel members in "multimillions." It can segment this large population in many ways, and it maintains panels for specific purposes. Its description of the panel (Figure 5-6) indicates that it has more than 1 million chronic illness sufferers worldwide. It offers a variety of other specialty panels as seen in Figure 5-6. Research firms that maintain panels can also develop special panels (samples, actually) for individual customers, either for a single research project or to be available over time. These panels represent groups of customers that are of special interest to some marketers and that may be

FIGURE 5-6   The Harris Poll Online interactive panel.

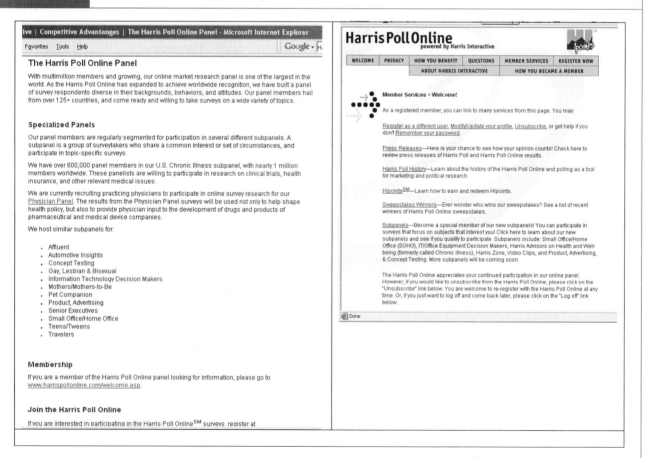

Source: http://www.harrisinteractive.com/advantages/hpolphanel.asp; http://www.harrispollonline.com/welcome.asp.

difficult or expensive to reach through conventional sampling techniques. The Harris Interactive Web site has a special page that panel members can use to manage their interaction with the firm (see Figure 5-6). This assists with panel member retention and lowers the cost of maintaining the panel.

Whether drawn from samples of populations or from panels, online surveys have potential downsides. Panels may not be representative, and their members may give biased responses. Web-based surveys obviously cannot reach people who are not online. Not all members of a sample will reply; and nonresponse bias is always an issue. When participation is obtained by some sort of online intervention—a pop-up box, for example—the bias inherent in the group that replies may be substantial.

One review of online data quality suggests that in some instances, such as product concept testing, the quality of online data may be equivalent to that of offline data. In applications like forecasting market share, offline research that allows non-Internet households to be included in the sample is preferable.[48] Another concern frequently voiced is the problem of verifying the identity of the person who responds to the questionnaire. Rather complex technical approaches are being used to ensure that the person who responds is the identified sample member who is providing honest answers.[49] These are valid concerns, and there will undoubtedly be additional developments to further ensure the quality of online data. Overall, the advantages of the online methodology are so great that research experts are predicting a major move away from telephone surveys, now the dominant method, toward online surveys. There is also a great deal of positive sentiment about the collection of qualitative data on the Web.

Qualitative Data Collection on the Internet—Personal Interviews and Focus Groups

Face-to-face interviewing was the methodology of choice when the marketing research industry was coming into prominence in the 1950s. Collecting data in this manner became increasingly expensive over time and increasingly subject to problems of nonresponse as women moved into the workforce in large numbers. Consequently, personal interviewing in the offline world is now mostly reserved for content experts, often in the early stages of a research project.

Focus groups gradually replaced personal interviewing as the preferred methodology for collecting data from consumers (and also business customers) in a face-to-face setting. Focus groups generally involve recruitment of participants based on a specific profile. Participants, generally six to twelve per group, gather in a central facility at an appointed time and engage in guided group discussion facilitated by a trained moderator. Focus groups produce rich data that arise not only from individual statements but also from the interaction among group members. It is subject to criticisms of small and nonrepresentative samples and possible moderator bias. Still, focus groups offer an unparalleled opportunity to probe the thoughts and opinions of target consumers and to hear responses in their own words, and they play an important role in contemporary marketing research.

The use of chat room functionality allows researchers to bring together prerecruited participants to engage in the type of guided discussion practiced in offline groups. Depending on the technology used, the number of participants can range from just a few to several dozen. The anonymity of the net may actually promote frank discussion in online focus groups. In any event, the technique is able to evoke rich discussion and insights. The Internet also provides a platform for showing, for example, graphics representing a new product or package design or animation of a rough advertising execution. The visuals can greatly improve the depth and quality of the insights obtained from the group.

Although online focus groups allow for cost-effective discussion between participants at scattered locations and for rapid analysis of results, there are some drawbacks. They primarily result from the lack of visual cues in the online environment. Facial expressions, body language, and nuances of speech—everything from hesitation to visible excitement—are important cues to both moderators and observers of offline focus groups. Once again, however, the speed and cost savings inherent in online focus groups make them an important part of the market researcher's toolkit.[50]

Internet technology has also revolutionized the assembly of secondary data from both internal and external sources. Secondary data represent the other major kind of conventional marketing research data.

5-7 Collection of Secondary Data Using the Internet

Two basic types of secondary data exist—internal and external. *Internal* data exist within the enterprise. As defined earlier, these are data that were not collected in the context of the current research project. Often, the data were not collected by the marketing department. Internal secondary data take many forms—from customer complaints to customer accounts to product return and servicing records. The issue for marketers is locating these data and obtaining them in a form that makes it usable for marketing purposes. Ways in which these data are being collected and used are discussed in Chapters 6, 7, 8, and 11 on customer acquisition, retention, and metrics.

External secondary data come from many sources. Census data provide statistical data about the nation's population with a completeness that is unmatched by any other source. Commercial data suppliers take this mass of data and transform it into useful information products that help marketers analyze population demographics by geographic area. Trade associations have long been a source of data about the industry they serve. There has also been an abundance of commercial research reports covering everything from specific market segments—affluent consumers, for example—to industry structure—a report on the home building industry, for example.

The Internet has not really changed these activities greatly. It has, however, expanded both their reach and their timeliness. Information is available over the Web, and many research reports can be downloaded, providing immediate access to important studies. As pointed out earlier, a lot of these commercial data are expensive, but the suppliers often provide free data as a promotional "teaser." They also offer free newsletters, which, although promotional in nature, give access to data that might not otherwise be known to the marketer. They also obviously provide a venue for advertising the paid reports.

There is another kind of secondary research that has received a big boost from the Internet, especially for do-it-yourself marketing researchers. There have been research suppliers that specialize in competitor research for many years, but their services are out of the reach of most small to medium-sized businesses. At this point throughout the world, most of the large and many of the small enterprises in any industry have Web sites. A few hours spent in intensive scrutiny of search engine results will reveal information about competitors both known and previously unknown. Tracking data on the Web sites of important competitors is a worthwhile activity. So is subscribing to their promotional newsletters, although the marketer may have to do this from a computer not identified as part of the corporate network. Both Web sites and corporate newsletters can offer early warnings of competitive activities.

Secondary data in the conventional sense, as we have discussed it here, is important and useful. It should not, however, be confused with marketing-specific data that can be captured in various ways from Web sites and other customer contact.

5-8 Online Data Capture

It is helpful to distinguish between two types of data that can be captured as a result of the activities of Web visitors and online customers. The nature of the data is different, and it is acquired in different ways.

5-8a Third-Party Internet Usage Data

Every time a person logs onto the Internet, and every mouse-click thereafter, a piece of behavioral data is generated. These data include site-specific variables such as how long a visitor spends on a site, what pages are visited, and the destination site as the visitor leaves. More general measures of Internet usage include how many Internet sessions a person conducts in a week or a month, the average length of each, and the average number of sites visited in each session. Some of these variables were shown in Table 5-1.

Stop for a minute and think about the differences in the variables just described. How long a visitor spends on the site, for example, is a piece of data that can be obtained from the operational records of the site. How many Internet sessions a person conducts in a given month requires knowledge of who that person is and access to records generated by his or her computer system. The enterprise could capture its own site-specific data if it chose to; measuring the activity of an identified person across many Web sites requires a substantially different kind of data collection activity.

The practical issue is that few sites attempt to collect and process their own usage data. The amount of data is enormous and must be extracted from operating systems and analyzed. It is easier, and in the end much cheaper, to obtain this data from suppliers who specialize in this important but arcane "clickstream" data capture. It also makes sense to obtain the general types of usage data from a supplier, most likely one that has an Internet panel as described in an earlier section. The subject of Internet usage statistics is so important that we will devote Chapter 11 to it in the context of measuring the effectiveness of Internet marketing programs. For now, it is sufficient to understand that these data are available and that can be acquired and used for various marketing programs. Recognize, however, that the site-specific statistics are for your own site, not for those of competitors.

Site usage data and other data about marketing programs on the Internet (for example, reports about the effectiveness of banner ads on other sites), as already noted, is most likely to be purchased from marketing data services. However, there is another type of data that has always been collected by the enterprise for sales and marketing operations. This is transactional data.

5-8b Transactional Data

This enterprise data is part and parcel of the transaction itself. Much of it is necessary to actually carry out the transaction, bill the customer, and update inventory records. Other types of data represent variables that marketing has identified or created to capture important facts about the customer and the transaction.

Transactional data include customer account data and data about each specific purchase. Customer account data consist of variables like customer name and bill-to address, acquisition source (catalog, banner ad, search engine, for example), and ship-to address. Many purchase-specific variables can also be captured. Common ones include **SKU** number for each product (the "stock-keeping number" that precisely identifies the model, color, size, and so forth, of the product and which is usually embedded in a bar code), date of purchase, total number of items, total value of purchase, channel (retail, catalog, or Web, for instance), method of payment, and many others.

SKU Stock-keeping unit; a unique numerical identifier attached to a product.

The level of detail at which the data are captured depends on the enterprise's current and future marketing plans. It is tempting to capture the largest possible number of variables at the finest level of detail (this is often referred to as the "granularity" of the data) on the grounds that the marketer doesn't know exactly what will be needed in the future and that it is possible to aggregate very detailed data but usually impossible to break out data that was collected at a higher level of aggregation. Although these are relevant issues, collection and maintenance of data is a significant marketing expense item, and unnecessarily detailed data are expensive to store and cumbersome to handle. It is therefore very important to carefully consider exactly what data will be captured from each customer purchase.

Database marketers have been wrestling with many other issues relative to the capture of transactional data for years. They include issues such as extracting data from accounting records in a form that is useful to marketers and whether to capture transactional data in real time or to extract data pieces in batches from the enterprise data repository. Many of the issues involve technical issues and organizational relationships as well as marketing requirements. The concept of capturing transactional data is relatively simple, but the technical and organizational issues often become very troublesome. These challenges can be overcome with time, resources, and organizational commitment, however. Time and resources are often scarce, but organizational issues and politics are usually the chief barriers to the successful capture and use of customer data.

The common conclusion among marketers in the field is that few firms capture customer transactions data for marketing purposes and then use it successfully to improve their marketing programs. There are many ways data can be used, but the ultimate goal, as described in Chapter 4, is to be able to calculate and use customer lifetime value. Many firms are in the process, but few have achieved the goal. What is especially striking about this conclusion is that transactional data have existed in business operating systems all along; the data just have not been captured and used. To further increase the pressure on marketers, there is another, less familiar, type of enterprise-specific online data that needs to be captured and used. These are data that originate in customer interactions with the enterprise.

5-8c Monitoring Customer Interactions

Cisco Systems, a B2B supplier of networking solutions, was one of the first to recognize the power of encouraging customer interaction on the site and using it to understand customer needs. Their customers are systems engineers who assemble and maintain complex, and usually customized, communications systems. They seem to enjoy communicating with other engineers and helping them resolve problems. This does two things for Cisco. First, it lessens the burden on their own customer support services, since customers often resolve one another's problems. Second, it gives them a set of forums they can monitor to understand customer problems and solutions. On their Network Professionals community page, they have more than thirty discussion forums in eight categories, including Network Infrastructure and IP Communications and Video.

Cisco nurtures these product-specific discussion forums in a number of ways besides just encouraging users to make posts. They encourage readers to rate the usefulness of posts on a 5-point scale from Extremely Helpful to Not Helpful. Posters are awarded points, and top point earners are listed on a special page, "Meet the Top Net Pros." They award a "badge" to members when they accumulate 100 points; some have accumulated several thousand points. They display all this "member appreciation" information, and each month they recognize members who have made important contributions. All of this provides a rich source of information about how customers are using Cisco products, and Cisco managers make use of it to understand problems and provide timely support information.

Auction site eBay has become famous for using data about customer activity on the site and direct customer feedback to both improve and expand its operations. Here are a few of the many techniques eBay uses:

- Customers are able to rate sellers and leave feedback about their transactions with them. These customer ratings are useful to other customers and to eBay in its constant effort to prevent fraud on the site.

- eBay maintains chat rooms and an Answer Center where customers can ask questions of one another.

- A Security & (dispute) Resolution Center contains extensive information and places to register complaints about things like unreceived orders.

- eBay maintains its own panel—the eBay User Experience panel—that recruits participants on the site. Members are then included in online surveys and are eligible for personal visits from eBay staff who are collecting feedback or for usability studies of the Web site.

Figure 5-7 shows an example of one of the community techniques. On the eBay discussion boards visitors can participate in discussions on dozens of different topics grouped by specific products, community help, eBay tools, general discussions and workshops. New topics are added frequently.

There are many other activities on the site and local clubs in many cities and states where eBay sellers and buyers can get together and trade experiences. eBay executives take their community seriously. According to CEO Meg Whitman,

the community has my e-mail address. It's meg@ebay.com. I read all my own e-mail—anywhere from 100 to 500 e-mails a day—many of which are from the community. So I have a pretty good pulse of what's happening out there. Also, at least a couple of times a week, I check the eBay discussion boards. I can get a real good pulse there. And I often sit in on Voice of the Customer groups [which bring in sellers and buyers and poll them on site features and plans].[51]

| FIGURE 5-7 | One aspect of community—the discussion boards. |

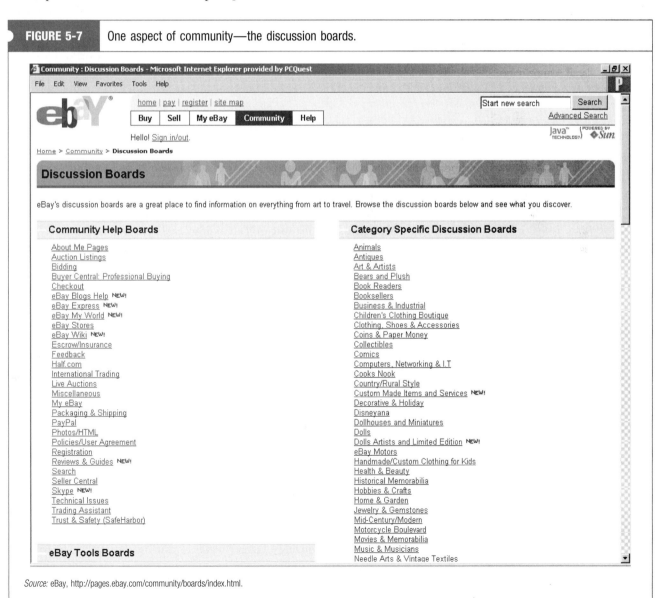

Source: eBay, http://pages.ebay.com/community/boards/index.html.

She adds that getting feedback from customers is much more efficient than trying to identify issues themselves.

But you may be thinking that Cisco Systems has a narrow target market of networking professionals and eBay has a unique business model. Their activities and results just aren't typical of other businesses. That is true only to a limited extent. Consider two things. First, as a customer, how often do you wish a retailer would listen to your problems and desires? Do you feel that businesses would be more successful if they did listen to customers' concerns? Second, why should marketers spend hundreds of thousands of dollars on marketing research before they mine the mass of rich data that is potentially available in their own customer records and Web sites—or before they make the effort to solicit unpaid customer feedback and to pay attention to what their customers are doing? Your answers are probably "Yes," and "They shouldn't do that!" However, like transactional data, capturing relevant customer interactions data and using the data wisely to inform marketing policies and programs is not a simple task. It also means that marketing and other top executives must listen to criticism, and that is never pleasant.

It is impossible to overstate the importance of the capture and creative use of online data, whether the data be usage, transactional, or customer feedback. It is equally difficult to overstate the difficulties of accomplishing this, especially in older, hierarchical organizations. Yet it is an essential competence for any enterprise that wishes to survive and prosper both on and off the Internet in the years to come. To illustrate these points, we conclude this chapter with a description of how various types of online research techniques can be used to support product development efforts.

5-9 Conducting Product Development Research on the Internet

Using the Internet to conduct research that supports the product development effort is currently in its infancy. Much of the early thinking is coming from academic researchers at Massachusetts Institute of Technology (MIT), Stanford University, and the University of California–Los Angeles (UCLA). The process that is being developed in MIT's Virtual Customer project consists of the following basic steps:

- Early in the product development process, a Web-based game called the "information pump" is used. It "provides incentives for truth-telling and thinking hard, thus providing new ways to verbalize the product features that are important to them."[52]

- Next, a large set of product features is screened quickly and inexpensively using an advanced statistical technique with the mind-numbing name of fast polyhedral adaptive conjoint estimation to identify the features that show most promise in further development efforts.

- As new product ideas move further through the development stage, virtual concept testing enables product development teams to test product concepts without actually building the product.

In conducting research throughout the various stages of the product development process, several innovative Web-based techniques are being used:

- Consumers are asked to make trade-offs that reveal the relative desirability of various product features. Long practiced in the offline world as the statistical technique called conjoint analysis, researchers can now use the Web to enhance the relevance of the data. This is done by taking advantage of the Web's ability to present products, product features, demonstrations of product use, and marketing elements like promotions in streaming multimedia formats.

TABLE 5-4	Web-Based Methods of Collecting Consumer Data about Products and Concepts

Method	Description of Respondents' Task
Web-based conjoint analysis (WCA)	Sort attribute-bundles by clicking on cards. To reduce the number of stimuli per screen, respondent presorts into three piles of cards.
Fast polyhedral adaptive conjoint estimation (FP)	Paired comparisons of attribute bundles. Respondent clicks radio buttons to express relative preferences between two stimuli.
User design (UD)	An "ideal" product is configured using drag-and-drop. Respondent trades off features against price or performance.
Virtual concept testing (VCT)	"Buy" from among competing concepts based on price and media-rich, integrated concepts. Analyzed as a two-attribute study.
Securities trading of concepts (STOC)	Each product is represented by a "security" and is bought and sold by respondents interacting with one another. Concepts can be richly depicted.
Information pump (IP)	Players formulate questions about product concepts and guess how others will react to their questions. Fine-tuned so that respondents think hard and tell the truth.

Source: Adapted from "The Predictive Power of Internet-Based Product Concept Testing Using Visual Depiction and Animation," http://www.anderson.ucla.edu/faculty/ely.dahan/content/predictive_power.pdf.

- Consumers can design their own virtual products "enabling the product development team to understand complex feature interactions and enabling customers to learn their own preferences for really new products."[53] This has been referred to as a **choiceboard**.[54]

- Stock market–like trading of virtual product concepts provides a new way to identify winning concepts before product prototypes are even produced.[55]

Table 5-4 gives a brief description of each technique, including the nature of the research task the respondent is asked to perform and the user interface encountered on the Web when performing the task. It will be useful to illustrate several of the techniques in the context of an actual research project.

To illustrate the viability of these techniques and to stress the fact that even relatively small companies can put them to good use, two Stanford University marketers designed a study of a new portable bicycle pump being designed by teams of Stanford engineering and MBA students. The essence of the project was as follows:

- Before beginning the design and prototype fabrication stage, the students used personal interviews with potential bicycle pump purchasers to identify five product attributes: size, durability, time for inflation, ease of inflation, and price.

- The five attributes were used in a trade-offs analysis to help the development teams understand the importance of each attribute and develop product concepts for testing. Figure 5-8 shows some of the visual stimuli used in the study for three of the products, AirStik, Epic, and 2wister. Some respondents saw a static depiction of the product while others saw an animated version. Both the static and animated versions of the product concepts were created using a commercial graphics program.

- When prototypes had been designed and built, the actual performance of each prototype was measured on each attribute.

- A final trade-offs analysis was conducted to estimate likely market shares for each of the nine new products against the two competitive products already available in the marketplace. Figure 5-9 shows the basic screen and a shot of the detail available if the respondent clicked on the product image.

The authors explain the research task as follows: Respondents express their preferences by clicking on the price tags below the eleven products in Figure 5-9. Each

choiceboard A customization technique in which people are asked to choose from a menu of options.

FIGURE 5-8   Static and animated product depictions.

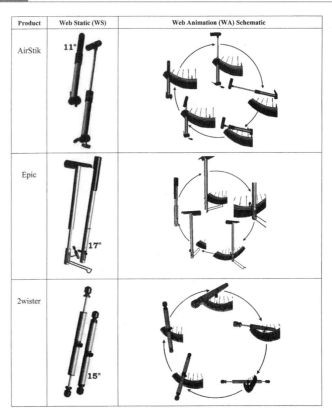

Source: "The Predictive Power of Internet-Based Product Concept Testing Using Visual Depiction and Animation," http://www.anderson.ucla.edu/faculty/ely.dahan/content/predictive_power.pdf.

FIGURE 5-9   Research task for trade-offs analysis.

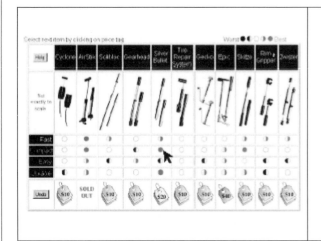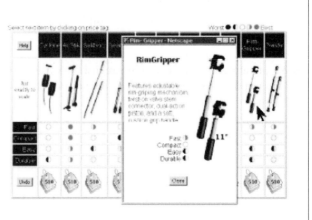

Source: "The Predictive Power of Internet-Based Product Concept Testing Using Visual Depiction and Animation," http://www.anderson.ucla.edu/faculty/ely.dahan/content/predictive_power.pdf.

TABLE 5-5	Predicted Market Shares of Bicycle Tire Product Concepts								
	Skitzo	**Silver Bullet**	**Epic**	**Rim Gripper**	**Gearhead**	**TRS**	**2wister**	**Gecko**	**Cyclone**
Physical (PP)	31.4	30.4	9.8	4.9	2.0	2.0	1.0	0.0	0.0
Animation (WA)	32.1	25.6	10.3	3.8	2.6	2.6	1.3	6.4	3.8
Static (WS)	27.6	32.2	11.5	2.3	1.1	1.1	0.0	2.3	0.0

Source: Adapted from "The Predictive Power of Internet-Based Product Concept Testing Using Visual Depiction and Animation," http://www.anderson.ucla.edu/faculty/ely.dahan/content/predictive_power.pdf.

product has three price tags below it—$10 on top, $20 in the middle, and $40 on the bottom. Initially the respondent chooses among all eleven products, each priced at $10. Suppose the respondent chooses AirStik. By clicking on the $10 price tag under AirStik, the selection is made and the price of AirStik goes up to $20. (The "Undo Selection" button enables the respondent to change his or her mind and return the most recently selected price tags to their original location.) The next selection for the respondent is therefore to choose among the eleven products with AirStik at $20 and all others at $10. In this case, suppose the respondent chooses Epic at $10. Epic's price increases to $20 and the next choice has nine products at $10 and the two others at $20, and so on. In Figure 5-9 the respondent has clicked on six price tags so far, the $10, $20, and $40 tags for AirStik, the $20 and $20 tags for Epic, and the $10 tag for Silver Bullet.[56]

- Finally, the ordering of the price choices produced statistics that allowed the researchers to compute the predicted market shares for each product as seen in Table 5-5. The row labeled "Physical" is the share prediction based on use of the actual physical prototypes. "Animation" is the group of respondents who saw the animated presentation of the concept, and "Static" identifies the group that saw the static presentation (see Figure 5-8). In the "Verbal" condition, respondents received only a verbal description of the product. The researchers concluded that both the static and animated product presentations did a better job of predicting than did the verbal-only descriptions. The verbal method consistently underpredicted the market share that would be achieved based on the actual performance of the bicycle pumps. They also pointed out that one product, Gecko, did receive a significantly higher score when either the animated or the static presentation was used. This was apparently because the computerized rendering made the product appear more attractive than it did when actually seen and handled.

The researchers also point out that both static and animated renderings produced essentially the same data, suggesting that the lower-cost static depictions could be relied on. In any event, the research suggests that, at the very least, virtual prototypes can be built and tested, reducing the number of physical prototypes that need to be built and therefore both the cost and time required by the prototyping stage.

This complex but interesting study illustrates a number of the potential advantages of product development research on the Web. Although they have no comparative data, the authors state that "firms can quickly generate multiple virtual prototypes and gather consumer preference data rapidly, and at very low cost."[57] It seems obvious that companies can indeed create virtual product prototypes more quickly and cheaply than they can make them using expensive and laborious techniques that often involve essentially hand-making the physical prototype. It is less obvious, but also true, that the complex trade-offs, questioning, and analysis can be greatly accelerated by interactive software that performs analytic routines and follow-on question development that, in the offline world, require several steps often separated by significant preparation time.

Summary

To understand Internet consumer behavior, it is necessary to expand on the traditional consumer decision process, putting it in a relational marketing context. It is also necessary to acknowledge that information acquisition as well as purchasing may be satisfactory outcomes on the net. Publicly available data about Internet consumers and their use behavior can help us understand the various stages. These data make it clear that the growth of the Internet is continuing around the world, with consumers showing more interest in online purchasing as the years pass. Still, online activities are heavily skewed toward communications, with relatively few consumers being active online purchasers. The ability of e-tailers to satisfy them is increasing, and the prospects for continued growth seem good.

Rarely, however, will the marketer's need for information about consumer behavior on the Internet be completely satisfied by publicly available data. This causes marketers to turn to their own data collection, either by means of online marketing research or by online capture of data about consumer use of the Internet and of the marketer's own Web site and the capture of data generated by transactions and by customer interactions with the enterprise. Conven-

tional marketing research techniques for the collection of both quantitative and qualitative data have been transferred onto the Web with considerable success. Online marketing research is comparatively quick and low in cost. The speed and quality of data preparation and analytics can also be greatly improved. The quality of results can also be enhanced by the use of techniques unique to the Web, such as computerized product renderings and the use of streaming media to present promotional material.

Wise capture and creative use of online data about consumers is one of the great challenges facing Internet marketers. Some data can be cost-effectively purchased from third-party data suppliers, but only the enterprise is privy to transactional data and it must capture data that provide "a 360° view" of the consumer.

Careful marketers will remain alert to public data and will be especially cognizant of data that reflect changes in their own industries. They will then move to answer their own specific and detailed questions about customers and prospects for their own products and visitors to their own Web sites. They will then use the data wisely and creatively to better serve their customers and to create greater value for all stakeholders.

Quiz

1. The model of consumer behavior on the Internet has the following important characteristic:
   a. It incorporates relationship marketing.
   b. It is entirely different from existing models of the consumer decision process.
   c. It requires metrics in addition to those available on the Internet.

2. Search behavior on the Internet _____.
   a. usually leads to an immediate purchase
   b. is usually conducted by brand name when people are interested in purchasing
   c. frequently leads to offline purchases

3. The primary Internet activity for most consumers can be described as _____.
   a. purchasing of goods and services
   b. communications and information search
   c. entertainment

4. Which of the following is a true statement about global Internet use?
   a. The United States leads in the number of people who have Internet access in their homes.
   b. In other countries, Internet use is developing in ways that are significantly different from historical patterns in the United States.

   c. The quality of e-commerce–related services has been decreasing in the United States.

5. Which of the following is a true statement about the digital divide?
   a. Consumers in the United States do not use public terminals to access the Internet.
   b. Studies show that households with higher levels of income and education are more likely to have Internet access at home.
   c. The digital divide has been documented only in the United States.

6. Which of the following characteristics can be used to describe a consumer Internet session?
   a. Length of the session
   b. Use of search engines
   c. Variety seeking

7. _____ is the name for the type of data derived directly from individual user mouse-clicks.
   a. Session data
   b. Primary data
   c. Clickstream data

8. Traditional methods used to collect marketing research data do *not* include _____.
   a. surveys

b. clickstreams

c. qualitative interviews

9. The term _____ describes a complete picture of a person's dealings with a specific business enterprise.

a. 360° view

b. primary data

c. interactions data

10. Advantages of conducting traditional marketing research on the Internet do *not* include _____.

a. opportunity to include rich media

b. automated data capture and reporting

c. access to many good e-mail lists

11. The marketing research technique that permits the collection of data about an individual consumer over time is _____.

a. survey research

b. consumer panel

c. sampling

12. _____ is a key type of data produced by online data capture.

a. Consumer purchase history

b. Consumer attitudes

c. Consumer demographics

Discussion Questions

1. What are the stages of Internet consumer behavior? What is the importance of the stages that come after "Purchase"?

2. What are the reasons most users access the Internet? Are there segments of consumers who might put entertainment at the top of their list? If so, who are they likely to be? Who is likely to be task-oriented?

3. What are some specific dimensions on which the global demographics of the Internet are changing? How do you expect these changes to affect use of the Internet?

4. What is the difference between online marketing research and online data capture? Be prepared to give an example of each.

5. *True or false:* Quantitative research is better suited to the Internet than is qualitative research. Be prepared to defend your position.

6. How does purchase history data differ from Internet usage data? Be prepared to give an example of each.

7. What are consumer interactions data, and why are they important to understanding and serving Internet consumers better?

8. The chapter states that organizational issues usually present the greatest barrier to successful capture and use of customer transactions data. Can you think of some ways in which organizational issues could impede the capture and use of marketing-relevant data?

9. Give a brief summary of some of the ways in which online marketing research can be used to improve both the speed and quality of new product development research.

Internet Exercises

1. Access the Internet to locate current statistics on consumer Internet use, including purchasing, in a country of your choice. You will find the references in the chapter useful in completing this assignment.

2. Select one of the three Web sites you are following for the semester. Using material from the site itself and from an Internet search, construct a detailed profile of the target market segment for the site. You may have to make some assumptions to make your profile reasonably complete; be specific about which elements are assumptions and the rationale for the assumptions you have made.

3. Again, select one of your three Web sites. Think about *(a) either the site itself or (b) a product or ser-*

vice that it sells, not both. As a marketer, what would you like to know (a) to improve the site or (b) to sell more of the product? Bring these to class in the form of "research questions," the issues a marketer wants to have resolved through marketing research.

4. Develop a scenario (a brief story) about a single-user session on the Internet—the purpose of the session, where the user goes, how long each site is visited how long each visit lasts (better?) and what types of pages are visited there, and why the visitor terminates the session, including anything special that happens in the course of moving around the net. Then come up with a list of data items that you believe would be generated by this session.

Notes

1. "Web Worldwide," accessed December 17, 2005, http://clickz.com/stats/web_worldwide/.
2. "Internet World Stats," accessed December 17, 2005, http://www.internetworldstats.com/stats.htm.
3. "USA Leads Broadband Subscriber Top 15 Ranking," November 14, 2005, http://www.c-i-a.com/pr1105.htm.
4. "2.14 billion Cell Phone Subscribers in 2005," May 20, 2005, Softpedia News, http://news.softpedia.com/news/2-14 billion-cell-phone-subscribers-in-2005-2120.shtml.
5. "Cell Phones to Ring in Slight Growth," May 9, 2005, CNET News, http://news.com.com/Cell+phones+to+ring+in+slight+growth/2100-1039_3-5700417.html.
6. "Internet Users Will Top 1 Billion by 2005," March 21, 2002, Computer Industry Almanac, http://www.c-i-a.com/pr032102.htm.
7. Donna L. Hoffman and Thomas P. Novak, "Marketing in a Hypermedia Computer-Mediated Environments: Conceptual Foundations," *Journal of Marketing*, 60, July 1996, pp. 50–68.
8. Deborah Fallows, "Reports: Demographics: How Women and Men Use the Internet," December 28, 2005, http://www.pewinternet.org/PPF/r/171/report_display.asp.
9. Carrie A. Johnson, "U.S.eCommerce: 2005 to 2010," September 14, 2005, Forrester Research, http://www.forrester.com/Research/Document/Excerpt/0,7211,37626,00.html.
10. "More Web Users Are Shopping Online," eMarketer, November 8, 2005, http://www.emarketer.com.
11. "The Digital Economy in Canada," April 16, 2004, http://strategis.ic.gc.ca/epic/internet/inecic-ceac.nsf/en/gv00237e.html.
12. "The Euros Are Coming!" eMarketer, July 12, 2005, http://www.emarketer.com.
13. "Belgium Online," eMarketer, November 7, 2005, http://www.emarketer.com.
14. "Ireland and Italy Online," eMarketer, December 27, 2005, http://www.emarketer.com.
15. "Europeans on an Online Spree," eMarketer, December 29, 2005, http://www.emarketer.com.
16. "Web Growing Faster Than Ever," eMarketer, October 13, 2005, http://www.emarketer.com.
17. "Who's Buying," BrandWeek, December 2, 2005, http://www.technologymarketing.com/bw/news/tech/article_display.jsp?vnu_content_id=1001613356.
18. Sean Michael Kerner, "Blog Readers Spend More Time and Money Online," ClickZ Stats, August 10, 2005, http://www.clickz.com/stats/sectors/demographics/article.php/3526591.
19. "Internet Retail Becoming a Woman's World," eMarketer, April 21, 2005, http://www.emarketer.com.
20. Lee Rainie, "Reports: Online Activities and Pursuits," Pew Internet & American Life Project, November 11, 2005, http://www.pewinternet.org/PPF/r/167/report_display.asp.
21. "Volume of Search Jumps 15 Percent in Past 5 Months," Nielsen//NetRatings Press Release, December 13, 2005, http://www.netratings.com/pr/pr_051213.pdf.
22. Suzy Bausch and Tracy Yen, "Online Shopping Grows 33% Year-over-Year during Sixth Week of Holiday Season," Nielsen//NetRatings Press Release, December 12, 2005, http://www.netratings.com/pr/pr_051212.pdf.
23. "comScore Study Reveals the Impact of Search Engine Usage on Consumer Buying," comScore Press Release, December 13, 2004, http://www.comscore.com/press/release.asp?press=526.
24. Search Before the Purchase," DoubleClick, February 2005, http://www.doubleclick.com/us/knowledge_central/documents/RESEARCH/searchpurchase_0502.pdf.
25. "DoubleClick's Touchpoints III," DoubleClick, July 2005, http://www.doubleclick.com/us/knowledge_central/documents/RESEARCH/dc_touchpointsIII_0507.pdf.
26. See a sample questionnaire at http://www.theacsi.org/ASSETS/sample_survey.pdf.
27. "Predictive Capabilities," http://www.theacsi.org/predictive_capabilities.htm.
28. "American Consumer Satisfaction Index Annual E-Business Report," FORESEE Results, August, 2005, http://www.foreseeresults.com/.
29. Enid Burns, "Customer Service Trumps Price," http://www.clickz.com/stats/sectors/retailing/article.php/3509301#table3.
30. Peter Bell and Pavani Reddy, "Rural Areas and the Internet," Pew Foundation, February 17, 2004, http://www.pewinternet.org/PPF/r/112/report_display.asp.
31. "Peer Pleasure: Teens Connect," MediaPost, March 24, 2005, http://www.centerformediaresearch.com/cfmr_brief.cfm?fnl=050324.
32. Amanda Lenhart, Mary Madden, and Paul Hitlin, "Teens and Technology," Pew Foundation, July 27, 2005, http://www.pewinternet.org/pdfs/PIP_Teens_Tech_July2005web.pdf.
33. Amanda Lenhart, Mary Madden, and Paul Hitlin, "Teens and Technology," Pew Foundation, July 27, 2005, http://www.pewinternet.org/pdfs/PIP_Teens_Tech_July2005web.pdf.
34. "Peer Pleasure: Teens Connect," MediaPost, March 24, 2005, http://www.centerformediaresearch.com/cfmr_brief.cfm?fnl=050324.
35. "Importance of Health Info Online to Take a Quantum Leap," MediaPost, March 9, 2005, http://www.centerformediaresearch.com/cfmr_brief.cfm?fnl=050309.
36. Susannah Fox, "Digital Divisions," Pew Foundation, October 5, 2005, p. 2, http://www.pewinternet.org/pdfs/PIP_Digital_Divisions_Oct_5_2005.pdf.
37. "All Visitors are Not Created Equal," McKinsey Marketing Practice, e-mail communication, December 7, 2005.
38. Bradley Johnson, "Marketing to American Luddites," *Ad Age Online,* March 7, 2005.
39. "Crossing the Digital Divide," eMarketer, November 1, 2005, http://www.emarketer.com.
40. Susannah Fox, "Digital Divisions," Pew Foundation, October 5, 2005, p. 3, http://www.pewinternet.org/pdfs/PIP_Digital_Divisions_Oct_5_2005.pdf.
41. "Crossing the Digital Divide," eMarketer, November 1, 2005, http://www.emarketer.com.
42. For a conceptual approach to online experimentation see A. Agrawal, J. Basak, V. Jain, R. Kothari, M. Kumar, P. A. Mittal, N. Modani, K. Ravikumar, Y. Sabharwal, and R. Sureka, "Online Marketing Research," *IBM Journal of Research and Development, Volume* 48, Number 5/6, 2004, http://www.research.ibm.com/journal/rd/485/basak.html.
43. For a good overview of marketing research basics see "The Research Methods Knowledge Base," http://www.social-researchmethods.net/kb/.
44. Troy Janish, "Talking 'Bout My Generation: The Evolution of Online Marketing Research," *Wisconsin Technology Network,* October 26, 2003, http://wistechnology.com/article.php?id=304.

45. "The Case for Online Research," eMarketer, November 11, 2004, http://www.emarketer.com.

46. "Conducting Online Research," CASRO, http://www.casro.org/faq.cfm.

47. Harris Online has an interesting demo that shows that essentially all types of survey questioning can be conducted online at http://survey.harrispollonline.com/w14975.htm.

48. Thomas W. Miller, "Can We Trust the Data of Online Research?" *Marketing Research,* Vol. 13, No. 2, pp. 26–32.

49. See, for example, the explanations to "How can I draw a sample of respondents?" and "How do I know whom I'm talking to?" on the FAQs page of CASRO, the Council of American Survey Research Organizations, http://www.casro.org/faq.cfm.

50. "What about qualitative research? Can Internet chat replace focus groups?" on the FAQs page of CASRO, the Council of American Survey Research Organizations, 1998, http://www.casro.org/faq.cfm.

51. "Meg Whitman on eBay's Self Regulation," *Business Week online,* August 18, 2003, http://www.businessweek.com/bwdaily/dnflash/aug2003/nf20030818_1844_db049.htm. Additional sources for this section included Robert D. Hof, "The People's Company," *Business Week e.biz,* December 3, 2001, EB15–EB16.

52. Ely Dahan and John Hauser, "The Virtual Customer: Communication, Conceptualization, and Computation," MIT working paper, September 2001, http://web.mit.edu/edahan/www/Virtual%20Customer.PDF.

53. Ely Dahan and John Hauser, "The Virtual Customer: Comm unication, Conceptualization, and Computation," MIT working paper, September 2001, http://web.mit.edu/edahan/www/Virtual%20Customer.PDF.

54. Adrian J. Slywotzky, "The Age of the Choiceboard," *Harvard Business Review,* January–February 2000, pp. 3–5.

55. See the Applied Marketing Science Web site for information on their ongoing research, http://www.ams-inc.com/.

56. Ely Dahan and V. Srinivasan, "The Predictive Power of Internet-Based Product Concept Testing Using Visual Depiction and Animation," *Journal of Product Innovation Management,* Vol. 17, No. 2, p. 105.

57. Ely Dahan and V. Srinivasan, "The Predictive Power of Internet-Based Product Concept Testing Using Visual Depiction and Animation," *Journal of Product Innovation Management,* Vol. 17, No. 2, p. 109.

Customer Acquisition: Brand Development and Online Advertising

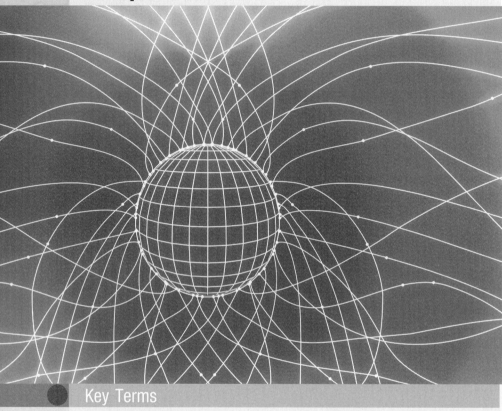

Source: © Getty

Key Terms

Learning Objectives

By the time you complete this chapter, you will be able to:

- Describe ways in which consumer media habits are changing.
- Discuss how brand development differs from direct response.
- Define major branding concepts.
- Understand how marketers are using online techniques to build and reinforce brands.

- List the major customer acquisition techniques, both online and offline.
- Identify the major online advertising formats.
- Explain ad serving.
- Describe the two techniques used to improve the targeting of online ads.

6-1 Customer Acquisition on the Internet

The way we think about customer acquisition in Internet space has changed as the Internet has matured. Those changes can be described as follows:

- Management pressure for accountability, in a return-on-investment sense, for all expenditures for customer acquisition
- Increasing knowledge about the power of integrated communications, with the Internet as an important part of the media mix
- Understanding of the power of the Internet as a branding medium
- Consumers' attempts to control their own media environment

In this chapter, we briefly discuss the changing media environment and then turn to a discussion of Internet branding and advertising. The next chapter discusses other customer acquisition techniques, including search marketing. Let's look first at the general outline of the new media landscape. Changing consumer habits, fueled by the growth of the Internet, are responsible for the change in the media environment.

6-2 Consumer Media Habits in the Internet Age

The Internet has helped consumers become accustomed to on-demand media that is available 24/7/365. It is not, however, the only factor. Consider for example, the phenomenal popularity of Apple's iPod. The iPod allows consumers to download their own music and create their own playlists. With the advent of **podcasting**, personal music players can do even more. An iPod or MP3 user signs up for **RSS** audio feeds, and when the content selected becomes available, the publisher pushes it to a podcasting aggregator, which then delivers it to the customer. The requested content then appears on the player automatically, and the customer can listen to it at his or her leisure. Will consumers who become accustomed to controlling their media content and use to this degree ever again be satisfied with an inflexible schedule of offerings from any medium? Many industry observers think not.

There are many media alternatives fueling consumer desire for on-demand content. Consider the following:

- DVDs offer large amounts of storage for entertainment and gaming applications.
- TiVo offers DVD-like access to television programming and the ability to fast-forward past advertising.

podcasting A service that uses RSS technology to download selected content to the user's iPod or desktop.

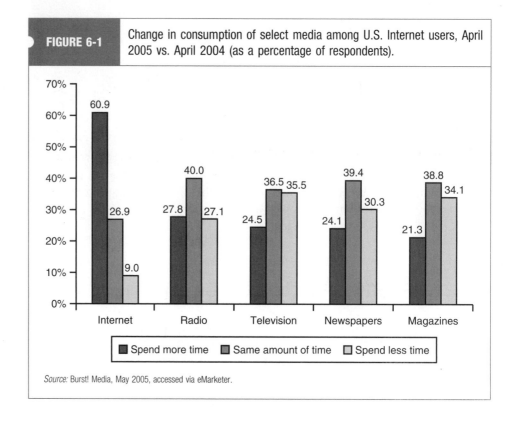

FIGURE 6-1 Change in consumption of select media among U.S. Internet users, April 2005 vs. April 2004 (as a percentage of respondents).

Spend more time ■ Same amount of time ■ Spend less time □

Source: Burst! Media, May 2005, accessed via eMarketer.

- Pay-per-view and v-ideo-on-demand television content allow viewers to watch what they want when they want without a wait.

- Content available via RSS feeds to mobile devices ranging from cell phones to portable computers to content players lets users acquire content as they need it.

And remember, streaming video on the Internet is becoming more and more available and popular as broadband becomes more widely available.

How has the new media landscape affected consumer media habits? Figure 6-1 indicates that the traditional media—radio, television, newspapers, and magazines— are experiencing less usage by 27.1% to 35.5% of U.S. Internet users. The Internet is the fastest-growing medium, with just over 60% of respondents spending more time using it than a year earlier.

Stanford University's Center for the Quantitative Study of Society examines time use among a representative national sample of Americans. Its most recent research finds that the average Internet user spends about 3 hours each day online (about 1 hour of which is at work), whereas the average respondent spends about 1.7 hours watching TV. For an average respondent, an hour on the Internet translates to 23.5 fewer minutes spent face to face with family members, 10 fewer minutes watching TV, and 8.5 fewer minutes sleeping.[1] A Pew Foundation report adds another dimension to changing consumer media habits: "The Internet was a key force in politics last year (2004) as 75 million Americans used it to get news, discuss candidates in emails, and participate directly in the political process."[2]

Consultant Tom Hespos recounts an experience that illustrates that the landscape in business-to-business (B2B) markets is changing also. The issue came to light when a client's **controlled circulation** trade publication began to show a decline in circulation. The client suspected competition from another print publication or perhaps from a specialized Web site. According to Hespos, this proved to be untrue:

> But that wasn't the case. Upon closer examination, we found that the publisher had debuted a PDF version of the magazine with enhanced functionality [....] and readers were opting to subscribe to [this] ... electronic version of the publication ... The

controlled circulation A type of business publication that is distributed free of charge to qualified members of a specific industry.

statistics on the electronic edition were astounding. For one, the electronic edition and the regular edition did not duplicate. At all. [. . . .] The publication's qualified circulation was opting for one or the other, not both ... Moreover, subscribers were writing to the publisher to express their views, stating their preference for the online version and asking the publisher to please ensure they no longer mailed copies of the magazine to their offices, but instead sent the subscriber a notification e-mail to let them know the instant that the online edition was available for download. [. . .] What looked on paper like a serious concern about audience migration turned out to be a terrific opportunity. When adding together the unduplicated audience of both print and online, the publisher was actually growing qualified audience at a healthy clip.[3]

This suggests that the changes in consumers' media habits are carrying over into their work lives. That is also true of the newer media that are full of consumer-created content.

6-3 Consumer-Controlled Media

User creation of content on the Web is not new. In fact, many of the earliest sites were personal Web pages like David Filo's page of URLs that eventually grew into Yahoo! Other early sites have retained more of their original character. Founded in 1995, craigslist was created as a community service in San Francisco and quickly became a popular place to post local items, such as apartments for rent or merchandise for sale. It became so popular that founder Craig Newmark was forced to incorporate in 1999. By late 2005, it served 190 cities in 36 countries.[4] Sites from Amazon to CitySearch encourage reviews of products and merchants. And, of course, there is eBay, the epitome of customer-created content.

In recent years, new applications have emerged to encourage consumers to create their own content. Some of the most popular include the following:

- Photo-sharing sites such as Flickr and Snapfish that offer a range of services, including uploading of digital photos, creation of interactive albums, and sharing with a list of friends.
- Sites that allow consumers to create news videos (http://www.current.tv/) or their own ads (http://www.adcandy.com).
- Sites that rely on users for content. dmoz, the Open Directory Project, has more than 70,000 volunteer editors who contribute links to the site. Wikipedia is an online encyclopedia whose English version has almost 900,000 articles on many subjects. Both these are nonprofit sites run by small paid staffs and depend on volunteers for content.
- Chat rooms and social networks where people can meet and interact with others. Friendster was one of the first and MySpace, where people can create individual spaces much like Web pages, has become wildly popular among teens.
- Social or personalized search applications such as del.icio.us (social bookmarks), digg (technology news), and Slashdot ("News for Nerds"[5]) that let users assign keywords (**tags**) that reflect their own interests to Web content. Social search has become so popular that it has spawned an engine to search the "tagosphere," the sites that allow users to create their own tags. Wink bills itself as "This isn't your Dad's search engine,"[6] an indisputable statement.

tags a user-supplied keyword or category name.

Young Internet users are especially active in content creation. The Pew Foundation estimates that 57% of teenage Internet users have "created a **blog** or webpage, posted original artwork, photography, stories or videos online or remixed online content into their own new creations."[7]

Blogs are not only popular among teenagers; they have become a staple of communication among many age groups and thrive in business as well as consumer markets. Technorati, a blog search service, reported that there were more than 23 million blogs in late 2005, with more being added daily. Internet users can build blogs free of charge on unpaid sites like Blogger or gain more editorial control over their content on paid sites like TypePad. The word *blog* is a corruption of *Web logs*, which aptly describes the content of many blogs. They reflect the personal thoughts and experiences of their authors. Some blogs develop substantial traffic; others would seem to be interesting only to their creators.

Blogging in the business world is controversial. Some corporations frown on employee blogs, and people have been fired over content their employers found undesirable. IBM and Microsoft actively encourage employees to blog, and Microsoft is said to use blogs for internal communications. General Motors Vice Chairman Bob Lutz has a popular and informative blog called FastLane. On the negative side, blogs written by dissatisfied customers can quickly spread unfavorable word of mouth, as Dell discovered to its dismay in the summer of 2005.[8] This kind of Internet content is so important that a primary duty of public relations has become monitoring everything written about the business on the Web, whether it is written by professionals or by customers.

Marketers have begun to advertise on blogs because they reach highly targeted audiences, such as technology professionals, that can be a good fit with target segments. Other personal media also reach very desirable targets like teenagers and young adults. Marketers are struggling to come up with creative ways to reach these consumers, who, after all, are using these communications techniques to control their own interactions. Traditional advertising is likely not to be welcome in that context.

The growth of these media adds another piece to the puzzle of appropriate media choice and integrated messages in today's complex communications environment.

6-4 Leveraging the Media Mix

All this consumer information gives the impression that people are leaving traditional media and flocking to the Internet in droves. Although this is true, many Internet users do not totally abandon traditional media vehicles. Figure 6-2 shows the specific

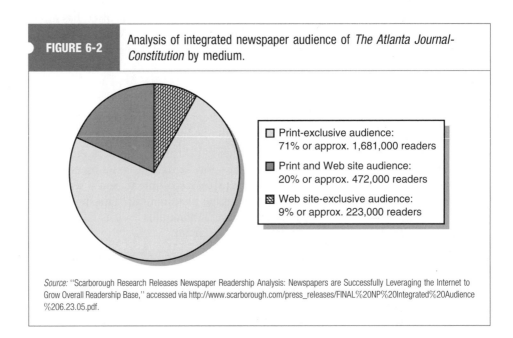

FIGURE 6-2 Analysis of integrated newspaper audience of *The Atlanta Journal-Constitution* by medium.

☐ Print-exclusive audience:
71% or approx. 1,681,000 readers

■ Print and Web site audience:
20% or approx. 472,000 readers

▨ Web site-exclusive audience:
9% or approx. 223,000 readers

Source: "Scarborough Research Releases Newspaper Readership Analysis: Newspapers are Successfully Leveraging the Internet to Grow Overall Readership Base," accessed via http://www.scarborough.com/press_releases/FINAL%20NP%20Integrated%20Audience%206.23.05.pdf.

example of *The Atlanta Journal-Constitution*. Only 9% read the newspaper only online, whereas 20% read it both online and in print.

According to Scarborough Research, which conducted the study, newspapers are leveraging the power of the Web to attract larger audiences, especially younger readers. Jim Wilson, the Director of Research and Audience Development at *The Atlanta Journal-Constitution*, comments:

> We no longer consider our print audience to be separate from our online audience. We provide our advertisers with multiple channels for reaching adults in Atlanta, and our reach within our marketplace is growing . . . For example, the audience for *AJC.com* and *AccessAtlanta.com* is significantly younger than the audience of the printed newspaper. While about 28 percent of the readers of the printed newspaper are between the ages of 18 and 34, over 38 percent of the Web sites' audience is in this age group.

Marketers have long understood that different media channels can reach different target audiences and have disparate effects on the people they do reach. Research firm Dynamic Logic conducted a study in which it measured the impact of adding magazines and the Internet to media plans that contained television only. Figure 6-3 shows results at different stages of the purchase process averaged over eight advertising campaigns. The Internet bar represents adding Internet to TV alone. The magazine bar shows the change if magazines are added to TV and Internet. The graph shows that all three media increased consumer brand awareness, preference, and purchase intent. In other words, each medium had an incremental impact, which is good news to the marketer who is spending incremental dollars.

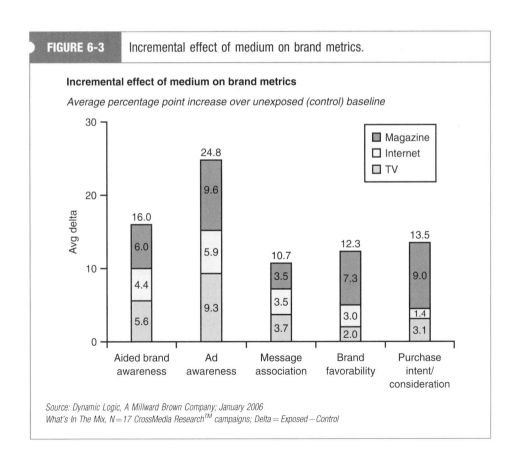

> **FIGURE 6-3** Incremental effect of medium on brand metrics.

Incremental effect of medium on brand metrics

Average percentage point increase over unexposed (control) baseline

Source: Dynamic Logic, A Millward Brown Company; January 2006
What's In The Mix, N=17 CrossMedia Research™ campaigns; Delta = Exposed – Control

aided brand awareness The ability of a respondent to identify a brand when prompted.

message association The ability of a respondent to recall some of the copy points of an ad to which he or she has been exposed.

purchase intent The self-reported likelihood that the respondent will make a purchase within a stated time frame.

ad serving The process of supplying advertising elements while a page is loading on a user's browser. Ads are served by an advertising network and are placed on the basis of user profiles.

Upon closer inspection of the data, the research firm also found the following:

- TV, Internet, and magazines each produced similar increases in **aided brand awareness**.
- TV and magazine produced greater changes than Internet in advertising awareness. The three media produced equal impact on **message association**, while magazines were better at increasing brand favorability and **purchase intent**. They speculated that this might be because the magazine ads had more product information.[9]

Ad serving firm DoubleClick conducted a similar study in which media impact was studied in ten different product categories. This study differentiates between the impact of the Web site alone and Internet Marketing, which includes both advertising and email marketing. They found that TV advertising was more effective, sometimes by a substantial amount, in raising brand awareness in five of the ten product categories studied. Travel was an exception in which the Web site was most effective in raising awareness. At another stage in the process the impact of media was different. They found that Web sites had the most impact on purchases in seven of the ten categories studied.[10]

Some of the most careful studies of adding interactive to the media mix are part of the Cross-Media Optimization Study (XMOS) of the Internet Advertising Bureau (IAB), the industry trade association. They take the concept of the impact of interactive one step further by searching for the optimal media mix. Two examples illustrate the opportunities:

- A study was conducted in conjunction with the introduction of Unilever's Dove Nutrium brand. The basic research design was to run print advertising only in week 1, add online in week 2, and television in week 3. Researchers collected brand-related metrics from 13,000 women over the 3-week period. The study concluded that keeping the total advertising budget constant but increasing online spending from 2% to 15% would produce an 8% increase in overall branding impact and a 14% increase in purchase intent without increasing the advertising budget.[11]
- When McDonald's introduced its Grilled Chicken Flatbread Sandwich in selected markets, it needed to raise understanding of "emotive" product attributes such as novelty and good taste and to drive purchase, especially among the primary target, adults 18 to 24. It added interactive marketing to a mix that included radio, print, and television. McDonald's found that by increasing online advertising, it was able to increase product awareness among the target market. Twenty percent of the people in that target are not heavy television users, but they are reachable online. In addition, the study found that television and radio advertising had little impact on the image attribute "combination of great flavors," but online marketing greatly increased perception of this attribute.[12]

These studies illustrate the complexity of media planning in the complex and rapidly changing media environment. Note that they both involve brands of traditional mass media marketers. This research also makes clear the importance of understanding the impact of the Internet on branding.

6-5 Building Internet Brands

Although there is much controversy swirling around issues relating to building brands on the Internet, there is no disputing one simple point: having a strong and trusted brand is essential to success on the Web. Visitors surf in from a variety of sources, ranging from search engines to affiliate links to offline promotions. They are reluctant to give their money to an entity with which they do not have an established relationship. A known and trusted brand gives the greatest possible reassurance that they will have a satisfactory purchase and use experience. This leads us to the concept known as brand equity.

6-5a Brand Equity and Brand Image

The strength of a brand is measured by **brand equity**. A number of definitions of brand equity exist, but the definition attributed to the Marketing Science Institute is comprehensive. It defines brand equity as:

> The set of associations and behaviors on the part of the brand's customers, channel members, and parent corporation that permits the brand to earn greater volume or greater margins than it could without the brand name and that gives the brand a strong, sustainable, and differentiated advantage over competitors.[13]

Brand equity is a concept that describes a financial asset as well as a competitive advantage. The issue for marketers is what activities and results are necessary to create a brand that becomes a source of both competitive and financial advantage.

The marketing issues are encapsulated in two concepts: *brand awareness* and *brand image*. Brand awareness has two levels. If consumers remember seeing or hearing about a brand, that is evidence of **brand recognition**. Recognition is measured by showing a representation (e.g., product, ad) and asking if members of the target group remember having seen or heard of it. Brand recognition is most likely to be achieved through repeated exposure to brand-related messages and images. Recall is considered a higher level of branding than is mere recognition. It involves being able to remember information about the product or brand.

Brand awareness alone is not sufficient to drive behavior when the product or service in question requires any significant level of involvement and information processing. The purchase of high-involvement products generally requires a brand image with strong and positive brand associations. Powerful incentives can compensate for some lack of strength in brand image, but not all. A strong brand image is essential for consumer comfort in an unfamiliar purchasing situation like the Internet. In Figure 6-3 this was referred to as brand favorability, and it was the last stage before the consumer developed purchase intent.

Low-involvement products, on the other hand, require less effort and involvement on the part of the customer who may take action on the basis of awareness alone. Low-involvement items can usually be equated to low-margin (convenience) products. Whether the brand is low involvement or **high involvement**, creating a trusted brand is a lengthy and expensive process, but it creates a lasting competitive advantage, especially in the impersonal environment of the Web.

6-5b Creating a Strong Brand on the Internet

Advertising executives Larry Chiagouris and Brant Wansley identify four stages in the brand-building process that are reminiscent of the advertising hierarchy of effects and stages in the media mix research just described (Figure 6-4).

brand equity The value of a brand, measured in financial terms.

brand image The advertising metric that measures the type and favorability of consumer perceptions of the brand.

brand recognition/brand awareness The advertising metric that measures the ability of target consumers to identify the brand under different questioning scenarios.

low involvement A purchase situation on which consumer spends little time or thought.

high involvement A purchase situation in which the consumer performs an information search and undergoes an extensive choice process.

> **FIGURE 6-4**   The four stages of brand building.

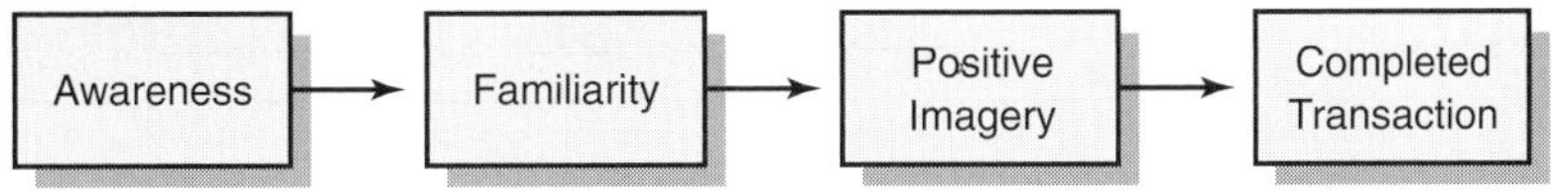

Awareness → Familiarity → Positive Imagery → Completed Transaction

Awareness represents a nodding acquaintance with the brand and, as noted, is measured by ability to recognize the brand or to recall being exposed to it. Familiarity suggests some knowledge of the product, its features, and services offered. It is measured by asking about recall of message points from the ad.

The next stage is the creation of a positive brand image. According to Keller:

> A positive brand image is created by marketing programs that link strong, favorable, and unique associations to the brand in memory. The definition of customer-based brand equity does not distinguish between the source of brand associations and the manner in which they are formed; all that matters is the resulting *favorability, strength,* and *uniqueness* [emphasis mine] of brand associations.[14]

The final stage in this model, the transaction itself, should be the beginning of a relationship, not the end of a process. Traditional brand building, however, has been done in the mass media, where the maintenance and deepening of relationships is difficult because of the inability of those media to address consumers based on their stage of relationship development. *The best brand building on the Internet will fuse the attention-getting power of the Web's interactive environment with the targeted relationship techniques of information-driven direct marketing. It will be tightly integrated with offline brand development activities.*

The marketing activities involved in good brand building are rather hard to separate into discrete stages, as the different terminology used by different authors suggests. However, the ideas about how one builds a good and trusted brand are the same. Good brand building in traditional media is rich in imagery and can address the stage in which the consumer finds himself at a given time. Let's look at two examples of using the unique strengths of the Web to develop strong imagery. Interestingly enough, both Gillette and BMW (see Cases in Point 6-1) are marketers of well-established offline brands.

Cases in Point 6-1   Gillette and BMW

Gillette, the maker of personal care products for both men and women, is a good example of mass distribution products that do not seem to lend themselves to being the stars of a Web site with a compelling branding message. Yet

Gillette has learned to use the interactivity of the Web to create a series of sites that draw visitors back. Figure 6-5 shows shots from the Mach3 razor site. It is full of Flash demonstrations and the sounds of racing cars. It offers a

FIGURE 6-5   Gillette's pages for the Mach3.

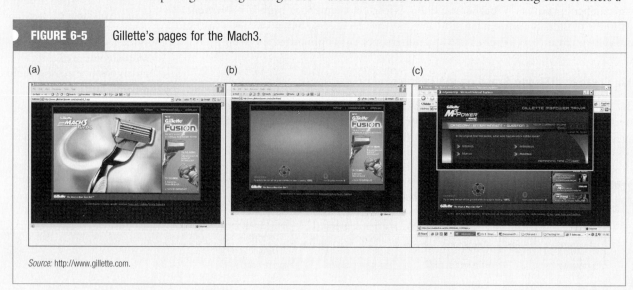

(a)   (b)   (c)

Source: http://www.gillette.com.

razor demonstration and features a great deal of interactive content, some of which seems only tangentially related to a razor. Yet the message of speed and power comes through on every page.

On the page that features British soccer star David Beckham, the visitor is challenged to keep the soccer ball in the air while the page loads. The visitor can then go to a Trivia section that has questions on sports, entertainment, music, or technology. The page also contains links to a contest as well as to pages that give more detailed product information. The corresponding site for the Venus razor for women (http://www.gillettevenus.com) uses many of the same techniques but places more emphasis on beauty and skin care tips. The Gillette sites (there are ten to twelve of them at any given time) often do not have a strong call to action, such as a coupon for a trial purchase of the razor. They do, however, support their mass market channels of distribution by providing "Where to Buy" pages.

Consider a different approach by another experienced offline marketer—BMW. *Advertising Age* describes the situation faced by BMW and its advertising agency, Fallon Worldwide, in 2000:

> [B]oth the BMW and Fallon people were growing increasingly concerned with their ability to reach their core market of overachieving, hard-working Bimmer buyers via traditional methods such as network TV.

Their research indicated that many were tech-savvy and had fast, reliable access to the Web. Most important, 85% of buyers had researched their car purchase on the Web before stepping into a showroom.[15]

BMW and Fallon needed to reach their target audience with a message that did not recall the yuppie arrogance of the 1990s and that emphasized performance without looking like all the other car ads on TV.

The solution was to create short, high-quality films to be played over the Internet. The innovative advertising approach created buzz in the industry; the use of internationally recognized movie directors helped generate buzz among the target audience. The series was entitled *The Hire* and eventually consisted of eight different films. The lead character in the films was called The Driver, played by actor Clive Owen. Each film featured a different BMW model.

The Promotion Marketing Council says that "The objectives of the BMW Films promotion were to make the brand relevant and cool to young customers between the ages of 25 and 44 who are entering the luxury car market, without alienating current owners, and to bring qualified buyers in the same demographic into the fold in a way to increase sales, especially of the bread-and-butter 3 Series."[16] The films won numerous advertising and film industry awards. More important, they were wildly successful among the primary target audience. During

FIGURE 6-6　BMWs *The Hire.*

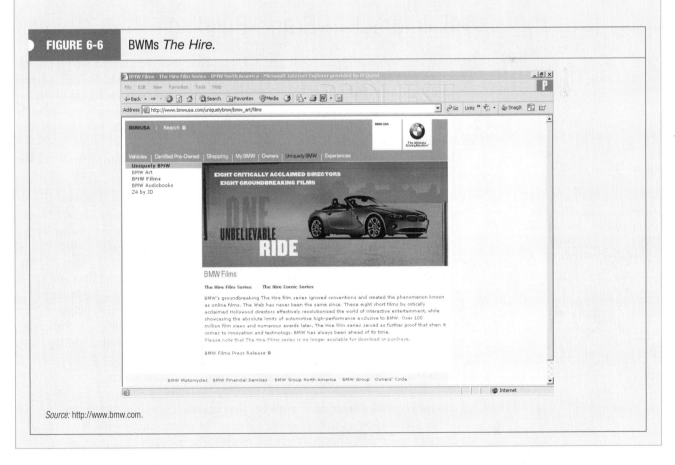

Source: http://www.bmw.com.

their initial 4-month run in 2001, the original films were viewed more than 11 million times, causing more visits than the Web site was designed to handle. They were responsible for large increases in relevant brand measures. In particular, a 77% increase was realized among members of the target audience who saw the films in the metric "BMW is a brand for people like me." Planned visits to BMW dealers soared, and 2001 sales increased by 12.5% without the benefit of a major product launch.[17]

By 2005 they were ready for a different approach. They turned the story line into a series of comic books from Dark Horse Comics. The comics were designed to continue the action theme of the films. Like the films, the comics were created by respected industry teams in order to give the entire series an aura of quality.

BMW continues to innovate in the arena of online video. They recently launched a line of short films to promote the Mini Cooper brand. The films feature a day in the life of a Mini Cooper Cabrio, the two roadies who drive it, and their bulldog companion. The Web site features the

trio and their Mini Cooper at different times of the day. It also offers a game called Hacky Sack and e-cards with scenes from the video clips. It is tightly integrated with information about the car itself, providing opportunities to get more product information and then resume watching the film, all accessible through their international Web site http://www.mini.com/com/en/general/homepage/index.jsp. In the United States Mini Cooper created a set of video clips called Hammer and Coop http://www.hammerandcoop.com/#. These videos feature a driver called Jim Turtledove and his car—the Coop. The edgy character is reported to have his own Second Life page and avatar and he encourages customers to share photos on his Flickr site.[18]

What both Gillette and BMW have done is to use the interactivity, immediacy, and involvement of the Internet to draw viewers to their site, where they deliver strong brand messages. These methods bear the stamp of the brand-building activities of both firms in mass media.

6-6 Interactive Brand Building

Pure-play e-commerce firms must build a brand on the Web, often supported by offline media. They are likely to make use of a wide array of interactive brand-building techniques to do so.[19] Canadian organic cosmetics retailer Saffron Rouge is a good example. The interactivity and the information richness of the site are immediately evident to the new visitor, who is presented with a pop-up with links to detailed information about Saffron Rouge (Figure 6-7).

The site makes use of powerful tools for building or supporting brands on the Internet. These include:

personalization The process of preparing an individualized communication for a specific person based on stated or implied preferences.

- *Personalization tools.* Like most Web sites, Saffron Rouge greets registered customers by name when they enter the site. It also offers an e-mail newsletter, "Inner Beauty." Unlike most sites, however, it tries to draw in the prospective customer immediately by responding to an e-mail newsletter subscription request by instantaneously sending the most recent issue of its newsletter.

  As the customer relationship deepens, the site captures customer data and is able to personalize newsletter content for the customer. This site goes further into such personalization, customizing marketing campaigns to her buying behavior. For example, a customer who has spent more than $500 over a lifetime but has not purchased for 9 months will receive a different marketing message than the customer who has only bought a total of $50 and has not purchased for 6 months.[20]

- *Purchase-process streamlining tools.* Saffron Rouge offers a shopping cart that can be saved if the customer does not wish to complete the transaction at that moment. It also offers the option to save customer information like mailing addresses and credit card numbers for use with later orders.

| FIGURE 6-7 | Saffron Rouge's Web offerings. |

Source: http://www.saffronrouge.com/site/home.html.

- *Self-service tools.* In many ways an e-commerce Web site is inherently a self-service activity. Skilled marketers use information and interactivity to encourage sales without additional human support but offer access to support when it is needed. On the Saffron Rouge site, clicking on any product image produces details on product use and ingredients and a link to the live chat feature if the viewer has further questions.

- *Customization tools.* Cosmetics do not seem to lend themselves readily to customized products because of testing and other regulatory issues. You might, however, enjoy visiting the BMW site and designing your own car.

- *Dynamic-pricing tools.* It is hard for users to see the degree to which prices are varied on a site, but it is becoming an increasingly common strategy. It may depend on data such as where the visitor lives (is there a retail store in the zip code that offers substantial competition in the cosmetics category?) or individual purchasing patterns (incentives to infrequent purchasers; reward programs for frequent customers). They can, however, see dynamic pricing in action on auction sites like eBay or on Amazon's auction pages.

- The prospect of creating *community* on the Web is of great interest to marketers. In the offline world, there are a few superb examples of brand communities that are full of brand evangelists who ardently spread the word about the brand. Chief

customization The process of producing a product, service, or communication to the exact specifications/desires of the purchaser or recipient.

dynamic pricing Having different prices to meet different market conditions at the same time.

community A group of like-minded people.

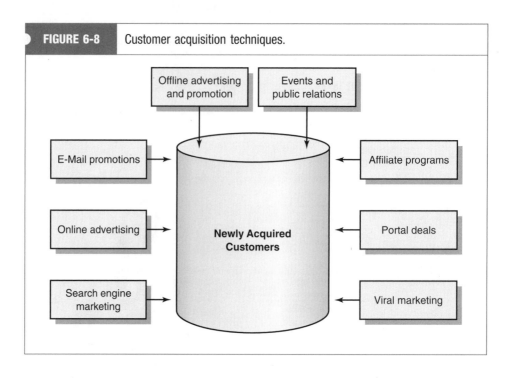

FIGURE 6-8 Customer acquisition techniques.

among them are the HOGs—the Harley Owners Group, who travel and interact together offline as well as on the Harley-Davidson Web site. In recent years, video gaming has moved onto the Web and offers an ideal opportunity for creating community around the various game platforms. Games.net (Figure 6-8) offers gamers the opportunity to meet and compete against people with compatible game platforms—a ready-made online community. Gamers tend to be avid about games and gaming and to enjoy talking about it with other aficionados. Games.net offers links to the blogs of members of the site where dialog can take place. This offers a popular type of *co-creation of content* on their site.

co-creation Customer participation in producing content for a site.

These four applications—Gillette, BMW, Saffron Rouge, and Games.net—have both similarities and differences. The most striking difference is that Gillette and BMW have major offline presences in terms of both promotion and retailing. Saffron Rouge is a brand that is being created on the Web, although they clearly also have the objective of building a retail chain. Games.net offers a richly interactive place for gamers to meet and a targeted audience for advertisers. All use interactivity well, and all provide information appropriate to the product category and target market. It is possible, although very expensive (as Amazon and eBay could tell you), to build a brand solely on the Internet. It is essential to support strong offline brands with appropriate Internet brand development techniques.

A strong brand is an important asset in all stages of the customer cycle—acquisition, conversion, and retention. In the same sense, every contact with the customer can be viewed as an opportunity to build positive brand associations. However, customer acquisition is where it all begins, and we turn now to a discussion of customer acquisition techniques.

6-7 Internet Customer Acquisition Techniques

Although there are a number of methods of acquiring new Internet customers in business-to-customer (B2C), B2B, and organizational markets, they fall into several basic categories, as shown in Figure 6-8.

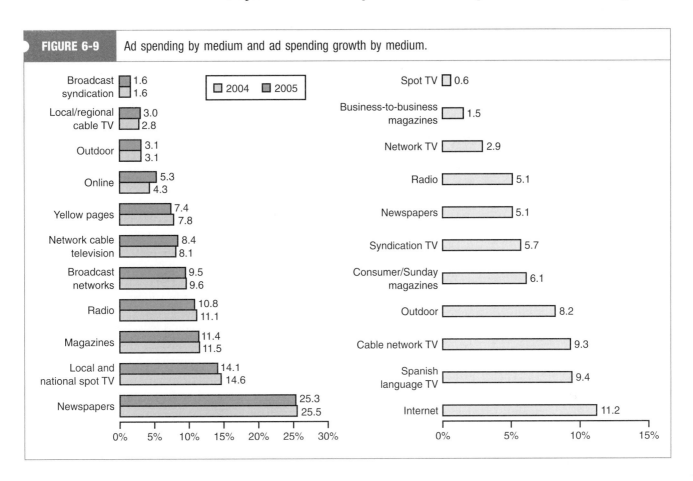

FIGURE 6-9 Ad spending by medium and ad spending growth by medium.

They are invariably used in combination with one another, as discussed earlier in the chapter. To better understand the complex issues of developing an effective media mix, it is necessary to understand the strengths and weaknesses of each medium. In the following sections, we discuss online advertising. In the following chapter, we discuss e-mail promotions, search engine marketing (SEM), and a number of other promotional categories. In so doing, we will keep in mind the fact that any and all of these techniques can and should be used in concert with the traditional tools of offline advertising and promotion. That is the essence of integrated communications strategies.

It is also important understand the subject in the context of overall promotional spending by marketers. Figure 6-9 gives two perspectives, expenditure by medium and rate of growth in spending by medium. You may be surprised to see newspapers as the leader, but notice that television is broken into several different categories. Notice also that online is a small proportion of the total. Figure 6-9 shows media spending by rate of growth. Internet is the fastest growing, with Spanish-language TV and cable TV close behind. According to the American Association of Advertising's Survey of Industry Leaders, there are several reasons for the rapid growth of online advertising. They include its ability to demonstrate return on investment (ROI), the ability of new ad formats to break through advertising clutter, the ability to engage in precise targeting, and the ability to complement and enhance the traditional media of advertising.[21]

6-8 Online Advertising

Two examples from the IAB illustrate the growing power of Internet advertising:

• When Universal Studios released the DVD of *E.T. the Extra-Terrestrial*, its promotional objective was to generate purchase interest among the target market of 25 to 49 year olds. It wanted to portray the film as one of the most beloved movies of all time and to communicate the fact that the DVD featured new footage and enhanced visual effects. The lion's share, 94%, of the budget went to television, with 6% being allocated to banner ads. Less than 1% was allocated to rich media ads that floated animations on top of Web pages, a technique called "overlay." The effectiveness study was conducted among people who were exposed to both the TV and the Internet ads. According to the IAB, "The most striking finding of this study was the effectiveness of the rich media component of the campaign. Although rich media was a small part of the budget, its results were dramatic, especially for the audience segment that was exposed to it in combination with TV and banner ads." Of those exposed only to the TV ad, 19.9% said they would definitely or probably buy the DVD. That compared with 22.7% who also saw a banner ad, and 25.4% who saw the TV and the rich media overlay. In addition, the key brand messages were also better remembered by respondents who had an opportunity to see the rich media ads. This led the IAB to conclude that the rich media overlay ads were the most cost-effective, despite the fact that their CPM (cost per thousand advertising impressions) was higher than either the banner or the TV ads. Further analysis indicated that the optimal media mix, in terms of reach not dollars, would have been 25% of the target audience reached through rich media overlay ads, 2% through banners, and 72% by television. This would have increased purchase intent by 2 points without increasing the advertising budget.[22]

- For two decades, the Ford F-150 pickup had been the best-selling vehicle in the United States, and the launch of a new model in late 2003 was an important event for Ford. It was supported with one of the largest-ever advertising campaigns in both English and Spanish on TV and radio, in print, and through outdoor advertising and direct mail. In the context of this large campaign Ford wanted to understand the effectiveness of the Internet in supporting branding impact and actual new vehicle sales and leasing. They ran standard online advertising units on the leading car-related sites, which were known to be visited by consumers who were researching cars in the early stages of their purchase process. For major portal sites, their agency developed a rich media page takeover ad they called a "digital roadblock." These ads appeared at the same time on high-traffic pages of AOL, MSN, and Yahoo! on two key days, one of which coincided with the mass media campaign launch. This ensured that a large portion of the online audience would see the ads. TV generated the highest reach and increase in purchase intentions but was less cost-effective than the other media. The online ads on the auto-related pages were the most cost-effective in terms of raising purchase intention. The roadblock online ads and the magazine ads were less cost-effective than the standard online ads but more cost-effective than television. IAB concluded that "The superior cost-effectiveness of the ads on auto-related sites, targeting specifically to an in-market car-buying audience, highlights the potential of the Web as a powerful medium for reaching prospects at the bottom of the 'sales funnel,' when they are close to making a buying decision."[23]

Notice that the so-called road block resulted from a particular approach to buying the advertising media. Specialized or highly targeted media buys are likely to become more common in the years to come. Some sites offer specific opportunities. For example, Boston.com, the online division of the *Boston Globe,* offers a Surround Session. What they are essentially doing is guaranteeing exclusivity to the advertiser for a specified period. All standard positions on a given page are reserved for a single advertiser. This might mean, for example, that the advertiser would have a leaderboard, a skyscraper, and a big rectangle (see Table 6-1) all on the same page at the same time. This exclusivity follows the visitor for four more

| TABLE 6-1 | Standard Internet Ad Formats |

Format	Size in Pixels
Banners and Buttons	
Full banner	468 × 60
Half banner	234 × 60
Micro bar	88 × 31
Button 1	120 × 90
Button 2	120 × 90
Vertical banner	120 × 240
Square button	125 × 125
Leaderboard	728 × 90
Rectangles and Pop-Ups	
Medium rectangle	468 × 60
Square pop-up	250 × 250
Vertical rectangle	240 × 400
Large rectangle	366 × 280
Rectangle	180 × 150
Skyscrapers	
Wide skyscraper	160 × 600
Skyscraper	120 × 600
Half-page ad	300 × 600

pages as he or she moves through the site, guaranteeing the advertiser five pages on which the individual visitor sees no other advertising.[24] Specialized media buys may become more common as more advertisers experiment with Internet advertising.

The *E.T.* and Ford research, as well as other campaigns that are part of the XMOS study, attests to the growing power of Internet advertising. This research also attests to its growing complexity. To understand this complexity, we first look at the basic online advertising formats. Then we look at online targeting techniques that may point the way to the future of online ads.

6-8a Online Advertising Formats

The IAB maintains the definitive—and ever-changing—set of standards for Internet advertising formats.[25] This includes elements such as size and guidelines for animation. However, many large publishers offer ad formats that are not included on the standard list, so it is important to carefully investigate individual sites. Sites that accept advertising usually have an online media kit that contains the usual information about the types of ads accepted, the pages on which various types can be placed, and programming specifications for the ads. What they do not usually contain, at least in the United States, is costs, although the *New York Times* recently added an online rate card.[26] There seems to be a greater likelihood that you will find a rate card on European sites.[27] There are two key reasons for the hesitation of sites to publish advertising rates on the Internet. First, most online campaigns are sold as packages, including more than one of the formats described in Table 6-1. Second, and probably more important, the volatility of the Internet advertising environment leaves most rates open to negotiation between advertiser and site.

Table 6-1 lists the basic ad formats and gives their size in **pixels**. All the standard formats can accept simple animation (animated **GIFs**) and **Flash**. Again, not all sites

pixel Short for picture element, a single point on a display screen or in a graphic image.

GIF An acronym for graphics interchange format, one of the common types of image files used on the Web.

flash An application development tool that allows programmers to create files with audio and streaming video that can be played on a Web browser equipped with the Flash player.

rich media Ads that can include video and audio.

offer interactivity in their ads. However, as the case histories given earlier suggest, so-called **rich media** is important in gaining attention and making a branding impact.

6-8b Rich Media

If you look in seven different places, you will find seven different definitions of rich media. Some writers define it according to the technology used. They point out that rich media can accept audio, video, and various kinds of animation, all of which is correct. eMarketer has a definition that takes a marketing perspective:

> Rich media advertising uses motion (animated or video), sound and/or interactivity to engage its audience. That engagement may simply be a better way to capture an individual's attention for direct response goals, or it may be a brand's attempt to build mindshare or weave its way into the consumer's heart.[28]

That definition suffices, especially because we probably have seen only the beginning of technology that can power rich media developments. We are also seeing the rollout of broadband around the globe, and the speed of broadband is necessary for the success of rich media. These ads must load quickly and play smoothly, or they risk annoying customers instead of engaging them.

Businesses commission ads with rich media, advertising agencies develop the advertising strategy, and specialized marketing services firms create the ads. Both the agencies and the services firms create an ever-changing landscape. To learn more about rich media formats and availability, visit a large content site or portal and investigate their advertising link. MSN has been a proponent of rich media from the beginning and has a directory of service providers whose products are accepted on the MSN site at http://advertising.msn.com/adproducts/3rdpartyrichmedia.asp. Good examples are usually available either on the MSN site or the client galleries of the services providers.

There are many examples of rich media success in addition to those of Gillette and BMW, cited earlier. Figure 6-10 shows shots from a complex campaign developed as part of a major promotional strategy initiative at General Electric (GE).

GE's "We Bring Good Things to Life" slogan was more than 25 years old, perhaps a bit tired, and seen as not suitable for the global enterprise it had become. Their advertising agency BBDO—in conjunction with its interactive unit, Atmosphere—developed a new slogan and a multimedia campaign around "Imagination at Work."

FIGURE 6-10   Ingenuity in GE's online marketing.

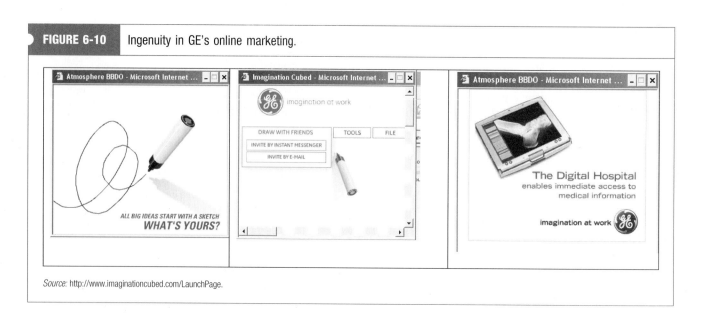

Source: http://www.imaginationcubed.com/LaunchPage.

The Internet creative team made extensive use of rich media in a variety of ways. The underlying GE brand positioning was "What We Can Imagine, We Can Make Happen." The campaign concept, shown in Figure 6-10a with a pen actively writing, was "All Big Ideas Start with a Sketch." Intervening frames invited the viewer to "Sketch Here." The final frame encouraged the viewer to create a sketch and share it with a friend (Figure 6-10b). Other executions were product oriented and featured products from various GE divisions. Some made use of the pen and some did not, but all had compelling visuals, as suggested by Figure 6-10c. All began with the GE logo and new "Imagination at Work" slogan and ended with an invitation to "Learn More" about the product category.

Atmosphere BBDO's Web site describes the response to the online campaign as "overwhelming." It increased customer perceptions of the GE brand on innovation-related attributes. Click-throughs that brought viewers to the GE.com site were in "the millions." The click-through rate (CTR) exceeded 10%, a higher rate than most campaigns achieve. The Pen banner and its associated viral marketing effort saw more than 5 million sketches created and e-mailed by consumers. These e-mails averaged more than an 80% open rate because of their viral nature (sent by friends) and the compelling content.[29]

As this illustration suggests, and as we discuss in detail in Chapter 11 CTRs are one measure, a direct-response one, of Internet advertising effectiveness. CTRs have shown a steady decline over several years. eMarketer quotes DoubleClick ad serving statistics as showing a non–rich media rate of 0.41% at the beginning of 2002, whereas the rich media CTR averaged 2.5%. By mid-2004, rates seemed to have become stable at a lower level, averaging about 0.22% for non–rich media and 1.7% for rich media. They attribute the stemming of the decline in CTR not only to the compelling nature of rich media formats but also to more attention to correct advertising frequency and better targeting by marketers.[30]

IAB summarizes some of the important research-based findings about ad formats and rich media as follows:

- *Different ad types* have varying effects on brand metrics, but bigger is usually better and may be more cost-effective.
- *Animation* improves brand metrics and lifts purchase intent when compared with standard banners. Rich media also outperforms static banners.
- *Video* improves brand metrics and lifts purchase intent when compared with standard banners.
- *Audio* improves "hard to move" brand metrics when done in an appropriate environment.[31]

The last statement about an "appropriate environment" is a reminder not to use intrusive advertising of any kind when and where it is likely to be annoying to the average viewer. It is also a reminder about the importance of targeting ads. Two types of targeting are in widespread use: contextual advertising and behavioral targeting. Before we discuss specific targeting techniques, however, it is important to understand how ads arrive on Web pages.

6-8c Ad Serving

Ads can be embedded in a Web page in the same sense that they are placed on a magazine or newspaper page. However, it is more common to serve ads separately from content. From the advertiser's point of view, it is important to target advertisements according to user profiles and to track the results of their ads. Because most Internet advertisers run ads on many sites simultaneously, these are not trivial tasks. From the publisher's point of view, it must fulfill the terms under which the advertising was sold. For example, the contract with the advertiser may require 100,000 CPMs over a 10-day period. The site could simply display the ad to the first

10,000 viewers each day, but that would not be optimum for either the advertiser or the publisher. If the contract was for 10,000 unique viewers each day, it would not be acceptable. In addition, it requires programming labor to swap ads in and out manually, and that is expensive and error prone.

Ad serving agencies provide the answer from both the advertiser's and the publisher's perspective. The agencies maintain the inventory of ads and serve them onto the site according to the contract between advertiser and publisher site. They can target ads by many variables, including location of the visitor, search keyword, daypart, or page on the site (sports or arts and entertainment, for example). The agencies offer specialized targeting services like contextual and behavioral advertising, which we discuss later in this chapter. They are able to handle rich media ads efficiently. They also have access to advertising networks that allow marketers to reach hundreds of small to medium-sized sites without dealing individually with each of them. Finally, the agencies provide media buying and ad tracking tools to allow media planners and marketers to deal effectively with the increasingly complex world of online advertising.[32]

When you stop to think about how difficult it is to serve the best ad from *both* the advertiser's point and the publisher's point of view, the magnitude of the task begins to become obvious. When you consider that the decision must be made and the ad retrieved from inventory and sent to the appropriate site while the site content is loading—a matter of seconds if the user has a broadband connection—another layer of complexity is added. This is only the most basic situation, not taking into account the more complex targeting techniques to be described in the next section. That explains why most sites of any size use ad serving technology of some kind.

Basically two kinds of ad serving services are available to marketers: third-party ad servers and site-side ad servers. Advertisers and their agencies use third-party ad servers to serve the ads that make up a campaign to the Web sites that have been chosen for the campaign. The ad serving agencies take care of the issues associated with actual serving of the ads and provide a consolidated set of reports to their advertiser clients. Site-side ad servers deliver ads to large publishers like the sites of newspapers who sell their own advertising. Not only do these services take care of the actual serving, they also control the advertising inventory, scheduling, and delivery. They provide reports to their clients, the publishers, who then make them available to their clients, the advertisers.[33]

If that's not confusing enough, another layer of complexity is added by the existence of the ad networks. An ad network may act as a media broker, reselling advertising inventory, usually remnant advertising of large publishers or ads of small firms who do not have media buying expertise. In this case the ad network identifies sites on which the advertising can appear and serves the ads to those sites. Other ad networks bring together a group of sites who partner with them to handle some or all of their media sales. In this case, the ad network looks for advertisers that are appropriate for the sites in their network. The existence of a network allows them to give advice to advertisers on how to reach target segments and then put together a set of sites that delivers that audience. Both types of networks provide reports on the reach and cost of the advertising and are able to make recommendations on how to improve the cost-effectiveness of the campaign. There are also networks that specialize in B2B advertising and networks that are emerging to serve new advertising markets such as blogs and podcasting.[34]

6-9 Targeting Online Ads

It has always been the job of media buyers to identify media vehicles that reach an identified target audience in a cost-effective manner and then to book space on those vehicles. Direct marketers, especially mail marketers, have long had the ability to develop and communicate individualized offers and messages to targeted market segments. However, the interactivity and trackability of the Web have advanced the ability of media planners to fine-tune audience segmentation and to target even small segments with relevant messages. An industry mantra has become "reaching the right person with the right message at the right time." E-mail marketing, discussed in Chapter 7, is one way for marketers to target and personalize their messages. Online advertising also offers two specific opportunities to target that go beyond what is possible in the offline world and begin to make the industry mantra a reality. These opportunities go under the headings of **contextual** and **behavioral** advertising.

6-9a Contextual Advertising

Search marketing expert Danny Sullivan says that "contextual advertising is when ads are delivered based on the content of a Web page being viewed, usually in an automated or semiautomated manner."[35] If the viewer is examining an article about online banking, the contextual advertising system delivers an ad for online banking. How is this really different from the media buyer placing an ad for online banking in the financial services section of the newspaper? The answer is that it is much more specific and targeted. The media buyer knows from experience and from research supplied by the newspaper that people go to the financial services section when they are looking for information about online banking and institutions that offer it. But people also go to the financial services section to read articles about financial markets, to check stock prices, to read world economic news, and so forth. The financial services pages are probably the most relevant location to reach a person is investigating online banking but they reach a great many readers who are not interested in online banking at the moment.

Contextual advertising "sees" the specific content a viewer is examining at a particular moment. It does do by examining keywords, and other items such as the URL, on the page. Based on its analysis of the most relevant keywords for the page, the contextual advertising provider serves an ad. Some examples include the following:

- The editorial content of the page is matched with text ads that look much like search listings. To do this, the contextual ad engine must boil down the essence of the page into the equivalent of a single search term.

- The editorial context results in a contextual ad unit being served as a pop-up or pop-under that consists of up to five relevant text ads.

- The keywords used by a visitor who is searching within a site trigger relevant contextual ads.

- The computer has what is euphemistically called a "helper application" installed. Based on the sites visited on actions taken, the helper application launches a window with text links from the contextual network.

The final example requires some explanation, because it sounds like the infamous Gator ads that popped up over Web pages without being sanctioned by the pages themselves. After several years of lawsuits and controversy inside the Internet advertising industry, Gator has disappeared into the GAIN network of behavioral targeting firm Claria and is no longer recognizable as an individual product. The firms that publicly offer ride-along ads describe their audiences as "opt in," meaning that they have agreed to accept ads in return for something else, perhaps free software. The software that is downloaded to the consumer's computer to enable this application is called **adware**. **Spyware** can have a similar function, but it is installed on the consumer's computer without permission and consequently delivers ads without the consumer's permission. Spyware can also have malicious purposes, such as the theft of personal financial information. Use of spyware is not considered acceptable by industry associations and firms that care about ethics and their public image.

contextual Ads that are displayed based on the content being viewed at the time.

behavioral Advertising displayed on the basis of anonymous Internet user profiles.

adware Programs installed on consumers' computers, with permission, that enable them to receive targeted ads.

spyware Programs installed on consumers' computers without their permission that assume partial control over the operating system.

Most contextual ads have been made up only of text and links, with the exception of the Overture search engine's ContentMatch program. In early 2004, Google announced a program to include image ads in their contextual advertising program, which is separate from their paid search advertising program, discussed in the next chapter. Google has continued to add more standard ad formats to the allowable contextual formats. Flash and animation are also allowed in these ads, which are served by Google onto content and search pages of participating Web sites. Google's influence on the industry is strong, and other large sites, including Yahoo!, have announced plans to test image ads in their contextual programs. Most contextual advertising is sold on the basis of keyword bidding, which is discussed in detail in Chapter 7.

Although the concept seems to make sense, contextual advertising has been controversial in the online industry. When compared with similar text ads that appear on search results pages, contextual ads have not performed well. The reason seems to be that paid search ads are seen only by active searchers who may be highly motivated to investigate and buy, whether the information comes from a paid or an unpaid listing. Contextual ads may be seen by visitors who are "merely browsing" and less likely to click through or to purchase. Contextual ads, however, may be a useful adjunct to paid search ads, reaching some qualified prospects who are not actively searching.[36]

Contextual targeting is based on the nature of the content the visitor is viewing. The second major type of targeting "product," behavioral targeting, is based on the nature of the visitor's Web activities.

6-9b Behavioral Advertising

Like contextual advertising, the concept of behavioral advertising is not new. Marketers have surveyed consumers, learning about specific product-related behaviors and lifestyles. Then they have developed segmentation strategies based on that information. Once again, the trackability of the Internet takes this marketing activity to a new level.

Behavioral targeting is based on the Internet visitor and current and past Internet behavior, not on the content of the pages he or she is viewing. eMarketer defines it as:

> The ability, through the use of anonymous data, to deliver ads to consumers based on their recent behavior: the Web pages they viewed, keywords they typed into a search engine, or products and services they shopped for online. Or a combination of all three.[37]

Large publishers, such as the *Wall Street Journal,* or marketing services firms that specialize in behavioral targeting, build and analyze large databases of consumer Web activities. The data is collected by placing cookies on Web browsers and results in the type of anonymous profile discussed in Chapter 4. The activities data are then analyzed and segments defined. The "tire kicker" (a person who is "just shopping," apparently) is often referred to in the industry as an illustration of a generic behavioral segment. Based on six to ten segment profiles, ads can be targeted to people who have recently engaged in the behavior on their next visit to the site or to a site in a network. An example will help explain the process.

American Airlines has reported successful use of behavioral targeting in an integrated marketing communications program that included TV, print, radio, messaging, and online advertising on fourteen Web sites. The program was designed to stress the relevance of the airline for business travelers in the face of price-oriented competition. The airline wanted to increase brand awareness and reach people who would be making business travel plans in the near future. American Airlines and its agency worked with WSJ.com—the online component of business newspaper the *Wall Street Journal*—and its behavioral targeting provider to test behavioral targeting as part of the campaign. The services provider had several travel-related segment profiles based on readership of WSJ.com travel content. These included segments called "Middle Seat," "Desktop

Traveler," and "Takeoffs and Landings." These segments were combined into a "Travel Seekers" segment for the purposes of this campaign. It is important to note that once a segment member was identified, the member could be "followed" around the site and served an American Airlines ad, no matter what section of WSJ.com he or she was reading. Identifying individuals who were members of the "Travel Seekers" segment was key to executing and evaluating the test. According to AdAge.com:

> Individuals in the travel-seekers group were served ads based on their behavior on WSJ.com. A control group, which had no demonstrated travel interest, was exposed to ads placed in the normal manner across the various sections of the site. The study compared these two groups.
>
> All visitors saw rich media, large-format ads, which featured testimonials from customers. They talked about the amenities American has that low-cost airlines lack, such as the ability to upgrade to first class; that AA flies often to many places around the world; and the benefits of a frequent-flyer program.[38]

The carefully controlled test produced useful results about behavioral targeting:

- Compared with the general run of site ads, the behavioral-targeted ads were seen by 115% more business travelers who take one trip a year.
- Among those who take five or more trips a year, the lift from behavioral over run of site was 145%.
- The behaviorally targeted group scored 3% better than the control group on aided brand awareness.
- They also scored better in message association, recognizing the message that American had 3,900 flights each day.

Using a metric of how much it cost to reach a member of the target audience, AdAge also found that it was 25% cheaper to advertise to the group that flew once a year and 45% cheaper to reach the group that flew five times each year. That takes into account the fact that WSJ.com charges a premium for behaviorally targeted ads.[39] A publisher like this can also take advantage of subscriptions and registrations on its site to identify visitors and to incorporate registration information into the behavioral profiles.

This case history describes behavioral targeting as offered by a large publisher, WSJ.com. According to eMarketer, the greatest amount of spending on behavioral by advertisers occurs on the sites of the so-called adware companies. These companies offer an incentive, often free software, to Web users to get them to download the software (adware) that accepts their advertising. This is purely an opt-in activity, although research shows that many people do not read the service agreements before they download and are consequently unaware of where the advertising is coming from.[40]

The third way, which is just emerging, to deliver behaviorally targeted advertising involves networks that are formed for that purpose. At the time of this writing, the behavioral networks are relatively new and untried. One of the largest behavioral suppliers, Tacoda Systems, already processes more than 100 billion data points each month for more than 100 million Internet users.[41] When its network is fully deployed, it expects to reach 50% of the Internet population in twenty-two standardized segments ranging from Auto Buyers to Travelers, Leisure.[42]

Internet technology has improved to the point that large behaviorally targeted campaigns are possible. For advertisers, they may improve reach and brand metrics and be cost-effective. For Web publishers they offer an opportunity to sell targeted ads on pages other than the relevant content pages. Still the targeting cannot be better than the profiles on which they are based. This seems to be an area in which there will be further developments of interest to both advertisers and the sites on which they advertise.

As advertising technology continues to develop, so does the consumer environment in which it must operate.

6-10 Trust in Online Advertising—or Ad Avoidance?

Because the Internet is a relatively new medium, there is relatively little information on trust in the medium or the advertising it contains. Research by PR firm Edelman provides insight when it asks respondents which medium they turn to first for trustworthy news. In all the countries for which data are available, the Internet is neither the source consulted first nor last (Figure 6-11). Edelman's continuing research on global trust of institutions has highlighted actions consumers are taking to exert more control over the media they consume. They describe the "democratization of media."

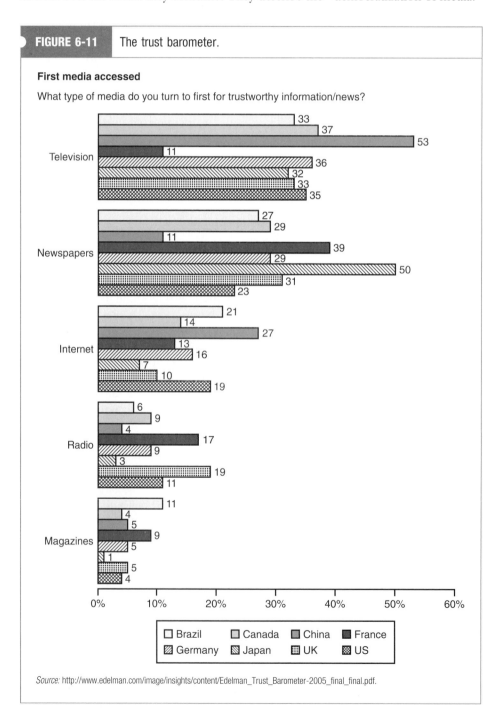

FIGURE 6-11   The trust barometer.

First media accessed

What type of media do you turn to first for trustworthy information/news?

Legend: Brazil, Canada, China, France, Germany, Japan, UK, US

Source: http://www.edelman.com/image/insights/content/Edelman_Trust_Barometer-2005_final_final.pdf.

On the media side, that includes media fragmentation and the ability of niche publishers to reach large numbers of people through pass-alongs and links to major outlets. On the consumer side, it includes the desire to be a part of the entertainment, not merely a passive recipient. New communications tools like blogs allow consumers to make their voices heard in ways previously unimaginable. They consider themselves to be empowered to demand accountability from corporations and media alike.[43]

One direct action that consumers can take is to reject **cookies** or to remove cookies that have already been set from their system. eMarketer reports a study that found consumers rejecting cookies at a rate of 2.84% in January 2004. By April 2005, that rate had risen to 12.4%. At that time, 16.9% of the cookies that were attempted by retail sites were rejected.[44] Internet Week quotes a study by JupiterResearch that found that 58% of Internet users have deleted cookies at some time and 39% delete them on a monthly basis.[45] ClickZ also reports on freeware called Greasemonkey, at this point for the open-source Firefox browser only, that allows users to change the way Web pages appear, including eliminating image ads from the page. Marketers, of course, continue to try to develop technology that permits them to capture the data they want in order to target and personalize Internet communications.

> **cookies** Lines of code placed on a user's computer that allow activity data to be collected anonymously.

A Pew Foundation study makes it clear that concern about adware and spyware is changing Internet user behavior. The study found that more than 91% of Internet users had made at least one change in their behavior as a result of concern over software intrusions. Among the changes:

- 81% have stopped opening e-mail attachments unless they are sure these documents are safe.
- 48% have stopped visiting particular Web sites that they fear will place unwanted programs on their computers.
- 25% have stopped downloading music or video files from person-to-person (P2P) networks for the same reason.
- 18% have changed Web browsers.

They note that there are significant gaps between people's perceptions and the reality of what is on their computers, quoting a study by AOL and the National Cyber Security Alliance in 2004. This research reported that 53% of respondents said they had spyware or adware on their computers, but actual scans found that 80% of their computers had these programs. Pew found that only 50% of respondents really understood what adware is. Many appear not to read the service agreements carefully before downloading and installing these programs.[46]

Summary

In its early days, the Internet was regarded as essentially a direct-response medium with capabilities that exceeded other direct-response media. However, as the Internet has matured, marketers have learned that it is also an effective branding medium. Research shows that the Internet can reach people who are not easily reached by other media. It can provide a lift in brand metrics as well as response when used in integrated campaigns with other media. Traditional mass media marketers are leading the way in testing the branding capabilities of the Web.

All customer contacts provide brand awareness and brand-building opportunities. At the same time, marketers must use these contacts to acquire customers. There are many techniques for customer acquisition. Online advertising is one. Numerous formats can be used for online ads. Static ads are losing popularity to rich media ads, which attract attention and deliver compelling messages. Most online ads are placed on Web sites by an ad serving system. The system tries to balance the requirements of the site with those of the advertiser. The site wishes to sell as many spaces as it has available on its site at the best possible rates. The advertiser wishes to reach the defined target audience with the right frequency at the lowest possible cost. Ads can be served directly to large sites or within networks of sites that have been brought into an alliance for that purpose.

As both technology and databases improve, it becomes possible to target ads with more precision. Contextual targeting is based on the content being viewed by the visitor at a given time. Most contextual ads are text based. Behavioral targeting is based on a user activity profile, either anonymous or merged with registration data. A visitor is followed through the site, and ads can be served based on the visitor's segment membership without regard to the content being viewed at any given time.

Both types of targeting require the compilation and use of consumer data, often without the consumer being aware that the data are being collected. That has led to consumer concerns and changes in behavior that may make it more difficult for advertisers to reach at least some Internet users.

Quiz

1. Media developments that appeal to consumers' desire to control their media experience include _____.
   a. on-screen television program listings
   b. blogs and other co-creation of Internet content
   c. belief that the Internet is the best source of news

2. The changes in consumer media habits do not seem to be affecting B2B markets.
   a. true
   b. false

3. The concept that describes the strength of a brand is _____.
   a. recall of advertising details
   b. brand personality
   c. brand equity

4. Internet advertising offers a way to reach consumers who are not _____.
   a. current users of the brand
   b. heavy viewers of TV
   c. willing to accept cookies

5. Tools for online branding *do not* include _____.
   a. price stabilization
   b. personalization
   c. self-service

6. Which of the following is a true statement about customer acquisition on the Internet?
   a. Internet advertising works well alone to acquire new customers.
   b. It is more expensive to reach qualified customers on the Internet than in any other medium.
   c. Internet customer acquisition activities should be tightly integrated with offline activities.

7. _____ is the advertising method that uses sound, motion, and interactivity to engage visitors.
   a. Flash
   b. Rich media
   c. Pop-ups

8. Ad serving is necessary for most sites because _____.
   a. matching site inventory to advertiser needs is complicated
   b. the software required is complex and expensive
   c. both a and b

9. The GE "Imagination at Work" campaign made use of _____.
   a. creative use of animation
   b. a viral message
   c. both a and b

10. _____ employs the kind of ad targeting that relies on anonymous profiles based on user activities.
    a. Behavioral advertising
    b. Lifestyle advertising
    c. Contextual advertising

11. Fear of adware and spyware is causing some Internet users to _____.
    a. stop using the Internet
    b. reject cookies
    c. complain to government agencies

Discussion Questions

1. Think about your own Internet use habits. Have you changed your use of other media? Why or why not? How do your own habits fit the media use attitudes and patterns described in this chapter?

2. What are some of the differences between ads that have primarily direct-response objectives and those that have primarily branding objectives?

3. A businessperson who is not an Internet expert asks you whether the Internet is useful for branding. What answer would you give, and how could you support it with illustrations?

4. What are the special techniques that enterprises can use in their brand-building process on the Web?

5. Why is ad serving an improvement over just placing an ad on a Web page and leaving it there?

6. What is rich media? What benefits does it offer the marketer? Does it have any downsides?

7. Is contextual advertising or behavioral advertising a better way to precisely target Web site visitors?

Internet Exercises

1. Visit a Web site you visit often, paying attention to the advertising this time. What kinds of ads do you see, and why do you think they were placed on this particular site? Close out of the site and come back several times in quick succession. What do you see going on with the ads? How does it illustrate concepts discussed in the chapter?

2. If you have not already done so, make a contact with one of the three Web sites you are tracking. You could register, ask for information, or even purchase a product if you wish. Think about the experience you have as you interact with the site. Then keep a log of contacts that are made because of your initiative. How does the site appear to be using the data from your contact(s)?

3. Visit the Web site of your local newspaper. Carefully examine the online media kit to understand what they offer that is the same as or different from the ad formats described in this chapter. Try your hand at developing an ad for one of the available formats.

Notes

1. Norman H. Nie *et al.,* "Ten Years after the Birth of the Internet, How Do Americans Use the Internet in Their Daily Lives," December 2004, http://www.stanford.edu/group/siqss/SIQSS_Time_Study_04.pdf.
2. Lee Rainie, John Horrigan, and Michael Cornfield, "Campaign 2004," http://www.pewinternet.org/PPF/r/150/report_display.asp.
3. Tom Hespos, "Consumers Abandon Channels, Not Publishers," June 28, 2005, OnLineSpin@MediaPost.com.
4. "craigslist facts & figures," accessed December 27, 2005, http://boston.craigslist.org/about/pr/factsheet.html.
5. http://www.slashdot.org.
6. http://www.wink.com.
7. Amanda Lenhart and Mary Madden, "Teen Content Creators and Consumers," November 2, 2005, http://www.pewinternet.org/pdfs/PIP_Teens_Content_Creation.pdf.
8. "Talkback: My Anti-Dell Blog," CNET News, July 24, 2005, http://news.com.com/5208-1042-0.html?forumID=1&threadID=396&messageID=57369&start=-1.
9. Dynamic Logic, "Comparing TV, Magazine and Internet Advertising Shows Incremental Impact and Specific Strengths," http://www.dynamiclogic.com. Dynamic Logic, A Millward Brown Company, is a leading marketing research company with expertise in measuring marketing effectiveness. Dynamic Logic's research products include: AdIndex® to analyze online ad effectiveness, CrossMedia Research™ to evaluate multimedia campaigns, MarketNorms®, a syndicated ad effectiveness database, and DigitalLink™, an online copy-testing solution developed jointly with Millward Brown. Founded in 1999, the company is headquartered in New York City with offices in Chicago, San Francisco, Rhode Island, London and Tokyo.
10. DoubleClick, "Touchpoints II: The Changing Purchase Process," March 2004, http://www.doubleclick.com/us/knowledge_central/research/advertising/
11. "Unilever's Dove Nutrium Bar," nd, http://www.iab.net/xmos/pdf/xmosdatadove.pdf.
12. "McDonald's® Grilled Chicken Flatbread Sandwich," nd, http://iab.net/xmos/pdf/xmosdatamcd.pdf.
13. Kevin Lane Keller, *Strategic Brand Management* (Upper Saddle River, NJ: Prentice Hall, 1998), p. 43.
14. Kevin Lane Keller, *Strategic Brand Management* (Upper Saddle River, NJ: Prentice Hall, 1998), p. 51.
15. Anthony Vignoni, "The Inside Story of BMW's Cyber-Cinema Ads," *Advertising Age,*July 23, 2001, http://www.adage.com.
16. Retail Marketing Council Case Studies, nd, http://www.pmalink.org/councils/RMC/case3.asp.
17. Retail Marketing Council Case Studies, nd, http://www.pmalink.org/councils/RMC/case3.asp.
18. "Auto Firms Try New Branding Strategies," February 24, 2007, http://www.slnn.com/article/automobile-marvel/
19. Based on Mary Lou Roberts, "Interactive Brand Experience," in Irvine Clarke III and Theresa Flaherty, *Advances in Electronic Marketing,* 2005, Idea Group, Inc., pp. 109–116.
20. Eric Krell, "The 6 Most Overlooked Customer Touchpoints," December 13, 2004, http://www.destinationcrm.com.
21. Sean Michael Kerner, "Online Media Spend Predicted to Double by 2007," November 8, 2004, http://www.clickz.com/stats/sectors/advertising/article.php/3432571.
22. "Universal: Release of E.T. on DVD," nd, http://iab.net/xmos/2004materials/UNI.pdf.
23. "All New Ford 2004 F-150 Brand Launch, Ford Tough," nd, http://iab.net/xmos/2004materials/2237%20XMOS%20Case_Ford.pdf with additional material from "Ford's F-150 Launch Increases Brand Awareness, Drives Sales," November/December 2004, http://www3.doubleclick.com/market/2004/12/dc/clientcorner.htm?c=0412_smr &id_lead=newsletter&id_source=newsletter_0412.
24. "Advertising Opportunities: Surround Session," http://www.boston.com/mediakit/ad_surround.html.
25. http://iab.net/standards/adunits.asp.
26. http://www.nytimes.com/marketing/adinfo/specs/rates.html.
27. See, for example, the online media kit of the *London Times,* http://www.tnl-advertising.com/brands/times-online/rate-card.aspx.
28. eMarketer White Paper, "Rich Media: At the Tipping Point," May 2005, p. 3.
29. "General Electric, 2004, http://www.atmosphere.net/thework.asp?cs=ge.
30. eMarketer White Paper, "Rich Media: At the Tipping Point," May 2005, p. 7.
31. "Final Rich Media Guidelines," September 2004, http://iab.net/standards/richmedia/pdf/RichMediaGuidelines.pdf.

32. For an interesting discussion of the evolution of ad serving see Tom Hespos, "Ad Serving Comes of Age," ClickZ, January 14, 2004, http://www.imediaconnection.com/content/2464.asp.

33. Eric Picard, "The State of Ad Serving," June 7, 2004, http://www.clickz.com/experts/ad/ad_tech/article.php/3363181.

34. Pete Lerma, "Campaign Brand Optimization," June 14, 2005, http://www.clickz.com/experts/media/agency_strat/article.php/3512216; Tessa Wegert, "Ad Networks: The Real Advantages," March 3, 2005, http://www.clickz.com/experts/media/media_buy/article.php/3486541.

35. Danny Sullivan, "Contextual Advertising in Context, Part 1," March 19, 2003, http://www.clickz.com/experts/search/opt/article.php/2114501.

36. Hollis Thomases, "Contextual Advertising with the Advertiser in Control," March 15, 2005, http://www.clickz.com/experts/media/agency_strat/article.php/3489546; Danny Sullivan, "Contextual Advertising in Context, Part 2, March 26, 2003, http://www.clickz.com/experts/search/opt/article.php/2169231; Kevin Lee, "Content is King, or Is It?" March 7, 2003, http://www.clickz.com/experts/search/strat/article.php/2077801.

37. Debra Aho Williamson, "What Comes Before Search?", September 2004, eMarketer White Paper.

38. Kris Oser, "Behavioral Targeting Boosts Airline's Internet Ad Results," May 17, 2004, http://www.adage.com.

39. Kris Oser, "Behavioral Targeting Boosts Airline's Internet Ad Results," May 17, 2004, http://www.adage.com.

40. Wendy Davis, "Study: Spyware Mystifies Consumers," May 17, 2005, http://publications.mediapost.com/index.cfm?fuseaction=Articles.san&s=30218&Nid=13480&p=276816.

41. Debra Aho Williamson, "What Comes Before Search?", September 2004, eMarketer White Paper, p. 5.

42. "TACODA Systems Introduces Guidelines for Standardized Behavioral Audience Segments," September 13, 2004, http://www.tacoda.com/documents/Standards_Guidlines_091304.pdf.

43. Richard Edelman, "The Relationship Imperative," *Journal of Integrated Communications*, 2003–2004 edition, pp. 7–13, http://www.medill.northwestern.edu/imc/studentwork/pubs/jic/journal/2004/JIC2004.pdf.

44. "Tossing Cookies," May 26, 2005, http://www.emarketer.com.

45. Antone Gonsalves, "Company Bypasses Cookie-Deleting Consumers," March 31, 2005, http://www.internetweek.com/showArticle.jhtml?articleID=160400749.

46. Susannah Fox, "Spyware," July 6, 2005, http://www.pewinternet.org/pdfs/PIP_Spyware_Report_July_05.pdf.

Customer Acquisition: Search, E-Mail, and Other Marketing Tools

Source: © Getty

Key Terms

algorithm (p. 177)

beta (p. 182)

cascading style sheets (p. 178)

deliverability (p. 188)

directory (p. 175)

javaScript (p. 178)

meta tag (p. 177)

opt-in (p. 187)

opt-out (p. 187)

organic (p. 177)

paid inclusion (p. 175)

paid placement (p. 178)

phishers (p. 191)

search engine (p. 174)

SEM (Search Engine Marketing) (p. 177)

SEO (Search Engine Optimization) (p. 177)

user intent (p. 181)

Web crawlers (p. 175)

Learning Objectives

By the time you complete this chapter, you will be able to:

- Discuss the reasons why search marketing is so important.
- Explain the difference between a directory and a search engine.
- Define SEM, SEO, organic search results, and paid inclusion.
- Identify the basic issues in keyword bidding.
- Explain the role of event marketing, publicity, affiliate programs, portal deals, and viral marketing in customer acquisition.
- Discuss reasons for the growing importance of e-mail marketing.
- Identify the basic steps in developing an e-mail marketing program.
- Recognize key provisions of CAN-SPAM laws in the United States and Europe.
- Describe the various levels of permission.
- List the steps involved in developing an e-mail marketing campaign.

7-1 Introduction

Chapter 6 discussed online advertising and how it is used for both branding and customer acquisition. We pointed out that multiple customer acquisition techniques (see Figure 6-9) are used by marketers in integrated programs spanning both advertising techniques and media. In this chapter, we discuss another acquisition technique that is enjoying explosive growth on the Internet—search marketing. We also discuss event marketing and public relations, affiliate programs, portal deals, and viral marketing. This chapter ends with a discussion of e-mail marketing techniques, which can be used for both acquisition, and even more effectively, for retention. Let's begin with search, the fastest-growing marketing activity on the Web.

7-2 The Growing Impact of Search Engines

search engine Software and algorithms, or a Web site based on search software, that allow users to search for content based on keywords they provide.

When the Pew Internet & American Life Project asked American consumers about their use of **search engines**, 32% of respondents said that they "couldn't live without them." Although that may be an overstatement, it epitomizes the role search engines have taken in the lives of Internet users. The study goes on to report that:

- 84% of U.S. Internet users have used search engines.
- the average Internet user performs thirty-three searches per month, a total of 3.9 billion searches on the twenty-five most popular search engines.
- on any given day, more than half the users who are online launch a search.
- more than one-third search at least once a day.
- 87% say they usually find the information they are searching for.[1]

Figure 7-1a shows that searchers look most frequently for information on specific topics, maps and directions, news and current events, general information, shopping, and entertainment, thus covering a wide range of subject matter on a daily basis. No wonder marketers have found opportunities for advertising in the medium. According to Figure 7-1b, marketers use these opportunities for branding, online sales, and sales lead generation for both manufacturers and dealers, to drive traffic to Web sites, and simply to provide content. The Search Engine Marketing Professional Organization (SEMPO) reports that marketers in the United States and Canada spent more than $5.75 billion on search marketing and advertising in 2005, which was a 44% increase in a single year. They forecasted that search marketing in North America will reach $11 billion by 2010.[2]

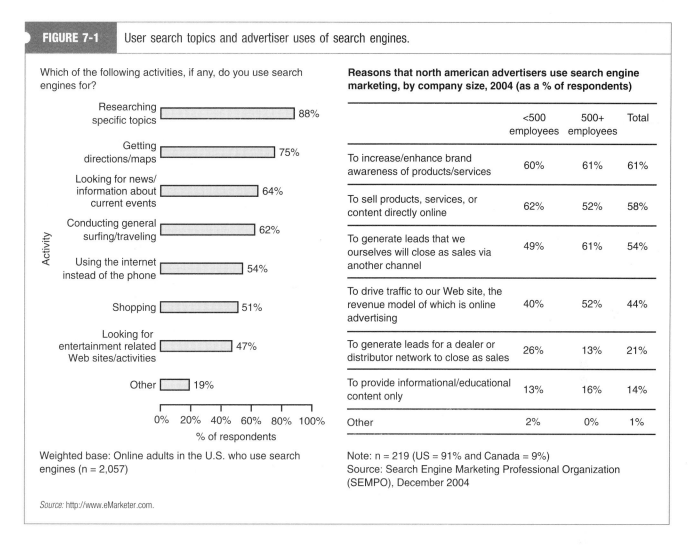

FIGURE 7-1   User search topics and advertiser uses of search engines.

Which of the following activities, if any, do you use search engines for?

Activity

Researching specific topics	88%
Getting directions/maps	75%
Looking for news/ information about current events	64%
Conducting general surfing/traveling	62%
Using the internet instead of the phone	54%
Shopping	51%
Looking for entertainment related Web sites/activities	47%
Other	19%

0% 20% 40% 60% 80% 100%
% of respondents

Weighted base: Online adults in the U.S. who use search engines (n = 2,057)

Reasons that north american advertisers use search engine marketing, by company size, 2004 (as a % of respondents)

	<500 employees	500+ employees	Total
To increase/enhance brand awareness of products/services	60%	61%	61%
To sell products, services, or content directly online	62%	52%	58%
To generate leads that we ourselves will close as sales via another channel	49%	61%	54%
To drive traffic to our Web site, the revenue model of which is online advertising	40%	52%	44%
To generate leads for a dealer or distributor network to close as sales	26%	13%	21%
To provide informational/educational content only	13%	16%	14%
Other	2%	0%	1%

Note: n = 219 (US = 91% and Canada = 9%)
Source: Search Engine Marketing Professional Organization (SEMPO), December 2004

Source: http://www.eMarketer.com.

7-3 The World of Search

The world of search is broader than just search engines, important though they are. It includes several types of search engines and also another major category, **directories** (Figure 7-2).

Directories were the first to emerge into public view. As discussed in Chapter 3, Yahoo! began as a directory in which Jerry Yang and Paul Filo listed their favorite Web sites. That is still the essence of a directory. At Yahoo!, for example, people scour the Web, looking for new sites to list. As you can imagine, this is a gargantuan task, and in recent years, it has been supplemented by automated searches for new listings. Directories can also be complied from existing sources. Switchboard.com, for example, uses a traditional direct marketing model, compiling listings from published sources. In fact, Switchboard.com calls it "the online Yellow Pages industry."[3] Open-source directories are built on the contributions of Internet users. The Open Directory Project (dmoz) describes itself as "the largest, most comprehensive human-edited directory of the Web. It is constructed and maintained by a vast, global community of volunteer editors."[4]

Directories like Yahoo! and Switchboard typify the traditional free listing model that we are accustomed to in offline directories of all types. Like the familiar telephone directories, online directories also provide an advertising opportunity. On Yahoo! this is called **paid inclusion**. Marketers use paid inclusion to be listed in a directory immediately instead of waiting the 2 to 4 weeks it ordinarily takes for the **Web crawlers**

directory On the Web, an index of Web sites and their contents.

paid inclusion Payment of a fee to ensure listing with a search engine.

Web crawlers An automated program that searches the Web for information. Also called bots, spiders, and agents.

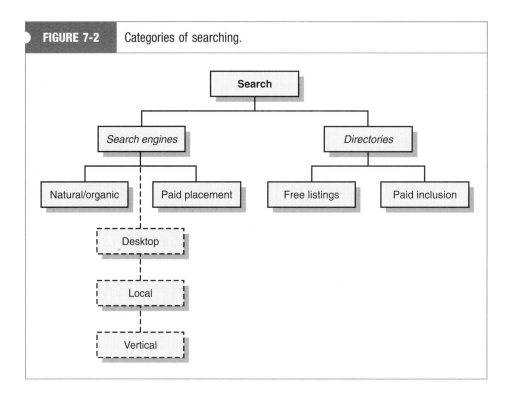

FIGURE 7-2   Categories of searching.

to find them. Paid inclusion can also be a way to provide visibility to pages deep in the site that are difficult for crawlers to index. In either event, Yahoo! is adamant that paid inclusion, or lack thereof, does not affect position in the free listings. Like any advertising, the paid inclusion listing runs out when the period is over unless it is renewed. However, during this time, the crawlers may have found and indexed the site, making it available in the free listings.[5] Variations are available on other directory sites. For example, Verizon's Superpages offers preferred placement, which does affect the order in which listings are displayed.[6] Not only is advertising on the directories different from the familiar display ads in print directories, it is executed differently by the various online directories.

7-3a Search Engines

Online directories seem to be overtaking their offline counterparts in many market sectors ranging from finding your former high school classmate to locating business services. Search engines, however, are the focus of attention because of their ability to organize and make accessible the vast amount of information on the Web. Exactly how they do this is highly technical and ever changing. John Batelle, Internet pioneer and author of a best-selling book about the industry, presents a good summary.

There are three basic components of a search engine. All search engines have a *crawler*, somes referred to as a spider or bot. The crawler scours the Web, moving from one link to another. It finds pages and sends them back to the search engine *index*. The index is a massive database that organizes Web content according to its own criteria. Whatever criteria it uses, the end goal is to produce relevant data for keyword search. The value of the search engine is based on the relevance of the results it returns. The third piece of the search engine is a *query processor* that takes the words typed into the search box, transmits it to the index and returns a search engine results page (SERP) to the user. The value, and therefore the popularity, of the search engine is determined by the relevance of those results.[7]

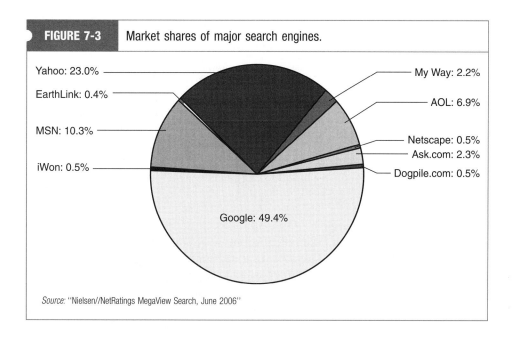

FIGURE 7-3   Market shares of major search engines.

Yahoo: 23.0%
EarthLink: 0.4%
MSN: 10.3%
iWon: 0.5%
My Way: 2.2%
AOL: 6.9%
Netscape: 0.5%
Ask.com: 2.3%
Dogpile.com: 0.5%
Google: 49.4%

Source: "Nielsen//NetRatings MegaView Search, June 2006"

There are a number of search engines with significant market shares as measured by number of searches conducted. Google is the leader in the overall search statistics shown in Figure 7-3. Yahoo! is the leader in local searches.[8] Each search engine has its own **algorithm** for ranking entries. These algorithms change over time, meaning that site ranks may change just because the way of determining site ranks has changed. All the search engine ranking algorithms are different, placing different weights on different characteristics. The exact ranking algorithm of any site is proprietary, although trade sources make educated guesses at the nature of the different algorithms.[9] Items that are usually included in the rankings are:

- The location and frequency (density) of keywords on the page
- The HTML title tag
- Content
- Quality and relevance
- The number of other sites that link to the page
- The number of click-throughs generated by searches.

There is also a piece of code called a **Meta tag** in the header of any Web site. The Meta tag often contains a sentence or two describing the site. Some search engines pay attention to the description in the Meta tag. Google, for one, completely ignores it in ranking the site although it does affect how the site is displayed on the search engine results page. That is one small example of the difference in ranking algorithms between different search engines.

7-3b Search Engine Marketing

SEMPO defines search engine marketing (**SEM**) as "the entire set of techniques and strategies used to direct more visitors from search engines to marketing Web sites." There are two basic aspects of SEM:

- **Organic** search engine optimization (**SEO**), which they describe as "using a range of techniques including augmenting HTML code, Web page copy editing,

algorithm A set of structured steps for solving a problem.

meta tag An HTML tag that provides information about the Web page, primarily for the use of the search engines.

SEM (Search Engine Marketing) All the techniques, including search engine optimization and paid placement, that are used to attract people from search engines to Web sites.

organic Search results produced by search engine spiders.

SEO (Search Engine Optimization) All the techniques used to cause a Web page to be highly ranked on one or more search engines.

site navigation, linking campaigns and more, in order to improve how well a site or page gets listed in search engines for particular search topics."

paid placement Paid ads that are displayed as a result of keyword searches.

- **Paid placement**, which involves "text ads targeted to keyword search results on search engines, through programs such as Google AdWords and Yahoo Overture 'Precision Match,' also sometimes referred to as Pay-per-Click (PPC) advertising and Cost-per-Click (CPC) advertising."[10] This is not the same as paid inclusion, which was discussed in the section on directories.

Paid placement does resemble the contextual advertising discussed in Chapter 6. It is indeed related because both use keyword targeting, but they are not the same.

Optimizing Organic Search

The results of organic search (also called natural search) show up in the main area of the search page. Exactly how they are displayed varies from one search engine to another, but they are always ranked by relevance based on the keyword or phrase chosen and provide the majority of the content on the page. Down the right side the searcher will generally see boxes with text images and links. Those are paid placements. There may also be a band of color across the top of the page that displays the highest-ranking paid placement ads.

As the definition of SEO suggests, practitioners work with the algorithms of the individual search engines to achieve the best possible ranking for the site or page on that particular search engine so their sites are listed at or near the top in the organic search listings. You may notice a problem here, however. Because the search engine algorithms are not disclosed, practitioners are working from what they believe the algorithms to be, based on their own experience and their own proprietary techniques for studying search engine rankings. This isn't a good place for amateur night, although nonprofessionals can certainly learn some of the main techniques and practice them.

A brief case history suggests the challenges involved. Home furnishings retailer Restoration Hardware lacked visibility in their retail sector. They had an in-house search marketing program but were not satisfied with the results, so they called on iCrossing, a supplier of search engine marketing services. Restoration Hardware wanted to increase the traffic of qualified prospects to their Web site, improve their conversion rate, and increase visibility on the major search engines. The agency identified the following problems:

javaScript Language that adds interactivity to static HTML pages.

cascading style sheets Essentially templates that define how elements of a Web page are displayed. They are "cascading" because multiple style sheets can be used to describe a single page.

- "Search engine spiders faced obstacles when scanning product pages of the Web site." Flash is the single biggest barrier to the spiders. Other Web site design and maintenance problems ranging from extensive use of tools like **JavaScript** and **cascading style sheets** to broken links can lower ranking or make the site invisible to the search spiders.

- "No site map on the client Web site." A detailed and accurate site map provides important assistance to the spiders.

- "Non-optimized navigation structure." The spiders need to be able to move through the site, understand the HTML code, and determine how to best index it. Anything that makes it difficult, like the extraneous HTML code inserted by some of the Web site development tools, impedes their progress.

- "Diluted link popularity of key category/product pages." Links are important to ranking. They need to be relevant and intact.

Although the total program of Web site revisions and measurement was carried out over a 12-month period, iCrossing was able to make revisions to the site within the first 4 months that resulted in measurable gains. They developed a site map for the Restoration Hardware site and delivered an optimized navigational structure. The following results were reported after the first quarter with revisions in place:

- "Conversions for non-branded search terms improved 236%." The assumption is that when people search by brand name they are far along in the purchase process and therefore conversion is easier. Nonbranded searchers are earlier in the process and more difficult to convert.

- "Unpaid search visitors converted at a rate of 40% higher than the paid search Web site visitors." It is always desirable to track the results of both unpaid (organic) and paid search. The desire is to get as much visitation as possible through organic search and then to add to that through paid search.

They also met the objective of increasing visibility and conversions on the three targeted search engines—AOL, Yahoo!, and Google.[11] Notice that it took several months for the changes to be made and for initial results to be seen.

Using Paid Placement

Paid placement is just the opposite of the complex technical issues required for organic optimization. It is set up to be easy for the average marketer to place an ad. The process used by Google has all the typical elements, although, again, not all search engines work in exactly the same way. They describe it as follows.

In the first step, the marketer specifies where the ad is to be displayed. Clearly, the marketer wants the ad to be displayed only in the languages and countries in which the business operates. Initially, paid placement on search engines caused the ad to be displayed whenever the relevant keyword was entered in the designated countries. However, the larger search engines now allow U.S. customers to choose from regions that closely correspond to the metropolitan statistical areas of the U.S. Census Bureau. That allows local businesses to take advantage of paid placement opportunities on the leading search engines.

The second step is to write the ad. It is limited to only a few words or characters, and writing extremely short advertising copy that is compelling enough to get viewers to click through is a challenge. Then the marketer chooses the keywords and completes the process by providing contact information and a credit card number. Paying for the ad is straightforward; bidding on keywords is the heart of issue when it comes to getting prominence for a search engine ad.

Bidding on Keywords

For best results, the search engines suggest listing at least twenty keywords for each ad. Each keyword will have a separate price that is based on its popularity. Some keywords may be priced out of the range of smaller marketers. Others may, however, appear to be quite cheap. There may be a minimum bid of, say, 5 cents. On some search engines, the minimum bid will actually be the lowest amount paid. Google, however, may set a higher minimum based on the popularity ("quality") of the word.

Figure 7-4 shows an example, taken from the Overture search engine, which is now owned by Yahoo! When a marketer uses the Keyword Selector Tool for "mobile phone," he or she finds that *cell phone* is the most popular term, with more than 2.7 million searches in the specified month. *Mobile phone* is not even on the list of several dozen terms that ends with *cellular phone Detroit* at 738 searches. Notice how many searches are conducted by brand. Some searchers also include their geographical location. So the marketer has learned a good deal already—the best keywords and the importance of brand in the cell phone market.

Then the marketer goes to the View Bids Tool, this time entering "cell phone." The table shows the current top bid to be $3.01 with a second advertiser right behind at $3.00. It then drops down to $1.33 for the third-ranked listing. Our marketer might be well advised to bid $1.34, especially if a high volume of click-through traffic

FIGURE 7-4 Yahoo! keyword selector tool and Yahoo! bid table.

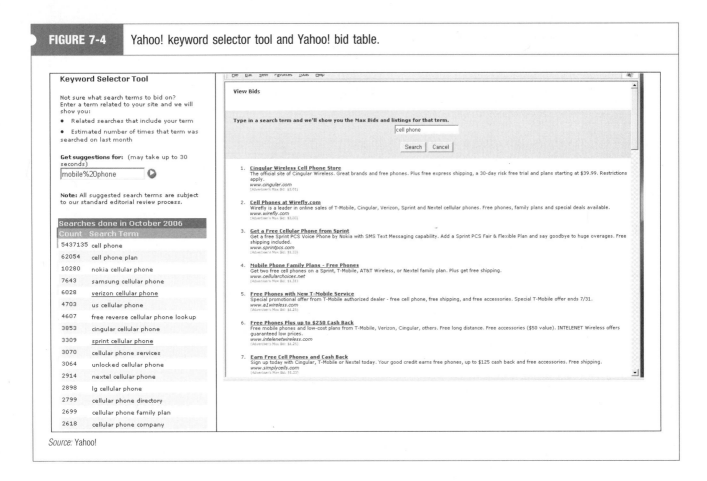

Source: Yahoo!

is expected, which is possible, given the popularity of the keyword. At $1.34, the marketer's ad would come up third, a highly visible position. And that is less than half the price of buying the highest rank. Of course, someone can bid $1.35, or even $3.02, at any time, changing the rankings of the ads. This is why paid placement programs need to be actively managed, but as you can see, it doesn't take a great deal of technical skill.

It is also important to recognize that paid placement is pay-per-click advertising. There may be a small set-up fee when the marketer initially establishes an account, but from then on, all charges are based on the number of clicks times the cost for each of the keywords. The marketer can set maximum charges by day or month to guard against higher-than-expected traffic or rapidly escalating keyword costs.

7-3c Specialty Search

Given the popularity of search among both Internet users and marketers, it is not surprising that special types of search are becoming available. Google was first to offer *desktop* search. Users download the relevant software and, in the process, give Google permission to index the entire contents of their hard drives. Once the indexing is completed, users have the option to search their own computers, including all files, e-mails, Web history, and chats. The search pulls up relevant items and provides icons that link directly to them in the computer's files. Desktop search results also show at the top of the page when the user does a Web search. It provides a convenience, especially to users who have many files stored on their computers. The idea of allowing any outside service onto their hard drive to categorize the data stored there makes many people nervous. Quoting from Google's privacy policy, "Your computer's content is not made accessible through Google Desktop Search to Google or anyone else without your explicit permission."[12] Each individual user must balance the convenience against the privacy concerns.

Local search is a rapidly growing activity. One study estimated that 70% of U.S. households use the Internet as an information source when they are shopping locally for products or services. According to the Kelsey Group, "This puts the Internet on par with newspapers as a local shopping information resource, with the Internet likely to surpass the impact of newspapers in the very near future."[13] Yahoo! was among the first not only to offer local search, based on the location specified by the user, but also to allow the user to view the search results on a map. Basic listings on Yahoo! Local are free, and they have offered local businesses incentives such as a free Web site to encourage submission of business listings. That incentive suggests the nature of the problem with local search. Many small businesses are not active on the Internet, and encouraging the millions of small firms to become active in ways that directly benefit their business and take advantage of the unique capabilities of the Web is a large task.

Optimizing local search is also providing a different challenge for search engine marketers. According to Justin Sanger, founder of an agency specializing in local search, a new type of SEO is emerging. He says it "was born as a result of major search engines Google, Yahoo!, MSN, and others segmenting their local search properties to create distinct local search engines. Major search engines decision to create distinct local search properties came as a result of an increased understanding of user intent. Combining their knowledge of **user intent** with a basic knowledge of local consumption patterns, the engines created unique local search results based on algorithms tailored for local search."[14] The search engines provide templates so that local businesses can provide the necessary information easily. They also encourage user creation of content, including ratings of businesses and comments. The ultimate objective is to give local search a rich content base that attracts business and searchers alike. It will provide a new challenge to marketing services providers, most of whom practice the traditional types of SEM and SEO described earlier. If search is the fastest-growing Internet marketing activity, it looks as if local search is the fastest-growing type of search.

user intent What the searcher is really looking for when a keyword is typed into a search engine

Another type of specialty search is *vertical* search. According to the *San Francisco Chronicle,* "By going vertical, search engine companies hope to reduce extraneous results for users by better guessing users' intent. A query for 'great white'—the name for an '80s rock band and a shark species—can get very different results on Google compared with an engine that specializes in academic material. Vertical search engines also can ask questions more quickly. Shopping search engines, for example, can ask up front the color, size and manufacturer of what you want to buy."[15] In other words, if you are on the academic search engine, you're probably going to get the listings for the shark species, not the rock band. This is so-called user intent. The user went to the academic search engine with a purpose—or so the search engine assumes.

Vertical search engines are springing up all over the place. Oodle helps you search the classified ads in selected cities. Technorati and BlogPulse specialize in the blogosphere. PodZinger provides search of podcasts. Teenja is for teenagers; GoBelle is for new moms. There are search engines devoted to travel and others devoted to shopping. Amazon's A9 search engine offers more that a dozen search categories, including movies, RSS feeds, and blogs. Amazon encourages specialized search engines to link to it in order to enrich its content and improve the relevance of its search results. Vertical search is still in its infancy, with other developments surely to come.

Other types of search tools are being introduced into the Internet market space with dizzying frequency. Yahoo! and Google, for example, both allow users to search images and news articles. Google has its Froogle shopping search engine. Video search is becoming commonplace. In early 2006, Yahoo! and Google had the largest shares in that space, followed by AltaVista and two specialized search engines, Singingfish and blinkx.tv.[16] Singingfish is a search engine that specializes in audio and video files. Blinkx operates across several content channels, one of which is video. Instead of keyword search, it conducts searches based on the content the user is viewing.[17]

beta The stage in the product development process in which a new product is released to a select set of users for testing.

Both Yahoo! and Google had personalized search services in **beta** in 2005. Personalized search allows users to apply their own tags to pieces of information and to store the tagged items for retrieval by like-minded individuals. Yahoo! also has a beta service called Yahoo! Answers that allows visitors to post questions to be answered by other visitors. These are both aspects of social networks as discussed in Chapter 6.

7-3d Search Summarized

This discussion has focused on search practices of consumers and the corresponding activities of marketers. There are aspects of search in business-to-business (B2B) applications that have not been covered. One example is enterprise search. Web sites, especially as they become moderately large, need a good search engine. Sites generally license that functionality, creating a B2B side of the market for the search engines. Enterprises are also interested in using search to organize and access data inside their own organization. Google, for example, has an enterprise version of its desktop search product that it offers to businesses.

Because the size of the Web increases by hundreds of pages each day, the importance of search to users, business-to-customer (B2C) and B2B alike, can hardly be overstated. Because having sophisticated and accurate search tools is important to Internet users, marketers and advertisers are close behind. You can expect two levels of change to affect SEM in the years to come. At a granular level, the search engines themselves will continue to tweak their algorithms to provide more relevant results. Search engine marketers will continue to scramble to keep up with those changes. At the level of the overall search marketplace, innovations such as vertical search, personal search, and others yet unseen will continue to proliferate for years to come.

Tapping into search technology is a key focus of Internet marketers at present. Other customer acquisition techniques, however, continue to evolve and remain an important part of the marketer's toolkit. Let us turn first to event-driven marketing.

7-4 Event-Driven Marketing

According to *Promo* magazine, marketers spent $166 billion on event marketing in 2004, almost 11% of their total marketing budgets. That was expected to increase to 25% of their total marketing spending in 2005.[18] Why is event marketing also on a growth trajectory?

Events have been a staple in offline marketing for product launches, to reach segments that are hard to attract through mass media, and to generate awareness and "buzz" in general. The ability of the Web to reach desirable market segments in a way that attracts attention has made it a natural for the staging of events. Witness the young woman who lived and dated on top of a Los Angeles billboard for 3 days in 2004. She used a wireless connection and Yahoo! Personals to schedule her dates. The event was watched live via Webcast, sponsored, of course, by Yahoo! Personals.

There are two basic types of events with which marketers can work. One is marketer-created events like the one just described. The other is an event in the life of the customer. Some events in the lives of each of us mark major transitions—graduation from college, the birth of a baby, and the purchase of a home are just a few. Events like these not only represent major changes in the way a consumer lives, and therefore the products he or she purchases, but also are matters of public record and therefore accessible to the marketer.

The American Association of Retired Persons (AARP) has been pursuing an event-driven strategy brilliantly for many years. It is virtually impossible for anyone in the United States to celebrate (or to try to ignore) his or her fiftieth birthday without receiving a mail message from AARP with congratulations on reaching the milestone and an offer to join AARP. Because the group has a wide array of benefits to offer to the still-working population as well as to those who have retired, the AARP has many reasons to continue to contact people in the target demographic with attractive offers for both products and services. Its database is so large that this type of event-driven contact is cost-effective.

Amazon.com's tenth anniversary showcased an event in its corporate history and made good use of its expertise in doing it. The Amazon.com home page featured things such as Halls of Fame for best-selling authors, musicians, and DVDs based on their own sales records. Video clips, posted on the company's home page, showed celebrities making deliveries of Amazon.com orders to surprised customers. For the grand finale, it presented a live concert in Seattle for 2,500 employees and customers. Called "A Show of Thanks," the concert was streamed live over Amazon's Web site.[19] Registered customers of Amazon were notified by e-mail of various aspects of the celebration and encouraged to take advantage of the events.

Other marketers use events with Internet aspects to reach audiences that are hard to reach through general media. It is also a good way to conduct sampling of a product in order to induce trials among the target market. Here are some other examples of event-driven marketing:

- Ford Motor Company tapped into the phenomenon of flash mobs—relatively spontaneous gatherings of people on the Web—to sponsor "flash concerts" to raise awareness about its 2006 Fusion sedan. Only users registered on the Ford site were notified by e-mail or instant messaging about the upcoming concerts.

- Diet 7-Up announced its reformulation with the Splenda sweetener by running a Free Ticket to Space Sweepstakes. Customers logged onto the 7up.com Web site and recorded a code found on the product in order to enter the contest, which was supported by a television advertising campaign.[20]

Event-driven marketing is part of a general trend away from mass media and toward new media and more experiential kinds of promotions. The Internet is proving to be an important facilitator or alternative to events carried out in the physical world.

Events have a close tie-in with publicity, either online or offline, as promotion for the event or buzz surrounding it. The field of public relations has been greatly changed by the Internet. Let's take a brief look at some of the ways in which this has occurred.

7-5 Generating Publicity

Staging events, issuing press releases, and arranging product placement in films and TV are all tools that public relations professionals use to generate unpaid media attention for products, services, and causes. Of those, the use of press releases appears to have been most changed by the Internet.

Writing press releases and distributing them to a firm's own media list or through a news wire is the stock and trade of public relations. It has always been important to write well when creating press releases, keeping in mind the interests of the target media, and to distribute them in a timely fashion to journalists who are likely to pick them up and use them in a feature article or even write an article around the subject of the press release. The challenge facing firms that use press releases exclusively has always been that journalists are deluged with press releases and drawing their attention to a particular one is difficult.

The Internet has provided journalists with an even richer source of information. According to a survey of journalists, 98% of journalists go online daily, 92% conduct research for articles online, and 73% go online to find press releases.[21] It behooves public relations practitioners to work to make their material visible online. Not surprisingly, the techniques used by such firms is similar to that of search marketing: the release must be written using the correct keywords in appropriate placement and density on the page and must be provided in a way that enhances the likelihood of search engines finding it. It is also important that the release include links to the relevant corporate site to provide more content and contact information to the reader.

Many public relations firms use Internet news services to distribute their press releases. These services have extensive media networks and can assist in appropriate targeting for each press release. It is especially important for the press releases to appear on the news services of the large portals like Yahoo! and Google. From there they will be picked up by other news and clippings services. Releases generally stay on the large portals for about a year.

Blogs are another way in which companies are reaching out for attention in places other than the paid media. Blogs that contain insight from individual personalities such as well-known journalists or groups, like the cast members of a particular television news program, have immediacy and can generate involvement by readers. A continuing tension exists between people having freedom of individual expression in this environment and the fact that the blog is identified with the corporate entity and reflects on its image. Large corporations are struggling with that issue. Corporate blogs represent a new development, and there are few guidelines except common sense to follow at present.

Event marketing and public relations are two closely related Internet promotional techniques. Now we turn to another acquisition technique, affiliate programs.

7-6 Affiliate Programs

We discussed affiliate programs as an Internet business model in Chapter 3. Because many of the prospects who enter a Web site as a result of an affiliate listing may be new customers, affiliate programs clearly qualify as a customer acquisition technique.

A survey by brokerage firm Piper Jaffray in 2005 found that "the vast majority of merchants asserted that affiliate marketing is the highest ROI channel vs. other forms of online advertising." Their respondents liked the pay-for-performance aspect of affiliate marketing and were including it in their online media mix along with other performance-based techniques such as paid search and contextual advertising. Piper Jaffray expected affiliate marketing expenditures to grow approximately 30% in 2005, in line with overall online ad spending.[22]

Affiliate programs follow the 80/20 rule. Only a small number of the affiliates produce the most click-throughs and most profitable sales. Consequently, affiliate programs need to be actively managed. Networks have grown up to serve the affiliate marketing sector by finding appropriate affiliates for merchants and publishers and relevant sites for small businesses who wish to participate in affiliate marketing. Marketing services firms will also assume the management of an affiliate system.[23]

Well-run affiliate programs can be a cost-effective portion of the marketing and advertising strategy.

7-7 Portal Relationships

In contrast to affiliate programs, portal deals have been criticized as unlikely to produce a return on large marketing investments. Portal placement deals generate both revenue for major portals and reach for advertisers. During the early days of the Internet, marketers were paying the large portals like AOL and Yahoo! millions of dollars for the right to be their retailer of choice or even the exclusive retailer of a particular product category on the site. Think of it as negotiating for a prime location in a shopping mall; the principle is the same. When the initial Internet boom ended, deals became more realistic, but they did not end altogether.

A recent example is the deal between Yahoo! and AutoTrader.com, a site for classified advertising for used cars. AutoTrader will become the only dealer to supply classified listings to the Yahoo! Autos page, although Yahoo! will continue to take listings from individuals. The financial details were not made public, but Yahoo! received a "marketing fee." In return, the AutoTrader brand will appear on every page of Yahoo! Autos, which is accessible from the Yahoo! home page. AutoTrader will also be promoted on other sites within the Yahoo! advertising network. The listings will benefit from newly enhanced functionality of the Yahoo! site—being able to search, save ads, compare products, and instant message other users. AutoTrader will continue to promote its listings through other relevant sites, including AOL and the car site Edmunds.com.[24]

Position is important, and portal deals help marketers achieve visibility on major portals. When the portal has other benefits to offer, such as a sizeable advertising network, the potential is enhanced. As long as portal deals produce a satisfactory ROI, they are likely to be a part of the Internet marketing toolkit of certain marketers.

7-8 Viral Marketing

Viral marketing is a promotion that, either by design or accident, catches on with Internet users and is passed from one to the other, multiplying the effectiveness of the original distribution. The classic viral e-mail is the series of Wazzzup Super Friends parodies. In case you missed it, clips of animated characters, including Superman and Wonder Woman, were edited so that they appeared to be delivering a Budweiser commercial. The creators of the clips insist that they sent them to only seven friends. Those people liked them and forwarded the clips to their friends. The rest is history. There is no count of how many people finally received them, but they became known worldwide and spawned many imitators.[25] Creators Philip Stark and Graham Robertson tried to build a business based on their success with the Super Friends clips, but it failed to find commercial success due to lack of long-term interest and concerns about copyright issues. This illustrates the difficulty of viral marketing. If it catches on, it can be explosive. If it doesn't, it sinks without a trace.

Many attempted viral campaigns have done just that. There have been some resounding successes, however. Burger King's "subservient chicken" ad was one of the greatest. It attracted more than 12.7 unique users who stayed on the site an average of 7 minutes issuing orders to an animation of a man in a chicken suit and watching it perform on cue.[26] Another wildly successful ad was Honda's cog in which a series of metal items engage in an amazing sequence of choreographed moves. Both attracted attention and viral activity. Both remain on the Web after the formal campaign ended. Burger King maintains the chicken site (http://www.subservientchicken.com), but reference to the corporation on the site is minimal. If a piece is too obviously a sales message, it simply doesn't go viral. The cog ad seems to have been posted independently at http://194.29.64.17/thecog/movie.html, probably because of its indisputable artistry.

Writing in ClickZ, consultant Heidi Cohen suggests three rules for creating messages that become viral:

1. "Find a promotional hook." Find creative ways to get consumers interested and involved, based on their interests, not yours as a marketer.

2. "Engage potential customers with a call to action that gets them to interact with your site." A contest or a survey on something light and fun, and only tangentially product related, can work.

3. "Maximize effect." The marketer needs to integrate the promotion with other aspects of the marketing plan by, for instance, linking it to the corporate Web site. This must be unobtrusive, however, and perhaps should even wait until buzz begins to build.[27]

It is not easy to create a marketing campaign that masks its corporate purposes in such a way that people pass it on to friends and coworkers and that perhaps even gets picked up by the media. Nevertheless, the potential power of viral marketing continues to generate efforts to develop planned viral programs.

The techniques we have discussed so far in this chapter—search, events, publicity, affiliate programs, portal deals, and affiliate marketing—are most often used in customer acquisition programs. To end this chapter, we turn to a technique used in both acquisition and retention—e-mail. This section discusses the basics of e-mail marketing and the regulation that governs it. We return to e-mail in the context of strategies for customer retention in Chapter 8.

7-9 E-Mail Marketing

E-mail as promotional activity has exploded in recent years, and most forecasters believe that its rapid growth is likely to continue for the foreseeable future. Why is this? E-mail offers marketers a fast, flexible, and highly controllable format. It is essentially direct mail on steroids, and a deep understanding of the nature of offline mail promotions is useful to the e-mail marketer. E-mails can be developed quickly, tested, and revised on the fly and can reach many Internet users in a short period. It is highly measurable. Compared with other types of Internet promotions, e-mail is cheap on a per customer contact basis. E-mail can be used by any marketer—B2C, B2B, or not-for-profit—who has an acceptable way to acquire an e-mail list of potential customers.

Customers, for their part, are active in the e-mail space. In late 2004, 81% of American Internet users reported sending e-mails multiple times each day and 33% reported using it "constantly." The average consumer reported receiving 308 e-mails per week. Nearly two-thirds of those were spam. Although only one in twelve e-mails was perceived to be permission-based, these consumers reported opening an average of 78% of the permission-based e-mail.[28] Although the latter is good news for marketers, the existence of spam continues to be an issue for e-mail marketers and recipients alike.

A February 2005 study by the Pew Foundation found that more than half of all Internet users complained that spam was a big problem. The problem is sufficiently serious that many users are changing their e-mail behavior. The study reported that:

- 28% of users with a personal email account say they are getting more spam than a year ago, while 22% say they are getting less.
- 21% of users with a work email account say they are getting more spam than a year ago, while 16% say they are getting less.
- 53% of email users say spam has made them less trusting of email, compared to 62% a year ago.
- 22% of email users say that spam has reduced their overall use of email, compared to 29% a year ago.
- 67% of email users say spam has made being online unpleasant or annoying, compared to 77% a year ago.

Those statistics also pose a problem for marketers. Many have come to rely on e-mail marketing as a cost-effective tool, not only for customer acquisition but also for customer development and retention. DoubleClick reports that 73% of research respondents made a purchase as a result of an e-mail, some online immediately, others online later; still others purchased offline at a later date. Almost 60% of those who redeemed online coupons did so offline using printouts.[29] These data are consistent with other research and monitoring statistics, which all testify to the power of e-mail marketing to influence consumer behavior.

Before we discuss e-mail campaigns, we need to address the issue of permission marketing.

7-9a Levels of Permission Marketing

The first issue relating to permission is that of spam. *Spam* is unsolicited e-mail. No responsible marketer uses or sanctions the use of spam. Ever. Period.

Direct marketers have been sending unsolicited mailings for many years. Many consumers do not like it, but unsolicited physical mail does not appear to arouse the same level of ire in consumers that spam e-mail does. There does not yet seem to be any definitive data on the issue, but anecdotally it seems that consumers regard spam as more intrusive than mail. It is also clear that reputable marketers do not want to be identified with spam in the minds of the consuming public.

In order not to be considered a spammer, the marketer must obtain permission from the customer or prospect before sending e-mail. There are four levels of permission:

1. *Opt-out* means that the visitor did not refuse to receive further communications from the marketer. This is an improvement over spam, but it does not represent a high level of commitment on the part of the visitor.

    Opt-out e-mail addresses are often collected via registration forms. The point is to make consumers take some explicit action in order *not* to receive further communications. The theory behind this seems to be that people may not bother to take the action, or be unaware that they could take it, and will therefore, almost by default, become members of the list. This is often operationalized by an already checked box saying in effect, "Please send me e-mail." Even if the choice is made to precheck the box, the accompanying statement must be clear about what the visitor is agreeing to. The statement should be unambiguous, and it should be located in a visible place. Under the CAN-SPAM law, all e-mails must have a clear option to unsubscribe.

    Opt-out represents, at best, passive agreement to receiving e-mail, but at present it represents the minimum acceptable standard. Opt-in is the preferred method by many marketers and observers of the field.

2. *Opt-in* means that visitors have actively chosen to receive further communications, usually by checking a box on a registration form. It represents active acquiescence, if not enthusiasm, about receiving future communications from the marketer. Consequently, members of opt-in lists should be more receptive to messages.

3. *Double opt-in* is a technique by which visitors agree to receive further communications, probably by checking an opt-in box on a site, and are then sent an e-mail asking them to confirm their consent by replying to the e-mail. The visitor has taken two actions, first indicating willingness to accept e-mail, then actively confirming it by replying to the confirmation. This should indicate an interested, potentially well-qualified prospect.

4. *Confirmed opt-in* is somewhere in between opt-in and double opt-in. The visitor actively acquiesces to receiving e-mail, again probably by checking a box. He or she is then sent a follow-up e-mail confirming the permission. No reply is required.

The opt-in/opt-out controversy is in part the traditional direct-marketing issue of fewer, better-quality leads versus more leads of lower quality. Marketers are often wise to choose quality over quantity in lead situations. The differences in the e-mail context have to do with both the economics and the relationships with potential customers. The cost of incremental e-mail is virtually zero, arguing for larger lists, even if they are less qualified. The annoyance factor is so high, however, that there is a strong argument for high-quality opt-in lists of prospects who are genuinely willing to receive marketer-generated communications.

opt-out Communication that has been passively requested by the Internet user. This is usually done by prechecking the communications request, requiring the user to uncheck it in order to avoid receiving the communication.

opt-in Communication that has been actively requested by the Internet user. It becomes "double opt-in" when the marketer sends an e-mail that requires the user to confirm the request before it is activated.

FIGURE 7-5   Examples of opt-in confirmation e-mails.

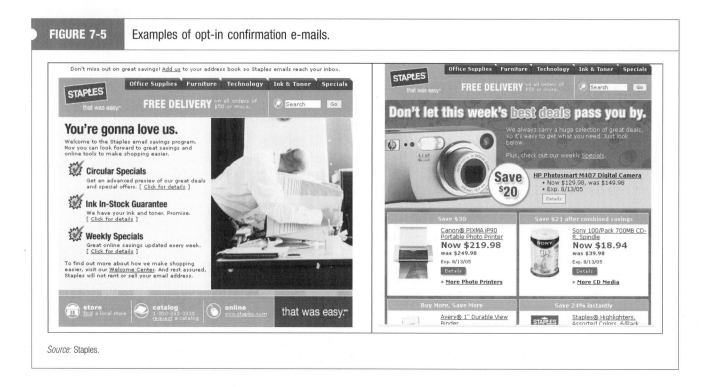

Source: Staples.

The one gray area is the marketer who has an e-mail list that was obtained without use of specific opt-in or opt-out authorization by the consumer. These lists should be converted to either opt-in or opt-out by means of one carefully constructed e-mail, perhaps including the use of incentives. There are relatively few e-mail lists like this that were collected in the early days of the Internet before e-mail protocol became something of an accepted standard. The existence of a small number of lists in this category should not be taken as an excuse for spam by other marketers.

Both the e-mails in Figure 7-5 are the result of a new registration on a site. Staples replied to a new registration with a welcoming sales message that linked to promotional areas on the site. Notice that at the top, it contains a message relating to **deliverability**, asking registrants to add the address to their address books so it will not be screened out by internet service provider (ISP) spam filters.

deliverability The ability to get commercial e-mail delivered to the intended recipient, primarily by taking the correct actions to avoid spam filters.

7-9b Developing an E-Mail Marketing Campaign

The Peppers and Rogers Group, whose expertise is in relationship marketing, summarizes the e-mail marketing process as it moves from analysis to action (Figure 7-6). Their process involves four steps:

- *Gather customer data.* This includes contact information, physical address or e-mail address, or both. The transactional data also include purchase history and a record of all customer interactions, as well as the types of information (offers) they wish to receive, their preferences for receiving it (frequency and communications channel), and their privacy preferences.

- *Derive customer insight.* Using the different types of information that have been captured about the customer, begin to understand what the customer needs and values. The most valuable type of understanding is what should come next in the purchase cycle—an extended warranty program for a recently purchased appliance, for example.

- *Suggest proactive action.* This is the point at which the process moves from analysis to action. E-mail programs are developed, executed, and refined based on the results of the programs themselves, captured in the customer database.

| FIGURE 7-6 | The e-mail marketing process. |

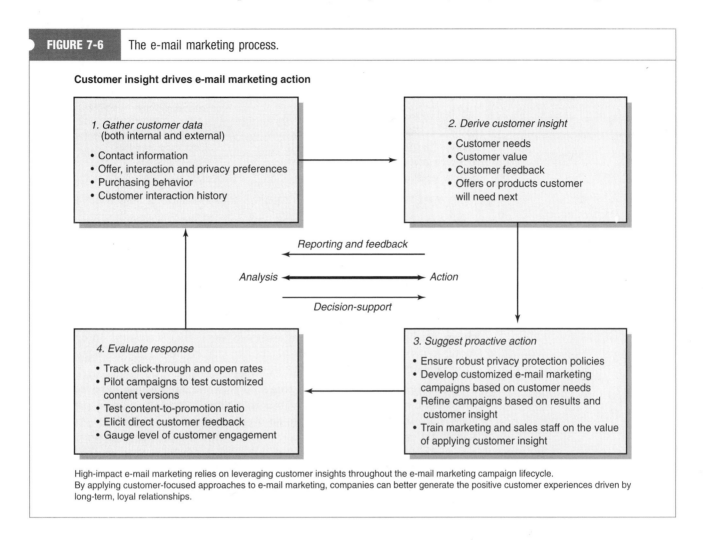

Customer insight drives e-mail marketing action

1. Gather customer data
(both internal and external)

- Contact information
- Offer, interaction and privacy preferences
- Purchasing behavior
- Customer interaction history

2. Derive customer insight

- Customer needs
- Customer value
- Customer feedback
- Offers or products customer will need next

Reporting and feedback

Analysis ⟷ Action

Decision-support

4. Evaluate response

- Track click-through and open rates
- Pilot campaigns to test customized content versions
- Test content-to-promotion ratio
- Elicit direct customer feedback
- Gauge level of customer engagement

3. Suggest proactive action

- Ensure robust privacy protection policies
- Develop customized e-mail marketing campaigns based on customer needs
- Refine campaigns based on results and customer insight
- Train marketing and sales staff on the value of applying customer insight

High-impact e-mail marketing relies on leveraging customer insights throughout the e-mail marketing campaign lifecycle. By applying customer-focused approaches to e-mail marketing, companies can better generate the positive customer experiences driven by long-term, loyal relationships.

- *Evaluate response.* In this step, program metrics are collected and analyzed to refine existing programs and suggest new strategies. Different approaches and content should be tested to see which perform better. It is also good to encourage direct feedback from recipients to further understand likes, dislikes, and desires.

The Peppers and Rogers Group presents an overview of the process that applies whether e-mail is being used for acquisition of prospects or relationship marketing to customers. Let's now turn briefly to a detailed set of steps for developing an e-mail campaign, which also applies to either acquisition or retention settings (Table 7-1).

- *Build or obtain an e-mail list.* Like Rome, e-mail lists are not built in a day, and list development needs to be an ongoing process, one begun well in advance of an actual e-mail campaign. Marketers who wish to be welcome in the inboxes of their customers obtain permission at one of the four levels just discussed. In direct marketing terms, this becomes their own "e-mail house list" and it is an essential foundation for permission-based e-mail marketing.

    If it is necessary to rent e-mail lists—and there are a considerable number available—the marketer should carefully investigate the source of the list, especially any privacy promises that were made to consumers as the list was constructed. Many privacy policies make it clear that lists will "from time to time" be shared with other marketers deemed acceptable to the list owner. When this is the case, both marketers are clearly within their legal rights.

TABLE 7-1	Steps in Developing an E-Mail Marketing Campaign

1. Build or obtain an e-mail list. 　a. Build a permission-based list 　b. Rent e-mail lists 2. Profile and segment the list. 3. Establish a communications schedule. 4. Develop specific program objectives. 5. Write compelling copy.	6. Structure your e-mail to be received and opened. 7. Create links to further information. 8. Make it easy for viewers to take action. 9. Test and revise the e-mail. 10. Measure results. 11. Integrate learning into next e-mail program.

However, that does not mean that the consumer is going to be thrilled about receiving e-mail from a company with whom he or she may have no relationship.

Lists for acquisition programs should be rented with care, from reputable list management agencies. Good lists will run from $100 to $300 per thousand, with established, performing lists closer to the higher end. Extremely cheap lists have been complied by software (bots) that search the Internet and snatch e-mail addresses in public places like chat rooms. They are the source of spam and should be avoided at all costs.

- *Profile or segment the list.* The customer/prospect database should have data, the volume of which grows over time, that allow a descriptive profile (middle-aged, high-income golfer living in an upscale suburb in the Midwest) or segmentation analysis that produces typical demographic (high-income, two-worker family with school-aged children) or lifestyle segments (patron of the arts). We return to the subject of segmenting the database as an element of relationship marketing strategy in Chapter 8. It is essential in order to know what communications to address to which segments of the list in order to get the best response.

- *Establish a communications schedule.* The ease of sending e-mail makes it tempting to send e-mail whenever the firm feels like it. With the exception of important "breaking news" types of notifications, which should be rare, the organization should establish a mailing schedule and stick to it. Better yet, it should ask subscribers for their preferences when they sign up. Then the marketer will send content that is relevant to each subscriber on the schedule the subscriber has dictated. That is the way to make e-mail welcome in the inbox.

- *Identify the target segment and communications objectives.* Each mailing should have its own specified target segment and specific objectives. Simply sending the same message to an entire list will not often be effective. Perhaps the business marketer is announcing a new product to users of that product line. The marketer of consumer credit cards may be delivering an offer of credit card protection insurance to new cardholders. The nonprofit marketer may wish to invite large donors and prospects to a special event showcasing the successes of the organization. The objective and the target segment must be a good fit, and the single campaign must fit into the overall communications and marketing strategies. Specify the action you want the recipient to take. You may, for instance, give the prospective large donor the option of calling a special phone number or visiting a special landing page to respond to the invitation.

- *Write compelling copy.* E-mail copy should be only as long as is necessary to convince the recipient to take the desired action. Often this action will be to click through on a link to go to a particular page on the Web site. The target pages should be carefully examined to make sure they are consistent with the objectives and message of the e-mail campaign. Writing short copy that persuades is not an easy task.

- *Structure your e-mail to be received and opened.* In their effort to control spam, ISPs have set up filters in an attempt to remove the offenders. In the process they capture many messages from legitimate marketers. The "from" header and the "subject" header are both important in this respect. The source must be clear and the subject descriptive.

- *Create links to further information.* One of the beauties of e-mail, whether text or HTML, is that links to more detailed information, usually on the Web site, are easy. Copy has to be written around the concept of linking. The Web site and landing page must be examined to ensure that they are ready to receive visitors from the e-mail.

- *Make it easy for readers to take action.* Marketers need to specify what it is they want recipients to do after they click through to the site. Do they want them to send for additional information? If so, create an e-mail link, or better, a form that requests a small amount of information about the requester. Is the objective to persuade recipients to donate to a charitable cause? If so, the links to material on the site need to make the case for the contribution, with multiple opportunities to click through to the form that accepts the donor's information.

- *Test and revise the e-mail.* E-mails can and should be tested using the techniques discussed in Chapter 4. Important things to test include the subject line and the offer. A test can be mailed to only a selected segment of the target list, or an A/B split can be used. Testing is a powerful tool, and it should not be overlooked.

- *Measure results.* E-mail service providers supply the most common metrics—received, opened, and clicked through are typical. Marketers can get more detailed results by creating special landing pages to receive the click-throughs and then tracking them through the site. Results will also include maintenance issues such as bounce-backs and unsubscribes.

- *Integrate learning into the next e-mail program.* Most organizations today will find themselves doing another e-mail campaign rather quickly. An ongoing challenge is how to use the results of one campaign to make the next one better. Some companies have developed formal programs for doing so, a subject to which we will return in Chapter 8.

This appears to be a rather formidable series of steps. However, the seasoned e-mail marketer, with the support of a well-maintained database and suppliers of the necessary services, can develop and launch an e-mail campaign in days if not hours. The speed, the relatively low cost, and the ability to target and measure will only fuel marketers' interest in effective e-mail marketing.

Because e-mail is open to abuse by spammers, **phishers**, and others who seek to dupe the unwary, legislation has been passed in an attempt to curb the worst abuses.

phishers Fraudulent emailers who engage in phishing by using emails that attempt to obtain personal data from consumers.

7-9c Requirements of the U.S. CAN-SPAM Act

This law, officially named "Controlling the Assault of Non-Solicited Pornography and Marketing Act," was passed in 2003 by the U.S. Congress in an attempt to curb unsolicited and, especially, offensive e-mail. Although it does not use the terms, it distinguishes between acquisition mailings by marketers and relationship mailings. Relationship mailings, or in the terms of the Federal Trade Commission (FTC), "a transactional or relationship message," are e-mails that facilitate a transaction or update an existing customer. As long as the content is not false or misleading, these e-mails are generally exempt from the provisions of CAN-SPAM. Acquisition mailings, however, come under the provisions of the law.

According to the FTC Web site, the main provisions of the law are:

- *It bans false or misleading header information.* Your e-mail's "From," "To," and routing information—including the originating domain name and e-mail address—must be accurate and identify the person who initiated the e-mail.

- *It prohibits deceptive subject lines.* The subject line cannot mislead the recipient about the contents or subject matter of the message.

- *It requires that your e-mail give recipients an opt-out method.* You must provide a return e-mail address or another Internet-based response mechanism that allows a recipient to ask you not to send future e-mail messages to that e-mail address, and you must honor the requests. You may create a "menu" of choices to allow a recipient to opt out of certain types of messages, but you must include the option to end any commercial messages from the sender.

  Any opt-out mechanism you offer must be able to process opt-out requests for at least 30 days after you send your commercial e-mail. When you receive an opt-out request, the law gives you 10 business days to stop sending e-mail to the requester's e-mail address. You cannot help another entity send e-mail to that address or have another entity send e-mail on your behalf to that address. Finally, it's illegal for you to sell or transfer the e-mail addresses of people who choose not to receive your e-mail, even in the form of a mailing list, unless you transfer the addresses so that another entity can comply with the law.

- *It requires that commercial e-mail be identified as an advertisement and include the sender's valid physical postal address.* Your message must contain clear and conspicuous notice that the message is an advertisement or solicitation and that the recipient can opt out of receiving more commercial e-mail from you. It also must include your valid physical postal address.[30]

  Commercial e-mail services help marketers abide by the provisions of the law. Most of them seem straightforward, but some are difficult to implement if the marketer has a large list. This is especially true of the requirements for removing e-mail addresses for individuals who have requested this be done—also known as "unsubcribes"—from the marketer's own list as well as those of any affiliates who may have been given access. If the list is to be rented, the unsubscribes must be meticulously purged from the rental list. Software that automates this process is desirable because errors must be avoided.

Other practices are also specified as unacceptable in the FTC implementation guidelines. Most are practices not used by reputable marketers in any event. They include so-called harvesting of e-mail addresses from other Web sites, a so-called dictionary attack in which the spammer uses computer algorithms to create e-mail addresses, using unauthorized networks, and other practices that mislead the consumer about the results of registering with a site. The last provision means, for example, that if a marketer needs to place a special piece of software on the registrant's computer so that he or she can receive e-mails in the desired format, the registrant must be explicitly notified of and agree to the placement of the software on the computer. That is an issue that can trip up even a marketer whose intentions are good.

7-9d CAN-SPAM in the European Union

The European Union (EU) Directive on Privacy and Electronic Communications was passed in 2002. It sets out guidelines for direct marketing in all media and requires that member nations of the EU harmonize their individual laws under the umbrella of the EU directive. E-mail is covered under the general policy directive, and the basic requirement is that people must opt-in to receive marketer-initiated communications in all electronic media. The "technology-neutral" laws resulting from the EU directive have been criticized as being unenforceable. The very generality of laws that attempt to cover the wide spectrum of electronic media makes it hard to be specific and therefore enforceable. The fact that the directive also covers the twenty-five members of the EU also creates difficulties. Finally, the fact that much spam received in Western Europe comes from outside that geographic area makes enforcement exceedingly difficult.

A 2004 study by Dutch researchers at the University of Amsterdam found that 80% of the e-mail sent to schools was spam and that more than half of those contain pornography. Dr. Asscher and his colleagues found that "the EU legislation on spam has a lot of potential to regulate and stop spam but currently that potential is simply not being realised. Says the study: 'The simple fact that most spam originates from outside the EU restricts the European Union's Directive's effectiveness considerably.' As a result the pan-Europe opt-in rule, which means spam only goes to those that choose to receive it, is rendered 'meaningless' said the study. Without similar anti-spam rules being adopted across the globe, the EU directives are not going to stop spam sent to European e-mail users from beyond the region."[31] That refrain sounds familiar to e-mail users around the globe.

For those interested in keeping track of the developments in privacy protection and antispam laws in Europe, the EU has a detailed and interesting site called "Europe's Information Portal," with a section on fighting spam.[32] Among other items on this content-rich site is a toolkit to be used by governments, regulators, and members of the industry in the continuing war against spam.[33]

Both the EU and the U.S. CAN-SPAM laws specify legal standards that marketers must meet. They are not, however, sufficient to ensure effective e-mail marketing.

The Golden *R*'s of E-Mail Marketing

Advocates of permission marketing argue that the requirements of CAN-SPAM are simply good business practice. In fact, many of them would argue that they represent minimal acceptable levels, not best practices. Some level of opt-in is considered more effective than opt-out. Many would go a step further, arguing that segmentation and personalization of content is a requirement for effectiveness. They speak disparagingly of "blast" e-mails that are sent to all members of a list, regardless of the relevance of the content.

E-mail boxes are crammed with spam, e-mails of dubious value to the recipient, and only a small number of communications that are welcome and that have a good chance of inciting to action. There is an approach marketers can follow to give their e-mails the best chance of being opened and acted upon, the three golden *R*'s of e-mail marketing:[34]

- *Relevance*. All content should be applicable to the recipient's needs and lifestyle. Content that is not relevant will not motivate the recipient to take action and it may tarnish the brand of the communicator.

- *Respect*. Relevant content cannot be generated without in-depth information about the recipient. In order to get the information and keep the trust of the recipient, the sender of e-mails must guard data from unwarranted or frivolous use.

- *Recipient control*. Go beyond simply obtaining permission to communicate with the recipient. Make the recipient an active partner in deciding what content he or she wants to receive and how often to receive it. That gives the content a much better chance of being seen as valuable.

Not only will following these three *R*'s give the e-mails the best possible chance of success, it will also, over time, contribute to the creation of brand that is trusted by the members of its target market.

Summary

The techniques for online customer acquisition may not be increasing in number, but they are increasing in flexibility and impact as the underlying technology becomes more robust and as more Internet users take advantage of them through broadband access. In addition to the many varieties of online advertising discussed in Chapter 6, marketers use search, events, publicity, affiliate programs, portal deals, and viral marketing as part of their acquisition programs. E-mail marketing is something of a hybrid technique. It has uses in customer acquisition, but it comes into its own as a customer relationship technique.

Search marketing has great impact, whether it is first optimizing a Web site so that it is easily visible to the search engines or then placing paid ads on search engine results. Search engines are also increasing in variety of use, with local and vertical search engines becoming important in specialized markets. They can streamline the user experience and make search more useful and accessible to niche and small business marketers.

Few marketers attempt to build their electronic marketing programs solely around the techniques of events, publicity, affiliate programs, portal deals, and viral marketing. They can, however, play useful roles in an integrated communications program. Among other things, they can offer higher levels of interactivity and reach target markets that are difficult to reach using standard techniques or offline media.

E-mail marketing for customer acquisition is marketing's version of a two-edged sword. It has genuine benefits when used in a permission marketing program. However, the volume of spam threatens to drown the efforts of legitimate marketers. Governments around the globe are attempting to stem the tide of spam.

Marketers' choices of customer acquisition techniques are rich, varied, and growing. The challenge is to use the correct techniques for the correct objectives at the correct time and to do so in a fully integrated online and offline communications program.

Quiz

1. Search engines have assumed a key role in the activities of Web users of all kinds.
   a. true
   b. false

2. A site that lists items by topic is called a _____.
   a. search engine
   b. directory
   c. paid placement

3. _____ is the development of Web pages in a manner that is friendly to search engine spiders.
   a. SEM
   b. SEP
   c. SEO

4. The objective of keyword bidding is to _____.
   a. get the best ranking for the lowest cost
   b. always be ranked first
   c. limit the amount of money the firm spends on search marketing

5. Event-driven marketing _____.
   a. is a purely online marketing technique
   b. is a purely offline marketing technique
   c. can be used effectively either on or offline

6. Offline promotional methods that can be used to attract prospects to a Web site do *not* include _____.
   a. affiliate programs
   b. event marketing
   c. public relations

7. _____ is the online technique that aims to encourage current customers to refer promotional material to prospective customers.
   a. reciprocal links
   b. online classified advertising
   c. viral marketing

8. Spam is only a minor annoyance to most Internet users.
   a. true
   b. false

9. The term used to describe the expressed willingness of consumers to receive further promotional material from the marketer is _____.
   a. opt-out
   b. registration
   c. opt-in

10. Acceptable e-mail marketing practices under the CAN-SPAM law include _____.
    a. sending unsolicited e-mail to prospective customers without giving them an opportunity to opt-out
    b. using correct identification of the sender in the header
    c. using spiders and other anonymous collection techniques

Discussion Questions

1. Why do you think search has become such an important part of the life of Internet users?

2. What options do marketers have when it comes to developing a search marketing strategy? Have you

been exposed to or participated in a marketing "event" recently either online or offline? If so, describe it and explain what you believe the marketer's objectives were.

3. Explain what a portal deal is. Why would a marketer expend some of her budget on this type of promotional activity?

4. Have you seen or participated in any viral marketing activity recently? If so, describe what it was and what motivated you to participate.

5. What is meant by *permission marketing*? Do you think it is an important concept to e-mail marketers?

6. Think about e-mail communications from marketers, perhaps some that you receive yourself. What makes them interesting and worth your time to open and read? Do you ever take any action as a result of the e-mails? Why or why not?

7. From your perspective, is the CAN-SPAM law working? Why or why not?

8. Assume that WilyMarketer.com is running an e-mail campaign to acquire new customers. It is considering two options. In either event, actual campaign management will be outsourced to an interactive agency. Which program would you recommend and why?

- Option A would use a high-quality rental list of 100,000 e-mail addresses. Direct costs under this option include the rental list at $250/m (per thousand names), and $10,000 for creative, program management, and reporting. If the e-mail campaign brings in 623 new customers, what is its customer acquisition cost?
- Option B would rely on banner advertising at $20 CPM, which has a predicted click-through rate of 1.5%. The campaign is designed to reach 100,000 viewers, and its creative, program management, and reporting costs will be $10,000. How many customers will it bring in, and what is the customer acquisition cost?

Internet Exercises

1. Choose a well-known branded product with which you are familiar.
   a. Identify at least ten keywords that a person might use to search for the product or the brand.
   b. Search for the product on at least two different search engines.
      i. What is the product's position in natural search?
      ii. What is its position in paid search?
   c. Use the Yahoo! keyword finder to learn how good your keyword choices were. Were there others that should have been in your top ten?
   d. What recommendations would you have for the managers of the product to help them improve their rankings on the search engines you studied?

2. Visit Amazon's Web site and investigate the process for becoming an Amazon affiliate (*associate* is the term they use). Does it seem simple and straightforward? Do you think it would be worthwhile for a small Internet retailer to become an Amazon associate? Why or why not?

3. If you have not already done so, sign up for an e-mail newsletter from one or more of the sites you are following. For the next few weeks, keep a log of the e-mail contacts that result. Pay special attention to how long it took for the site to confirm/welcome you and the nature of the confirmation communication.

Notes

1. Deborah Fallows and Lee Rainie, "The Popularity and Importance of Search Engines," August 2004, http://www.pewinternet.org.
2. SEMPO, "Search Engine Marketers Spent $5.75 Billion in 2005," January 9, 2006, Press Release, http://www.sempo.org/news/releases/Search_Engine_Marketers.
3. "About Us," http://www.switchboard.com.
4. http://dmoz.org/
5. Danny Sullivan, "Buying Your Way In," November 22, 2004, http://www.searchenginewatch.com.
6. "More Advertising Solutions," accessed 1/11/06, http://my.superpages.com/spweb/portals/customer.portal?_nfpb=true&_pageLabel=bp_more&promo=adsol.
7. John Battelle, *The Search* (New York: Penguin, 2005), pp. 19–25.
8. Sean Michael Kerner, "Yahoo! Trumps Google in Local Search," August 12, 2005, ClickZStats, http://www.clickz.com/stats/sectors/search_tools/article.php/3527176.
9. Google has a generic explanation of its algorithm at http://www.google.com/newsletter/librarian/librarian_2005_12/article1.html.

10. SEMPO, "The State of Search Engine Marketing 2004," http://www.sempo.org, p. 4.

11. "Case Study: Restoration Hardware," http://icrossing.com/company_we_keep/case_studies/restoration_hardware.htm.

12. "Google Desktop Search Privacy Policy," http://desktop.google.com/privacypolicy.html.

13. "New Research by The Kelsey Group and ConStat Indicates 70% of U.S. Households Now Use the Internet When Shopping Locally for Products and Services," March 22, 2005, http://www.kelseygroup.com/press/pr050322.htm.

14. Justin Sanger, "A New Form of Local Search Optimization, Part I," July 7, 2005, http://www.clickz.com/experts/search/local_search/article.php/3517776.

15. Verne Kopytoff, "New Search Engines Narrowing their Focus," April 4, 2005, http://www.sfgate.com/cgi-bin/article.cgi?file=/c/a/2005/04/04/BUGJ9C20VU1.DTL&type= printable.

16. "Hitwise: Video Search," January 12, 2006, iMediaConnection, http://www.imediaconnection.com/content/7811.asp.

17. "About blinkx," accessed 1/12/06, http://www.blinkx.com/content/about.php.

18. Betsy Spethmann, "Buzz Gets Louder," April 1, 2005, http://promomagazine.com/mag/marketing_buzz_gets_louder/.

19. KOMO Staff, "Amazon Celebrates its 10th Anniversary," July 16, 2005, http://www.komotv.com/stories/38011.htm.

20. "Event Marketing," http://promomagazine.com/event/.

21. Middleberg/Ross Survey, quoted by David Berkowitz at "Leveraging Search for Greater Impact in Your Public Relations Programs Conference," December 14, 2004.

22. Safa Rashtchy, "The Silk Road," July 5, 2005, http://www.piperjaffray.com/popup.aspx?id=1092.

23. "Affiliate Marketing: A Primer," August 3, 2004, http://www.clickz.com/resources/adres/the_basics/article.php/3389931.

24. Pamela Parker, "AutoTrader.com Inks Portal Deal with Yahoo!" January 5, 2005, http://www.clickz.com/news/article.php/3454571.

25. Some of the Budweiser clips and other ads and e-mail advertising parodies are archived on http://www.adcritic.com.

26. Heidi Cohen, "Create (and Measure) Buzz," December 23, 2004, http://www.clickz.com/experts/crm/actionable_analysis/article.php/3450681.

27. Heidi Cohen, "Create (and Measure) Buzz," December 23, 2004, http://www.clickz.com/experts/crm/actionable_analysis/article.php/3450681.

28. "DoubleClick's 2004 Consumer Email Study," http://www.doubleclick.com/us/knowledge_central/documents/RESEARCH/dc_consumer_email_0410.pdf, 2. Deborah Fallows, "CAN-SPAM a year later," April 2005, http://www.pewinternet.org/pdfs/PIP_Spam_Ap05.pdf.

29. "DoubleClick's 2004 Consumer Email Study," http://www.doubleclick.com/us/knowledge_central/documents/RESEARCH/dc_consumer_email_0410.pdf, 7.

30. "The CAN-SPAM Act: Requirements for Commercial Emailers,"http://www.ftc.gov/bcp/conline/pubs/buspubs/canspam.htm.

31. "European Spam Laws Lack Bite," BBC News, April 28, 2004, http://news.bbc.co.uk/1/hi/technology/3666585.stm.

32. http://europa.eu.int/information_society/policy/ecomm/todays_framework/privacy_protection/spam/index_en.htm

33. http://www.oecd.org/document/24/0,2340,en_2649_22555297_34804568_1_1_1_1,00.html.

34. Based on a concept suggested by Bill Nussey, *The Quiet Revolution in Email Marketing*, (New York: iUniverse, Inc., 2004).

Customer Relationship Development and Management

Chapter Outline

Source: © Getty

Key Terms

Learning Objectives

By the time you complete this chapter, you will be able to:

- Explain the importance of customer retention.
- Describe the difference between relationship and transactional marketing.
- Discuss the concept of customer relationship management and the marketing functions on which it is based.

- Understand why CRM is an ongoing process.
- Be able to list key components of that process.
- Understand what is necessary to make CRM work.

8-1 Introduction

In 1996, Frederick Reichheld published a seminal volume titled *The Loyalty Effect.*[1] The book's chief argument was that businesses were paying too much attention to—and spending too much money on—customer acquisition. In the process they were overlooking the greater profitability to be gained from maximizing the value of their customer base. The book struck a responsive chord among managers who found the prospect of more cost-effective, more accountable marketing extremely appealing. It launched the marketing mantra of the late 1990s, "It costs seven to ten times as much to acquire a new customer as it does to maintain an existing one." It also firmly established customer relationship management (CRM) as a core process of the marketing discipline. Reichheld's argument for CRM was compelling because it was based on empirical data about customer value across industries, both consumer and business-to-business (B2B).

In addition to the high cost of customer acquisition, the advocates of relational approaches point to additional positive outcomes:

- The average company loses half its customers every 5 years.
- Reducing defections by 5% can increase profits by 25% to 85%, depending on the industry.
- As many as 85% of customers who defect say they were satisfied with their former supplier.
- Customers who are extremely satisfied are six times more likely to repurchase than customers who are merely satisfied.
- A satisfied customer will tell five people, whereas a dissatisfied customer will tell nine.[2]

8-2 The Importance of CLV

The relationship argument relies on the concept of customer lifetime value (CLV) to demonstrate the profit impact of relationship strategies. Figure 8-1 documents the importance of relationship maintenance in the online apparel industry. After accounting for acquisition costs, the consultants identify three revenue streams associated with each customer—each one's *base* spending amount, the *growth* of spending as the customer persists with the marketer, and the revenue generated by customer *referrals*. In this example, breakeven on acquisition costs occurs after 1 year; in other industries it tends to be longer because of higher acquisition costs and longer purchase cycles. The general pattern, however, holds true across industry sectors in both consumer and business

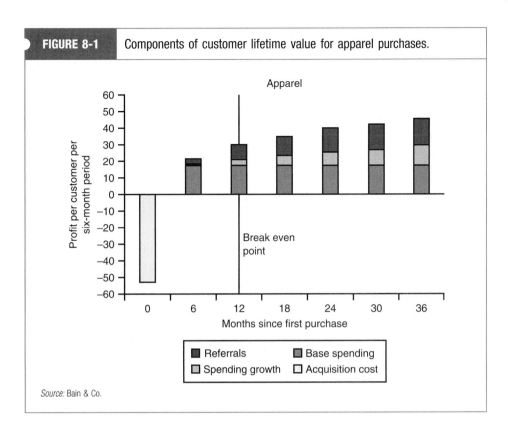

FIGURE 8-1 Components of customer lifetime value for apparel purchases.

Apparel

Profit per customer per six-month period

Months since first purchase

Break even point

■ Referrals
□ Spending growth
■ Base spending
□ Acquisition cost

Source: Bain & Co.

markets.[3] It emphasizes the importance of caring for customers in a way that causes them to return and to concentrate more of their purchases with the marketer.

Each of the revenue streams makes a contribution to CLV as the customer persists. In the case of the apparel industry, the data indicate the following:

- The average repeat customer spent 67% more in months 31 through 36 of the relationship than in the initial 6 months.

- An average apparel shopper referred three people to the online retailer's site after the first purchase. After ten purchases, the shopper had referred a total of seven people.

- Loyal Web customers also expressed willingness to buy other product lines from the online retailer. "For example, almost 70 percent of Gap Online customers said they would consider buying furniture from the Gap. And 63 percent of online grocery shoppers would buy toiletries and OTC [over the counter] drugs from their online grocers."[4]

Although the economics of the relational concept are persuasive, implementing it requires a complete reversal in the way traditional marketers think about and perform their jobs. Change of this magnitude is always difficult, and such has been the case with relational strategies. In order to understand the issues, we need to contrast the older transactional model to the relationship model.

8-3 The Transactional vs. the Relationship Perspective

Consumer marketers in the traditional mass media environment have really had no choice except to pursue a transactional approach. These marketers ordinarily did not have direct contact with their customers. Consequently, they could not identify their customers as individuals and attempt to develop an ongoing relationship with them.

The mass media did not facilitate identification and tracking of individual customers and prospects. The customer relationship, if there was one, was owned by an intermediary in a channel of distribution. These two factors created a powerful barrier to the establishment of direct relationships by marketers who produced the products and services. In addition, the large up-front investment required to build a product-specific customer database could not be justified by the small gross margins provided by many frequently purchased consumer products.

B2B marketers had different but no less serious issues. They typically dealt directly with their customers through field sales forces. Sales representatives tended to feel that they had ownership of the customer relationship and to be reluctant to provide detailed data to a centralized customer database. Even if that reluctance did not exist, contact with customers often took place in various units, including field sales, the telephone call center, field service, and technical support. To make the situation even worse, if the customer purchased items from more than one division or product line within the company, multiple and confusing customer contact points existed. What did not usually exist, however, was a data repository that permitted a complete view of the customer relationship with the firm. On the positive side, however, sales reps were often able to recognize customers who were transactional in nature, usually because they were price sensitive. Relationship customers had stronger ties with the firm, perhaps because they required customized products or specialized services. Reps who recognized the difference could, on an individual basis, allocate their time and effort according to the value of the customer relationship. There was not, however, a lasting record of customer actions that formed the basis for strategy planning and execution.

Many nonprofit organizations have experienced the same CRM issues. They need to retain and upgrade both members and donors. Some have extensive member databases built from their direct-mail marketing efforts. Others have little in the way of member data beyond name and address. Many have members and donors who predate the Internet and who have never been asked for e-mail addresses. Moving to Internet-based member retention programs has been difficult for many. However, as more nonprofit organizations become adept at the use of the Internet, and especially as they acquire new prospects or members from Web-based contacts, CRM efforts are becoming a major part of nonprofit marketing strategies also.

Whether in the business-to-customer (B2C), B2B, or nonprofit marketplaces, the basics of transactional and relational approaches are similar (see Figure 8-2). Transactional marketing is centered around products and single economic exchanges. Marketers engage in one-way communication in the mass media, targeting market segments identified by conventional marketing research. The primary goal of traditional marketing is generally stated in terms of market share. The approach is product-focused, not focused on a customer-oriented value proposition as discussed in Chapter 3.

When the marketing process moves to a relational approach, the focus shifts to customers and their relationship cycle with the organization. Customer needs and the expertise needed to meet them become key. Communications become targeted at individuals and contain personalized content. Goals are focused on growing customer value, not market share. CLV, which incorporates both revenue and cost to serve the customer, becomes a key metric, as do customer satisfaction, loyalty, and employee satisfaction. In implementing the CRM strategy, two-way communication becomes the norm with project-based marketing research taking a backseat to meaningful, ongoing dialog with the customer. Seamlessly satisfying customer

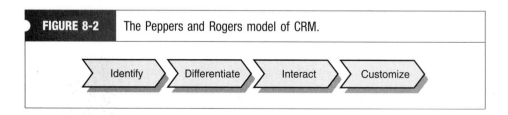

FIGURE 8-2   The Peppers and Rogers model of CRM.

Identify   Differentiate   Interact   Customize

experience becomes the vision that guides all marketing activities and permeates the entire organization.[5]

8-3a A CRM Model

CRM consultants Don Peppers and Martha Rogers have long espoused a model that captures the essence of customer relationship management (Figure 8-2). Their view is an information-driven one, with every step in the process adding to the customer database that is essential to drive CRM strategy and programs. The steps are as follows:

- *Identify* your customers by individual or household name and address or e-mail address.
- *Differentiate* them according to their needs and their actual or potential value.
- *Interact* with customers based on their own needs. From the organization's perspective, the interactions should become more cost-effective. Each interaction should be used as an opportunity to increase the store of data about the individual or household.
- *Customize* at least some aspects of the organization's dealings with the customer. This could be things such as tailored communications and specialized offers that allow the enterprise to recognize the customer as a valued supporter and that present opportunities for growing the value of the individual customer.

The concept of relationship marketing is extremely attractive. After all, marketers have been preaching the virtues of customer orientation for many years. As a result, marketers of all kinds have taken many different paths in their search for strong and lasting relationships with their customers. However, B2B marketers have an additional issue to deal with, and out of their efforts have come the term in widespread use today, *CRM*—customer relationship management.

8-4 The Foundations of CRM

Although much controversy surrounds the use of the term *CRM* today, there is little disagreement on how the discipline originated. In the 1980s, there was growing recognition among business marketers that the cost of a single sales call was spiraling out of control. Figures quoted were typically in the hundreds of dollars for one sales call. Marketers needed a way to make their field sales forces more efficient without risking their ability to grow sales. They turned to **sales force automation** in an attempt to offer more cost-effective service to customers while decreasing their overall sales costs. According to Moriarty and Schwartz, some of the sales force automation tools include the following:

- Sales force productivity tools such as call reporting and checking order and inventory status
- Direct-mail **sales lead generation** campaigns that include mail fulfillment of product information
- Telemarketing, often to follow up the sales leads generated by direct mail
- Sales and marketing management tools including sales forecasting and reporting.[6]

This is another information-driven marketing application. In this case, lower-cost media are used to generate (direct-mail) and **qualify** (telemarketing) sales leads. Field salespeople are given access to a comprehensive customer/prospect database, which is also used for sales and marketing management applications. The result should be better customer service at lower cost to the enterprise.

sales force automation Processes, and the software that supports them, that permit salespeople to work more effectively both in and out of their offices by providing electronic access to important documents and customer data.

sales lead generation The process of identifying prospective purchasers.

qualify To determine whether a prospective customer is likely to make a purchase at some time in the future.

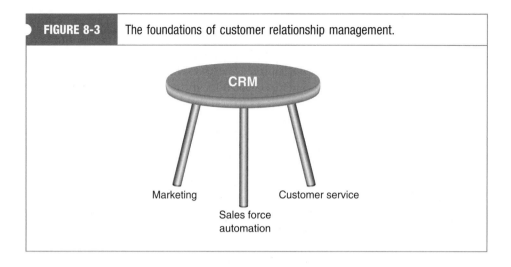

FIGURE 8-3   The foundations of customer relationship management.

CRM

Marketing

Sales force automation

Customer service

Early systems focused on the sales force, with marketing developing and executing direct-mail campaigns, and sophisticated call centers using the customer/prospect database to qualify leads and provide customer service. This has led to the "three-legged stool" concept of CRM portrayed in Figure 8-3. The sales force productivity "leg" has little application in the B2C marketplace, but the concept itself and the marketing and customer service components are entirely applicable. The term *CRM* has been adopted to describe relational marketing in both the B2B and B2C spaces despite the differences just described. It is also the term used to describe retention marketing in the nonprofit space.

8-5 Three Approaches to CRM

To better understand the complexity of the CRM undertaking, let's look at three brief case histories that illustrate the diversity of the firms engaging in CRM and of the CRM systems they have developed.

8-5a Lands' End

Lands' End (http://www.landsend.com), the well-known catalog retailer of classic casual clothing, established its Web site in 1996 on principles developed as a result of their successful direct marketing experience. According to an executive at the time, "Because we've been a direct merchant for 36 years, the customer service, the fulfillment operation—all of that was in place. It was very easy to add a front-end Web site."[7]

Lands' End, established in 1962 as a catalog operation, is now a successful multichannel retailer. It now features three types of retail stores, "inlets," "not quite perfect" stores, and airport stores. Since its acquisition by Sears in 2002, its products are also featured in Sears stores. The multichannel experience is enhanced by a link on Web site home page called "As Seen in Stores!" that features merchandise currently displayed in the stores. Although the catalog is still its revenue mainstay, the Lands' End Web site has become a hub of retail operations and a model for innovative customer service and relationship marketing.

The site's special features encourage visitors to browse, buy, and return. The "My Virtual Model" feature creates a "virtual dressing room" in which the shopper can select a body type and "try clothing on" the virtual model to see whether a given fashion will be flattering. During the summer buying season, there is a special version, the Swim Finder, to help shoppers find the best swimsuits for their body types. If the customer is still having trouble finding the right product, there is a live chat feature accessible on the Customer Service page that allows customers to exchange text messages with a customer representative in real time. Product images can be provided to the customer during the chat session. For even more individualized service, the customer can ask for a Specialty Shopper by phone or chat. This person will help find the needed products and can keep a file of sizes, preferences, and contact information for future reference.

If the shopper is still unable to find just the right product, Lands' End offers a line of custom garments. At the time of this writing, the offerings for women included jeans, chinos, blouses, and jacket. Since introduced in about 2002, the number of custom offerings has continued to increase, so it is reasonable to assume that Lands' End considers it successful. From the customer's point of view, the custom products are not significantly more expensive than regular counterparts, they arrive quickly, and the customer's measurements are retained for future orders.

Lands' End describes itself as the world's largest volume apparel Web site. It has achieved this by adhering to its customer service heritage and constantly innovating to deliver an exceptional shopping experience, both important components of overall CRM.

8-5b Yellow Transportation

Yellow Transportation (http://www.myyellow.com) is a freight company headquartered in Overland Park, Kansas, serving the B2B marketplace. Until 1998, its customer service consisted of an 800 number for shipment scheduling and tracking. The company knew it was important to migrate customer service to the Web. "We want our customers to be able to communicate with us any way they want to. If we were going to migrate to the Web, we knew that it had to be as good as or better than working with a customer service representative," said Paul Marshall, senior director of customer support.[8] This has become even more important as gasoline prices have increased from 2003 on and Yellow's customers turned to the Internet for cost-saving options.

The Yellow Transportation Web site (Figure 8-4) has numerous applications that provide a variety of services to customers. They can track shipments in process, get prices for planned shipments, and obtain a number of useful reports. Customers can also create their own "My Yellow" page and specify parameters such as regular shipping time and pickup address. Yellow also offers chat capability on the Web site. A subsidiary, New Penn, is piloting a system that offers real-time shipment status from the time a product is picked up until it is delivered. According to the New Penn Vice President of Marketing, "Historically, customers have not been able to start tracking a shipment until the day after it has been shipped. With NP-Connex, customers can actually begin tracking the shipment from the moment it is picked up, or before if the bill of lading and pickup were created at www.newpenn.com." Customers can also receive status updates by e-mail for especially sensitive shipments.[9]

The basic functions are easily accessible from the Online Tools home page (see Figure 8-4), which features the recognizable Yellow logo. When visitors click through to the Online Tools page, they find self-service tools listed by category. Many of the tools have demonstrations available to assist users in the sometimes complex planning and paperwork necessary to expedite shipments. The home page offers a Site Enhancements page to help customers keep abreast of the new self-service features that Yellow introduces with some regularity.

Frequent addition of useful functionality on a site is an important way to keep customers coming back and retaining loyal customers in the face of competition. It also landed Yellow Transportation on the Fortune magazine's 2005 list of most admired companies, ranking first in the transportation industry.[10] In 2004, Yellow received Carrier of the Year and Innovator of the Year awards from Wal-Mart for its contributions to supply chain excellence.[11]

chat Provides the capability of real-time conferencing on a LAN or on the Internet by typing on the keyboard.

FIGURE 8-4 The Yellow Transportation home page.

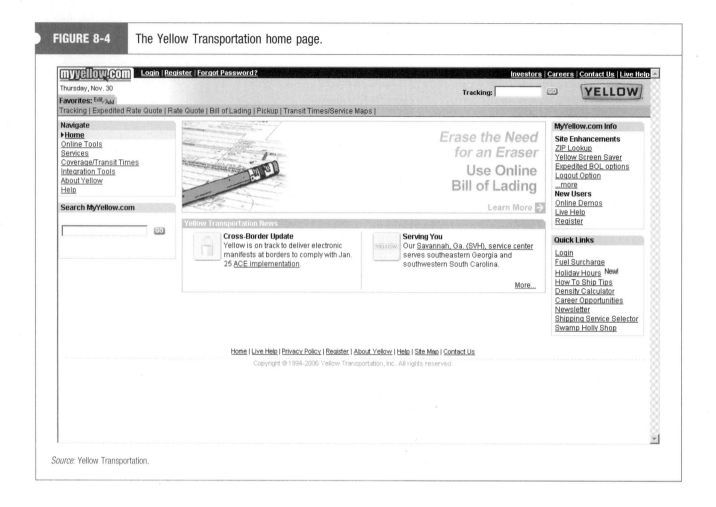

Source: Yellow Transportation.

8-5c ASPCA

The nonprofit American Society for the Prevention of Cruelty to Animals has become an adept user of the Internet in carrying out its mission of "providing effective means for the prevention of cruelty to animals throughout the United States."[12] The ASPCA is a venerable organization, founded in 1866 by Henry Bergh and modeled on England's Royal Society for the Prevention of Cruelty to Animals, which dates back to 1840.

Like many nonprofits, the ASPCA saw the potential of the Internet to extend its reach and impact, but early efforts were tentative. In 2002. the society revamped its Web site (Figure 8-5) and strengthened its e-mail marketing program.

The Web site has extensive content to support responsible pet "parenting" and care in addition to its work to prevent cruelty. It urges visitors to join its efforts by becoming a member, by donating online, and by signing up for e-mail communications. Incentives for providing an e-mail address include the following:

- Ability to send e-cards
- Weekly e-mail newsletters
- Information relevant to animal protection in the registrant's state
- Access to the archives of *ASPCA Animal Watch* magazine
- ASPCA rewards program
- Special offers from the ASPCA online store[13]

The list of e-mail addresses had grown to more than 250,000 by 2003. It consisted of members and visitors who registered on the Web site.[14] Online donations also increased with the new Web site, averaging about $62, as compared with $19.20 by mail.[15]

Source: ASPCA.

Visitors who register on the site are required to provide a name, e-mail address, and information on whether they currently own a cat, dog, or other pet. They are also asked whether they are an animal shelter professional, an educator, or an animal health or behavior specialist. Providing a mailing address and telephone number is optional. Using this profile information, ASPCA is able to target e-mails to cat or dog owners or to animal health professionals. Its relationship marketing agency reports on the results of a personalized e-mail campaign conducted in November 2003.

This particular appeal was to sponsor a pet by sending a donation to the organization. It was sent to both past donors and nondonor registrants who had provided profile information. According to Convio, "An overall 'Help us find safe homes for the holidays' message was altered slightly in the subject line to personalize it for the dog people and the cat people, and the order of appearance of dogs or cats on the message was different based on which category of recipient was receiving the message." They also tested a neutral message, targeting neither cat nor dog owners. The response rate averaged 230% higher among donors (see Figure 8-6) for the personalized message. Among nondonors, the personalized message achieved an 85% higher response.[16] This is a simple profile, but the power of relevant personalization is great in the nonprofit arena, just as it is in the for-profit one.

The business case is clear for the use of relationship marketing in businesses and nonprofit organizations of all kinds. It is not, however, easy to do. Achieving relationship marketing success requires a disciplined process. Let's turn to an overview of the process necessary to make relationship marketing work.

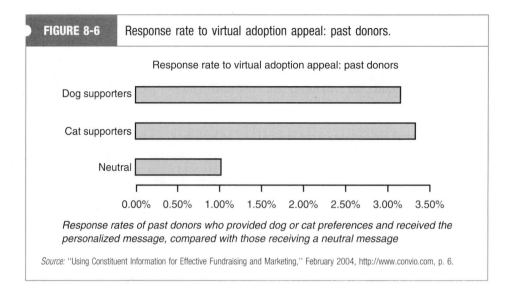

FIGURE 8-6   Response rate to virtual adoption appeal: past donors.

Response rate to virtual adoption appeal: past donors

Response rates of past donors who provided dog or cat preferences and received the personalized message, compared with those receiving a neutral message

Source: "Using Constituent Information for Effective Fundraising and Marketing," February 2004, http://www.convio.com, p. 6.

8-6 The Process of Customer Relationship Management[17]

The reason that CRM requires considerable discipline is twofold. First, relationship marketing requires significant changes in the way marketing is done. The emphasis must move from promotional campaigns and marketing research projects to ongoing dialog that is captured and stored in a customer database. Second, it must be treated and managed as an ongoing process, not as a series of discrete events. This is the antithesis of the way most marketing managers are measured, using metrics such as market share, sales growth, and expansion of customer base. The result is that for CRM to succeed, changes in organizational thinking and action must go beyond the marketing department to the highest levels of the corporation. This degree of change is not easy, and it requires a clear vision of the requirements and potential achievements of the CRM process.[18]

Figure 8-7 represents the process. It is a closed-loop process in which each customer contact is captured and represented in the customer database and in which all marketing programs are information driven.

Successful CRM cannot exist outside the context of the business unit's overall marketing strategy. The economics simply will not work unless the business identifies high-value customers (initially based on marketing research if no database is available), individually or by market segment, targets those customers, and develops marketing strategies and programs that specifically meet their needs. This is a genuinely customer-centric approach; target customers are identified first, and the value proposition, encompassing all aspects of the marketing mix, is then developed. It, too, is the antithesis of the traditional marketing model in which products are developed and it becomes the job of the marketing department to market and sell those products.

The customer database is the focal point of both design and execution of a CRM strategy. The database is developed and used to develop models including customer lifetime value and response to various types of promotional efforts. As programs are developed and executed, additional data are captured to enrich the database, to allow performance measurement of individual programs or customers, and to continually refine critical marketing models.

Program execution also comes from the database. Outbound programs, which could be e-mail promotions or marketing programs supported by physical world promotional media such as direct mail, are planned and implemented with reliance on the database. One of the types of discipline necessary to make CRM work is to compel all programs to rely on the database. Often the pressure to get programs out the door

> **FIGURE 8-7**   The CRM process.

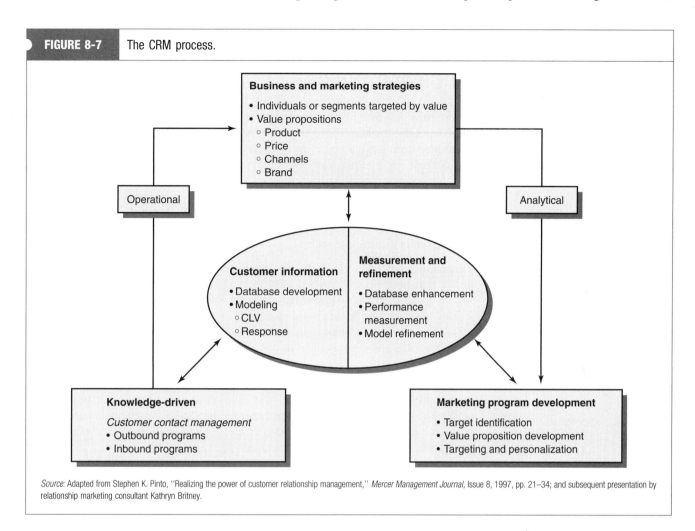

Business and marketing strategies

- Individuals or segments targeted by value
- Value propositions
  - Product
  - Price
  - Channels
  - Brand

Operational

Analytical

Customer information

- Database development
- Modeling
  - CLV
  - Response

Measurement and refinement

- Database enhancement
- Performance measurement
- Model refinement

Knowledge-driven

Customer contact management
- Outbound programs
- Inbound programs

Marketing program development

- Target identification
- Value proposition development
- Targeting and personalization

Source: Adapted from Stephen K. Pinto, "Realizing the power of customer relationship management," *Mercer Management Journal,* Issue 8, 1997, pp. 21–34; and subsequent presentation by relationship marketing consultant Kathryn Britney.

causes marketers to want to forgo the front-end analytics and simply e-mail the entire list. The economics of the Internet, as we have often noted, makes that a seductive argument. However, damage to the relationship can be caused by an onslaught of untargeted, irrelevant marketer-originated communications. Airlines, for example, know the residential location of their frequent flyers, and if they have mined their data warehouses intelligently, they may have been able to ascertain clear flight patterns for individual customers. Why, then, are airlines e-mailing their frequent fliers with promotional offers that originate in cities in which they do not live and to which they do not travel? The cost of sending these messages may not be high, but the longer-term damage to the customer relationship (the "trust" referred to by Reichheld and Schefter) may be significant. In other words, consumers ask, "How can I trust a company that appears to know nothing about me, even though I have transacted with that company?"

It is essential that **inbound** programs also depend on the customer database. If a company offers Web-enabled customer service and support, the database is an integral part of meeting customer needs in those areas. Telephone call centers and Internet-based chat also rely on the customer database for real-time data that allow representatives to provide seamless service to customers on the basis of full knowledge about their dealings with the firm, both past and present.

None of these knowledge-driven programs or strategies are viable, however, unless we can selectively reach identified targets with content and messages custom-tailored to each. The Internet provides an especially powerful medium for targeting customers with personalized content.

inbound Communications that originate outside the enterprise and that are destined for a person or unit inside it.

8-7 Targeting, Personalization, and Customization

As we prepare to discuss this key competency of Internet marketing, we enter another semantic thicket. These three important terms—targeting, personalization, and customization—are used often, in many contexts, with many shades of meaning. When defined by various authors, they often give different definitions.[19] The distinction between "personalization" and "customization" is especially fuzzy, with some authors using them interchangeably and some attempting to give more precise meanings. For the purpose of our discussion in the remainder of this chapter, we give the terms the following meanings, which are helpful in teasing out the specific ways in which marketers can use the techniques:

- Targeting refers to directing marketing communications to individuals or businesses that have been identified as valid prospects for acquisition or retention for the good or service. Targeting can be visible, as when a marketer sends an e-mail newsletter with personalized content to a customer who has given permission for this type of communication. It can be invisible to the receiver, as when targeted ads are served onto a Web site without the visitor's explicit knowledge.

- Personalization involves the creation of specialized content for a prospect with a known profile by choosing from an array of existing content modules. In addition to the e-mail newsletter, just described, personalization occurs when a visitor registers on a Web site like Yahoo! and creates a My Yahoo! page by choosing the content he or she wants from extensive lists presented by the site.

- Customization is the creation of new content, services, or even products based on the needs and wants of an individual customer, either business or consumer. Internet marketers like NIKEiD are offering the ability to customize products. Others, like iTunes, are offering customers the ability to customize their own user experience.

Note that this terminology defines customization rather tightly, calling into question the way in which the term is often used by Internet marketers. Even so, there is still a gray area in which goods or services are configured to customers' orders from a set of components or services. This is represented by manufacturing processes like Dell's and NIKEiD's and has been called *mass customization* in discussions in both the academic and trade press.[20] With few exceptions, Internet marketers are not engaging in customization at this level, and we can therefore center our discussion on targeting and personalization. In so doing, we are not missing any important marketing issues because the processes used to identify and reach prospective customers with offers for truly customized products are the same as the ones used to identify customers in order to target them with personalized content.

8-7a Targeting and Profiling

Direct marketing, again, provides the foundation concepts for *targeting* on the Internet. Direct marketers in the physical world have long used mailing or telephone lists as their primary targeting mechanism. As noted in the preceding chapter, e-mail lists are now available and are likely to grow in both size and number in the coming years. For the present, however, good lists (translated as opt-in lists) are expensive and short. If the right type of rental list is available, it can be useful to the Internet marketer, especially in the acquisition process, as discussed in Chapter 7. For retention purposes, however, the issues are different. The process that supports relationship marketing in either the physical or the cyber worlds is represented in Figure 8-8. The

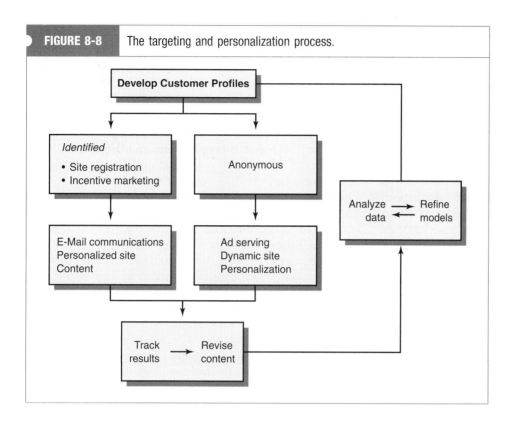

FIGURE 8-8 The targeting and personalization process.

chief difference between the two is that Internet marketers are able to capture more data faster and to revise their content on a more frequent, even real-time, basis.

Targeting in CRM programs is most often accomplished by developing **customer profiles** and using them either to identify customers who are appropriate to receive a particular offer (the more traditional approach) or to identify customers who represent sufficient value, either as individuals or as a segment, to warrant the development of a unique value proposition (a CLV-based approach).

Two types of profiles are available to marketers. *Anonymous* profiles are created without knowledge of the identity of the prospective customer. They are developed from clickstream data and perhaps enhanced with other data that belong to the marketer or are purchased from a third-party supplier. Cookies are the most common way to develop anonymous profiles. A **cookie** is a small text file that is placed on a user's hard drive. Whenever a computer makes a request to a Web server, that server has an opportunity to set a cookie. The file stores a string of tagged data items that describe user activities. For instance, a click-through on a banner ad may result in a cookie being set. That cookie can be used for tracking movement on the site after the click-through, for creating a user profile, or to manage the serving of ads to the user. A cookie is also set when a user selects personalization options on a Web page. However the cookie is set, when the user contacts the Web site again, the cookie is automatically activated. In general, a cookie can only be read by the server that sends it and can track activity only on one Web site, including where the visitors come from and where they go as they exit. Cookie files can be located by the user and disabled, but that may prevent access to some Web sites. It will also erase any personalization the user has done.[21]

Identified profiles are compiled from data that are explicitly provided by a known prospect. This is often done by asking the visitor to register on a Web site and to provide profile information in the process. Also, infomediaries offer incentives in return for customer information, which they then sell to marketers. Companies that offer coupons from participating manufacturers over the Web are an example of this type of information product.

customer profile
A description, primarily quantitative, of an individual or segment using specified demographic, lifestyle, and behavioral characteristics.

cookie A few lines of code that a Web site places on a user's computer to store data about the user's activities on the site.

registration A process requiring a visitor to provide identifying personal information in order to receive communications or other benefits from a Web site.

The fastest way for a firm to build its own house list and to create its own identified profiles is **registration** on the Web site. This sounds simple, but it has to be done carefully. The process itself must be carefully thought out. And, of course, people must first be attracted to the site using acquisition techniques described in the previous chapters.

The registration form must be carefully designed for ease and speed of completion. A new registrant may have little, if any, existing relationship with the organization and will divulge only minimal information. Techniques that prevent errors, like pull-down lists, are also desirable. Even so, the form may not be completed unless there is an incentive. The incentive may be tangible, as on the many B2B sites that require visitors to register to get information of some type, perhaps to download a white paper. It may be intangible, as when the not-for-profit offers the ability to "customize our newsletter to reflect your interests." There may be services offered to the registered visitor that are not available to the general public, as in the ASPCA case.

Note two things about the common strategy of providing an information incentive. First, the registrant should receive instant gratification, either by clicking on a link to download or by automatic e-mail provision of the report. Making the person wait for something to arrive invalidates many of the special advantages of the Internet. If the information comes on a scheduled basis, not on demand, automate the process to immediately send a "thank you" e-mail (for an e-mail newsletter subscription, for example), as shown in the Saffron Rouge example in Chapter 6. Second, this is a classic direct marketing lead generation process. Consequently, enough information should be gathered to begin to categorize the desirability of the prospect. At the same time, the information should not be so detailed or complex that the visitor does not complete the form. Abandoned forms can be tracked. If there is a consistent point at which the form is being abandoned, it signals a problem with the information gathering that should be corrected immediately.

The basic rule is to gather only the information genuinely needed by the marketer to make the next communication effective. As the relationship strengthens, more information that is more detailed and more personal can be collected. Just like politeness in the physical world, do not presume too much on a brief acquaintance! There should be a relationship program plan from the beginning that specifies the data needed and the stages in which it will be collected. In the absence of a plan, data collection is just a "fishing expedition," which is unlikely to be valuable to the marketer and is highly likely to be annoying to the prospective customer. However, both the data collection and the relationship marketing strategy should be flexible and should be examined at every step for possible improvements.

The other method of using profiles to target identified prospects is to use the services of a third-party firm that specializes in targeted and behavioral marketing programs. Current practice is for the supplier of the service to make the contact, thereby keeping the prospect's identity private. As in traditional direct marketing, only if the prospect responds to an offer does the marketer obtain direct access to the customer. CoolSavings, which distributes coupons and other promotions for many manufacturers, provides a good example of how this process works (Case in Point 8-1).

8-7b Personalized E-Mail and Site Content

Whether the marketer uses a service provider or manages e-mail programs internally, the e-mails should go out to a list of targeted prospects. If a service provider like CoolSavings is used, it sets the schedule for initial customer contact. If the marketer manages its own e-mail, it also controls the schedule of customer contact, which is desirable. With either option, the contact schedule is marketer controlled.

If, however, the marketer chooses *personalized site content* as all or part of the relationship program, the communication must await the visitor's return to the site. Three basic types of personalized site content are in use at present:

Case in Point 8-1   Targeting Consumers at CoolSavings

An illustration of how these suppliers of Internet marketing services operate is provided by Q Interactive, which describes itself as an interactive marketing services provider that helps marketers connect with their customers via its consumer savings site, CoolSavings, and affiliate sites in its advertising network. In 2005 CoolSavings' database contained over 12 million active households. The activity of these households generated over 5 billion data points to be used in analytic and predictive modeling efforts on behalf of their customers. Customers include consumer products companies of all kinds, many of them major brands who have historically relied heavily on newspaper inserts and direct mail to distribute coupons, samples and other offers.[22]

Large consumer products brands are attracted by the targeting services offered through CoolSavings. These services include collection of consumer preferences, tracking and analysis of consumer activity, and predictive modeling. One type of predictive modeling is provided for customers who extend so-called soft offers, offers that require later payment and often a large up-front incentive. These include magazine publishers and music companies. The predictive modeling allows them to increase the number of qualified leads, customers with a high propensity to follow through and pay for the products.[23] They also offer partnership programs to customers. For example, in 2004 CoolSavings designed a program for the Kroger supermarket chain and consumer products Gatorade and ESPN that allowed consumers to accumulate points for free Gatorade products and ESPN gear. Shoppers who had a Kroger loyalty card entered the program by registering on the Kroger Web site. The loyalty card already tracked coupons selected on the Web site. The registration allowed Kroger to capture the email addresses of participating customers. CoolSavings managed the database for Kroger. Its ability to track purchases at the product level allowed Kroger to target electronic coupons to consumers based on their purchasing behavior.[24]

CoolSavings acquires new customers in many ways—banner advertising on major portals and paid search listings are key sources of new customers. When the new user clicks through to the CoolSavings home page (Figure 8-9a), she sees many cost-saving incentives and a simple registration form. Filling out the registration form (Figure 8-9b) takes her to a preference page where some items are opt-in and some are opt-out. When the preferences page is submitted, a series of specific offers follows. For example, if the registrant opts in to the Walt Disney World vacation planning kit offer, its preference page requests information specific to vacation planning including when, for how long, how many children, and the children's ages. The series of preference pages may be substantial, but once completed, the consumer is ready to start receiving emails with a variety of selected offers.

FIGURE 8-9 | The CoolSavings home page and preferences page.

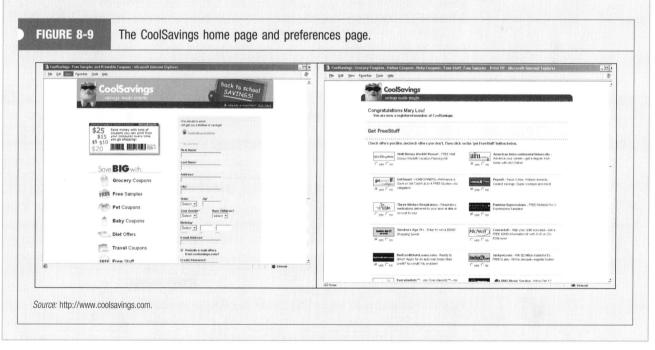

Source: http://www.coolsavings.com.

1. **Rules**-based personalization chooses content on the basis of known characteristics (Weather.com provides geographically appropriate content to registered users) or characteristics or information made available at the time of the visit. For example, the "Purchase Circles" on Amazon.com use characteristics such

rule See *decision rule*.

as the registered address of the customer to say something like "The new Harry Potter book is popular with Boston residents this week." It can also identify the corporate site from which the visitor is coming and say, "The new edition of *Data Mining for Dweebs* is popular at the AtoZ Corp. this week." Rules-based algorithms can link several characteristics, but they are usually fairly straightforward.

2. User-controlled personalization allows the user to choose the content elements to be displayed. Businesses are increasingly encouraging customers to create their own personalized entry page containing the information they access most frequently (for example, the My Yellow option as shown in Figure 8-4).

3. Information-driven personalization uses complex profiles and models to assign content instead of simpler **decision rules**.[25]

decision rule A statement that takes the form "If . . . then," specifying an action to be taken, given the occurrence of a particular event.

User-controlled personalization obviously remains unchanged until the user decides to modify it. Rules-based personalization can also be relatively static, with rules and associated actions being established in advance and merely executed at the time of the visitor's arrival on the site. Information-driven personalization occurs in real time and is more complex in concept and execution. The software builds a profile almost instantaneously when the visitor hits a site. It can use many types of data, depending on what is available and the level of identification of the visitor—everything from clickstream data to transactional data from the customer database. As the visitor moves around the site, the profile is updated. It also stores information, perhaps in the customer database and perhaps on a cookie on the visitors own computer, in preparation for the next visit. Virtually any aspect of site content can be served to the visitor on the basis of the profile—the products to be displayed, incentives to be offered, and characteristics of the offer itself, including price.

Personalized site content can be a powerful tool. However, as previously noted, it has to wait for the visitor's arrival. Internet marketers can combine the two tools of targeted, personalized e-mail and individualized site content in a relationship program. Figure 8-10 shows two different examples. In Figure 8-10a, ChoiceStream, a supplier of personalized Web site solutions, shows how a music page can be personalized for even a first-time visitor, using predictive models and only a few data points about the new visitor. This is a good example of dynamic content that does not

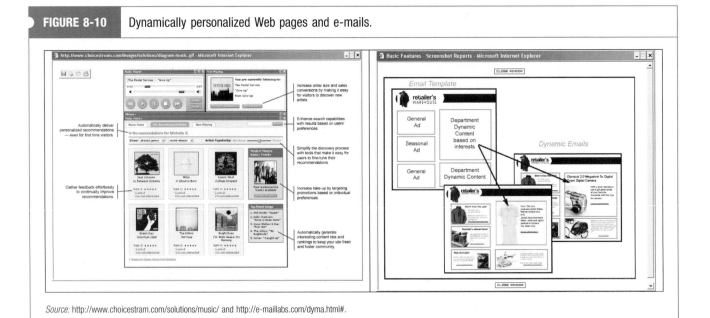

FIGURE 8-10   Dynamically personalized Web pages and e-mails.

Source: http://www.choicestream.com/solutions/music/ and http://e-maillabs.com/dyma.html#.

depend on a registration or return visit but attempts to solidify the connection with a visitor even on the initial visit.

Figure 8-10b shows how an e-mail can be personalized with content relevant to the recipient based on his or her profile, stated preferences, and Web site and e-mail response activities. The importance of relevant content to users who have their choice of Web sites and an inbox full of e-mail can hardly be overstated.

Both of these processes—the CRM process itself and the subprocesses of targeting and personalization—imply a continuous, closed-loop process of data capture, information-driven programs, and knowledge refinement. One additional technique is widely used to increase the momentum and power of relationship marketing. That important technique is the loyalty program.

8-8 Customer Loyalty Programs

Loyalty programs are familiar and ubiquitous. Businesses from the corner pizza parlor to the urban department store to the international hotel chain have loyalty programs. Consumers and business travelers have wallets full of their cards. Incentives range from "Buy nine and get the tenth one free" to free airline tickets to rental car upgrades and many others.

Several different airlines have taken credit for inventing the programs in the l970s. In any event, loyalty programs began there and quickly spread to other industries. The upside was that customers continued their patronage in order to receive their rewards. This created an opportunity for marketers to construct detailed databases chronicling the activities of their frequent customers. The downsides were that the programs were more expensive than many marketers originally estimated and more difficult to administer. Adding expiration dates and restrictions to programs helped with the cost issues but increased the administrative burden. Nevertheless, loyalty programs have become a staple of the marketing strategies of firms such as Britain's Tesco supermarkets.

Tesco, Britain's second-largest food retailer, began its loyalty program in 1995, when its growth had plateaued. By 2005, the program covered 10 million households in the United Kingdom and Asia. It captures data on 85% of store sales and links them to individual household profile data. All these data are captured in a data warehouse and analyzed with sophisticated data mining tools, as discussed in Chapter 6. Using the customer insights from these data, Tesco has branched out into nonfood retailing, offering everything from DVDs to travel and legal services. It also offers a broad array of financial and telecommunications services.

From the beginning of the Club Card program, Tesco has used the data for segmentation analyses. Over time, the data have produced more detailed and actionable segments. Segments include cost-conscious, mid-market, and up-market demographic groupings. From a lifestyle perspective they have identified healthy, gourmet, convenience-oriented, family living, and other similar segments. Each of these demographic or lifestyle segments can be further segmented into small segments with homogeneous characteristics. Tesco tailors mailings to the known interests of these segments, sending 4 million customized member magazines each quarter. Coupons distributed in these magazines are redeemed at a rate of 20% to 40%, a rate much higher than the industry norm. Tesco attributes this to the relevance of the coupons to each individual customer, not to higher-value coupons.

In one 5-year period in the 1990s, Tesco sales increased by 52%, a rate higher than the industry average. It is now the number one food retailer in Great Britain, with a market share that has increased from 16% at the time of the Club Card introduction to 27% for the 2003 fiscal year. According to Professor Don Schultz, "They are way beyond rewarding customers and retention; they are using data to drive business decisions."[26]

Consultant Arthur Hughes offers recommendations for successful programs. According to him, loyalty programs should:

- be easy to use.
- provide immediate rewards.
- have value from the customer's perspective.
- be aimed at customers whose behavior the company is trying to change.
- be limited to what the company can afford to spend.
- have a published exit strategy.[27]

Whether you call them loyalty programs or frequency programs or reward programs, they should be only one component of a planned and information-driven CRM program. In this context, they can become a useful component of a comprehensive program.

In fact, each of the techniques we have discussed can be a useful part of a comprehensive CRM program. The real difficulty, however, is putting them together into a successful, ongoing CRM process. At present, many enterprises are working to implement successful processes, but few, if any, have yet come close to achieving the potential of CRM.

8-9 The CRM Failure Rate

Installing a CRM system in a large enterprise can be expensive. In 2004, IDC interviewed representatives of more than thirty large corporations in the United States and Europe. They found that the median investment in a CRM application prior to start-up was $426,000 and that the median total cost of the system over its first 5 years was $1.2 million. The majority of their respondents reported recouping their initial investment in CRM. Of the respondents, 58% experienced a payback period of 1 year or less, 35% paid back the investment in 1 to 3 years, and 8% achieved payback in 3 years or more.[28]

At about the same time, IBM was sounding a warning note that is consistent with much of the industry conventional wisdom, saying:

> To the chagrin of many companies—from those with billions of dollars in annual revenues to small businesses with less than US$50 million in annual revenue—CRM has yet to achieve the promised ROI that made it so appealing in the first place. In many cases, customers have yet to notice a decisive difference at all.[29]

Their research estimates that fully 85% of companies, large and small, that were included in this survey were not fully satisfied with their CRM results.[30] That may suggest the triumph of excessively high expectations over the metric of return on investment used by IDC.

CRM is not easy to implement. The data requirements and the technology can be daunting, but that is only a small part of the reason that many CRM projects fall short. The overriding reasons fall under the general heading of "organizational issues," ranging from lack of strong and consistent leadership from top management to failure to achieve buy-in from people throughout the organization. Bell and his colleagues identify seven barriers to successful CRM. Using cases in the hospitality industry as their bases, they point to issues, some of which we have already discussed, and others that need to be considered. Their barriers are as follows:

- The need for individual level data. They point out that traditional direct marketers have long been building and using customer databases, giving them something of a head start over traditional mass media marketers in this area.
- The need to track customers as assets. This is a familiar refrain; the importance of customer value to the overall profitability of the enterprise.
- The need to build models to accurately forecast future revenue. The issue here is different industries, with different basic types of customers. The "lost-for-good"

customer might be a cable TV subscriber whose defection means the loss of their entire revenue stream. The "always-a-share" customer is one who either splits purchasing between two or more suppliers—for example, a customer who regularly shops two different supermarkets—or who has a measurable probability of returning after defection—for example, a customer who changes cell phone service providers from time to time.

- The need to maximize CLV. This is the other side of the familiar CLV refrain; the importance of managing customers in a way that grows their asset value to the enterprise.

- The need to align the entire organization around customer management, not product management. This is a seismic change in the organizational mindset of traditional marketers and of organizations as a whole. The difficulty of orchestrating such a change cannot be overstated.

- The need to respect the sensitivity of customer information. With the collection of customer data comes a major responsibility—keeping the data accurate and secure. Anything less than total success in this aspect of the endeavor damages, perhaps permanently, the trust the customer has in the enterprise.

- The need to migrate CRM from a cost-saving effort to one that focuses on improving customer service. If the objective is seen only as saving money, CRM efforts will fall short of their goal of optimizing customer experience.

The CGI Group, a supplier of business process improvement services, provides a "top ten list" of reasons why CRM projects fail that makes some of the same points (Table 8-1). They point to the importance of a CRM strategy that is integrated into the overall business strategy. The development of a comprehensive strategy will help customize the installation to the needs of the enterprise, not simply implement a cookie-cutter solution. It will include examining all customer interfaces and getting customers' input into how they want and need to be served. Technology must be regarded as an enabler, not a solution. Objectives must be established and appropriate metrics identified. CRM must be regarded as a process; it must include the alignment of the entire organization around a customer-centric philosophy. Finally, they emphasize the importance of leadership from top management and of buy-in from employees throughout the organization. Stop and consider this list for a moment; all the items, in one way or another, describe the way an organization approaches and reacts to a CRM initiative.

Keeping CRM focused on the enterprise's vision of how it wishes to interact with and to be perceived by its customers is necessary to overcome barriers and avoid failure drivers. The generic vision for CRM can be described as a "seamlessly satisfying customer experience."

TABLE 8-1	Top Ten Reasons for CRM Failure

CRM initiative is launched without a comprehensive strategy.
CRM strategy is not integral to the business strategy.
CRM methodology is based on what worked for another company.
CRM is launched without concern for effective enterprise and customer interfaces.
CRM is launched without customer input.
CRM is considered an information technology (IT) project instead of a business initiative that leverages technology.
CRM is launched without defined objectives and metrics.
CRM is considered a one-time event.
Organization lacks a customer-centric culture.
There is lack of top management leadership and employee buy-in.

Source: Adapted from: "The Top Ten Reasons CRM Projects Fail," 2004, CGI Group, Inc.

8-10 The CRM Vision—Seamless Customer Experience

The CRM vision is to provide the customer a totally satisfactory experience—through every distribution channel the enterprise employs, by means of any communications channel the customer chooses to use, at any time. In an era of multichannel marketing, that is a tall order indeed.

Figure 8-11 suggests the nature of both the problem and the opportunities. Merchants can offer access through their retail stores, Web sites, telephone call centers, direct mail and catalogs, and self-service kiosks such as automated teller machines (ATMs). Field service technicians, the people who repair your refrigerator at home or copier at work, also represent the enterprise and can, in fact, present up-sell and cross-sell opportunities if they are properly trained and motivated. B2B marketers also have field sales forces as another important channel. No single marketer, B2B or B2C, is likely to use all these channels of distribution. However, most now offer a set—branch banks, a Web site, a telephone customer service center, and ATMs, supplemented with occasional direct-mail promotions, would be typical for a retail bank, for example. Most nonprofits have mail, telephone, and Web site contacts as well as personal contacts of various types. An industrial concern would be likely to have a field sales force, a Web site, printed catalogs, a telephone call center, and field service technicians. Each of these channels represents a "customer touchpoint." Each of these touchpoints provides an opportunity to serve the customer well—through information, transactions, or service. Each customer contact sends a message about the brand—positive or negative. Technology can assist in both these dimensions.

Figure 8-11 also lists the technologies that are in most common use in CRM applications today. Some have already been discussed. A customer at Lands' End, for example, can receive a catalog in the mail, investigate a purchase on the Web site, and either call the telephone center or activate a chat session to ask a question about the

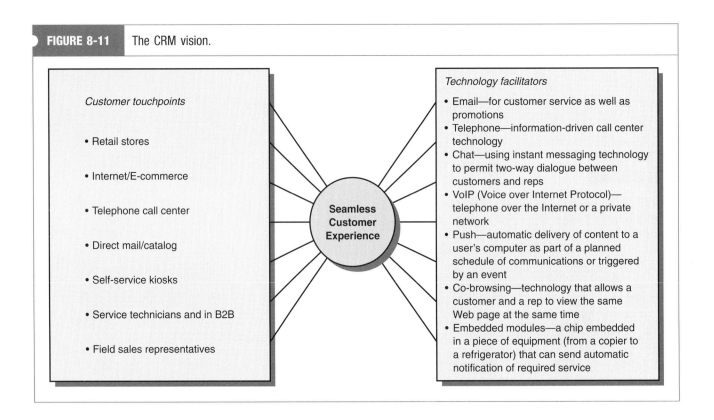

| FIGURE 8-11 | The CRM vision. |

Customer touchpoints

• Retail stores

• Internet/E-commerce

• Telephone call center

• Direct mail/catalog

• Self-service kiosks

• Service technicians and in B2B

• Field sales representatives

Seamless Customer Experience

Technology facilitators

• Email—for customer service as well as promotions
• Telephone—information-driven call center technology
• Chat—using instant messaging technology to permit two-way dialogue between customers and reps
• VoIP (Voice over Internet Protocol)—telephone over the Internet or a private network
• Push—automatic delivery of content to a user's computer as part of a planned schedule of communications or triggered by an event
• Co-browsing—technology that allows a customer and a rep to view the same Web page at the same time
• Embedded modules—a chip embedded in a piece of equipment (from a copier to a refrigerator) that can send automatic notification of required service

merchandise. The Lands' End customer service rep can push additional information to the customer immediately or open a Web page that they can browse together. These technologies all can be applied in either B2C or B2B environments. Embedded modules are an emerging technique, discussed in Chapter 3 as the machine-to-machine business model. Consider the possibility that your refrigerator might notify the field service technician of a potential problem before it actually stops functioning. We return to this issue in the final chapter as an aspect of wireless technology.

The CRM issue is that the customer may contact the enterprise at any time, through any of the channels, using any one of several available technologies (really communications channels). The marketer's job is to deliver the right product, service, or information—consistently and correctly—no matter when, where, or how the customer makes contact. Furthermore, the product, service, or information should be delivered by the agent—anyone from a call center representative to a field service technician—with whom the customer makes the initial contact. Referring the customer from one person to another in the organization in order to try to get information or settle an issue is the antithesis of "seamless customer experience."

You should easily recognize that executing this level of CRM is highly information intensive. It will take sophisticated software and IT systems to provide that information to each customer touchpoint in real time. That leads to the easy assumption that good software is the answer. As is true in all areas of Internet marketing, good software is necessary, but not sufficient. It is necessary to:

- capture and maintain the necessary customer data. We have already discussed marketing, technological, and organizational issues related to data capture and maintenance.

- have processes and systems, especially back-end ones, that function efficiently. If a bank, for example, attempts to automate a mortgage application and approval process that does not work in the physical world, we can facetiously observe that the automated process will make more errors faster than the manual system. Alternatively, we can simply say that, at best, the money spent on software and hardware to automate the system will have been wasted and, at worst, chaos will have been created.

- have organizational resources and commitment to support the arduous work involved—work that involves the active cooperation of many functional units in the typical organization.

Writing in the *Harvard Business Review,* Bain consultants Rigby, Reichheld, and Schefter say, "Executives often mistake the easy promise of CRM software for the hard reality of creating a unique strategy for acquiring, building relationships with, and retaining customers."[31]

Their solutions, as all the perspectives presented in this chapter, are centered around acquiring and retaining high-value customers, developing the right value proposition, ensuring that all business processes are functioning properly, and motivating employees at all customer touchpoints. These are organizational and strategy issues; CRM systems can implement strategies, but they cannot devise them. The enterprise must do the demanding work that goes all the way from identifying high-value customers and learning how to increase their value to reengineering processes if necessary to learn how to keep customers from defecting. At that point, the enterprise knows what it needs to do, and it has a foundation for choosing suppliers of CRM software, systems, and integration services to assist them in implementing their strategies.

Summary

Practitioners of CRM are often heard to say that "CRM is a journey, not a destination." The process of learning about the customer is never ending; so are the marketing activities that make use of customer knowledge. In addition, there will undoubtedly be more technologies to add to the menu of CRM program options. Not only is

CRM one of the most important aspects of contemporary marketing, it is also one of the most challenging.

The discipline of relationship marketing focuses on customer retention and the reactivation of lapsed customers on the premise that it is less expensive to maintain existing customers than it is to acquire new ones. True CRM is based on the three disciplines of sales force automation, marketing, and customer service. However, the term, along with *e-CRM,* is universally used to describe relational marketing in B2C as well as B2B markets.

Specific CRM techniques range from segmentation approaches to highly personalized one-to-one programs. Different approaches may be appropriate for different businesses because of the nature of their products and target segments. Whichever specific approach is used, it is important to remember the value of building trust over time and of respecting the privacy of the customer. Opt-in permission marketing techniques are essential elements of relational marketing processes.

To implement CRM programs on the Web, a substantial amount of customer knowledge is necessary. This knowledge is embedded in profiles of individual customers or visitors to the Web site. Profiling is done either anonymously or for identified customers. Although anonymous profiling has obvious relevance in the early stages of a potential customer relationship, it also has important privacy implications that should not be overlooked by the marketer. One way to avoid privacy issues is to develop value-added programs, such as frequent customer reward plans, that deepen relationships over time and lead to willing revelation of additional information on the part of loyal customers. Identified profiles can be developed when the visitor or customer provides personal information, usually through registration on a site or making a purchase from it.

Marketers have a menu of options in terms of the channels they will use and the technologies they will implement. The CRM vision is to integrate the chosen channels and technologies in such a way that the customer can make contact whenever he pleases, through whatever channel he prefers at that particular time (the customer touchpoint), and receive the information or service he desires without delay, errors, or being transferred from one enterprise agent to another. This is the "seamless customer experience." It represents both the opportunity and the challenge facing CRM programs of all types.

Quiz

1. Among the arguments for the importance of customer retention are that _____.
   a. a satisfied customer does not talk about the firm and product
   b. it costs at least seven times as much to acquire a new customer as it does to retain an existing one
   c. reducing customer defections will increase sales but not necessarily profits

2. _____ is *not* a way in which relationship marketing differs from transactional marketing.
   a. Long-term focus instead of short-term perspective
   b. Customer dialog instead of isolated marketing research projects
   c. Networked organizations instead of hierarchical organizations

3. _____ is one of the elements of the Peppers and Rogers CRM model?
   a. Differentiation
   b. Analysis
   c. Involvement

4. The CRM process _____.
   a. is driven by customer information
   b. makes segmentation obsolete
   c. is useful only for outbound marketing programs

5. The foundations of a CRM program include _____.
   a. customer service and e-mail marketing
   b. sales force automation and customer service
   c. marketing and promotion

6. Analytical CRM includes _____.
   a. capturing and storing data in a customer database
   b. developing specialized value propositions
   c. both a and b

7. What function do cookies perform in the targeting and personalization process?
   a. Identify the visitor's e-mail address
   b. Store data that enable the site to deliver relevant content
   c. Collect data about the visitor's activities on all Web sites

8. A/An _____ profile can be developed when a person registers on or buys something from a Web site.
   a. identified
   b. anonymous
   c. statistical

9. _____ is *not* a component of the targeting and personalization process.
   a. Anonymous profiling
   b. The ability to customize content for an individual customer
   c. Customization of products to meet customer needs

Discussion Questions

1. Explain, in your own words, the importance of relationship marketing and how it differs from transactional marketing.

2. Customer relationship marketing is generally considered to have its foundations in three marketing functions. Explain what the functions are and what each contributes to a CRM program.

3. What is the relevance of customer lifetime value in the discussion of CRM?

4. Discuss the process of implementing CRM, paying special attention to the importance of customer data in the process.

5. Targeting, personalization, and customization are three different but related CRM concepts. Define each, clearly explaining why they are different from one another and giving an example of each.

6. Profiling is essential to good targeting and personalization on the Web. Do you agree or disagree? Explain why or why not.

Internet Exercises

1. Visit one B2C and one B2B Web site. Examine each carefully, identifying as many relationship-building techniques as possible. Do you find extensive differences between the B2C and B2B sites? Be prepared to discuss your findings, and the similarities and differences between programs on the two sites, in class.

2. By now you are probably receiving communications from at least one of the Web sites you are tracking. Are they doing it well or not? How would you assess the effectiveness of this part of their CRM program?

3. Look back at the log you have kept of the contacts from a particular site. In general, what are they learning about you from these interactions? Specifically, what data might they have added to your record in their database?

4. You probably have a loyalty card for a supermarket, gas station, restaurant, or retail store. If you do not, interview a friend or family member who does. What data can be collected from the customer's use of the card? How could the retailer or the manufacturers who supply the retailer use the data? Are they using it to strengthen the customer relationship? How?

Notes

1. Frederick F. Reichheld, The Loyalty Effect (Boston: Harvard Business School Press, 1996).

2. Joe Giffer, "Capturing Customers for Life," Cambridge Technology Partners, http://www.ctp.com.

3. For a discussion of customer value in services markets, see Valarie A. Zeithaml, Roland T. Rust, and Katherine N. Lemon, "The Customer Pyramid: Creating and Serving Profitable Customers," California Management Review, Vol. 43, No. 4, Summer 2001, pp. 118–142.

4. Sarabjit Singh Baveja, Sharad Rastogi, Chris Zook, Randall S. Hancock, and Julian Chu, "The Value of Online Customer Loyalty," Bain & Company, April 1, 2000.

5. Youngme Moon, "Interactive Technology and Relationship Marketing Strategies," 1999, Harvard Business School Publishing; S. Nelson, "The Eight Building Blocks of CRM Strategy," June 25, 2003, Gartner Group.

6. Rowland T. Moriarty and Gordon S. Schwartz, "Automation to Boost Sales and Marketing," Harvard Business Review, January–February 1989, pp. 100–108.

7. "10 Companies That Get It," Fortune, November 8, 1999, p. 116.

8. "Power to the People," August 15, 2000, CIO Magazine, http://www.cio.com.

9. "New Penn Introduces NP-Connex," April 2005, http://www.corporate-ir.net/ireye/current#current.

10. "2005 Most Admired Companies," Fortune, http://www.fortune.com/fortune/mostadmired/subs/2005/number1/0,23159,00.html.

11. Yellow Transportation Receives Carrier of the Year and Innovator of the Year Awards from Wal-Mart, June 2004, http://www.corporate-ir.net/ireye/ir_site.zhtml?ticker=yell&script=460&layout=-6&item_id=590484.

12. http://www.aspca.org.

13. http://www.aspca.org.

14. "Using Constituent Information for Effective Fundraising and Marketing," February 2004, http://www.convio.com.

15. Kristin Bremner, "ASPCA Puts Some Bite into its Online Fundraising Efforts," DM News, April 29, 2002.

16. "Using Constituent Information for Effective Fundraising and Marketing," February 2004, http://www.convio.com.

17. For a more detailed discussion of the process of CRM, see Russel S. Winer, "A Framework for Customer Relationship Management," California Management Review, Vol. 43, No. 4, Summer 2001, pp. 89–105.

18. See Roland T. Rust, Katherine N. Lemon, and Das Narayandas. Customer Equity Management (Upper Saddle River, NJ: Pearson Prentice Hall, 2005), especially Chapter 2, p. 30.

19. For a discussion of competing definitions, see Don Peppers and Martha Rogers, "Is It Personalization or Customization?" Inside1to1, June 20, 2000, http://www.marketing1to1.com.

20. See, for example, James Gilmore and Joseph B. Pine II, "The Four Faces of Mass Customization," *Harvard Business Review*, 1997.

21. For more information on cookies, primarily from the user perspective, see http://www.cookiecentral.com.

22. "Corporate Overview," http://phx.corporate-ir.net/phoenix. zhtml?c=120944&p=irol-homeProfile&t=&id=&.

23. "CoolSavings, Alliant Cooperative Data Solutions Launch Lead Generation Solution," *DM News*, January 26, 2005, http:// info.coolsavings.com/news/intheNews.asp?CS=undefined.

24. "A loyalty program that goes from web to store and back again," *Internet Retailer*, October 10, 2004, http://info.cool-savings.com/news/intheNews_arch.asp?view=10142004_ir& CS=http%3A%2F%2Fwww101%2Ecoolsavings%2Ecom%2F-scripts%2FWelenroll%2Easp%3FSessionID%3D1418828126.

25. David Smith, "There Are Myriad Ways to Get Personal," *Internet Week*, May 15, 2000, http://www.techweb.com.

26. Betsy Sphethmann, "Loyalty's Royalty," *Promo*, March 1, 2004, http://promomagazine.com/mag/marketing_loyaltys_royalty/index.html. Other sources for the Tesco Club Card program include Bill Millar, "Is Customer Loyalty in the Cards," Peppers & Rogers Group, October 1, 2001, http:// www.1to1.com/View.aspx?DocID=20021;"Tesco Has Links with the Corner Shops of England's Past," Seklemian & Newell, March 2005, http://www.loyalty.vg/pages/CRM/case_stu-dy_14_Tesco.htm.

27. Arthur Middleton Hughes, "How the Safeway Savings Club Built Loyalty," *Journal of Database Marketing*, Vol. 7, No. 3, February 2000, p. 216.

28. "New IDC Study on Implementing Customer Relationship Management Applications Reveals Impressive ROI," February 2, 2004, http://www.idc.com/getdoc.jsp?containerId=pr2003_12_22_135532.

29. "Global CRM Study 2004," IBM, http://www-1.ibm.com/services/ondemand/business/global_crm_study_2004.html.

30. "Doing CRM Right," IBM, http://www-1.ibm.com/ services/ ondemand/business/global_crm_study_2004.html.

31. Darrel K. Rigby, Frederick F. Reichheld, and Phil Schefter, "Avoid the Four Perils of CRM," *Harvard Business Review*, February 2002, p. 9.

Customer Service and Support in Web Space

Source: © Getty

Key Terms

Learning Objectives

By the time you complete this chapter, you will be able to:

- Explain the evolutionary stages of customer service provision.

- Understand the role of customer service in creating a sustainable competitive advantage.

- Explain the importance of integrating customer service with other customer-facing enterprise activities.

- Identify themes that recur in discussions of providing exceptional customer service.

- Describe the various channels used to deliver customer service.

- Discuss the steps involved in developing a strategic customer care program.

- Identify technologies that can be used to deliver customer service and support.

When we discussed the subject of customer relation management (CRM), we said that CRM has three foundations—sales force automation, marketing, and customer service. We also said that customer service was such an important element that we would devote an entire chapter to it. As we do that, we should remember the importance of two other aspects of CRM— seamless customer experience and the 360-degree view of the customer. An example will illustrate not only the key role of customer service but also the necessity to integrate customer service with other CRM elements in order to provide quality customer experience.[1]

9-1 A Customer Encounter of the Frustrating Kind

DSL Digital subscriber line, technology that greatly increases the transmission capacity of ordinary telephone lines; one type of broadband transmission.

modem Device that allows a computer to transmit data over a standard telephone line.

Technology writer Kimberly Hill lives and works in the Midwest. Some time ago she received a mail brochure touting **DSL** service through her local telephone service provider, Ameritech. She was interested but not convinced, even though the offer included an incentive of a $150 MasterCard cash card.

Two days later, an Ameritech contact center representative called to close the sale. In response to her questions, the sales rep told Kimberly she could move the **modem** to her new home in a few weeks and that it could be used with both her Mac laptop and her desktop PC. Kimberly wanted to think it over but realized that the rep was commissioned, so she invited him to call back the next night for her decision. He didn't call back the next night—or ever.

As the incentive offer neared expiration, she called Ameritech. Another rep gave her the same answers; yes she could move the modem and yes the service would work with both computers. She made arrangements for the modem kit to be sent to her current address and scheduled the installation of her phone and DSL service at the new address.

When the kit did not come, she called Ameritech, and after talking with a customer service rep and a customer service supervisor (not one of the sales reps she had spoken with to place the order), she found that her order had been put on hold until service was activated at the new address.

A week later, at her old address, she unexpectedly received a DSL modem kit. When she tried to install it, she found that it was missing the installation CD-ROM. The customer service rep who answered her call told her she didn't actually need the installation software. She called back and a second rep, Chris, told her that the modem she had received didn't work with Macs. He would send her a new kit and software, and she would need to return the first modem kit in order to avoid being charged for two. The rep gave her a return authorization number and suggested that she keep the UPS tracking number. He arranged to activate DSL service at her new home the next day, on November 13. Kimberly points out that there were multiple problems in trying to fulfill her order. She continues:

> I do see an overall pattern. Marketing and sales did what they thought was their job, and customer support did what they thought was theirs.
>
> I say this because I received that slick brochure, was enticed by the $150 MasterCard cash card offer and then received a call two days later to follow up. That's a solid, well-timed campaign, and it worked.
>
> Unfortunately, the sales representatives were misinformed or poorly trained and answered my questions about moving incorrectly. Perhaps they also answered my Macintosh questions incorrectly—that is yet to be determined.[2]

Does Kimberly's story sound familiar? Most of us could probably recount similar experiences. Some of us have eventually resolved our problems. Others have probably just given up. But few of us have had the follow-on experience that Kimberly had. But then, we don't write for a widely circulated Internet newsletter. Let's continue with Kimberly's narrative:

> A couple of weeks ago, Ameritech president of consumer markets Kathy Coughlin had a pretty tough start to her day, thanks to a message from her company's attorney. It seems he saw my CRMDaily column about the difficult time I had ordering DSL (digital subscriber line) service from Ameritech.
>
> [Coughlin and her director of DSL operations] called me to find out more about the situation—they're Ameritech, after all, so they know my phone number.[3]

A series of phone calls followed, first with the operations director, then a conference call with both the president and the operations director. Kimberly recounted her experience in detail and felt the two executives were really listening. She was told that there were business rules (ways to handle an issue) that covered a customer's move, but both sales and customer service reps were not properly trained on the issue. The same was true of the Mac plus PC situation, but in that case not only did the reps need better training but product information sent to the customer needed to be improved.

These things went wrong despite the fact that all managers in the consumer division are required to listen to customer service calls every week, that Ameritech conducts regular customer satisfaction surveys, and that the DSL group holds weekly meetings to try to coordinate technical and customer service issues. Kimberly concludes with the reminder that often managers who "talk the talk" about customer service are not the front-line services people who struggle on a daily basis to provide it.

Has the situation changed in recent years? A 2007 study of sixteen consumer brands by Forrester found all sixteen failing the test of their cross-channel review methodology. Among the anecdotes they collected were:

- When a researcher called one large retailer for information on an order, the automated system politely stated that the customer's complete satisfaction was a priority, said "Goodbye," and hung up.

- Upon contacting the sales department at another large retailer for a product recommendation a live salesperson told the researcher to call back and ask for tech support. When the researcher called back and asked for tech support, the call was transferred to sales.

- The Web site of a mobile phone services provider provides a form for sending email inquiries to customers who have a registered account. Unfortunately when a researcher tried to use it, he found that the password for the account had been sent by text message to a phone that had not yet been received.[4]

All these stories are ones with which many of us can identify. Beyond the all-too-common frustrations of trying to obtain customer service that works, they make two important points:

1. Quality customer service cannot exist in isolation from other customer-facing functions. All these functions must be integrated into a single system, seamlessly providing products, service, and support.

2. As we will discuss in detail, technology is essential to provide cost-effective customer service to all segments all the time, especially in the fast-paced global world of the Internet. However, human beings are still at the heart of effective customer-facing systems. And, unfortunately, organizational issues still present some of the greatest barriers to the effectiveness of those systems.

Keeping those two issues in mind, let us look first at the degree to which customer service impacts e-businesses and then at applications that illustrate effective customer service strategies.

9-2 The Importance of Customer Service and Satisfaction

A recent study for consulting firm Accenture surveyed consumers in the United States and United Kingdom about their experiences in ten service industries. Although many companies in these industries have been investing in customer relations programs, almost two-thirds of the respondents did not believe that customer service had improved much in the last 5 years.

Does their lack of satisfaction make a difference? When asked if they had switched service providers, 19% of retail customers said they had. Across all ten industries, 10% of consumers had switched providers. The two top reasons were poor service or product quality (61%) and lower prices (46%).[5]

Lack of satisfaction is costing companies who do not provide a satisfactory customer experience, including customer service. Research uses data based on industry studies to illustrate the size of the problem. Studies in the insurance industry indicate that as many as 40% of policyholders may experience a service problem or failure in a given year. The results are shown in Figure 9-1. As is typical in customer service and satisfaction studies, some of the customers who experienced problems did not report them, in this case 20% of the people who had experienced problems with their insurance. Only 10% will not repurchase, but keep in mind that the insurance provider has lost hundreds of opportunities to identify problems and, presumably, to correct them. Notice that if the customers were satisfied, they intended to repurchase. Of those who were mollified (only partially satisfied), only 5% will not repurchase, whereas 40% of those who were dissatisfied declared their intent not to repurchase. The result was 274 lost customers out of a total of 6,000. They do not estimate the dollar value of the lost customers, but insurance customers represent a continuing stream of revenue, so you can imagine that their value is high. This analysis also shows something else that is noteworthy about customer satisfaction: it is not the fact that customers experience a problem that is critical to their defection; it is the fact that their problem is not satisfactorily resolved. That places the onus for customer retention squarely on the customer service function. When a business meets that challenge, its profitability can be significantly increased, as shown by Harrah's Casinos (Case in Point 9-1).

9-2a The Impact of Improved Customer Service in B2B Markets

A study of the impact of CRM on the profitability of high-technology firms provides additional detail and insight into the importance of customer service in the business-to-business (B2B) space. Another study for Accenture found that excellent CRM

FIGURE 9-1 The financial impact of customer service problems.

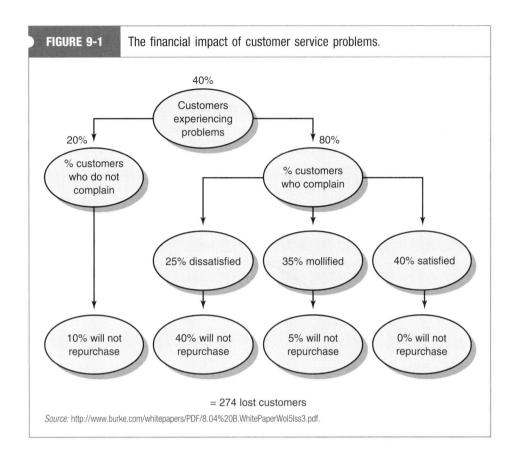

Source: http://www.burke.com/whitepapers/PDF/8.04%20B.WhitePaperWol5lss3.pdf.

Case in Point 9-1 The Impact of Improved Customer Service at Harrah's

One business that demonstrates the financial impact of improved customer service is Harrah's Casinos. We discussed their information-driven program to increase customer value in Chapter 4. Improving customer service was an important part of the program. According to chief executive officer (CEO) Gary Loveman:

> Casino service generally is disappointing all around. Service is hard to deliver in a casino. Employees are under strict rules to ensure there is no corruption. For example, dealers might want to give you a hug but can't, because you might slip something into their pockets. It's not like a hotel.

Proactive measures were taken to improve customer service at all the properties. Mr. Loveman continues:

> [B]eginning in 1999 we started paying out a bonus to every nonmanagement employee of the casino if his or her property improved its customer service scores by 3 percent over the same period a year earlier. And as long as the property is at 80 percent of its operating-income plan or higher, everyone gets a bonus. We've paid out $40 million in bonuses to employees across the system—

anywhere from $75 to $300 each, each quarter.... In the employee areas there are graphs to let them know their service numbers, which are based on customer satisfaction surveys. The data come in each week, and employees check to see how they're doing.

The customer satisfaction surveys are important, both as overall measures of satisfaction and also as a driver of customer value. Harrah's is able to directly attribute increases in customer value to the improvement in customer service. Mr. Loveman says:

> We can track the customers who fill out surveys. We can track their gaming behavior, so we can assess whether a player who rates us better this year than last year also plays more. And the answer is remarkably positive. The people who get happier with our service play much more with us, and the people who become unhappy play much less with us. *Market by market, where our profitability and revenues greatly exceed our relative market position, there's no question but that the results are largely service driven* [emphasis mine].[6]

continued

Case in Point 9-1   *Continued*

Figure 9-2 quantifies the relationship between satisfaction and CLV. Decreased customer satisfaction by as much as 2 points over the previous year results in a decrease of 10% in CLV. At the other extreme, an increase of 2 points in customer satisfaction results in an increase of more than 20% in CLV.

FIGURE 9-2   The value of satisfied customers at Harrah's.

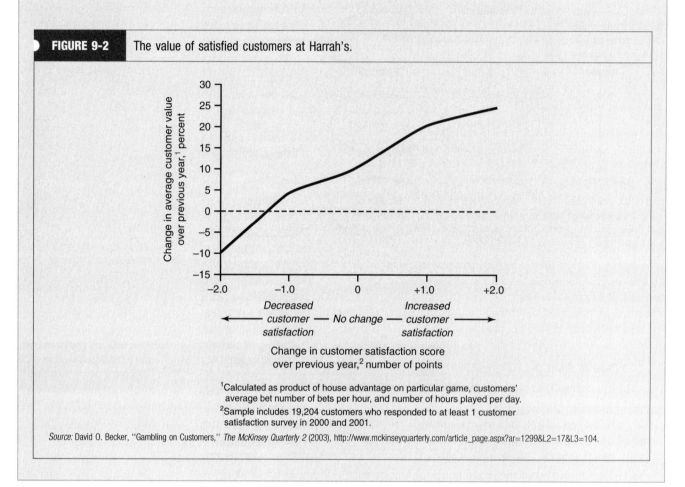

[1]Calculated as product of house advantage on particular game, customers' average bet number of bets per hour, and number of hours played per day.

[2]Sample includes 19,204 customers who responded to at least 1 customer satisfaction survey in 2000 and 2001.

Source: David O. Becker, "Gambling on Customers," *The McKinsey Quarterly 2* (2003), http://www.mckinseyquarterly.com/article_page.aspx?ar=1299&L2=17&L3=104.

performance could improve a company's return on sales by as much as 64% over merely average performance. Ten CRM capabilities accounted for fully half the improvement in return on sales. Of those, five are clearly customer service capabilities:

- Strategically manage large account customers (ranked number 4).
- Develop effective customer service systems (ranked number 6).
- Proactively identify customer problems and communicate resolution options (ranked number 7).
- Leverage customer information from the service process (ranked number 8).
- Prevent customer problems via customer education (ranked number 9).

For every billion dollars in sales, Accenture estimated the impact on increased profitability as follows:

Customer service	$42 million
Sales and account management	$35 million
Marketing	$34 million[7]

Although the importance of customer service seems irrefutable, technology in general and the Internet in particular have made enormous changes in the way customer service is delivered. It has become more than a pleasant smile and a cheerful answer to a question. Customers demand more comprehensive customer service and support at the same time technology enables companies to provide them in a cost-effective manner. The Internet may also have contributed to increasing customer expectations about service quality. Throughout the global economy, the enduring chorus of complaints about customer service suggests that most companies are either not getting the message or have not mastered the techniques.

9-2b What Do Consumers Want?

Because most of our data come from consumers, it is reasonable to ask what consumers want in terms of customer service. According to data from knowledge management firm Primus, online consumers expect:

Timely response to inquiries	45%
Informative content	22%
Communication with a real person	17%
Product displayed clearly and prominently	14%
24-hour availability	14%[8]

Consumers not only expect good service but also expect to be able to access service through multiple channels. The channels include personal service in retail stores, on the telephone, and through self-service on Web sites. E-mail is also an important channel for customer service.

Software provider eGain conducted a study in 2004 in which researchers posed as customers and made e-mail inquiries that indicated interest in purchasing a high-value product or service. E-mails were sent to 300 large U.S. and Canadian retailers and travel and hospitality, financial services, e-business, telecom, and consumer electronics firms. More than 100 of the firms did not respond at all. In addition, the study reported that:

- only 15% of companies sent any form of acknowledgement of the query.
- 39% of the sample did send a response within 24 hours.
- only 17% of the companies in the sample responded with a complete and accurate answer.
- 6% of the sample did not even offer e-mail contact.[9]

The cost of poor service is enormous and increasing. It is realized in two ways:

- Lost sales. E-tailers can measure the number of shoppers who abandon a shopping cart before purchasing. What about the customers who couldn't find what they wanted in 5 minutes and just left?
- Higher customer service costs. For example, Fidelity Investments found that an automated customer service inquiry costs about $1, whereas a telephone call handled by a human being costs about $13. Fidelity saw its call volume increase from about 97,000 calls to 700,000 in just a decade, of which 75% are handled by an automated system.[10]

These are consumer data, but there is no reason to suggest that the expectations of business customers are not equally demanding and ever-increasing. Business customers are, after all, consumers in their off hours. It might even be reasonable to suggest that these same consumers, in their business customer roles, may be even more demanding. It therefore behooves marketers to make provision of customer service part of their overall strategy.

9-3 The Evolution of Customer Service Strategy

The Internet not only is a key reason why the expectations of both business-to-customer (B2C) and B2B customers are rising but also can be a way in which their expectations can be met in a cost-effective manner. Figure 9-3 suggests an evolution in the way customer service is delivered that has the potential to improve service without increasing the cost of providing it. It involves, first, moving away from total reliance on telephone call centers for live customer service to customer service provided on the Internet, either with or without direct human intervention. Whether live customer service is used or whether self-service over the Web is the norm, notice that the first two stages are essentially reactive. The customer must ask; then service will be forthcoming.

The final step in the evolution is to provide service proactively, before the customer even asks, perhaps even before the customer is aware of needing it. This has variously been called "anticipatory" or "preemptive" customer service. Whatever the terminology, the aim is to prevent problems, not just resolve them once they occur. One way of going about it is to use rules-based automation. This involves routines such as, "*If* the customer has purchased Model Y, *then* send Update Y2." The business may notify the customer by e-mail that an update is available. This is usually done with software to ensure that the customer is aware of and agrees to the modification of the software. The other way is to **push** content to the user. Many sites now offer the option on notices or alerts when something relevant to the customer happens. For example, the Wall Street Journal Online offers desktop alerts on subjects selected by the subscriber. These appear on the desktop without any action being taken by the subscriber.

As we will see throughout this chapter, firms of all kinds are moving to provide more service over the Web. Few, however, are anywhere close to taking full advantage of the opportunities offered by the Internet to deliver satisfying customer service at a reasonable cost. Even fewer are supplying limited types of anticipatory customer service and support.

push Technology that allows preselected data to be distributed to the user's computer at preselected time intervals.

9-3a Customer Service Channels

Figure 9-3 also includes the main channels that are used to deliver customer service:

call center Department within an organization that handles telephone sales and/or service.

- The *telephone,* usually represented by formal telephone **call centers**. Call center workers are generally not well paid, and many would argue that they often are not well trained. In addition, call center work is high stress, even if it is limited to inbound calls and does not include outbound cold calling. When customers place inbound calls, often there is something wrong, and at the very least, they want something. Calls are often monitored, as you have probably heard in the required

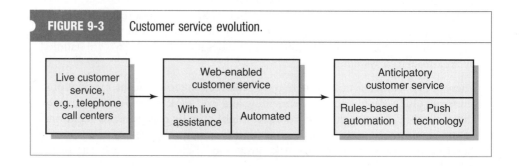

> **FIGURE 9-3** Customer service evolution.

customer notification. The result is not only high stress but also high turnover. Conventional wisdom in the industry indicates that turnover of 100% per year is not unusual in call centers. Is that likely to produce sound and caring customer service? The kindest answer is that it is hard to do so under those circumstances.

Calls that cannot be handled satisfactorily by the front-line rep are referred to a supervisor who is better trained and consequently more expensive. This is referred to in the industry as escalation. The hope is that the supervisor is capable of rendering better service in all cases except those in which a technical expert is needed. Many industrial and high-tech firms, for example, have identified engineering personnel who have the personal characteristics as well as the technical expertise to satisfactorily deliver customer service over the telephone. Whether volume is sufficient to assign engineers full-time to a telephone center or whether they are simply summoned to take calls that cannot be handled by nontechnical personnel, this is an expensive way to provide customer service. Highly technical, specialized B2B firms have often found, however, that assigning knowledgeable engineers to customer service is well worth the cost in customer satisfaction and retention.

- *Web-based* customer service. Customer service can be delivered in two ways over the Web. One includes the assistance of a live person. This includes e-mail, instant messaging, and chat. The second way is to completely automate the process, resulting in customer self-service. The first level of automated service is the ubiquitous **FAQs**. Other types include searchable knowledge bases and Flash or video demonstrations. Web-based service is available at all times, and that is a major advantage. It is also entirely consistent, as service delivered by humans is not. To the extent that customers like to be in control of their own service and support requirements, many have developed a preference for self-service.

FAQ Frequently asked question.

Notice that the first two stages of customer service evolution are reactive. The customer asks for service or support and the business is expected to provide it. That alone is a large order. To recognize potential problem before they occur and provide anticipatory service is a major undertaking.

9-3b Cost of Customer Service by Channel

Many enterprises are making a major effort to migrate customer service requests to the Internet. The compelling reason is cost. In a 2004 article the following costs are quoted:

A telephone inquiry handled by a live person	$9.50
An e-mail handled by a live person	$5.00
Live chat, where one rep can handle several customers at a time	$5.00
E-mail in which a live person is supported by an automated e-mail management system (discussed in Chapter 13)	$2.50
Interactive voice response (**IVR**) with no human intervention	$1.10
A Web site inquiry	$.50
Automated e-mail	$.25[11]

IVR Interactive voice response; automated telephone systems in which customers key in or speak data and responses and the system responds with a combination of recorded voice messages and real-time information from databases.

Because the volume of contacts between firms and their customers continues to increase, the issue of costs is important. The Gartner Group found that:

- interactions with consumers are growing at the rate of 15% per year.
- e-mail alone is growing at 20% per year, whereas self-service inquiries are growing at 25% per year.

Most customers, however, have not yet turned to the Web for service. In 2004, the Yankee Group found that:

- 77% of customer interactions still occurred through the telephone call center.
- only 13% were handled by IVR.
- online self-service and e-mail each made up 4% of total service requests; only 2% were handled through Web chat.[12]

Businesses vary a great deal in the extent to which they have adopted a proactive stance toward customer service and technologies to implement it. A 2004 study by the Aberdeen Group suggests that the types of technologies do make a difference. Firms that Aberdeen labels "Best in Class" are much more likely to use a wide range of electronic technologies, including short message service (SMS) and e-mail alerts, self-service using knowledge bases, chat, and automation of inbound e-mail. They are also more likely to use case management (identifying and tracking specific queries) and careful scripting of telephone representatives.

Some customers, however, still seem to be reluctant to turn to the Web for customer service. This may be an issue for some B2B marketers, but it is likely to be more of an issue in consumer markets where consumers are less accustomed to thinking about the Web for delivery of customer service. When it comes to purchasing on the Web, the marketer can offer incentives, often price discounts or free merchandise, to encourage customers to use the lower-cost channel. Positive incentives do not seem to be as easy when it comes to customer service. Consequently, marketers tend to turn to negative tactics in the customer service arena. Fees are the most common, either on a pay-per-use basis or as a paid service contract. Although customers may not be wildly enthusiastic about service fees, they are effective in encouraging customers to use low-cost methods before they resort to paying for the higher-cost ones. How much and when to charge for service becomes a strategic issue in the long run, because it can have a direct bearing on the quality of service and the level of customer satisfaction. That makes customer willingness to engage in self-service an important issue.

9-4 A Word About Self-Service

There may be more to the issue of when to use self-service technologies than incentives or charges. A study of more than 800 service encounters that involved self-service technology revealed that there were instances when consumers actually preferred self-service. They included:

- when consumers experienced a sudden need. A consumer who recognized a need for cash and was able to fill it immediately at an ATM was satisfied with the encounter.
- when self-service performed better than alternatives. This included situations in which the self-service technology was easy to use, was preferable to dealing with service personnel, saved time or money, and was found at the time and place the customer wanted it.
- when it simply did its job. Customers were satisfied with self-service when it fulfilled their need and let them go on about their business.

On the other hand, there were clear situations in which customers were not satisfied with the use of self-service technology. They were:

- when the technology failed.
- when the process itself didn't work. It is nice to be able to fill out a credit card application online, but if something happens and the application doesn't get processed, the consumer is not happy.

- when the self-service technology or process is poorly designed. The customer who has already filled out an application online and is asked to fill out a second one on paper is definitely not happy.

- when the customer is responsible for the failure. Some of the technology is so complex that the customer simply cannot figure it out, resulting in a failure.

The overall impression left by this piece of research is that self-service technologies have a great deal of potential to deliver satisfactory customer experience if they are carefully designed and if customers are trained in or guided through their use.[13]

The experience of firms that have made customer service an integral part of their strategies shows that implementing customer-centric service provision systems is a major undertaking for corporations, no matter what their age, size, or business sector. The Dow Chemical Co., a Michigan-based maker of chemical, plastic, and agricultural products, has been cited for excellence in electronic customer service in forums ranging from *Business Marketing Magazine,* to *CIO Magazine,* to *Advertising Age.*

9-5 Getting Closer to Customers at Dow Chemical

Dow's Customer Interface Initiative is only one part of its overall e-business strategy. That strategy is encapsulated in a two-phase corporate transformation process that began in 1993. In 1999, after a trial in two of its fifteen businesses, Dow implemented its Six Sigma continuous quality improvement program globally. The objectives of the Six Sigma process were to create a corporate culture that would be hospitable to customer service initiatives as well as to cut costs and improve productivity. In the years following its implementation, Dow has continued to deploy Six Sigma methodology throughout the corporation, crediting it for "productivity gains, opportunity growth, and cost savings."[14]

Part of the original process was a Customer Interface Initiative designed to collect information from all customer contact points into a centralized database. Customer contact points include the Web, a telephone service center, field sales offices, and a telesales center. Dow set out to ensure that, no matter what the most recent contact point had been, the representative has access to a record of the customer's last ten transactions. The customer database also enables Dow to analyze the purchasing behavior of individual accounts, assigning them to segments like needs-based, price, convenience, or relationship. A different offer is developed for each segment; for example, handling inventory management for a convenience-oriented buyer.

The initiative also included an extranet, MyAccounts@Dow, that delivers services to registered customers. Services include online access to order entry, order status, account history, and payment information. It also gives customers access to the technical and product support database. The information captured from these interactions allows Dow to customize communications about new products and the use of existing ones. By 2005, Dow had more than 6,000 registered users of myaccount@dow and registered more than 10,000 visits to the site each month. The site accounts for annual sales of more than $2 billion.[15]

Throughout, Dow maintains a focus on the customer. According to the program leader:

"Dow continues to invest much time and resources into organizing its people and process around our customer," said Mack Murrell, then-director of Customer Interface for Dow. "We will strive to continue to invest in technologies to streamline our customer touch points and make it easier, faster and more convenient for them to do business with Dow."[16]

The phrase "make it easier, faster and more convenient for customers to do business with Dow" has become something of a mantra within the corporation, reappearing with great frequency in material by and about Dow. Quality professionals call this "talking the talk," and it is important to disseminate the message of quality customer service throughout the organization. It is worthless, however, unless personnel at all customer touchpoints also "walk the walk." Let's look at an organization that has done just that from the very beginning.

9-6 A Proud Tradition of Customer Service at Eddie Bauer

Eddie Bauer established his retail store in 1920 in Seattle. An avid sportsman, the store was called Eddie Bauer's Sports Shop. By 1922, he had a formal customer service creed:

> To give you such outstanding quality, value, service and guarantee that we may be worthy of your high esteem.

His business philosophy included an unconditional guarantee, which was relatively unusual at the time. This philosophy served him well when he began a mail order catalog in 1945. Successful mail order retailers have always understood that, lacking an in-store experience, which can have important social dimensions, top-quality customer service is essential to mail order success.

After Eddie Bauer's retirement in 1968, growth accelerated with the opening of new stores and the addition of specialty catalogs. The first international catalog was launched in Germany in 1993, followed by three stores and a catalog in Japan in 1994. By 1995, there were stores in Germany and other European countries. The company also underwent ownership changes during this period, first being sold to General Mills and later to Spiegel. Despite growth and management changes, the customer service philosophy of Eddie Bauer has been kept alive within the company and is featured on the Web site and in the catalogs.

The 1996 Web site was one of the early entrants into the e-retail category. Today it features a series of online catalogs and e-mail notifications. To facilitate ordering from either the paper or the online catalog, there is a Catalog Quick Order feature. There is also a store locator feature that emphasizes the multichannel nature of Eddie Bauer's business. The customer service page, which is accessible from every other page in the site, lists many self-help options, including the following:

- Order status and history, which allows customers to track their order
- Delivery information
- Easy returns
- Size charts with instructions for measuring for a correct fit
- Gift cards and e-gift cards
- Watch repair
- Monogramming services.

If self-help does not answer the question, contact information is provided. Most important, it offers access to a human representative, which is critical for customers who have tried self-help but not found the needed problem resolution.

The signs of customer service commitment visible on the Web site are impressive. Eddie Bauer is also well regarded for keeping its promises to customers. It should be just that simple. If customer service is poor, it is a difficult and lengthy process to turn it around. British Airways is one of the classic cases in this respect.

9-7 Using Technology to Provide Customer Service at British Airways

Instead of having a fortunate heritage of commitment to customer service, British Airways had just the opposite. Consider the following quote from an employee:

> I remember going to parties in the late 1970s, and if you wanted to have a civilized conversation, you didn't actually say that you worked for British Airways, because it got you talking about people's last travel experience, which was usually an unpleasant one.[17]

British Airways' inattention to customer services issues was rooted in its history. The airline we know today as British Airways was formed when the British Airways Board assumed control of two separate state-run airlines, British European Airways (BEA) and British Overseas Airways Corporation (BOAC). Both airlines retained their own boards of directors and management structure, with the British Airways Board providing an extra level of hierarchical policy control. Both BEA and BOAC saw themselves as government agencies that represented British pride and tradition and both had management groups primarily made up of military veterans. Their sense of business mission was often described as being limited to getting the aircraft into the air and down onto the ground on time. Even profitability was secondary, and the recession of the late 1970s reduced revenues and increased costs to a point that the survival of the airline was threatened.

In 1981, Sir John King was appointed chairman with the expectation that he would reverse the financial fortunes of the airline. Among the management appointments he made was that of Sir Colin Marshall, the CEO of Avis Rent A Car, in 1983. Although he had no airline experience, Sir Colin understood customer service and its importance in the marketing of travel services. He quickly undertook a quality management program that generated increases in productivity throughout the business and was a key part of the airline's return to profitability by the late 1980s.

Customer service, however, was still an unresolved issue. According to Charles Weiser who was brought in to deal with the situation:

> When I joined British Airways' customer relations department in 1991, I found an operation virtually untouched by the quality revolution that had caused the airline's reputation and fortunes to soar. The department took more than 12 weeks on average to respond to customer correspondence, it lost 60% of calls from customers on any given day, and the cost of compensating customers with grievances was rising rapidly.[18]

The first step was to train employees to stop arguing with customers about the facts of the case and to set about resolving their complaint. The overriding goal was long-term customer retention, not short-term cost savings. The eventual outcome was a four-step process:

1. Apologize and take ownership of the problem.
2. Respond quickly. British Airways research showed that as many as 50% of customers defected if complaints were not resolved within 5 days.
3. Assure the customer that the problem is being resolved.
4. Do it by telephone. Remember the time was the early 1990s, and the alternative was mail. Both the speed and the personal contact were deemed important in retaining the customer.[19]

There was ongoing investment in training and information systems to support customer service throughout the company. British Airways even made an effort to *generate customer complaints,* because it knew that many dissatisfied customers do not complain. Customer service did improve. Further research showed that for every £1 invested in customer retention efforts there was a return on investment (ROI) of £2.

In 1995, Sir Colin Marshall discussed the airline's efforts and results up to that point with the *Harvard Business Review.* Some of the points he made included the following:

- The basic price of entry in the airline industry has five points: getting passengers where they want to go, doing it safely, having the desired routes, providing nourishment, and letting them build up frequent flier miles. These are things customers take for granted, not things that make them satisfied or loyal customers.

- In all customer segments, there are travelers who will pay a small premium in price for superior service.

- Customers don't buy an object; they buy an experience. British Airways tries to make the travel experience seamless, personal, and caring.

- In order to meet the service-driven standards that customers want, British Airways listens carefully to its most valuable customers.[20]

The airline also continues to invest in technology that improves customer service. This has included the following:

- E-ticketing that eliminates paper ticketing and speeds airport check-in

- Online check-in through the Web site

- Self-service kiosks that operate in multiple languages in major airports, allowing customers to select seats, print receipts and boarding passes, and check luggage (Figure 9-4)

- A Fast Bag Drop service for customers who have used either the online check-in or the kiosk at the airport

- A partnership with mobile services provider Vodafone that allows customers to access many services from their cell phones (Figure 9-4)

The British Airways experience represents an odyssey lasting more than 20 years in search of exceptional customer service. As their foray into wireless applications illustrates, it is an odyssey that never ends. New technologies become available to improve the overall customer experience, and the customer becomes ever more demanding as

FIGURE 9-4   British Airways customer service amenities.

Source: British Airways.

time goes on. Customer experience should be the key focal point. Providing good customer service is a natural outgrowth of customer focus, whether the entity is a corporation, a nonprofit, or a government agency.

9-8 e-Government: The State of New York Department of Motor Vehicles

Like other states and national governments, the state of New York offers many e-business services to citizens and companies that wish to do business with the state. According to the site, "From reserving a camp site to purchasing a MetroCard, it can be done online here."[21] One of the busiest pages is that of the Department of Motor Vehicles (DMV). It receives almost 19,000 hits each day, allowing citizens to obtain driver's licenses and vehicle registrations and to access other vehicle-related services. Automation software was installed to allow citizens to find answers to questions online and to reduce the number of e-mails that were manually processed. Their software provider reports that benefits of the system have included the following:

- At least 97% of users find the information they need.
- The volume of e-mail inquiries has decreased by 80%.
- The easy-to-use and up-to-date knowledge base has reduced the number of telephone calls and visits to DMV offices.
- Much of the repetitive routine is handled online, allowing support staff to focus on customers who need individualized attention.

This type of success was achieved only after intensive effort to initially build a knowledge base and to continue to improve it on the basis of customer usage patterns. For example, Internet customer relations manager George Filieau found that many users were sending e-mail even though the answers to their questions were available on the site. As a result, the DMV changed the navigation of the site so that knowledge base items became visible before the customer was able to send an e-mail. The number of visitors who found immediate answers to their questions increased from 94% to the current 97%. This high rate of self-service reduces customer service costs and eliminates e-mail backlogs, giving citizens quick answers to their queries.[22]

9-9 Customer Service Themes

Each of the organizations discussed here has followed a different path to arrive at customer service excellence. Taken together, these case histories illustrate a number of aspects of providing exceptional customer service. These are some of the recurrent themes:

- Excellent customer service cannot be delivered by a single department acting in isolation from the rest of the organization.
- Providing superior customer service is a long-term endeavor. If a customer service culture must be built in an organization that does not have one, it takes time and effort plus a substantial infusion of corporate resources.
- The customer service culture should pervade the entire organization. Customer service skills and philosophy should not be limited to a narrowly defined customer service department.

- Creating a culture of customer service is virtually impossible in an organization that does not follow at least some of the tenants of quality. The Dow case refers specifically to their Six Sigma program, and British Airways began their progress back from the brink of bankruptcy with a quality management program.

- Quality programs emphasize collection of data about processes ("what gets measured gets managed"). This is especially important for "softer" parts of the organization, such as marketing and customer service.

- Technology offers many opportunities to improve customer service, including allowing customers to access the services they want when and where they want them.

- Technology also makes it possible to offer customers multiple channels for accessing customer service.

- Even in the Internet age, however, customers want to know that they can access a competent and caring human being when necessary.

- It is helpful when the provision of customer service is done with a clear objective in mind. Cost savings are a desirable outcome, but improving customer experience is a better long-term objective.

Above all, what these case histories illustrate is that it is difficult to build an organization that consistently delivers outstanding customer service. That is why customer service excellence can form the centerpiece of sustainable competitive advantage.

These examples also make it clear that developing, introducing, and continuing to execute a successful customer service strategy is an ongoing process. It is helpful to see the steps in the process laid out early in the journey. Consultancy PricewaterhouseCoopers (PwC) has been studying how enterprises achieve excellent customer care for a number of years. Their perspective goes beyond simply pleasing customers to making customer care an important component of good strategy and the profitability it achieves.

9-10 The Pillars of Strategic Customer Care

PwC concludes that there are three stages, each with substages, in the process of developing strategic customer care (Figure 9-5). In Stage I, companies focus on customer acquisition and learning about their customer base. Stages II and III represent customer relationship management strategies of ever-increasing intensity. Stage II companies place emphasis on segmenting the customer base and learning to serve each segment more effectively. In Stage III, companies are able to use technology to offer consistent customer care at all times and all customer touchpoints. PWC describes organizations that have achieved customer care excellence as follows:

> Stage III organizations have realized that they cannot be all things to all people. While most customers are potentially profitable, some customers offer more long-term promise than others. The ability to predict who these customers are is a necessary

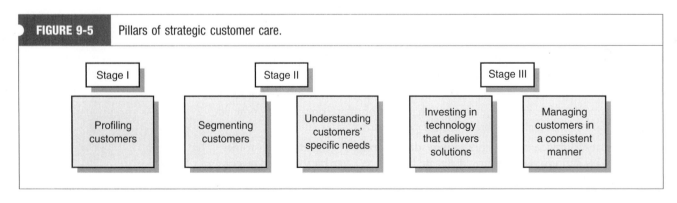

FIGURE 9-5   Pillars of strategic customer care.

Stage I	Stage II		Stage III	
Profiling customers	Segmenting customers	Understanding customers' specific needs	Investing in technology that delivers solutions	Managing customers in a consistent manner

skill on the upward path to strategic customer care. By wisely applying the right technology and information tools (remember, technology is not a solution in its own right), companies at the strategic level of customer care exercise a core level of service for *all* their customers and a distinctive, optimized level of care for their *best* customers.[23]

The first three steps—profiling, segmenting, and understanding customers' needs—should all sound quite familiar. We discussed profiling in Chapter 4 as a data-driven way of identifying segments of customers with the highest potential customer lifetime value (CLV). We continue to emphasize the importance of customer focus and customer knowledge. Putting it in this context emphasizes that this knowledge is most valuable when it is acquired for specific, high-value customer segments.

9-10a Stage III: Technology and Strategic Customer Management

To fully realize the potential of CRM and strategic customer care, the enterprise needs to progress to steps four—investing in the right technology—and five—managing customers in a consistent manner. Most of the technologies in common use and on the horizon vary by the channel in which they are used. An exception is *document imaging*, scanning documents into a database where they can be indexed by keyword and made available to any application. Document scanning ensures that all data are included and avoids the errors inherent in a manual entry process and is often used to incorporate historical data into the database.

Telephone-Related Technologies

Technologies that are commonly used to enhance the productivity of telephone call centers include the following:

- *Interactive voice response.* All of us are familiar with the menu of choices presented to us when we dial into the main telephone numbers of most large organizations. They can be profoundly annoying and frustrating, but they also represent a type of automation that can deliver major cost savings. If the menu options are a good fit with the customer's needs in dealing with the business and if the number of first-level options is kept to no more than four to six, the annoyance factor can be minimized.

- *Intelligent call routing.* The software that controls telephone call centers can recognize incoming numbers and route calls to the most appropriate representative based on a set of user-supplied decision rules. When they are well executed, call routing systems are essentially invisible to the customer and provide specialized and personalized service.

  call routing Automated telephony systems that route calls to appropriate service agents based on data such as caller's telephone number or data provided by an IVR system.

- *Call recording.* Recording calls permits real-time supervision in a call center environment and allows supervisors to review calls with reps at a later time as part of training activities. Recording also acts as proof of what has transpired during a call and can be especially important in situations, such as dealing with financial services, where there are legal requirements for information provision prior to purchase.

- *Help desk/problem-tracking software.* *Help desk* is the generic term used to describe the technical services support group in a high-tech firm. A help desk is staffed by people who are trained to answer routine questions themselves and to refer difficult questions to the appropriate expert. Help desks are supported by software that can manage incoming requests and queue them, send automatic acknowledgments, maintain a knowledge management database that holds technical information and results of past requests, and provide a variety of management reports. Early help desks were telephone-oriented. Today many of the queries come in by e-mail.

  help desk The group in an organization that provides support for both hardware and software. The term is also used in connection with specialized software that supports help desk operations.

Internet-Related Technologies

The Internet offers many technologies that can make customer service and support more accessible to the customer and more productive to the firm. They include the following:

- *E-mail response management systems* (ERMS). As the term suggests, this is software that helps organizations manage large numbers of e-mail messages coming into generic addresses such as info@atomicdog.com. The software usually contains filters that route mail to reps based on keywords in the message content. Software modules can also perform functions such as sending automatic messages or routing a stream of continuation messages to the same rep. The software also can also provide a variety of management reports.

embedded service module A device, usually a chip, that is part of a product and that is used to provide remote monitoring and diagnostics of the product's performance.

- *Embedded service modules*. Mainframe computers and servers, as well as many other electronics like medical devices, have long had embedded hardware and software that provide ongoing diagnostics. Some of this has been called *self-healing;* in other words, the equipment fixes itself, either by code built in to the embed itself or by intervention from a remote operator. Alternatively, the embedded devices can signal the operator to summon a service technician, as in the elevator example of machine-to-machine business models in Chapter 3.

- *Wireless applications*. When users make wireless devices a part of their lifestyles, those devices tend to go everywhere with them—home, work, and travel. That makes them ideal for delivery of customer service. As Internet-enabled wireless devices become more widely available, more customer service applications will be migrated to the wireless environment. Some will merely consist of mobile access to existing customer services. The more interesting ones will take advantage of the wireless Web.

- *Push and polite push*. Push is the technique of sending content to a recipient without the person having to ask for it. "Polite" push takes advantage of unused network time to load without interfering with the application the user has accessed. Push technology is currently being used to make time-sensitive information available to field sales and field technical support forces. New developments or information simply shows up on their handheld device. Push is also used to provide alerts and updates to customers. For example, antivirus software systems generally put out alerts to all registered customers when a dangerous new virus emerges. Polite push is appropriate when the content is less sensitive—a video clip demonstrating a new functionality just added to an existing application, for example.

streaming media Technology that permits a Web site to deliver continuous audio or video or both to a user's computer.

- *Streaming media*. Streaming media, now primarily used for entertainment and promotional applications, also has potential application in the customer service arena. Video is very useful in customer service situations where demonstrations are needed, such as the "connect widget x to gadget y" difficulties that exist in both consumer and business markets. Companies often have helpful videos available, but as downloads they take much too long to be viable in most instances. Streaming video, however, can overcome the slow download syndrome, present useful information, and perhaps even prevent a service call. The marketer can make the streaming instructional clip available on the Web site for customer self-service or can make it available as part of a consultation with a service representative.[24]

Technologies like these do not exist in isolation. Consider the powerful combination of politely pushing streaming media content to a user's always-on mobile device. That sounds like marketing nirvana. The danger in this particular marketing paradise is the frequently repeated warning that marketers must not overstep customer-defined boundaries in supplying content to mobile devices.

- *Agent technology.* This is the contemporary manifestation of so-called **artificial intelligence**, a concept that has been around almost since the dawn of the computer age. Internet technology resource CNET points out that there is not a commonly accepted definition of the term, but it is generally used to describe software that automates certain computing functions and then applies preestablished decision rules to give the appearance of exercising judgment on behalf of the user. An application in the Internet infrastructure is the search bots that constantly travel the Web, examining the HTML tags on Web sites and indexing the sites for the major search engines. A visible application is a service like Ask.com (formerly Ask Jeeves) (http://www.ask.com), a search engine that permits users to enter their questions in natural language. A great deal of artificial intelligence or **expert systems** technology is involved in applications like this. However, if you have used one, you may find the term *intelligence* somewhat inappropriate because they often do not work very well. In this as in many other instances, though, the technology will undoubtedly improve and present more opportunities.

  Software firms continue to try to develop solutions that can interact with customers in the guise of a human being. The idea of being able to deliver customer service in a personal manner by means of an intelligent agent, one that can make choices such as answering customer questions, is attractive. Figure 9-6 shows a virtual character encouraging citizens to use electronic filing for their income taxes and providing some basic instruction about how to do it. This agent is presenting the message in Spanish. A different character delivers the message in English. The software companies love to point out that these company representatives work around the clock and never take a coffee break!

- *Voice activation.* Finally, consider another technology that has been inexistence for a long time but is just now coming into its own. Speech recognition has

agent A piece of software that triggers an activity when a specified event occurs. Agents or bots perform a variety of repetitive tasks on the Internet, ranging from searching for content for the search engines and directories to searching for product offerings by e-merchants to provide comparison prices for users.

artificial intelligence Applications that exhibit human-like intelligence and behavior and have the ability to learn from experience.

expert system A branch of artificial intelligence that uses rules and knowledge obtained from human experts and incorporated into a knowledge base to solve problems.

FIGURE 9-6   Virtual character on Internal Revenue Service Web site.

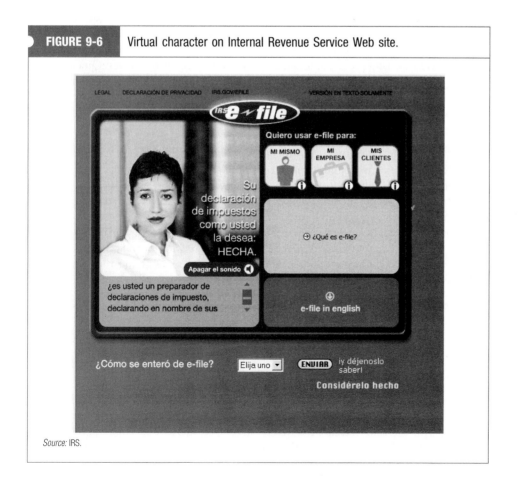

Source: IRS.

been expensive, hard to use, and not terribly accurate. Its primary use to date has been in disability services applications. It is probably wireless technology that has stimulated further development of voice recognition because the keyboards on wireless devices are small and difficult to use. Voice activation will greatly increase the ease of use of these devices.

9-10b Step Five: Strategic Customer Management

Once the appropriate technology solutions have been implemented, the final phase of the process is to put a strategic customer management program in place. We have discussed that in the context of high-CLV customers and customer segments. The Safeway case history in Chapter 4 emphasized the importance of segmenting customers by value and developing individualized marketing and customer service strategies for each segment. British Airways is an example of a service business that interacts with individual customers and that can, with the proper data in hand, treat each one according to their value to the firm. Strategic customer management leads to a program of differentiated customer service. Customer service is one of the pillars of CRM, as discussed in Chapter 8. When customer service strategies are developed for different customer segments it can, however, present a problem for low-value customers.

9-11 The Dark Side of Differentiated Customer Service

Business Week stated the issue succinctly in an October 2000 cover article, "Why Service Stinks." The article points to the consistent decline in customer satisfaction in most consumer sectors as measured by the University of Michigan consumer satisfaction index, which we discussed in the preceding chapter. It quoted Len Berry, a Texas A&M marketing professor and one of the codevelopers of the ServQual index of service quality, as seeing " 'a decline in the level of respect given to customers and their experiences.' "[25]

The article takes a dim view of the practice of strategic customer care that we have just described. It asserts that:

> For the first time, companies can truly measure exactly what such service costs on an individual level and assess the return on each dollar. They can know exactly how much business someone generates, what he is likely to buy, and how much it costs to answer the phone. That allows them to deliver a level of service based on each person's potential to produce a profit—and not a single phone call more.
>
> The result could be a whole new stratification of consumer society. The top tier may enjoy an unprecedented level of personal attention. But those who fall below a certain level of profitability for too long may find themselves bounced from the customer rolls altogether or facing fees that all but usher them out the door.[26]

The author uses examples including better service for frequent fliers on the airlines and ever-increasing fees for financial services customers who do not meet certain minimum revenue standards. The article ends with advice to the individual consumer on improving his or her customer profile. It concludes, "These days, the best way to ensure good service is to make yourself look like a high-value, free-spending customer."[27]

Both perspectives are clearly valid. Segmented and differentiated customer service can reduce costs, raise revenues by retaining customers, and increase corporate profitability. It can also decrease the quality of service, increase its cost—or both—for some customers. Is there anything that can be done to resolve the inherent conflict?

9-12 Building Anticipatory Customer Service

The issues of the cost and effectiveness of customer self-service, important though they are, still do not make full use of the Web's potential to deliver high-quality customer service at a lower cost to the marketer. That is the anticipatory service concept of being proactive, not simply waiting passively until customers request service. To do this, companies must anticipate potential problem areas before they become troublesome, develop solutions, and provide service that exceeds customer expectations.

Forrester Research says that a firm needs to do three things in order to implement anticipatory customer service:

1. Build customer scenarios, using data including call center reports, e-mail logs, chat transcripts, and Web site software that can report unusual volumes of activity and uncover patterns in day-to-day service queries. Use the scenarios to determine where intervention can prevent problems, such as common customer mistakes in placing orders.

2. Make customer service pervasive by fulfilling common requests before the customer even asks and ensuring that service is readily available throughout the value chain.

3. Design the service process for "seamless escalation." Translated, this means firms must guide customers to the service they need without having to move through frustrating layers of information that does not fit the needs of the customer.[28]

Consider, for example, two scenarios. The first could have been stimulated by examination of customer search patterns on a Web site, and perhaps filled out by qualitative marketing research. The consumer is Bob, an avid woodworker, who has recently purchased the hottest new model of belt sander and now needs a specific belt for it. You may have experienced some of the situations represented in this scenario:

> Rather than driving all over town looking for a particular sanding belt, Bob decides to try the Internet. After logging on to the Web site of his favorite hardware store, Bob has to search for sanders, which are not given as a major category in the catalog listings. He types "belt sander" into the search engine, which unfortunately takes him to the page that offers "gravel, tan bark, and sand fillers." Frustrated, he laboriously navigates his way through the catalog listings until he stumbles upon belt sanders and ultimately sanding accessories. Though the site sells his model of sander, they don't offer sanding belts made by that manufacturer. Do the belts that are listed even fit his model, he wonders? How can he find out? He considers sending an email, but he'd like to receive the belt by the weekend, when he plans to work on his new table. With some companies, it could take that long just to get an email reply. He decides to call the company, which leads to a long wait on the phone and finally, the opportunity to reiterate all of his steps to the customer service agent, who ultimately helps him order the sanding belt. Hanging up, Bob vows that next time he'll just drive to the store—or pick up the phone. His unsatisfying Web experience has driven him back to the traditional avenues of the brick-and-mortar environment—and away from the Internet.[29]

Notice the pattern that could have been uncovered from analysis of activity on the Web site. The visitor searched, but did not click through on items listed. Instead, he returned to a previous page and searched through several additional pages. He then left without making a purchase. That is what the data unequivocally tell us.

The scenario itself is somewhat embellished but not unrealistic. It suggests strongly that much of the expensive work that has gone into the development of the Web site has been wasted. At best, it functioned as an online catalog, to which the consumer could refer as he placed an order by telephone. At worst, it performed so poorly that the consumer is unlikely to return to the site any time in the near future.

What would it take to turn the situation around and provide the seamlessly satisfying experience? Consider the following scenario:

> Bob logs on to his favorite online hardware store looking for a sanding belt. At the site, he uses an automated guide that lets Bob describe in plain English what he's looking for, then takes him to the correct page, which displays several options and conveniently offers a targeted ad for a sale-priced lathe. Bob clicks one of the belts into his shopping cart, along with some tongue oil, a new thermostat, and the lathe—as a woodworker, he's been planning to get one for a while and this special is too good to pass up. But since they don't offer Bob's brand of sanding belts, he'd still like to ask some questions about whether the one he chose will fit his sander. Bob's shopping cart includes a button titled "Got a Question About Your Order?" Based on the value of the items in Bob's shopping cart, Bob is considered a premium customer. Pressing the button opens up an instant messaging session in which the service agent takes Bob to a page that gives him helpful information about which sanding belts will work with his sander. Bob sends his order and promptly receives an email confirmation with order number, total cost, and shipping date. If he wants to modify his order, he can do so easily by email. Bob logs off, another satisfied customer who can't understand why everyone doesn't shop on the Web.[30]

What did it take to accomplish this? Quite a bit, actually. The site incorporates a natural-language query system that matches the question to the best solution using keywords and decision rules. It's very nice if it works, but it takes a lot of fine-tuning to make that happen. It suggests a profile that indicates that Bob is a woodworker or it suggests a well-calibrated ad serving process that matches his query to a complementary product with considerable precision. Notice that the button for instant messaging does not appear until the shopping cart is activated—or to be precise, until the shopping cart is loaded with an expensive product. The instant messaging feature is available only to customers whose planned purchase warrants real-time service. We can easily imagine that other customers will be relegated to e-mail. The transaction is completed with compulsory automatic confirmation of the purchase. Because the scenario indicates he can modify his order, it seems clear that he has access to order status information if he desires to track it.

The customer's experience is seamless and satisfying and that is the good news. The bad news is that it is very hard work on the marketer's part to provide this level of customer service. Note that it also provides a valuable opportunity for the customer to upgrade his purchase. It is a very effective sales and service system. If it were easy, everyone would be doing it. That is why exceptional service provides sustainable competitive advantage.

Summary

Providing superior customer service is an important part of a CRM strategy. Data from various sources emphasize that service is important to both customer loyalty and profits in B2C and B2B markets. It also points out that customer service is a multifaceted construct that includes not only service recovery but also issues such as timely delivery and provision of information that makes it easier for customers to use the product.

Anecdotal evidence helps us appreciate the complexity of the customer service issue and the necessity to engage in a process of continuous improvement in order to develop and maintain excellent customer service. The process includes making sure that business systems work and implementing technology to deliver service when appropriate. The examples also stress the key role of organizational factors in creating a successful customer service system.

Delivering good customer service has also become an information-driven activity. It requires segmenting and profiling customers, identifying and targeting high-CLV segments, developing differentiated service programs for different customer segments, and giving all segments seamlessly satisfying experiences appropriate to their value.

To make customer service cost effective, technology must be part of the equation. One aspect of technology implementation is to offer customer-driven self-service opportunities. Self-service, when it works well, can be satisfying to customers at the same time it reduces the marketer's costs. There are myriad technologies in widespread use today and on the horizon that offer interesting opportunities for delivering customer service. None of the technologies are cheap, and marketers must make careful trade-offs between what customers need and the technology solutions they offer.

Offering superb customer service and targeting customer segments with the appropriate level of service are both essential to marketing success in the global Internet economy. The ability to deliver exceptional customer service has the potential to produce sustainable competitive advantage that no other strategic marketing variable can match.

 ## Quiz

1. Among the benefits that exceptional customer service confers on enterprises that can deliver it are _____.
   a. decreased cost of customer acquisition
   b. sustainable competitive advantage
   c. elimination of the need for measuring customer satisfaction

2. Customer service capabilities include _____.
   a. leveraging customer data to better understand customer needs
   b. adjusting prices to increase customer satisfaction
   c. assigning service representatives to specific customer accounts

3. Customer needs relative to customer service include _____.
   a. ability to communicate with a real person
   b. advance notification about the nature of customer service policies
   c. minimal content

4. _____ represents the final stage in the evolution of customer services practices within an enterprise.
   a. Moving some customer service activities to the Web
   b. Providing live customer service
   c. Anticipating and delivering service and support before the customer recognizes the need

5. _____ is one currently available technology for delivering customer service.
   a. Live chat
   b. Integrated back-end systems
   c. Landing pages

6. _____ is *not* an acceptable part of a process for delivering exceptional customer service.
   a. Resolving the customer's issue in a timely fashion
   b. Assuring the customer that the problem is being resolved
   c. Locating and assigning blame for the problem

7. Themes that recur frequently in the discussion of customer service include _____.
   a. the recognition that quality management concepts are ineffective in the area of customer service
   b. the need to invest time and resources in providing good customer care
   c. the high cost of exceptional customer care

8. Steps in developing a strategic customer care program include _____.
   a. segmentation analysis of the customer base
   b. outsourcing parts of the customer care program
   c. moving to service delivered entirely by human agents

9. Which of the following is *not* a true statement about customer reactions to various types of customer service practices?
   a. Customers tend to react favorably to good self-service options.
   b. Customers expect their first contact to be with a live person
   c. Customers want options for accessing customer service.

10. _____ is the result of analysis and segmentation by customer value.
   a. Proactive customer service
   b. Differentiated customer service
   c. Automated customer service

Discussion Questions

1. Throughout the chapter, reference is made to exceptional customer service as the basis for sustainable competitive advantage. Do you agree with this perspective? Why or why not?

2. The Internet has the capacity to increase customer expectations about service levels and also to be the vehicle that delivers service that meets or exceeds

those expectations. Take a position on this statement and be prepared to discuss it.

3. Moving all service delivery to the Web where customers can access it when they need it is the most important aspect of building a successful customer service program. Do you agree or disagree? Why?

4. What is anticipatory customer service? What role can it play in successful customer service delivery?

5. Can you identify any ethical issues that are inherent in sophisticated customer service programs?

6. Think about organizational issues and their impact on the delivery of exceptional customer service. Have you encountered any instances of customer service in which people in the same organization seemed to be giving you different information or advice? Why do you think this happened?

Internet Exercises

1. Find a reason to contact a Web site (e.g., asking for information, searching for support for a previously purchased product or service). Keep track of the timeliness, correctness, and completeness of the responses. Be prepared to describe them and to characterize your overall experience.

2. Identify a Web site that has a significant customer self-help component. Web sites for consumer software and consumer electronics companies are especially good candidates, but there are many others. Think of a specific problem or question that you might have in relation to this product. Visit the site and try to solve the problem or answer the question.

Be prepared to describe the nature of your experience and your degree of overall satisfaction.

3. Visit the Web sites you are tracking. Learn as much as you can about their customer service policies. Be alert to how easy it is to find the information you would need as a customer and how complete it appears to be. Note any aspects of the way the site provides customer service that look like they are particularly good or especially problematic. Establish several criteria that identify good service policies. Rank the sites according to your perception of their customer service policies and practices. Be prepared to discuss your criteria and rankings in class.

Notes

1. Many students will wonder about the relationship between the issues covered in this chapter and their study of services marketing. The latter deals with the marketing of service products. Customer service, as we are discussing it in this chapter, might be best understood as "service recovery" (meeting a customer need for information or assistance, solving a customer problem, or correcting an error in service delivery) in the services marketing models. Customer support can then be understood as providing information or learning opportunities to customers in order to prevent future problems. Support and service are provided through the same channels of communication.

2. Kimberly Hill, "Customer Service Outrage: Ameritech Delivers DSL at Snail's Pace," November 15, 2001, http://www. crmdaily.com.

3. Kimberly Hill, "Customer Service Response: Ameritech on the Line," December 18, 2001, http://www.crmdaily.com.

4. Hein, Kenneth. "Sixteen Brands Receive Failing Customer-Support Grades," February 19, 2007, http://www.brandweek.com.

5. "Frustrated and Fleeing," eMarketer, August 1, 2005.

6. David O. Becker, "Gambling on Customers," *The McKinsey Quarterly,* 2003, Number 2, http://www.mckinseyquarterly.com/article_page.aspx?ar=1299&L2=17&L3=104.

7. "How Much Are Customer Relationship Capabilities Worth?" 2001, http://www.accenture.com.

8. Jeanette Brown, "Service Please," *Business Week E.Biz,* October 23, 2000, p. EB 50.

9. "Major Corporations Not Handling E-Customer Relations Well," eMarketer, August 31, 2003.

10. Diane Brady, "Why Service Stinks," *Business Week,* October 23, 2000, p. 122.

11. Jeffrey F. Rayport and Bernard J. Jaworski, "Best Face Forward," *Harvard Business Review,* December 2004, pp. 1–11.

12. "Realizing the True Value of Online Self-Service and eBilling," August 2005, Seibel Systems.

13. Matthew L. Meuter, Amy L Ostrom, Robert I. Roundtree, and Mary Jo Bitner, "Self-Service Technologies: Understanding Customer Satisfaction with Technology-Based Encounters," *Journal of Marketing,* Vol. 64, July 2000, pp. 50–64.

14. "Six Sigma: The Way We Work to Improve Productivity, Cost Control and Efficiency," nd, http://www.dow.com/commitments/prosperity/six.htm.

15. "eBusiness @ Dow Delivering Results," nd, http://www.dow.com/ebusiness/results/milestone.htm.

16. "The Dow Chemical Company Receives CIO-100 Award for Excellence in Customer Service," Press Release, August 15, 2000, http://www.dow.com. Additional sources for this section included "Dow Names Third Among Top 10 Swith-E Aware Winners for Excellence in Electronic Customer Service," Press Release, February 10, 2000, http://www.dow.com; "The Dow Chemical Company's E-Business Strategy," Press Release, June 19, 2000, http://www.dow.com.

17. John P. Kotter, "Changing the Culture at British Airways," Harvard Business School, No. 9-491-009, 1990, p. 1.
18. Charles R. Weiser, "Championing the Customer," *Harvard Business Review,* November–December 1995, p. 113.
19. Charles R. Weiser, "Championing the Customer," *Harvard Business Review,* November–December 1995, pp. 113–116.
20. Steven E. Prokesch, "Competing on Customer Service," *Harvard Business Review,* November–December 1995, pp. 101–112.
21. "e-bizNYS," 2005, http://www.nysegov.com/e-bizNYS.cfm?displaymode=normal&fontsize=100&contrast=lod&content=about.
22. "State of New York Department of Motor Vehicles," 2004, http://www.rightnow.com/news/article.php?id=724.
23. "The Route to Strategic Customer Care," Pricewaterhouse-Coopers, 1998, http://www.pwcglobal.com.
24. Michael Hurwicz, "Streaming Media Gets Down to Business," *Network Magazine,* October 5, 2000, http://www.networkmagazine.com.
25. Diane Brady, "Why Service Stinks," *Business Week,* October 23, 2000, p. 120.
26. Diane Brady, "Why Service Stinks," *Business Week,* October 23, 2000, pp. 120–121.
27. Diane Brady, "Why Service Stinks," *Business Week,* October 23, 2000, p. 128.
28. Forrester Research, "Tier Zero Customer Support," December 1999.
29. "Building eCustomer Relationships One Interaction at a Time," Brightware, Inc, June 2000, http://www.brightware.com, p. 7.
30. "Building eCustomer Relationships One Interaction at a Time," Brightware, Inc, June 2000, http://www.brightware.com, pp. 7–8.

Evaluating Performance and Opportunities

Developing and Maintaining Effective Web Sites

Chapter Ten

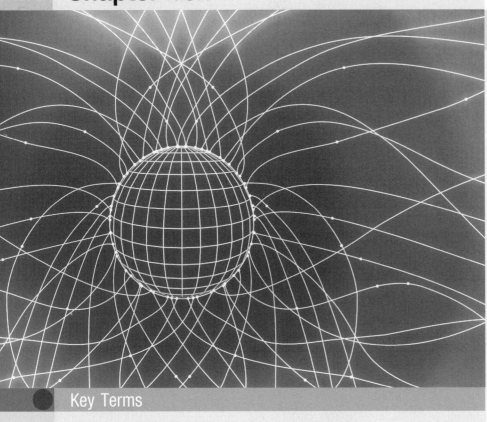

Source: © Getty

Key Terms

accessibility (p. 261)

alt tag (p. 259)

experiential (p. 253)

heat map (p. 256)

persona (p. 270)

repurpose (p. 255)

usability (p. 249)

Learning Objectives

By the time you complete this chapter, you will be able to:

- Explain each step in the Web site development process.
- Identify important issues in Web site design.
- Discuss ways in which overall customer satisfaction with Web sites can be measured.
- Explain the concepts of usability and customer experience.
- Understand what is involved in the redesign of a major Web site.
- Identify major cost elements involved in initial development of a site or redesign and relaunch.

10-1 Introduction

As Internet marketing has entered the economic mainstream, Web sites have attained new status and maturity. The environment is no longer "everyone must have one" but has moved toward carefully crafted objectives, execution for **usability**, and measurement of effectiveness. The marketing aspects of creating and maintaining customer-effective sites are covered in this chapter. Measurement is the subject of the following chapter.

usability The ease with which users are able to perform desired tasks on a Web site.

10-2 The Role of Web Sites

There are two key, but not mutually exclusive, roles a Web site can play in marketing strategy. It can be a channel for providing information, a channel for generating sales, or both. In the 10-year history of the commercial Internet, the use of Web sites as an "electronic brochure" has faded, and marketers have come to understand—and generally to take advantage of—the reach and interactivity of the Internet to meet a variety of marketing objectives. Some of the generic objectives that justify the existence of an enterprise Web site include the following:

- To provide cost savings, especially in promotion and customer service
- To increase sales revenue
- To increase the visibility of the enterprise
- To advertise products and services
- To aid in brand development
- To provide customer service
- To generate sales leads
- To retain customers
- To build an online community

The Direct Marketing Association adds that the percentage of firms that consider the major benefit of interactive media to be cost savings has increased from 43% to 56% between 2002 and 2004. The percentage of firms that find the primary benefit to be increased revenues has increased from 31% to 45% during the same period.[1] This implies that most firms are looking for tangible returns from their Web sites in either cost savings or revenue enhancement.

On the customer side of the equation, uses of the Internet have become more varied and a more integral part of the lives of business-to-customer (B2C) and

TABLE 10-1	U.S. Consumer Online Buying Breakdown, 2001 to 2007

Year	Buyers Ages 14+ (in millions)	Average Annual Retail Purchase per Online Buyer (excludes online travel)	Online Retail Sales (in millions; excludes online travel)
2001	65.3	$524.43	$34,263
2002	77.2	$573.75	$44,287
2003	85.7	$653.17	$55,996
2004	94.9	$748.23	$71,006
2005	102.2	$860.03	$87,937
2006	108.9	$954.74	$103,977
2007	115.0	$1,053.21	$121,077

Source: http://www.eMarketer.com, October 2004.

TABLE 10-2	Product Research Resources Used by U.S. Multichannel Shoppers, December 2004 (as a percentage of respondents)

Store	41%
Web site	38%
Circular/advertisement	10%
Catalog	3%
Shopping comparison Web site	3%
Competitor store Web site	3%
Recommendation from friend	2%
Call center representative	0%

Note: n = 4,000+ consumers.
Adapted from: ForeSee Results, January 2005.

business-to-business (B2B) customers alike, as discussed in Chapter 5. Further evidence is found in the growth of online retail sales. In 2003, the U.S. Department of Commerce reported $56 billion in online retail sales and $69.2 billion in 2004, a growth rate of 23.5%. Online B2C sales are expected to continue to increase at a decreasing rate. eMarketer estimates they will reach $139 billion by 2008, with a growth rate of 16.7% between 2007 and 2008.[2] Growth is seen on all available measures. Table 10-1 shows that the number of adults who purchase on the Web and the size of their average annual purchases continues to increase. Table 10-2 shows the importance of the Web as a source of product research, almost matching the importance of retail stores. The importance of multichannel shoppers is even greater, with research suggesting that multichannel shoppers purchase more frequently and in greater amounts. One study found that shoppers at J.C. Penney who purchased only on the Internet averaged $157 each year, whereas those who purchased only in stores averaged $195. Customers who purchased both at retail and on the Internet averaged $485, whereas those who purchased on all three channels—store, Internet, and catalog—averaged $887.[3]

Other research shows that more consumers are responding to nonprofit direct mail by going to an organization's Web site—20% in 2005 versus only 9% in 2002.[4] Whatever the market space, Web sites are playing a key role in marketing strategy. However, if the Web site suffers from poor design or execution, does not give visitors what they want, or is not easy to use, its failure may nullify the best-designed strategy. Marketers therefore need to have a clear understanding of what makes a Web site effective for its users—consumer, business, or nonprofit.

Marketing managers must establish clear marketing and communications objectives for the site, identify the target market and its needs, monitor site planning and development, see that the site is meticulously tested for both technical quality and visitor usability, and ensure that it is updated frequently and accurately. They must, in other words, treat it as they would any other critical marketing activity. A Web site should not be viewed as a tool of the information technology (IT) department but rather as a tool of marketing and organizational communications.

None of this is meant to diminish the importance—and the difficulty—of designing and building a first-class Web site. The technical issues are numerous, complex, ever changing—and mostly beyond the scope of this chapter. It is, however, highly recommended that marketing students acquire some firsthand knowledge of Web development tools, either through formal classes or by using some of the many excellent free sources available on the Web itself. Marketers who have even a rudimentary knowledge of technical issues will be more competent to deal effectively with the technicians responsible for Web development and maintenance. The work of the technical specialists is demanding, but marketing must lead the way to a Web site that achieves marketing objectives. Otherwise the Web site will be full of technical sound and fury but possess little commercial value.

This chapter deals with the process of developing a site and the characteristics that make it attractive and useful from the customer's perspective. As you read this chapter, bear in mind that this is a discussion of marketing strategy as it relates to Web sites, not one about "cool" or "favorite" sites. It is about what works, and that is often a different issue—as we make clear later in this chapter—from what is "cool" from a technical or aesthetic point of view. The perspective of "what works" is so important that Chapter 11 considers in detail the issues involved in measuring and evaluating site effectiveness on an ongoing basis.

Let's start the discussion of sites that accomplish business objectives by taking a look at the steps involved in the site development process.

10-3 The Web Site Development Process

Figure 10-1 summarizes the steps that are essential to the establishment of an effective Web site. It begins with the establishment of site objectives, which, in turn, should flow directly from the marketing objectives and the corporate objectives of the enterprise.

10-3a Establishing Site Objectives

The nature of the objectives will depend on whether the site is intended to be primarily informational or whether it is transactional in nature. There are many possible generic objectives, as discussed at the beginning of this chapter. The individual enterprise must take these generic objectives and develop them into specific, measurable objectives for the particular Web site.

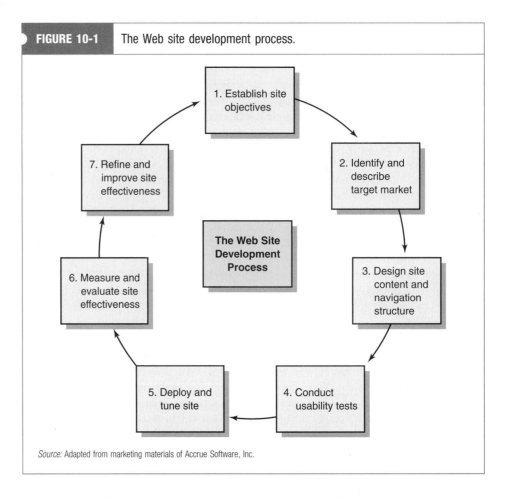

FIGURE 10-1   The Web site development process.

Source: Adapted from marketing materials of Accrue Software, Inc.

If a site is informational in nature, objectives might be based on the

Awareness → Knowledge → Conviction → Purchase → Evaluation

hierarchy that is familiar in the mass media advertising environment. The argument would be that the Web site could be used to make potential customers aware of the product and service offerings of the business, to convey detailed knowledge about product use, and to develop an intent to purchase. The Web site might then connect the prospect with the party that would facilitate the transaction. Some retail chains follow this model by providing basic information and store locator services that drive visitors into the retail store. Some manufacturers of business products choose not to create channel conflict by having a transactional Web site. They present product information and direct potential customers to the nearest dealer or distributor.

Characterizing this as a communications hierarchy process, however, has a major drawback—whether the market space is B2B or B2C. It overlooks the fact that the Internet is inherently a direct-response mechanism and risks ignoring important functions that can be included in Internet marketing activity that are difficult to carry out in the traditional mass media.

First, mass media communications do not ordinarily include a call to action. The interactive nature of the Internet makes it highly desirable to ask the prospect to take some action. If it does not appear reasonable to close a sale—a consumer shopping for automobiles or a businessperson gathering information on enterprise software applications, for example—an effort should be made to obtain the visitor's name and e-mail address for further promotional activity. This makes an informational Web site into a sales lead generation process, which is an accountable type of marketing activity that can help provide return-on-investment (ROI) justification for the expense of having a Web site.

Second, a communications hierarchy approach is likely to overlook the desirability of obtaining information about the prospect. Offering an incentive in return for information about the prospect or requiring registration to enter some of the deeper pages in the site are two ways of accomplishing this. On the Web, informational incentives often work well and have little incremental cost. The *New York Times* has done a good job of packaging content in various ways—from newsletters called "Your Money" and "Movie Update" to offers for "Great Getaways" or for the "Sophisticated Shopper"—that it uses to persuade people to register on the site. The white papers and webcasts that are a prominent feature of the marketing efforts of many B2B marketers act as informational incentives to get people to register for the site. Whatever the tactic used to obtain information that identifies visitors to the site, the ability to do so is one of the important characteristics of the Internet.

Finally, the communications hierarchy approach ignores the very nature of the Internet, in which customers choose the content to which they want to be exposed instead of having it presented to them by mass media. As a result, the task of creating awareness on the Internet is quite different from the situation mass media advertising faces in the physical world. As discussed in Chapters 6 and 7, there are many ways of bringing prospects to a Web site for the first time, some of which are online methods and some of which occur offline. The common theme is that few visitors just stumble onto a Web site by accident; most are brought there by some planned marketing or search technique. This implies that initial awareness is most likely to be created off the Web site, with provision of information taking place on the site itself.

Different objectives lead to different types of Web sites, often visually as well as operationally. Figure 10-2a is a site from Lipton, a division of Unilever. According to the agency that developed the site:

> Real Branding worked closely with Lipton and its agency partners to create an integrated strategy that would reposition and enable Lipton.com to serve as the seamless online hub for all Lipton marketing efforts. Under this new strategy, all Lipton marketing efforts are wrapped in the "Tea Can Do That" positioning and drive users online. Once directed to Lipton.com, the promise of "Tea Can Do That" comes to life in the form of **experiential** content that demonstrates Lipton's promise.[5]

experiential A term that implies learning through experience; a product with features that facilitate learning through experience.

These strategic objectives make a strong case for the Web site of a traditional consumer products company being key to positioning while providing a great deal of persuasive informational content. The site has a store locator service and offers the opportunity to purchase online.

Silicon Solar Inc. is a multichannel retailer of environmentally-friendly solar products including lighting, solar panels and water heaters. It serves consumer and wholesaler markets and has an active affiliate program. Its site is designed to facilitate e-commerce transactions from each of their channels. Figure 2b shows one of the product pages from their garden lighting section. The thumbnail visuals on the main product page offer pop-ups with additional product details and the opportunity to purchase directly from the product detail page. The site supports easy navigation with a detailed product directory in the left-hand column on all pages. Silicon Solar fosters its positioning in the fast-growing renewable energy market by sponsoring a Solar Forum where customers can connect with other users, product specialists and industry experts. This type of virtual community helps newcomers make product decisions, provides educational opportunities, and gives Silicon Solar continuing insight into the interests and activities of their customers.

Good Web site objectives take into account the overall marketing objectives of the enterprise and provide a strong foundation for measuring site effectiveness. They also take into account the special capabilities of the Internet to provide information or to make shopping easy. In establishing objectives, marketers also need to be keenly aware of the needs and preferences of the target market. As a result, a concurrent task is identifying and describing the target market.

FIGURE 10-2   A Branding Site and a Transactional Site.

(a)   (b)

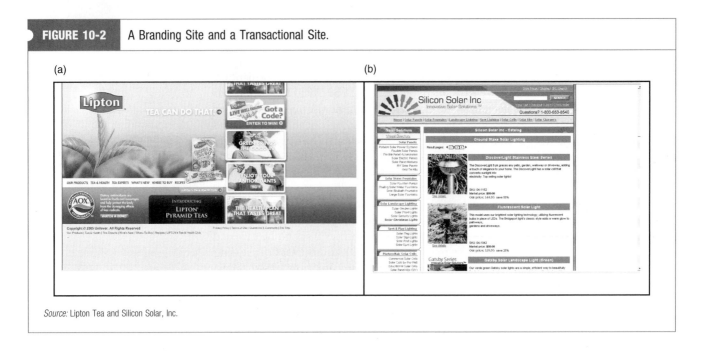

10-3b Identifying and Describing the Target Market

Marketing is clearly responsible for the important step in the Web development process of identifying and describing the target market. The marketing function understands how the objectives relate to a specified target market. Marketing is also the location within the firm of detailed knowledge about the needs, attitudes, and shopping behaviors of market segments targeted by the business.

It is important that marketers share this information with all who are involved in designing and building the site. Think about it. Should an entertainment-oriented site that is targeted to teenagers look and interact like an entertainment-oriented site that is targeted to older adults? You'll undoubtedly agree that it should not and that content, visual appearance, and interaction should all be designed with a specific target market in mind. It is the marketer's job to see that the site is geared to the identified target market by sharing information about the target market with Web designers and developers. These data include the demographics, lifestyles, and—very importantly— Web use behaviors of the identified target market. Both the marketers and the Web technicians must then work together to translate what is known into a target-market-appropriate Web site.

The nature of the product as well as the specific target market also make a difference. The marketing director of a hospital in Southern California reports on the results of using a focus group to test competing approaches to site design as follows:

> [M]y colleague had focus-group tested the four color extravaganza against a much simpler, content-rich two-color document...The group participants liked the simpler, content-rich stuff. "With all the fancy pictures and glossy design, you look as if you've just got money to burn," they said. "It's not very responsive to the consumer's need for information."[6]

Members of the target market for any health care application are probably looking for information with a serious purpose in mind. The site must be responsive to both the need for information and the attitude with which the target visitor enters the site. That implies that content should not be chosen on a whim or even on the basis of what is readily available. It should instead be chosen with a deep understanding of what the

| FIGURE 10-3 | Reebok's site targeting PSP users. |

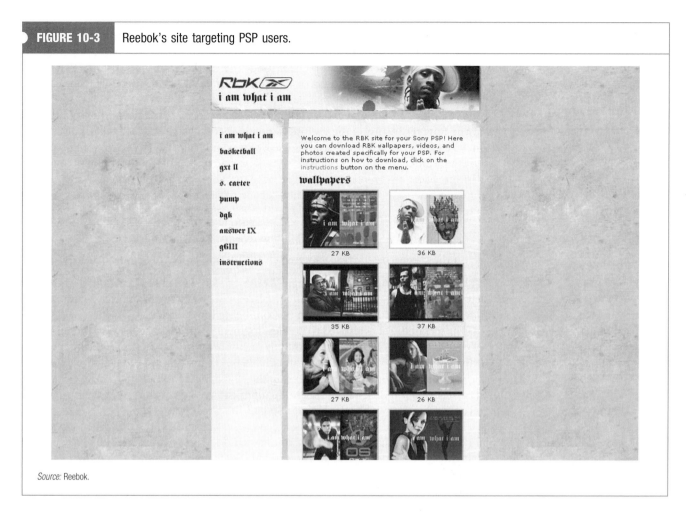

Source: Reebok.

target market wants and expects. The same is true of the design and visual appearance of the site. It should be entirely appropriate to the objectives of the site as well as to the target market and its purpose in visiting the site.

Figure 10-3 shows the home page of the site set up by Reebok to market their products to customers of the Sony Playstation Portable (PSP). The site is viewable through the PSP browser. It offers videos, wallpapers, athletic tips, and interviews with athletes. ClickZ describes it as "a sort of PSP portal to all of Reebok's various campaigns, allowing device users to access content tailored to the PSP."[7] They add that in the early phase virtually all the content is **repurposed** from other Reebok marketing activities. Reebok and its interactive agency plan to keep a close eye on the site, and if it catches on, they may develop site-specific content. Clearly this is a niche site, aimed at a very specific target market, one that is of great interest to the marketer.

Once the target market, its profile characteristics, and its reasons for visiting the Web site are determined, the next step is to design site content and the navigational structure. This step will guarantee optimum accessibility of the content to the target market.

repurpose Jargon for taking content from one corporate communications piece and with only minor revisions using it for another communications activity, often the Web site.

10-3c Designing Site Content

Identifying the necessary content and the appropriate manner of presentation are other marketing tasks. The content of the site is something that, at first glance, appears quite straightforward. Marketers, after all, in every business except a startup have experience in developing mass media advertising and marketing support material, such as brochures and catalogs. However, content on the Web is not that straightforward.

For one thing, Internet marketers believe that most viewers skim instead of reading word by word. This means that copy must be laid out in short blocks, preferably in columnar fashion. When the copy is long, the marketer should assume that many visitors will not scroll down far or will not jump to a continuation page and should place key content accordingly.

Even more provocative is a series of studies that focus on content pages conducted by the Poynter Institute, the Estlow Center at the University of Denver, and Eyetools, Inc. The carefully designed studies use eye-tracking cameras in the ongoing study of how consumers read news on Web sites. The cameras allow the researchers to record with precision the movement of a respondent's eyes on a Web page. Results from a series of studies indicate that, in the absence of specific design elements:

- eyes first land in the upper left of the page, especially if attracted by a headline.
- users usually look at only the first few words of headlines.
- on these news pages, respondents tended to look at five headlines before clicking.

That information has led to dividing a Web page into sixteen quadrants, with the upper left being highest priority for content placement, roughly the middle being second priority, and roughly the right and bottom being lowest priority.[8]

heat map A visual metric that shows which parts of a Web page perform best, that is, receives the most attention for the longest period.

The technology has also led to the development of **heat maps**, visual representations of eye activity on a Web page. The red to orange areas in Figure 10-4 indicate the most activity, and the blue to black, the least. The visual also shows the page break on the viewer's browser (often referred to using the newspaper terminology "above the fold"). It also shows a mouse-click, which identifies the area on which the viewer's eye was focused when he or she left the page.

The unexpected finding of the early eye-tracking studies was that when entering a Web page, more than half the readers included only text (no graphic elements) in their first three eye fixation clusters. The researchers also indicated that when the first three glances on a page included a graphic element, the element was more likely to be a photograph or a banner ad, not an informational graphic or other type of artwork.[9] This contradicts conventional wisdom, which says that graphics are first to attract the viewer's attention, and supports those who argue for the primacy of content in Web applications.

It also argues for the importance of well-written copy on Web sites. The more task-oriented and the more hurried the viewer is, the more likely he or she is to leave as a result of poor content or poor navigation. It is also important to recognize that visitors enter the site at different times and on different pages—not necessarily the home page. Content must be relevant, make sense even if it has been archived for a long time, and repeat key points without sounding repetitive. And—of critical importance—visitors must be able to find it easily. This is the job of the content design and the navigation structure.

10-3d Designing the Navigational Structure

The first step is to design the content structure. The grammatically questionable but meaningful phrase "to architect the information structure" is increasingly used to describe this process.[10] The implication is that there must be a coherent structure to the content of a site, usually one that is hierarchical in nature. This enables visitors to move around the site in a manner that fits each person's individual need to merely examine summary information or to drill deeper into the site in search of detailed information about a specified topic. At the same time site designers or information architects plan a careful and comprehensive structure. They should adhere to a premise often referred to as KISS—"Keep It Simple, Stupid." One way of implementing the KISS rule is to try to see that the visitor is never more than three mouse-clicks away from desired information. A common reason that visitors leave a site is that they cannot find the information they want with what they consider reasonable effort. Enabling them to do that is the job of the navigation structure.

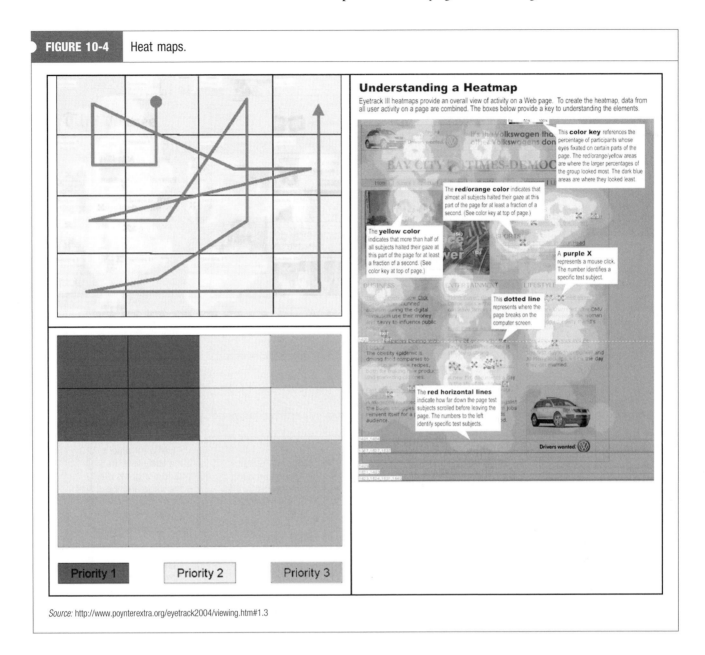

FIGURE 10-4 Heat maps.

Source: http://www.poynterextra.org/eyetrack2004/viewing.htm#1.3

The navigation structure defines the manner in which visitors move around the site. Or, quite simply, the navigation structure determines how easy it is to get from one place to another on the site and for the visitor to find what he or she needs. It may determine whether the user stays on the site or leaves, perhaps never to return.

Figure 10-5 shows two highly recommended steps in developing the navigational structure of a Web site. The first is to develop a simple graphical flow chart that shows the structure of the site. It shows the home page, second-level pages that are the entry points to major content areas of the site, and the succeeding levels that provide more detailed types of content. There may be more levels than shown here, but going beyond three or four levels creates a complex site that may be difficult for visitors to navigate. Even though the graphical hierarchy appears deceptively simple, it ensures that the connections are logical and it gives an overview of the navigational task that will face visitors. It is a step that must not be overlooked.

The next step is to develop mockups of pages. A detailed mockup called a wireframe is shown in Figure 10-5. This shows the type, placement, and size of each piece of content on the page. It also provides notes to guide the technical part of the development process.

FIGURE 10-5   Web site hierarchy and planning.

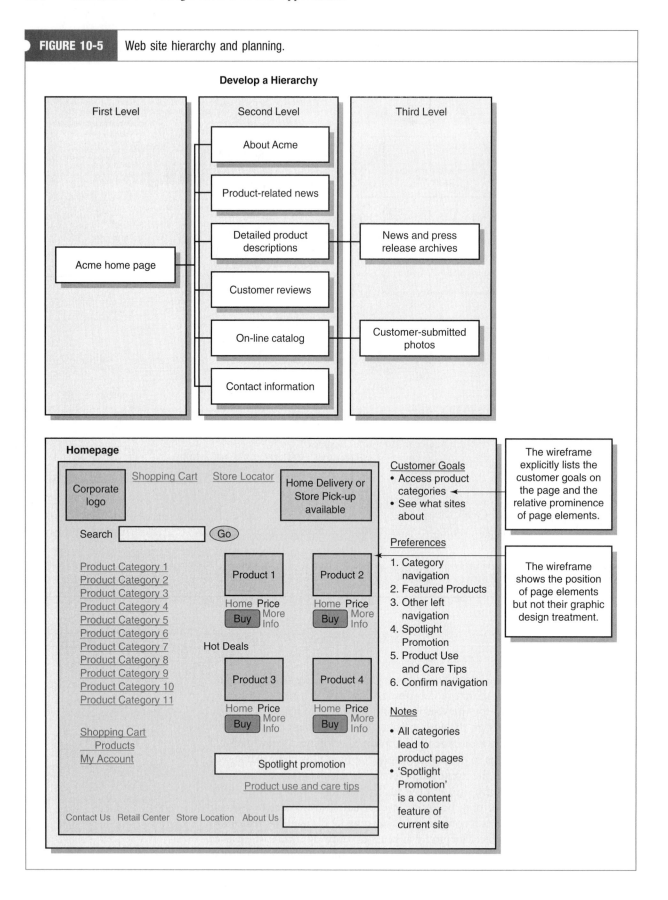

At least two rules need to be followed in designing a navigation structure for any Web site. The first is to ensure that all key information appears on every page. Be sure that visitors always know where they are within the site. Many people consider it desirable to provide a link to the home page on every page within the site so that visitors can simply start over if the path becomes a bit torturous or if they realize they are on the wrong path. This can be done by using the corporate logo as a link, which fulfills two functions—branding information and the return to home page link. If that is done, the same rule holds true as it does when any icon is made into a link. Be sure that visitors can easily identify it as a link, either by text below it or by using an **alt tag**. The alt tag also serves an important function for visitors whose browsers cannot display the graphics.

The second rule is that navigational structures must be simple and intuitive. That is, they should be clear and obvious to the visitor. The visitor should be able to navigate the site without instructions by following familiar Web conventions (like the corporate logo as a link to the home page) or simple logic. Another way of expressing it is to say that the navigation structure should be designed with the visitor in mind, not necessarily according to the way managers and marketers are used to thinking about their corporate information. The navigational structure is commonly expressed by navigation bars (often shortened to "nav bars") at the top of the page, a navigation menu in the left column of the page, and text links at the bottom of the page. Another navigational aid is "breadcrumbs," a bar at the top of each page showing the path the visitor has followed to reach this location in the site. Breadcrumbs look like:

Home > About Acme Corp > Press Releases

This is a simple and useful device for letting visitors know where they are at all times.

If all else fails, the visitor should be able to do two things. The first is to refer to a site map using one of the text links that should be at the bottom of every page. The site map performs another important function, making it easier for search engines to index the site. The second thing is that there should be one or more links to the home page on every page in the site. It should be recognized, however, that having to resort to the site map or return to the home page is a failure in terms of customer-friendly Web sites.

Developing the nagivational structure and the overall visual design for the site is a complex creative process that has no set rules. There are, however, rules of thumb and many good site designs that should be studied by Internet marketers. The Digital Gallery of the New York Public Library is a good example (Case in Point 10-1).

> **alt tag** An HTML tag (formatting instruction) displayed as a call-out bar that describes a graphic element for the benefit of people who have text-only browsers.

Case in Point 10-1   The New York Public Library Digital Gallery

New York Public Library—Extending the Reach of the Library

Figures 10-6a and 10-6b show the home page and a third-level page from the digital gallery of the New York Public Library. It is simple, is visually appealing, and illustrates a number of the rules for good site design. Some of the issues that can be seen from an examination of the site include the following:

- The *content* is specialized and offers a service to the Web population that was impossible before the advent of the

Internet. It was developed as a separate entity with a link to the main site of the New York Public Library.

- Trying to organize this material into the main site, which offers myriad typical library services, would have been difficult and might have resulted in a confusing site.
- The target market for this site is narrower that that for the main library site and can be better attracted and served with the minisite.
- The site is rich with images, but it loads smoothly.

continued

FIGURE 10-6 Examples from the New York Public Library digital gallery.

Source: NYPL.

- It is organized into seven categories, which are listed on the upper left side of the home page, the most visible location according to the eye-tracking studies. The "Explore" bar just above lists the seven categories and remains at the top of each page when the visitor leaves the home page.

- Several search options are available. There is a general search box. There are search links to directories of names of artists and others, to a detailed subject listing, and to the libraries whose collections have been digitized for this site.

- The home page is set up in *columns,* basically a three-column structure on the home page. Columnar organization makes it easier to engage in the skimming that is characteristic of viewers of Web pages. It also makes it essential to chunk content into short paragraphs or blurbs such as the "Curator's Choice," middle left on the page. Without this kind of organization, the page becomes a dense mass of text, unlikely to be read by visitors.

- *Navigation* is well thought out. Second-level pages contain a brief paragraph about each collection in a major category shown on the home page. Each has links to a more detailed description of the source and nature of the collection and to a listing of the entire contents of that particular collection.

- They also do an excellent job of three other important navigation concerns:

  - They have a "breadcrumb" bar at the top of each page. On the product page in the figure it shows that the visitor went from the home page to the Cities and Buildings page, to the Collections Guide page, and is now on the Contents page. Visitors also want to be able to get back to the home page quickly and easily.

  - Each page has a link back to the home page—the identification text at the top left of the page.

  - There are text links at the bottom of the site to support pages, including a site map.

- *Color* is another important design issue. This site uses the plain white background that designers recommend for readability and fast downloading. A red border highlights site branding and navigation tools and is visually consistent with the main library site. Beyond that, the emphasis is on the digital content of the site.

- The *font* is a contemporary sans serif font, perhaps Arial or Verdana. Sans serif fonts lack the little lines at the tip of letters (A) as opposed to fonts with serifs (T). Sans serif fonts give a clean, crisp look and are generally recommended for Web pages. The font size is large enough to be easily read with normal browser settings.

- *Scrolling* is an annoyance that should be avoided whenever possible. The home page is not long and requires only a little scrolling to see the entire page. The second-level and some of the third-level pages are rather long because they have a great deal of content. The site is sized to fit horizontally into any monitor that is set to normal pages, no matter what the size of the monitor itself.

There is a link in small font to a text-only version of the site. This is important to visitors who have older browsers or a type of browser that does not handle graphics well. It is

also important to persons with physical challenges who may have special types of readers or browsers. Designing sites for **accessibility** by the physically challenged is good business practice. It is required of sites of organizations that accept federal funds, which includes most colleges and universities. Your school's site may have a page describing accessibility accommodations. The federal accessibility guidelines can be found on the Accessibility page of the Usability.gov site at http://www.usability.gov/accessibility/index.html.

The NYPL Digital Gallery site seems to follow rules of good site design and navigational structure in a manner appropriate to its objectives and target market. However, no set of rules can capture the gestalt of what makes a Web site work in the eyes of its target customers. So here comes another "trite but truism"—the only way to find out what customers and prospects think is to ask them! That is the nature and purpose of a *usability test*. We discuss the process for conducting usability tests in detail in the next chapter.

10-3e Deploying and Tuning the Site

This stage, deploying and tuning, is essentially a technical one. The site itself should be fine-tuned, compressing images to make them load faster, checking links, and in general making sure that the site works as quickly and smoothly as possible. It is then ready to be uploaded to a host server (a computer that manages requests from browsers and returns HTML pages from the Web site in response to those requests) on the World Wide Web. Uploading requires working closely with the Internet service provider (ISP) or hosting service to ensure that the site meets all its technical requirements. The host will deal with technical issues such as load balancing and distributing content for faster access, but the company must continually monitor site performance.

> **accessibility** Web site design principles that allow physically challenged people, who may need special devices such as screen readers or voice recognition software, to successfully use the Web site.

10-3f Measuring, Evaluating, and Improving Site Effectiveness

Technical monitoring will be conducted by the IT department. Marketing is responsible for measuring and evaluating the *business effectiveness* of the site, a topic Chapter 11 discusses in detail. The evaluation metrics will provide information that points to areas in which it is possible to refine and improve site effectiveness. Possible improvements that surface as a result of site evaluation range from infrequently accessed pages to abandoned shopping carts to navigation paths that indicate difficulty in locating content. Continuous improvement should be the motto for Web sites. If improvements can be made without radically revising the site, they should be implemented immediately. When the burden of proof generated by the evaluation metrics and various kinds of user satisfaction measures warrants it, a full-scale redesign and relaunch of the Web site should be undertaken.

Looking back over this process, it should be abundantly clear that the initial steps in Web site development rely heavily on marketing for structure and guidance, whereas technical design, function, and usability concerns tend to predominate in later stages. One of the worst mistakes Internet marketers can make is to simply turn the process over to the technical experts and say "design us a Web site." The result is almost certain to be a Web site loaded with technical bells and whistles but without a marketing objective in sight. Yet this is what happens all too often in companies of all types and sizes.

The entire Web site development process, then, should focus on the marketing objectives of the site and the usability and user satisfaction required for the accomplishment of the objectives.[11] The process should be seen as an iterative one, with usability tests at various stages signaling either the need for more work or readiness to proceed to the next stage. A research-based approach tends to exhibit the following set of steps:

- Exploratory research (most often qualitative research as discussed in Chapter 5) to determine how customers want to use the site should come first, before the development of site strategy and objectives. This may lead to the construction of personas, which is described in a later section of the chapter.

- Concept testing should be used to refine design and navigation concepts and the design of individual pages. Respondents are questioned about the tasks they expect to perform on the site and whether concepts such as navigation bar structure will facilitate task accomplishment.

- *Prototyping,* the creation of page mockups, should be done before design concepts are finalized. We discuss concept testing and prototyping in the next chapter in the context of usability testing. A prototype will generally have some of the main functionality in place, such as links to other pages, but will not have all functions such as search bars and shopping carts actually working.

- **Beta testing** should be done before a new site or major component redesigns are released to the public. Beta testing is the process of asking experts and existing customers to try a product before it is offered commercially. In the Web development process, this is done by putting the site on a server that does not have a World Wide Web address. For the test, beta subjects can then be directed to a site that is not publicly available but is complete and fully functional.

- Once the site is deployed on the Internet, customer feedback and usage statistics should be used to continually monitor and improve site performance. The example of eBay's ability to listen to and act on feedback from its customers, discussed in Chapter 6, Chapter 5 provides an excellent model for this important activity. We discuss usage statistics in the next chapter. Customer feedback and usage statistics provide the knowledge required for continuous improvement of the site.

- Ongoing exploratory research that serves to document how visitors are using the site and possible changes in customer requirements brings the knowledge-gathering process full circle and may, at some point, suggest that major site revisions are in order. Likewise, as new technology becomes available, sites may be redesigned to do things that were not previously possible.

10-3g Site Usability Criteria

Qualitative research is invaluable in investigating the needs and behavior patterns of the target market of a specific Web site. So are surveys like the customer satisfaction study reported earlier. Another approach is to develop a set of questions or criteria that can be used to rate sites. Forrester Research has developed a set of criteria that describe the effectiveness of the user experience on a given site. They have tested it on both B2C and B2B sites. The twenty-five criteria are listed in Table 10-3.

The criteria were factor analyzed into four dimensions. The first is the *value* of the content to the user. The second is the effectiveness of the *navigational structure.* The third is the *presentation* of the site—details that range from the wording and graphics of the site to the effectiveness of the icons and clues such as breadcrumbs that help visitors interact with the site. The fourth dimension is *trust,* which identifies elements of site functioning that make it dependable in the eyes of users. Rationale for the importance of some of the items is given in the right-hand column. It all boils down to making it easy for visitors to use the site and accomplish the tasks that brought them there.

The Forrester methodology uses carefully trained experts to rate sites on a 5-point scale on each of the twenty-five criteria. A study in 2003 found a great deal of variance between the customer experience provided by a sample of B2C sites. Some of the well-known sites generally performed well, but all had some areas in which they failed to provide a satisfactory experience.[12] Just over a year later, they compared 139 B2C sites with 31 B2B sites. The performance of the B2C sites consistently surpassed that of the B2B sites. Forrester recommended, among other issues, that B2B sites needed to

TABLE 10-3	Forrester's Web Site Methodology, Version 4

Value

1. Is essential content available?
2. Is essential function available?

Sites don't need the most content and function. Instead, they need the mission-critical content and function users require for goals such as buying goals, for example buying a coat, getting sports tickets, booking a vacation, or reserving a test drive.

Navigation

3. Do menu categories effectively set user expectations?
4. Do menu categories expose or describe their subcategories?
5. Is the menu structure flat?
6. Do site menus provide multiple paths to critical content or function?
7. Are keyword-based searches comprehensive and precise?
8. Does search present results in a useful interface?
9. Is the site accessible to the physically impaired?
10. Is the site accessible to the visually impaired and hearing impaired?

Exposing subcategories clarifies the meaning of poorly named categories and helps flatten the menu's structure. Business results include improved look-to-buy rations and increased page views.

Rollover menus that snap shut during natural mouse movements cause users to miss their targets and click the wrong choices. Fixing this flaw improves usability for everyone, not just the disabled.

Presentation

11. Does the site use language that's easily understood by target users?
12. Does the site use graphics, icons, and symbols that are easily understood by target users?
13. Is text legible?

Online readers prefer 12-point fonts over 10-point fonts. Users read 12-point font faster than 10-point, too.

14. Are navigation elements easily recognizable at a glance?
15. Do page layouts use space effectively?

Poorly designed layout grids create unused and unusable expanses of white pixels. The resulting ''trapped negative space'' displaces content, ads, and navigation.

16. Are controls, settings, and data fields presented in a logical order?
17. Does the site provide location cues?
18. Are interface elements consistent?

Trust

19. Is contextual help available at key decision points?

Firms can deflect call center costs by providing answers online. This tactic works best when users find help integrated into pages when and where it's needed.

20. Does the site explain how personal data are kept secure?

Consumer confidence in online security fell in 2002 and has not improved in 2003. Sites can ease concerns by linking to easily understandable security policies wherever personal information is requested.

21. Do users have control of their personal data?
22. Is the site consistently fast?
23. Is the site reliable?
24. Does the site recover well from errors?
25. Does site functionality give feedback?

Adapted from: Forrester Research Criteria for Web Site Usability, ''The Best and Worst of Site Design, 2003.''

make better use of Web analytics to evaluate the effectiveness of their sites and assign priorities to improving the most glaring problems.[13]

Shopzilla, formerly BizRate, takes a different approach. This company administers pop-up surveys following e-commerce purchases, and it allows customers to come to the site and rate e-merchants. It uses these data for two purposes. When it has a sufficiently large sample of ratings for a particular e-retailer, it rates their services on the site. It also uses the data as the bases of marketing research products it sells to marketers. Their fifteen quality factors are shown in Table 10-4. Eight of the items are measured immediately upon checkout by the pop-up and the other seven are measured by e-mail after a sufficient time has elapsed for fulfillment to take place.

TABLE 10-4	The Shopzilla Quality Factors

Source	Rating	Explanation
At checkout	Ease of finding what you are looking for	How easily you were able to find the product you were looking for
At checkout	Selection of products	Types of products available
At checkout	Clarity of product information	How clear and understandable the product information was
At checkout	Prices relative to other online merchants	Prices relative to other Web sites
At checkout	Overall look and design of site	Overall look and design of the site
At checkout	Shipping charges	Shipping charges
At checkout	Variety of shipping options	Desired shipping options were available
At checkout	Charges stated clearly before order submission	Total purchase amount (including shipping/handling charges) displayed before order submission
After delivery	Availability of product you wanted	Product was in stock at time of expected delivery
After delivery	Order tracking	Ability to track orders until delivered
After delivery	On-time delivery	Product arrived when expected
After delivery	Product met expectations	Correct product was delivered and it worked as described/depicted
After delivery	Customer support	Availability/ease of contacting, courtesy and knowledge of staff, resolution of issue
After delivery	Would shop here again	Likelihood to buy again from this store
After delivery	Overall rating	Overall experience with this purchase

Adapted from: http://www.bizrate.com/content/ratings_guide.html.

Their items are typical retail satisfaction measures that include ease of finding the products and prices, e-commerce issues such as shipping costs and options, and fulfillment issues such as delivery and customer service.

Whatever measures are used—and more options are covered in the next chapter—it is important to meet or to even exceed customer expectations. If the Web site does not satisfy expectations, visitors will leave, and many will never return. Even if that has become a trite statement, it is true, and there is no reason to doubt that it will continue to be true. There is simply too much competition on the net both in terms of products and services and in terms of competition for the user's attention. Second chances are rare in Internet marketing; the pressure is great to do it right the first time. Marketers have turned to the concept of customer experience to provide an overall framework to guide their efforts.

10-4 Providing a Rewarding Customer Experience

The concept of customer experience is not new to service marketers. Valarie Zeithaml and Mary Jo Bitner point out that customers evaluate products and services according to the properties of their offering. One category of properties is *search qualities*, attributes that lend themselves to evaluation prior to purchasing, such as color, style, and price. *Experience qualities* can be discerned only during the use of the product or service. Airline travel and restaurant meals are examples of service products that must be purchased and consumed before their characteristics can be evaluated. Goods may also have *credence qualities*, properties that cannot be accurately evaluated even after consumption. Services like repairs on your computer can be evaluated only indirectly—does it work or not—but there are often lingering doubts about the quality of the repair and its cost. Zeithaml and Bitner point out that most tangible products are high in search qualities, whereas services are more likely to be high in credence qualities. Both products and services can be high in experience qualities. Automobiles, for example, have a high component of experience qualities, and in their image-building efforts, automobile marketers tend to play up the experiential components. Many services, such as vacations, are inherently experiential. The quality of the customer's experience with the product or service is a key determinant of satisfaction with it.[14]

That makes it important to understand the nature of customer experience and what marketers can do to engineer satisfactory experience. Rayport and Jaworski, whose basic reference point is the physical world, suggest that there are four dimensions of a customer interface that work together to create customer experience:

- *Physical presence and appearance.* Physical presence is an attribute of products and services in the offline world, but appearance is a characteristic of Web sites. Note how different the appearance is between, say, the branding site and the transactional site portrayed in Figure 10-3. Contrast them with the Reebok PSP site in Figure 10-4. Each promised a different experience, one based on the nature of the target market and the task it expects to complete on the site.

- *Cognition.* This is the thinking/knowledge aspect of the experience. It may be driven by information, as when information in the customer database allows the service rep or the Web site to provide a personalized and satisfying experience.

- *Emotion or attitude.* Emotional or attitudinal aspects are characteristics of human beings, but a Web site can convey some of those aspects visually.

- *Connectedness.* This dimension implies the ability of all people or elements to work together to provide satisfactory experience for the customer. Effective teamwork can also be enabled by information that keeps everyone moving in the same direction.[15]

Rayport and Jaworski give a number of examples in which machines are able to outperform human beings at the customer interface. Consider the Netflix site. Its physical appearance is attractive and welcoming. It knows more about movies, especially about your personal preferences, than any person could be expected to know. This is because all the necessary elements of the site are connected to the customer database, to the content database of the site, and probably to other specialized Netflix databases. The site allows members to connect with their friends to recommend and discuss movies. Although the site can't display emotion, it is unfailingly polite and welcoming to the visitor, no matter the day or hour.

Berry, Carbone, and Haeckel describe the process as one of giving off clues of various kinds. One set of clues relates to functionality. Can a Web site that is frequently down or that provides outrageous information when you conduct a search be trusted with your credit card number? Their second set of clues relates to the sensory experience—sights, smells, voices. In the multichannel environment, the site can drive customers to a retail store in which sensory experiences can be provided. The site can suggest some of the experiential characteristics with logos, pictures, and other visuals that evoke the store experience. These authors say:

> To fully leverage experience as part of a customer-value proposition, organizations must manage the emotional component of experiences with the same rigor they bring to the management of product and service functionality. The way to begin that effort is by observing customers and talking to them about their experiences in order to gain a deeper understanding of the clues they're processing during their encounters with the company.[16]

As these two sets of concepts suggest, the importance of customer experience and the activity of staging consumer experiences are not new or unique to the Web. Many good service marketers practice elements of experience marketing—the chocolate on the pillow of the turned-down bed in the Ritz-Carlton Hotel or the greeter at the door in a Wal-Mart store are both examples. Some retailers have incorporated experiential marketing into their operations in innovating and entertaining ways. An enterprise renowned for its ability to stage compelling customer experience in the physical world and an effective portrayal of experiential characteristics on the Web is Disney.

10-4a Multichannel Customer Experience at Disney

In the physical world, the company that epitomizes the customer experience has to be Disney. Its theme parks are the best and most visible example of Disney's attention to the quality of the customer experience. The experience begins with the physical design of the parks, which ensures that the visitor is transported into a controlled environment where jarring notes can be kept to an absolute minimum. The grounds are meticulously maintained, as you know if you've even thrown down a candy wrapper there and seen a worker snatch it up immediately. The concern with maintenance and physical appearance extends to extensive plantings, which are changed regularly to keep them fresh and in bloom. It even extends to the design of the entrance, which is slightly uphill as visitors enter, creating a towering vision of the Sleeping Beauty's castle. Coming out at the end of the day, the downhill incline creates an easy walk for weary visitors.

The concern with total customer experience continues with careful employee selection and intensive training—except that they are not considered employees; they are "cast members." Training includes elements beyond customer service basics, including topics such as staying in character and drawing visitors into the experience of rides and other activities. There's another exception to common practice here, however. Consumers who come into the park are not considered customers or even visitors; they are guests. Cast members begin the day with the rallying cry, "Showtime!"

The Disney home page is designed around a series of islands, reminiscent of the theme parks, that represent different Disney products and services—from hotels at the parks, to the Disney shop, to Disney mobile services. Each island has a set of links available through a mouse-over. These links take the visitor deeper into the site, to content of her choosing. The links are repeated on the tabs at the top of the page, giving two ways to navigate the site. The site is very large, covering Disney movies, videos, and television programs. Pull-down menus at the bottom of the site help the visitor navigate through other major portions of the site. Text links at the bottom of the page, in addition to offering corporate information, permit the visitor to switch to "Disney Online Lite," which lacks some of the functionality and allows the viewer to remove Disney Motion, its proprietary video player. The visitor is given a great deal of assistance in navigating a complex site and also is allowed considerable control over the nature of his or her experience on the site.

When the visitor clicks on the Destinations link and chooses Disney World, that person is asked to "Choose Your Experience." The page that opens—complete with music and a Flash presentation—depends on which category you choose from options, including Preschoolers, Teens, Romance and Relaxation, and others. It's not quite like being there, but it does convey some of the magic. However, if you have a slow connection, you can view a low-bandwidth site that has the content but less of the magic.

10-4b Direct Experience at the San Diego Zoo

Another site that offers many experiential elements is that of the San Diego Zoo (Figure 10-7). It features a Flash introduction with pictures of appealing animals and Zoo visitors enjoying them. At the "fold," it has a series of banners, in this case their own house advertising. Attracting members is important, as is increasing revenue from the Zoo store. The final banner offers opportunities to book travel and hotels through

FIGURE 10-7   The San Diego Zoo Flash introduction page.

Source: San Diego Zoo.

the Zoo site, which provides affiliate revenue for the Zoo. In the image captured here, visitors are encouraged to print their own admissions tickets online, thereby avoiding the often-long lines at the Zoo gates.

The Zoo is very adroit at taking advantage of its current animal stars. At the time of the introductory screen capture, there was an infant panda who was both the subject of video clips and featured in a Zoo blog. Polar bears are another consistent crowd-pleaser at the Zoo; they are featured in one of the ads and in a video clip. When visitors go to the home page, they find more pictures and the practical information visitors need—directions, hours, and maps of exhibits. Special programs, such as an opportunity to see the Zoo at night during the summer, are featured along with other visitor information such as dining opportunities. The main navigation bar, which has pull-down listings of second-level pages, is the same one seen at the top of the introductory page. Below there is a second navigation bar containing specifics for visitors.

The Zoo takes great advantage of interactivity with webcams and videos. A zebra named Robert, who is especially personable, is a performer in Zoo TV ads. Clips of Robert's most quotable remarks are found along with the ads in which he stars on the TV page. The Zoo's blogs (it refers to them as Weblogs) are interesting. Actually, it is a single blog structure with different paths. Visitors can narrow the blog entries seen to their particular interest, choosing from seven categories that range from conservation to giant pandas. The blog entries are written by Zoo experts, and comments and questions from readers are solicited. Questions are answered when possible on the blog. Links to more detailed information, to videos, and to webcams are frequently seen. The only issue is that the Weblogs are hard to find, not being intuitively included in any of the navigation aids on the home page. Overall, however, this Web site is a virtuoso performance in terms of structure, content, and performance.

Take a moment to think about the different sites that have been used to illustrate this chapter. They have different objectives, have different appearances, and give their visitors different experiences. The nature of the experiences will be based on the tasks the visitor expects to perform on the site. All sites need to provide their visitors with satisfying experiences, ones that make them likely to return, maybe even to recommend the site to a friend.

10-5 Resources for Web Site Development

There are few road maps for the Internet marketer in search of ways to create a satisfying, rewarding, and even exciting experience for the Web site visitor. Four things that good marketers do on a regular basis will be helpful:

- Think carefully about the marketing objectives for the site. Is the visitor experience contributing to the attainment of the objectives? Even better, think about it from the visitor's point of view. What should a visitor "take away" from the site—not just in terms of information obtained but also in terms of the feeling and overall attitude with which the visitor leaves the site?

- Be alert for marketing activities that focus on experience and learn from them, whether they are competitors or in a totally unrelated business sector. The Rebook PSP and Disney examples in this chapter are perfect examples.

- Track some Web sites on a regular basis. These should include not only your direct competitors but also some "idea" sites. You may learn a great deal from totally unrelated sites, such as a B2B marketer who follows some entertainment sites like Sony.com or a fantasy football league like ESPN's.

- Talk to your customers, frequently and comprehensively. Do not, however, expect that they will simply present you with great new ideas for improving the experience on your Web site. They will be able to tell you what they like, what they don't like, and other things you might do. The latter will usually be things they have seen elsewhere that could be adapted to your site. Although this can be useful, it is not likely to produce new ideas. The marketer has to develop the truly innovative ideas from a deep understanding of customer likes, dislikes, and expectations.

Some of the suggestions for change that come from customer feedback and monitoring may result in incremental improvements to the Web site. These improvements can be made as their desirability is confirmed and may or may not be announced to consumers. As long as the improvements and refinements simply improve the customer experience and do not change the way the customer uses the site, they probably can be done without fanfare. At some point, however, Web sites may deem it necessary to do a complete redesign and relaunch. Even successful sites like that of Staples may opt for a complete remake of their site.

10-6 The Relaunch of Staples.com

Corporations are not often forthcoming about the reasons they have chosen to do a major site relaunch or how much it costs. There are, however, two basic reasons for an extensive site redesign. One is that site metrics, the voice of the customer, or both point to major difficulties in using the site. For example, if the site metrics, a topic discussed in Chapter 11, show that many people are leaving from the product pages without making a purchase, the firm should question customers to find out why. The answer will often be, "We can't find what we want." That is a strong indicator that the

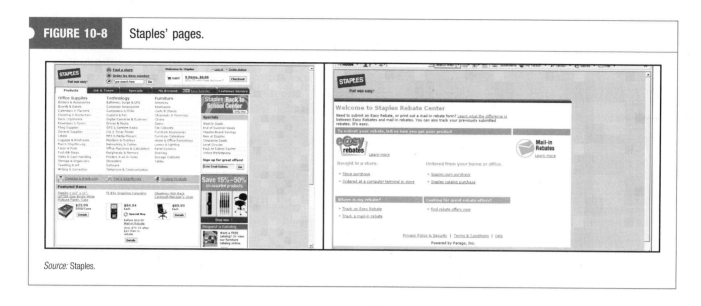

FIGURE 10-8 Staples' pages.

Source: Staples.

site needs to be redesigned. The second possibility is that new technology has become available that enables functionality on the site that was not previously available. An example is the "print your own admission ticket" function on the San Diego Zoo site. At first glance, printing something like an admission ticket or a manufacturer's coupon to be redeemed in a retail store does not seem like a major technological issue. However, after reflection you will probably realize that extensive security systems are necessary to let you print valid zoo or concert admissions tickets and keep the hackers from printing invalid ones that are indistinguishable from real. Marketers want to offer functionality like printing tickets that makes purchasing easy and convenient for their customers.

Staples did not say precisely why they decided on a major redesign, but they are clear about the strategy they are pursuing. The basis of the strategy is seen in their brand promise "We make buying office supplies easy" and the "That Was Easy" slogan used in all their channels—store, Web site, telephone call center, and catalog. The redesign was focused around three themes:

- Easy to Find
  - Through usability research with customers, they reduced the number of product categories from twenty-four to seventeen. The site handles more than 40,000 items, so categorizing them in a customer-intuitive way is not easy. See Figure 10-8 for a product page example.
  - Information is furnished on *Learn More About* and *Help Me Decide* pages to help shoppers make the right choice.
  - The navigation structure has been revised to focus more on the products and information that customers access most frequently.
- Easy to Order
  - Easy Reorder lists that record past purchases. New functionality makes it easier to select multiple items from a list and add them to a shopping cart.
  - When products are ordered, other "Necessary and Recommended" suggestions are presented.
- Easy to Check Out
  - An Easy Rebates feature (Figure 10-8) lets customers submit rebates online with no paper processing or mailing. A tracking number is returned by e-mail so that the customer can keep track of the rebate as it is processed.
  - The information available for tracking orders has been increased.[17]

Taken individually, most of these features are not unique; other sites have one or more of them. What sets a relaunch like this apart is the careful research and planning. Staples is known to have a usability laboratory in which it continuously tests and refines the design and operation of the site. For example, for the relaunch it conducted card sorting research (described in Chapter 11) with more than 5,000 customers in order to reduce and refine the product categories listed on the home page.

The Staples research team used other tools, both qualitative and quantitative, to segment customers. They rode on delivery trucks, visited customer job sites, monitored telephone service reps, and conducted focus groups. They have a 35,000-member customer panel that was used to produce samples for surveys. The result was a set of seven customer segments. Two of those became the focus of the site redesign. **Personas** were built around these two key segments. Lisa Listmaker is an office manager whose goal is to get the purchase done as quickly as possible. She has a standard order list complete with item numbers. She shops most often at Staples.com but also uses the catalog and the nearest retail store. The "Easy to Order" features are important to Lisa, who wants to get everything done at once, quickly and efficiently.

persona A hypothetical person whose characteristics are those of a segment of users.

Sammy Specific runs a small business and does not plan carefully for office purchases. He doesn't shop by item number, but he does know the products he needs by brand or type. The "Learn More About" and "Help Me Decide" informational pages make his purchasing easier. Both Lisa and Sammy use the "My Account" functionality to list previous purchases and to do things like sort them by product, date, or total amount.[18]

Would you like to know whether you are more like Lisa Listmaker or Sammy Specific? Take the brief survey posted as "quiz" at the bottom of the Staples multimedia press release http://www.prnewswire.com/mnr/staples/21229/. Or do you just think this is a bit silly? The use of personas is considered an advanced Web design technique. It gives guidance to designers: "Would Sally like this function?" and "What would she use it for?" It also gives the technical personnel—programmers and others—the sense of real persons for whom they are creating Web pages. One positive outcome is to keep designers and programmers from filling a site up with aspects that are not used by many visitors and that make site functioning slower or navigation more difficult or both.

Careful, thorough customer research; an umbrella strategy; and clear objectives are the marks of a site design or redesign that has a high probability of providing satisfactory customer experience.

10-7 How Much Does It Cost?

The question, How much does it cost?, is one that everyone would like to have answered. Current data are not readily available, but a number of generalizations can be made. First, you are probably aware that there are many sources of free Web site templates and free or inexpensive Web hosting. Unique domain names are not free, but they are available at low cost. If site templates are provided by a reputable supplier, they usually work pretty well and they may meet the needs of individuals or small businesses. The templates, however, are not very flexible, and you may soon find yourself wanting to do something that is available only as a purchased service. Do you see a marketing strategy there? As far as the Web hosting is concerned, if it is free, your site will undoubtedly be subjected to ads served by the host. Depending on your purpose that may be acceptable, but it should be expected.

At the other extreme, Web sites can cost hundreds of thousands of dollars to develop, and a million or more if major hardware purchases like high-volume servers are required. Costs can, in general, be broken down into design, programming, specialized software, dedicated hardware, consultants, and systems integration. One reason that costs are hard to come by is that most sites are built using a mix of purchased services and in-house labor. Each firm needs to take a hard look at its in-house capabilities and how much time the necessary specialists will be able to devote to site development. Then it can begin to identify the purchased services it will need and to develop estimates of costs.

Careful attention to all the details can result in an acceptable Web site for a few thousand or perhaps a few tens of thousands of dollars. There is, however, one rule of thumb that has existed since the beginning of the commercial Internet and appears to be as true today as it was in the mid-1990s. *Maintenance of the site will cost from three to five times as much each year as the original development costs.* This is a daunting figure to many managers. However, if the Web site is not well maintained and continuously improved, it may do more harm than good to the reputation of the organization.

Whatever manner the marketer uses to establish a Web presence, it is imperative to remember that the expectations of customers are constantly increasing. Whether B2C, B2B, or nonprofit, they expect a quality site in terms of both usability and aesthetic appeal. To be part of the Internet economy, the marketer must find a way to meet customer expectations about the site itself and the fulfillment and customer service that supports it. Anything less may do fatal damage to an Internet business or lasting harm to a bricks-and-mortar brand.

Summary

This chapter sets forth a marketing perspective on building and maintaining Web sites without understating the effort and expertise needed for successful technical design, programming, and implementation. Marketers are primarily responsible for the initial stages of Web site development in which objectives are established, the target market is identified and described to all participants, and the information architecture and navigational structure of the site are outlined. They are also responsible for working closely with technical professionals during actual site development and closely monitoring the site for visitor usability and consistency with business and marketing objectives.

The first step in ensuring that the site meets visitor expectations is technical usability—does the site work smoothly, and are visitors able to find the information they want? This is a behavioral measure, and it is measured by usability testing. The second step is visitor satisfaction. As a purely attitudinal measure it can be measured by conventional marketing research techniques. Satisfaction can also be implied from a number of site-generated statistics, such as shopping cart abandonment and site stickiness. The most comprehensive level is the overall customer experience. The aim should be to

move visitors through a series of stages that begin with functionality and progress through intimacy, internalization, and finally evangelism.

A variety of measures, monitored on a regular basis, will be necessary to understand the dimensions of experience on a particular site and to continuously improve the experience for the target visitor. Taken together, effective Web site development and adequate ongoing maintenance are complex and difficult tasks.

At some point, market development or the availability of new technologies may make the complete redesign of the site desirable or even necessary. This will initiate the Web site development process once again. It will be no less demanding than the original development of the site, and as the Staples example suggests, it can be time-consuming and expensive. A complete site redesign may be taken as a marketing opportunity to stage a highly visible relaunch, one that draws attention to the improved customer experience available on the site.

A firm can establish and maintain its Web presence in alternative ways. The option chosen should provide the best long-term fit with company objectives, availability of necessary resources, and the firm's level of commitment to a meaningful Web site.

Quiz

1. When setting objectives for a Web site, marketers must be concerned about _____.
   a. the role of the site in overall marketing strategy
   b. a Web site that offers entertainment to visitors
   c. making sure the Web site is equipped to conduct e-commerce

2. Typical Web site objectives include _____.
   a. providing information for employees
   b. creating "buzz" about the new site
   c. providing customer service and support

3. The nature of Web site objectives will depend on _____.
   a. how visitors are going to be attracted to the Web site
   b. tasks visitors expect to perform on the site
   c. the types of hardware and software that will be used

4. In developing the site navigational structure, it is important to _____.
   a. turn it over to technical personnel who have the necessary expertise
   b. construct a hierarchical diagram of site structure
   c. have every page represented on the main navigation bar

5. Which of the following are true statements about the content of a Web site?
   a. It can be taken directly from the enterprise's other marketing materials.
   b. Most visitors will only skim the content.
   c. Content must be determined by how much information the Web site is able to store.

6. Among the Web design elements that help create a satisfactory customer experience are _____.
   a. dramatic and attention-getting graphics and other visuals
   b. pages that have a lot of text and are able to answer all the visitor's questions
   c. multiple navigation aids like breadcrumbs and different colors for followed links

7. It is important for marketers to measure and evaluate _____.
   a. the business effectiveness of the site
   b. the level of satisfaction with the customer experience on the site
   c. both a and b

8. A _____ is a partially functional Web page that target customers can evaluate.
   a. prototype
   b. wireframe
   c. beta site

9. Among the types of testing that marketers can do to improve their Web sites are _____.
   a. concept testing, beta testing, and monitoring customer feedback
   b. prototyping, exploratory marketing research such as focus groups, and beta testing
   c. both a and b

10. Which of the following are true statements about customer experience on a Web site?
    a. Customer experience describes what happens to users on a single visit to a site.
    b. Marketers can do little to affect the nature of customer experience on a Web site.
    c. The components of good customer experience may be different in various channels.

11. Among the requirements for successful multichannel marketing are _____.
    a. presenting information in channel-appropriate ways
    b. eliminating conflict between channels
    c. keeping online and offline marketing activities separate

12. Which of the following is a true statement about Web site maintenance costs?
    a. Maintenance costs will not begin to occur for several years after a site is developed.
    b. Yearly maintenance costs may be several times the size of initial development costs.
    c. Maintenance costs are not a concern of marketers.

Discussion Questions

1. *True or false:* It is imperative that marketers play the leading role in all stages of the Web site development process. Take a position on this statement and be prepared to defend your answer.

2. What are the steps involved in developing a Web site? What should the marketer's role be in each step?

3. The chapter makes frequent references to both testing and conventional marketing research. What testing and research techniques are appropriate in the Web site development process, and what is the role of each?

4. What is the best way to assess customer satisfaction with a Web site?

5. Explain the concept of "consumer experience." What is its relevance to Internet marketing? Contrast that with the role of the consumer experience in the offline retailing environment.

6. How does a marketer know when a site should simply be improved upon and when it should be completely redesigned and relaunched?

Internet Exercises

1. Think of some specific ways in which a Web site can support the marketing strategy of an existing business. Locate a Web site that illustrates some of them and be prepared to discuss the points of strategy integration between the offline and online marketing efforts.

2. Identify a Web site that you judge to have major experience components. Spend some time on the site and be prepared to discuss your experience in class. Pay special attention to whether or not you believe the experience components contribute in a meaningful way to achievement of site objectives.

3. Study the site plan of your school's Web site, either by examining the site map or by dissecting its navigational structure. Propose an interactive or experiential element that you believe could be usefully added to the site. Be specific about the target audience that you wish to engage in the interactivity or visitor experience.

4. Choose one of the sites you are tracking and do a careful assessment of the degree to which it is either easy and pleasant or difficult and frustrating to navigate. Develop a set of criteria that you consider important in assessing whether a site provides good navigation or not.

5. Visit a site that you would describe as being local in nature. What are the main content elements of the site? How does it attempt to serve a primarily local market? Can you think of ways in which the site could be improved?

Notes

1. "The DMA 2004 Ecommerce Report," August 2004, http://www.the-dma.org.
2. "ERetail Sales Pick Up Speed," eMarketer, August 31, 2005.
3. "The Changing Role of the Catalog for Multichannel Retailers," DoubleClick, 2004.
4. "Direct Mail's Success in Non-Profit Space," eMarketer, January 31, 2005.
5. "Tea Time," August 30, 2005, http://www.imediaconnection.com/content/6628.asp.
6. Susan Solomon, "Hey Marketers, Content's Back in Style," ClickZ Network, December 5, 2000, http://www.clickz.com.
7. Pamela Parker, "Reebok Reaches Out to PSPers with Site," August 30, 2005, http://www.clickz.com/news/article.php/3530971.
8. "Viewing Patterns for Homepages," nd, http://www.poynterextra.org/eyetrack2004/viewing.htm#1.3.
9. Marion Lewenstein, "Study Snapshot Suggests Serendipity Lives Online," August 18, 2000, Poynter Institute, and "A Deeper Probe Confirms Findings," July 12, 2000, http://www.poynter.org.
10. A useful reference can be found in the Information Architecture Tutorial at http://hotwired.lycos.com/webmonkey/design/site_building/tutorials/tutorial1.html.
11. For a detailed manual on designing and developing Web sites from a customer usability perspective, see http://www.usability.gov.
12. Harley Manning, "The Best and the Worst of Site Design 2003," September 2003, Forrester Research.
13. Bruce D. Temkin, "B2B Sites Fail the Usability Test," January 12, 2005, Forrester Research.
14. Valarie A. Zeithaml and Mary Jo Bitner, *Services Marketing* (New York: McGraw-Hill, 1996), pp. 57–59.
15. Jeffrey F. Rayport and Bernard J. Jaworski, "Best Face Forward," *Harvard Business Review*, December 2004.
16. Leonard L. Berry, Lewis P. Carbone, and Stephan H. Haeckel, "Managing the Total Customer Experience," *Sloan Management Review*, Spring 2002, pp. 85–89.
17. "Staples Launches New Staples.com for Easy Online Ordering," Press Release, July 27, 2005, http://investor.staples.com/phoenix.zhtml?c=96244&p=irol-newsArticle&ID=735662&highlight=.
18. "Staples Launches New Staples.com for Easy Online Ordering," Press Release, July 27, 2005, http://investor.staples.com/phoenix.zhtml?c=96244&p=irol-newsArticle&ID=735662&highlight=; Susan Kuchinskas, "A Staples.com Even 'Lisa Listmaker' Could Love," InternetNews.com, February 28, 2005, http://www.internetnews.com/ec-news/article.php/3486026.

Measuring and Evaluating Web Marketing Programs

Chapter Eleven

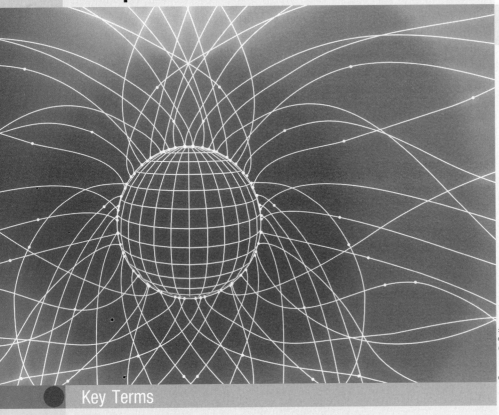

Source: © Getty

Key Terms

Chapter Outline

Learning Objectives

By the time you complete this chapter, you will be able to:

- Explain the importance of usability testing.
- Describe some of the technical issues covered in analysis of site performance.
- Identify the reasons why traffic and audience measurement are a central issue in Internet marketing.
- Understand the process of collecting data from server log files, coded pages, and user panels.
- Define key traffic and audience metrics and the purpose of each.
- Identify some of the issues in measuring the impact of online advertising.

11-1 Introduction

From the beginning of this text, we have discussed the important role that information plays in all aspects of Internet marketing. There are many types of and many uses for the vast quantity of information that is available on the Internet. One key part of that information is the clickstream of data that is produced by user activities on the Web. Although these data are essentially a by-product of Internet activity and therefore have little, if any, incremental cost of production, they are not in a form that is usable to marketers. Marketers need to know what data are available, what metrics are needed, and how to obtain them. Those topics comprise the major part of this chapter.

Before dealing with the quantitative metrics that are available, we look at a mostly qualitative approach to information about Internet marketing effectiveness. The subject of Web site usability was broached a number of times in Chapter 10. We begin this chapter with a discussion of the methodology of usability analysis. Later in the chapter, we discuss the manner in which metrics and usability studies interact.

In the meantime, however, consider a scenario that suggests how much information is available and some of the uses to which these data can be put.

11-2 Sally Shops for a Fishing Rod

Sally's father's birthday is approaching. She wants to look for a particular brand of fishing rod as a gift. All she knows about fishing is that her father likes it; she has no idea where to try to purchase the rod. She enters the name of the branded product, "Fish-Friendly fly rod" into a search engine and is rewarded with about twenty Web sites that purport to carry the item. Scrolling through the first page of listings, she sees nothing outstanding, so she clicks on the first listing. Listing One turns out to be a highly specialized retailer, and "fly rods" are one of the listings on the left-hand navigation bar. Pulling down the menu, she sees the Fish-Friendly brand and goes directly to it. They show the particular rod that her father wants but note that the item is out of stock and will not be available for another 2 weeks. That's not soon enough, so she goes back to the search page and clicks on the second listing. Listing Two turns out to be the site for a retailer of everything from basketballs to tents. After several tries, Sally finds "fishing gear" under "outdoor recreation" and separate pages for four different types of fishing rods. "Fly rods" is one, so she clicks on it. No Fish-Friendly rods are listed, however. Back to the search page. The third try does turn out to be a charm; Listing Three has the rod in stock, and she places the order. It's going to be a gift shipment directly to her father, so that's two forms to fill out, but after a couple of tries she gets it all right and submits the order. The order is quickly confirmed, and a promotional item on the confirmation page suggests that she consider subscribing to a fly-fishing magazine. That

clickstream The complete data record, made up of mouse-clicks, of consumer activity on the Internet during a specified period, usually the duration of a visit to a single Web site.

server log Record kept at the server level that records each file requested from a Web site.

sounds like something her father would enjoy, so she clicks on the offer box, which takes her to the magazine site. Two more sets of forms, and she has ordered the subscription for her father. Satisfied, she moves on to check her e-mail.

One of the facts of Internet life is that every mouse-click Sally made on this shopping expedition (the **clickstream**) has been recorded on one or more **server logs**, the operating records of the system. The marketing task is to determine how these data can be used to fine-tune existing marketing strategies and devise new ones. Consider the following possibilities:

- Listing One can tell how many orders it has lost as a result of the out-of-stock condition.

- Listing Two can tell that visitors must look through several pages to find the desired item. One way of ascertaining this is to see that they are following circuitous paths through the site instead of going straight to the product.

- Listing Three captured two customer names, one of whom is a gift-giver and one of whom, based on current knowledge, is a fly fisher.

- Each of the three firms can tell that Sally arrived on their page from a search engine page. The magazine site can tell that she arrived by way of Listing Three. That could be important for a number of reasons, but if the sporting goods firm is an affiliate of the magazine site, it is owed an affiliate commission, which must be tracked.

The ability to log, retrieve, and analyze every mouse-click has important implications for marketers:

1. The data point to possible usability problems that need to be examined and corrected.

2. The data are used to generate site effectiveness measures that are essential for a number of marketing purposes. These "metrics" are used in managing the site. They are key in determining advertising rates for the site. They are also essential to understanding the impact of various Internet marketing programs like e-mail and online advertising campaigns.

3. They provide a mother lode of data that can be mined to develop an in-depth understanding of visitor behavior on the site. These data can be used to improve the site and to guide the way to useful new site features and marketing programs.

4. The fact that these data exist is becoming widely known to Internet users. Although they may not entirely understand all the ramifications of its use, they are concerned about a perceived loss of personal privacy. This subject is covered in Chapter 12, so this chapter focuses entirely on the marketing management uses of the data.

11-3 Ways to Evaluate Web Site Effectiveness

In Chapter 10 we used the term *Web site effectiveness.* It is important to take a moment for a high-level view of that term, because it can have different but equally important meanings. Figure 11-1 lays out the issue.

Unfortunately, the term *Web site effectiveness* is strategically appropriate when used in three different but related ways. The one with which we are already familiar is site usability, which we discussed in terms of its importance to the customer experience in the preceding chapter. This is the way visitors look at the site, the way they gauge its ease of use and value to them. This perspective cannot be overlooked. It is also a

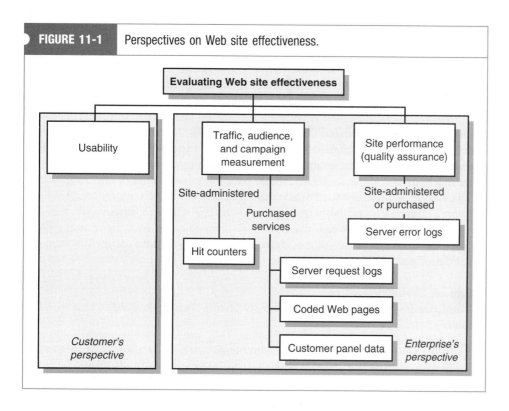

FIGURE 11-1 | Perspectives on Web site effectiveness.

perspective that has a clear relation to the business effectiveness of the site. If visitors find the usage experience satisfactory, the site has a greater chance to be successful in the long run. This is the purpose of **usability testing**, which we acknowledged in the previous chapter as an important part of the Web development process. In the next section, we examine the methodology of usability testing.

The second is traffic and audience measurement, the term used to describe a set of techniques used to provide effectiveness data vital to marketing management. We discuss traffic and audience measurement techniques in detail in this chapter. The third perspective is that of site performance. This involves data that are needed by site technicians to gauge and improve site performance. Even though it is the responsibility of the technical side of the Web team, marketers should be familiar with the basic approaches, which we cover along with other purchased metrics.

It is appropriate to look at usability testing first, because its greatest value comes prior to the actual deployment of a site or a redesign. In advertising terms, it is a **pretesting** technique used to ensure that the site functions according to user expectations before the site is made available to all visitors. It also can and should be used on an existing site from time to time, especially if other metrics suggest site problems.

11-3a Usability Testing

First, it is important to be clear about what usability testing is and is not. It is *not* conventional marketing research, although it may incorporate some research techniques into the testing process. It is, in fact, more similar to the testing done by direct marketers or in advertising laboratories than to the marketing research typically used by mass media marketers.[1] In addition, usability testing should not be confused with the testing of communications appeals, which should be part of the enterprise's overall marketing communications program if not of the Web site development process itself.

Usability testing is exclusively designed to see if the site works in a user-friendly fashion according to the expectations of members of the target market. Site performance (**quality assurance** is another frequently used term), as portrayed in Figure 11-1, is a different

usability testing Ensuring that it is easy for visitors to navigate and, in general, to find desired content quickly and efficiently on a Web site.

pretesting As used in advertising, to conduct research on a promotion before it is used in the marketplace with the purpose of improving its effectiveness.

quality assurance Synonymous with quality control in manufacturing; procedures for ensuring the correct performance of software.

issue that requires different metrics. Usability tests are essentially qualitative, and *they are performed by target site users, not by technicians.*

The undisputed guru of Web usability is Jakob Nielsen. Now a consultant, he was with both the original Bell Labs and IBM before moving to Sun Microsystems, where he was lead usability engineer for the establishment of the first Sun Web site in 1994. His personal Web site (http://www.useit.com) is filled with information about usability testing and is updated frequently. Nevertheless, some of the most instructive material on the site dates back to his early experiences with Sun in the mid-1990s. This supports the assertion that usability testing has strong foundations in basic testing approaches, many of them originating in psychology laboratories and adapted for specific uses in applications such as advertising evaluation and computer hardware and software design. Even a cursory inspection of Dr. Nielsen's site further indicates that much of his current activity involves spreading the word about usability testing to Web managers around the world and railing against those who ignore (or are ignorant of) principles of good design for usability.

Stages of Usability Testing

It is not overly simplistic to divide usability testing into three general categories as follows:

concept testing Research performed on the idea behind a product or a communications program.

- **Concept testing** is the earliest stage and reflects none of the actual site programming. In testing at this stage, one or more concept boards are shown to respondents, who critique it from the perspective of how logical they perceive it to be and how easy they think it would be to use. Concept tests are useful at a very high level to prevent egregious design flaws and to give general guidance to the designers about what customers and prospects expect and what they think about the design concepts presented to them. This type of testing can be done relatively quickly in a focus group setting. Because it requires only the development of concept boards, it is also relatively cheap. Remember that the concept boards are testing the design of major pages on the site and the degree to which they communicate the desired corporate image and specific communications objectives, not the communications appeals themselves.

- Prototype testing is the second level. At this point in the development process, the site design is complete and at least some parts of the site are fully functional. Testing a prototype affords an opportunity to get reactions to the appearance of the site and to get some information about the degree to which the site structure is consistent with customer expectations. The earlier prototype testing is conducted, the more visual appearance and structure can be changed without increasing the development time and cost of the site. Early testing, however, implies that much functionality is probably not operating and that the test will be somewhat artificial. The marketer must carefully assess the trade-off between early and more complete testing.

- Full usability testing indicates that the site has been uploaded to a server and is fully functioning, even though it is not accessible to the general public. Dr. Nielsen has a page on his site that shows a testing setup in detail, the major elements of which are reproduced in Figure 11-2. The setup shows a single testing station with a computer on one side and other research tasks set up on tables facing the computer.

The Methodology of Usability Testing

Many of you will see the commonalities between the usability testing lab and psychology labs in which you were a test subject at some time in your academic career. The setup is simple and, except for the two-way mirror shown in Figure 11-2b, can be replicated in a space like a corporate conference room without great effort or expense. If marketing and Web development personnel want to view the usability test,

> **FIGURE 11-2**   Usability testing stations.

Source: "Usability Testing of WWW Designs," May 1995, http://www.useit.com/papers/sun/usabilitytest.html.

alternatives are to use a commercial focus group facility or to video for remote viewing. The test itself can be administered by one person, or one researcher can be assigned to each respondent to give instructions and to probe comments in a focus-group fashion. The researchers must be scrupulous in not giving information or conveying attitudes to the respondents.

The setup itself shows great care and attention to detail.

- It is being videotaped to give a complete and detailed record of the session. It you look carefully, you also see a lavaliere microphone next to the computer that will record all the comments made by the respondent during the session.

- One concept board is shown in Figure 11-2, probably the home page. They found that it damaged easily, so the researchers taped it down and covered it with protective film.

- There is a separate setup for **card sorting**. This research task involves giving subjects a deck of cards, each with a single information item, in random order. The subject is asked to sort the cards into sets that "fit together," but the researcher is careful not to explain *how* they should fit together. The subject sorts the cards into as many or as few piles as deemed necessary. The researcher then asks the subject to explain what the topic category is and why each informational item fits into that category. This is a way of understanding how customers view proposed content, for example, into which categories they place various products. This sounds simplistic, but customers often suggest an organizational framework that is different from the way management views its own products and services.

card sorting A research technique in which respondents place individual items written on cards into piles that represent similar content.

focus group The qualitative marketing research technique in which a group, usually six to twelve people who fit a particular profile, are brought together to discuss an issue under the guidance of a skilled moderator.

In this procedure, you may recognize a process similar to a marketing research **focus group**. The two techniques have many of the same advantages and disadvantages, among them the opportunity to get a great deal of information from a few carefully selected respondents and the care that must be taken by the person conducting the test not to bias the responses of the test subject.

The main focus of a usability test is to ask test subjects to perform tasks that simulate what a visitor would want and expect to do on the site. In a more recent research project in which Dr. Nielsen and his colleagues tested twenty e-commerce sites, he explained the various types of tasks. First, test subjects were simply asked to explore the site for a few minutes to see what they believed the purpose of the site was. The second task element was to ask them to locate a specific product on the site. For example, on one home products site they were asked to locate the cheapest toaster. For the third task element, test subjects were given a more open-ended task. An example was, "Pretend that you have just moved from Florida to a cold climate and that you don't own any winter clothes. Please buy what you will need to be able to go for a walk in freezing temperatures."[2] The fourth task was for the users to answer specific questions about customer service on the site, for example, whether the customer could cancel an order after placing it.

In this research project, each Web site received attention for 35 to 40 minutes. This is considerably less than the 1 hour or more spent when a single site is being tested. Dr. Nielsen notes that after 2 hours, both the test subjects and the facilitators are sufficiently tired, so further useful results are unlikely, no matter how many or how few sites are being tested.

Usability Testing and the Pareto Curve

Usability testing should not be considered an option or a luxury. Even the best designed Web sites invariably have problems that are quickly detected by users. Even the so-called cosmetic problems will produce an inferior user experience.

pareto curve A plot of number of occurrences against percent of total; the source of the 80/20 rule.

The need for testing is often questioned on the grounds of both time and expense. Nielsen makes a strong case for the affordability of user testing by constructing a **Pareto curve** (Figure 11-3), which shows that more than 75% of a site's usability problems can be identified with five user tests and that 100% will be found by testing fifteen users.[3] He also states that, with experience, the tests can be completed in 2 workdays if user recruiting has been outsourced to a commercial marketing research firm.[4]

The message should be that eliminating or skimping on usability testing is a false economy. It should be a standard part of the launch of any new Web site, whether it is

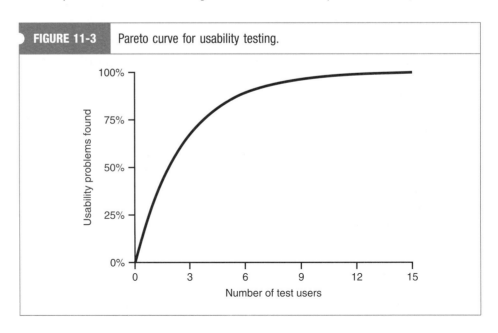

> **FIGURE 11-3**   Pareto curve for usability testing.

completely new or a redesign. It should also be done when other site metrics indicate usability problems, as is explained in the next section.

One important decision the marketer will have to make is at which stage in the development process the usability testing should be done. The earlier it is done, the easier it will be to make fundamental changes. At the same time, the lack of functionality in early-stage testing makes it somewhat artificial. On the other hand, if the functionality is nearing completion, considerable time and money have been invested in the site and it will be harder to make major changes. The issues involved in testing a prototype versus a fully functioning site suggest that several small-scale tests at various mileposts along the way might be more productive than any single larger-scale test.

Usability testing may also be conducted at various points in a site's life cycle. As the site grows and additional pages are added, usability may be compromised. Site metrics, as we will discuss later in the chapter, may also suggest that there are usability problems.

The basic process of usability testing has not changed since the early days of the Internet, but technology can provide enhancements. The computer on which the prototype site is installed can be fitted with software that records each mouse-click the user makes. This is referred to as "clickstream data," and it provides a rich database for analysis of usage patterns, especially convoluted paths and dead-ends that exist in the Web site navigation structure. If desired, the user's eye movements can also be tracked by using the type of camera described in the preceding chapter. This also provides rich data about actual usage, but it cannot be done meaningfully until pages are essentially complete.

The marketer's decisions, then, include at what points in the development process to do usability testing and how many data collection methodologies to use at each one. Different data collection methods and types of questioning are likely to be appropriate at different points. For example, concept boards are most useful in very early stages of development, whereas eye-tracking data require pages that are complete with both text and graphics. This is another strong argument for multiple usability tests at various points in the development process.

Usability testing joins creative site design to make up the two primary techniques that marketers use to ensure an enjoyable and satisfying visitor experience on the Web site. It should be regarded as an integral part of the development process. At some point, though, the Web site is going to be pronounced "ready for prime time" and is going to be launched into the public domain. At that point, it becomes extremely important to have in place a set of site metrics and reporting tools that measure the attainment of site communications and business objectives.

11-4 Enterprise Metrics for Evaluating Web Sites

Site metrics fall into two basic categories: measures of business performance and measures of site performance. The business effectiveness measures provide data by which marketers can judge the success of various parts of the site itself and of Internet marketing programs. They are key to managing Internet marketing activities and demonstrating return on investment (ROI) on those activities.

The effectiveness measures can be used in many ways. It is critical to set clear purposes and objectives before the analysis of metrics begins. The La Quinta chain of inns and hotels provides a good example. The enterprise launched its original Web site in 1997. The site quickly became its most cost-effective channel for booking visitors to various properties. New and returning visitors can check availability and make reservations at inns across the country, view their existing reservations online, and manage benefits from their loyalty program, "Returns" (Figure 11-4). The Web site

Source: http://www.lq.com.

relaunch was intended to make it easier for customers to carry out these tasks and for the business managers at La Quinta to understand customer usage patterns and to make rapid revisions to better meet their needs.

Specifically, they needed to know who their visitors are, where they come from, how they use the site, and how to best encourage them to book a room using the site. They choose various metrics services from WebTrends to meet their particular needs. Ted Schweitzer, vice president of e-commerce for La Quinta, said, "We needed to be able to track our campaigns and our conversion paths to make sure the site was doing what we intended."[5] They need to first attract visitors to their Web site and, once there, convert them by getting them to register for a room. In order to attract visitors, they use online advertising, including banners and paid search. Their pages are optimized to attract visitors through organic keyword search. They needed to not only be able to measure click-throughs from each of these acquisition methods but also to see which method produced the most conversions. From their segmentation analyses, they place targeted advertisements and run both direct-mail and e-mail campaigns for niche travel markets. Here also, they need to be able to measure response from both online and offline channels and to determine which channels produce the highest conversion rates. "I can see not only if a particular program had a response rate, but if it had a converting response rate, which is key."[6] The vice-president of e-commerce sums up the importance of Web metrics by saying, "Online marketing is the most effective [sic] of our advertising dollars. With WebTrends, the results of our marketing campaigns are in black and white—tangible and touchable. This is especially helpful in evaluation performance of niche site marketing and those sites that require annual subscription payments for participation."[7]

These kinds of measures of business effectiveness are vital to marketing managers. Measures of site performance give directions to the technicians who maintain the site.

In the words of the Web site development process, this is tuning of the site to maintain and improve the manner in which it functions. Let's turn briefly to site performance. We will then devote the remainder of the chapter to discussing the source, nature, and use of the business effectiveness measures.

11-4a Web Site Performance

Figure 11-5 shows a report of the performance of a single Web page, the page itself, and each file on it. Timing starts from the time the URL (http://www.alertsite.com) is translated into the Internet protocol (IP) address—the **DNS** Lookup on the legend at the bottom of the chart. That occurs when the URL is accessed, and the more detailed printed report shows that it required 0.0024 seconds to look up the IP address on the network. Then the page starts loading, file by file. For each file, the webmaster can see how many seconds it took to connect with the file, how long it took for the first byte of

DNS Domain Name System; the process for converting the name of a Web site into its IP address.

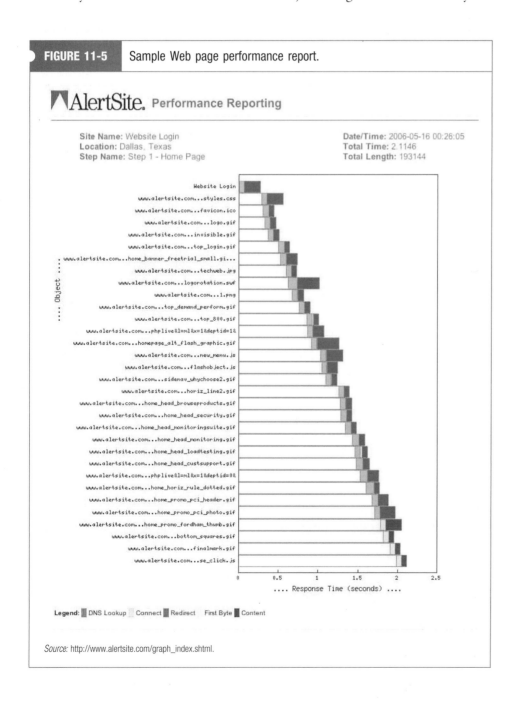

FIGURE 11-5 | Sample Web page performance report.

Source: http://www.alertsite.com/graph_index.shtml.

redirect Sending one URL to another Internet address.

information to load, and how long it took for content to load. Notice that many of the files are graphics—GIFs or JPEGs—and do not have significant text content. There is also no **redirect** on this page as there is when, for instance, a firm has been purchased and the original URL is redirected to the home page of the new owner. It took 1.3902 seconds for the page to load completely, which would be acceptable to most users. Reports like this are available in real time; that is, the webmaster can call up a status report for any page—or many other elements of Web functionality—at any time.

This type of data is clearly of great use to the Web technicians, but it provides little direct benefit to marketers. Marketers should be concerned about the smooth functioning of the site, but it is the job of the webmaster to make it happen. Marketers are concerned with the traffic and audience data because this information has direct relevance to marketing programs.

11-4b Collecting Traffic, Audience, and Campaign Data

An important measure of the business effectiveness of a site is the number and quality of its visitors. Site effectiveness can also, of course, be measured by sales if it is a transactional site. However, both content and transactional sites rely heavily on traffic and audience measurement for the reasons described at the beginning of this chapter: to manage and to improve the site, to establish advertising rates, and for other marketing purposes such as persuading other sites to link or to become affiliates. The relevant measures can be defined as follows:

- Traffic data describe activity on the site. These data include metrics such as number of visitors, sessions, and page views.

- Audience data describe both the *behavior* of people on the site—where they come from, what paths they take through the site, and whether they take desired actions—and the *people* themselves using both anonymous and identified profile data as described in Chapter 4.

There are three basic ways of collecting those measures from the site itself—**hit counters**, server log files, and **coded Web pages**. It is important to understand the basic technology they entail before looking at the statistics they generate.

hit counter A piece of software inserted onto a Web site that measures the number of visits to the site.

coded Web page A technique in which a small image, usually a 1-pixel transparent image (called a pixel tag or transparent GIF), is placed on a Web page. Used in conjunction with a cookie on the user's computer, the image returns data about user activity on the Web page.

page view A page actually seen by a visitor; currently measured as a page being delivered to the visitor, which is not exactly the same thing.

unique visitor An identifiably distinct, although not necessarily identifiable, visitor to a Web site within a specified period.

Hit Counters
A hit counter is a small piece of software that can be added to a Web site to provide a few basic metrics. Site development tools like FrontPage have hit counters that can be inserted as part of the process of building the site. Others can be found free on the Web. Older ones are visible meters on the site; newer ones may not be visible to the visitor. A hit counter is a few lines of HTML code that are placed on each page in the site that the owner wants to measure. Many sites provide free hit counters in the hope that the Web site owner will purchase reporting services or more complex hosted counters.

Figure 11-6 shows a sample of one of the many reports that can be obtained from a hit counter. For each day of a specific week of a specific month, it shows the number of pages that have fully loaded (**page views**), the number of **unique visitors**, and the number of visitors who return. There are multiple ways in which sites can identify unique visitors, which is discussed in a later section of this chapter. The figure also slows the main navigation bar of the site. It gives an idea of how many reports can be obtained from the relatively simple technology of a hit counter.

Whether the marketer chooses a simple hit counter or a more comprehensive Web analytics application, there are two basic ways of collecting the clickstream data—server log files and coded pages.

Server Log Files
As the name suggests, server log files are created by the server that houses the Web site. Each time a browser requests a file in order to build a Web page, it generates an

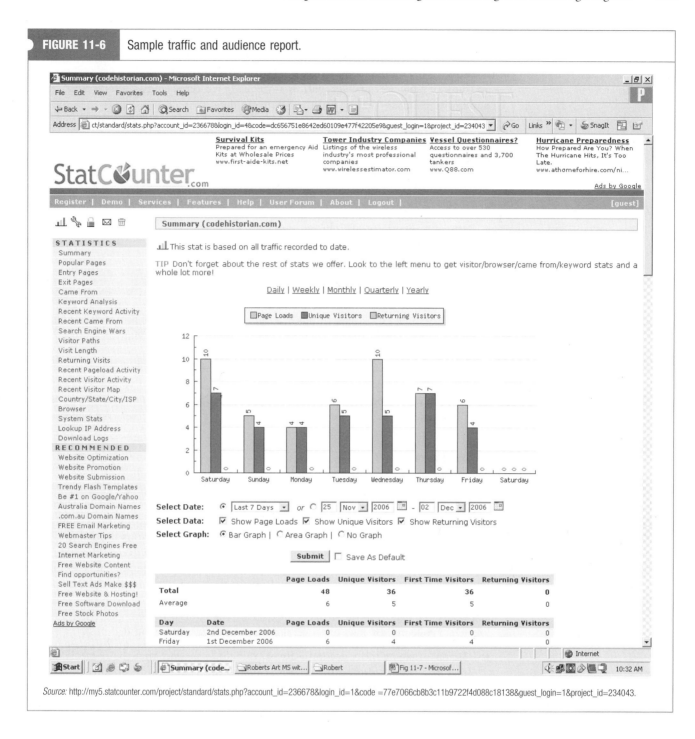

| FIGURE 11-6 | Sample traffic and audience report. |

Source: http://my5.statcounter.com/project/standard/stats.php?account_id=236678&login_id=1&code =77e7066cb8b3c11b9722f4d088c18138&guest_login=1&project_id=234043.

entry in the *server request log.* That sounds like a simple and straightforward statement, but it has enormous implications. Each graphic on a Web page is a separate file, and there can be several content files on a single page, as shown in Figure 11-5. So, for example, consider a simple Web page has three graphics and one content block. Each time that Web page is accessed, four hits are registered on the server log. Yes, that's correct; *a hit is counted for each file on the page,* no matter how many or how few.

To further complicate the situation, what the server registers is the requester's IP address. Every computer linked to the Internet, whether it is a server or recipient (client) of information, must have such an address. Some addresses are permanent, but if the user is linked by a dial-up connection the address is dynamic, meaning that it is assigned only for the duration of that session. These addresses are made up of as many as twelve numbers separated by periods in a configuration like xxx.xxx.xxx.xxx. So think of a big spreadsheet, with many rows, each representing a served file, and a number of columns that record the following data:

- The IP address of the requesting computer
- Date and time of request
- Code indicating whether request was successful or not
- Number of bytes of data transferred
- Referring site
- Type and version of Web browser making request
- Operating system of computer making request[8]

Now think about how big that spreadsheet is going to get and how quickly!

No marketer wants to spend time understanding the arcane language of server log files, much less trying to make sense of the millions of requests a busy site gets each day. There are many software applications that will take the server log data and translate it into reports that are relevant to marketing decisions. Many hosting services provide basic Web analytics as part of their package.

Server logs are maintained as part of running the site, so it is natural that these data were the first to be used to evaluate site effectiveness. More recently, however, another type of data collection has emerged. It involves implanting a tiny file of some sort on the Web page itself. This file sends data directly back to the server. We will use the general term *coded pages* to describe this process.

Coded Pages

The use of coded pages is a new method of collecting data, on the "browser (user's) side" of the information transaction instead of on the "server side." The typical file used to implement coded pages is 1 **pixel** by 1 pixel, and it is placed on the Web page itself, where it usually is invisible. There is no consistency of terminology between the marketing services firms offering this service. Various terms have been used to describe it, including *data tag, pixel tag,* and *transparent GIF.* The term *Web bug,* although less flattering, is also used. The tag is part of the page that is requested by and served to the user's browser. The file then sends data back to the server. Working with cookies, the tag can send back detailed information about the visitor's activity on the page. On the surface, the data are the same as those collected by a server log. Data collected by tags has several advantages over server log data:

- The data may be more accurate. Reasons include the fact that the user's IP address may change during the session, causing the server log to, in effect, record different visitors instead of the same visitor. Most browsers are able to **cache** Web pages, allowing them to be recalled without going back out onto the Internet. This speeds the visitor's surfing session considerably, but it means that multiple requests for the same page in a single session are not recorded in the server logs. The data tags can also be programmed so that they do not recognize automated requests, for example, requests for shopping bots that travel around the Web looking for prices. It is also possible to program the tags so that they do not return data unless the complete page is viewed.
- Data collected by Web bugs has smaller storage requirements because it stores only relevant data, not all the site operating data stored by server logs.
- When data are collected in this manner, it permits real-time processing and viewing of site metrics. Server log data, on the other hand, must be transferred to a separate analytics system for batch processing. It can be made available quickly, but not in real time.[9]

pixel One dot in the matrix of dots that makes up the display on a monitor.

cache High-speed storage for data that is referenced frequently.

To collect detailed information about visitor activity, tags must be used in conjunction with cookies. Cookies themselves have become controversial, although the general Internet public seems less aware of coded pages in general.

Cookies

Cookies are small data files that are stored on the user's computer and transmitted back to a Web server. One function of a cookie is to identify visitors. If no other information is available, the cookie assigns a unique number to identify the visitor. This allows, for example, the visitor to be recognized when he or she returns to the site, making it possible to serve ads or content based on data provided by the cookie. If the visitor has registered on the site, a personal greeting can be displayed upon entering the site. Several types of cookies exist:

- Session cookies are effective for only one visit. They are placed when the visitor enters and expire upon leaving the site.
- Persistent cookies remain for a specified period, a year perhaps, and then they expire.
- Third-party cookies are set by an outside services provider like an ad serving firm or a metrics service.
- First-party cookies are set by the Web site itself.

Cookies can also be set to retrieve personal information or not.

As Internet users have become more aware of cookies, some have begun to take action. A JupiterResearch study in early 2005 reported that 39% of users delete their cookies every month.[10] Third-party cookies are the focus of particular concern by many of these users, and some are setting their browsers to reject all third-party cookies. This makes applications like ad serving and metrics less effective. As a result, many Web marketers are switching to first-party cookies, which are more costly to maintain but are more acceptable to users.[11]

11-4c Panel Data

The process for using panel data to generate site effectiveness data is the same as using panels in the general marketing research process discussed in Chapter 5. The first step is to recruit a statistically representative panel of Internet users who agree to participate in the data collection. The size of the panel is determined by traditional statistical criteria, including the size of the universe to be sampled and segments that are to be broken out of the aggregate data. Specialized software is downloaded onto the participant's computer to record the clickstream data. The software is polled at regular intervals to upload the data.

Suppliers of this type of measurement service argue that there are three main benefits of this type of data as opposed to server logs. First, the source of the data is unambiguous, which it often is not with server logs. For example, international IP addresses can be difficult to identify precisely in terms of their source. Second, a person who uses the Internet from both home and work is two separate people according to server logs, but carefully planned and maintained panel data can overcome this issue. Third, the measurement firm can collect demographic and behavioral data from panel households that can be very useful in reporting and analytics. Because server logs identify most users by dynamic IP addresses, it is not possible to use much third-party data to enhance it. Getting visitors to register on the site, however, can overcome this difficulty to some extent.

Marketers need to have a basic understanding of the methods used to collect traffic and audience data, but their primary job is to select the metrics that can accurately evaluate the effectiveness of the Web site and Internet marketing campaigns. Let's turn now to a discussion of the metrics that are available.

11-5 Variables Used to Measure Web Site Traffic, Audiences, and Marketing Campaigns

Whatever the method of data collection, the same set of variables can be measured. The definitions that follow are generally accepted within the Internet industry:

- Traffic measures simply document site activity:
  - Hits: the number of files requested
  - Impressions: the number of times an ad banner is requested by a browser
  - Page views or deliveries: the number of times a Web page is requested
  - Sessions: the amount of activity on a site during a specified period
  - Click-throughs: the number of times visitors come to the site by clicking on an ad
- Audience measures provide data about the people who visit the site:
  - Visitors: the number of people who visit a site
    - Total (includes multiple visits) or unique (different people) during a specified time frame
    - Unidentified (anonymous) or identified (registered or customer)

  - Unduplicated audience: the visitors that are unique to a Web site
  - Behavior on the site
    - Number of page views
    - Session time
    - Path through the site
    - Shopping cart abandonment
    - Entry page (many visitors do not enter through the home page)

There are many other traffic and audience variables that can be measured. You should be aware that there is no clear dividing line between traffic and audience measures, but traffic always implies general information about site activity while audience always implies information about the demographics and behaviors of visitors to the site. In addition, there are measures of marketing campaign effectiveness:

- Campaign measures provide data about the effectiveness of marketing efforts.
  - By communications channel: e-mail, mail, online banners, and so forth
  - By offer: free shipping versus 25% off, for example
  - Search effectiveness by keyword

And, again, these are only a few of the campaign measures that can be tracked.

Notice that the campaign measures have the ability to integrate measures about offline activity (direct mail, for example) or activity off the Web site (search keywords, for example). Results are shown in terms of metrics like page views, number of visitors, number of unique visitors, and sales revenue. For multichannel marketers, the ability to see reports that cover all types of marketing activities across all their channels is essential.

To be meaningful, all these measures must be taken during a specified period. That leads to an almost endless set of metrics that can be produced, depending on the needs of the marketer. Some common metrics follow:

- Average number of visits per day
- Number of page views per month

- Average visitor session length last month
- Number of hits for each hour of the day
- Paid search results for the most recent 7-day period

And so it goes—almost infinitely.

The issue for the marketer is to determine, out of the almost infinite number of reports available, what reports are really needed and affordable. The "almost infinite" issue is a very important one. So many metrics and reports are available that the marketer quickly starts drowning in them unless he or she keeps a careful focus on the objectives of sites and campaigns. Chapter 10 pointed out that establishing Web site objectives are an important part of the site development process. Because the Web is an interactive medium, objectives tend to be action-oriented. We also indicated that objectives could be communications-oriented, which most marketers would characterize as either branding or information provision objectives. *The way to choose the correct measurement metrics out of the plethora available is to ask which ones are needed to measure the achievement of site objectives.*

11-6 Traffic, Audience, and Campaign Metrics

Internet marketers must choose metrics that correspond to their objectives, whether the objectives are transactions or communications-oriented. Server logs, coded Web pages, or panels can be used to collect the necessary data. The critical issue is putting it into a format that marketers can interpret and use for decision-making purposes. As already noted, it would be theoretically possible to perform this task internally, but this requires specialized programming and analytical talent that few companies have. The option chosen by most is to purchase reporting services from a marketing agency of some kind. Internet advertising agencies can provide reporting capabilities. The other choice is to turn to a marketing services firm that provides reporting and analytics.

Many firms supply Web analytics—some as part of a larger bundle of services, some as their primary business activity. Most offer either hosted solutions or software licensing. Hosted solutions demand less in the way of information technology (IT) expertise and resources, and they are the choice of many Internet marketers. However, if the marketer needs to customize the metrics in ways that are not readily available, there is no choice but to license the software so that it can be revised as needed.

11-6a Report Dashboard

Figure 11-7 shows one type of presentation that allows marketers easy, real-time access to important reports directly from their desktop. Called a **dashboard**, it is displayed in a window on the marketer's desktop. The example in Figure 11-7 shows that the marketer has selected Sales by Product SKUs of his DVD line. There is another view available, a text-only "ticker" that, in this case, shows sales revenue by product subcategory. The data are essentially in real time, although like any other continuous information provision (stock market tickers, for example), there may be a short time delay.

If the marketer wants further detail about any one of the reports available from the dashboard, he or she signs into WebTrends and accesses the report desired. Figure 11-8 shows one of the detailed reports on search engine marketing. It is called drill-down because the marketer is "drilling down" into the details behind the summary reports available on the dashboard.

dashboard Customizable display of summary data on a computer screen. Because the summary data are always present on the specified screen, it prevents the user from having to activate a function or program or visit another Web site to obtain data.

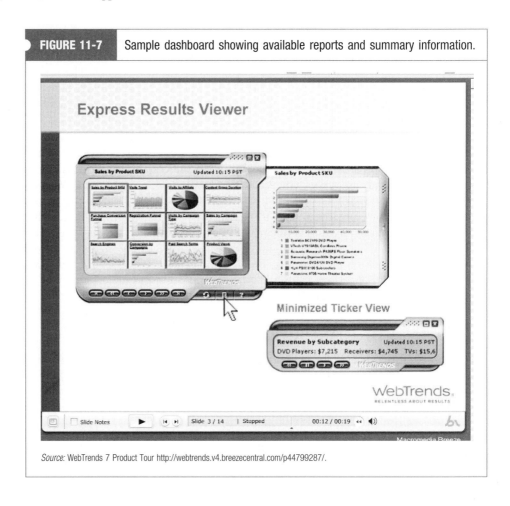

Source: WebTrends 7 Product Tour http://webtrends.v4.breezecentral.com/p44799287/.

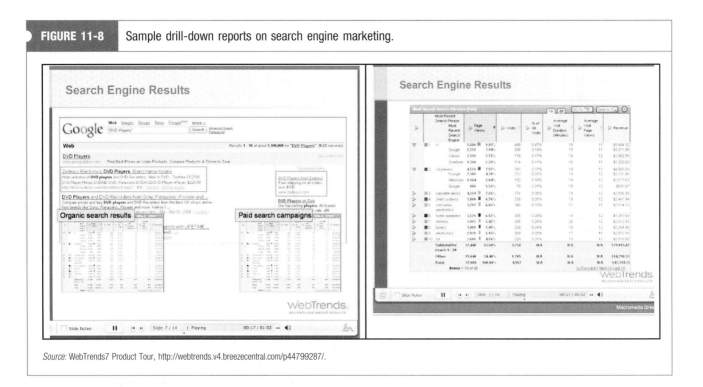

Source: WebTrends7 Product Tour, http://webtrends.v4.breezecentral.com/p44799287/.

In this case, the report shows how well the DVD player category is faring on Google search pages. The first panel shows the results by keyword for both organic search and any paid campaigns the marketer currently has on Google. The second panel shows results of paid search ads. The first expanded entry shows the search term "TV," and the number of recent searches on Google, Yahoo!, and Overture. The metrics reported are page visits, number of visits, the percentage of all visits to the TV page that the search engine ads generated, the average duration of the visits, the average number of pages viewed per visit, and the revenue produced by this set of visits. Notice that the second keyword campaign for DVD players is running on Froogle, AltaVista, and Google. The same metrics are reported. Notice also that there are many more paid search campaigns that can be expanded to provide this level of detail.

11-6b Marketing Campaign Reports

To get an idea of the number of reports available in a single category, consider the control panels shown in Figure 11-9. The main report panel shows the many types of reporting available. The campaigns item is expanded, showing the many reports available in that single category. The figure shows the calendar feature, which allows the marketer to select any day, week, month, or other specific time period for the report. It also shows that the marketer can produce comparative reports by selecting two time frames for comparison of a particular reporting item. The Campaigns report itself can be configured from many online and offline possibilities ranging from direct mail to advertising on specified sites to affiliate referrals—and many more. The many types of reports available multiplied by the many metrics that can be displayed multiplied by the time periods that can be selected produce a staggering number of reports available to the marketer.

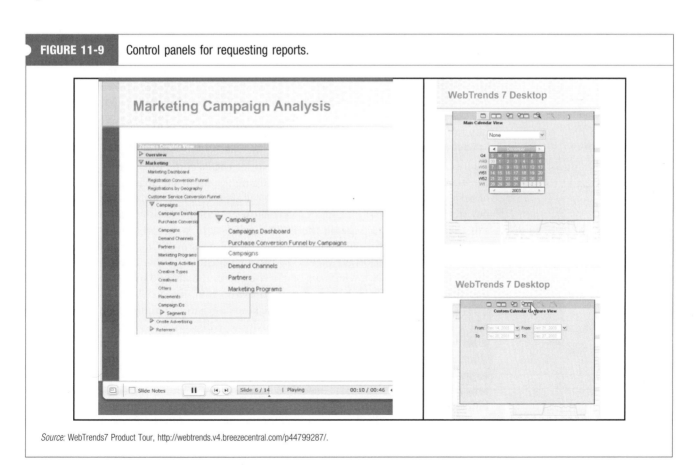

> **FIGURE 11-9**   Control panels for requesting reports.

Source: WebTrends7 Product Tour, http://webtrends.v4.breezecentral.com/p44799287/.

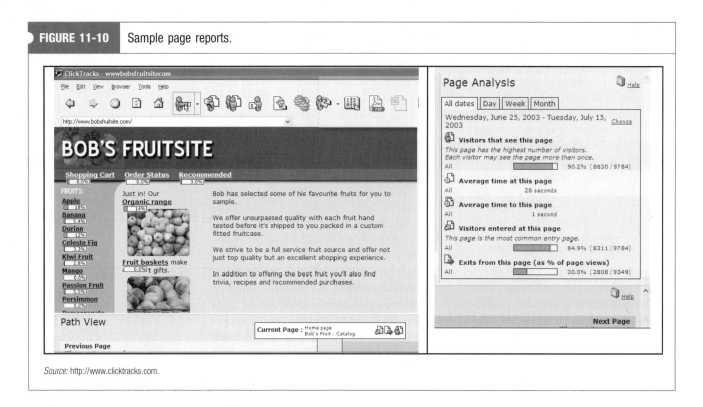

Source: http://www.clicktracks.com.

Although the metrics themselves are fairly standard, the analytics services firms have many ways of presenting them and configuring useful combinations of metrics.

11-6c Browser-Based Reports

Figure 11-10 shows a different way of presenting basic information, in this case about the home page of a hypothetical Web site. The report is shown in browser format. To access it, the marketer who subscribes to the service simply enters any page in the site, and data will be displayed. The data that are overlayed on the page represent the percentage of visitors who click through on each link on the page. The right panel shown in Figure 11-10 presents other data relevant to this page, including the number of visitors who see the page, how much time they spend, where they came from, and where they go when they exit the page. Notice the calendar tabs at the top that allow the marketer to choose the desired time frame for the Page Analysis report. Another panel shows the specific sites from which the visitors come, search engines, affiliates, newsletters, and so forth. The final one shows the destination of each visitor as they exit the page, either a page on the Bob's Fruit Site or some other site.

The entry point, the path visitors follow through the site, task completion, and the exit point are all important pieces of information for the marketer. Think back to the verbal scenario with which we began the chapter. Sally had to retrace her steps on one site due to inefficient navigation and exited two sites when she could not find what she needed on product pages. Those kinds of visitor difficulties become obvious when the marketer is able to string individual visitor data together to trace paths completely through the site.

11-6d Path Analysis

Figure 11-11 shows the basic steps that would result in successful task completion, in this case a purchase. The concept is straightforward. As is often the case, the actual data appear more complex. The center arrows in Figure 11-11 show the basic steps. The data to the left show the entry points to that step; the data to the right show the exit points.

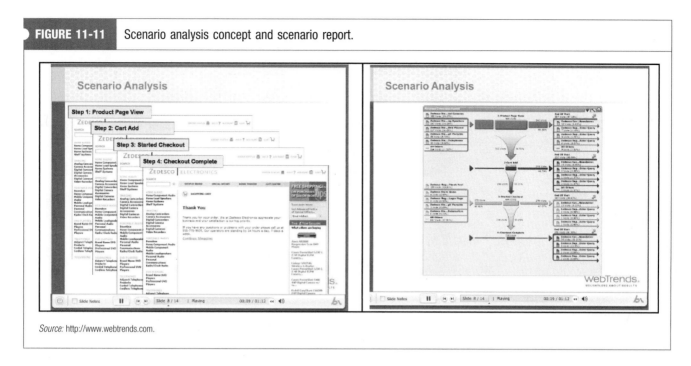

FIGURE 11-11   Scenario analysis concept and scenario report.

Source: http://www.webtrends.com.

In general, people who are backtracking are experiencing navigational problems, especially if they return to the home page or the site search function. Visitors exiting the page for another page in the site may still be looking for the product they want. Visitors who exit for another site have abandoned the shopping task, at least for the moment. Marketers need to examine each data point with care. Some will immediately suggest issues like faulty navigation or high shipping prices. Others will suggest possible problems, but either the exact nature of the problem or its solution is not entirely clear. At that point, the marketer should employ usability research or conventional marketing research to determine what the problem is and how best to resolve it.

11-6e Segmentation by Behavior and Channel

There are many other ways of looking at visitor behavior on the site. Being able to segment visitors, by behavior pattern or by information provided by the visitor, is important to many types of marketing decisions. Figure 11-12 shows the pages viewed by male visitors to a site. If there is a difference between the pages most viewed by demographic groups—say men, women, and teenagers—the site will be able to charge more for advertising that is able to target a specific demographic. Think back to the discussion of behavioral segmentation in Chapter 6. That provides examples of segmentation that do not rely on demographic data provided by the visitor but are dependent on site metrics to uncover behavior patterns and develop segmentation strategies that take advantage of visitor behavior patterns.

A final example shows a report that is able to show multichannel behavior. It is shown in the form of a "conversion funnel." This is an often-used concept, especially among direct marketers, that shows the number of potential customers who begin the purchase process, the number who remain at each stage in the process, and the number who complete the purchase task.

Figure 11-13 shows conversion from two different communications channels. The advertising channel on the left shows a different pattern of acquiring and converting qualified sales leads than does the e-mail channel on the right. The costs per initial response vary—$42 for the advertising channel and $24 for the e-mail channel. The cost for acquiring a qualified lead is $3.81 for advertising and $2.40 for e-mail. The conversion rate is 26.19% for advertising and 15.62% for e-mail. Notice that the two conversion funnels are different at each step, meaning that no single metric gives the

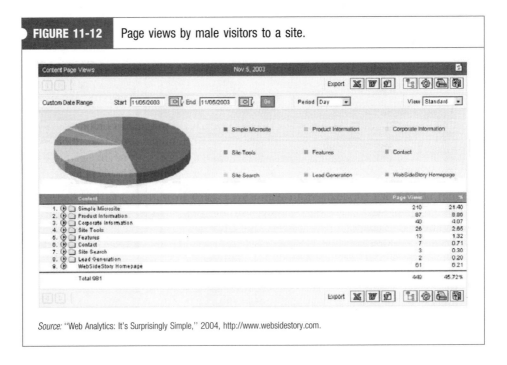

FIGURE 11-12 | Page views by male visitors to a site.

Source: "Web Analytics: It's Surprisingly Simple," 2004, http://www.websidestory.com.

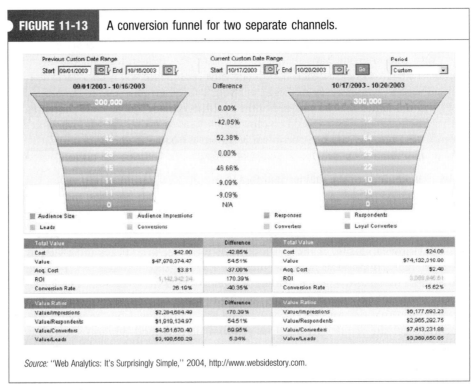

FIGURE 11-13 | A conversion funnel for two separate channels.

Source: "Web Analytics: It's Surprisingly Simple," 2004, http://www.websidestory.com.

total picture. The ROI on marketing expenditure for e-mail is more than 170% of that for the advertising channel in this example.

Tracking customer behavior across multiple channels is even more difficult. We know that many consumers still research products online and purchase at retail. Business-to-business (B2B) customers may receive and respond to an e-mail promotion, with the sale being closed by a field salesperson. Tracking activity across multiple channels requires the ability to identify individuals when they are active in either channel, the ability to collect data from both channels, and an analytics system that can take data from two sources and present it in a comprehensible format.

Reports similar to those just shown can be generated for a single site from panel data. Panel data also have the ability to generate competitive intelligence in the form of data about behavior on other sites. They also can be used to generate industry-wide or Internet-wide data. We should therefore take a brief look at the type of information that is available from panel data.

11-7 Metrics Based on Panel Data

Clickstream data based on server logs and coded Web pages provide metrics for all users of the Web site or sites of a single business, large or small. On the other hand, panel data are obtained from the clickstreams of carefully selected panels of Internet users. That permits comparisons of activity across Web sites. The use of panel data allows the accumulation of a great deal of background demographic, lifestyle, and activity data from panel members, as we discussed in Chapter 5.

Nielsen//NetRatings is perhaps the best-known name in this space because it is descended from Nielsen Media Research, which is the source of television ratings data. Data for the Nielsen//NetRatings reports comes from a sample of "nearly one million people in the United States, United Kingdom, France, and Germany."[12] Nielsen//NetRatings releases data on top sites in several categories to the public each week, but detailed data are available only to clients on a subscription basis.

Households are contacted using established random sampling techniques from the marketing research industry. Once an Internet user has agreed to become a panel member, a special piece of Java-based software is installed on his computer to record each click. This is similar in concept to the recording devices that collect TV rating data. Not only does it give statistically representative data from a relatively small sample, it also creates a panel that is available for custom research studies. For example, if a client wants to study some aspect of senior citizen use of the Internet that is not covered by commercially available reports, he or she may turn to a firm that maintains a user panel. The owner of the panel can identify members based on criteria supplied by the client, recruit them to participate in a special research project, and provide the custom data and usually a report to the client. This kind of segment-based data collection is usually prohibitively expensive except in a panel environment.

Collecting data about Internet use, however, faces a particular issue that is not found in the traditional marketing research environment. People use the Internet at work for both work and professional purposes. Measurement of Internet traffic is not complete without data collected in the workplace, but collecting that data represents unique problems. Most employees have to obtain the permission of their systems administrator to install unapproved software on their computer. Systems administrators do not like outside software on their systems. Employees may also be concerned about the possibility of managers getting access to the record of their personal Internet use at work. Consequently, cooperation rates for at-work data collection are considerably lower than for at-home collection. Nielsen//NetRatings uses conventional marketing research techniques to oversample and weigh sample data in order to compensate for sampling problems like this. They also make special efforts to obtain employer cooperation for at-work monitoring.

11-7a Examples of Panel-Based Reports

Because they capture the data directly from the computers of users instead of taking the data from enterprise server logs, companies that provide panel data can provide more varied reports. In particular, they can furnish competitive data that give businesses insights into the marketing activities of their competitors and the effectiveness of competitor marketing programs. Figure 11-14 shows some of the types of reports that Nielsen//NetRatings can provide. Figure 11-14a is a report of the most-visited sites in Australia for August 2005. The metrics presented are unique

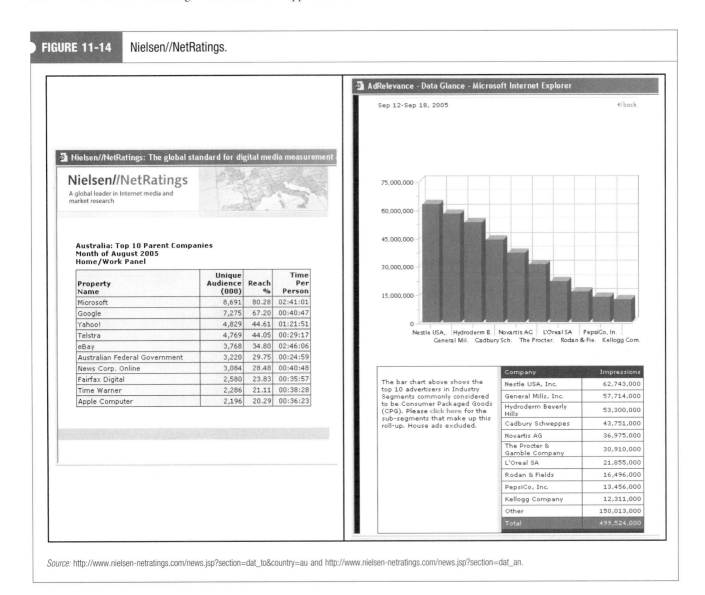

FIGURE 11-14   Nielsen//NetRatings.

Source: http://www.nielsen-netratings.com/news.jsp?section=dat_to&country=au and http://www.nielsen-netratings.com/news.jsp?section=dat_an.

visitors, penetration of the Internet user universe, and the time spent per visitor. Figure 11-14b gives U.S. coverage. It reports data on the ten largest consumer package good advertisers for 1 week in September 2005. The metrics in this report are the traditional advertising impressions measure.

Since clients sometimes prefer to obtain all their metrics data from a single source, Nielsen//NetRatings also offers Web site metrics like those discussed in earlier sections of this chapter. The point is for marketers to be able to get a complete view of what is taking place on the Internet, in various countries in which they do business, in their industry, and for their own Web site, whether they choose to purchase metrics from various suppliers or from a single source.

11-8 Measuring Internet Advertising Effectiveness

There is disagreement about which metrics are best, and much of it is related to how advertising rates should be set. There are two basic types of advertising rates, both offline and online: rates based on how many people are *exposed* to the ad and rates based on how many people *respond* to the ad. Advertising exposure, operationalized as advertising impressions, is the traditional offline measure. **CPM** (cost per thousand advertising impressions) expresses the advertising cost per 1,000 advertising impressions. Offline, this could be either ad impressions or page impressions, but it is a familiar way to purchase media, and many advertisers are comfortable with it.

The most familiar response metric is **CPA** (cost per action) or **CPC** (cost per click). It is generally operationalized as follows:

- Cost per click-through
- Cost per order (synonymous with cost per sale and cost per conversion)
- Cost per lead
- Cost per qualified lead[13]

As local advertising and search begin to gain prominence on the Web, another kind of response metric has emerged—pay per phone call advertising. According to one industry observer: "Consumers are accustomed to making phone calls to contact local businesses and local businesses are similarly used to closing leads over the phone," said Kelsey Group analyst Greg Sterling. "A performance-based online medium that delivers calls rather than clicks therefore makes sense for the local market."[14]

A study by local advertising consulting firm Kelsey Group estimated that this market could reach $1.4 billion by 2009 depending on pricing and availability. It seems ideas for both local customers and local businesses from plumbers to lawyers who are more accustomed to having customer contact come in over the phone than on a Web site.

Direct marketers like response-based charges, although relatively few advertisers offer them at present. It seems obvious, doesn't it, that paying for results is better than just paying for exposure? Not necessarily. It depends on the cost of the CPC or pay-per-click (PPC) ads and the response rate the marketer expects to get. Sites generally charge more for CPA than for CPM, so the answer to "Which price is lower—CPM or CPA?" is not obvious. It's probably the wrong question anyway.

The right question is, "Given my objectives, what are the correct metrics—exposure or action?" If the objectives are transactional—sales or lead generation—then the marketer needs to measure those directly, which is relatively easy. It may also make sense to pay for advertising on a CPC or PPC basis, since that is the nature of the metrics being used, but effectiveness metrics and advertising rates are not the same thing.

If the objectives of a marketing program are brand-oriented—for example, brand awareness or recall of brand promises—then advertising reach and effectiveness are the important metrics. The meaning is clear. *Metrics must be chosen to measure specific marketing program objectives.* Not all marketers need the same metrics; in fact, the same marketer may need different metrics at different times. This makes the choice of metrics an important activity for marketers, one that should be part of the initial campaign planning process, not an afterthought.

11-9 The Need for Good Internet Metrics

Like so much else on the Internet, the metrics used to measure effectiveness are still a moving target. There are methodologies yet to be developed. Partnerships between suppliers who collect different types of metrics are becoming common, allowing marketers to measure cross-channel activities. There are almost infinite amounts of data to be mined, analyzed, and interpreted for marketing decision purposes. The issues are complex and often not well understood, even by Internet marketers themselves, as shown in Table 11-1. Only 5% of Web marketers say they are "very confident" in the measurement of their Web marketing activities. This was related to the issues surrounding cookies discussed earlier in the chapter.

CPM Cost per thousand advertising impressions; the primary pricing mechanism for many media, including the Internet.

CPA Cost per action; a media pricing mechanism based on the number of visitors who take a specified action, for example, clicking through on an ad or making a purchase.

CPC Cost per click from an ad or referring Web site.

TABLE 11-1	Level of Confidence in Measuring Web Marketing Efforts According to Business Professionals Worldwide, May=June 2005 (as a % of respondents)

Very confident	5%
Moderately confident	26%
Fairly confident	43%
Flying blind	26%

Source: WebTrends, June 2005.

Consumers are concerned about cookies, and some are deleting them, as noted earlier. It also appears that many marketers are not entirely familiar with Web site policies that impact this issue. According to a WebTrends study quoted by eMarketer:

- 39% of respondents said they have "no idea" what method their Web site is currently using to identify unique visitors.

- only 19% of respondents utilize legitimate first-party cookies—the recommended best practice to track unique visitors.

- 13% identify visitors by IP address only—a largely inaccurate method to track visitors and their behavior.

- only 20% have a comprehensive set of metrics to measure campaign performance.

- 52% are still only looking at click-through rates or *nothing at all.*[15]

The ability to track and measure activities is one of the unique capabilities of the Web. If marketers are not using appropriate traffic, audience, and campaign metrics, they are missing out on a major benefit conferred by the Internet. In the Internet economy, this will quickly become a competitive disadvantage.

The complexity of the subject notwithstanding, it is important for all Internet marketers to have at least a user-level understanding of what metrics are available and what is most appropriate for their purposes. In the case of programs with sales objectives, the need for behavioral measures is unequivocal. When programs have branding objectives, metrics must be chosen to assess the effectiveness of the branding effort.

It is important to emphasize that the site metrics discussed in this chapter represent *aggregated data* that are crucial to the evaluation of the effectiveness of Internet marketing programs and Web sites. *Individual-level data* are required to drive Internet marketing programs that require targeting and personalization, as described in Chapters 7 and 8.

If the quantity of data and the various ways in which they can be analyzed and used appear to represent a great challenge, that is a correct perception. When considering the magnitude of the challenge, however, it is also important to remember that the very nature of the Internet creates expectations that marketing activities there will be tracked and measured with the end goal of understanding promotional ROI. It is easy to predict that technology will offer other options for measuring the effectiveness of integrated marketing communications as time goes on. For example, a new program was announced by Yahoo! and Marketing Management Analytics in late 2005. Their approach to metrics will allow marketers to better understand the impact of their online marketing activities on customer offline purchasing behavior.[16] Developments like this will assist the marketer to better understand the effectiveness of current programs and to improve future programs, both online and offline.

Summary

There are two different perspectives on the effectiveness of Web sites and Internet marketing programs. The user perspective is concerned with the usability of the Web site itself, which, in turn, leads to a satisfying user experience. Usability testing techniques are well established and should be made an integral part of the site development process. With planning, this can be done without massive expenditures of either time or money. Testing should also be done on established sites when the quantitative site metrics suggest there may be usability problems.

There is a large set of metrics that describe the activities of Internet users with respect to the Web site, Internet marketing programs, and offline marketing efforts of Internet marketers. Site performance metrics, obtained from server error logs, are important to the technicians whose job is to keep the site working smoothly but have little direct relevance for marketers. Marketers focus on traffic, audience, and campaign metrics in order to provide information about site visitors and to measure marketing campaign effectiveness. These metrics are obtained from server request logs, coded pages, or from Internet consumer panels. Internet enterprises, large and small, usually outsource the collection and reporting of these metrics to marketing services firms that have the specialized software and expertise required for this demanding endeavor.

The use of traffic, audience, and campaign metrics to gauge effectiveness presupposes that marketers have clear marketing objectives. These objectives may range from provision of information to customer service to sale of products. When the objectives are transactional in nature, behavioral measures in the form of traffic and audience metrics are needed. When there are branding objectives, marketing research is required to measure the attitudinal variables that are used to assess the effectiveness of branding efforts, both online and offline.

The number of metrics and the many ways in which reports can be configured from them add up to a deluge of possibilities that can inundate the unwary Internet marketer. Initial program planning should include not only a careful consideration of objectives from a marketing point of view but also a clear understanding of the metrics that will be necessary to assess the effectiveness of the program.

Quiz

1. _____ is the name given to the data points created by all mouse-clicks made by a visitor.
   a. Analytics
   b. Clickstream
   c. Database

2. Which of the following is a true statement about the nature of participants in a usability test?
   a. Fifteen participants can identify virtually all the usability problems.
   b. Participants need to have a high level of computer expertise.
   c. A large sample is required.

3. A site that is partly or fully functioning but that has not yet been released to the public is called a _____.
   a. concept site
   b. prototype
   c. model

4. Which of the following is a true statement about Internet metrics?
   a. Hit counters provide useful data about the characteristics of the audience that visits a site.
   b. Marketers and IT technicians are both direct users of Web site performance statistics.
   c. Usability data assess how well the site works from the customer's perspective.

5. Which of the following data items is *not* recorded by server request logs?
   a. The site from which the visitor was referred
   b. The e-mail address of the requesting computer
   c. A code that indicates whether the request was successful or not.

6. Metrics that describe Web site traffic and audience include _____.
   a. hits and identified visitors
   b. hits and server logs
   c. unduplicated audience and consumer panels

7. _____ is an Internet metric that has the same meaning as it has in the offline world of mass media advertising.
   a. Session length
   b. Impression
   c. Unique visitors

8. The best way to assess Internet usage patterns of individuals both at home and at work is to use _____.
   a. consumer panels
   b. special measurement software
   c. cookies

9. _____ is another name for a pixel tag.
   a. Spider
   b. Transparent GIF
   c. Index

10. _____ is a way of paying for Internet advertising based on results, not mere exposure to the ad.
    a. CPM
    b. CPA
    c. GRP

Discussion Questions

1. The term *metrics* is commonly used by Internet marketers. Be prepared to explain your understanding of the meaning of the term.

2. *True or false:* Internet marketers need to decide whether they will conduct measurement from a visitor usability perspective or from a traffic and audience measurement perspective. Be prepared to defend your answer.

3. The term *hit counter* implies that all this technology can do is measure the number of people who enter a site. Based on the discussion in this chapter, is that an accurate perception? Why or why not?

4. Describe the similarities and differences between server log, coded Web page, and panel data. Which do you think is most useful?

5. What are some of the specific metrics that measure Internet traffic, audiences, and campaigns? Which ones do you think are most important?

6. What kinds of variables are needed to measure the effectiveness of branding efforts on the Internet? Where are these measures obtained?

7. Do you believe that most commercial Web sites have metrics that are used to improve customer experience and enhance their marketing effectiveness? Do you have any personal experiences that support your view on the issue of Web metrics?

Internet Exercises

1. Conduct a partial usability analysis of your school's Web site. Describe two tasks that you believe the target audience wants to perform on the site. Go to the site and attempt to perform both tasks. Record your experience for each, noting the time it took to perform each task. What recommendations would you make to the webmaster of the site based on your test?

2. Visit a Web site that offers reporting services to Internet marketers and explore the types of reports they offer in more detail. Several sites are discussed in the chapter, and you can find others by searching the net. Be prepared to discuss several specific reports that a marketer can obtain from this site. Look for pricing information for these reports.

3. Using one of the sites you are tracking, prepare a careful summary of the objectives you believe that

site has. In doing so, keep in mind that the objectives of the site may be a subset of the marketing and business objectives of the organization. When you are satisfied that the set of objectives is complete, list the corresponding metric or metrics that would be needed to measure each objective. Present this information in a table that shows objectives and the corresponding metrics.

4. Using a Web site with which you are familiar, develop a scenario that tells the story of how one user segment would behave on a visit to the site. When you are satisfied that your scenario represents behavior of one segment adequately, identify the metrics that would be useful in ascertaining if the segment's needs are being met and if the customer experience for this segment is satisfactory.

Notes

1. See "Chapter 10, Testing Direct Marketing Programs," in Mary Lou Roberts and Paul D. Berger, *Direct Marketing Management,* 2nd ed. available for free download at http://www.marylouroberts.info for a detailed description of the direct marketing testing process.

2. Jakob Nielsen, Rolf Molich, Carolyn Snyder, and Susan Farrell, *E-Commerce User Experience* (Fremont, CA: Nielsen Norman Group, 2001), p. 337.

3. The formula used is $N(1(1 - L)^n)$, where N is the total number of usability problems, L is the proportion of usability problems found by testing a single user, and n is the number of users tested. "Why You Only Need to Test with 5 Users," http://www.useit.com/alertbox/20000319.html.

4. "Cost of User Testing a Web Site," http://www.useit.com/alertbox/980503.html.

5. "La Quinta Turns Lookers into Bookers with WebTrends OnDemand," 2005, http://www.webtrends.com/Customers/CaseStudies/LaQuintaTurnsLookersintoBookerswithWebTrends OnDemand.aspx.

6. "La Quinta Turns Lookers into Bookers with WebTrends OnDemand," 2005, http://www.webtrends.com/Customers/CaseStudies/LaQuintaTurnsLookersintoBookerswithWebTrends OnDemand.aspx.

7. "La Quinta Turns Lookers into Bookers with WebTrends OnDemand," 2005, http://www.webtrends.com/Customers/CaseStudies/LaQuintaTurnsLookersintoBookerswithWeb-TrendsOnDemand.aspx.

8. Richard Hoy, "Traffic Analysis Solutions for Small Business: Part 1," June, 9, 2000, http://www.clickz.com.

9. "Log Files Versus Data Tags," 2001, http://www.buystream.com.

10. Dave Morgan, "Making the Cookie Case to Consumers," March, 24, 2005, http://www.clickz.com/experts/crm/actionable_analysis/article.php/3492071.

11. David Kesmodel, "When the Cookies Crumble," September, 12, 2005, The Wall Street Journal Online.

12. "MegaPanel®," Nielsen//NetRatings, nd, http://www.netratings.com/downloads/MegaPanel.pdf.

13. For more detail on the background and use of these metrics, see the New Media page on the Medill School of Journalism site, http://newmedia.medill.northwestern.edu/courses/nmpspring01/orange/cpc/index.shtml.

14. Mike Shields, "Pay-Per-Phone Ads to Hit $1.4 Billion," *Media Week,* June, 22, 2005, http://www.adweek.com/aw/search/article_display.jsp?schema=&vnu_content_id=1000966078.

15. "Advertising Up, Confidence Shaky," June, 9, 2005, http://www.emarketer.com.

16. "Yahoo! and MMA to Offer Measurement Service to Enable Marketers to Optimize Advertising Spend Across Media," Marketing Management Analytics Press Release, December, 16, 2005, http://www.mma.com/relevantnews/Press%20Release_MMA_Yahoo_Dec%202005.pdf.

Social and Regulatory Issues I—Consumer Data Privacy

Chapter Twelve

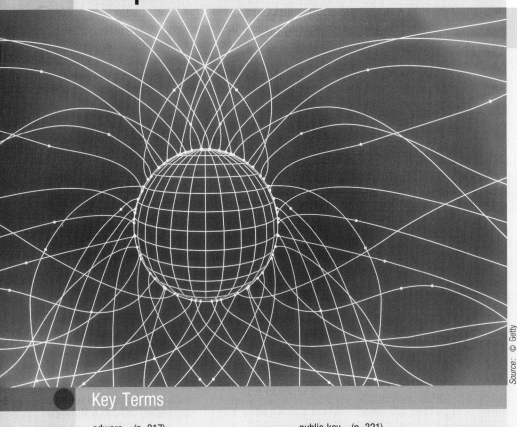

Source: © Getty

Key Terms

adware   (p. 317)
biometrics   (p. 322)
encryption   (p. 321)
pfarming   (p. 317)
phishing   (p. 317)

public key   (p. 321)
secure sockets layer   (p. 322)
spoofing   (p. 317)
spyware   (p. 305)

Chapter Outline

Learning Objectives

By the time you complete this chapter, you will be able to:

- Discuss trust as a facilitator of Internet activity.
- List some of the concerns consumers have about the privacy of their personal data.
- Describe some of the actions businesses are taking to guard the privacy of their customers.
- Identify the Fair Information Practices Principles.
- Discuss self-regulation and regulatory action to protect privacy in the United States and the European Union.

- Discuss major consumer concerns about security.
- Explain the nature of security issues from the perspective of the enterprise.
- Identify key issues that relate to intellectual property on the Internet.

12-1 Introduction

From the origin of the Internet as a project sponsored by the U.S. Department of Defense to its current status as a global network, the relationships between Internet users, governmental agencies, and the public at large have often been strained. The Internet boasts a tradition of free speech and a *caveat emptor* attitude toward information and activities that take place there. However, as the Internet has evolved into a mass medium with users of all ages and degrees of technological sophistication, there has been greater concern over protection of users. Public policy makers all over the world have evidenced this concern.

There are a variety of consumer protection issues that have either arisen or become more urgent because of the Internet. This chapter examines three key issues: the privacy of personal data, the security of data and transactions, and the protection of intellectual property on the Internet. It considers customer attitudes and behaviors with respect to privacy and security issues. It also considers both corporate and governmental reactions to the various issues.

The ability of business and government to assure citizens that their data are safe and being used properly affects the degree to which people trust those institutions. That is especially true on the Internet, where consumer power and access to information has reached an all-time high.[1] We should therefore begin by briefly considering the importance and role of trust as a facilitator of Internet use and e-commerce activity.

12-2 The Role of Trust in Facilitating Internet Activity

The corporate scandals that peaked in 2002 brought attention once again to the issue of trust in our institutions—government, business, and media. A study of trust in several countries around the globe by the Edelman Annual Trust Barometer found differences, some of them substantial, between countries in the degree to which they trusted business, government, the media, and nongovernmental organizations to do the right thing. Looking at Figure 12-1a, however, it is clear that in most countries, trust in most of the institutions falls below the 50% level. When they asked questions about trust in various media (Figure 12-1b) the level of trust was again low, falling well below one-quarter of the respondents in many countries. Again, there were differences from one country to another, but in general, television and newspapers were most trusted, followed by the Internet, with radio being the least trusted medium in most of the

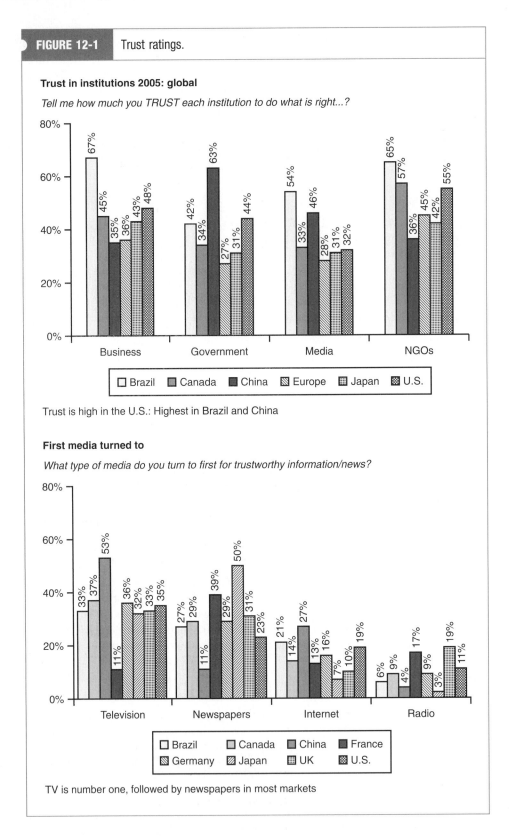

FIGURE 12-1   Trust ratings.

Trust in institutions 2005: global

Tell me how much you TRUST each institution to do what is right...?

Trust is high in the U.S.: Highest in Brazil and China

First media turned to

What type of media do you turn to first for trustworthy information/news?

TV is number one, followed by newspapers in most markets

countries surveyed. Edelman concludes that trust is shifting from institutions to a network of personal sources, colleagues, friends and family, like-minded individuals, and experts, including physicians and academics.[2] This is not an isolated result. In its ongoing Consumer Internet Barometer survey of 10,000 U.S. households, The Conference Board found only 27.2% of their sample reporting trust in the Internet.[3]

This lack of trust in the Internet does seem to matter. In Chapter 11 we discussed Internet users' concern over cookies and the fact that some users are deleting cookies. A study by the Annenberg Center at the University of Pennsylvania also found that 65% of their respondents had deleted cookies at one time or another. In addition:

- 43% had used filters to block unwanted e-mail.
- 23% had used software to block **spyware** on their computer.
- 17% had used software that hides the user's identity from sites being visited.

Of greatest concern to marketers should be the study's finding that experienced Internet users were more likely to say they knew a lot about stopping Web sites from collecting personal data without consent and more likely to take all available actions to control the use of their personal information.[4]

Milne and Culnan, in a study of who reads privacy policies, list other privacy actions taken by readers of privacy policies. They found that:

- 87% had refused to give information to a Web site because it was too personal or unnecessary.
- 84% had asked to have their name and address removed from marketing lists.
- 81% had asked a Web site not to share name or personal information with other companies.
- 66% had decided not to use a Web site or to make a purchase because they were unsure of how personal information would be used.
- 32% had set their browser to reject cookies.
- 32% had supplied incorrect information to a Web site when asked to register.[5]

The fact that people are willing to take a wide range of actions to protect their personal information and that their actions could hinder the efforts of marketers is cause for concern. On the other hand, writing about "The Trust Imperative," Massachusetts Institute of Technology (MIT) marketing professor Glen Urban points out that there are positive advantages in building trust in the customer base. He identifies those advantages as follows:

- Reduced customer acquisition cost. He argues that the advertising of trusted brands will receive greater attention. In addition, customers will be more loyal to trusted companies, reducing their need to acquire large numbers of new customers to replace defecting ones.
- Higher profit margins. Customers are willing to pay a premium for products or services from a trusted supplier.
- Growth. Trusted companies will be more successful in selling more to their existing customers and in converting visitors to customers.
- Long-term competitive advantage. A trusted brand and strong relationships based on understanding of customer needs will contribute to long-term success.[6]

Accenture agrees, saying that "If companies are to use today's revolutionary technologies effectively to fuel economic growth, they must meet the privacy challenge head-on. Today, privacy and trust have become critical aspects of any business imperative."[7] They identify the dimensions of trust as follows:

- Security—protection of personal information against misuse or theft
- Data control—the consumer has control over who has access to personal data and when, as well as what they are permitted to do with it
- Personal access—the consumer has control over who contacts him or her and how
- Benefit—the uses of the data provide value to the consumer as well as to the business

spyware Software that sends information about Web activities back to its Web site.

Accenture urges companies to start now to become a trust leader in their industry. This involves building a reputation, often over a considerable period of time, for being responsible and effective in the use of personal information about consumers and business partners. Because trust exists throughout the value chain, creating it involves careful planning about exactly how the company wishes to be regarded and what it must do to achieve that regard. Once a trust plan is developed, it should be articulated as a set of published trust policies that set standards of behavior within the organization and between the organization and its business partners. Accenture emphasizes the importance of understanding what trust means to customers, especially in "high-trust" industries, including financial services and health care, which we discuss in a later section of this chapter.[8]

The fact that trust can only be built, action by action, over a period of time emphasizes Urban's contention that trust can provide long-term competitive advantage. That advantage would accrue to companies who pay immediate attention to the importance of being a trusted entity in both business-to-customer (B2C) and business-to-business (B2B) markets. He adds, "Trust is hard to earn—and easy to lose."[9]

With an understanding of the importance of trust and the role of data protection and privacy in creating it, we can turn to an examination of the issue of data privacy in the United States and globally.

12-3 Data Protection and Privacy on the Internet

Writing in the *Journal of Interactive Marketing*, Harvard professor John Deighton points to the increasing vulnerability consumers feel as a result of the way business is done on the Internet. According to Deighton:

> In the physical world, they (consumers) can choose to be anonymous, trading cash for goods and moving on with no trace of their identity left behind. When they trade in cyberspace, anonymity is not an option. They have to say who they are, how to get back to them, and what their credit record is worth, or the transaction falls apart. They will give this information only if they are confident that it will not be used against them. If they are not sure of that, they know full well that there are many other ways to do business, and they will cast their vote to defer the arrival of the digital age.
>
> Deeper insight into the human need for privacy, then, is perhaps as important to the blossoming of the interactive marketing industry as any single factor. We need to understand why so often people want to be let alone, and why sometimes they do not. Marketing fundamentally, of course, is about meeting customer needs. In the matter of privacy, what are the needs that are met and not met?[10]

In this section we examine what is known about consumer privacy concerns in the United States and other Internet economies, as well as what responses have been made by business and regulatory agencies in the United States and the European Union (EU).

12-3a Consumer Attitudes toward the Privacy of Their Personal Data

There have been studies of consumer attitudes about the privacy of personal data since the beginning of the Internet. Both the Pew Foundation and the Annenberg Center at the University of Pennsylvania have conducted studies with statistically valid samples of Internet users. The Annenberg Center repeated its 2000 study in 2003, providing data on how attitudes have changed (Table 12-1).

TABLE 12-1 Concerns about Privacy of Personal Data

Pew % of Sample Who Are Concerned		Annenberg % of Parents in Sample Who "Agree Strongly" or "Agree"		
	2000		2000	2003
Businesses and people you don't know getting personal information about you and your family	84%	I should have a legal right to know everything that a Web site knows about me,	95%	95%
Someone might know what Web sites you've visited	31%	I am nervous about Web sites having information about me.	73%	72%
Your e-mail will be read by someone besides the person you sent it to	27%	When I go to a Web site, it collects information about me even if I don't register.	59%	57%
		I trust Web sites not to share information with other companies or advertisers when they say they won't.	50%*	37%
		Web site policies are easy to understand.	53%*	45%

*2003 score significantly higher than same question in 2000 study.

Adapted from: "Trust and Privacy Online: Why Americans Want to Rewrite the Rules," Pew Internet & American Life Project, 2000, p. 4; "Americans and Online Privacy: The System Is Broken," Annenberg Public Policy Center of the University of Pennsylvania, 2003, p. 18.

The Pew study in 2000 asked questions about a number of social issues, data privacy among them. The three questions related to privacy are shown in Table 12-1. By far, the greatest level of concern users had was about businesses and people getting personal information about themselves and their families. The Annenberg study segmented parents and nonparents. Table 12-1 shows results for parents in 2000 and 2003. As you might imagine, there were some differences in responses to these items between parents and nonparents, with parents expressing slightly more concern than nonparents. These differences, however, were not statistically significant. This sample was adamant about their right to know what data Web sites have and was nervous about the sites having information. They know that sites can collect information even if they have not registered. They are not particularly trusting that sites will keep their privacy promises. That is the negative item about which concern significantly increased between 2000 and 2003. They also do not find Web site privacy policies easy to read, although the positive news on that item is that more find them easy in 2003 than they did in 2000.

12-3b Knowledge about Privacy Practices

The Annenberg study points out that even though Internet users express concern about their personal data, they tend to be naive about what companies are actually doing. Some of their findings follow:

- Sixty-six percent of respondents who were confident about their understanding of privacy policies believe (incorrectly) that having a privacy policy means that sites won't share data.

- Respondents do not understand the flows of data collected by marketers, in particular that marketers are able to connect separate pieces of data. According to the report, when they presented respondents with an explanation of the way sites track, extract, and share information to make money from advertising, 85% of adults who go online at home did not agree to accept that kind of information practice from even a valued site.

  - Of all respondents, 54% would neither accept the common practices nor pay for site content in lieu of having data collected, once the practices were explained.

- Sixty-four percent of respondents had never searched for information about how to protect their information on the Web.

- Forty percent said they know "almost nothing" about stopping sites from collecting data. Twenty-six percent know only "a little," and only nine percent say they know "a lot."[11]

A study that dealt with direct marketing practices without specific reference to the Web had similar findings. Dommeyer and Gross developed scales to measure knowledge about direct marketing practices related to privacy, awareness of ways of protecting personal data privacy, and use of strategies designed to protect personal data. Their respondents were not particularly knowledgeable about marketing practices, confirming results of earlier studies. Awareness of privacy protection systems was relatively high. However, scores on the protection scale, which measured actual use of the systems, were the lowest of all three scales. The authors concluded that consumers needed information, not only on protection strategies but also on how to easily implement them.[12]

Lack of proactive action on the part of consumers was also seen in the study by Milne and Culnan of how frequently people reported reading Web site privacy policies. They found that:

- 4.5% always read privacy policies.
- 14.1% read them frequently.
- 31.8% sometimes read them.
- 33.3% rarely read them.[13]

The study by Milne and Culnan found that consumers who read privacy policies were likely to take privacy actions, as described in earlier. The relatively small number who do read privacy policies always or frequently suggests that few people are taking the privacy actions available to them.

The picture that emerges is of widespread concern among consumers about the nature and use of the data companies have about them. At the same time, there is lack of knowledge about the overall nature of business data collection and about what can be done to prevent data abuses. These data imply that few consumers are taking advantage of actions that can protect their own personal data. They also imply that there are different groups of consumers with respect to privacy and privacy-related segments.

12-3c Privacy-Related Segmentation

An early study identified three privacy-related segments:

- *Privacy fundamentalists* who are extremely concerned about the use of their data and unwilling to provide data to Web sites under any conditions.
- *Privacy pragmatists* who tended to be less concerned in a general sense. They were also more willing to accept laws or Web site privacy policies as meeting their concerns.
- *Marginally concerned* consumers who had only mild concerns and were ordinarily willing to provide data to Web sites. They were, however, eager to remove their names from mailing lists.[14]

At about the same time, the Pew Internet & American Life study found that Internet novices who had been online for 6 months or less, parents, older Americans, and women were more concerned about privacy issues than other demographic groups of Internet users. Because other aspects of Internet use change the longer a user has been online, it is reasonable to expect that concern about privacy will change also, and the Annenberg study discussed earlier showed some specific changes.[15]

The three basic segments appear to have persisted. A 2003 Harris Poll found the following:

- *Privacy pragmatists* increased from 54% in 1999 to 64% in 2003.
- *Privacy unconcerned* declined from 22 % to 10% over the same period of time.

- *Privacy fundamentalists* appear to have remained relatively stable at 26%.[16] As early as 1993, Ellen Foxman and Paula Kilcoyne identified the two key dimensions of the privacy issue as consumer *control* over the release of information and the *degree of their knowledge* about collection and use of their personal information. Writing in a special privacy issue of the *Journal of Marketing and Public Policy* in 2000, Kim Sheehan and Mariea Hoy added three more dimensions that help explain the level of concern about privacy—*sensitivity of the information, familiarity with the entity collecting it,* and *whether compensation is provided.*[17] All these dimensions are controllable to the Internet marketer, from the establishment of a known and trusted brand name to attention paid to collecting only needed information and to informing the consumer about the collection and use of information.

Each of these dimensions takes on special prominence when the Internet users are children.

12-3d Regulation of Children's Privacy Issues

Parents and other concerned citizens attach special importance to protecting the privacy of children while they are on the net. Children lack the knowledge and maturity to share the privacy concerns of adults, and they tend to be willing to share information readily, especially if an incentive is offered. According to a study by the Annenberg Public Policy Center reported by eMarketer in May 2000, nearly 75% of teens believed it was acceptable to reveal family data on the Internet in exchange for a gift.

This study found parents to be generally positive about their children's use of the Internet, although they expressed concern over the children's willingness to divulge information and some of the content that was available to them on the net. Their concern seems justified by some of the findings of the study, which revealed:

- 65% of youngsters are willing to give out the name of their favorite stores.
- 54% are willing to give out the names of their parents' favorite stores.
- 44% are willing to give out the type of car the family drives.
- 39% are willing to give out the amount of their allowance, whether their parents talk a lot about politics, and what they do on the weekend.
- 26% are willing to give out what their parents do on the weekends.[18]

There is a regulatory tradition of considering children a vulnerable group in terms of marketing and advertising, and these data suggest it is appropriate to extend it to the Internet. In 1997, the Federal Trade Commission (FTC) brought the first-ever privacy complaint against the GeoCities Web site, which alleged that the site had violated its own privacy policy. Its violations were alleged to be especially serious in the case of its children's community. The issue was said to be that GeoCities collected data from children in return for free Web site hosting and turned that data over to third parties who used it in ways inconsistent with GeoCities' posted privacy statements. The complaint was settled in 1999, just after Yahoo! announced its acquisition of the site. The consent decree specified a rigorous set of privacy practices that GeoCities agreed to follow for 10 years.[19]

This move by the FTC was followed by the passage by Congress in 1998 of the Children's Online Privacy Protection Act (COPPA). The major provisions of the act required Web sites that knowingly collect information from children younger than age 13 to:

- provide parents notice of their information practices.
- obtain prior parental consent for the collection, use and/or disclosure of personal information.

- provide a parent, upon request, with the ability to review the personal information collected from his or her child.

- provide a parent with the opportunity to prevent the further use of personal information that has already been collected, or the future collection of personal information from that child.

- limit collection of personal information for a child's online participation in a game, prize offer, or other activity to information that is reasonably necessary for the activity.

- establish and maintain reasonable procedures to protect the confidentiality, security, and integrity of the personal information collected.[20]

In 2001, the Annenberg Center celebrated the first anniversary of COPPA by examining the privacy activities of the 162 sites with the highest percentage of child visitors younger than 13 years of age. The study concluded that "they often did not live up to the spirit and sometimes even the letter behind the rules." They added, "Privacy policies are typically too unclear and time-consuming to realistically encourage parents to confidently guide their children's Internet experiences."[21]

12-3e Regulation of Privacy in the Financial Services Sector

An example of regulation with broad impact is the Gramm, Leach, Bliley Act (GLBA), which became law in November 1999 and was scheduled to take full effect in July 2001. According to Robert Pitofsky—who was then chairman of the FTC—the law:

> requires a financial institution to disclose to all of its customers the institution's privacy policies and practices with respect to information it shares with both affiliates and nonaffiliated third parties and limits the instances in which a financial institution may disclose nonpublic personal information about a consumer to nonaffiliated third parties. Specifically, it prohibits a financial institution from disclosing nonpublic personal information about consumers to nonaffiliated third parties unless the institution satisfies various disclosure and opt-out requirements and the consumer has not elected to opt out of the disclosure.[22]

The law requires that each year consumers must be notified about the specific privacy policy of the institution and offered an opportunity to opt out of certain types of information collection and transmission. Anecdotal evidence in various settings suggests that few consumers read this information with care and even fewer take the opportunity to opt out of the specified data collection and transfer activities. It also requires that corporations take proactive steps to ensure the safety of consumer data.

12-3f Regulation of Privacy in the Health Care Sector

Health-related information is another area of special consumer concern. In 1996, Congress added a provision on privacy of medical records to the Health Insurance Portability and Accountability Act (HIPPA). The provision required that, if Congress did not pass a comprehensive law on the privacy of medical data within 3 years, the U.S. Department of Health and Human Services (HHS) would be required to develop a set of regulations to deal with misuse and disclosure of medical records. No law was passed, and in 1999, a set of rules was issued for public comment by HHS, with a final revision issued in December 2000. The new administration, recognizing the public concern about this issue, agreed to let the rules take effect as scheduled in April 2001. The rules give patients greater control over their health information, including access to their medical records; restrict the use and release of medical records; ensure the security of personal health information; and provide penalties for the misuse of personal health information.[23] One visible result has been the posting of data policies in the offices of health care providers and the requirement that each patient sign a statement asserting that he or she has read and understands the provider's data privacy policies.

COPPA, GLBA, and HIPPA could have important ramifications as models for regulation of other industry sectors. In addition, they have a direct effort on marketing services firms that serve the regulated sectors. They will affect database use throughout the industry as well as list brokers, who will be asked to certify that the lists they are renting are from organizations whose practices comply with the regulations. Had the attacks of 2001 not occurred and diverted attention from general consumer privacy issues, there might have been more regulatory attempts in the intervening years.

12-3g Privacy Issues Going Forward

In the wake of the attacks on the World Trade Center in September 2001, the issues surrounding privacy have changed in some respects. The Patriot Act (the common title for the unwieldy "Uniting and Strengthening America by Providing Appropriate Tools Required to Intercept and Obstruct Terrorism") was passed in late 2001. The act has numerous aspects,[24] some of which directly speak to the collection of data about individual people and their activities on the Internet. A number of the privacy sites have extensive discussion of the pros and cons of the act,[25] but the potential impact on marketing is less clear. The Annenberg study asked three specific questions that relate to issues raised by the Patriot Act (Table 12-2). They show support when the issue of terrorism is included in the question but also suggest concern about the degree to which the government is collecting data about its citizens.

Increasing levels of concern among the public have stimulated a proposed new law—the Personal Data Privacy and Security Act of 2005. It would increase the criminal penalties for identity theft and the buying and selling of Social Security numbers. It would also require that consumers be notified when the security of their data has potentially been breached.[26] The likelihood of regulation increases if the public is not satisfied with the steps business is taking to protect their data and to use it in ways of which they approve. We therefore turn next to an examination of the actions U.S. corporations have taken to reassure their customers that they are acting in their best interests.

12-3h Response of U.S. Business to Privacy Concerns

Businesses in the United States have argued strongly for self-regulation as the best approach to meeting consumer privacy concerns. They have been supported in their preference for self-regulation by trade associations and by the stated preference of the FTC for self-regulation. This places the burden squarely on individual enterprises and alliances of firms with similar perspectives.

TABLE 12-2	Attitudes toward Governmental Collection of Data about Internet Users

Attitude Statements	Percent Who "Agreed" or "Agreed Strongly"
Because of the war on terrorism, the government needs to make it easier for law enforcement to track users' online activities without their knowledge or consent.	66%
U.S. government agencies are collecting information about me online without my knowledge or consent.	52%
In the interest of national security, the federal government should have the technology to find out what anyone is doing on the Internet at all times.	45%

Adapted from: "Americans and Online Privacy: The System Is Broken," Annenberg Public Policy Center of the University of Pennsylvania, 2003, p. 19.

In the absence of laws, it is up to each Internet enterprise to develop its own privacy approach. Two types of privacy disclosures can be enlisted in order to come up with comprehensive privacy guidelines:

- A *privacy policy notice* is a comprehensive description of a site's privacy practices. To be acceptable, it must be located in a single, readily identifiable place on the site. It must be easily accessible by a single link or icon. The link should be present on the home page, and it is also desirable to have it in a visible location when information is being collected, for example, on registration pages.

- An *information practice statement* is a discrete statement that describes a specific information practice from which a potential use of the information can be inferred. Examples include:

  "Click here if you want to be informed about future offers of this nature."
  "We will not share your information with any other organization."

In 1998, the FTC examined commercial Web site and found that although more than 85% of the sites collected user information, only 14% of the sample Web sites provided any disclosure about their information practices.[27] The study was repeated in 2000 and found improvement in the percentage of sites that had some type of information disclosure.[28]

The Consumer Respect Group, a privacy consulting organization, has developed twenty-one items that measure Web site practices with respect to privacy. Among the findings of their 2005 study were that:

- only 42% of the 464 corporate Web sites examined scored "good" for their policies toward sharing of collected personal data.
- 72% scored "poor" for their policies toward reusing personal data for marketing purposes.
- 64% of companies had privacy policies that scored "good" on clarity and are written to be understandable by the consumer.
- only 23% of companies had policies that were considered "good" for allowing users to destroy personal information stored on corporate databases.[29]

In their 2000 study, the FTC found that only 20% of the sites had fully implemented the four Fair Information Practices Principles, an important standard for acceptable privacy policies.

12-3i The Fair Information Practices Principles

The Fair Information Practices Principles have become an important international standard in the field of data privacy. They have evolved over the last quarter century as a result of analyses by governmental agencies in the United States, Canada, Australia, and Europe and are widely accepted in regulatory frameworks around the world. The principles are as follows:

- *Notice/awareness.* Customers should be given notice before information is collected in order to allow them to make informed decisions about what to divulge. Notification should include identification of the entity collecting the data, uses to which it will be put, with whom data will be shared, nature of data collection (including voluntary and involuntary), methods of collection, data security measures, and consumer rights with respect to collection and use of data.

- *Choice/consent.* Consumers should be given control over how information will be used for purposes beyond the current transaction. This includes both internal use of the information, such as putting it in a database, or external use, such as transferring it to a third party.

- *Access/participation*. The consumer should be able to view data about himself or herself and ensure that the information is accurate and complete.

- *Integrity/security*. Integrity describes the accuracy of the data, specifically that anyone who accesses the data at a given moment receives exactly the same data. Security refers to the managerial and technical measures that protect the data from unauthorized access and use.

- *Enforcement/redress*. There should be a mechanism in place to enforce these principles of privacy protection and to provide remedies for injured parties.[30]

Although these fair information principles provide a strong conceptual framework for privacy action by businesses, they do not provide sufficient guidance for the majority of firms who lack internal expertise in this area. In addition, businesses would benefit from greater understanding of privacy issues on the part of consumers, and consumers would feel more confident if privacy approaches were sanctioned by a trusted third party. This has led to the establishment of various industry-supported privacy organizations.

12-3j Privacy Organizations and Seals

As part of the industry effort to achieve effective self-regulation, a number of organizations have either been formed or have added a privacy initiative to the services they offer. In general, these organizations can be characterized as nonprofits that specialize in the privacy arena or trade organizations that support the privacy actions of their members. The best-known of these organizations include:

- TRUSTe, which is a nonprofit organization founded by concerned businesses and supported by member dues. Its primary activity is the licensing of Internet businesses that develop and display a privacy policy that meets the standard established by the Fair Information Practices Principles. Web sites that have an accepted privacy policy are entitled to display the TRUSTe "trustmark." To increase the impact of the trustmark, a campaign of consumer education has been undertaken by the member companies. Licensees can also have their privacy policies and practices audited by the organization. TRUSTe accepts complaints and questions about the privacy practices of its licensees from the general public and investigates the issues raised. They have a special program and seal that indicates compliance with the provisions of the COPPA legislation. Information about their activities, including investigations, can be found on their Web site, http://www.truste.org.

- BBBOnLine, which is a program of the Better Business Bureau. BBBOnLine has long been active in mediating disputes between consumers and businesses, especially at the local retail level. It has both a privacy seal program, which also incorporates the Fair Information Practices Principles, and a reliability seal. It also has a separate seal for sites that serve children younger than 13 years of age. Its reliability seal certifies that firms are members of their local Better Business Bureaus and have agreed to stated principles covering truth in advertising and consumer dispute resolution. Complaints can be filed on the Web site, http://www.bbbonline.org. The site also offers consumer information and a search function that helps consumers locate businesses that are certified by BBBOnLine.

- the Online Privacy Alliance, which is a nonprofit alliance of businesses that want to promote a safe and trusting environment on the Internet. They provide guidelines for privacy policies and support third-party seals of approval but do not offer their own certification mechanism. The Web site, http://www.privacyalliance.org, is a good source for articles about privacy issues in the United States and Europe.

- trade associations that serve specific industries. These associations are also active in promoting acceptable privacy practices by their members. The Direct Marketing Association (DMA) offers both information and guidance on developing a privacy policy (http://www.the-dma.org/privacy/privacypolicygenerator.shtml). The DMA offers tools for creating privacy policies for businesses in general and for businesses that come under the provisions of COPPA and HIPPA. The American Bankers Association (http://www.aba.com/Industry+Issues/gr_pr_legislative.htm) offers privacy policy guidelines for its members. The Interactive Advertising Bureau requires that its members post privacy policies that conform to the Fair Information Practices Principles (http://www.iab.net/standards/privacy.asp).

- organizations and Web sites. There are a number of other organizations and Web sites that are resources for information about privacy issues. They include the Electronic Privacy Information Center (http://www.epic.org), the Electronic Frontier Foundation (http://www.eff.org), and the Privacy Rights Clearinghouse (http://www.privacyrights.org). Government agencies like the Department of Commerce and the FTC are also information resources.

- the EU Web site, which deals with data protection issues and regulations inside the EU (http://europa.eu.int/comm/justice_home/fsj/privacy/).

- the FTC's Kidz Privacy site. Kidz Privacy is a special site for children and about children's privacy matters (http://www.ftc.gov/bcp/conline/edcams/kidzprivacy/index.html). On a related subject, the FTC also has a special Web site with information about spam (http://www.ftc.gov/spam/).

All this activity, however, begs the question of whether self-regulation is working sufficiently well to forestall legislation. Most industry leaders and regulators in the United States still voice strong support for self-regulation. However, many other countries have taken a regulatory approach toward Internet privacy from the beginning, believing that self-regulation is insufficient to protect the public. In the next section, we look at privacy activities in other major Internet-using countries.

12-3k Privacy Regulation in Various Internet-Using Countries

Privacy is a concern in countries around the world, but it is not safe to assume that the concerns are the same from one country to the next. The marketer who is conducting business globally must be aware of consumer concerns and actions as well as of the regulations in each country. Although the regulations are generally based on the Fair Information Practices Principles, their degree of severity varies among countries.

The legislation with the most widespread impact is the European Union Directive on Protection of Personal Data. It was adopted in 1995 by the Council of Ministers and took effect on October 28, 1998. Unlike the United States, the EU has a declared preference for regulation in the area of personal data privacy and has a record of action that dates back to the Council of Europe Convention in 1981. The 1995 directive was aimed at bringing the protection of personal data into the Internet age. Its purpose was to ensure that data could move freely between the member countries of the EU while guaranteeing a stated level of privacy protection.

The directive establishes a principle of *informed consent,* which requires that consumers be informed about the existence and nature of data collection and processing. It specifically requires that data be collected only for specified, explicit, and legitimate purposes and that the data are to be stored only if it is relevant, accurate, and up to date. It also establishes a principle of *fairness,* by which individuals are given the option of whether or not to provide information. The directive has provisions for *flexibility,* meaning that there can be some differences in the laws passed by the member states to implement the directive. In the case of differences, the law of the state in which the data processor is located applies. The directive also establishes arrangements for *monitoring* by independent authorities.

The rights granted to data subjects under the directive are as follows:

- Right of access to data
- Right to knowledge about where data originated
- Right to have inaccurate data corrected
- Right of recourse in the event of unlawful processing
  - Legal processing is defined by consent, contract, legal obligation, vital interest of the data subject, and balance between the interest of data processors and data subjects.
- Right to withhold permission to use data in certain circumstances, for example, the sending of direct marketing material

The directive also regulates data transfer to non-EU countries to ensure that EU rules are not circumvented. In order for data transfer to take place, the non-EU countries must ensure an adequate level of data protection. For countries like the United States that have considerably lower legal standards for personal data protection, this has been a looming problem.

After years of negotiations, the United States reached a "Safe Harbor" agreement with the EU in the summer of 2000. In the simplest terms, the two governments agreed that data transmitted into the United States from the EU would be protected under U.S. law and that government agencies would monitor compliance.

In practical terms, this means that firms that agree to abide by the self-regulatory principles (which are those of the Fair Information Practices Principles) will register annually with the U.S. Department of Commerce. This will immunize the company from having to comply with the EU Data Protection Directive but will allow it to conduct Internet commerce with companies inside the EU. The U.S. Department of Commerce oversees the program[31] while the FTC and the judicial system have authority to impose sanctions on firms that violate the agreement. The government agencies are working with TRUSTe, which has developed an EU Safe Harbor Privacy Seal as a visible symbol of compliance with the program.

The Safe Harbor agreement is an important step forward. However, other countries, such as Canada and Australia, have passed stringent privacy laws that exceed those of the United States. It is possible that these differing laws may, in time, result in other agreements that bring more consistency to privacy regulation and ensure the free flow of electronic commerce around the world. In the meantime, it behooves corporations to be aware of privacy sensibilities and legal structures in all the countries in which they do business. This is a tall order, but it is necessary to prevent damaging privacy incidents.

From the data presented in this part of the chapter, it is clear that trust is important to the success of Internet business. It is equally clear that trust in the ability of institutions to protect personal data is not high in various parts of the world. The other issue of special import to the creation and maintenance of trust in Internet businesses is that of the security of personal data. We now turn to a discussion of the business and marketing issues that relate to the security of data and transactions.

12-4 Consumer Data Security Breaches

Theft of consumer data from databases owned by businesses and governments is not new. It predates the Internet. The Internet, however, has given hackers and thieves a path that leads directly to the boundary of the organization. At that point, the organization must have a firewall and other network security devices to keep unauthorized users out and fulfill their responsibility to keep consumer data secure, as specified by the International Fair Information Practices Principles (FIPP) and laws like GLBA.

Breaches of data security tend to make the news. Some may be only mischievous, as when Microsoft reported that a hacker was able to move around parts of the Microsoft network almost at will during a 12-day period in October 2000.[32] That followed an announcement a few months earlier that hackers had gained access to the account and personal information of what AOL described as "a very small number of accounts."[33]

In February 2005, the issue once again burst into the news when ChoicePoint, a firm that provides verification services to credit card companies, announced that personal data of as many as 140,000 accounts was compromised. In this case, it was not done by hackers; the theft was carried out by fraud artists posing as legitimate businesses.[34] The sensitive nature of the information attracted a great deal of public notice and the damage did not end with the original incursion. In November 2005, ChoicePoint reported that a total of 162,000 accounts were actually affected. As many as 750 credit card customers became victims of identity theft as a result.[35]

Unfortunately, the ChoicePoint theft was not an isolated event. The Privacy Rights Clearinghouse, a nonprofit organization, posted a chronology that began with the ChoicePoint incident in February 2005 and is still active. In January 2006 it listed security breaches that could have exposed personal data at the rate of several each month. Some of the incidents involved only a few hundred to a few thousand data records. Others had the potential for compromising 1 million or more accounts. This list includes a number of financial services providers, retailers, and health care providers. It includes several state government agencies and many colleges and universities. The largest single exposure occurred when more than 40 million accounts were obtained through hacking at CardSystems, a firm that processes credit card accounts for large issuers, including MasterCard and Visa.[36] Large credit card issuers, including American Express and Visa, announced their intentions to sever their relationships with the firm after its admission that it had not adequately protected consumer account data. The chronology also makes clear that hacking is not the only security issue. Numerous lost or stolen computers are listed, as are e-mails and mailings that exposed personal data, and even one instance where personal data was displayed at gas stations. By January 2006, the Privacy Rights Clearinghouse had counted 52,064,352 accounts that had possibly been compromised. That did not include a December 2005 incident in which a computer tape containing mortgage data was lost and later found by the delivery firm.[37] The beat goes on, and enterprise information technology (IT) security experts have many issues with which they must deal.

Many consumers have received notification from financial services providers that their accounts may have been compromised. Many more have read the accounts in the media. The result is significant and growing concern about the security of personal data.

12-4a Consumer Concern about Security

Just as consumers consistently report concern about the privacy of their personal data, they also express concern about the security of their transactions. In June 2005, The Conference Board found that:

- 54% of Internet users surveyed are more concerned about the security of their personal data on the Internet than they were a year ago.
- 42% say their level of concern has not changed.
- 4% are less concerned than they were a year ago.

They were concerned both about financial transactions and online purchases. The level of concern varied by age group, with 49% of users younger than 35 being extremely concerned about the security of their data when they made financial transactions online and 63% of those 55 and older being extremely concerned about the security of online financial transactions.

These respondents are changing online behaviors as a result of security concerns. According to The Conference Board:

- nearly 70% have installed additional security software.
- 54% now opt out of special offers.
- 47% are purchasing less online.[38]

Specific concerns include spyware, adware, and identity theft.

12-4b Spyware and Adware

Spyware and **adware** are both marketer-initiated actions. Spyware works in the background as consumers move around the Web, tracking their movements and recording things like keywords used in searches. Adware is a particular type of spyware that continually pops up ads on a user's screen using the behavioral techniques described in Chapter 6.

In many cases, spyware is simply used to create anonymous profiles. In other cases, it may be much more intrusive, for example, repeatedly changing the consumers opening page to a specific Web site despite the consumer's efforts to specify another page or resisting all efforts to stop the advertising pop-ups. Spyware is often placed in the process of receiving a free download. The presence of spyware may, in fact, be specified in the service agreement the consumer must sign before the download begins. Based on all we know, it seems reasonable to assume that most consumers do not read the agreements carefully and that, in all likelihood, if they understood the implications, they would not accept the spyware programs. In fact, a Pew Foundation survey found that 73% of Internet users say they do not always read user agreements or other disclaimers before downloading or installing software.[39]

In terms of reported knowledge about these issues, they found that:

- 78% say they understand what spyware is.
- 52% say they understand what adware is.

After being given a careful definition of the two terms, 43% said a piece of spyware, adware, or both had been placed on their computer. The accuracy of that self-reported statement is questionable. They quote a 2004 study by AOL and the National Cyber Security Alliance, which stated that 53% of respondents reported having spyware or adware on their computers. When the computers were scanned, with their permission, the study found that 80% of the machines actually had spyware or adware present.[40]

Of these users, 91% have made changes in their online behavior in an effort to prevent unauthorized downloads:

- Eighty-one percent have stopped opening e-mail attachments unless they are sure the documents are safe.
- Forty-one percent have stopped visiting particular Web sites that they think might download unwanted programs.
- Thirty-four percent have stopped downloading software. (Another 33% say they have never downloaded software.)
- Twenty-five percent have stopped downloading music or video files from peer-to-peer (P2P) networks. (Another 48% said they had never done so.)
- Eighteen percent have changed Web browsers.[41]

There are other threats to security in addition to spyware and adware. Three of the important Web-related ones go under the colorful names of **phishing**, **pfarming**, and **spoofing**.

adware Software that inserts ads onto the viewer's screen.

phishing E-mails that attempt to obtain personal information by making fraudulent claims.

pfarming Creating fake Web sites that are similar to legitimate business sites.

spoofing Creating false identities in order to evade rules for conducting business and communications on the Web.

12-4c Phishing, Pfarming, and Spoofing

Adware and spyware result from marketer-initiated efforts. A variety of other techniques are used by fraud artists to obtain the personal data of consumers.

- *Phishing* is the practice of using fraudulent e-mails in an attempt to get information like consumer account numbers and passwords. These come in the form of an e-mail that purports to be from a recognized financial services provider. Often they inform customers of that provider that there is a problem with their account and that they need to provide information to clear it up. From the consumer standpoint, the rule is simple. *Never provide personal information in response to an incoming e-mail.* That should be enough to protect the consumer, but unfortunately it is not.

- *Pfarming* also attempts to obtain personal data, but it does so in a different way. Perpetrators hack into the DNS (Domain Name System) servers that provide the Internet protocol (IP) addresses for URLs and thereby allow users to access Web sites on the Internet. They hijack some of the pages and create a site that looks much like the original. Because they have gained unauthorized access to the DNS server, they can direct the user to the fake site and trick him or her into divulging personal information. Because the sites look real, this fraud is hard for consumers to detect. This technique is widely used to scam charitable donations after any disaster by using sites that resemble sites of legitimate charities. For example, ABC news reported that a site called http://www. AirKatrina.com was raising money by claiming to be flying evacuees out of the region for medical treatment.[42] The ".com" is a clue that it is not a nonprofit organization, so is the very fact that it was new. As soon as the FTC verifies a scam, they can and do shut these sites down under antifraud laws, which apply on the Internet just as they do offline. In the meantime, they obtain both money and personal information from unsuspecting consumers.

- *Spoofing* is the general term that describes a situation in which a person, computer program, or Web site is able to masquerade successfully as another. Spoofing requires that the criminal first identify the IP address of the trusted Web site. Then it must waylay individual data packets and modify their identifying headers so that it appears that they are coming from the trusted Web site. That sounds difficult to do, but there are apparently many poorly written IPs that make it possible for people with technical expertise to tap into the telecommunications stream that comprises the traffic of the Internet.

Both phishing and pharming can be considered as specific types of spoofing.

Whatever the method used to steal personal data, the possible outcome is identity theft. Identity theft implies that a thief has obtained access to information that allows him or her to pose as another individual, doing things like using the other person's credit cards or bank accounts. It poses a direct threat to consumers' financial well-being and is a topic of considerable and growing concern.

12-4d Identity Theft

The FTC reports that 3.2 million U.S. citizens are victims of identity theft each year. It costs consumers and businesses about $52 billion annually. Victims are forced to spend an average of 30 hours restoring their credit.[43] When asked if they were concerned about identity theft, 21% replied they were very worried and another 44% were moderately worried.[44]

InsightExpress found that 85% of Americans believed that identity theft could happen to them. They believe that online is the most dangerous (37%), compared

TABLE 12-3	Avenues of Identity Theft

Ways Americans Think Identity Theft Could Happen to Them	% of Americans Agreeing
Stolen wallet	86
Accessing a credit card number on the Internet	65
Identifying information on Internet sources	64
Stolen mail from an unlocked mailbox	64
"Dumpster diving" in trash bins for unshredded documents	58
Fraudulently accessing credit reports	56
Obtaining your name and Social Security Number from personnel or customer files in the workplace	54
"Shoulder surfing" at ATM to capture PIN numbers	46

Source: InsightExpress, April 17, 2004, http://www.insightexpress.com/pressroom/release_042704.asp.

TABLE 12-4	Steps Taken to Protect against Identity Theft

Steps Taken by Americans Actively Trying to Prevent Identity Theft	% of Americans Actively Trying to Prevent Identity Theft
Avoid giving my Social Security Number out	87
Shred or destroy ban and/or credit card information	83
Shred or destroy any credit card or other direct-mail offers	81
Create passwords containing numbers and letters	61
Avoid buying or making donations over the phone	58
Purchase goods online only from a reputable Web site	56
Install a computer firewall at home	52
Read the privacy statements and/or bank liability clauses	50
Check my credit report more frequently	38
Only use one credit card for purchases	31
Avoid shopping online	31
Avoid using my debit/check-cashing card for purchases	20
Subscribe to an identity theft protection program	11

Source: InsightExpress, April 17, 2004 http://www.insightexpress.com/pressroom/release_042704.asp.

with telephone (34%) and in-store purchases (10%). At the same time, they are aware that there are many ways that identifying information can be stolen. According to Table 12-3, consumers are aware that identity theft can occur in various ways, ranging from a stolen wallet, to thieves stealing their trash, to people looking other their shoulders at the automated teller machine (ATM). Concern about the Internet is high on the list, however; 65% were concerned about credit card numbers being stolen on the net, and 64% were concerned about other types of data theft there. When asked what actions they were taking to prevent identity theft, actions directly related to the Internet again were not at the head of the list. Still, 56% report that they will buy online only from reputable Web sites, whereas 31% avoid shopping online altogether (Table 12-4).[45]

Identity theft is clearly a serious problem, and Internet marketers should take all possible steps to prevent it. There are many ways in which corporate security can be breached and personal identity threatened. Let's now turn to an examination of the methods and the steps business is taking to protect themselves and their customers.

12-4e Business Concerns about Security

Security is an issue that has become important in the minds of managers in recent years. In 2005, it was estimated that e-commerce revenues would be decreased by $2.8 billion in fraudulent transactions alone. For middle-sized to large e-tailers, that amounted to 1.8% of their e-commerce revenues.[46]

There are two basic security issues. One is protecting systems from *natural disasters*, such as floods and fires. This requires secure storage off-site and is a well-developed security industry service long used by firms like banks who must keep extensive records of important documents.

The information technology industry has, from its beginnings, recognized the necessity of protecting systems from *human intrusion*—the second basic security issue. Your own school probably has relatively strong systems in place to protect private records such as student grades and to protect communications systems like e-mail. The standing joke among academic IT people is that the better the computer sciences program at a school, the more layers of security the institution's computers and network must have. The reason is, of course, a significant number of highly skilled students who may take pleasure in hacking into systems, either to do mischief like changing grades or just to prove they can do it. Whatever the motivation, hacking into academic systems is one Information Age version of a student prank.

Whatever the venue, it is easier to protect a physical data center where you can put equipment behind locked doors and have authentication systems to regulate who enters. It becomes more difficult to protect corporate networks because there are many more points of entry. It is even more difficult to provide security once a network is connected to the Internet because it provides a highway for potential intruders right up to the communications doorway of the organization. Adding to the magnitude of the security problem, there is increasing use of wireless devices to access the corporate network from outside its firewall.

Marketers attempt to protect against fraudulent transactions in a number of ways. One is to have a human being review orders for suspicious entries. Larger retailers use address verification systems and other technologies in an attempt to prevent fraud. You may have noticed, for instance, that more e-merchants are asking for the verification number on the back of the credit card when placing an order online.

We should look at the types of threats from the perspective of business, government, and nonprofit organizations. It is also helpful to look at the types of people or groups who are the potential sources of threats. Finally, we conclude this section with a brief examination of the types of steps that are being taken to protect consumer data from unauthorized access and use.

12-4f Types of Threats against Business Networks

Consultants at Gartner asked IT managers about security issues. They found that organizations continued to increase their spending on security in 2005. The issues they are defending against are shown in Table 12-5.

Like consumers, businesses are concerned about viruses and worms that jam systems and carry unauthorized software, hacking, identify theft and phishing, spyware, spam, and viruses that infect mobile systems. There are some threats that are not common in the consumer space:

- *Denial of service* refers to an outside attack that makes a Web site unavailable to users. This is generally done by sending a huge volume of communications that

TABLE 12-5	Critical IT Security Threats Cited by Organizations in North America, May 2005 (based on a 10-point scale)

Viruses and worms	7.6
Outside hacking or cracking	7.1
Identity theft and phishing	7.0
Spyware	6.8
Denial of service	6.6
Spam	6.3
Wireless and mobile device viruses	6.2
Insider threats	6.2
Zero day threats	5.9
Social engineering	5.9
Cyberterrorism	5.6

Source: http://www.eMarketer.com.

tie up the computing resources of the site under attack. It can be accomplished by illicitly seizing networks and programming them to send massive numbers of repetitive communications.

- *Insider threats* include malicious activities ranging from alteration to destruction to theft by disgruntled employees.
- *Zero day threats* are intrusions into systems that are made on the day the public is made aware of, or even before they know about, a vulnerability in a major piece of software, often the operating system. The attack occurs before the maker of the software has an opportunity to make a security patch available, perhaps even before IT administrators are aware of a potential problem.
- *Social engineering* is a term with meaning that extends beyond the Internet. It describes the manipulation of legitimate users to obtain sensitive information from them in person, over the phone, or on the Internet. Both phishing and pfarming fall under the broad category of social engineering.
- *Cyberterrorism* is simply the transfer of terrorism onto the Internet, using any of the techniques we have described in this section of the chapter.

The Cyber Security Institute conducts an annual survey for the Federal Bureau of Investigation (FBI) on issues relating to the security of information systems. In 2005, it received responses from 700 private corporations, government agencies, and educational institutions and other organizations. They found that viruses remained the largest source of security-related financial losses for these organizations. Web site incidents, although small in the magnitude of financial loss, had greatly increased in number over the preceding year.

Figure 12-2 shows that the same technologies that consumers should be using against intrusion into their computer systems are the ones used by almost all organizations who responded to the survey. Firewalls and antivirus software were in almost universal use. Many also use special software located on their network and on servers to detect attempted or actual intrusions. Passwords and smart cards for identification purposes are also important. In addition, they used other important technologies:

- **Encryption** is the use of mathematical algorithms to code or scramble data so it cannot be recognized without being decoded.
- **Public key** Information refers to systems that provide for the verification of identity (that a Web site is the site it says it is, for example) by a trusted third party. This

encryption Using mathematical algorithms to encode data for security in transmission or storage.

public key A security device that can be sent by ordinary communications methods like e-mail.

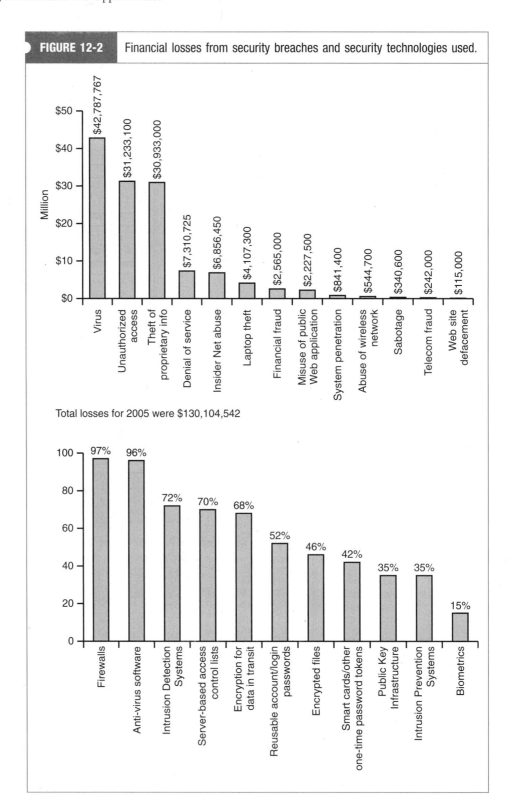

FIGURE 12-2   Financial losses from security breaches and security technologies used.

Total losses for 2005 were $130,104,542

secure sockets layer Internet security protocol that validates the identity of a Web site and makes it safe to send financial information like credit card numbers.

biometrics Using a biological characteristic, for example, a fingerprint or voiceprint, to authenticate the identity of a person.

permits the exchange of information in a secure fashion. PKIs are essential to the operation of the **Secure Sockets Layer** (SSL), which secures e-commerce transactions on the net.

• **Biometrics** refers to the use of some physical characteristic to identify a user and admit him or her into a physical location or a computer network.

Biometrics that are coming into use to prevent unauthorized access to systems include fingerprints, voice prints, and cameras that scan the retina of the user's eye.

Corporations, government agencies, and nonprofit organizations all stand to lose financially from criminal activities that violate the security of their networks. They stand to lose even more if they lose the trust of their customers, their donors, and the citizenry in general. All organizations that hold any amount of customer data have a fiduciary responsibility for the protection of that data. It is a responsibility that organizations are taking with increasing seriousness, even as cybercriminals become more ingenious in their attempts to breach security systems.

There is one additional type of activity we need to examine before concluding this chapter. It does not usually include breaches of security, but it does involve potential theft of a possession. The subject is the thorny one of intellectual property on the Internet.

12-5 Intellectual Property

Napster is clearly the poster child of the intellectual property controversy on the net. As most students know, Napster was the home of software that makes it possible to download music over the Internet. It is the prime example of the consumer P2P business model, first attracting media attention when it slowed the computer systems of several universities in the United States so severely that it was banned from many campus networks. Napster not only drew media attention, it also attracted the ire of the recording industry. At the end of 1999, several record companies filed suit, essentially to prevent Napster from facilitating the distribution of copyrighted music.

At its height, it is estimated that 30 million people were registered with Napster. In 2000, Bertelsmann AG, a European media conglomerate, acquired Napster with the intention of turning it into a subscription service.[47] Under that business model, Napster continued to exist but failed to thrive. Its place has been taken by a host of other file-sharing products, with Kazaa the apparent market share leader in MP3 downloads and BitTorrent leading the way in use for downloading large files like videos.[48]

Consumers tend to view downloading of music and other intellectual property over the Internet as simply obtaining something they want. Figure 12-3 shows that 75% of Internet users surveyed did not want downloading of music for personal use to be considered illegal. At the same time, they believe that downloading music for resale should be illegal.[49] If consumers seem somewhat conflicted about the legality of downloading music, and perhaps other digital items, industry is not. A study for the Business Software Alliance estimated the value of pirated software in 2003 to approach $30 billion worldwide.[50] The Recording Industry Alliance estimates that the music industry loses approximately $4.2 billion to piracy worldwide each year.[51] The Digital Millennium Copyright Act was passed to attempt to deal with these issues in a way that protects consumer access to information while simultaneously protecting the interests of owners of intellectual property.

12-5a The Digital Millennium Copyright Act

The Committee on Intellectual Property Rights and the Emerging Information Infostructure of the National Academy of Sciences points out that from the time of Thomas Jefferson, access to information has been a cornerstone of American democracy

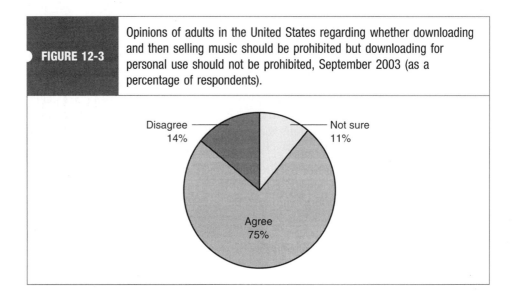

FIGURE 12-3

Opinions of adults in the United States regarding whether downloading and then selling music should be prohibited but downloading for personal use should not be prohibited, September 2003 (as a percentage of respondents).

Disagree
14%

Not sure
11%

Agree
75%

and of the educational system. Public libraries have made printed material available to any citizen at virtually no cost. One hallmark of this system is that one published item is available to only one person at a time.

However, when that same content is published electronically, there is no theoretical limit to the number of people who can access it simultaneously. That leads to the worst nightmare of musicians and authors and their publishers—that electronic publishing will ultimately lead to the sale of only one book or recording. The rest would simply be copied.

After years of international discussion about intellectual property issues as they pertain to electronic products of all kinds, the U.S. Congress passed and the president signed the Digital Millennium Copyright Act in 1998. It has many provisions that affect Internet users, libraries, Web sites, and educational institutions. Among the provisions are to make it a crime to circumvent the antipiracy codes built into most commercial software or to make or sell code-cracking devices. Libraries and educational institutions receive certain exemptions that allow them to make copyrighted material available to authorized users. However, Internet service providers (ISPs) are required to remove material that constitutes copyright infringement from customers' Web sites, and webcasters are required to pay licensing fees to recording companies.[52] Given the data in Figure 12-3 it appears that enforcement of the law at all levels will present great difficulty for some time to come.[53]

The issues are also difficult because the interests of various stakeholders clash with little obvious ways of reconciling them. In addition, traditional practices and laws vary in different countries around the globe.[54] As with privacy, there are important differences in approach between the United States and the EU.

12-5b Intellectual Property Regulation in the European Union

In February 2001, the European Parliament approved a directive that is supposed to protect the rights of copyright holders by allowing them to use technical methods such as encryption to prevent unauthorized copying. The European Commission (EC) has issued a series of recommendations on how to implement the directive, including one in early 2005 that recommends strategies for legitimate online distribution of music products. The EC maintains a Web page that chronicles their deliberations on the thorny issue of intellectual property on the Web at http://europa.eu.int/comm/internal_market/copyright/management/management_en.htm.

12-5c Other Approaches to Protecting Intellectual Property

Many companies around the world are working on technological solutions to various intellectual property issues. However, protection of intellectual property requires more than technological fixes. Management must also exercise skill and vigilance to protect important corporate assets in an ever-changing world. From a broader social point of view, online intellectual property protection is a public policy issue that needs to be approached on several fronts. It involves legal and regulatory concerns that must be dealt with. There are also consumer needs for control and flexibility in their acquisition and use of products that should be considered. At the same time, there is a need for better consumer understanding of the subject of intellectual property and the responsibility of consumers in helping to maintain a free and fair marketplace. To add the final complication, in the field of intellectual property, as in all other aspects of regulation of the Internet, technology advances so quickly that it is impossible for regulatory efforts to keep pace.

In this spirit, there are attempts to deal with the issue by striking a balance between traditional copyright law and an environment in which there is no protection at all for intellectual property. You might think of the traditional posture as "all rights reserved." The intent of newer initiatives is to provide widespread access to intellectual product in a "some rights reserved" environment. A well-known manifestation of this activity is the Creative Commons, a nonprofit organization that attempts to help producers manage their intellectual property rights under existing copyright law.[55] Discussion about open access publishing continues in academia and can be followed on various Web sites.[56] Government agencies are also interested in the approach, as evidenced by a new requirement that recipients of National Institutes of Health grants publish under open access terms as well as in refereed academic journals.[57]

An eventual solution to the dilemma of protecting owners' rights while allowing access to material is likely to require activities on numerous dimensions—social, legal, and technical. Managers who have responsibility for intellectual products will need to pay close attention to developments.

Summary

The social and regulatory issues that pertain to the Internet are many and varied. In this chapter, important concerns related to the protection of personal data, data security, and intellectual property were reviewed. These issues are recognized in Internet-using countries around the world, although the reaction in individual countries to each issue may vary. This is true even at the most basic level of preference for industry self-regulation versus a regulatory approach.

Trust is essential to success in the Information Age, especially for businesses who rely on the Internet. Whatever the status of current regulation, trust is an issue between the organization and its customers. Building trust is hard to do; it can be destroyed by a single event. The importance and the fragility of trust combine to make it another potent source of competitive advantage on the net.

The Internet has caused intense focus on the issue of privacy of personal data on the Internet. Consumers in many countries are concerned, although they do not necessarily have in-depth knowledge about the subject or examine privacy policies that are posted on the Web. In general, consumers tend to be concerned about practices like unwanted communications and use of their data by companies other than the one to which they furnished the data and its use for purposes other than the original. They want to know what company policies are with respect to data and other important aspects of their dealings with a company. The perceptions of privacy and the actions consumers are most likely to take in the face of privacy concerns differ from one country to the next, creating a difficult situation for the global Internet marketer.

Maintaining security on the Internet, especially the safety of databases with consumer information, is a complex technical issue. Marketers have a large stake in it. Keeping data safe and informing the consumer about security practices in a way that builds a trusting relationship should be a marketing focus.

The maintenance of intellectual property rights is also of direct concern to marketers. In many instances, it affects the products or services they have for sale. The Internet makes it easy for users to transfer material, and protecting it from unauthorized copying is both a technical and a business model issue. Consumers evidence little concern about intellectual property issues, exacerbating the problem. Neither technological or legal solutions alone appear to hold the answer to the intellectual property dilemma.

Dealing with these concerns is an ongoing issue because new challenges continue to arise. Successfully coping with them demands a combination of technology and management vigilance.

Quiz

1. Actions taken by consumers to protect the privacy of their data include _____.
   a. boycotting Web sites
   b. starting e-mail campaigns
   c. deleting cookies

2. The dimensions of trust on the Internet include _____.
   a. organizations that monitor behavior of Web sites
   b. security of personal data
   c. public relations activities of enterprises

3. A privacy-related segmentation of consumers includes _____.
   a. privacy unawares
   b. privacy fundamentalists
   c. privacy protectors

4. Consumers tend to consider _____ information as being sensitive.
   a. health-related
   b. goods and services purchased
   c. Web sites visited

5. In the United States, laws have *not* been passed regulating the collection and use of personal information about _____.
   a. financial activities of consumers
   b. people older than 65 years of age
   c. information collected from children

6. _____ is the agreement that allows e-commerce between the United States and EU despite the difference in privacy policies.
   a. Safe Harbor
   b. Information Agreement
   c. Treaty of Rome

7. The software that tracks consumers' activities on the Web, usually without their knowledge, is called _____.
   a. traceware
   b. spyware
   c. openware

8. Among the security problems often experienced by businesses are _____.
   a. consumer refusal to provide data
   b. laws that restrict security efforts
   c. identity theft and phishing

9. Which of the following are *not* true statements about intellectual property issues on the Internet?
   a. P2P file sharing is acceptable in the eyes of copyright law.
   b. The Internet has magnified the problem of protecting intellectual property.
   c. Consumers show little concern for intellectual property protection.

10. Intellectual property can be protected by _____.
    a. technological solutions
    b. management vigilance
    c. both a and b

Discussion Questions

1. The increasing use of the Internet around the world has heightened consumer concerns about the privacy of their personal data. What is the nature of the concerns, and what are their implications for Internet marketing activities?

2. Businesses are doing all they should to protect the privacy of their customers and to inform them about privacy issues. Do you agree or disagree? Why?

3. What are the Fair Information Practices Principles? Why are they important?

4. Compare and contrast the approaches taken by the EU and the United States to protect data privacy for their citizens.

5. What do you think are consumers' chief concerns about security on the Internet? Do you agree that these concerns are well founded?

6. What do enterprises need to do to protect their own assets and the data entrusted to them by their customers?

7. How has the Internet increased both the importance and the difficulty of protecting intellectual property?

8. What is your own feeling about the importance of the intellectual property issue, both on and off the Internet?

Internet Exercises

1. Conduct your own privacy survey, using the Web sites you are tracking and others that you visit frequently. Do they all have a privacy policy? Do the policies you find seem to meet the requirements of the Fair Information Practices Principles? Why or why not?

2. Visit the Web sites of at least two privacy organizations. Carefully study what they do and be prepared to discuss this material in class. As you do this, pay attention to what their target market seems to be—consumers, businesses, or other institutions.

3. Conduct informal interviews with consumers to evaluate how much they seem to know about various Internet security issues. Evaluate the degree to which they seem to be taking actions to protect their own information security.

4. Conduct informal interviews with friends to see how they feel about file-sharing services for music in par-

ticular and the issue of intellectual property on the Web in general. Try to find out whether they are using sites that allow them to download music or other files free of charge. Be prepared to discuss your informal findings and to speculate about the degree to which your peer group engages in potentially questionable practices with respect to intellectual property rights.

5. Research the privacy and security policies of your school. Do you think most students are aware of these policies and understand the reasons for them? Do you think most students agree with them? Why or why not?

6. Interview one of the librarians at your school about policies regarding fair use of intellectual property in general and issues related to electronic documents in particular.

Notes

1. Glen L. Urban, "The Trust Imperative," MIT Working Paper 4302-03, http://ssrn.com/abstract=400421, p. 1.

2. "Trust Shifting from Traditional Authorities to Peers, Edelman Trust Barometer Finds," January 21, 2005, http://www.edelman.com/news/allnews.asp.

3. "Consumer Internet Barometer™," press release, June 23, 2005, http://www.consumerinternetbarometer.us/press.cfm.

4. "Americans and Online Privacy: The System Is Broken," Annenberg Public Policy Center of the University of Pennsylvania, 2003, p. 26.

5. George R. Milne and Mary J. Culnan, "Strategies for Reducing Online Privacy Risks: Why Consumers Read (Or Don't Read) Online Privacy Notices," *Journal of Interactive Marketing,* Vol. 18, No. 3, Summer 2004, p. 22.

6. Glen L. Urban, "The Trust Imperative," MIT Working Paper 4302-03, http://ssrn.com/abstract=400421.

7. "The Economic Value of Trust," *Accenture Outlook,* 2003, Number 3, p. 34.

8. "The Economic Value of Trust," *Accenture Outlook,* 2003, Number 3, pp 32–41.

9. Glen L. Urban, "The Trust Imperative," MIT Working Paper 4302-03, http://ssrn.com/abstract=400421, p. 4.

10. John Deighton, "The Right to Be Let Alone," *Journal of Interactive Marketing,* Vol. 12, No. 2, Spring 1998, p. 3.

11. "Americans and Online Privacy: The System Is Broken," Annenberg Public Policy Center of the University of Pennsylvania, 2003, p. 3.

12. Curl J. Dommeyer and Barbara L. Gross, "What Consumers Know and What They Do: An Investigation of Consumer Knowledge, Awareness and Use of Privacy Protection Strategies," *Journal of Interactive Marketing,* Vol. 17, No. 2, Spring 2003, pp. 34–51.

13. George R. Milne and Mary J. Culnan, "Strategies for Reducing Online Privacy Risks: Why Consumers Read (Or Don't Read) Online Privacy Notices," *Journal of Interactive Marketing,* Vol. 18, No. 3, Summer 2004, pp. 20–21.

14. Lorrie Faith Cranor, Joseph Reagle, and Mark S. Ackerman, "Beyond Concern: Understanding Net Users' Attitudes about Online Privacy," AT&T Labs-Research Technical Report TR 99.4.3, April 14, 1999, http://www.research.att.com/library/trs/TRs/99/99.4/.

15. Lee Rainie *et al.,* "Trust and Privacy Online: Why Americans Want to Rewrite the Rules," August 20, 2000, http://www.pewinternet.org, p. 16.

16. "Most People Are 'Privacy Pragmatists,' Who, While Concerned, Will Sometimes Trade It Off for Other Benefits," March 19, 2003, Harris Online, http://www.harrisinteractive.com/harris_poll/index.asp?PID=365.

17. Kim Bartel Sheehan and Mariea Grubbs Hoy "Dimensions of Privacy Concern among Online Consumers," *Journal of Public Policy & Marketing,* Vol. 19, No. 1, Spring 2000, pp. 62–73.

18. "Kids Think Giving Out Information on Net OK," May 30, 2000, http://www.emarketer.com.

19. Mary Lou Roberts, Geo-Cities (A) and (B), *Journal of Interactive Marketing,* Winter 2000, pp. 60–72.

20. "Children's Online Privacy Protection Rule: Notice of Proposed Rulemaking: Federal Register Notice," nd, http://www.ftc.gov.

21. Joseph Turow, "Privacy Policies on Children's Web sites: Do They Play by the Rules?" The Annenberg Center for Public Policy of the University of Pennsylvania, March 2001, p. 12.

22. Prepared Statement of the Federal Trade Commission on "Recent Developments in Privacy Protections for Consumers," October 11, 2000, http://www.ftc.gov.

23. "Protecting the Privacy of Patients' Health Information," Department of Health and Human Services, May 9, 2001, http://www.hhs.gov.

24. See full text and other details on the Library of Congress site, http://thomas.loc.gov/cgi-bin/query/z?c107:H.R.3162.ENR:.

25. See, for example, The Electronic Privacy Information Center, http://www.epic.org/privacy/terrorism/usapatriot/, and the Privacy Rights Clearinghouse, http://www.privacyrights.org/links.htm.

26. Kimber Spradlin, "National Standards for Privacy Law," CNET News, October 11, 2005, http://news.com/Data+privacy+standards%2C+American+style/2010-1029_3-5892395.html?tag=carsl.

27. Federal Trade Commission, "Privacy Online: Fair Information Practices in the Electronic Marketplace," May 2000, p. i.

28. "Advertising and Marketing on the Internet," Federal Trade Commission, September 2000, p. 4.

29. "The Consumer Respect Group 2005 Privacy Report Focused on How Corporations Treat Online Consumers," Consumer Respect Group, Q3 2005, http://www.customerrespect.com/default.asp.

30. Federal Trade Commission, "Privacy Online: A Report to Congress, Part III," June 1998, http://www.ftc.gov.

31. To view the documents that constitute the Safe Harbor Privacy Framework and to access a list of companies that have self-certified compliance with the provisions, see http://www.export.gov/safeharbor/.

32. "Microsoft Responds to Security Issue," press release, October 29, 2000, http://www.microsoft.com/presspass/features/2000/oct00/10-27security.mspx.

33. Jim Hu, "AOL Security Breach Exposes Personal Info," CNET News, June 16, 2000, http://news.com/AOL+security+breach+exposes+personal+info/2100-1023_3-242034.html.

34. "ChoicePoint Tricked into Disclosing Info on 140,000 People," CNN, February 15, 2005, http://money.cnn.com/2005/02/17/technology/personaltech/choicepoint/.

35. "ChoicePoint Filing: 17,000 More May Be Fraud Victims," November 8, 2005, *Atlanta Business Chronicle*, http://atlanta.bizjournals.com/atlanta/stories/2005/11/07/daily25.html.

36. "A Chronology of Data Breaches Since the ChoicePoint Incident," The Privacy Rights Clearinghouse, October 5, 2005, http://www.privacyrights.org/ar/ChronDataBreaches.htm.

37. Robert McMillan, "Troubled CardSystems to Be Sold," IDG News Service, September 23, 2005, http://www.infoworld.com/article/05/09/23/HNcardsystems_1.html.

38. "Consumer Internet Barometer™," press release, June 23, 2005, http://www.consumerinternetbarometer.us/press.cfm.

39. Susannah Fox, "Spyware," Pew Internet & American Life Project, July 6, 2005, p. 6, http://www.pewinternet.org.

40. Susannah Fox, "Spyware," Pew Internet & American Life Project, July 6, 2005, p. 3, http://www.pewinternet.org.

41. Susannah Fox, "Spyware," Pew Internet & American Life Project, July 6, 2005, p. 13, http://www.pewinternet.org.

42. "Katrina Scams Surprise Law Enforcement Officials" ABC News, October 10, 2005, http://abcnews.go.com/WNT/HurricaneKatrina/story?id=1190014&page=1.

43. "Losing Your Life Online," eMarketer, March 22, 2005; Grant Schulte, "Agencies Warn of Scam Artists," *Houston Chronicle*, October 6, 2005, http://www.chron.com/cs/CDA/ssistory.mpl/business/3384143.

44. "Financial Insights Consumer Banking Survey," quoted in "Losing Your Life Online," eMarketer, March 22, 2005.

45. "Identity Theft Robs Consumers of Peace-of-Mind," Insight-Express, April 17, 2004, http://www.insightexpress.com/pressroom/release_042704.asp.

46. Susan Kuchinskas, "Fraud Chewing E-Commerce Profits," Internet News.com, November 10, 2005, http://www.internetnews.com/ec-news/article.php/3563061.

47. "Napster Audience Surges Ahead of Appeal," Reuters, October 2, 2000, http://www.techweb.com.

48. Robert P. Lipschulz and John Clyman, "P2P Programs: Popular and Perilous," PC Pitstop, nd, http://www.pcpitstop.com/spycheck/p2p.asp

49. "Most Still Side with Music Downloading," eMarketer, February 10, 2004.

50. "Piracy Study," BSA/IDC, July 2004, http://www.aladdin.com/pdf/hasp/BSA_IDC_Piracy_study_July_2004.pdf.

51. "Anti-Piracy," nd, Recording Industry Association of America, http://www.riaa.com/issues/piracy/default.asp.

52. The UCLA Online Institute for Cyberspace Law and Policy, "The Digital Millennium Copyright Act," http://www.gseis.ucla.edu.

53. For a good summary and a useful set of related links, see the Electronic Privacy Information Center, "Digital Rights Management," http://www.epic.org/privacy/drm/.

54. For a detailed examination of the issues from a global perspective, see the *Primer on Electronic Commerce and Intellectual Property Issues*, World Intellectual Property Organization, nd, http://ecommerce.wipo.int/primer/primer.html.

55. See "Frequently Asked Questions," Creative Commons, http://creativecommons.org/faq#Is_Creative_Commons_against_copyright?

56. See, for example, "Lawrence Lessig," http://www.lessig.org/bio/short/, and the site of Stevan Harnad, http://www.ecs.soton.ac.uk/harnad/.

57. John Savarese, "The Impact of Electronic Publishing," *Campus Technology*, January 4, 2006, http://www.campus-technology.com/article.asp?id=17723.

Leveraging the Marketing Knowledge Asset

Source: © Getty

Key Terms

automation (p. 332)

collaborative (p. 334)

data (p. 330)

expertise (p. 330)

explicit knowledge (p. 331)

information (p. 330)

intranet (p. 342)

knowledge (p. 330)

profile (p. 339)

protocol (p. 338)

queue (p. 347)

query (p. 344)

structured questions (p. 344)

tacit knowledge (p. 331)

template (p. 334)

work flow (p. 334)

Learning Objectives

By the time you complete this chapter, you will be able to:

- Explain the concepts of data, information, and knowledge.
- Define explicit knowledge and tacit knowledge.
- Describe ways in which knowledge-based systems can help human agents do their work.
- Describe ways in which knowledge-based automated marketing systems can improve customer experience.
- Identify the elements of customer contact protocols.
- Understand some of the challenges facing marketers in developing knowledge-based systems.

13-1 Introduction

The success of Internet marketing programs not only rests on sound business models and strategies but also depends on superb execution in a fast-paced and demanding environment. Increasingly, superb execution is dependent on equipping workers with instantaneous access to information needed to perform their tasks and on automated marketing programs of many kinds. To improve the learning and decision making of human beings and to develop automated systems that are effective in meeting business and customer needs, enterprises are turning to the discipline of knowledge management.

13-2 The Knowledge Management Continuum

information Data that have been processed into more useful forms using techniques that range from simple summary formats to complex statistical routines.

knowledge Information to which human expertise has been added.

data Raw, unprocessed facts and numbers.

expertise Skill or knowledge.

The American Productivity & Quality Center defines knowledge management as "the systematic process of identifying, capturing, and transferring information and knowledge people can use to create, compete, and improve."[1] This definition uses the terms **information** and **knowledge**, but not the term **data**. This is consistent with the way we have used these important terms throughout the text.

Figure 13-1 portrays the concept in marketing research terminology. "Knowledge" in this sense is a continuum. It begins with *data* collected in any of the ways discussed in Chapter 5, from traditional marketing research to transactional data captured in the context of various marketing activities. Raw data are subjected to *analytic routines* in order to transform them into *information* that is useful for decision-making or operational purposes.

According to this concept, organizational knowledge is formed when information is combined with **expertise**. Expertise is a human characteristic; the second definition in

> FIGURE 13-1   The knowledge continuum.

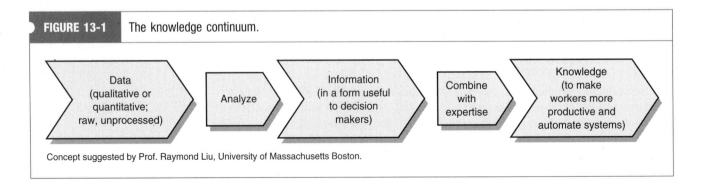

Concept suggested by Prof. Raymond Liu, University of Massachusetts Boston.

the *American Heritage Dictionary* is "skill or knowledge in a particular area."[2] The knowledge that the enterprise needs to capture and manage is therefore a combination of factual information and the expertise that is resident in skilled workers at all levels of the organization. Knowledge can be either *tacit* or *explicit*. **Explicit knowledge** is more readily available. It is the knowledge of skilled workers that can be articulated, communicated to others, and, if necessary, incorporated into marketing decision support or automated marketing systems. The time and cost required to build those systems should not be underestimated, but it is something that enterprises know how to do.

Tacit knowledge, on the other hand, is the property of skilled workers. They may be able to articulate exactly what it is they do to perform a task well. For example, a salesperson may be able to lead a trainee through rather precise steps used to close a sale with a hesitant customer. On the other hand, some workers evidence excellent task performance without being able to articulate exactly how they do it. This is often true of successful customer service agents. For instance, why is it that one counselor can tell you that you cannot take a course at this time and you walk away angry and frustrated, whereas another counselor delivers similar information at another time and you walk away understanding this is a necessary rule, maybe even in your best interest. The two counselors may be enforcing exactly the same set of rules, but one is able to make them palatable and another is not. This kind of experience with customer service representatives is common, and it is difficult to extract just exactly what the successful rep does and train the unsuccessful rep to do it just as well. *Making all customer encounters as successful as the best customer encounters is the great challenge facing marketers.* It is especially crucial to online marketers, for whom customer expectations, as noted throughout this text, are high and rising.

Embedding knowledge in systems is a path many marketers hope to follow in order to meet the challenge. In the customer relationship management (CRM) and customer service chapters, we discussed in considerable detail *what* leading edge enterprises are doing to provide satisfying experiences for their customers in all their channels. Now it is time to delve in more depth into *how* these enterprises are utilizing knowledge management systems to accomplish this challenge.

explicit knowledge Knowledge that has been or can be articulated in a relatively straightforward manner.

tacit knowledge Knowledge that has not been articulated; often subconscious and relatively difficult to communicate to other people.

13-3 Knowledge Management in Marketing[3]

Knowledge management has many applications throughout the business world, from airline yield management to transactional fraud detection to control of national power grids.[4] Marketers are interested in a narrower set of activities that focus on integrating front- and back-office services and delivering information to customer service personnel and decision makers when and where they need it. They are concerned about the customer experience and realize they must deliver it seamlessly through multiple channels at times and places demanded by the customer. This requires marshalling all the resources of the enterprise to create usable knowledge from the multiple types of customer data described in Chapter 5 and the expertise of best workers. The key word here is *usable*. How do we take the ever-growing streams of customer data from all sources and fashion them into knowledge that is usable in two key ways?

- To enable human agents to do their work better, faster, and in a way that provides maximum customer satisfaction
- To create automated systems that perform at least as well as the most skilled human agent

Furthermore, how do we develop systems that encourage customers to use the most effective and cost-efficient methods of obtaining the products, services, and support they need?

automation Replacing manual tasks and processes with computers and computer-controlled equipment.

Many suppliers of software and services have at least partial technology solutions for knowledge management in applications, such as customer service and **automation** of marketing processes. There do not seem to be any enterprises that have fully implemented knowledge management solutions with the goal of providing a seamless customer experience. Many are in the process of implementing at least partial solutions, but no enterprise has yet fully achieved the goal. However, as we pointed out in the discussion of CRM in chapter 8, a vision of what such a solution would look like does exist. The desired outcome is relatively easy to visualize in a financial services setting. Let's examine a scenario that suggests how this could work. The technology is all currently available, but the automation and integration challenges are so great that few companies approach this ability to provide a seamless customer experience.

13-4 Leveraging Knowledge at a Hypothetical Bank[5]

In a number of applications, knowledge-based systems make a great deal of sense. These involve decisions that are repetitive, are made frequently, and for which data are available electronically.[6] Credit applications are a prime example. Let's construct a hypothetical scenario in which a young couple applies for their first mortgage. This scenario does not require any technology that is not currently available. However, few companies have sufficiently integrated their front-end and back-end business processes and presented them to the customer in a way that provides this type of seamless service.

13-4a The Application

Consider a hypothetical young couple—Frank and Sally—who are about to purchase their first home and want to prequalify for a mortgage. On Saturday evening, they look at Web sites of several banks and online financial services providers. In the end, however, they decide to start with the large national bank where they have individual checking accounts and a joint brokerage account. They hope their relationship with the bank will smooth the mortgage process. They fill out the application, giving basic financial information about themselves and about Sally's home-based business. They send off the application and cross their fingers, hoping for success. What they don't realize is that given all the choices consumers have, the bank's chances of converting any applicant to a mortgage customer are slim. Their bank, however, has spent the last several years building an integrated system in an attempt to make the process as quick and efficient as possible.

Figure 13-2 is an example of a screen that might be triggered for a customer in a similar situation. It gives a consolidated view of the customer's accounts with the bank—a checking account, a cash reserve account, and a managed assets account. Several services are offered on the top bar—adding another account, applying for a loan, and ordering checks. At the bottom is a link to the customer's account information so that updates can be made as needed. The bar on the left provides access to several types of information about the bank and its services. So far, this sample page is similar to personalized pages available on Web sites of many kinds. It is, in fact, another use of the technology that created your "My Backpack" screen when you purchased the electronic version of this book. Individualized customer screens display information specifically for that consumer, in this case, the course number, book link, and other data relevant to your account with Atomic Dog. This is simply a display of customer account data, configured in an easy-to-use format. Data can also be used for customer-relevant promotion as shown in Figure 13-2, where the customer is being offered a low rate of interest on a loan. The assumption is that the bank has prequalified the customer to know there is a high probability that the loan application

> **FIGURE 13-2** Customer screen with knowledge-based component.

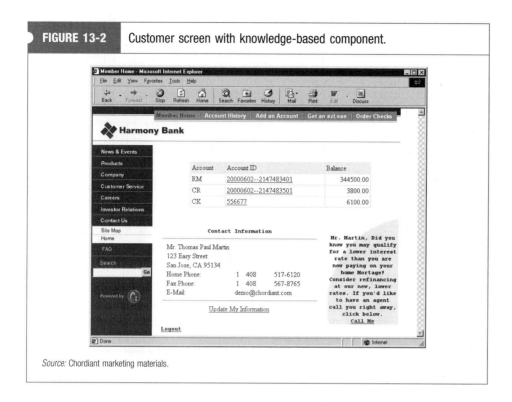

Source: Chordiant marketing materials.

would be accepted. Otherwise, the offer is a waste and may do more harm than good to the customer relationship. There is a Call Me link at the bottom of the text box so that the customer can use live chat to request more information. That makes it easy for the customer to take action on the offer.

The contents of the screen show that the bank has considerable information about the customer and is using it in ways that have a good chance of being productive. The bank has prepared a polite greeting for this hypothetical customer when he arrives at the Web site. Beyond that, it demonstrates respect for his business by recognizing his status as a customer and offering both standard and targeted services that are appropriate to his situation.

13-4b The Response

Imagine that the door has been opened courteously via an online contact. Now the bank's task is to persuade the customer to walk through it. In the case of the mortgage application scenario, this means being responsive to Frank and Sally's application.

So assume that the bank is able to recognize them as customers, quickly assess their potential value, and reply accordingly. The application with the relevant financial information is processed through the bank's knowledge management system. It identifies them as customers who individually maintain substantial minimum balances. The joint savings account where the down payment for their house resides is also present on their consolidated balance sheet. In addition, the knowledge portal recognized Sally's business as a commercial customer. And finally, the application shows that they are looking for a substantial mortgage.

Frank and Sally are categorized as "moderate value, high growth potential" based on the data the bank has. The system automatically pulls a current credit report on the couple, and it returns a high credit score. All together the data identify them as valuable customers. Two actions are taken immediately on that Saturday night. First, a personalized sitelet is constructed for them with information like that in Figure 13-2. This goes a step further because it is a Web page that contains their name in the URL and has links to all basic information, such as the bank's FAQs about mortgage applications.

It also has links to all relevant documentation, including their application. Second, their value justifies a live customer service representative. Her name is Jessie, and a button that opens a live chat with her is added to the sitelet. The bank has found this to be useful in both customer conversion and retention. All this is done automatically, using many applications, all relying on event-driven software. In this case, the trigger is the mortgage application, which activates a series of decision rules.

In this case, we can see two decision rules in action:

- *If* a customer of low to moderate value is applying for a conventional mortgage, *then* send automatic e-mail response MAC1. The automatic e-mail identified might be a personalized e-mail that greets the customer courteously by name, thanks him or her for completing the application, and gives a time frame for notification of loan approval. The copy of the e-mail message is written, identified by number, and stored in a file to be retrieved as needed. The customer's name from the appropriate box on the form is dropped into the e-mail message, and the automatic reply is sent almost immediately after the form is received. Everything is standard except the applicant's name.

template A document structure into which content can be dropped.

Software firms refer to these as **templates**—prepared documents into which personalizing information and targeted offers can be inserted. The decision rules specify what the insertions will look like.

In Frank and Sally's case, a different and more personalized response was triggered.

- *If* a high-potential customer is applying for a large mortgage, *then* send automatic e-mail response MAJ3. This e-mail contains the URL for the personalized sitelet and emphasizes the contact information for Jessie, the live customer service rep. At the same time, it updates Jessie's customer log with the name and account number of the newly assigned customer.

13-4c The Reaction

work flow An automated system that electronically routes documents to the next person in the process.

Although the bank's knowledge-driven **work flow** was hard at work, Frank and Sally watched a celebratory movie and went to bed early to prepare for a day of house hunting on Sunday. Before leaving the house, Sally checked the couple's e-mail account. To her surprise, the e-mail from the bank was there, welcoming their application and giving the URL to their sitelet. Frank and Sally are both impressed with the speed and efficiency with which the bank accepted their application. By the time they return home late that evening, there is an e-mail from Jessie, also automatically generated, thanking them for their application and expressing willingness to assist in any way she can.

The next day Jessie follows with an e-mail that tells Frank and Sally exactly what supporting documentation and financial information is needed to complete their application. They can post all the information directly to their sitelet, speeding the process and making it more accurate. Jessie wrote this e-mail herself, but she was guided in its construction by the bank's knowledge management system. It retrieved all the data the bank had about the couple, matched it against what was needed in the application process, and specified only data that the bank did not already possess in any of its customer divisions. This prevented Frank and Sally from having to provide information they had already supplied in other dealings with the bank.

13-4d The Automated Work Flow

collaborative Working together; often refers to software that supports people working together over time and distance.

In addition to corresponding with Frank and Sally, the work flow system automatically identifies tasks that must be performed, assigns responsibility and due dates for each task, and establishes a **collaborative** database file that can be accessed by all bank personnel who have an assigned role in processing the application. The documents in the database are automatically updated whenever a task is performed, and all participants have access to up-to-date information about the process.

The automated system, called a work flow, speeds the process, reduces errors inherent in manual data entry and processing of forms, and provides a transparent process that can be viewed by all participants. It is a method for accomplishing necessary tasks in a quick and orderly manner, and it also communicates important information to all involved.

Figure 13-3 shows a high-level view of a work flow for this process. It is high level because it gives an overview of the complete work flow, not the details of each component. For example, "Automated review of customer history" probably requires only a few steps. The nature of the application (mortgage) and the data submitted (Frank and Sally's employment history and financial data) activate the necessary decision rules to specify the data needed. For instance, whether Frank and Sally have overdraft protection on their personal checking accounts is probably not important; that Sally has a commercial account with the bank is. At each step in the mortgage approval process, a set of decision rules determines the actions to be taken and the nature of communications to Frank and Sally. This appears to be a relatively simple process, but specifying all the decision rules—getting each rule correct and being sure there is a rule to cover every feasible situation—is demanding.

When the application is complete and at least a minimal amount of the necessary documentation has been submitted, the loan approval process is triggered. This is a financial process, not a marketing one. It is also a back-end process, not a customer-facing one, although the result of the process certainly affects the customer. The loan approval process is a complex one with many steps to be completed. For instance, one separate and identifiable step is verification of the applicant's employment and salary. It also triggers other subprocesses. For example, checking the applicant's credit rating may involve several steps, including getting account information and releases from the applicant, obtaining a report from a credit rating agency, checking with the applicant's landlord, and thoroughly examining the applicant's record on all accounts held with the bank. Finance's main objective is to protect the bank against credit risk; marketing's is to grant as many loans as possible. The design of a process that provides the best possible result from both perspectives is important. Efficient functioning of this step in the process is important to marketing, but it is the responsibility of finance.

13-4e The Question

As the work flow continues with the automated process, Frank and Sally have found a house they like and are thinking about specific mortgage terms. They wonder whether they should pay 2 points in return for a lower interest rate. It is too late in the evening for live chat, so they e-mail Jessie. The next day, they receive a reply with an answer to their specific question and a link to the rate calculator on the bank's site. Jessie offers to make an appointment for live chat if they need it. Frank can participate from work and Sally from her home office if they need to engage in a three-way conversation. This can be quicker and more effective than a stream of e-mails in some instances.

Frank and Sally are a young couple with straightforward financial requirements. Jessie has experience with older couples who have more complex needs. In one instance, she was able to bring a financial planning expert into the live chat to advise a retired couple on structuring a mortgage within their existing estate plan. She is proud of the system the bank has established that allows her to meet complex customer needs, often in real time.

The work flow graphic in Figure 13-3 illustrates the many types of dialog involved in this particular work flow. A great deal of it is electronic, from the time Frank and Sally enter the Web site and complete a mortgage application to the use of a personalized sitelet to provide a complete overview of the process to their e-mail communication with Jessie. Much of it is automatic, with each event triggering an update to their sitelet. However, there are points in the process where other types of communication are warranted and that should be built into the process.

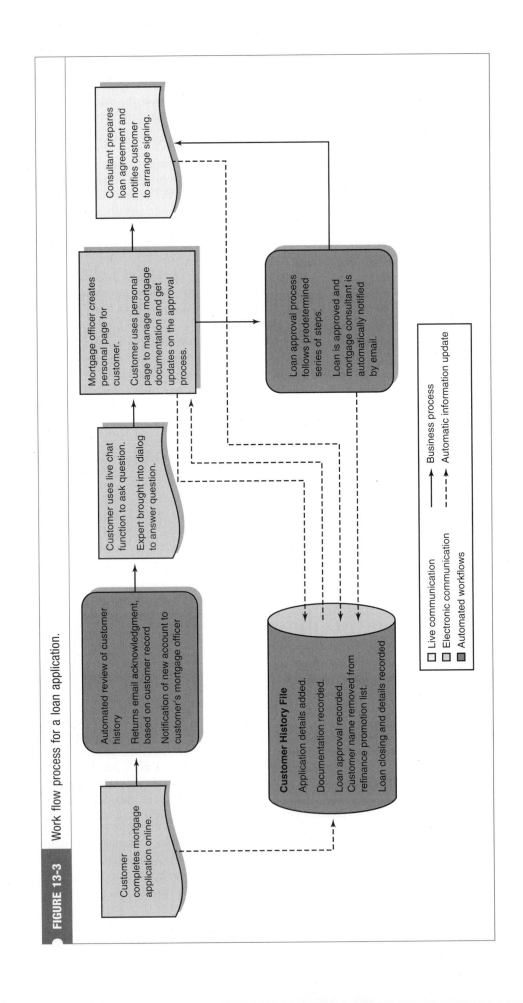

FIGURE 13-3 Work flow process for a loan application.

Customer completes mortgage application online.

Automated review of customer history

Returns email acknowledgment, based on customer record

Notification of new account to customer's mortgage officer

Customer uses live chat function to ask question.

Expert brought into dialog to answer question.

Mortgage officer creates personal page for customer.

Customer uses personal page to manage mortgage documentation and get updates on the approval process.

Consultant prepares loan agreement and notifies customer to arrange signing.

Loan approval process follows predetermined series of steps.

Loan is approved and mortgage consultant is automatically notified by email.

Customer History File

Application details added.

Documentation recorded.

Loan approval recorded.

Customer name removed from refinance promotion list.

Loan closing and details recorded

☐ Live communication

☐ Electronic communication

☐ Automated workflows

→ Business process

- - - → Automatic information update

336

13-4f The Loan Approval

With that in mind, let's conclude the scenario with a positive result for Frank and Sally.

About a week later, while Jessie is out of town attending a conference, she gets a message on her cell phone that the mortgage has been approved. At the first opportunity, she takes out her laptop computer and reviews the status of all the key events. She verifies that Frank and Sally have received the loan amount and the interest rate they requested and that all the documentation is in order. That evening she places a phone call to Frank and Sally to offer her personal congratulations on the approval of their loan. All the details are shown on their sitelet and ready to be shared with their real estate agent. The loan agreement will be available in about 2 days, and if they wish, they can use verified digital signatures instead of having to physically come to the bank to sign the papers. Frank and Sally are please with the speed and efficiency of the process from beginning to satisfactory ending. Another bond of loyalty has been forged between them and the bank.

According to CRM gurus Don Peppers and Martha Rogers, this scenario portrays many of the characteristics customers are searching for in dealing with financial services institutions. One of their studies identified the major factors that create customer loyalty in the financial services sector:

- *Tailoring products to customers' needs.* Frank and Sally were offered the size and type of mortgage that met their personal requirements.

- *Providing a personal contact.* Frank and Sally could do most of what they needed to do 24/7 through the personalized sitelet. However, when they needed live assistance, Jessie was there to answer questions or find someone who could.

- *Anticipating customers' needs.* As soon as Frank and Sally submitted the application, the system was at work to determine the appropriate communications style and the best offer that could be made to them. The personalized sitelet provided one centralized contact point where needs and progress could be monitored by the applicants and all the bank personnel who were involved in the process. Frank and Sally did not expect this kind of individualized communications. Exceeding customers' expectations is a hallmark of superior services marketing.

- *Making customers feel appreciated.*[7] Throughout the process, Frank and Sally received all the information that was relevant to their application and were treated with the respect due established customers of the bank.

Remember that at this time, the scenario is hypothetical. This kind of customer care is still a work in progress at leading enterprises and only a wistful aspiration at others. The technology does exist, however, to do everything in the scenario. The barriers exist in other areas. These kinds of systems—whether they are decision support

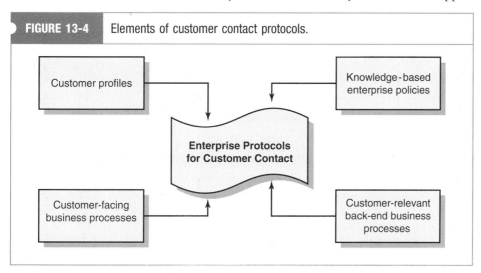

> **FIGURE 13-4** Elements of customer contact protocols.

systems that help human agents perform better or automated systems that improve internal processes or offer self-service to customers—represent organizational change, which is always difficult because it changes the way people do their jobs. They also require integrating disparate data and information systems from around the enterprise. Major integration projects are technologically challenging. They are time-consuming and often very expensive. They also require the cooperation of groups within the enterprise who may be accustomed to working separately, not **collaboratively**. So as we discuss the steps in creating knowledge-based customer **protocols** within marketing (Figure 13-4), recognize that these systems can have profound organizational impact.

protocol A set of rules that govern the sending and receiving of data.

13-5 Developing Customer Contact Protocols

The field of knowledge management is so new that it has no commonly accepted vocabulary, so we need to define terms with care. The key terms used in explaining the concept of customer contact protocols are as follows:

- *Protocol.* Think of a protocol as a detailed set of guidelines for using knowledge from several sources to provide the products, services, and support customers need. This is broader than the technical usage, which according to TechEncyclopedia refers to "rules governing transmitting and receiving of data."[8] It is closer to the way scientists use the term to mean a detailed set of procedures to be used in conducting a scientific experiment or procedure.

- *Policies.* The term *policy* is being used in the strategy sense, as a definition of how the enterprise intends to treat a specific group of stakeholders, in this case customers.

- *Back end.* This term has been used throughout the text to refer to the internal, non–customer-facing systems of the enterprise.

- *Business processes.* Davenport and Short offer a definition that illustrates the difficulty of pinning down this concept. They define businesses processes as "a set of logically related tasks performed to achieve a defined business outcome." They go on to say, "A set of processes forms a business system—the way in which a business unit, or a collection of units, carries out its business."[9]

Although the definition makes sense, it doesn't do a great deal to help us identify a business process. Davenport and Short go on to give criteria and some examples. The criteria are, first, that each process must have "customers," either external or internal. Second, processes usually cross functional (marketing and accounting) or organizational (manufacturer and supplier) boundaries. Their examples include the following:

- Developing a new product
- Ordering goods from a supplier
- Creating a marketing plan
- Processing and paying an insurance claim
- Writing a proposal for a government contract

Ordering goods from a supplier, for example, typically involves multiple organizations and functions. For example, the end user, purchasing, receiving, accounts payable, and supplier organization are all participants. The user could be viewed as the process's customer. The process outcome could be either the creation of the order or, perhaps more usefully, the actual receipt of the goods by the user.[10]

This discussion indicates that there are core business processes, such as new product development, that are present in most enterprises. Certain processes are also present only when the business model requires them. For instance, if a merchant does business only from a retail store, she does not need a fulfillment process. On the other hand, if her business model includes a transactional Web site, she needs a fulfillment process that includes a picking (locating items in stock), packing (in shipping containers), and shipping (delivering to carrier) subsystem. The fulfillment system would be linked to the enterprise's inventory management system, a core business process.

For a given business, what the business processes are, what specific elements and subsystems each contains, and what the linkages are between various systems are empirical questions. If the processes have not been documented, it can be done by interviewing the people who perform the tasks at each step in the process, identifying the elements of the process, and specifying how the elements connect to one another. The output is usually a flowchart of the process. The work flow diagram in Figure 13-3 is an example of a sales process for a residential mortgage loan, for example.

The definition and empirical documentation of businesses processes is not a trivial matter. Processes have become the key unit of analysis for improving quality and for implementing automated systems. It is not the individual step in the process that is most important; it is the smooth functioning of the entire process that is critical for success. Think about it this way: no matter how well the Web site and the customer care systems in the banking scenario function, if the loan approval function breaks down or presents endless hassles to the customer, the overall experience is not going to be satisfying. In the scenario presented in this chapter, Frank and Sally might have decided to do business with another institution if the loan approval process got bogged down. At the very least, they might not have come out of the process feeling any loyalty to the bank. Consequently, it is critical for marketing and finance to work together to make sure the whole loan process is seamless and satisfying to the customer.

Let's now look at how these concepts apply in the construction of consumer contact protocols.

13-5a Constructing Customer Profiles

We have used the term *customer* **profile** often throughout this text, and we all understand that we mean a description of an individual or a segment of consumers. Let's look briefly at a detailed profile to understand how profiles are constructed and used in the online environment.

profile In marketing and marketing research, a description of a person or segment.

Table 13-1 shows a profile for John Golfer, a hypothetical customer of a golfing equipment Web site. Because it is identified, we can assume that it came from registration on the site. There are several things to keep in mind about this profile:

- The data are in ranges in typical marketing research style. There is no reason for the marketer to know that Mr. Golfer made $82,521 last year, and he probably wouldn't divulge the information precisely anyway.

- It is already relatively long, and there are other blocks of information the marketer would like to have. Chief among those are his media use habits. Does he read any golfing magazines? What other magazines and newspapers? What about his Internet use behavior—amount, type, related sites visited?

- Even without additional data, this profile stretches the amount a customer should be invited to provide at one time without major incentives. It is important to ask for only a small amount of information initially and to ask for more as the relationship develops. This requires careful setting of information priorities.

- Mr. Golfer was very cooperative. He answered a lot of questions. Did he decline to provide an address and telephone number? Or did the Web site not ask those questions, preferring to fill them in when he makes a purchase instead of arousing suspicion about its motives for asking?

TABLE 13-1	Hypothetical Profile of an Identified Golfer

Demographic Characteristics

Gender	Male
Age	45 to 55
Income	$75,000 to $100,000
Occupation	Marketing Director
Marital Status	Married
Children Under 18 in Household	2
Geographic Area	Midwest

Contact Information

E-Mail Address	JGolfer@ISP.net
Mailing Address	_____
	_____
Home Telephone Number	_____

Golfing Behavior

Number of Rounds per Month	3 or fewer
Member of Private Club	No
Total Golf Spending per Year	Under $1,000
Average Score	Above 100
Number of Years an Active Golfer	More than 20

Related Behavior

Number of Out-of State Trips per Year	15 to 20
Business	15 to 20
Pleasure	1 to 5
Number of Trips to Golf Resort per Year	Less than 1
Frequency of Golfing on Business Trips	Sometimes
Frequency of Golfing on Pleasure Trips	Almost Never
Other Activities (1 to 2 times per month)	
Tennis	Yes
Handball	No
Squash	Yes
Swimming	No
Running	No
Baseball/Softball	Yes
Soccer	No
Basketball	No
Other	No

Source Data

Acquisition Type	Web site registration
Referral Source	Banner advertisement

Contact Data

Monthly Newsletter	Yes
Promotional Offers	Yes
Offers from Partners/Affiliates	No

- More generally, what about the problem of missing data? Three approaches are commonly taken by marketers:

1. Be patient. As just suggested, some data can be obtained over time in the normal course of business. Also, the marketer can ask for additional data at a time when its relevance is clear.

2. The marketer can model from his or her own data and supply ("infer") missing data. Assume for a moment that Mr. Golfer did not fill in the travel

data—how many trips, business trips, personal trips, golf resorts, and the likelihood of playing golf while traveling for business and pleasure.

In order to make inferences about the data, the marketer must take the following steps. First, identify the segment into which Mr. Golfer falls. Let's assume he falls into the "occasional/low value" segment based on golfing frequency, amount spent, and no private club membership.

The model would then use other variables to infer his travel behavior. For example, members of this segment who hold a title of director or vice president and make between $75,000 and $100,000 have a 10% probability of taking fewer than ten trips per year, a 20% probability of taking ten to fifteen trips per year, a 50% probability of taking fifteen to twenty business trips per year, and a 20% probability of taking more than twenty trips per year. The fifteen to twenty trips per year category has the highest likelihood of being correct for Mr. Golfer, and we could insert that data into Mr. Golfer's profile. It is important to label it as an inference, rather than customer-supplied data, but it is now there to be used for analytics or to drive marketing programs. In this case, the inference "got it right," but that is often not the case.

What if Mr. Golfer had not given his age, and we went through the same modeling process to estimate it? Assume that Mr. Golfer is actually 38 years old and the model predicted 55 to 65. We might then send him a promotional e-mail for a new "mature adults" golfing community being built in his area. At best, his regard for the Web site goes down, because they are not successfully targeting their communications. At worst, he is insulted and decides not to do business with the Web site.

Actually, the model should not have made such a bad prediction if the data item "2 children under 18 in the household" was also available. Models, however, do not always get it right, and the marketer must decide whether he is willing to assume the risk of a wrong answer. The alternative is to exclude Mr. Golfer from any age-related promotion, and the marketer usually wants to make his or her list as large as possible. Whether to use inferential data or leave the item blank is not a straightforward choice, and the marketer should make it with care.

3. The third option is similar, but it uses data from third-party data suppliers. For example, Internet behaviors might be important to a program being planned. The site does not have the data and does not think asking for additional data from its registered users is feasible at the moment. It might choose to purchase data from one of the suppliers of panel data discussed in Chapter 6. The panel has extensive background data on its members and has a good chance of providing a close match of the Web site's profile data. For example, the site might be interested in purchasing Internet use data for golfers who play more than six times per month and belong to a private country club. The question is whether the panel will be able to produce a sufficiently large number (sample) of golfers who have these characteristics to give a stable estimate of the desired Internet behaviors. The issues of sample size and stability of estimations require the attention of a statistician who is skilled in sampling applications. The practical fact is that if the characteristics are relatively broad so that they apply to numerous golfers, a panel of reasonable size should be able to produce a satisfactory sample and provide data that meet the marketer's needs.

Profile data, then, are one important element of a customer contact protocol. The profile may be used directly, as when a golfer requests information about whether to have a beloved club repaired or whether it should be replaced. Sadly, our Mr. Golfer is a low-value customer, and he will probably be referred to FAQs and a self-help database. The data in the profile are also used for analytics that deepen the information about the site's customer base and to plan and execute marketing programs, as just described.

However, do not let this description lead you to visualize marketers who have hundreds of thousands of customer profiles stored in their databases. First, although data storage is not exorbitantly expensive, costs begin to add up when this much data are stored. Second, it is no more expensive to create a new profile from stored data when it is needed than it is to update an existing profile, and there may be less chance of error. So think of this, again, as a template—the profile items are specified, and the actual data are filled in at the time of use. This is the preferable solution, although when profiles are needed for live interaction, it puts heavy demands on the dependability and speed of internal systems.

Profiles represent an important use of data and are essential to the development of a knowledge-based marketing system. The key to advanced systems, however, is the incorporation of knowledge into the system.

13-6 Embedding Expertise in a Knowledge-Based Protocol

In order to understand what needs to be done and how, we must return to the concepts of explicit and tacit knowledge.

13-6a Explicit Knowledge

intranet An enterprise Web site that serves the needs of employees.

Explicit knowledge exists in written form in policy manuals, training materials, handbooks and guides, product specification sheets, price lists, and other corporate material. The steps are first to locate all relevant material and then to incorporate it in the correct format into the system. Corporate **intranets** (internal networks) are very helpful in locating relevant material, because much of it has already been posted there. The interviews that document the process can also identify what the relevant explicit knowledge is and how the workers access it.

Incorporating this qualitative information into information systems is a challenging but reasonably well understood technological task. For automated systems it must be stored in databases in appropriate formats and linked to templates. For instance, a Web page or a template would be built to display product information. The product specifications would then be stored in formats dictated by the display template.

Figure 13-5 illustrates the concept. The page lists all 101 phones that are available in the Boston market at a particular time. It allows the user to select price levels, physical dimensions, operation time, carrier, brand, and many other features. This is a great deal of data, but it can be captured, stored in a product database, and called out as required by the user's selections. Notice that those selections create a behavioral profile for the user, although they do not request personal data. Data are retrieved and displayed on the basis of the profile. Maintaining a database of this size and complexity is obviously a tall order. However, it does not require the use of knowledge as we have defined it to help the cell phone purchaser in making a decision.

Displaying qualitative information in a template—and keeping it functioning and totally accurate—is a great deal of work, but it is not leading-edge technology. When you let visitors ask their own questions, instead of giving them a very structured choice, it gets more complicated. Figure 13-6 shows two Web sites that in their own ways incorporate what might be considered tacit information.

13-6b Tacit Knowledge

Ask Jeeves, now Ask.com, is a well-known search engine that allows users to make their queries in natural language. In Figure 13-6 a user asked, "What is an environmentally friendly building?" The results are displayed in typical search format

FIGURE 13-5 Cell phone selector page.

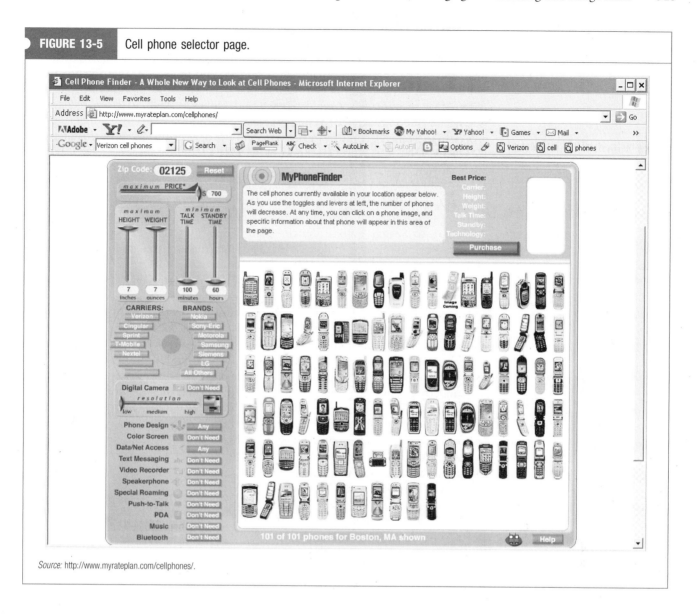

Source: http://www.myrateplan.com/cellphones/.

FIGURE 13-6 Different kinds of search results.

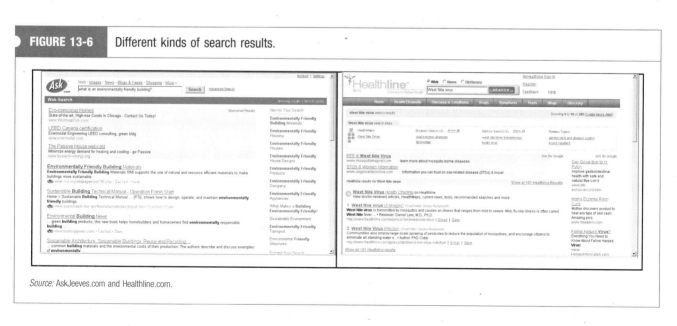

Source: AskJeeves.com and Healthline.com.

as discussed in Chapter 7. Stop and think for a moment about how complex it is to take spoken language and translate it into code that a computer can understand and use to produce structured search results. Applications of natural language processing can be found in many devices and activities, ranging from an automobile telematics system that recognizes spoken language and replies in kind to voice recognition systems for customer service to computer-based learning systems. As natural language processing systems become more accurate and the devices that support them become affordable, you can expect to see more applications. The Ask Jeeves results page has a relatively new feature, seen on the left-hand bar. It allows the user to "Narrow Your Search" or "Expand Your Search." That's not entirely different from what you see on other search engines. However, these two sections are not keyword driven, as they are on other search engines. Instead they are categorized on the basis of related concepts. According to Search Engine Watch, "Ask Jeeves uses clustering technology that identifies 'communities' on the web that have information related to your query, and pulls the meaningful concepts from those communities into the lists of suggestions."[11] Although the tool is automated, there is clearly an element of human knowledge and perhaps even judgment built into it.

Figure 13-6 shows a Web site into which human knowledge is built in a different fashion. Healthline is one of the growing number of specialized (vertical) search engines. As the name suggests, it has a number of useful features, from searchable images to the "health map" feature shown at the bottom left of the screen. The very simplicity and straightforwardness of its presentation camouflage the sophistication of the underlying information structure. Health-related information is somewhat difficult to search for and even more difficult to understand when you find it. Much of it is presented using medical terminology, which has the advantage of being precise but the great disadvantage of often being incomprehensible to the layperson. Quoting Search Engine Watch again, "Healthline addressed that problem by mapping a medical taxonomy over hundreds of common lay terms for diseases, medications and other health related terms. When you search, lay terms are translated and relevant medical information is presented."[12] To do that—and to get it right—requires great knowledge and precision, both of which have to be built into the search engine in order to produce the correct answer to the question.

13-6c Querying the Knowledge Base

query In information systems, requesting information from a database.

Questions, or **queries**, to a database represent a continuum from highly structured to totally unstructured. Marketing research and other information applications identify three basic types of questions—structured, semistructured, and unstructured. Consider these examples of questions of each type.[13] As you do so, think about the implications of providing an automated answer to the question. Will it be simple retrieval of data from a database, or will it involve the application of human expertise to understanding the question, identifying the appropriate answer, or both?

structured questions In marketing research, a question that can be answered by choosing one of a prespecified set of responses.

1. *A highly **structured question** asked by a sales manager.* "Which products did customers in the Northeast region purchase most frequently last month?" This requires that the correct data items for the correct period of time be retrieved from the data repository. Data warehouses include tools that permit this type of natural-language query, dictionaries for defining terms, and report formats for returning the information to the manager (e.g., table, bar chart, pie chart). There is not much to define here; "customers," and "last month" are standard. However, what does the questioner mean by "Which products?" Two, five, one hundred? The system would return its own query about the number of products to be included in the report and produce the report based on the answer.

2. *A semistructured question asked by a marketing manager.* "What is the next product we should offer to the low-value/occasional golfer segment?" Given

that the questioner has specified the customer segment, several definitions or specifications are still needed. The most important is the criteria that determine the next addition to the product line. Is it only the highest potential profit? Is the company interested in expanding its offerings to women, who make up a growing number of segment members? Does "next product we should offer" refer to an existing product around which we will construct an offer? Or does it mean what kind of new product should we develop?

Just specifying the terms in the question does not resolve all issues, however. Does the firm have a profitability model of past offers that permits the identification of not only the most profitable offers but also the factors that contributed to profitability in the order of their impact? If so, would it be reported as model output (probably the result of a regression model in this case), forcing the decision maker to interpret the results for himself or herself? Or would it be produced as a text report that explains the meaning of the model output? Building an offer profitability model is no small task for the statisticians, and the difficulty of building a model pales beside the difficulty of constructing a report template that can accurately report the results of even a straightforward statistical model.

3. *An unstructured question from the marketing vice president.* "How effective was our last marketing campaign?" An unstructured question requires extensive definition and specification of terms. By effectiveness, do we mean profitability, number of new customers acquired, improvement in brand image, or what? Producing an answer would also require a different model for each type of marketing campaign. Each model would require revision depending on whether the variable to be predicted was profitability, customer acquisition, or something else. A less easily quantified dependent variable like "improvement in brand image" might require extensive additional model building.

Publicly available sites such as Ask Jeeves (Ask.com) and Healthline show that progress is being made in making knowledge available through natural-language queries. More progress is probably being made in corporations, but they are often unwilling to divulge information because they see these systems as being a foundation for future competitive advantage.

If all this complexity exists in the realm of explicit knowledge, what about tacit knowledge?

13-6d Capturing Tacit Knowledge

An initial step in constructing systems that incorporate tacit knowledge is to collect it directly from the people who possess it. This is, at best, time-consuming and expensive. At worst, it may be next to impossible. Some experts may have difficulty articulating what they actually do.

One study found that in complex systems, no single expert fully grasped the components and their interrelationships with one another. They identified a number of reasons for the incompleteness or inaccuracy of the information collected from experts:

- Some parts of the system may not be visible and therefore are not part of the worker's expertise.

- Some details may be known to other participants in the system but not to the expert being interviewed.

- The expert may find it impossible to verbalize tacit knowledge in a meaningful way.

- It may be desirable to withhold some knowledge, either in the interest of control over the job or because it is counter to organizational policies.
- The expert may make adjustments to situations without even realizing it and therefore be unable to report them as knowledge.[14]

If it is necessary to study multiple experts in order to obtain tacit information, techniques developed by social psychologists and organizational behaviorists can be used. They involve extensive observation of the work group, developing a code for each task or activity, and then using those codes to map the work processes. These methods are time and labor intensive and require highly trained observers to collect the data.

Pentland and Rueter use the term *organizational routines* to describe the way in which work processes are structured in a task unit. They go on to say:

> Routines are difficult to study because they are essentially complex patterns of social action. Our tools for characterizing the variable properties of static objects are well developed, but our tools for characterizing the sequential structure of patterns of action are not.[15]

Their research, however, demonstrates the ability to capture work processes in a telephone call center help desk with considerable specificity. It seems likely that marketers will be forced to turn to some technique for mapping communications networks and group dynamics in order to fully capture tacit knowledge. It does not appear, however, that many organizational resources have been employed in this effort in recent years. The implication is that marketers have made considerable progress in capturing explicit knowledge and transferring it to human agents and automated systems in usable formats. We are, however, only on the threshold of being able to capture and utilize tacit knowledge.

Let's, then, end this chapter with a discussion of an existing marketing application that makes use of many elements of knowledge management discussed in this chapter—automated e-mail systems. This type of system is a clear indication of how far we have already come in embedding knowledge in the most advanced marketing applications.

13-7 Automated E-Mail Campaign and Response Systems

We discussed in other chapters the extent to which e-mail is growing, as both an acquisition and a retention technique. We also pointed out that e-mail provides a cost-effective communications channel for marketers, although it is not the cheapest of all those available. One reason for the growing use and cost-effectiveness of the e-mail channel is the ability to automate many types of e-mail messages. Table 13-2 summarizes ways in which knowledge is currently being used to make e-mail more effective and more efficient. No single vendor offers all these functions, but they are all available and in use by high-volume e-mail marketers. As the cost of the technology has come down, they have also become available to small to medium-sized business from software suppliers who specialize in smaller volumes.

Outbound campaigns can benefit from automated construction of permission-based databases that are automatically updated when people subscribe or ask to be taken off the list or when e-mails are returned. Many kinds of rules-based personalization are offered. Rules can be based on customer knowledge, as discussed in earlier parts of this chapter. They can also be based on previously successful offers or

TABLE 13-2	Knowledge-Based E-Mail Functionality

Outbound E-Mail Campaigns	**Inbound Response Management**
Build permission-based e-mail databases	Intelligent routing and queuing of messages
Segment databases on the basis of profiles	Automated personalized acknowledgments based on message content
Manage subscriptions, unsubscribes, and returned e-mails (bounce-backs)	Tag messages that require special attention
Personalize e-mail messages	Suggested responses to human agents
Personalize offers based on customer profiles and product inventory levels	Systems that learn from responses made by expert agents
Offer targeted discounts based on profiles, inventory levels, and product classes	
Target e-mail campaigns based on customer profiles	Construction of response templates
Collect behavioral data, such as amount spent on last purchase or category of product purchased	Reporting by message type, message volume, agent productivity, and other variables in real time
Pretest e-mail offers and messages	
Send triggered messages (e.g., seasonality, customer events such as birthdays)	Use data mining tools to analyze trends in customer communications
Include targeted ads	
Analyze and report in real time	

Sources: http://www.doubleclick.com, http://www.siebel.com, http://www.teradata.com, and http://www.egain.com.

even on inventory levels by product category. Rules can also drive targeting to individuals or customer segments, event-based messages, and inclusion of targeted advertising in e-mail messages. E-mail campaign products are available that allow for quick testing of e-mail campaigns and reporting results by many categories of performance metrics, as discussed in Chapter 11.

Outbound campaigns go out in batches—small for short lists or highly targeted campaigns to very large for messages with broad applicability. Inbound e-mail comes in individually. It includes everything from customer questions and service requests to responses to marketer-generated e-mails. The management issues for inbound e-mail are therefore somewhat different, but once again knowledge can make the process quicker and more accurate.

Inbound functionality includes the ability to route e-mail to the most qualified agent and to place it in the **queue** of messages based on its urgency. It can add a special tag if the message requires special attention, perhaps from a supervisor. This is done by special software that uses natural-language processing capability. The software recognizes words and phrases and examines types of words and message construction. This type of software can make suggestions to human agents about appropriate responses, making them more productive. Some of the software products can "learn" from the responses of expert human agents. Vendors can also supply automatic response templates that can be filled in based on the content and nature of the message. The inbound e-mail management software also provides sophisticated real-time reporting capabilities by message type, e-mail volume, agent productivity, and other identified metrics. Some use keyword search functionality to categorize messages by content and analyze trends in customer messages.

By now you are now well aware that none of this automation happens by accident. It requires both extensive data and sophisticated analysis to make it a reality. It also requires that marketers make careful choices between entirely automated processes, human agents supported by extensive knowledge bases, and judicious combinations of both.

queue A line of objects or people.

Summary

The emergence of the Internet as a significant business channel has increased the pressure on marketers to develop strategies, execute programs, and provide customer care with speed and precision. Throughout the text, we have emphasized that it is essential for all these activities to be information driven. We have also discussed myriad ways of collecting data on the Internet and some of the analytics necessary to transform it into useful information to support marketing decisions.

In this chapter, we take the concept a step further: to the transformation of information into marketing-relevant knowledge. This knowledge is necessary to make human agents, especially those who have direct customer contact, more proficient and more productive. It is also a fundamental part of customer-facing automated marketing systems.

To create knowledge from information, we must add human expertise to information systems. This requires the incorporation of explicit knowledge that already exists in the written documentation of the enterprise. This is detailed and demanding work, but systems that contain explicit enterprise knowledge are at work in many organizations today. The next level is to incorporate tacit knowledge—the know-how of individual skilled workers.

Tacit knowledge has usually not been documented, and it is a difficult thing to do. Even the workers who are most skilled at performing a specific task may be unwilling or unable to verbalize exactly what they do. Enterprises do not yet seem to be incorporating substantial amounts of tacit knowledge into information systems.

This chapter illustrates that marketers can use knowledge-based systems for a variety of internal purposes. Technology is available to incorporate knowledge into customer-facing systems in many ways. As yet, few enterprises have extensive knowledge-based customer-facing systems. Great effort is required to build systems to support specific processes such as a mortgage loan application. Much of the effort involves integrating many formerly disparate information systems within the enterprise so that they work smoothly together to provide a seamless customer experience.

Separate applications, however, are being used, often with considerable success. Automated e-mail systems are arguably the best example in marketing at present. They require both sophisticated technology and a great deal of customer-relevant knowledge to perform well. Automated e-mail may be a harbinger of what we can expect from other knowledge-based marketing systems in the future.

Quiz

1. Which of the following are true statements about knowledge?
   a. Knowledge includes both information and human expertise.
   b. Knowledge is produced by analyzing primary and secondary research data.
   c. *Knowledge* and *information* are essentially synonymous terms.

2. _____ is knowledge that can be articulated and communicated to others.
   a. Empirical
   b. Explicit
   c. Tacit

3. For marketers, the benefits of knowledge management systems include _____.
   a. creating automated systems that perform at least as well as the most skilled workers
   b. replacing human agents
   c. creating systems that are indistinguishable from human agents

4. A mortgage application is a good candidate for an automated knowledge management system because _____.
   a. data can be made available electronically
   b. it involves a great deal of repetitive processing
   c. both a and b

5. Which of the following is a true statement about the hypothetical mortgage application process described in the chapter?
   a. Frank and Sally are required to submit all the necessary data with their application.
   b. Some parts of the process are completely automated, and some support the work of human agents.
   c. Because the loan is a legal document, all parties must have paper copies.

6. Which of the following are true statements about work flows?
   a. Work flows are most useful in automating back-end processes.
   b. Work flows provide a parallel information flow for physical flows of goods.
   c. Work flows improve the accuracy of processes.

7. Customer contact protocols include _____.
   a. back-end processes
   b. business strategies
   c. policies that are based on strategies

8. Elements of customer profiles may include _____.
   a. product-related behaviors
   b. data identifying source of customer acquisition
   c. both of the above

9. Which of the following is *not* a true statement about knowledge-based policies?
   a. It is easier to incorporate explicit knowledge than tacit knowledge into knowledge-based policies.
   b. Qualitative information cannot be incorporated into policies.
   c. Policies can be used to support customer interaction through automated systems and human agents.

10. Which of the following are functions that an automated e-mail management system can include?
    a. Learning from responses made by human agents
    b. Creating personalized e-mail messages
    c. Both a and b

 ## Discussion Questions

1. Be prepared to discuss how data are transformed into information and then into knowledge. Thinking about your own Internet experience, choose one specific data item that could be produced as a result of a particular interaction. Describe how it could be transformed into information for a specific marketing use and whether its usefulness could be enhanced by the addition of expertise of some kind.

2. Again thinking about your own Internet experience, can you think of a specific encounter in which information or knowledge clearly improved your interaction with a human agent? Can you think of an encounter in which the human agent lacked the information or knowledge to make your experience satisfactory? Be prepared to discuss both positive and negative experiences and what could have transformed a negative encounter into a positive one.

3. Have you had experience with automated e-mail replies? Have they been satisfactory or not? Why? Are you sure you can tell whether an e-mail is an automated reply or whether it was prepared by a human agent?

4. What do you think the future holds in terms of knowledge management and use in marketing applications?

 ## Internet Exercises

1. Choose an economic sector other than financial services. Construct a customer interaction scenario that involves seamless use of human agents and automated systems to meet the customer's needs quickly and with precision. Be specific about where information and knowledge are used in the information systems described in the scenario.

2. Using a Web site with which you are familiar, choose a customer-facing business process that is executed on the site. It could be a transaction, a customer search for information, a customer request for service, or another kind of relevant interaction. Diagram the process with as much detail as you can. Be as clear as you can about where the customer-facing process has to bring in other customer-facing or back-end processes to work successfully.

3. Using a site referenced in the chapter, or one that you find yourself through a search, select an article about a recent development in knowledge management and be prepared to discuss its contents in class. The article may or may not be directly relevant to marketing. If it is not directly relevant, think about whether there may be future marketing applications of this knowledge-related concept or technique.

 ## Notes

1. http://www.apqc.org/km/. For an extensive collection of resources on knowledge management, see the page of the Business Processes Resources Center at Warwick University, http://bprc.warwick.ac.uk/.

2. http://education.yahoo.com/reference/dictionary.

3. Readers who follow technology developments will see the similarity to artificial intelligence and specifically to expert systems technologies that were the subject of intense interest a number of years ago. Knowledge management is essentially synonymous with expert systems. KM is the preferred terminology at the moment.

4. For a good overview, see Thomas H. Davenport and Jeanne G. Harris, "Automated Decision Making Comes of Age," *Sloan Management Review*, Vol. 46, No. 4, Summer 2005, pp. 83–89.

5. This scenario is based on an idea suggested in "Knowledge Management in Action: Three Scenarios," Lotus Development Corporation White Paper, January 2001, http://www.lotus.com/km. (Note: This disappeared from the Web after the Lotus site merged into IBM's.)

6. Thomas H. Davenport and Jeanne G. Harris, "Automated Decision Making Comes of Age," *Sloan Management Review*, Vol. 46, No. 4, Summer 2005, p. 84.

7. "Financial Services Institutions Lose Millions Annually in Profit Opportunities, Reports LOMA and Peppers and Rogers Group," January 15, 2002, http://www.1to1.com.

8. http://www.techweb.com/encyclopedia/.

9. Thomas H. Davenport and James E. Short, "The New Industrial Engineering: Information Technology and Business Process Redesign," *Sloan Management Review*, Vol. 31, No. 4, Summer 1990, p. 12.

10. Thomas H. Davenport and James E. Short, "The New Industrial Engineering: Information Technology and Business Process Redesign," *Sloan Management Review*, Vol. 31, No. 4, Summer 1990, p. 13.

11. Chris Sherman and Gary Price, "Ask Jeeves Serves Up New Features," Search Engine Watch, May 26, 2005, http://searchenginewatch.com/searchday/article.php/3507871.

12. Chris Sherman, "Curing Medical Disorder," SearchDay, No. 1161, October 17, 2005.

13. For an empirical study of corporate efforts in this type of information provision, see Thomas H. Davenport *et al.*, "Data to Knowledge to Results," *California Management Review*, Vol. 43, No. 2, Winter 2001, pp. 117–138.

14. Gabriel Szulanski and Sidney Winter, "Getting It Right the Second Time," *Harvard Business Review*, Reprint RO201E, January 2002, p. 64.

15. Brian T. Pentland and Henry H. Rueter, "Organizational Routines as Grammars of Action," *Administrative Science Quarterly*, Vol. 39, 1994, p. 484.

The Future—Wireless and Convergence

Chapter Fourteen

Chapter Outline

Source: © Getty

Key Terms

Learning Objectives

By the time you complete this chapter, you will be able to:

- Identify important adoption theory concepts that apply to the diffusion of technological innovations.

- Describe the environment variously called pervasive computing and ubiquitous computing.

- Discuss the basic outlines of the wireless market in the United States, Europe, and Japan.

- Identify the strategic drivers of and barriers to the adoption of wireless technology.

- Discuss the implications for mobile advertising and commerce.

- Explain the meaning and implications of digital convergence.

14-1 Introduction

In 1996, the Internet burst on public consciousness and ignited a firestorm of activity. In the intervening years, both pure-play Internet firms and traditional mass media marketers have made the Internet a key element in marketing strategies. They have done so not because the Internet is interesting technology but because it has become part of the everyday life of consumers and businesses around the globe. In the years to come, there is every reason to believe that the Internet will continue to penetrate virtually every aspect of our personal and business lives. Marketers will be continually challenged to keep up with developments and integrate them into their communications and e-commerce activities.

The purpose of this chapter is to present a perspective on two unfolding Internet developments of special importance to marketers: the related topics of the wireless Internet and converged devices that access it. In evaluating these developments, we need to keep in mind that this is an ongoing process of developing innovative new products and services and facilitating their diffusion in the marketplace. There are three key concepts from innovation and diffusion theory that we should keep uppermost in our minds as we cover this material: the adoption process, the diffusion process, and the characteristics of a product that encourage adoption.

14-2 Consumer Adoption of Innovations

The *consumer adoption process* is a generally accepted conceptualization of the stages a consumer goes through when confronted with a new product or service (Figure 14-1a) According to the adoption process, the consumer must first become aware of the product; then develop an interest in it; perform some prepurchase evaluation; and then try the product, either as a consequence of a purchase or of a marketer-sponsored promotion or incentive. Two important stages follow trial. First, the consumer must decide to purchase/continue purchasing the product, which can be behaviorally identified as adoption. A harder to discern stage is that of internalization, in which the product has become an integral part of the consumer's lifestyle. The internalization stage is particularly important in the case of technology. Products or services with a high component of technology often require that consumers undergo a substantial learning process in order for it to be used successfully. Only if consumers are willing to undertake the learning process, and only if that process is successful, is the product internalized and becomes an integral part of the consumer's life.

Closely associated is the concept of the diffusion process (Figure 14-1b) It is a communications model and as such it consists of four elements: the innovation, communication channels, time, and the social system within which the innovation is spreading. With time on the horizontal axis and number of adopters (defined as

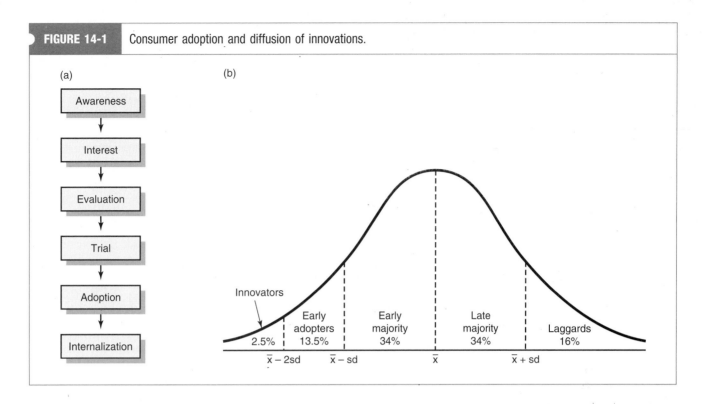

> **FIGURE 14-1**   Consumer adoption and diffusion of innovations.

(a)

Awareness

↓

Interest

↓

Evaluation

↓

Trial

↓

Adoption

↓

Internalization

(b)

Innovators

Early adopters

Early majority

Late majority

Laggards

2.5%   13.5%   34%   34%   16%

$\bar{x} - 2sd$ $\bar{x} - sd$ $\bar{x}$ $\bar{x} + sd$

first-time purchasers) on the vertical axis, the concept shows a process that is normally distributed around a population mean.

The third concept describes product characteristics that affect the ease of generating trial and adoption. These are widely accepted in the marketing literature as being:

1. relative advantage—the degree to which product benefits are perceived to be superior to those of existing products.
2. compatibility—the degree of consistency between the new product and consumer's perceptions of and behaviors toward existing members of the product category.
3. complexity—the extent to which the new product is difficult to learn to use.
4. trialability/divisibility—the extent to which the new product can be tried on a limited or modular basis.
5. observability/communicability—the degree to which the new product's benefits are evident to or can be communicated to the prospective customer.

The degree to which an innovative product or service possesses these characteristics determines the ease with which it is adopted and diffused throughout the population.

Reporting on a global conference held in 2004, IBM suggests that innovating in the Internet age is different in three important ways:

1. Innovation occurs with greater rapidity across product types and national boundaries.
2. It requires collaboration across scientific and technical disciplines.
3. The traditional concept of intellectual property is being questioned. It needs to evolve from being a possession that is hoarded to being a productive asset that is invested or even shared to encourage further progress.[1]

Figure 14-2 shows the shape of adoption curves for a number of innovations. Older ones like the automobile and telephone were slower to diffuse through the population than newer ones like the Internet and cellular phones. In this fast-paced environment, marketers must develop and successfully commercialize new products. That has never

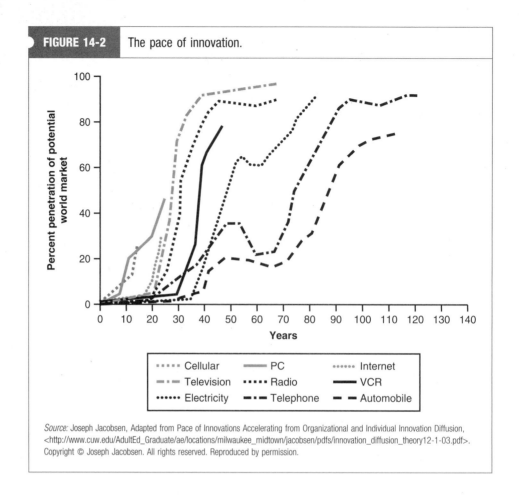

FIGURE 14-2 The pace of innovation.

been easy. It becomes more difficult in an environment where major technological changes occur with lightning speed.

We should apply what we have learned in the early stages of the Internet to improve our chances of picking winners among the emerging technologies and products. Keeping this in mind, this chapter focuses on three key points:

- The emerging computing environment, which is interchangeably called either pervasive or ubiquitous computing
- The next major technology to take advantage of the Internet—wireless
- Digital convergence

Let's start by taking a look at the environment in which this is going to take place. Whether it is called ubiquitous computing or pervasive computing, it describes an Internet environment different from the one with which we are currently familiar.

14-3 Pervasive Computing

The pervasive computing concept existed long before the commercial Internet. This powerful concept implies that a single person has access to myriad computing devices to assist in performing all sorts of daily tasks.

Computing pioneer Mark Weiser of Xerox's PARC research laboratory has been working on the concept since the early 1990s. His vision is based on the idea of making computing power available in virtually every aspect of everyday living and making the computers themselves invisible to the user. This is different from the environment that surrounded either mainframe or desktop computers. There the focus was on the computer itself and on making it do the task the user wanted to accomplish.

The focus of the early pioneers was to enhance the world of everyday activities by using embedded devices that perform without human intervention. In a 1991 article for *Scientific American,* Weiser described a world in which "doors open only to the right badge wearer, rooms greet people by name, telephone calls can be automatically forwarded to wherever the recipient may be, receptionists actually know where people are, computer terminals retrieve the preferences of whoever is sitting at them, and appointment diaries write themselves. No revolution in artificial intelligence is needed—just the proper imbedding of computers into the everyday world."[2]

A few years later, IBM elaborated on the vision, using the synonymous term *pervasive computing.* According to IBM:

> Pervasive computing aims to enable people to accomplish an increasing number of personal and professional transactions using a new class of intelligent and portable devices. It gives people convenient access to relevant information stored on powerful networks, allowing them to easily take action anywhere, anytime.
>
> These new intelligent appliances or "smart devices" are embedded with microprocessors that allow users to plug into intelligent networks and gain direct, simple, and secure access to both relevant information and services. These devices are as simple to use as calculators, telephones or kitchen toasters.[3]

The word that gives most people pause in descriptions like this is *simple.* We are all familiar with devices that are difficult to learn to use, complex software applications that require extensive study, and ancillary devices that are difficult to connect to the system or network. Some of us never even gained confidence in our ability to program our VCR to record a program that we want to watch later or to successfully program all the functions on our cell phone. In other words, we have a great deal of experience to suggest that new technologies are usually not simple, especially in the early stages of their development or user adoption. Complexity can retard the diffusion of an innovation.

14-4 The Pervasive Challenge

Marketers must seize the opportunities presented by the changing technological environment and develop new products and services that successfully take advantage of it. There are already a number of examples of successful applications of one or more aspects of the technology. Let's briefly look at some of them.

14-4a Speedpass—RFID-Based Payment System

ExxonMobil's Speedpass system has issued more than 6 million devices to customers who benefit from the ease and speed of payment it offers at nearly 11,000 retail gas stations and convenience stores in the U.S., Canada, Singapore and Japan. The Speedpass device is described as a "wand", transponder, or fob (see Figure 14-3). The customer waves it in front of the Speedpass symbol on the gas pump or the store cash register to activate a transaction.

The technology used is an rfid transponder (the wand) carried by the customer. A reader inside the pump or inside the store verifies the customer's system ID, processes the transaction, and prints a receipt if the customer opts to generate a receipt (there is an option to not have a receipt printed). The customer's credit card number and other personal information are not stored in the Speedpass signal system and therefore cannot

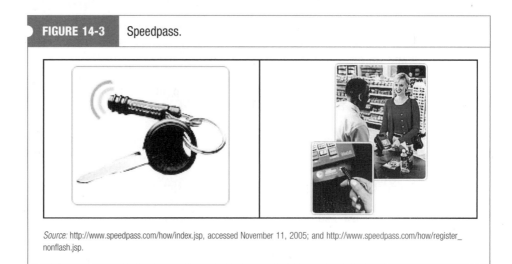

FIGURE 14-3   Speedpass.

Source: http://www.speedpass.com/how/index.jsp, accessed November 11, 2005; and http://www.speedpass.com/how/register_nonflash.jsp.

be accessed during transmission. Personalization information including the credit card to be used and whether the customer wants a printed receipt is part of the central database system.

Customers like the system, and ExxonMobil has developed infrastructure to support it that apparently has excess capacity or is easily scalable or both. It can also be used to pay for car washes at gas stations, and more than 450 car washes in the US can actually accept Speedpass at the Car Wash entrance as well.[4] This is a good example of a well-established technology evolving into a newer one in ways that meet customer needs for convenience and security.

14-4b British Airways—Innovative Technology to Service Customers

British Airways has been a leader in deploying mobile services for its customers to supplement onsite services like the check-in kiosk pictured in Chapter 9. Mobile services include flight schedules that can be downloaded to mobile devices or desktops. They also include the ability to check in for flights remotely from either fixed or mobile devices and to access wireless broadband (**Wi-Fi**) in selected British Airway lounges.

Wi-Fi Technically, a wireless communication protocol; in lay terms, often used to refer to the ability to access the Internet via wireless hotspots or access points.

One channel used by BA to deliver customer service is created by a partnership with British mobile services supplier Vodafone. Working with Vodafone allows BA to deliver mobile services without owning a mobile network. Users and perform tasks ranging from accessing flight information to monitoring their Executive Club accounts from their phones. The service is available free of charge as part of the Vodafone live! service for 3G phones. It is accessible through their Travel and location menu without subscription or registration on the part of the user.

The Vodaphone partnership allows British Airways to provide services that it could not afford to provide on its own. From the perspective of Vodafone the British Airways services are one part of an extensive menu of broadband wireless services that include music downloads, games, text messaging and video calling. Many of those services are the result of partnerships with content providers. This illustrates an important principle about wireless marketing. Marketers of products or services want to provide mobile services, but few will want to build networks to deliver them. They will partner with providers of mobile networks to provide services. That creates a win-win situation for both product marketer and network provider. It also suggests a complex environment for marketing application of pervasive computing technology.

14-4c BNSF Railway—Making Field Workers More Productive

Mobile applications are important to many businesses that need to increase the productivity of their field sales or service forces. The Burlington Northern Santa Fe (BNSF) railway uses a mobile solution to manage more than 32,000 miles of track in twenty-eight states and two Canadian provinces. It is described as a long-haul carrier, transporting goods that span the gamut from grain to mineral products to consumer goods to aircraft parts. With a territory that covers a large geographic area and 6,000 field service workers servicing the tracks, access to data and communications is vital to ensure a smoothly functioning transit system.

Crew foremen and inspectors are the point people in track maintenance and repair efforts. Their work is often performed far from offices in geographically remote locations. Before the wireless solution was implemented, the field supervisors had to return to their hotels in the evening before sending data to or retrieving data from corporate headquarters. Internet access was usually slow dial-up, and broken connections were frequent. When that happened, users often lost an hour or more of data entry and had to start over again. Clearly BNSF needed a better solution to enter and retrieve data and to access various types of corporate information and communications.

The technology solution included wireless notebook computers and several special-purpose software solutions. In urban locations, communications can be handled over Wi-Fi networks; in rural areas, they use cellular data services, transmitted over their own microwave links in the most remote areas. The wireless system allows them to access various enterprise systems like technical manuals and work orders and to send and receive status reports from the site. Authorized users specify their personal information needs on the corporate portal. The relevant data are pushed to their laptop as soon as they become available.

BNSF's railmaster says that "my desk is basically 194 miles long—as long as my territory. I can do my office work at any location in my territory instead of going back to my office at the end of the day. There's little lag time between when I learn something and when I can pass the information on to the person who needs it."[5] That adds up to an hour or two each day for each mobile worker—hours rescued from paperwork drudgery that can be devoted to more productive activity.[6]

14-4d Las Vegas—Using Your Cell Phone at the Parking Meter

Wireless parking meters were introduced a number of years ago in Europe and Australia. They have more recently been installed in a few American cities, including Las Vegas (Figure 14-4) The city touts them as an improvement in the "parking experience" because users no longer have to carry a pocket full of coins. The parking meters accept most debit and credit cards. After registering with the system, the user can pay by cell phone. The phone can be programmed to call when time on the meter is about to expire. The user can add time to the meter by calling on the cell phone and receive a statement of usage charges for expense account reimbursement. The meters also have the potential to use smart cards that can store data and value in advance of transactions.

From the perspective of the city using them, the meters are expensive to install. The *Las Vegas Tribune* reported that the meters there, which can be used in either English or Spanish mode, cost more than $4,200 each before installation. Each meter can serve up to ten parking spaces. The meters are supposed to increase the municipal revenue stream by rejecting bad coins, being less vulnerable to damage, and providing an electronic audit trail for all transactions at the meter.

A potential drawback of the system is the small size of the transactions. Credit card service fees charged to the merchant, in this case the municipality, could far exceed revenues. To solve this problem, a specialized type of intermediary has emerged. These intermediaries aggregate the **micropayments** and bill the consumer using an

micropayments Payments for electronic purchases of low-ticket products or services that are uneconomical under traditional payment mechanisms like credit cards.

FIGURE 14-4   Wireless-enabled parking meter.

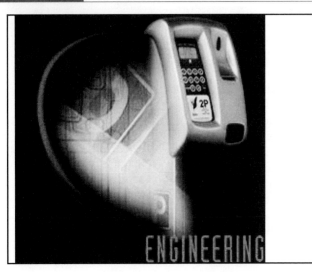
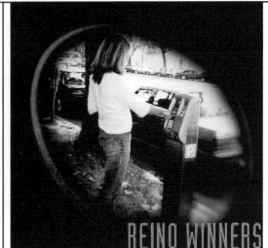

Source: http://www.multibay.com/, accessed November 7, 2005.

existing payment system, usually a credit card. Micropayments first became an issue in the music downloading industry, and the technology has been transferred to the mobile payments market where it will enable other types of small transactions.[7] From the user perspective, it means that customers will be able to sign up for payment systems that will allow them to make purchases without entering payment data for each transaction. Both the time involved and the difficulty of entering data on the keyboards of small mobile devices require that some type of payment system be used. Speedpass illustrates a proprietary payment solution; the service is also offered by independent micropayments specialists.

These four case studies describe an emerging environment that differs in important respects from the communications and commerce environment of the early Internet days. It has been described as *a*ccess *a*nywhere, *a*nytime, to *a*ny *a*uthorized user on *a*ny Internet-enabled device—the six A's of pervasive computing. Let's look at the strategic implications of this emerging environment for the marketers of today and tomorrow.

14-5 The Mobile Marketplace

The mobile environment will place more stress on marketing systems even as it offers new opportunities to engage customers. Marketers must be prepared to meet customer needs for content wherever and whenever they need it. That means serving the needs of users one at a time, not communicating with segments of customers. It also means providing content and services when users desire them, not when it is convenient for marketers. The marketing requirements for effectively serving the mobile marketplace are referred to as the 6 As—Access to Anyone who is Authorized, Anytime, Anywhere on Any Internet-enabled device (Table 14-1).

Being effective in this environment will require that databases be updated frequently if not actually in real time. The British Airways flight tracking system must reflect current data at all times. The Las Vegas parking system must record the current status of all parking meters in use at any given time and make it available to citizens on request. Only if the databases are completely up to date can the marketers meet their customers' needs for current content and transactions based on them.

TABLE 14-1	Dimensions of the Pervasive Computing Environment	
Dimension	**Marketplace Implications**	**Marketer Requirements**
Access	Information instantaneously available, either through actively accessing the network or through passive provision by embedded devices	Large and constantly updated databases of content
Anyone	Inexpensive and/or embedded devices make pervasive computing readily available to most people around the globe	Increased market size; may also increase the number of small transactions
Anytime	Users able to access data and communications at any time, not just when they are seated at their desks	Be prepared to respond to customers instead of initiating customer communication
Anywhere	Wireless networks blanket first urban areas and then outlying regions, bringing access to residents and travelers	Increasingly high customer expectations for content and service
Any Internet-enabled device	Communications and data no longer limited to fixed desktop machines but available on a large number of small portable devices	Different display and revision of content necessary for mobile devices
Authorized	Networks able to provide secure access when required for communications and transactions	Security and authentication that is understood and trusted by customers

Customer expectations are increasing, not only in terms of availability of current content, but also in terms of the customer's ability to access it from any location. Mobile networks are being aggressively built out, but not all services that an individual user expects from specific providers may be available at all places. British Airways, for example, is able to provide wireless hotspots in only selected locations in European airline terminals. It has been difficult to deploy wireless services inside terminals because all the structural steel and the many other communications systems produce a great deal of interference. Expectations that are not met result in dissatisfied customers, even though the reasons may be beyond the control of the marketer.

Migrating services to devices with small screens and tiny keyboards is not easy. A derisive term has been invented to describe what must not be done. A *screen scrape* is an attempt to simply copy a screen for display elsewhere. It is not possible to take all the content and graphics from full-sized Web site screens and transfer them to smaller devices. Every screen must be redesigned for usability on mobile devices. That is a labor-intensive task, and it may require design techniques that differ from those that make existing Web sites engaging.

Finally, some of the tasks users want to perform require secure processing. Speedpass emphasizes the security of its RFID-based system in all its promotional material. Whether the user wants to purchase an airline ticket or simply add another hour on the parking meter, the transaction has to be easy to initiate and the processing must be secure. Business-to-business (B2B) users will require that all their corporate communications be secure, even those that are not especially sensitive.

The mobile marketplace represents the wired Internet on steroids. Everything will happen more quickly; many things will happen more frequently. It will require new approaches on the part of marketers to effectively make use of the technology. Let's now turn to a brief description of the technology with which they will work in developing applications of all sorts.

14-6 The Evolution of Wireless Technology

If a world where computing is pervasive has been envisioned for more than two decades, why are all these technology applications becoming available now? The answer is partly that the technology that was once only envisioned is now available. Even more important is the fact that the cost of the technology has declined to the point where it is usable in many everyday applications. We discussed one example, RFID tags, in Chapter 2.

> **TABLE 14-2**   Evolutionary Stages and Standards of Wireless around the Globe
>
> - 1G—First-generation wireless telephones are an obsolete technology. They were analog devices that offered relatively poor quality and could carry only voice transmissions.
> - 2G—Second-generation wireless technology is digital and can handle both voice and data transmissions. That includes e-mail and Web pages. Speeds for both voice and data transmission are about 14.4 kbps (kilobits per second—a kilobit is 1,000 bits of data).
> - 2.5G—Second-generation-plus wireless is an intermediate step. It will involve the enhancement of existing technologies that improve the transmission of e-mail and wireless access to Web pages.
> - 3G—The third generation is the technology the wireless world is waiting for because it will eventually offer speeds equivalent to broadband. Speeds are expected to start at about 56 kbps—about the speed of a good dial-up modem—and eventually reach 2 mbps (megabits per second—a megabit is 1 million bits).
> - 4G—Standards for 4G are in their infancy, but it is expected to be able to reach peak download speeds of 1 gbps (gigabit per second—a gigabit is 1 billion bits).

The other enabling technology is the wireless Internet. Wireless communications have diffused throughout the world and are a commonplace aspect of everyday life. However, only now has wireless technology advanced to the point where the Internet can be accessed efficiently using wireless devices. You can boil this down to a single word: *broadband*.

Early wireless devices, first-generation analog and second-generation digital, were slow, as described in Table 14-2. Think of the slowest dial-up computer connection you have ever used, and those speeds, or even lower, are the speeds of 1G and 2G wireless transmission. 2.5G, especially in the United States, is an interim solution, but it is only with the deployment of true broadband in the form of 3G systems that the Internet will become truly accessible through wireless devices. 4G systems are only in the planning stage, and they are not expected to be widely available until late in this decade.

Third-generation systems have been deployed more rapidly in Japan, Korea, China, India, and Europe than in the United States. Reasons include the following:

- *Early adoption of the wired Internet in the United States.* Users who have good access to and are satisfied with the wired Internet are less likely to rush to adopt wireless (United States).

- *Lack of landline telephone infrastructure in developing countries.* It is faster and cheaper to deploy wireless service, and that is the option frequently chosen in areas where landline infrastructure is not already present (China, India).

- *Compact geographic areas with dense populations.* This makes wireless deployment cost-effective even if landline service is available (Europe).

- *A cultural environment that is unusually receptive to electronic products.* The most visible manifestations of this have included the rapid adoption of cell phones and video games (Japan, Korea).

- *Greater standardization of wireless transmission in other countries.* Europe's GSM standard and Japan's i-Mode are not the only wireless protocols in their respective geographic areas; they are more ubiquitous than the standards in the United States, as shown in Table 14-3.

- *Political barriers to the granting of wireless licenses.* The United States has been slower than most other countries to make broadband spectrum available to wireless service providers. Because they have not been able to license sufficient bandwidth to offer broadband services, the wireless carriers have been restricted to offering service at speeds lower than 3G.

> **TABLE 14-3**   Wireless Standards in Various Countries

The many wireless transmission protocols present a confusing alphabet soup to the nontechnical reader. Here are brief definitions of the most commonly used standards:

- In the United States, each carrier is free to choose its own transmission protocol. The most commonly used is Code Division Multiple Access (CDMA). Voice conversations are digitized and tagged with a code and transmitted over a radio frequency. The mobile phone uses the code to pick the right conversation off the airways. CDMA can carry data at low speeds of about 14.4 kbps.

- Time Division Multiple Access and Global System for Mobile Communication (TDMA) is the other standard widely used in the United States. It allows the carrier to divide a single radio frequency into multiple time slots, allowing a single channel to support multiple transmissions at the same time. Data speeds are slow, only 9.6 kbps.

- There is more standardization in Western Europe, where the Global Standard for Mobile Communications (GSM) standard predominates. The standard is based on TDMA technology. Phones that use GSM technology utilize Smart Identity Module (SIM) smart cards that contain the user's account information. The programmability of the smart card makes the phone useful in many nations, allows personalization, and facilitates renting and borrowing of phones.

- In Japan, the national cellular carrier NTTDoCoMo uses the i-Mode standard. i-Mode is its proprietary standard and provides services like Web access, e-mail, messaging, and personal calendars. Transmission speed was initially only 9,600 kbps but will increase as new generations of technology are rolled out.

- Wi-Fi describes the use of the 802.11 communications protocol to make wireless local area networks (LANs) available to users in a given area. These areas are known as wireless hotspots. They are being deployed around the world and provide wireless access for a wide range of devices.

This adds up to a more advanced wireless environment in countries other than the United States. Marketers can look to those countries for indications of how the mobile economy is developing. As we discussed in Chapter 5, the United States has been the leader in the development of the wired Internet, but it is unlikely to ever gain a leadership position in wireless. Landline communications and desktop personal computers are too universal and broadband wireless has been too slow for that to happen. The good news from the perspective of marketers is that they can look to experiences in other countries to inform their own mobile marketing strategies.

14-7 Use of Wireless Content and Services

According to Telephia, a firm that collects wireless audience data from a panel of wireless users, there were 191 million wireless users in the United States in mid-2005. Only 4.8% of them access e-mail on their devices,[8] although the Pew Foundation had earlier estimated that 28% were "wireless ready." That is, they used laptops or cell phones that were wireless enabled.[9]

Table 14-5 shows what mobile services and Web sites wireless users accessed in addition to e-mail. These are people "on the go," so their use of weather, search, sports, and news services is not surprising. Perhaps more unexpected is that the heavy users of these services are in the 35 to 54 age range. The picture changes, however, when the categories are entertainment, gaming, and Internet portals. The heaviest users of these categories are younger people in the 25 to 34 age range. They access their information and entertainment on major Web sites with which they are presumably familiar from their fixed Internet use (Table 14-6).

Mobile content is not all Internet-based. Table 14-6 shows that wireless users are making increasing use of the functions on their mobile phones by engaging in activities like text messaging, checking their e-mail, and downloading mobile games. These activities can all be supported by the wireless services provider; they do not require access to the Internet. Slightly less than 11% of the respondents in the September 2005 survey of U.S. mobile users addressed content using an Internet

TABLE 14-4   Top U.S. Mobile Internet Categories, June 2005

Web Site Category	Subscriber Reach	Subscriber Age Breakdown (% of audience for the category)			
		18–24	25–34	35–54	55+
E-mail	4.8	19	29	41	11
Weather	3.9	20	28	43	10
Search	2.9	24	30	32	14
Sports	2.5	18	30	32	14
News/politics	2.1	14	22	45	18
Entertainment	2.1	18	42	33	6
City guides/maps	2.1	23	34	36	8
Games	2.1	21	40	34	5
Portals	1.4	4	47	33	17
Business/finance	1.2	20	17	41	21

Adapted from: http://www.clickz.com/stats/sectors/wireless/article.php/3547651.

TABLE 14-5   Top U.S. Mobile Internet Web Sites, June 2005

Web Site	Subscriber Reach (%)	Average Sessions per User per Month
The Weather Channel	2.5	6.2
Yahoo! Mail	2.4	6.3
MSN Hotmail	2.1	6.0
Google Search	2.1	7.4
ESPN	1.8	7.3
Yahoo! Search	1.4	5.4
MapQuest	1.1	4.8
CNN	1.1	8.0
AOL Mail	1.0	2.8
Yahoo! Driving Directions	1.0	3.1

Adapted from: http://www.clickz.com/stats/sectors/wireless/article.php/3547651.

TABLE 14-6   U.S. Mobile Subscriber Monthly Consumption of Content and Applications McMetrics Benchmark Survey, September 2005

Activity	Projected Monthly Reach (000s)	Percent U.S. Mobile Subscribers
Sent or received text messages	55,762	30.8
Retrieved news and information via browser	19,642	10.9
Purchased ring tone	15,624	8.6
Used photo messaging	14,929	8.2
Used personal e-mail	10,748	5.9
Used mobile instant messenger	9,457	5.2
Used work e-mail	6,129	3.4
Purchased wallpaper or screen saver	5,927	3.3
Downloaded mobile game	5,315	2.9

Adapted from: http://www.mmetrics.com/press/PressRelease.aspx?article=20051031-benchmark.

TABLE 14-7	Type of Content Mobile Phone Users Worldwide Expect to Access in 12 Months, by Region, May–June 2005 (as a % of respondents)			
	Asia-Pacific	**Europe**	**North America**	**South America**
Ring tones	73	20	27	25
Multimedia images	56	16	13	13
Music	55	15	13	28
Games	49	15	11	30
News	31	15	15	23
Sports clips	29	7	7	10
Video clips or movie previews	25	7	7	10
Full-length feature films	11	8	3	8

Adapted from: eMarketer, July 15, 2005.

browser. Table 14-7 shows content data from regions around the globe. It shows mobile phone users in the Asia-Pacific region and South America to be more active in accessing most types of content than are users in Europe and the United States. Consumers in the Asia-Pacific region are much more likely than others to access entertainment content that requires broadband access, such as movies and videos. Ring tones, clearly not an Internet service, are popular worldwide. News is also consistently popular around the globe, and that may imply use of the wireless Internet.

What emerges is a picture of an industry in the growth stage around the world. Some geographic areas are more advanced than others, and growth rates vary. We need to keep this in mind as we look at the opportunities for mobile advertising and marketing.

14-8 Mobile Advertising and Marketing

If consumers around the world are able to send and receive content on their cell phones and other wireless devices, can marketers be far behind? Marketers are, of course, eager to explore the options for wireless communications and transactions. Some marketers, especially in Europe, have been using text messaging to communicate with consumers for a number of years. Globally, most mobile phones are capable of sending and receiving text messages without accessing the wireless Internet. British text messaging services supplier TextAlert estimates that 150 billion text messages were sent worldwide in the last quarter of 2004. In the United Kingdom alone, more than 2.5 billion text messages are sent each month. The U.S. market is smaller, with just over 5 billion messages sent each month in 2004, but that number was expected to double in 2005.[10]

14-8a Cell Phone Promotions

The early wireless promotional efforts used short messaging services (**SMS**), brief text messages that cannot contain images or graphics. It is easy for marketers, working through a supplier of text messaging services, to set up lists of customer phone numbers and send text messages directly to them. For example, "You can buy the new Harry Potter DVD today at VideoStop." If you are a user of SMS messaging, you know that text messaging has developed its own shorthand that goes something like, "u cn bi . . ." that may or may not be used in promotions, depending on the target market. Text messaging has evolved and now includes **MMS**, multimedia messaging services. MMS messages can include graphics, sound, and video, as well as brief text.

Figure 14-5a shows an SMS screen from a Snapple summer sweepstakes promotion. Snapple printed 225 million numbers inside Snapple bottle caps and

SMS Short messaging services; text messaging services for cell phones

MMS Multimedia messaging services; rich-media messaging services for cell phones.

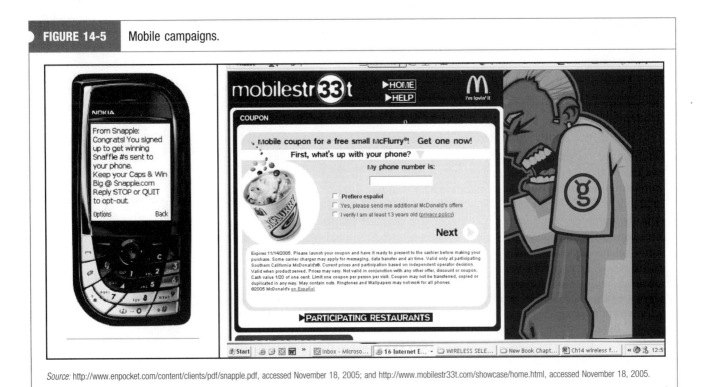

FIGURE 14-5 Mobile campaigns.

Source: http://www.enpocket.com/content/clients/pdf/snapple.pdf, accessed November 18, 2005; and http://www.mobilestr33t.com/showcase/home.html, accessed November 18, 2005.

announced three winning numbers each week for 12 weeks. The campaign was carried out on TV, in print, and on Snapple's Web site, as well as through the mobile channel. Opt-in mobile customers received notices of winning numbers on their cell phone. Notice that in the sample screen, users are being reminded that they opted in for this message and are being given the option to opt out. If they replied to "CAPS" on the mobile phone, they were connected to the Snapple mobile channel. There they found communications options, including the ability to forward information about the promotion to friends, making the promotion viral. Winning numbers were announced in other media at about 10 p.m. On the mobile channel they were announced at noon, targeting the peak consumption time for the product.[11]

McDonald's used MMS in Southern California for a trial promotion of its McFlurry drink product. The screen shown in Figure 14-5b uses an advanced Java platform that requires equally advanced cell phones. Consequently, they also had an SMS version and an intermediate version to make the campaign available to as many consumers as possible. When consumers accessed the site shown in Figure 14-5b and clicked on the coupon link, they were asked a series of questions to verify the capability of their cell phone and to ensure that they were at least 13 years old (to satisfy the requirements of the Children's Online Privacy Protection Act [COPPA]), and they were given a Spanish-language option. Completing the series of questions (some of which are shown in the pop-up in Figure 14-5b and providing a cell phone number qualified a consumer for the campaign. Coupons were then delivered to the consumer's cell phone.[12]

The next stage is the inclusion of video in MMS messages. Figure 14-6 gives an example of an early use of this channel. In this campaign from British mobile services supplier Enpocket, Barclay's Bank is sponsoring video clips of football matches (soccer games to American fans). The clips are available as part of the Vodafone Live! service that was described in the British Airways customer service application earlier in the chapter. Two leading British firms are using mobile services in different ways to promote their brand. Both use an existing mobile channel instead of establishing their own. This is one glimpse of the future of mobile promotional efforts.

A different approach to cell phone–delivered video is being taken by Jeep, and it may be a forerunner to what other major consumer brands will do. Using the network

FIGURE 14-6   Enpocket advertising.

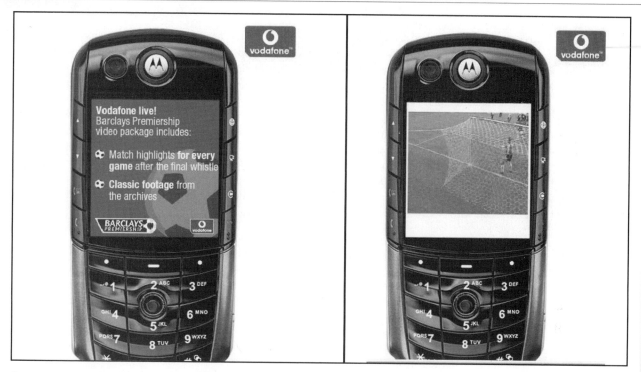

Source: http://www.enpocket.com/campaigns3g/campaigns3g.html, accessed November 18, 2005.

of a supplier called MobiTV ("Live Television. Anywhere. Anytime."),[13] Jeep is running ads about once an hour on eighteen different mobile channels. In addition, it has launched its own channel, which will "repurpose" content from a Web site. The Jeep channel will run a continuous loop of episodes of "The Mudds." These are short films made for the Internet that feature a fun-loving, mud-splattered family that drives a Jeep Commander.[14] The films have their own site (http://wearethemudds.com/index.html), which sometimes can be seen linked to other travel and adventure sites.

Other mobile devices like laptop computers, tablets, and personal digital assistants (PDAs) are also candidates for wireless promotions, but so far they have not received much attention. Reasons may include the fact that wireless laptops and tablet computers have full-screen access to the Internet and all its promotional activities. PDAs do not appear to represent a growing market, and they are primarily used by business and professional people. Consequently, they may not provide an attractive venue for most marketers. The iPod, however, is a different story.

14-8b iPod Promotions

Marketers are eager to explore opportunities for advertising that might be presented by podcasting. In 2004, The Diffusion Group reported that there were only 800,000 podcast subscribers in the United States. They predicted that the number would grow to 4.5 million in 2005, 32.9 million in 2008, and 56.8 million by 2010.[15] Not only is the potential market large, podcasts reach highly targeted audiences. As has been true with other innovative products, the early market has tended to be made up primarily of young males. However, iPods and consequently podcasts are diffusing through other market segments with a speed reminiscent of the steepest curves in Figure 14-2[16] Case in Point 14-1 describes a groundbreaking commercial sponsorship that was acquired by a teenage female podcaster.

Case in Point 14-1   Podcasting Nature's Cure

In one early example, the podcast of 15-year-old Martina Butler secured commercial sponsorship by Nature's Cure, a maker of acne treatment products. The podcast is called "Emo Girl Talk" and features the teen angst and activities of an emo girl. (For the uninitiated, *emo* is emotionally charged punk rock.) Martina hopes "that my success paves the way for more teens to have their voices heard and that more companies will recognize us as an important consumer force." Marketers are, in fact, eager to reach this demographic, but often find it difficult. Nature's Cure VP of Marketing, Dana Doron, points out that "reaching teens requires being in-touch with what's important in their world. . . . There are a number of teens now listening to podcasts. Sponsorship is an excellent way to increase our brand awareness in an environment that is meaningful and credible to teens." John Houghton is president and founder of MobileCast Media, a firm that specializes in audio downloads for the teen market and was responsible for the Emo Girl sponsorship. He agrees with many other advertisers who find that the teenage audience is especially difficult to reach through traditional communications media. He finds that "teens and young adults are increasingly turning to new media such as podcasts, which are downloaded to a mobile device or computer."[17]

Young people are not the only market segment that can be selectively reached by podcasts. Paige and Gretchen are young mothers who host "Mommycast" from their Northern Virginia homes. Their audience is obviously other young mothers, another desirable demographic. Dixie Paper Products, which makes disposable paper products like plates and cups, agreed to sponsor Mommycast. Audience and sponsor seem to be made for one another.[18]

Burger King experimented with the new video iPod channel by creating its own podcasts and inviting users to download them when the device was only a few weeks old. The videos were reported to be shots of customers wearing Burger King masks that the customers had submitted via the Burger King Web site. They were available for download from an edgy site called Heavy.com that specializes in both audio and video downloads. Within days, *Advertising Age* reported that consumers had created their own video that was also available for free download at the Heavy.com site, which it describes as a "male-dominated, video-rich site." Featuring a parody striptease that ends with a shot of a man in a Burger King mask, it had recorded 4.1 million downloads in just a brief period of time, qualifying it as highly viral. Henry Assad, chief executive officer (CEO) of Heavy.com, defends the racy video by saying, "When users create content with their cultural icons, it's not always in line with the strategy of the advertiser, but it's really important because sometimes the consumers are more in touch with how to propagate a brand than the marketer is." An unidentified Burger King spokesperson added that the "brand is part of the popular culture, and that the chain had no control over the video's content."[19] Was Burger King sanguine about being featured in an X-rated video because it appeals to their primary target market, males 18 to 34?

These mobile promotional applications show the evolution of the technology and consequently the creativity that can be employed.[20] What does this say about accomplishing sales in the medium?

14-9 Wireless Transactions

Wireless transactions, or mobile marketing, is in an even earlier stage than promotional activity. The ability to conduct transactions has been severely limited by bandwidth, security issues, and the availability of products that are suitable for download in the mobile channel. Again, however, a few adventurous marketers are finding effective uses for the medium.

Figure 14-7 shows several screens from the process of downloading a digital ticket for a rock concert in Sydney, Australia. The customer orders the ticket through an

FIGURE 14-7 Mobile downloading of a concert ticket.

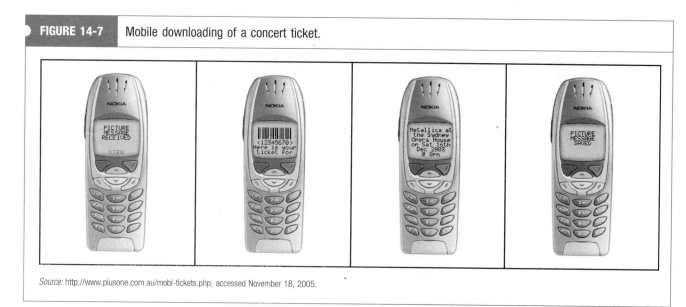

Source: http://www.plusone.com.au/mobi-tickets.php, accessed November 18, 2005.

existing ticketing system, so no new payment vehicles are needed. When the ticket is ready, the vendor sends a picture message that begins the process represented in the figure. The cell phone user is told that a ticket is waiting, and the bar-coded digital image is downloaded to his or her phone. At the concert venue, the saved screen with the bar-coded ticket is simply scanned over the existing POP scanning system. It appears to be a simple transition from phone to Internet to wireless for both the customer and the merchant. The service intermediary says that among the advantages of mobile ticketing are cost savings over paper tickets, ease of delivery, single redemption eliminates the risk of the message being forwarded to other cell phones, multiple in-venue redemptions, i.e. entry, and discount at concession stand, and increased ability to track and monitor the volume of sales in real time. This same technology can be used to deliver coupons or other promotional devices.[21]

Mobile advertising and marketing is expected to show growth in the United States and around the world. In 2005, eMarketer made projections of year-over-year spending growth in the United States at three levels—conservative, moderate, and aggressive. From 2006 through 2009, they conservatively estimated spending growth on both marketing and advertising campaigns to grow at about 22% per year. The moderate growth projection averaged about 26%, and the aggressive projection was for more than 30% per year spending growth in the mobile marketplace.[22] The dollar amounts will still be a small part of the overall marketing budget, but the increasing focus on reaching targeted segments over wireless devices is clear. The road ahead is not, however, without important barriers that marketers will have to overcome.

14-10 Barriers to the Use of Wireless

Wireless use is growing rapidly throughout the world, more so in some regions than others, as has already been noted. In late 2005, the Judge Management School at Cambridge University and the A. T. Kearney consulting firm released the eighth report in their tracking study of wireless adoption and use. They surveyed 4,000 mobile users in twenty-one countries. Among their key findings were the following:

- More than half of respondents reported being able to access multimedia services, including mobile e-mail and the Internet.
- Camera phones represent 36% of all handsets worldwide and 85% in Japan.
- Worldwide, 59% of phones have color screens. Highest penetrations are Japan, 92%; China and South Korea, 72%; Europe, 59%; Scandinavia and Australia/New Zealand, 58%.

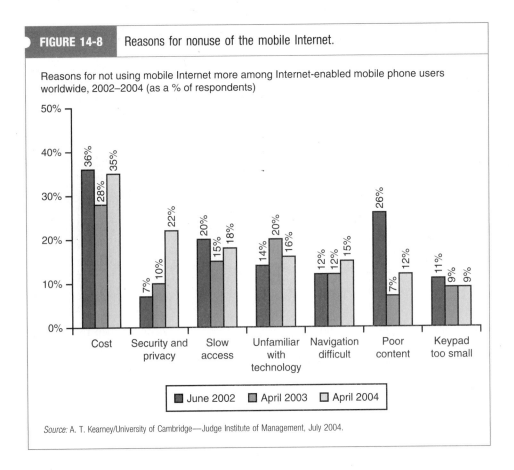

FIGURE 14-8   Reasons for nonuse of the mobile Internet.

Reasons for not using mobile Internet more among Internet-enabled mobile phone users worldwide, 2002–2004 (as a % of respondents)

Legend: ■ June 2002 ■ April 2003 □ April 2004

Reason	June 2002	April 2003	April 2004
Cost	36%	28%	35%
Security and privacy	7%	10%	22%
Slow access	20%	15%	18%
Unfamiliar with technology	14%	20%	16%
Navigation difficult	12%	12%	15%
Poor content	26%	7%	12%
Keypad too small	11%	9%	9%

Source: A. T. Kearney/University of Cambridge—Judge Institute of Management, July 2004.

- Users are most likely to access e-mail over their mobile phone once a week or even once a month, although some use it multiple times each day.

- Worldwide, 32% of users download or send pictures or video at least once a month, and 33% had downloaded music during the past year.

- Mobile gaming is also experiencing increasing use, but the frequency is lower than that of music.

- Seventeen percent of users would be willing to pay to watch TV on their mobile device.

- Two-thirds would like to be able to access news and sports.

- Almost two-thirds say that new functions and services are easy to use.[23]

There are, however, still reasons for nonuse of advanced services, as shown in Figure 14-8.

Consumers around the world find cost a barrier to the use of mobile services. Their concerns about security and privacy and with navigation difficulties have grown between 2002 and 2004. Speed of access is still a problem, and so is the size of the keypad. Overall, these barriers have been fairly stable as the mobile Internet has begun to diffuse. That suggests the nature of the tasks ahead for marketers.

14-11 Strategic Drivers of Wireless Technology

The much-anticipated rollout to 3G networks is increasing the speed of cell phones and other mobile devices, but barriers remain, especially when mobile is compared with wired broadband. Wireless content and mobile commerce (m-commerce) services will only be successful if they take the inherent differences into account. The strategic drivers that will enable them to operate successfully in this environment are as follows:

- *Context*. This means providing necessary information when and where the customer needs or wants it. The content trigger is in the hands of the customer, not of the marketer. Context in the wireless environment has two dimensions:

  - *Localization*. Through various geographic systems, the location of the user can be identified and information specific to that location can be provided. A consumer driving down the highway can be beamed information about attractions in the area.

  - *Personalization*. The customer can select not only the type of information desired but also the frequency of information provision. For example, the consumer may select specific stocks and specific price levels at which he or she wishes to be notified.

- *Time sensitive*. Screens are small and storage is limited, so information must be provided at the time appropriate to the customer, not convenient for the marketer. As a customer passes a store in a shopping mall, he or she may be willing to receive a coupon for a purchase in that store, which can be saved or retained on the screen until the customer shows it when checking out the purchase.

- *High value*. The coupon will have to have a reasonable value in order to make it welcome in the wireless context.

- *Voice activation*. There are many situations, driving in particular, in which it is not safe—and in many locales, not legal—to use the keyboard of a mobile device. Voice activation is the solution in these situations.

- *One-click payment mechanisms*. Consumers are not going to be willing to enter credit card information on mobile keyboards and may be uncomfortable with the idea of their credit card data being transmitted wirelessly. They are not likely to be willing, either, to have numerous vendor-specific accounts, especially for micropayments. A system in which payment is easily and securely authorized and billed to a single account will be necessary to enable frequent use of m-commerce services.

- *Security*. Users must be assured that data transmissions are secure, and authentication services must be provided in a way that is suitable for the devices. Embedded devices that identify the owner are one possibility. Smart cards that can be inserted and removed to protect encoded information are another.

- *Privacy*. In addition to protecting personal data, providers of content and services will have to be sensitive to download times, lack of storage, and the fact that users are paying for airtime. They must not abuse technological capabilities like geographic locational services.

- *Expanded permission marketing*. Marketers will have to extend the concept of Permission Marketing beyond simple opt-in scenarios. They must find out what kind of information consumers are willing to receive, how often they are willing to receive transmissions, and where they are willing to receive it. This means an accurate customer database that is updated in real time.

It also means that marketers must be vigilant in trying to stop mobile spam before it gets a major foothold in the marketplace. Earlier chapters have described the ire of consumers who receive spam on their conventional systems. E-mail sent to desktop systems does not cost the consumer, nor is it a significant user of scarce computing resources in most instances. Still, consumers hate it. It does not seem unreasonable to predict that they will hate unsolicited wireless advertising even more because it is even more intrusive. The fledgling industry is attempting to deal with the issue.

14-12 Wireless Industry Self-Regulation

Marketers are concerned about preventing mobile spam and the damage it can do to consumer perceptions of the industry. In 2004, the Mobile Marketing Association was formed, combining European- and U.S.-based trade organizations into one. They have published a code of conduct, which includes the following:

- *Choice.* Consumers are required to opt in to each marketing program. Segmentation- or location-based messaging is prohibited unless consumers have provided verifiable personal data for that specific program.
- *Control.* Consumers must easily be able to opt out of any message stream.
- *Customization.* Data should be collected and used to send relevant messages and to restrict messages to categories specifically requested by the consumers.
- *Consideration.* The consumer must receive something of value for being willing to receive the advertising.
- *Constraint.* The MMA explains that "the marketer, content provider, or aggregator must provide a global 'throttling mechanism' capable of managing the number of messages received by an individual consumer. The purpose of the throttle is to effectively manage and limit mobile messaging programs to a reasonable number of programs, defaulted to a maximum of 2 new campaigns per week." They add that the consumer may opt in to additional messages.
- *Confidentiality.* The marketer must have a privacy policy that meets TRUSTe's standards and abide by their electronic list policies.

Notice that these six categories are similar to the Fair Information Practices Principles discussed in Chapter 12. The implementation, however, is much more restrictive than the practices that are sanctioned on the wired Internet. The MMA provides detailed implementation guidelines at http://www.mmaglobal.com/ bestpractices.pdf.

The code of conduct is only binding on MMA members, but it is nevertheless an important step in the very early stages of mobile marketing. As stated, it applies to business-to-customer (B2C) marketing only. However, there is already evidence that B2B customers want the same kind of protection from unsolicited wireless advertising. B2B customers are easily able to reach marketers with complaints about unsolicited messages, and the value of their business may convince B2B marketers to police their own activities without much outside pressure.

The examples in this chapter have suggested that some innovative marketers are meeting the requirements of the strategic wireless drivers and are exhibiting creativity in the way they approach target segments in the mobile channel. They are merely the vanguard of change to come. A host of powerful forces is converging to change the way marketers and advertisers do business. The convergence of multiple, often incompatible, media into a seamless source of communication, information, entertainment, and marketing may be the biggest development we can look forward to over the next few years.

14-13 Digital Convergence

Like many other technologies discussed in this text, which have taken longer to diffuse through the mass market than initially expected, convergence has been discussed for at least two decades. Syracuse University's Convergence Center defines convergence as "the power of digital media to combine voice, video, data, text, and money in new applications, devices and networks."[24] It is driven by the desire of consumers and B2B users to perform a variety of tasks on the go. The primary ones appear to be the following:

- Phone calls
- Internet access for content like news, weather
- Take, export, and e-mail pictures
- Music and video downloads
- Games
- Search, especially local

Early concepts often centered around a single device that would meet all consumer needs. In the household it might be a "super TV" that broadcast content, accessed the Internet, and controlled various household systems to provide user convenience, security, and energy conservation. It would be controlled by one or more devices such as a handheld remote in the home and a dashboard console in the car. For users on the go, digital convergence would be represented by a single lightweight portable device that would enable them to complete desired tasks from any location.

14-13a Device Convergence

Whatever the configuration, the vision of a single, all-encompassing device has not materialized for a number of reasons. Bandwidth is still a hindrance for transmitting full-length video over the Internet. Making a highly functional device with a useful screen and keyboard that is actually lightweight has proved to be a challenge.

The Mobile Individual

Instead of a universal device, myriad multifunction devices have been introduced into the mobile marketplace in recent years. Some typical configurations include the following:

- Cell phones with **GPS** positioning technology accessible by local **911** systems
- Camera phones, most of which have access to e-mail and to the Internet
- Phones that open to reveal a full-function keyboard and a color display screen
- Phones with Bluetooth (short-range wireless) capability, allowing them to communicate with other wireless devices in range
- PDA devices primarily designed for high-volume e-mail that include other functionality like phone and Internet access
- Tablet PCs, lightweight laptop PCs that have the capability of deciphering hand-written notes recorded with a **stylus** on the screen
- A ballpoint pen that includes a computer and small camera with educational programs for children 8 to 14 years of age
- Game players that include functions from Internet access to MP3 players for music
- Touch screens in places like kiosks and taxis that provide content and Internet access

GPS Global Positioning System; a satellite-based system for accurate location of a signal anywhere on Earth.

911 The national emergency response number in the United States.

stylus A pen-shaped device used to either point or draw.

There are many possible combinations of the functionality that most mobile consumers and workers want. The variety of possible functions has made it difficult to combine them all into a single device that is both portable and usable.

The Wireless Household

The single all-encompassing device has not been perfected for the household either. There are, however, some interesting examples of convergence:

- A refrigerator that can monitor contents and use the Internet to place reorders for home delivery

- A refrigerator that includes a TV and a home message center
- A washing machine that can access the Internet to download programs for new fabrics or washing problems
- TV that permits pausing of the current program and other DVD-like features
- Home theatre that includes DVD-like features, Internet access, and the ability to display and organize photos

As in the market for individual mobility, there are many possible combinations of functionality for entertainment, learning, and management in the household. Once again, the issue is what functions to incorporate into what devices and how to tie them together into a seamless household network.

There is more. The electronic marketplace does not stop with converged hardware devices for individual or household use. Media is converging in a way that opens vast new possibilities.

14-13b Media Convergence

During the years preceding the Internet, and culminating in furious activity during the Internet bubble, media mergers and acquisitions occurred throughout the global media industry. This activity was fueled both by the need to compete globally and also by the desire to integrate activities across traditional and electronic media channels. Some of the major consolidations included the following:[25]

- CBS records, a division of the Columbia Broadcasting Company, was acquired by Japan's Sony Corp. in the late 1980s.
- During the 1990s, Canada's Seagram's, formerly best known for leading brands of spirits, engaged in aggressive acquisition of media firms, including Universal Studios and record companies in Europe and the United States.
- Seagram's itself was acquired by French media conglomerate Vivendi in 2000.
- The history of media acquisitions by German media giant Bertelsmann AG goes far back. In the 1960s, they expanded into other European countries by purchasing print media. In the 1970s, it was music; in the 1980s, it was broadcasting. In 1995, they partnered with AOL to set up AOL Europe.[26]

The most significant event in this wave of consolidation was clearly the merger of AOL and Time Warner, owner of many media properties, including CNN, in January 2001. Like many of the other media mergers just chronicled, this huge combination has gone sour. By late 2005, there were rumors that Time Warner might divest itself of the AOL property. Instead, in December, AOL announced that Google would purchase a 5% share of AOL for $1 billion in an agreement that involved significant **cross-marketing** between Time Warner and Google.[27]

Whether it is the difficulty of making media acquisitions work or whether it is the fluidity of the current communications environment, the pattern of convergence has undergone a major change in the new millennium. It is now characterized more by partnerships than by acquisitions.

This movement attained maturity in July 2005, when promoter Bob Geldof organized a series of concerts around the globe to raise awareness of poverty in Africa. The concerts were held simultaneously in London, Paris, Berlin, Rome, and Philadelphia. They were televised and broadcast on terrestrial radio and satellite radio. AOL streamed the concerts live and made them available on demand for another 6 weeks. This represented an unprecedented coming together of media in support of a single event. That was partly because of the efforts of Geldof and U2's

cross-marketing Partnerships or divisions of a corporation that market and promote the products of one entity to the customers of another.

Bono to achieve cooperation from many sources, but it was also because technology had reached a level of maturity that made an undertaking of such complexity possible.[28]

Later that month, AOL announced a partnership with XM Satellite Radio and AEG, a provider of sports and entertainment content. The network was designed to serve the more than 100 million subscribers to AOL around the world and the growing network of satellite radio subscribers. Some of the entertainment content would originate from sports and entertainment venues operated by AEG. Network Live Founder and CEO Kevin Wall called it the "network of the future, delivering digital programming to consumers who are hungry for live programming."[29] AOL, MSN, and Yahoo! all have radio networks, with Yahoo! alone reaching almost 2.5 million individuals every day in late 2005.[30]

They were not through yet. In October 2005, AOL announced the premier of a "made for the Internet" reality show, The Biz.[31] In November, they announced an agreement with CBS news to provide video and text news coverage on the site.[32] These developments all occurred within the span of a few months. They attest to the newly felt power of media convergence.

AOL was not alone. In November 2005, Yahoo! announced a partnership with Clear Channel Malls, an offshoot of the Clear Channel radio outdoor advertising corporation, to display news in the food courts of selected malls in New York and Los Angeles. The large, full-motion video screens were to carry sports, entertainment, and financial news provided by Yahoo! Advertising space would be available.[33] At about the same time, CNN and Daimler Chrysler Motors announced an agreement for Chrysler to sponsor the *Time* magazine Person of the Year issue and related announcements on CNN. In addition to TV and print coverage, media used were expected to include online, podcasting, video-on-demand, and interactive TV.[34] At the beginning of 2006, CNN began to actively promote a new content subscription service called Pipeline in twenty-five countries across the globe. The commercial-free service provides four channels of live video ("pipes") at any given time, as well as headlines, archives, and search functionality.[35] This service offers a larger selection of content in a commercial-free environment in addition to CNN.com's free advertising-supported video service. Both are available on demand, giving consumers access to and control over news content whenever they want it. Through the availability of RSS feeds, podcasts, and mobile news alerts, CNN is also moving in the direction of "wherever they want it" for news content.

The major television networks are offering streamed newscasts over the Internet just a few hours after live broadcast. They are offering entertainment programming a few hours after broadcast for a small download fee. Magazines and major urban newspapers and television stations are offering free podcasts. TiVo, perceived as the archenemy of television advertising, is partnering with large advertising agencies to make keyword search available on TV.[36] At the 2006 Consumer Electronics Show, Intel announced new technology and new partnerships based on it. The new Viv computer chip blurs the line between the PC, TV, and mobile devices by allowing content to be moved from one to another in a seamless fashion. Intel's initial partners included satellite TV provider DirecTV and actor Morgan Freeman's broadband production company ClickStar. They announced that Freeman's next movie would be available for broadband download almost as soon as it was released to theaters, bypassing the usual DVD stage.

This is only the beginning. When it will become a stable and well-organized media environment is unclear. In the meantime, marketers are going to have to be content with a chaotic media environment.[37] This environment is full of risk, but it will reward marketers who assess it correctly and take innovative actions to reach highly targeted audiences in highly selective media.

Summary

It is not yet clear what forms the converged hardware or the converged media of the future will take. Yet one thing does seem clear, even in the very early stages. It is not the device; it is not the specific media entities who come together for a specific event or business venture. It is the network—the Internet—that makes all these developments possible.

Some of the network will be wired. More and more will be wireless as time goes on, especially in countries that have limited Internet access at present. Different infrastructure requirements and cultural issues will impact the speed and nature of developments. From the beginning of the text we have described the evolution of the Internet

into "Internet 2." There are many opinions about when and what "Internet 2" will be. It is likely to be more open, more transparent, and more reliant on a variety of services. It is also likely to provide opportunities not yet envisioned for people to find information and to link to one another in all kinds of collaborative activities.

The second stage of the Internet is unlikely to be a finished product any time soon. It is sure to present a day-by-day challenge for marketers. The growth and development of Internet marketing will be an integral aspect of that challenge as consumers and businesses alike increasingly rely on the network to support multiple aspects of their daily activities.

Quiz

1. The adoption stage in which a new product has become a part of the user's lifestyle is called _____.
   a. permanent adoption
   b. loyalty
   c. internalization

2. _____ is a product characteristic that determines ease of adoption.
   a. Relative advantage
   b. Sustainable advantage
   c. Substitutability

3. Which of the following is *not* a true statement about pervasive computing?
   a. It is a result of computing power embedded in a variety of devices.
   b. Internet-enabled wireless devices must have the same level of functionality as desktop computers in order to be successful.
   c. Pervasive computing will allow more personalized user communications.

4. Among the strategic implications of pervasive computing is the fact that _____.
   a. marketers must wait for customers to contact them
   b. marketers must be able to contact customers near the time and place of purchase
   c. content will become less important than context

5. _____ is likely to be a high-volume use of the wireless Internet in the near future.
   a. M-commerce
   b. SMS services
   c. Advertising messages

6. Which of the following is a true statement about advertising in the wireless environment?
   a. Consumers will not be interested in receiving any type of advertising content on their wireless devices.
   b. Marketers must engage in expanded permission marketing.
   c. Advertising-sponsored business models will be common.

7. Strategic drivers of wireless technology include _____.
   a. localization
   b. larger screens
   c. new methods of advertising

8. Barriers to the adoption of wireless technology include _____.
   a. total cost of ownership
   b. fast download speed
   c. too much content

9. _____ is the term used to describe multiple media woven into a seamless communications network.
   a. Wireless networks
   b. High-definition television (HDTV)
   c. Digital convergence

10. Media convergence implies _____.
    a. that large media companies will buy other large media companies
    b. an expanding set of strategic partnerships in the media industry
    c. that everyone will have to buy new communications devices

Discussion Questions

1. Explain the nature of the consumer adoption process. How is it different from the concept of diffusion of innovations?

2. Using a technological innovation of your choice, explain how well its characteristics fit with those that increase the ease of diffusion.

3. Define *pervasive computing* in your own words. What changes is it likely to bring about in the way marketers approach the Internet?

4. List some of the ways wireless technology can be used to by consumers for convenience and entertainment. What are some ways it can be used to increase productivity in B2B markets?

5. Be prepared to describe the strategic drivers of wireless adoption and to give an example of each.

6. What are some of the barriers to adoption of wireless technology?

7. What are some of the marketing implications of digital convergence? What industries do you think will be most affected by it?

8. What is meant by *media convergence*? What are some recent examples of partnerships between media? In particular, are you aware of partnerships between media that might otherwise be considered competitors for consumer attention and advertising dollars?

Internet Exercises

1. Identify a market space that interests you. It could be anything from household use of converged devices to educational applications of handheld devices to use of pervasive computing in a specific industry sector. Construct a scenario (story) that describes in detail the applications that might pertain to this specific segment and the way in which users would interact with devices and tasks.

2. Identify two or three Web sites that offer mobile services. It will be helpful if they are drawn from the three sites you are following or services that you personally use. Find out as much as possible about the nature of the services offered. Be prepared to discuss both their potential usefulness and how willing you believe consumers or businesses will be to use these services and even to pay for them.

3. Explore a portal of your choice—either one of the major ones or a specialized one that serves a particular type of activity or industry. What types of mobile services do they offer?

4. Visit a local content site. It might be a local newspaper or a local search site or another type of site that focuses on a local area. Does it offer mobile services? Do you see evidence of partnerships with other media?

5. You may have already been assigned to evaluate the effectiveness of the three Web sites you are following as independent marketing entities. Now find out as much as you can about the strategy of the three firms. Be prepared to discuss how you see their Internet marketing strategy fitting into both their corporate and their marketing strategies.

Notes

1. "Global Innovation Outlook 2004," IBM, http://t1d.www-306. cacheibm.com/e-business/ondemand/us/pdf/IBM_ GIO_ 2004.pdf, p. 5.

2. Mark Weiser, "The Computer for the Twenty-First Century," *Scientific American*, pp. 94–10, September 1991. Available online at Weiser's personal Web site, http://www.ubiq.com/ hypertext/weiser/SciAmDraft3.html, accessed November 11, 2005.

3. "What Is Pervasive Computing?" nd, http://www-3.ibm.com.

4. Speedpass Fact Sheet, "No Cash? No Card? No Problem! New Speedpass Features Allow Stop & Shop Customers to Pay and Save All in One," nd, http://www.speedpass.com; Nora Mancuso, "McDonald's to Expand E-Payment System," May 29, 2001, *E-Commerce Times*, http://www.newsfactor.com; Texas Instruments, "Retail Applications," nd, http://www.ti. com/rfid/docs/applications/pos/retail.shtml.

5. "BNSF Railway Company: On the Track to the Information Edge," *CIO Magazine*, June 2005, http://www.cio.com/ sponsors/061505sybase/?page=1.

6. Additional sources for this section include "BNSF Railway," Sybase Case Study, nd, http://www.sybase.com/detail?id= 1034175; "BNSF Facts," nd, http://www.bnsf.com/media / bnsffacts.html.

7. Ted Russel, "Las Vegas and Citizens Likely to Be Winners," May 13, 2005, http://www.lasvegastribune.com/20050513/ headline1. html; "New Parking Meters Will Make Doing Business Downtown Easier," November 7, 2005, http://www.lasvegasne-vada.gov/business/5530.htm;"About mPark," nd, http://www. mparkusa. com/mpark/lasvegas.jspx; "Peppercoin Partners with Reino in Parking-Meter Technology Rollout," October 5, 2005, http://boston.bizjournals.com/boston/stories/2004/10/04/ daily28.html.

8. Enid Burns, "The Utilitarian Life of the Internet," ClickZ, September 9, 2005, http://www.clickz.com/stats/sectors/wireless/article.php/3547651.

9. John B. Horrigan, "28% of Americans Are Wireless Ready," Pew Internet Project Data Memo, May 2004, http://www.pewinternet.org/pdfs/PIP_Wireless_Ready_Data_0504.pdf.

10. "Introduction to Text Messaging," nd, http://www.textalert.com/t3/skins/default/docs/marketingGuide/marketing Guide.asp.

11. "Snapple: Case Study," 2005, http://www.enpocket.com/content/clients/pdf/snapple.pdf.

12. "McDonald's Goes Mobile," Creative Showcase, November 3, 2005, http://www.imediaconnection.com/content/7191.asp.

13. http://www.mobitv.com/.

14. Alice Z. Cuneo, "Jeep Launches Own Mobile Phone TV Channel," *Advertising Age*, December 12, 2005, http://adage.com/news.cms?newsId=47113.

15. "Podcast Projections," eMarketer, November 18, 2005.

16. "Searching for the Pod of Gold," *Business Week Online*, November 14, 2005, http://www.businessweek.com/magazine/content/05_46/b3959131.htm.

17. "15-Year Old Podcaster Secures Major Sponsorship," PR Newswire, November 17, 2005, http://prnewswire.com/cgi-bin/stories.pl?ACCT=SPIMUS.story&STORY=/www/story/11-17-2005/0004218730&EDATE=THU+Nov+17+2005,+11:46+AM.

18. "Podcasts Reel in Major Sponsors," *MarketingVox*, November 18, 2005, http://www.marketingvox.com/archives/2005/11/18/podcasts_reel_in_major_sponsors/.

19. Kris Oser, "Burger King Icon Used in Strip-Tease Viral Video," November 18, 2005, http://adage.com/news.cms?newsId=46838.

20. For other examples see Fareena Sultan and Andrew Rohm, "The Coming Era of 'Brand in the Hand' Marketing," *Sloan Management Review*, Fall 2005, Vol. 47, No. 1, pp. 83–90.

21. "Introducing Mobile Tickets," PlusOne, nd, http://www.plusone.com.au/mobi-ticket.php, accessed November 19, 2005.

22. "Where Is Mobile Marketing Headed?" eMarketer, February 4, 2005, http://www.emarketer.com.

23. A. T. Kearney and Cambridge University, "Mobinet 2005," October 2005, presentation, http://www.atkearney.com/shared_res/pdf/Mobinet_2005_Detailed_Results.pdf.

24. Convergence Center, http://dcc.syr.edu/index.htm, November 21, 2005.

25. See "Who Owns What," *Columbia Journalism Review*, http://www.cjr.org/tools/owners/, for extensive information on media ownership.

26. "History," http://www.bertelsmann.com/bertelsmann_corp/wms41/bm/index.php?ci=178&language=2.

27. Julia Angwin and Kevin J. Delaney, "AOL, Google Expand Partnership, with a Key Ad Sales Provision," *Wall Street Journal*, December 21, 2005, http://online.wsj.com/article/SB113512324965227926.html.

28. "Live 8 Concerts to Fight Poverty," CNN.com, July 26, 2005, http://www.cnn.com/2005/SHOWBIZ/Music/05/31/live8.geldof/; "Live 8 Internet, Television and Radio Broadcast Information," About.com, nd, http://philadelphia.about.com/od/calendarofevents/qt/live_8_media.htm.

29. AOL Press Center, "AEG, America Online And XM Satellite Radio Join Forces with Executive Producer of Live 8, Kevin Wall, to Create 'Network Live,' the First Multi-Platform Digital Entertainment Company for Live Programming," July 12, 2005, http://media.timewarner.com/media/newmedia/cb_press_view.cfm?release_num=55254409.

30. "AOL Online Radio Reaches over Two Million in Morning Drive Time," Center for Media Research, December 9, 2005, http://www.mediapost.com.

31. AOL Service, "AOL Music Presents Series Premiere of Online Reality Show 'The Biz' on Thebiz.com," October 18, 2005, http://media.timewarner.com/media/newmedia/cb_press_view.cfm?release_num=55254464.

32. AOL Service, "CBSNews.com to Make Latest Video and Text Programming Available on AOL News," November 9, 2005, http://media.timewarner.com/media/newmedia/cb_press_view.cfm?release_num=55254472.

33. "Clear Channel, Yahoo Partner for Mall Advertising," *MarketingVox*, November 21, 2005, http://www.marketingvox.com/archives/categories/media_convergence/index.php.

34. "Chrysler 'Person of the Year' Campaign Uses Web, Podcasts, Wireless," *MarketingVox*, November 21, 2005, http://www.marketingvox.com/archives/2005/11/21/chrysler_person_of_the_year_campaign_uses_web_podcasts_wireless/.

35. "CNN.com Launches Broadband Video News Service," CNN.com, December 5, 2005, http://www.cnn.com/2005/TECH/internet/12/05/pipeline.

36. Brian Steinberg and Nick Wingfield, "TiVo Users Can Soon Search for Ads," November 28, 2005, *Wall Street Journal*, http://online.wsj.com/article/SB113314789302107860.html.

37. Bob Garfield's columns in *Advertising Age* and broadcasts on National Public Radio provide one expert's commentary on the changing media scene, which he calls the "chaos scenario." They began on April 4, 2005, and continue in both media at irregular intervals.

Glossary

80/20 rule Pareto principle. The rule of thumb that states that 20% of a phenomenon (customers) tends to product 80% of the results (profits).

911 The national emergency response number in the United States.

A/B split Presenting one offer, creative execution, and so forth, to one group of customers or prospects and another version of the same offer, creative execution, and so on, to another group of customers.

accessibility Web site design principles that allow physically challenged people, who may need special devices such as screen readers or voice recognition software, to successfully use the Web site.

acquisition The process of obtaining new customers.

ad serving The process of supplying advertising elements while a page is loading on a user's browser. Ads are served by an advertising network and are placed on the basis of user profiles.

adware Software that inserts ads onto the viewer's screen.

adware Programs installed on consumers' computers, with permission, that enable them to receive targeted ads.

affiliate A Web site that agrees to post a link to a transactional site in return for a commission on sales made as a direct result of the link.

agent A piece of software that triggers an activity when a specified event occurs. Agents or bots perform a variety of repetitive tasks on the Internet, ranging from searching for content for the search engines and directories to searching for product offerings by e-merchants to provide comparison prices for users.

aided brand awareness The ability of a respondent to identify a brand when prompted.

algorithm A set of structured steps for solving a problem.

alt tag An HTML tag (formatting instruction) displayed as a call-out bar that describes a graphic element for the benefit of people who have text-only browsers.

anonymous profile A customer profile created without knowing the name or e-mail address of a Web site visitor from data captured during Web site visits.

application programming interfaces A set of programming tools including small modules of software and communications protocols used as building blocks in building software applications.

Applications Services Provider (ASP) Provides access to software-based services to clients.

ARPANet Stands for Advanced Research Project Agency, originally an arm of the U.S. Department of Defense. In the 1950s, the Agency developed a connected system of computers that formed the basis of the modern Internet.

artificial intelligence Applications that exhibit human-like intelligence and behavior and have the ability to learn from experience.

auction A preexisting business model that operates successfully on the Internet by announcing an item for sale and permitting multiple purchasers/suppliers to bid on them under specified rules and conditions; see also *reverse auction*.

automation Replacing manual tasks and processes with computers and computer-controlled equipment.

baby boom The population cohort born between 1945 and 1963.

back end The activities that are required to satisfy the customer after a sale is made, including fulfillment and customer service.

bar codes The printed, machine-readable set of black lines and white space that identifies products according to the universal product code (UPC).

barter Trading goods or services without money changing hands.

behavioral Advertising displayed on the basis of anonymous Internet user profiles.

beta The stage in the product development process in which a new product is released to a select set of users for testing.

biometrics Using a biological characteristic, for example, a fingerprint or voiceprint, to authenticate the identity of a person.

blogs Short for Web logs; records of personal experiences posted on the Web and publicly accessible.

brand A name, term, sign, symbol, design, or a combination thereof intended to identify the goods and services of one seller or a group of sellers and to differentiate them from those of the competition.

brand equity The value of a brand, measured in financial terms.

brand image The advertising metric that measures the type and favorability of consumer perceptions of the brand.

brand recognition/brand awareness The advertising metric that measures the ability of target consumers to identify the brand under different questioning scenarios.

broadband High-speed transmission over telecommunications networks.

browser A program that allows a user to connect to the World Wide Web by simply typing in a URL.

build-to-inventory The generic business model in which demand is forecasted and products are made and stocked in inventory based on the forecast.

build-to-order A business model, most often attributed to Dell, in which products are built only after an order has been received.

business plan Written statement of how an owner, often an entrepreneur, intends to execute all business functions to successfully achieve objectives.

cache High-speed storage for data that is referenced frequently.

call center Department within an organization that handles telephone sales and/or service.

call routing Automated telephony systems that route calls to appropriate service agents based on data such as caller's telephone number or data provided by an IVR system.

card sorting A research technique in which respondents place individual items written on cards into piles that represent similar content.

cascading style sheets Essentially templates that define how elements of a Web page are displayed. They are "cascading" because multiple style sheets can be used to describe a single page.

channels of distribution The intermediaries through which products and information about transactions move in the course of a single exchange.

chat Provides the capability of real-time conferencing on a LAN or on the Internet by typing on the keyboard.

choiceboard A customization technique in which people are asked to choose from a menu of options.

clickstream The complete data record, made up of mouse-clicks, of consumer activity on the Internet during a specified period, usually the duration of a visit to a single Web site.

cluster analysis Classifying objects or people into mutually exclusive and exhaustive groups on the basis of two or more classification variables.

co-creation Customer participation in producing content for a site.

coded Web page A technique in which a small image, usually a 1-pixel transparent image (called a pixel tag or transparent GIF), is placed on a Web page. Used in conjunction with a cookie on the user's computer, the image returns data about user activity on the Web page.

collaborative Working together; often refers to software that supports people working together over time and distance.

collaborative filtering Software used to make recommendations based on the stated preferences and purchase history of other visitors to the site.

community A group of like-minded people.

complex experimental design Test designs that permit testing of more than one variable at a time without sacrificing statistical validity.

concept testing Research performed on the idea behind a product or a communications program.

consortia B2B marketplaces sponsored by a group of otherwise competitive enterprises in a specific industry.

contextual Ads that are displayed based on the content being viewed at the time.

controlled circulation A type of business publication that is distributed free of charge to qualified members of a specific industry.

convenience sample As the name suggests, a sample that is easy to obtain; convenience samples do not permit generalization to a larger population, as random samples do.

conversion The process of moving a prospect from consideration to purchase.

coordination costs The costs incurred in transmitting information that permits economic exchange.

cookie A few lines of code that a Web site places on a user's computer to store data about the user's activities on the site.

cookies Lines of code placed on a user's computer that allow activity data to be collected anonymously.

CPA Cost per action; a media pricing mechanism based on the number of visitors who take a specified action, for example, clicking through on an ad or making a purchase.

CPC Cost per click from an ad or referring Web site.

CPM Cost per thousand advertising impressions; the primary pricing mechanism for many media, including the Internet.

cross-marketing Partnerships or divisions of a corporation that market and promote the products of one entity to the customers of another.

customer lifetime value The net present value of a future stream of net revenue from an identified customer.

customer profile A description, primarily quantitative, of an individual or segment using specified demographic, lifestyle, and behavioral characteristics.

customer value The worth of a single customer to the enterprise.

customization The process of producing a product, service, or communication to the exact specifications/desires of the purchaser or recipient.

cycle time The time from beginning to completion of a business process; for example, the time it takes to fill a customer's order.

dashboard Customizable display of summary data on a computer screen. Because the summary data are always present on the specified screen, it prevents the user from having to activate a function or program or visit another Web site to obtain data.

data Raw, unprocessed facts and numbers.

database A set of files (data, video, images, etc.) organized in a way that permits a computer program to quickly select any desired piece of content.

data mining The analytic process and specialized analytic tools used to extract meaning from very large data sets.

dealer An intermediary in B2B channels of distribution that is roughly equivalent to the retailer in business-to-customer channels.

decision rule A statement that takes the form "If . . . then," specifying an action to be taken, given the occurrence of a particular event.

default A value or setting that is automatically in effect unless the user changes it.

deliverability The ability to get commercial e-mail delivered to the intended recipient, primarily by taking the correct actions to avoid spam filters.

directory On the Web, an index of Web sites and their contents.

discount rate The interest rate at which a person or a business borrows money. In the calculation of CLV a substantial risk premium is usually added to the market interest rate.

distributor An intermediary in B2B channels of distribution that is roughly equivalent to the wholesaler in business-to-customer channels.

DNS Domain Name System; the process for converting the name of a Web site into its IP address.

domain name A unique name on the Internet.

DSL Digital subscriber line, technology that greatly increases the transmission capacity of ordinary telephone lines; one type of broadband transmission.

dynamic pricing Having different prices to meet different market conditions at the same time.

e-commerce Buying and selling goods and services online.

electronic data interchange The general term used to describe the digitizing of business information like orders and invoices so that they may be communicated electronically between suppliers and customers.

electronic product code Made up of header information, manufacturer identification, product identification, and serial number in a way that provides unique identification number for more than 16 million manufacturers and SKUs as compared to 100,000 manufacturers and SKUs for the Universal Product Code (UPC).

embedded service module A device, usually a chip, that is part of a product and that is used to provide remote monitoring and diagnostics of the product's performance.

encryption Using mathematical algorithms to encode data for security in transmission or storage.

enterprise resource Planning that integrates all aspects of the business from manufacturing resource planning and scheduling through service functions like human resources.

excel macros Functions or formulas that have been created and saved inside an Excel worksheet so that they can be called and executed as needed.

experiential A term that implies learning through experience; a product with features that facilitate learning through experience.

expertise Skill or knowledge.

expert system A branch of artificial intelligence that uses rules and knowledge obtained from human experts and incorporated into a knowledge base to solve problems.

explicit knowledge Knowledge that has been or can be articulated in a relatively straightforward manner.

extranet A corporate information system that is made available to business partners who are able to access portions of the system for which they have passwords.

extranet Corporate networks linked together to share designated information.

FAQ Frequently asked question.

flash An application development tool that allows programmers to create files with audio and streaming video that can be played on a Web browser equipped with the Flash player.

focus group The qualitative marketing research technique in which a group, usually six to twelve people who fit a particular profile, are brought together to discuss an issue under the guidance of a skilled moderator.

friction The economic term that describes the presence of information search and transactions costs, which do not add value, in a channel of distribution.

front end All the marketing and promotional activities that occur before a sale is made.

gen X The population cohort born after the Baby Boom, in the 1960s and 1970s. There is considerable debate about the exact beginning and ending dates.

gen Y The population cohort born between 1981 and 1995.

geodemographic The analysis of demographic data by zip/postal code to find market segments.

GIF An acronym for graphics interchange format, one of the common types of image files used on the Web.

gigabyte One billion bytes of data; a byte is a binary unit that holds one character of data.

GPS Global Positioning System; a satellite-based system for accurate location of a signal anywhere on Earth.

heat map A visual metric that shows which parts of a Web page perform best, that is, receives the most attention for the longest period.

help desk The group in an organization that provides support for both hardware and software. The term is also used in connection with specialized software that supports help desk operations.

high involvement A purchase situation in which the consumer performs an information search and undergoes an extensive choice process.

hit counter A piece of software inserted onto a Web site that measures the number of visits to the site.

hosting Locating a Web site on the servers that will make it available to the Internet. Hosting can be done internally or by specialty suppliers that offer hosting and associated services such as Web metrics.

HTML Hypertext markup language, one of the foundations of the common Internet platform. HTML describes the structure of Web documents using a type of coding called tags.

hypertext Allows one document, or one portion of a document, to be linked to another.

inbound Communications that originate outside the enterprise and that are destined for a person or unit inside it.

incentive A reward offered by a marketer to a prospective customer in return for furnishing information or making a purchase.

incidence A marketing research term that describes how often a particular characteristic occurs in a specified population.

infomediary Intermediary in channels of distribution that specializes in the capture, analysis, application, and distribution of information.

information Data that have been processed into more useful forms using techniques that range from simple summary formats to complex statistical routines.

information product A commercial product that consists solely of data.

infrastructure stack A term used to describe the various layers of hardware, software, and purchased services that make up the network on which the Internet runs.

interactive Media or channels that permit two-way communications, for instance, between a marketer and potential customer.

intranet An enterprise Web site that serves the needs of employees.

intranet Corporate network accessible only to employees and outsiders with authorization.

inventory turns The number of times inventory is sold (turns over) in a year.

IVR Interactive voice response; automated telephone systems in which customers key in or speak data and responses and the system responds with a combination of recorded voice messages and real-time information from databases.

JavaScript Language that adds interactivity to static HTML pages.

just in time A set of production management techniques that requires production close to the time of demand, reducing work-in-process inventory and the overall cost of production.

knowledge Information to which human expertise has been added.

knowledge worker A person who uses brains, not brawn, to earn a living. Most Internet-related workers fall into this category.

landing page A Web page designed to receive visitors who are coming to the site as a result of a link from another site.

legacy Existing information systems, usually ones running on mainframe computers or minicomputers.

licensing Legal permission to own or use a product or piece of content.

logistics The business function that controls the flow of products, information, and other resources from their point of production to the place where they are needed for further production or for sale.

low involvement A purchase situation on which consumer spends little time or thought.

machine-to-machine (M2M) A business model in which automated systems allow computers and specialized devices to communicate with one another without direct human intervention.

many-to-many A communications system in which there are many recipients of communications and many sources of those same communications.

margin (gross margin) Essentially sales minus cost of goods sold; margin is the amount that must cover operating expenses, including marketing expenses, and profit.

market segment A portion of a total market that is homogeneous in terms of demographics, behaviors, lifestyles, or other variables of interest to the marketer.

mass media Media that are characterized by large audiences and relatively few sources of messages, often referred to as one-to-many communications channels.

message association The ability of a respondent to recall some of the copy points of an ad to which he or she has been exposed.

meta tag An HTML tag that provides information about the Web page, primarily for the use of the search engines.

Metcalfe's Law In 1994, Robert Metcalfe, inventor of Ethernet and one of the founders of the 3Com Corp., stated that the power of a computer is proportional to the square of the number of computers that are connected to it. That results in a geometrical increase in value each time a new computer is connected to the network.

micropayments Payments for electronic purchases of low-ticket products or services that are uneconomical under traditional payment mechanisms like credit cards.

mirroring Using information to present a complete and timely picture of activities in the value chain.

MMS Multimedia messaging services; rich-media messaging services for cell phones.

MMS Wireless telecommunications services that allow graphics, audio clips, and video clips to be transmitted over cell phones.

modem Device that allows a computer to transmit data over a standard telephone line.

monetize Jargon used to describe the concept of first creating a content-rich Web site and then being able to sell advertising to support it.

Moore's Law In 1965, Gordon Moore, one of the founders of Intel, predicted that computing power would double every 18 months while the cost of producing it fell by 50%. That prediction has been borne out, and the result is a reduction of roughly 60 million times in the cost of storing a single item of data.

multichannel Using more than one channel of distribution to reach the customer.

network A system that transmits voice, data, and video between users.

net present value The current value of a future revenue stream.

node A communications junction or connection point.

open source Freely available content that is produced collaboratively by volunteers.

operating system The master piece of software that runs the computer and all the applications used on it.

opt-in Communication that has been actively requested by the Internet user; it becomes "double opt-in" when the marketer sends an e-mail that requires the user to confirm the request before it is activated.

opt-out Communication that has been passively requested by the Internet user. This is usually done by prechecking the communications request, requiring the user to uncheck it in order to avoid receiving the communication.

organic Search results produced by search engine spiders.

page view A page actually seen by a visitor; currently measured as a page being delivered to the visitor, which is not exactly the same thing.

paid inclusion Payment of a fee to ensure listing with a search engine.

paid placement Paid ads that are displayed as a result of keyword searches.

pareto curve A plot of number of occurrences against percent of total; the source of the 80/20 rule.

peer-to-peer model Transmission of files directly from one user to another.

persona A hypothetical person whose characteristics are those of a segment of users.

personalization The process of preparing an individualized communication for a specific person based on stated or implied preferences.

pfarming Creating fake Web sites that are similar to legitimate business sites.

phishers Fraudulent emailers who engage in phishing by using emails that attempt to obtain personal data from consumers.

phishing E-mails that attempt to obtain personal information by making fraudulent claims.

pixel One dot in the matrix of dots that makes up the display on a monitor.

pixel Short for picture element, a single point on a display screen or in a graphic image.

platform The hardware and software architecture, including the operating system, on which computers run.

podcasting A service that uses RSS technology to download selected content to the user's iPod or desktop.

portal A large site with multiple services, ranging from news to directories to searches, that acts as an entry point onto the Internet.

predictive model Relevant variables and associated response factors or probabilities are used to estimate the likelihood of occurrence of a specific behavior, given the existence of a given level of the specified variables.

predictive modeling Using relevant variables and associated response factors or probabilities to estimate the likelihood of occurrence of a specific behavior, given the existence of a given level of the specified variables.

pretesting As used in advertising, to conduct research on a promotion before it is used in the marketplace with the purpose of improving its effectiveness.

profile In marketing and marketing research, a description of a person or segment.

profile A summary of the distinctive features or characteristics of a person, business, or other entity.

proprietary systems Software or networks that are the exclusive property of the firm that developed them and that cannot be used by others without permission.

protocol A set of rules that govern the sending and receiving of data.

public key A security device that can be sent by ordinary communications methods like e-mail.

purchase intent The self-reported likelihood that the respondent will make a purchase within a stated time frame.

push Technology that allows preselected data to be distributed to the user's computer at preselected time intervals.

qualify To determine whether a prospective customer is likely to make a purchase at some time in the future.

quality assurance Synonymous with quality control in manufacturing; procedures for ensuring the correct performance of software.

query In information systems, requesting information from a database.

queue A line of objects or people.

redirect Sending one URL to another Internet address.

registration A process requiring a visitor to provide identifying personal information in order to receive communications or other benefits from a Web site.

regression Statistical technique that predicts the level of magnitude of a dependent variable based on the levels of more than one independent variable; also called *multiple regression.*

repurpose Jargon for taking content from one corporate communications piece and with only minor revisions using it for another communications activity, often the Web site.

retention Preventing existing customers from defecting to another supplier.

retention Preventing existing customers from defecting to another seller.

revenue model The way or ways in which a firm makes its money from marketplace transactions.

reverse auction Auction in which there is a single purchaser with multiple suppliers bidding for the opportunity to supply the product or service.

RFID Radio frequency identification tags; tiny computer chips that can be affixed to any item of merchandise which then transmits data to a radio transponder.

RFM Recency × Frequency × Monetary value; a direct marketing model for assessing the worth of a customer.

rich media Ads that can include video and audio.

RSS (Rich Site Summary or, more commonly, **Really Simple Syndication)** Technology that allows the owner of content to share it with other Web sites.

rule See *decision rule*.

sales force automation Processes, and the software that supports them, that permit salespeople to work more effectively both in and out of their offices by providing electronic access to important documents and customer data.

sales lead generation The process of identifying prospective purchasers.

Sarbanes Oxley Act U.S. law passed in 2002 that mandates standards for financial disclosure and corporate governance.

scalable The degree to which an information system can grow with demand without completely replacing the system.

search engine Software that allows users to search for content based on keywords.

search engine Software and algorithms, or a Web site based on search software, that allow users to search for content based on keywords they provide.

secure sockets layer Internet security protocol that validates the identity of a Web site and makes it safe to send financial information like credit card numbers.

SEM (Search Engine Marketing) All the techniques, including search engine optimization and paid placement, that are used to attract people from search engines to Web sites.

SEO (Search Engine Optimization) All the techniques used to cause a Web page to be highly ranked on one or more search engines.

server A computer from which other computers request files.

server log Record kept at the server level that records each file requested from a Web site.

six sigma The quality management technique that results in near-perfect products, technically results that fall within six standard deviations from the mean of a normal distribution.

skip patterns The marketing research term that describes survey questions that branch; that is, the next question is dependent on the answer to the previous one.

SKU An identifying code assigned by the retailer that describes a specific item by product, size, color, flavor, or any other relevant feature.

SKU Stock-keeping unit; a unique numerical identifier attached to a product.

SMS Short messaging services; text messaging services for cell phones

spoofing Creating false identities in order to evade rules for conducting business and communications on the Web.

spyware Software that sends information about Web activities back to its Web site.

spyware Programs installed on consumers' computers without their permission that assume partial control over the operating system.

streaming media Technology that permits a Web site to deliver continuous audio or video or both to a user's computer.

structured questions In marketing research, a question that can be answered by choosing one of a prespecified set of responses.

stylus A pen-shaped device used to either point or draw.

supply chain the downstream portion of the value chain, the channel from suppliers to producers.

syndication Sale of content to multiple customers, each of whom then integrates it into their own products.

tacit knowledge Knowledge that has not been articulated; often subconscious and relatively difficult to communicate to other people.

tags A user-supplied keyword or category name.

TCP/IP Transmission Control Protocol/Internet Protocol, the communications protocol (standard) of the Internet. It permits the accurate transmission of messages over otherwise incompatible networks.

telecommunications The network of copper land lines, fiber-optic cables, and wireless transmitters that allows voice, data, text, graphics, and video to be transmitted over long distances.

telematics Sending, receiving, and storing data using telecommunications devices.

template A document structure into which content can be dropped.

total cost of ownership How much it actually costs to own a piece of technology, including items like the original cost, upgrades, maintenance, technical support, and training.

transaction costs The costs of making and fulfilling sales, often referred to as "friction" in channels of distribution. They include both search and distribution costs.

unique visitor An identifiably distinct, although not necessarily identifiable, visitor to a Web site within a specified period.

UPC Universal Product Code; codes embedded in bars and printed on items of merchandise. The codes can be read by checkout and handheld scanners.

usability The ease with which users are able to perform desired tasks on a Web site.

usability testing Ensuring that it is easy for visitors to navigate and, in general, to find desired content quickly and efficiently on a Web site.

user intent What the searcher is really looking for when a keyword is typed into a search engine

value chain The integrated channel that stretches from suppliers through the producer and on to the end users.

value (customer value, customer perceived value) Essentially the usefulness (economic utility) of the product less its price.

value-added network Connectivity between computer systems that adds additional functions to ensure the quality and security of the data transmitted.

value-added services Services that make the original product more valuable and help generate additional revenue.

value proposition Customer value delivered to a specific target market.

vertical markets Business markets that concentrate on a specific industry sector or business function.

virtual value chain The term given to an integrated supply chain in which all transactions are conducted electronically.

visibility The ability to obtain supply chain information, especially about goods in transit, in an easy and timely fashion.

Voice Over Internet Protocol (VOIP) Internet telephony; the ability to make calls over any IP network.

Web crawlers An automated program that searches the Web for information. Also called bots, spiders, and agents.

Web services Applications that allow enterprises to exchange information over the Internet using open (public) standards; this permits otherwise incompatible systems to interact with one another without human or programming intervention.

Wi-Fi Technically, a wireless communication protocol; in lay terms, often used to refer to the ability to access the Internet via wireless hotspots or access points.

work flow An automated system that electronically routes documents to the next person in the process.

XML Extensible markup language; like HTML, XML uses tags to code documents—technically, it defines data elements on a page; practically, it allows the creation of documents that can be filled out and transmitted electronically.

Y2K The acronym given to the fear that, because of short-sighted design of early computer programs, many software applications for critical businesses like utilities and banks would cease to function at midnight on January 1, 2000.

Index